PUBLIC POLICY
PERSPECTIVES AND CHOICES

PUBLIC POLICY

PERSPECTIVES AND CHOICES

Charles L. Cochran
United States Naval Academy

Eloise F. Malone
United States Naval Academy

McGRAW-HILL, INC.

New York   St. Louis   San Francisco   Auckland   Bogotá   Caracas   Lisbon
London   Madrid   Mexico City   Milan   Montreal   New Delhi
San Juan   Singapore   Sydney   Tokyo   Toronto

This book was set in Times Roman by Better Graphics, Inc.
The editors were Peter Labella and John M. Morriss;
the production supervisor was Kathryn Porzio.
The cover was designed by Yael Dresdner.
Project supervision was done by The Total Book.
R. R. Donnelley & Sons Company was printer and binder.

PUBLIC POLICY

Perspectives and Choices

This book is printed on acid-free paper.

2 3 4 5 6 7 8 9 0   DOC   DOC   9 0 9 8 7 6 5

ISBN 0-07-011528-1

Library of Congress Cataloging-in-Publication Data

Cochran, Charles L.
    Public policy: perspectives and choices / Charles L. Cochran,
Eloise F. Malone.
      p.   cm.
    Includes bibliographical references and index.
    ISBN 0-07-011528-1
    1. Policy sciences.   I. Malone, Eloise F.   II. Title.
H97.C6   1995
320'.6—dc20   94-33885

ABOUT THE AUTHORS

Charles L. Cochran is a professor of political science and past chairperson of the department at the U.S. Naval Academy. He holds a B.S. degree from Mount St. Mary's College and a Ph.D. from Tuft's University. He has authored numerous articles, contributed several chapters to books, and edited and co-authored a book on civil-military relations. He has served as a consultant to the Departments of Energy, Commerce, and Transportation. He has also worked at the Defense Intelligence Agency. He has served on the editorial board of the *Journal of Political and Military Sociology*. Professor Cochran is married and has four adult-aged children.

Eloise F. Malone is an assistant professor of political science at the U.S. Naval Academy, Annapolis, Maryland. She received her B.A. from the Pennsylvania State University and her Ph.D. from the American University. Professor Malone previously worked at the U.S. Department of State where she analyzed public opinion. She teaches courses in American Government, Political Philosophy and Research Methods. At the Naval Academy, Professor Malone has been actively involved in the use of computer applications in political science research and teaching. She continues to pursue research activity on French Canadian politics.

For Mimi and Our Children,
Christy, Collie, Cassie,
and Chip
C.L.C.

For Dave and Our Children,
Jim, Mike, and Katherine
E.F.M

CONTENTS

PREFACE   xv

1 Basic Concepts in Public Policy   1

    WHAT IS PUBLIC POLICY?   1
    OPPORTUNITY COSTS   2
    SOCIAL CHOICE   4
    SOCIAL JUSTICE   8
    POLITICS AND ECONOMICS   11
    PUBLIC POLICY TYPOLOGY   12
    PUBLIC POLICY AND ECONOMIC ORGANIZATION   15
    WHY GOVERNMENTS INTERVENE   16
    CONCLUSION   21
    Questions for Discussion   22
    Key Concepts   22
    Suggested Readings   23

2 Methods and Models for Policy Analysis   24

    POLICY ANALYSIS AS A SUBFIELD OF POLITICAL SCIENCE   24
    PUBLIC POLICY AND THEORY   30
    THE POLICY-MAKING PROCESS   38
    CONCLUSION   57
    Questions for Discussion   57
    Key Concepts   58
    Suggested Readings   58

ix

3 Rational Public Choice   59

  INTRODUCTION   60
  PUBLIC INTEREST THEORY OF GOVERNMENT   62
  THE CAPTURE THEORY OF GOVERNMENT   63
  PUBLIC CHOICE THEORY   64
  COST-BENEFIT ANALYSIS   64
  POLITICAL ENTREPRENEURS   66
  BALLOTS AND DECISION MAKING   69
  VOTING AND THE POLITICAL MARKETPLACE   78
  INTEREST GROUPS—ADDED MUSCLE IN THE POLICY MARKET   80
  THE BUREAUCRATIZATION OF THE POLITY   83
  CONCLUSION   85
  Questions for Discussion   86
  Key Concepts   86
  Suggested Readings   87

4 Public Policy in a Strange New World   88

  DECLINING FAITH IN GOVERNMENT   89
  THE CULTURAL-HISTORICAL HERITAGE   94
  THE CONSTITUTIONAL CONVENTION AND THE GOVERNMENT
     IT CREATED   96
  FEDERALISM AND THE SCOPE OF THE CONFLICT   107
  POLITICAL PARTIES   111
  DIVIDED GOVERNMENT   112
  CONCLUSION   123
  Questions for Discussion   123
  Key Concepts   124
  Suggested Readings   124

5 Economic Theory as a Basis of Public Policy   125

  INTRODUCTION   125
  ADAM SMITH AND CLASSICAL OPTIMISM   126
  CLASSICAL MALTHUSIAN MELANCHOLY   130
  THE HAUNTING SPECTER OF KARL MARX   132
  THE REALIST CRITIQUE OF KEYNES   133
  THE ECONOMY: STABLE OR UNSTABLE?   142
  ADVANTAGES OF GOVERNMENTAL INTERVENTION
     TO CORRECT MARKET FAILURES   148
  CONCLUSION   149
  Questions for Discussion   150
  Key Concepts   150
  Suggested Readings   150

6   **Economic Policy: Crunch Time: Strategies for Tight Budgets and New Social Needs**   **151**

INTRODUCTION   **151**
POLICY INSTRUMENTS   **151**
THE POLITICAL ECONOMY OF DEFICITS   **155**
POLICY IMPLICATIONS OF THE DEFICIT   **161**
THE POLITICS OF THE DEFICIT   **165**
TAX POLICY AS A PARTIAL SOLUTION   **173**
CONCLUSION   **187**
Questions for Discussion   **188**
Key Concepts   **188**
Suggested Readings   **189**

7   **The Politics and Economics of Inequality**   **190**

INTRODUCTION   **191**
EQUITY AND EQUALITY   **191**
THE FUNCTIONALIST THEORY   **194**
TRENDS IN INEQUALITIES OF INCOME AND WEALTH   **199**
ETHICS AND DISTRIBUTIVE JUSTICE   **206**
MEASURES AND DEFINITIONS OF POVERTY   **210**
POLICIES TO FIGHT POVERTY   **213**
CONCLUSION   **222**
APPENDIX   **223**
Questions for Discussion   **224**
Key Concepts   **225**
Suggested Readings   **225**

8   **Crime: The Policy Quagmire**   **226**

HOW MUCH CRIME?   **226**
CRIME: A DEFINITION   **232**
CAUSES OF CRIME: WHAT DO WE KNOW?   **232**
CHARACTERISTICS OF THE CRIMINAL JUSTICE SYSTEM   **234**
INGREDIENTS OF VIOLENCE: DRUGS, GUNS, AND POVERTY   **242**
WHITE COLLAR CRIME   **251**
CONCLUSION   **252**
Questions for Discussion   **254**
Key Concepts   **254**
Suggested Readings   **254**

9   **Crisis in Housing Affordability**   **255**

HOUSING POLICY AND THE "AMERICAN DREAM"   **255**
HOUSING AND POLITICAL TRENDS   **258**

THE HOMELESS 266
HOUSING AFFORDABILITY 274
CAUSES OF THE LOW-INCOME HOUSING CRISIS 275
U.S. HOUSING POLICY 278
RENT CONTROL 284
CONCLUSION 287
Questions for Discussion 288
Key Terms 288
Suggested Readings 289

10 **Educational Policy: Low Grades for National Effort** 290

INTRODUCTION 290
FEDERAL SPENDING ON EDUCATION 291
THE STRUCTURE OF AMERICAN EDUCATION: AN OVERVIEW 293
EDUCATION: A QUASI-PUBLIC GOOD 295
TRENDS IN AMERICAN EDUCATION 306
ASSESSING FACTORS IN LEARNING 307
THE BRITISH EFFORT AT SCHOOL REFORM 320
DROPOUT PROBLEMS 321
FEDERAL POLICY IN ELEMENTARY AND
   SECONDARY EDUCATION 326
POSTSECONDARY EDUCATION 327
CONCLUSION 328
Questions for Discussion 329
Key Concepts 329
Suggested Readings 329

11 **Health Care: Diagnosing a Chronic Problem** 331

INTRODUCTION: THE GROWING CONSENSUS ON THE NEED
   FOR CHANGE 331
HEALTH CARE EXPENDITURES: THE HEART OF THE PROBLEM 333
IMPERFECT MARKETS: IMPACT ON HEALTH CARE PRICE,
   SUPPLY, AND DEMAND 337
A CLOSER LOOK AT THE MALADIES OF AMERICAN HEALTH CARE 341
TYPES OF MEDICAL INSURANCE COVERAGE 345
ORGANIZATIONAL CHANGE 364
THE UNINSURED 365
PUBLIC DISSATISFACTION: THE GROWING CONSENSUS
   FOR REFORM 370
CHOICES IN POLICY ALTERNATIVES 370
CONCLUSION 379
Questions for Discussion 380
Key Concepts 381
Suggested Readings 381

12 Environmental Policy: Domestic and International Issues   382

INTRODUCTION   382
EMERGING ENVIRONMENTALISM   383
MARKET FAILURE AND THE ENVIRONMENT   387
ENVIRONMENTAL PROTECTION AND RATIONAL CHOICE   389
POPULATION   398
POLICY RESPONSES   402
ETHICS AND ENVIRONMENTALISM   406
CONCLUSION   407
Questions for Discussion   407
Key Concepts   408
Suggested Readings   408

13 American Foreign Policy   409

INTRODUCTION   409
THE SETTING OF AMERICAN FOREIGN POLICY   410
CHARACTERISTICS OF AMERICAN FOREIGN POLICY   410
AN AMERICAN SENSE OF DESTINY AND MORAL SUPERIORITY   411
PRAGMATISM   411
AMERICAN FOREIGN POLICY MAKING   413
THE GLOBAL ACTORS   420
COMING IN OUT OF THE COLD WAR   426
FOREIGN POLICY AFTER THE COLD WAR   434
FUTURE CHALLENGES AND FOREIGN POLICY   436
ETHICAL CONCERNS AND FOREIGN POLICY   436
NATIONALISM AND ETHNIC CONFLICT   438
ECONOMIC THEMES   439
CONCLUSION   443
Questions for Discussion   444
Key Concepts   444
Suggested Readings   444

INDEX   447

PREFACE

Why We Wrote *Public Policy: Perspectives and Choices*

This book is about the theoretical foundations and practical realities of public policy. In it we present public choice theory to help students analyze and evaluate contemporary policy issues. Understanding the implications of public policy choices is essential for every educated citizen. For over two centuries, the United States has been an inspiring example to the rest of the world representing what an informed and involved citizenry could achieve. Democratic government has come to be regarded as a positive instrument in promoting the general welfare. This has prompted many nations with non-democratic pasts to turn to participatory government and market solutions to resolve policy dilemmas.

At the same time, however, many Americans have become increasingly detached from public life. Attacks on the institutions of American government as *the problem* make it extraordinarily difficult to craft compromises needed to produce effective policies. Unfortunately this tactic is increasingly used by assorted groups to block policies inimical to their interests. Political pundits and politicians often focus on symbols leading to polarization and paralysis, rather than on the substantive issues that might lead to consensus and real problem solving. The ability to assess the perspectives of liberal and conservative ideologies that sometimes work against collective responsibility and to assess proposed policy alternatives is enhanced if one has a grounding in policy theory.

Public policy, as a discipline, is optimistic. It is based on the profoundly significant belief that the citizenry in a democratic society can take responsible actions to improve the national well-being.

The Plan of This Text. What Is Different?

Introductory public policy textbooks often ignore basic concepts used by policy analysts and social scientists. Some begin by encouraging students to discuss controversial substantive issues without any development of theory, while others study public policy merely as process, or encourage the use of model(s) with which to examine policy. Although political scientists have long used these approaches, interdisciplinary techniques in recent decades have contributed important new understandings. We believe it is important for students to be thoroughly grounded in the application of such concepts as opportunity costs, production possibilities, market failures, the median voter, and externalities among others. The first five chapters provide a tour of the basic elements of a "political scientist's way of thinking" about policy issues, while always keeping in mind that politicians pay more attention to voters than to policy analysts.

These chapters contain applications dealing with fundamental aspects of issues including scarcity, rational self-interest, the tragedy of the commons, the free rider problem, market **and** government failures, and other issues relating to the political, economic, and philosophical basis of public policy. Although the leading professional journals in public policy now routinely deal with these topics, they are frequently ignored in public policy texts. We believe that these topics should be presented as an essential part of the "core" of public policy that students will remember long after the course is over.

We think these principles are important because they are fundamentally very logical, but often misunderstood by intelligent laypersons. Almost every idea in public policy can be explained clearly in language understandable to the average reader. We have done our utmost to accomplish this task. At the same time we try to avoid oversimplification of the complexities of many policy issues. All texts in public policy proffer a variety of "real world" issues of public policy. We try to elevate the policy problem by high-lighting political, philosophical, or economic problems that underlie the issue. We find that policy issues that are interwoven with theoretical perspectives and choices work well.

The world is changing rapidly. And it is shrinking. In the past it made sense for texts to treat public policy in America in isolation from international comparisons or linkages. Today what goes on in the rest of the world has a far greater impact on a variety of policy issues in the United States than was the case 50 years ago. Other countries have faced the same policy dilemmas as the United States and frequently they have made different policy choices that can inform U.S. policy alternatives.

Finally we have tried to emphasize that, although capitalism appeals to the individual's self-interest, public policy goes beyond the narrow appeal to individual self interest, to the larger purpose to "promote the general welfare." All capitalist societies recognize that market failures contribute to outcomes that are unacceptable. Individual welfare is inextricably bound up with the general welfare of others. The study of public policy involves the thoughtful use of interdisciplinary insights and empirical evidence in pursuit of "social justice." Government involvement is inevitable. The goal is for wise involvement. Responsive government must be based on a broad consensus of the citizenry to provide wise policy.

Acknowledgments

We are indebted to so many people for their help in writing this book that it is difficult to know where to begin thanking them. Our parents imparted a strong sense of social justice and fairness to us. We were also encouraged by them to be informed about political issues and to always be open to new ways of seeing things. This debt cannot be repaid, only acknowledged.

Second, our spouses, Mimi and Dave, have encouraged us in this undertaking. They have also taken an active part in reading each draft and made detailed comments and suggestions for improvement.

Others have helped in numerous ways from checking footnotes to tracking down sources. Among them we owe special thanks to Barbara Breeden, Dr. Katherine Dickson, William McQuade, Mary Ellen McQuade, Barbara Yoakum, Florence Todd, Kari Horney, and George Rush. Debra Janes spent hours recovering a lost computer file and for this we are extremely grateful. Many of our colleagues helped by providing information, sources, articles, and, frequently unknowingly, through conversations that stimulated new ideas, or resulted in the modification of our own. They have contributed to making this a better book and have saved us from many errors. Among them are: John Fitzgerald, Robert Bender, Arthur Rachwald, Clair Morris, Eric Fredland, Tom Zak, Karl Lamb, and Bob Rau.

Throughout the entire process there were many reviewers who read and reread our drafts and made many helpful comments: William Arp, III, Louisiana State University; Robert Bartlett, Purdue University; Dennis Daley, North Carolina State University; David Davis, University of Toledo; John Hird, University of Massachusetts–Amherst; Michele Hoyman, University of Missouri–St. Louis; Karen Hult, Virginia Polytechnic Institute; Susan Hunter, West Virginia University; Gary Klass, Illinois State University; Eugene McGregor, Indiana University; Mark Peterson, University of New Mexico; Terrel Rhodes, University of North Carolina; Evan Ringquist, Texas Tech University; David Robertson, University of Missouri–St. Louis; Susan Tenenbaum, Baruch College; and R. Lawson Veasey, University of Central Arkansas.

Several parts of the book were classroom tested by midshipmen at The United States Naval Academy, students at The Johns Hopkins University, and at Central Michigan University. These students made helpful comments which we have tried to incorporate in the final draft of the manuscript.

Particular acknowledgment must be made to those at McGraw-Hill who have been extremely thoughtful and helpful throughout the entire process of producing this text. Rose Arlia was extremely enthusiastic and helpful from the very beginning in getting our manuscript on the road. Peter Labella, the political science editor, guided the project through each step. He has always been available for advice and direction and has managed to keep us on track. Annette Bodzin has been extremely helpful in turning the manuscript into the final product. Finally we have been most fortunate that Lester Strong edited our manuscript with painstaking care and saved us from many mistakes. We are deeply indebted to him for his suggestions for improvement of the final draft. For any errors that remain, the authors blame each other.

Charles L. Cochran

Eloise F. Malone

PUBLIC POLICY
PERSPECTIVES AND CHOICES

BASIC CONCEPTS IN PUBLIC POLICY

We begin this book by introducing you to the vocabulary of public policy. The following pages define concepts students need to know to understand the policy process. The driving force pushing public policies is scarcity and rational self-interest. In a diverse society embracing different values and points of view, interests collide and compromises are unavoidable. The policy analyst must deal with practical questions of who will gain and who will lose by any given policy. Will government intervention improve upon a market solution? The analyst must also be aware of the need to examine the ideas regarding normative values of what is good for society as a whole.

WHAT IS PUBLIC POLICY?

Public opinion polls confirm that people worry about their economic well-being more than any other concern. People worry about educating their children and meeting mortgage payments. They worry about the high cost of health care, the needs of an elderly parent, the threat of unemployment. These concerns cut across age groups. Students worry about finding a job when they graduate, paying their rent, making insurance payments. Many people express concern for economic problems like federal budget deficits, taxes, and inflation. Many are increasingly aware that personal well-being is somehow related to broader social trends. This relationship is the domain of public policy, though few really understand how the public policy process works or how it affects them personally.

Public policy consists of political decisions for implementing programs to achieve societal goals. These decisions hopefully represent a consensus of values. When analyzed, public policy consists of a plan of action or program and a statement of objectives, in other words, a map and a destination. The objectives statement, the destination, tells us **what we want to achieve with policy**. Objectives also describe **who** will be affected by policy. Public policy program statements, the map, **outline the process or the necessary steps to achieve the policy objectives**. They tell us **how** to do it. For example, a newly proposed public policy for national health care would include an objective statement explaining why a health care policy matters along with a detailed health care program or procedure. The program might be "managed competition," or perhaps a "Canadian single-payer" program. Usually, the program stage is when the rubber hits the road and people are forced to face up to the values and principles they espouse.

Ultimately public policy is about people, their values and needs, their options and choices. The basic challenge confronting public policy is the fact of *scarcity*. We cannot have everything we want. Unfortunately available resources are limited, while for practical purposes human wants are limitless. Scarcity is an ever present attribute of the human condition. Because of the combination of limited resources and unlimited wants, we must choose among the goods and services to be produced and in what quantities. Because of scarcity, there is a need for governmental organizations (such as the Departments of Education, Energy, Defense, Health and Human Services, or Treasury, and so forth) to allocate resources among competing potential users. Conversely, if there were no scarcity, we would not have to make choices between which goods or services to produce.

Poverty and scarcity are not synonymous. Scarcity exists because there are insufficient resources to satisfy all human wants. If poverty were eliminated, scarcity would remain because even though everyone might have a minimally acceptable standard of living, society still would not have adequate resources to produce everything people desired.

OPPORTUNITY COSTS

Public policy focuses on the **CHOICES** individuals and governments make. The saying that **there is no such thing as a free lunch** indicates that, because of scarcity, choices must be made which preclude other alternatives.[1] This may seem an obvious point, but many often assume that there **is** a free lunch. For instance many people speak of "free public schools," or the need for "free medical care," or "free highways." The problem is that "free" suggests no opportunities forfeited and no sacrifice. This is not the case, however, as the resources that provide education, health care, or highways could have been used to produce other goods.

Whenever we make a choice, there is a cost. This cost equals the value of the most desired goods or services forgone. In other words, to chose one alternative means that we sacrifice the opportunity to choose a different alternative. For example, when you decide to enroll in college rather than get a job, the opportu-

---

[1] The statement is accurate when referring to the market in the long run. However, it is not necessarily true in the polity in the short run. There are many public policies in which taxes paid by some people are redistributed to provide benefits for others. For example middle-income taxpayers may provide funds for food stamps for the poor. Those providing the largesse for others usually want spending reductions, while the recipients of the benefits favor more resources.

nity cost of college includes not only the cost of tuition and other expenses, but also the forgone salary. The **opportunity cost** of any government program is determined by the most valuable alternative use. A fixed amount of money, say $100 billion, can be used to buy military goods, or an equivalent amount of social goods (education or health care), but it cannot be used to purchase both goods simultaneously. A decision to have more of one good is also a decision to have less of other goods.

The opportunity cost principle can be illustrated. Figure 1-1 summarizes the hypothetical choices in what political economists call a production possibilities curve. This **production possibilities curve (PPC)** or **production possibilities frontier (PPF)** provides a menu of output choices between any two alternatives. **Think of it as a curve representing tradeoffs.** It illustrates the hard choices we must make when resources are scarce, or the opportunity costs associated with the output of any desired quantity of a good. It also illustrates the indirect effect of **factors of production** defined as land, labor, and capital. Our ability to alter the mix of output depends on the ease with which the factors of production can be shifted from one area to another. For example, with the collapse of communism the government is trying to shift production from the defense industry to the civilian sector.

In Fig. 1-1 the economy is at point *A* but conservatives want to pull it to point *B* while liberals prefer point *C*, resulting in a political struggle. Both could get the quantity they want through economic growth (point *D*). Even at point *D* both soon find that their wants are greater than the scarce resources available. And the tug-of-war would soon begin on the new PPF. *Note:* Efficient points lie on the PPF. The economy cannot operate outside its production frontier with current resources and technology. It is not desirable to operate inside the frontier. Note that point *E*

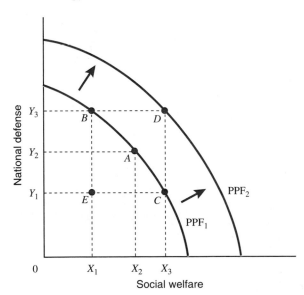

FIGURE 1-1
Changing tradeoffs between goods. Economic growth indicated by a shift from PPF$_1$ to PPF$_2$ (where PPF = production possibilities frontier). Both liberals & conservatives get more. *(Source: Adapted from Roger A. Arnold,* Macroeconomics, *West Publishing, New York, 1989, p. 30. Reprinted by permission. Copyright 1989 by West Publishing Company. All rights reserved.)*

is a feasible output combination but not a desirable one. Why? Because by moving to *B*, for instance, the economy could produce as much social welfare as at *E* but it could also produce considerably more national defense. Or by moving to *C* more social welfare could be produced without sacrificing the production of defense. Production at point *E* means that the economy's resources are not being used efficiently.

As we move more factors of production from the production of national defense toward social welfare, we must give up ever-increasing quantities of defense in order to get more social welfare and vice versa. **This is so universal a phenomenon that it is referred to as the law of increasing opportunity costs**. It states that the opportunity cost of producing additional units of one good increases as more resources are used to produce that good. Or, stated differently, in order to get more of one good in a given period, the production of other goods must fall by ever-increasing amounts.

Production possibilities are not fixed for all time. As more resources or better technology becomes available, production possibilities increase. As population increases, the number of potential workers increases production possibilities. An improvement in the quality of the labor force, such as through improved education, or investment in new plants and equipment, can also increase production possibilities. The outward shift of the PPF is at the heart of an increase in economic growth. This also means a reduction of opportunity costs and a potential increase in an overall standard of living.

The points along the production possibility curve or frontier indicate that many bundles of goods can be produced with the same resources. Consequently, movement along the PPF demonstrates that most changes in public policy are modest or **incremental** shifts. Policy changes are usually, but not always, relatively small, and are typically made with **current conditions** in mind. Hence the best predictor of what the federal budget will be next year is the current budget. The decision to change the budget is made at the **margin**. Essentially, **decisions at the margin** mean that we focus on the effects of small changes in particular activities. Policy makers usually consider marginal not total benefits and costs and, as a result, we are not faced with all-or-nothing choices.

Studying the PPF helps us see that choosing what mix of goods and services to produce is the essence of public policy considerations. A nation may face a guns-versus-butter choice in a period of high threats to national security, and environmental protection versus health care might come to the fore in peacetime. Shifts outward in the PPF represent growth; however the production possibilities curve says nothing about the desirability of any particular combination of goods and services. To understand this, we have to know more than **what choices have been made**. We must also know **why and how individuals and groups make choices** and **who benefits**.

SOCIAL CHOICE

Resource scarcity sets up the conditions for social choice. It is important to emphasize that choices are ultimately made by individuals. The press may report that "the Congress passed a bill," or that "a divided Supreme Court decided . . . ," but these are summary expressions of a group decision-making process. Actually a majority of the **individual** members of Congress voted for a bill, or a majority of the **individual** members of the Court decided a case before it. The mechanism for aggregating individual choices to arrive at collective decisions is democratic majority rule. The democratic process translates the private interests of individual human beings into group decisions. Interested individuals freely express their preferences and decide, in the aggregate, what the public policy decision will be. However, as we shall examine later, public opinion and the voting process may provide very weak guidance to political elites.

While individual choice is the basic unit of public policy analysis, there are often situations in which we treat an organization such as a government agency, a lobbying group, or even a family as a **black box**. A black box is a gadget whose output is known even though its internal workings are not completely known. Mechanisms such as television sets or computers are, for most, black boxes. In the public policy realm, in some instances we will open the black box to examine exactly how and why certain individual and group decisions are made. It is of crucial importance that as students of public policy we understand what goes on within the black box of the "political system." We need to know how policy is produced within the institutional processes of the political environment and how voters, interest groups, and political parties behave.

Rational Self-Interest

The conventional view of policy making in America is that people act on the basis of self-interest in public and private affairs. The "public interest" may be understood as the entirety of these individual preferences expressed as choices. Society is improved when some people's preferences can be satisfied without making other people worse off. Usually we assume the economic market will serve best to improve society. Public policies are needed when they make improvements more efficiently than the market.[2] This is not a statement of how public policies are actually made, but how they are justified.[3]

Individuals may make decisions using a variety of methods from reasoned logic to flipping a coin to tradition. Public policy is interested in purposeful **rational** choice. In this sense, **rational behavior** simply means making choices the consumer believes will maximize personal satisfaction or utility. Adam Smith simply described this as "the desire of bettering our condition" which begins at birth and never leaves until we go to our graves.

Since the concept of **rational self-interest** is often the source of misunderstanding, it is important to clarify its meaning.[4] Rational self-interest means that individuals have preferences. People **intend** to act in such a way to achieve those

---

[2] As an economic term, efficiency is defined as maximizing output at the lowest possible cost.

[3] Robert B. Reich, *The Resurgent Liberal and Other Unfashionable Prophecies* (New York: Vintage Books, 1989), p. 259.

[4] For an excellent summary of rational self-interest, see Henry Demmert, *Economics: Understanding the Market Process* (New York: Harcourt Brace Jovanovich, 1991), pp. 4–6.

preferences when the expected benefits exceed the extra costs of available choices. Rational behavior does not mean that individuals never make what, in retrospect, was a bad decision. Sometimes people, even intelligent people, make mistakes. But only a self-destructive individual will knowingly choose an inferior alternative to a more preferred one. The concept of rational self-interest also suggests that an individual would never **knowingly** choose a higher-cost means of achieving a given end when a lower-cost alternative is available. In short, people will attempt to **maximize** the difference between the expected benefits and the costs of their choices.

Rational self-interest also suggests that **individuals will react to alterations in costs and benefits in predictable ways**. If the cost of health care rises in real terms (adjusted for changes in inflation), less will be demanded. Drivers will buckle their seat belts if the perceived benefit (reduced risk of injury) outweighs the cost (the time spent buckling and the discomfort of the restraint). But, if the cost of their use is viewed as exceeding the benefit, seat belts will remain unbuckled. People will try to reduce costs and increase benefits to themselves.

Rational self-interest arouses ambivalence in many people. It evokes images of reason and informed decision on the one hand, but on the other hand suggests a sophisticated self-centered behavior. **Rational self-interest is not the same as selfishness or greed.**[5] It does not deny altruism. Individuals may act out of altruism in working in soup kitchens or in homeless shelters. However, rational self-interest does suggest that the altruistic behavior of individuals will be affected by changing perceptions of costs and benefits. For example, if tax deductions for charitable contributions are reduced or eliminated, such contributions will decline. Conversely increasing the tax benefit for charitable contributions will result in their increase.[6] The corollary to the point that rational self-interest does not coin-

[5] It is important to note that selfishness and self-interest are not the same. An individual who suffers a broken arm in a fall and seeks medical attention is acting in his or her self-interest, but we would not accuse that individual of being selfish because of that action. By the same token, obeying the law may well be in one's self-interest, but it is not selfish conduct.

Selfish conduct is behavior that disregards the interests of others in situations in which their interests should not be ignored. For example, to take an abundant supply of food on a camping trip is not selfish, but to refuse some of one's excess food to a hiker who has been lost and without food for days would be selfish.

[6] Opinions regarding what motivates individual choices are often raised in public policy discussions. There is an often heard contention that there are no truly altruistic acts. **Unselfish** acts, such as volunteering to work in a soup kitchen to feed the hungry, make people **feel morally correct** by giving them a clear conscience. Thus actions are altruistic only at a superficial level. Upon closer examination, the motivation to act "altruistically" is really to achieve the self-satisfaction of thinking of one's self as being a good person.

To derive satisfaction from helping others does not make one selfish. The unselfish person **does** derive satisfaction from helping others, while the selfish person does not. The truly selfish person is unconcerned about the suffering of others. It is sophistry to conclude that, because an individual finds satisfaction in helping to feed the poor, she or he is selfish. If we ask **why** someone gains satisfaction from volunteering to work in a soup kitchen, it is because the individual cares about other people, even if they are strangers; the volunteer does not want them to go hungry, and is willing to take action to help them. If the individual were not this kind of person, he or she would receive no satisfaction in helping others; this feeling of satisfaction is a mark of unselfishness, not of selfishness. See James Rachels, *The Elements of Moral Philosophy* (New York: McGraw-Hill, 1986), pp. 56–60.

cide with selfishness is the observation that rational self-interest does not mean individuals are motivated solely by the pursuit of material goods. Individuals may be motivated by love, justice, power, and other abstract influences. It is still true, however, that economic welfare may often be the basis for achieving even many nonmaterial goals.

Rational self-interest does not mean that people make the best decisions. Mistakes will still be made. Decisions are usually made under conditions of limited information. The costs associated with acquiring all the relevant information may be too high, or the information required for utility-maximizing behavior may not be available. For example, a government may formulate foreign policy based on intelligence findings. These intelligence findings are the best information available about another country's policies. Failures of foreign policy occur when there is an incorrect assessment of the intelligence information, resulting in mistakes and failures in that foreign policy.

When the full range of information needed to make a truly rational, self-interested choice is unavailable or too great for a person to adequately assimilate, then the **process of choice** rather than the outcome of the process can still be considered rational. Behavior may be procedurally rational when it is the outcome of appropriate, though incomplete, consideration based on incomplete information.

None of the foregoing is meant to suggest that individuals consciously calculate benefits and costs before selecting an alternative. Rational self-interest describes **behavior** not **thought processes**.[7] A physicist would describe the forces involved in achieving balance in riding a bicycle quite differently than the average adolescent riding one. However, the child riding a bike will act as if he or she has a physicist's understanding when, in fact, he or she does not.

Rational self-interest is an assumption about the way people **do** behave, and is not a judgment about how they **should** behave. The term "rational" does not indicate approval or disapproval of the goal itself.

The Tragedy of the Commons

Any discussion of rational self-interested behavior should point out that individual rationality and group rationality are not identical and may even be opposed. To understand this dilemma, we consider a metaphorical story written by biologist Garrett Hardin. Hardin asks us to assume that several farmers use a common pasture to graze their sheep. The total number of sheep grazing this pasture is at the maximum sustainable amount of grass the pasture can yield to maintain the sheep. It is in the farmers' collective interest not to allow any additional sheep to graze in this pasture and to try to secure an agreement among themselves to that effect.

But, since the sheep are the sole means of livelihood for each farmer, the number of sheep each farmer has directly relates to the income his family has. For each farmer, therefore, the rational strategy is to sneak additional sheep into his flock to graze in the common meadow. The farmer clandestinely breaking the agreement

[7] Rachels, *The Elements of Moral Philosophy*, pp. 5–6.

Calvin and Hobbes

by Bill Watterson

will obtain the whole benefit of the additional sheep. The cost in overgrazing will be shared by all the farmers, though each individual's cost will be small.

Each farmer has an incentive to act according to a short time horizon to improve his personal well-being. But at some point in the future this behavior, though individually rational, will result in the disintegration of the entire common from overgrazing. The individual farmer is seeking immediate large gains over what appear to be smaller losses in the remote future. **The moral of the metaphor is that individual rational self-interested behavior to maximize private gain may be suboptimal in the long run.**

The story concerns what policy analysts call "the public interest" and what economists call "collective goods." The ideas revealed in the "Tragedy of the Commons" undermine Adam Smith's laissez-faire assumption that self-interested behavior will maximize social benefit. Many of those who identify themselves as *libertarian* in the 1990s were drawn from conservative circles and the "New Left" of the 1960s and 1970s, both of which groups applied the same laissez-faire logic to politics that others applied to economics.

More importantly, public policy originates in our understanding of the public interest. Appealing to that public interest is difficult because it mirrors the disagreement among competing concepts of social morality and justice. In many situations there may be no conflict between acting in one's self-interest **and** the interest of others, or the common good, simultaneously. More frequently, however, if people act in their narrow self-interest, it becomes impossible to achieve the common good. A healthy public spirit, the social form of altruism, sometimes referred to as social responsibility, is essential for a healthy democracy. A willingness to accept the general interest as one's own is what President Kennedy referred to when he said, "Ask not what your country can do for you, but what you can do for your country."

SOCIAL JUSTICE

Public policy analysis is by its very nature **normative**. Normative analysis raises questions about what policy **should be**. Questions about what "ought" to be shape the dissatisfaction felt over current policy, as well as the proposals for a "preferred" policy in the future. Normative policy analysis is concerned with how the individual justifies the use of state authority to pursue one purpose rather than another.

Because self-interest inevitably conflicts with the interest of others, it is impossible to achieve an absolute moral consensus about appropriate government policy. A fundamental problem is that the American polity lacks a practical agreement on the meaning of justice. The result is that conflict and not consensus is at the center of modern politics and public policy.

To illustrate the problem, consider a controversy between two individuals. One individual, Joan, is concerned with what she believes is the arbitrary nature of the distribution of wealth and income. She is particularly distressed over the accompanying inequality of power between those with considerable wealth and those without. She concludes that the poor are virtually powerless to improve their condition, while the wealthy are able to increase their wealth and power with ease. The great inequalities in wealth and power are considered **unjust** by Joan. She concludes that government efforts to redistribute wealth in the direction of the poor through taxes is demanded by simple justice. This help by government activity will lead to greater individual freedom and justice. Joan therefore decides to vote for political candidates who support such taxes and her notion of justice.

The second individual, Robert, has worked hard all his life to achieve certain goals in life. These include financial independence that permits him to purchase a house, to travel, to send his children to college, and sufficient investments to permit a comfortable retirement. He now finds his goals jeopardized by proposals to raise taxes to reduce the deficit and to provide housing for the indigent. He regards these policies that threaten his goals as **unjust** because they deprive him of his financial resources against his will. He believes that justice demands the full entitlement of each person to the fruits of his or her own labor, and that each individual should have the complete rights to use and control them.

If the economy is growing rapidly enough, Joan's projects may be implemented without threatening Robert's goals. In that case they may both vote for the same political candidates. But if the economy is stagnant, and either Joan's or Robert's policies must be sacrificed to the other, it becomes clear that each has a view of justice that is logically incompatible with the other. In such cases each will use their competing concepts of justice to promote incompatible social goals.

John Rawls has received considerable attention for his treatise *A Theory of Justice*,[8] in which he addresses the question of what constitutes a just distribution of goods in society, what kinds and how much. He holds that principles of just distribution may limit legitimate acquisition. If applying principles of just distribution requires a redistributive tax or the taking of property through eminent domain, that acceptance of the taking of property is the price that must be paid to achieve a broader justice in the community.

---

[8] John Rawls, *A Theory of Justice* (Cambridge, MA: Harvard University Press, 1971).

Robert Nozick argues in his book *Anarchy, State, and Utopia* in response to Rawls that each individual has a right in justice to the product of his or her labor unless or until that individual chooses to give some part of it to another person (or to a central authority for redistribution).[9] If the result of individual acquisition is a gross inequality between individuals, justice requires that the disparity be accepted.

The price to be paid for justice in each definition must be paid by another group. Neither of these contending principles of justice is socially neutral.[10] American culture has no accepted rational criterion for deciding between rights based on lawful entitlement versus claims based on need. However, Rawls and Nozick both suggest rational principles to appeal to the contending parties. Some, like Rawls, define justice in relation to an equitable distribution in society. For them, justice is based upon a consideration of the present-day distribution. Justice should have priority over economic efficiency. This leads them to an appeal against absolute entitlement. Others, like Nozick, argue legal acquisition of wealth and income in the past is alone relevant; present-day distribution is irrelevant.[11] They appeal against distributive rules to a justice based upon entitlement.

Neither Rawls or Nozick refer to what is **deserved** based upon justice. But concepts of what is **deserved** or **merited** are implied. Nozick argues that individuals are **entitled** in justice to their wealth and property, and not that they **deserve** that wealth and property. However, groups supporting this position invariably argue that they are entitled to what they have acquired through their efforts, or the efforts of others who have legally passed title to them. Rawls protests on behalf of the poor that their poverty is **undeserved** and therefore unwarranted. The child born to the migrant worker is no less deserving than the child born to a family of wealth and privilege. Rawls called this the "natural lottery." Both complain about perceived **injustice**.

The debate over taxes further illustrates this difference in values between distributive justice and entitlement theory. The modern opposition to any tax increases or government expenditure policies originates in the strongly negative attitude toward taxation among those who must pay them. Taxes, they argue, are paid primarily by the haves, while benefits accrue primarily to the have nots. Many of the more fortunate members of society oppose all taxation, but their opposition to the redistribution of wealth through tax policy is not put so crudely.

---

[9] Robert Nozick, *Anarchy, State, and Utopia* (New York: Basic Books, 1974). This work is in part a response to John Rawls. The extension of Nozick's thought leads to a view that the only form of economic life compatible with individualism is laissez faire capitalism.

Nozick's position is in the tradition of writers in the anarcho-capitalist tradition. His response to Rawls has attracted more comment than the writings of others with similar views.

[10] See Alasdair Macintyre, *After Virtue: A Study in Moral Theory*, 2nd ed. (Notre Dame, IN: University of Notre Dame Press, 1984), especially Chap. 17, "Justice as a Virtue: Changing Conceptions," for an excellent comparison of the theory of John Rawls and Nozick's countering view.

[11] Nozick's critics point out that his thesis assumes that legitimate entitlements can be traced back to rightful acts of earliest acquisition. Based upon that criterion, however, there are few legitimate entitlements as most property has been inherited from those who originally used force or theft to steal the common lands of the first inhabitants.

A concern for liberty, the requirements of justice, efficiency, or the virtues of laissez faire capitalism are the most frequently cited justifications. Indeed it is perhaps naive to expect the privileged to respond sympathetically to policies that transfer resources from themselves to others, particularly since there is no community consensus on virtue. The affluent attack government as an arbitrary, profligate, liability that is only held in check by relentless attention to its defects and efforts to hold it in check. Those with the temerity to promise increased services for the needy are promptly labeled "big spenders."

The Rawls-Nozick philosophical debate is an extension of the economic and political rift between different groups in society. Not only is there no value consensus in public policy, but modern political competition is a less violent form of civil war.

POLITICS AND ECONOMICS

How societies decide to utilize their scarce resources is determined by a variety of factors, along with values, including the history, culture, socioeconomic development, and forms of government and economic organization of those societies. The classic definition of political science is that it is a study of **"Who gets what, when, and how in and through government."**[12] Consequently, politics involves the struggle over the allocation of resources based on the values of the society. **Public policy is the outcome of the struggle in government over who gets what.**[13] Economics has been defined as **"the science which studies human behavior as a relationship between ends and scarce means which have alternative uses."**[14]

These definitions of the two disciplines of political science and economics have a great deal in common. Both are concerned with studying human behavior in competition for scarce resources. Public policy exists at the confluence of these disciplines (see Chap. 2). As such, any definition of public policy will reflect these origins. Most definitions of public policy are rather imprecise, and we will offer only a working definition. For our purposes **public policy** includes **actions of government to convert competing private objectives into public commitments, as well as decisions *not* to take action. Public policies are purposeful decisions made by authoritative actors in a political system, recognized because of their formal position, as having the responsibility for making binding choices among goals and alternatives for the society.**[15] Public policy is a form of government control usually expressed in a law, a regulation, or an order. Since it reflects an intent of government, it is backed by an authorized reward or incentive or a

[12] Harold Lasswell, *Politics: Who Gets What, When, How* (Cleveland: Meridian Books, 1958).
[13] Thomas R. Dye, Harmon Zeigler, and S. Robert Lichter, *American Politics in the Media Age*, 4th ed. (Pacific Grove, CA: Brooks/Cole, 1992), p. 2.
[14] Roger A. Arnold, *Macroeconomics* (St. Paul, MN: West Publishing Co., 1989), p. 6.
[15] See Larry N. Gerston, *Making Public Policy: From Conflict to Resolution* (Glenville, IL: Scott, Foresman and Co., 1979), pp. 4–6. See also Jay M. Shafritz, *Dictionary of American Government and Politics* (Chicago: The Dorsey Press, 1988), p. 456.

penalty. The laws reflect the expedients of policy in the struggle as politicians respond to the articulated will of the voters.

The assumption voiced in the Declaration of Independence that individuals create government to secure their rights poses a paradox in contemporary American public policy. Men and women can advance their individual freedom only by giving up the anarchistic freedom of no government. **Government policy must be coercive and constrain the individual in order to promote the general welfare and secure order and predictability.** People organize out of a dread fear of uncertainty.

PUBLIC POLICY TYPOLOGY

One practical means of categorizing policies is based upon the technique of control used by policy makers. Three categories of control are **patronage, regulatory, and redistributive policies.**[16]

Patronage (or promotional) policies include those government actions that provide incentives for individuals or corporations to undertake activities they would only reluctantly undertake without the promise of a reward. As distinct from policies that threaten punishment for noncompliance, this kind of policy motivates people to act by using "carrots." Not surprisingly, it is the recipients of the rewards who often convince the government to subsidize individuals or corporations to act. **These promotional techniques can be classified into three types: subsidies, contracts, and licenses.**

The use of subsidies has played a central role in the history of the United States. Alexander Hamilton wrote in his *Report on Manufactures*, one of the first policy planning documents in the administration of George Washington, that subsidies for American business should be provided by "pecuniary bounties" supplied by the government. Subsidies to business quickly became commonplace in America, ranging from land grants given to railroad companies to cash subsidies for the merchant marine fleet, for shipbuilders, and for the airline industry. Other subsidies to businesses have included loans to specific companies like the Chrysler Corporation or the recent broader savings-and-loan "bailout."

Subsidies have also been provided to individuals through such policies as land grants to farmers in the nineteenth century, or the current tax deductions allowed for interest on home mortgage payments.

Subsidies are typically made possible through the largesse of the American taxpayer. Since the cost is spread out among all the population, each person bears only a minuscule portion of the whole cost. There is little opposition to these kinds of subsidies. The threat of their removal can arouse intense reactions from their recipients, for whom their loss could entail significant financial hardship. However, subsidies are often attacked as "pork-barrel" programs, so every effort is

---

[16] See Theodore Lowi, "American Business, Public Policy, Case Studies and Political Theory," *World Politics* (July 1964), pp. 677–715. See also by the same author, *The End of Liberalism: The Second Republic of the United States* (New York: Norton, 1979).

made to tie such projects to some "high national purpose" (such as military defense) to avoid that label.

Contracting is also an important means of promoting particular policies. It can be used to encourage corporations to adopt certain behaviors, such as equal employment opportunity, which they might otherwise find burdensome.

In the same way, governments can through licensing grant the privilege of carrying on a particular activity. Licensing allows corporations or individuals to conduct a business or engage in a profession (e.g., a licensed pilot) that without the license is illegal. The government is therefore also able to regulate various sectors of the population and the economy through this process.

Regulatory policies allow the government to exert control over the conduct of certain activities. If patronage policies involve positive motivation (the use of carrots), then regulatory policies involve negative forms of control (the use of "sticks"). The most obvious examples of regulation techniques include civil and criminal penalties for certain behaviors. The immediate example that comes to mind is regulating criminal behavior. Other forms of regulated conduct are not necessarily criminal or immoral in themselves, but may have negative side effects. These activities are regulated not to eliminate the conduct, but to deal with the negative side effects. For example, a public utility may provide a community with the "desired good" of electricity, but there is a strong probability it will seek monopoly profits. The conduct of the utility is "regulated" rather than "policed" in a criminal sense in that the company is given an exclusive license to provide electrical energy to a given geographical area but in return the government holds the right to regulate the quality of service and the rates charged.

Other forms of regulatory policies that generate more controversy include environmental pollution, consumer protection, or employee health and safety concerns. Tax policy often may have as its primary purpose not raising revenue but regulating a certain type of behavior by making that behavior too expensive for most individuals or companies to engage in. By taxing a substance like gasoline, tobacco, or alcohol, the government encourages a reduction in the consumption of these products. Likewise, "effluent taxes" may raise the price of goods and services that pollute, which encourages companies to reduce their pollution to reduce or avoid the tax.[17]

Regulatory decisions frequently reallocate costs for those affected. Unlike promotional policies that appear to provide only benefits and thus to have only win-

---

[17] Taxation for the purpose of discouraging certain conduct or eliminating certain activities is often opposed on the grounds that the affluent can buy the right to behave in a manner that is prohibitive to the less wealthy. The charge is correct in that the affluent may be less deterred by the higher price of gasoline, alcohol, tobacco, or other products that cause pollution, than will the poor who may be eliminated from the market by the repressive features of the tax. However, exercising the right to buy the products will make the wealthy poorer. It should also be pointed out that, by discouraging the purchase of certain products, public health should improve and the environment become cleaner. The repressive nature of the tax may also be beside the point if the extra amount that the affluent pay exceeds the value we place on the harm caused by alcohol or tobacco consumption, or if a cleaner environment caused by less consumption of gas or other products that cause pollution results in the transference of real income to the population as a whole.

ners, regulatory policies are usually thought of in terms of winners and losers because the losses they cause are as obvious as their benefits.

Redistributive policies control people by managing the economy as a whole. The techniques of control involve fiscal (tax) and monetary (supply of money) policies. They tend to benefit one group at the expense of other groups through the reallocation of wealth. Changing the income tax laws in the 1980s, for example, significantly reduced the taxes of upper-income groups compared to other income groups in the society, although lower-income groups were taken off the tax roles altogether. The result was a decline in the middle class.[18] Since those who have power and wealth are usually reluctant to share those privileges, redistribution policies tend to be the most contentious. Many past policies aimed at redistributing wealth more equitably, even when initially successful, faced severe obstacles in their long-term viability. The 1960s' Great Society and War on Poverty programs are the most obvious examples. Programs with widely distributed benefits such as Social Security have enjoyed more success, because of the larger number of prople with a stake in their success.

Fiscal policy uses tax rates and government spending to affect total or aggregate demand. Each particular approach to taxing or spending can have a different impact on the overall economy, so political entrepreneurs often propose or initiate policies with the goal of achieving specific impacts. For example, President George Bush, faced with a sluggish economy in an election year, proposed a policy of stimulating the economy by cutting taxes to increase demand (and thereby employment). He also proposed cutting taxes on capital gains, a policy that would have benefited primarily higher-income people, with the claim that it would encourage real investment.[19]

Monetary techniques used by the Federal Reserve Board (the "Fed") also try to regulate the economy through policies directed at changing the rate of growth of the money supply or at manipulating interest rates (for more on this see Chap. 6).[20]

---

[18] See Richard Morin, "America's Middle-Class Meltdown," *The Washington Post*, December 1, 1991, p. C1. Reporting on several studies Morin stated that "the boom years of the 1980s were a bust for fully half of all Americans. At the same time, the safety net of social programs for the nation's poor was replaced by a safety net for the rich, speeding the decline of the middle class."

[19] **Capital gains** is the realized increase in the value of an asset. **Real** investment refers to the accumulation of real capital such as machinery or buildings rather than to financial investment (which refers to the acquisition of such paper instruments as bonds).

[20] The Federal Reserve System's control over the money supply is the key aspect of U.S. monetary policy. The Fed has three primary levers of power. The first concerns the reserve requirement. The Fed requires private banks to keep some fraction of their deposits in reserve. The reserves are held in the form of cash or as credits in the bank's reserve account at its regional Federal Reserve Bank. By changing the reserve requirement, the Fed can directly affect the ability of the banking system to lend money. The second lever concerns the Fed's discount rate. On occasion, private banks must go to the Fed to borrow some reserves. This is called "discounting" when the Fed lends reserves directly to the private banks. By raising or lowering the discount rate, the Fed changes the cost of money for banks and their incentive and ability to borrow. The third, and most important, lever involves the Fed's open-market operations, which directly alter the reserves of the banking system. When the Fed buys bonds, it increases the deposits (reserves) available in the banking system. If the Fed sells bonds, it reduces the reserves and restricts the amount of money available for lending.

PUBLIC POLICY AND ECONOMIC ORGANIZATION

Command and Market Economies

If political science is the study of who gets what, when, and how, then public policy may begin by examining the current state of affairs of who already has what, and how it was obtained. Two basic types of economic systems have emerged to deal with the problem of administering societal needs in response to scarcity. **Command (or planned) economies** are characterized by government ownership of nonhuman factors of production. Since the government allocates most resources, it also makes most of the decisions regarding economic activities. **Pure market (or capitalistic) economies** are characterized by private ownership of the nonhuman factors of production. Decision making is decentralized and most economic activities take place in the private sector.

Of course the real world is much more complex than these simple definitions indicate; there are simply no examples of pure capitalism or pure command economic systems. While there are some examples that are closer to the definitions than others, it is not possible to draw a line between pure capitalism and pure command (or socialist) economies and place countries squarely on either side.

Mixed capitalism combines some features of both types of economic organization. **Mixed capitalism** is a system in which most economic decisions are made by the private sector, but the government also plays a substantial economic and regulatory role.

What, How, and for Whom to Produce?

The major distinction between command and market systems can be viewed in terms of how they answer the three questions of what, how, and for whom to produce. In a command economy, the "what to produce" question is decided by the government in its overall economic blueprint. In a market society, **individual consumers** answer the "what" question; the government ignores it. Production of goods is in response to demand or "dollar votes."

The system must next decide how the goods will be produced. In a command economy, government planners decide how to produce the goods by issuing orders to the managers of state-owned enterprises. In a market economy, the "how" question is again ignored by the government. How goods are produced is answered by the available technology and the entrepreneurs' profit-motivated desire to produce most efficiently. Prices are the signals in a market economy for what and how to produce goods.

Clearly economic systems that rely on command are significantly less efficient than those that rely primarily on the market. Most noteworthy in this regard is the former Soviet Union, which became notorious for shoddy goods, shortages and surpluses in the market, absenteeism among the labor force, and an overall lack of innovation in products and production techniques. By the early 1990s, the standards of living in the command economies of the Soviet Union and Eastern Europe were falling further and further behind those of the economies of the United States, Western Europe, and Japan. Mikhail Gorbachev finally proclaimed that he supported the dismantling of the command economy in favor of **"mixed capitalism."**

Finally, in command economies the government determines to whom the goods will be distributed. In theory this occurs according "to one's needs." In practice it has often been charged that what is produced is distributed according to political or party loyalty. In a market economy, on the other hand, to whom the goods are to be distributed is again ignored by the government and public policy. The goods are distributed to those having what can be labeled as "rationing coupons." Dollar bills serve as rationing coupons. If you have sufficient dollar bills, you can purchase whatever you **demand** in the marketplace: food, Jaguar cars, health care, education, or homes. If you do not have these rationing coupons, the system will not recognize your needs, since entrepreneurs respond only to those having the means to demand (i.e., those willing and able to pay for the good in question). Thus, members of a pure market system would have to be willing to watch people starve to death in the streets, unless those starving could prevail upon some private charity to provide minimum support.

Since command and market systems have glaring weaknesses, we find that they rarely exist in a pure form. While command systems are very inefficient, pure market systems do not allocate resources in a way that most people are willing to tolerate. Hence **mixed capitalism** in the United States, and increasingly in the rest of the world, is the basis for an increasing number of politicoeconomic organizations. John Maynard Keynes, as Chap. 6 develops, was the theoretician of a partnership between government and private enterprise. In Keynesian economics, government is responsible for initiating policies that lead to full employment, while ownership of the means of production and profits remain in private hands.

The perceived legitimate public policy role for government is much greater in those countries emerging from command economies, or other varieties of socialism, than in countries living under mixed capitalism that evolved from more libertarian origins such as the United States. The American political and economic system begins with a bias in favor of a **laissez faire** attitude, which has come to mean a minimal role for government in private lives and distributional policies.

This is significant because, as we shall see, the existence of certain public policies that are taken for granted in many nations (such as a system of national health care) may be challenged as not even legitimate for government to consider undertaking by many people in the United States.

WHY GOVERNMENTS INTERVENE

What possible justification can there be for the government to displace the role of the individual in providing goods and services, especially if we agree that a market system is the most efficient system devised for the production of goods and services at the lowest possible prices? Often and perhaps usually the market does achieve the goal of being the most efficient method for resource allocation. There are situations, however, when markets fail to achieve the ideal economic efficiency. In a very literal sense, in fact, markets always "fail" because economic efficiency is a fabricated definition based upon a normative model of how the world **should** be. Perfect economic efficiency is a figment of the imagination. Market failure indicates that supply and demand forces have resulted in a mix of output that is different from the one society is willing to accept. It signifies that we are at a less than satisfactory point on the production possibilities curve. Some cases of market failure are so extreme, and the potential for corrective public policy action sufficiently available, that most people would support some form of governmental intervention to achieve a better output mix. Because of these limitations, no country relies exclusively on the free market to make all of its socioeconomic policy decisions.

Public Goods

Consumers in the marketplace express their collective answer to the question of *what* to produce by offering to pay higher or lower prices for certain goods, thus signaling their demand for those goods. The market mechanism works efficiently because the benefits of consuming a specific good or service are available only to those who purchase the product. A **private good** is a good or service whose benefits are confined to a single consumer and whose consumption excludes consumption by others. If it is shared, more for one must mean less for another. For example, the purchase of a hamburger by one individual effectively excludes others from consuming it. If the purchaser shares the hamburger with someone else, the portion shared cannot be consumed by the purchaser.

Certain other products in our society do not have the characteristic of private goods because they never enter the market system, so the market does not distribute them. These **public goods are indivisible and nonexclusive**—that is, their consumption by one individual does not interfere with their consumption by another. The air from a pollution-free environment can be inhaled by many people simultaneously, unlike a hamburger which cannot be consumed simultaneously by many individuals. No one can be excluded from the use of a public good. You can be denied the use of your neighbor's swimming pool, but you cannot be denied the protection provided by the nation's national defense network. If the national defense system works, it defends everyone under its umbrella whether they have contributed to its purchase or not.

Another characteristic of **public goods is that they can be provided only by collective decisions**. The purchase of private goods depends on an individual decision as to whether to spend one's income on hamburgers or swimming pools. But it is not possible for one person to decide to purchase national defense, dams, or weather services. The decision or agreement to buy a public good and the quantity of it to buy is made collectively.

There are few examples of pure public goods, but air pollution control and national defense come as close to meeting the characteristics that define public goods as anything can. Other examples that do not meet the criteria as clearly but nevertheless have enough of the characteristics to qualify as public goods in need of collective, governmental provision on grounds of economic efficiency include police protection and education. Police protection generally provides a safer environment for everyone living in an area even if one does not contribute to the purchase of that protection. Education is a similar good. The primary beneficiary of an education is the person educated. However, there are secondary benefits to society of a better educated work force. Moreover, the amount of education allotted to one person does affect the amount left over for others. The same could be said for highway space or the administration of justice.

The communal nature of public goods leads to a major problem in public policy known as the **free rider**. A free rider is someone who enjoys the benefits of someone else's purchase of a public good while bearing none of the costs of providing it. If we **both** will benefit from national defense, good public education, or pure air, the question arises as to who should pay for it. Each individual has an incentive to avoid payment, hoping to take a free ride on other people's "purchase." As a result, all parties will profess little interest in purchasing the good, hoping others will step forward, demand the good, and pay for it. This is a rational response for individuals with limited resources. Everyone will benefit from the good by more than their proportionate cost, but they would benefit even more if others paid the entire cost. Thus the good will not be purchased unless the government makes the purchase and requires everyone to pay his or her fair share through mandatory taxes.

How do we determine how many and what mix of public goods the government should purchase? By relying on a specific means of public decision making: voting. Because voting is a very imprecise mechanism that limits us to a "Yes" or a "No" for candidates, it does not make any distinctions regarding the myriad of issues that must be acted on collectively. Nor does it register the intensity of preferences by various individuals or groups. Therefore, we sometimes find ourselves with an oversupply and sometimes with an undersupply of public goods. But it is clear that the market mechanism cannot determine a desirable level of the output of public goods, and some kind of political technique of making public policy decisions must be used.

Not everyone agrees that turning the decision making over to the public policy mechanism of government constitutes a good solution. Many people believe that governmental processes to alter production choices or to redistribute goods and services do not promote efficiency. Therefore, in their view, whatever the deficiencies of market mechanisms, the market is still to be preferred over government intervention in matters of distribution.

Some **conservatives** tend to believe that some **public goods** could be treated as **private goods** and brought into the market system while reducing the role of government. For example, tolls could be charged on all roads and bridges for their maintenance. This would limit the building and repair of highways to the amount of demand expressed by those paying the tolls. We might charge an admission fee sufficient to pay for the services provided in "public parks," thereby reducing the number of those needing those services.[21] "Public libraries" could charge fees for their services to provide the budgets needed for salaries and the purchase of books and materials. "Public transportation" in cities could be required either to charge the fees necessary to operate profitably or to reduce their service, producing only that amount of service demanded by those paying the fares. According to conservatives, other areas of government operations could also be reduced through "privatization." For example, the operation and maintenance of prisons could be contracted out to private companies rather than being staffed by public employees.

The privatization of public goods and services in this manner would certainly produce them more or less as if they were private goods. However there are many difficulties associated with this approach. First, there are the technical difficulties of making some public goods private. How do you make national defense a private good? Also, this approach offends our sense of justice and equity. Do we really think that national or state parks should exist to be enjoyed only by those with sufficient income to pay for their upkeep?

Externalities

Market failure is closely associated with the characteristics of public goods. **Externalities** are the effects, either positive or negative, of the output of goods and services on a third party (someone other than the immediate producer or consumer), or put another way the difference between the private and social costs of a market activity. Whenever externalities are present, the preferences expressed in the marketplace will not be an accurate measure of the good's value to society. We experience market failure.

Imperfect Information

As noted, the market system is built on the assumption that individuals are **rational** and do not act capriciously, and that they have roughly accurate information about the market. Without adequate correct information, people cannot make decisions in their rational self-interest. In fact, most people do not have adequate information to make rational decisions. Developing or finding the information has a significant opportunity cost associated with it. Very few people have the resources or time to do a complete research job.

---

[21] See, for example, Dan Bechter, "Congested Parks—A Pricing Dilemma," *Monthly Review*, Federal Reserve Bank of Kansas City (June 1971). Overcrowding at public parks may reflect a distortion in the recreation market by charging too little for their use. It is suggested that such low pricing amounts to a misallocation of resources. Raising the price would help "clear" the market and relieve congestion. If the price of visiting national parks were increased, more people would substitute other leisure activities.

Information, then, can be considered a public good, or a good with positive external effects. Once the information is provided, it can be shared by any number of people. Once in the public domain, it is impossible to exclude anyone from using it. Information is a positive externality.

Manufacturers of consumer products, such as cigarettes, do not have an interest in advertising the health hazards associated with the use of their products. But ignorance about those hazards can be reduced by informing consumers, through mandatory labels on cigarette packages, that smoking is dangerous. The manufacturers may still advertise their cigarettes. But the mandatory labels attempt to mend omissions in the market system by introducing information so that individuals can make better choices.

Many people believe the government has a role in researching and disseminating various kinds of information relevant to consumer choices. For instance, the government might investigate and publicize information about the safety of different consumer products such as cars, ingredients in drugs, food additives, microwave ovens, and other potentially dangerous products.

There is a debate regarding how this remedy for market failure should be applied. **If** you accept the proposition that the individual is the best judge of his/her own welfare, then many argue that governmental actions should be limited to the **provision of information**. The government, having produced the information, should **not regulate the behavior of individuals**, according to this view. Once people have been supplied with all the relevant information, they should be permitted to make their own choices—to consume dangerous substances (e.g., to purchase tobacco products), or to purchase potentially dangerous products. Only if the risks extend beyond the user—meaning negative externalities exist involving third parties—may there be an argument for expanding the role of government beyond providing information. For example, those in favor of the right to a smoke-free work environment argue that the spillover effect of inhaling secondary smoke is hazardous to nonsmokers's health.

This view of the informational role of government is not followed consistently in practice. For example, the Pure Food and Drug Act prohibits the sale of certain harmful products but does not provide the option of informing consumers of the product's harmful effects.

Equity and Security

Public goods, externalities, and ignorance all cause resource misallocation. They result in the market mechanism failing to produce the optimal mix of output. Beyond a failure of *what* to produce, we may also find that *for whom* the output is produced violates our sense of fairness.

In general, the market mechanism answers the question of for whom to produce by distributing a larger share of output to those with the most rationing coupons (dollars). While this method is efficient, it may not accord with our view of what is socially acceptable. Individuals who are unemployed, disabled, aged, or very young may be unable to earn income and need to be protected from such risks inherent in life in a market economy. Government intervention may be sought for income redistribution through taxes and programs like unemployment compensation, Social Security, Medicare, and Aid to Families with Dependent Children (AFDC), which shift these risks to taxpayers as a whole.

Redistribution of income to reduce inequities also falls under the theory of public goods because it adds to public security. Without some redistribution, we could expect more muggings and thefts to occur as people sought to escape the consequences of poverty. Moreover, leaving inequalities of wealth solely to market mechanisms would produce the phenomenon of the free rider again. Some individuals would no doubt contribute to charities aimed at reducing poverty, and everyone would benefit from somewhat safer streets. But those who did not so contribute would be taking a free ride on those who did.

Society is therefore forced to confront tradeoffs between the efficiencies of the market system and our views of justice and equity. For example, it is true that current policies of unemployment compensation and welfare benefits may be structured in ways that prolong unemployment by a high benefit-reduction rate that decreases incentives to find employment, but those policies are solving other problems. Programs like Social Security reduce the incentive to save money, which provides capital formation for greater economic growth, but they too answer social needs we have been unable to provide for in other ways.

Every society has to deal with the question of what constitutes an equitable distribution of income. It is clear that no government policy is neutral on the question. Income distribution tends to reflect the biases of governments ranging from traditional laissez faire economics to theories of planned economies. The political process by which any society governs itself must ultimately decide what constitutes an acceptable inequality of wealth and income.

CONCLUSION

1 The crux of all of our public policy problems is to be found in the hard reality of limited (scarce) resources. The free market has proven a superb device for efficiently producing goods and services, based upon individual rational self-interest. Problems of scarcity, which are universal, require intervention. This suggests that solutions, whether left to market forces or government intervention, reflect values. There are a variety of possible solutions reflecting the biases and choices of the individuals proposing them.

2 It is important to keep in mind that efforts to relieve market imperfections (failures) by public policy will also be flawed. Just as the market solution falls short when measured against its ideal performance, so do government solutions fail when measured against their ideal aims. The question is whether government, which was created to "promote the general welfare," will provide solutions that will be less imperfect than market mechanisms.

3 Some people are so distrustful of government because of its inherent defects that they believe government cures are worse than the "market disease" that calls them forth.

4 Others argue that government may be the only actor that can improve market efficiency or alter economic and social costs, risks, and income distribution in a positive way. They argue that these problems can be solved, but that *most* solutions mean someone must accept significant economic losses. No one willingly accepts a loss. So people struggle to veto any solution that would impact negatively on them, or at minimum have the cost transferred to someone else, or another group. The effect is to produce "veto groups" waiting to aggressively fight any proposed public policy that would result in a loss to their position. Often, the political struggle that results causes a larger cost than gain for those attempting to effect the change. The result is often political and economic paralysis.

5 However, not all public policy solutions must be **zero-sum** solutions, where one group's net gains must be offset by another group's losses. There are non-zero-sum solutions. Achieving those usually involves increasing economic growth so there is more for everyone. But even this solution requires the intervention of government in the form of industrial policies, and many people see this as just another effort to have government provide a remedy no more promising than any the market itself can provide. The major economic competitors of the United States, including both Japan and Germany, have incorporated industrial policy as a key component of their public policies, but it is a controversial issue in the United States.

QUESTIONS FOR DISCUSSION

1 If society desires health care and a clean environment for everyone, why does the free market not provide it?
2 Explain the difference between self-interest and selfishness.
3 Explain how scarcity, choice, and opportunity costs are related and make public policy inevitable.
4 Is reliance upon the market to resolve policy issues inherently conservative, or is it inherently progressive?
5 Explain the different types of economic organization and how they answer the questions of what, how, and for whom to produce.

KEY CONCEPTS

Equity
Externalities
Free rider
Laissez faire
Mixed capitalism
Opportunity costs
Patronage techniques
Private goods
Production possibilities

Public goods
Pure market capitalism
Rational self-interest
Redistributional techniques
Regulatory techniques
Scarcity
Tragedy of the commons
Zero-sum

SUGGESTED READINGS

Henry J. Aaron, Thomas E. Mann, and Timothy Taylor (eds.), *Values and Public Policy* (Washington, DC: The Brookings Institution, 1994).

David R. Berman, *American Government, Politics and Policy Making*, 3rd ed. (Englewood Cliffs, NJ: Prentice-Hall, 1988).

Henry Demmert, *Economics: Understanding the Market Process* (New York: Harcourt Brace Jovanovich, 1991).

E. J. Dionne, Jr., *Why Americans Hate Politics* (New York: A Touchstone Book, Simon & Schuster, 1991).

Lawrence J. R. Herson, *The Politics of Ideas: Political Theory and American Public Policy* (Prospect Heights, IL: Waveland Press, 1984).

Stuart Nagle, *Public Policy: Goals, Means and Methods* (New York: St. Martin's Press, 1984).

Robert B. Reich, *The Resurgent Liberal and Other Unfashionable Prophecies* (New York: Vintage Books, 1989).

Steven E. Rhoads, *The Economist's View of the World: Government, Markets, and Public Policy* (New York: Cambridge University Press, 1990).

Mark E. Rushefsky, *Public Policy in the United States: Toward the Twenty-First Century* (Monterey, CA: Brooks-Cole, 1990).

Andrew Shonfield, *In Defense of the Mixed Economy* (New York: Oxford University Press, 1984).

Lester C. Thurow, *The Zero-Sum Society: Distribution and the Possibilties for Economic Change* (New York: Basic Books, 1980).

Jim Tomlinson, *Public Policy and the Economy Since 1900* (New York: Oxford University Press, 1990).

2

METHODS AND MODELS FOR POLICY ANALYSIS

Although public policy has been recognized as a subfield of political science for only a few decades, the study of ways to "promote the general welfare" goes back centuries. Policy is made in the present, based upon the past, with the purpose of improving the well-being of society's future. It utilizes both normative and scientific methodologies to achieve this. Public policy is action-oriented. The purpose of studying public problems is to provide insight into a range of policy options in order to take some control over the future.

POLICY ANALYSIS AS A SUBFIELD OF POLITICAL SCIENCE

Public policy emerged as a prominent subfield within the discipline of political science in the mid-1960s. In a broad sense, the analysis of public policy dates back to very early civilization. **Policy analysis** describes investigations that produce accurate and useful information for decision makers.

Considering how political science fits into the taxonomy of intellectual disciplines helps students appreciate the scope and the methods of public policy analysis. In the Middle Ages all study was under the rubric of philosophy, which means "to seek wisdom." As shown in Fig. 2-1, philosophy in medieval times was divided into two parts: moral philosophy and natural philosophy. Moral philosophy focused on human existence and has come down to us as the **humanities**. The subject matter of the humanities is our social world, or in other words, the human condition and human values. The social world reflects the nature of the human

24

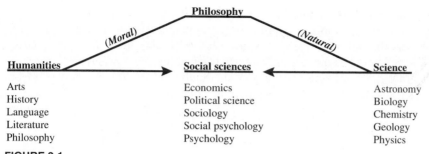

FIGURE 2-1
Schematic of relationship of disciplines..

beings that created it. Because the social world is a projection of human nature, individuals can no more completely understand or control it than they can completely understand and control themselves. Indeed, it is the very intimacy of the human involvement with the social world that inhibits both the comprehension of and authority over it.[1]

Natural philosophy has evolved into the natural sciences. Since it is focused on the outside world that can be observed, weighed, and measured, it is viewed as being **value-free**. It is a paradox that the natural world, which humans did not create, is much more susceptible to human understanding than is the social world, which is created by humans themselves. Through the discovery of the laws by which the universe is ordered, people can look back into the past and project into the future. Through this understanding, they can control and even harness the forces of nature as they wish.

More recently, a new set of disciplines existing between the humanities and the natural sciences, the social sciences, have matured and have made significant contributions to our understanding of human society through the systematic study of various aspects of the human condition.

The social sciences have a split personality. They not only exist between the humanities and the natural sciences, but they borrow freely from both. The social sciences developed from the historic cultural values and conditions of the social community. At the same time, they borrow the methods of the natural sciences. Many believe that political science, of which the study of public policy is a subfield, exists at the confluence of the social sciences. It is not an independent discipline within the social sciences. In their view, a political scientist focuses on the political ramifications of the other social sciences.

As a consequence, political scientists use methods of investigation that span the

[1] Hans J. Morgenthau, "The Purpose of Political Science," in James C. Charlesworth (ed.), *A Design for Political Science: Scope, Objectives, and Methods* (Monograph 6) (Philadelphia: The American Academy of Political and Social Science, 1966), pp. 67–68.

range of intellectual and scientific disciplines. The criterion for using a particular method is whether the tools of inquiry from the other discipline match the particular problems the political scientist is addressing. (It should be noted in passing that political science is not the only social science that uses a borrowed toolbox, and this practice of utilizing a toolbox of methodologies borrowed primarily from the physical sciences has caused considerable concern.[2]

Statistical inference is widely used in public policy, as is historical inquiry. Many statistical procedures have been adjusted to fit the kinds of information public policy experts deal with. Likewise, the use of historical investigation is somewhat different when undertaken by those interested in public policy than when carried out by a historian. Students of public policy must study the present with an understanding of the past for the purpose of guiding the future. In this regard, no part of humanity or civilization is beyond their concern.

The political scientist's perspective, scholarly interests, and manner of thought are heavily influenced by the society of which he or she is a member. Every society has biases that encourage an acceptance of and conformity to its political culture. However, the political scientist's obligation to seek the truth about the world of politics will necessarily result in he or she being the messenger of things that society will not want to hear.

A civilization's prevailing socioeconomic culture and the political institutions that grow out of that culture contain an elaborate articulation of the culture's ideals which are pursued through the political system. Existing political systems are usually defended by conceding that they have problems, but that those problems can best be dealt with in terms of the existing system. Consequently, a society that styles itself Marxist, like the People's Republic of China, cannot allow a searching investigation into the assumptions upon which communist theory is based. A society based upon a caste system, or other types of ethnic or racial discrimination, cannot accept such issues as proper subjects for scientific inquiry. Likewise, in republican forms of government, it is taken for granted that the voting mechanism of the nation reflects fairly the "will of the people." Consequently, republics whose economies are basically capitalist in nature are biased against inquiries regarding the goal of equal distribution of property in Marxist societies, as they are against inquiries regarding the unequal distribution of property in capitalist societies.

Since every society fosters support for the premises upon which the community is based, a commitment to truth in studying a society leads to questioning and controversy regarding the values and institutions of that society. In 1966, Hans J.

---

[2] The concern is that humans are the makers of tools which shape their environment, guide their vision, and help make their destiny. When people use these tools on themselves and other people, it is important to ask how these tools affect their vision of humanity. Charles Hampden-Turner in *Radical Man: The Process of Psycho-Social Development* (New York: Anchor Books, 1971) argues that the scientific method has a very conservative bias when applied to the human environment.

Morgenthau, a renowned political scientist, summed up this aspect of political inquiry in a statement that is valid today:

> A political science that is neither hated nor respected, but treated with indifference as an innocuous pastime, is likely to have retreated into a sphere that lies beyond the positive or negative interests of society. The retreat into the trivial, the formal, the methodological, the purely theoretical, the remotely historical—in short, the politically irrelevant—is the unmistakable sign of a "noncontroversial" political science which has neither friends nor enemies because it has no relevance for the great political issues in which society has a stake.[3]

This is of particular concern for public policy scholarship which has two main concerns, positive and normative policy analysis.

Positive Policy Analysis

One major concern of policy analysis is what might be called **positive policy analysis** or a concern with understanding how the **policy process** works. This aspect strives to understand public policy **as it is**. It also endeavors to explain how various social and political forces would change policy. Positive policy analysis tries to pursue truth through the process of testing hypotheses by measuring them against the standard of real-world experiences.

Positive policy analysis usually deals with assertions of cause and effect. A disagreement over such analysis can usually be resolved by examining the facts. For instance, the following is a positive statement: "If the U.S. government raises interest rates, then consumers will borrow less." We can check the validity of this statement by measuring it against real-world observations. Other positive policy statements such as "If long-term welfare recipients were required to finish their high school education as a condition of continuing to receive their welfare checks, a high percentage would develop employable skills and become self-sufficient," may be tested by setting up an experiment within a state. The results may confirm or refute the statement.

On occasion policy experiments are possible, particularly when the government is anxious to address questions of efficiency. But policy analysts usually do not have the luxury many natural scientists possess of being able to freely conduct experiments. At best, many social science experiments are difficult to carry out. People do not willingly let themselves become the laboratory subjects for someone else's experiment. For instance, if one were to hypothesize that federal grants to states for education could be significantly reduced without affecting student achievement levels, it would be impossible to get any state or school district to agree to forgo federal funds. The risk would be too great. So policy analysts must conduct this kind of study by examining the factual evidence of funding levels in

[3] Morgenthau, "The Purpose of Political Science," p. 73.

different states and trying to estimate the effects of per pupil funding in comparable areas.

Human Behavior and Predictability

The policy sciences deal with the behavior of people, which is not so neatly categorized as other phenomena. How do you find order with so many variables that cannot be isolated? A variation of this view holds that human beings are the least controllable or predictable of subjects for scientific inquiry.[4] However, even if one accepts the argument of the great complexity of the social sciences, one cannot conclude that the discovery of relationships is impossible, only that there are more variables **making it more difficult to discover the critical ones**.

Another argument runs that, while the natural sciences deal with inanimate matter subject to natural laws, the social sciences focus on humans with free will and passions not subject to such laws. Consequently, generalizations formulated in the social sciences lack predictive power. It is true that free will and passions like love, hate, pride, envy, ambition, and altruism are more unpredictable in their effects on human behavior than natural causes on the behavior of atoms. All of these influences, which are extremely difficult to understand, interact within individual humans, and affect human behavior. Nevertheless, having free will and passions does not mean that individuals do not act rationally on the basis of their values, disposition, character, and external restraints, and that these actions cannot be understood.[5]

As an example of the difference between the natural and social sciences, **if** hydrogen and oxygen are mixed under specific conditions, **then** water will result. However, if the government decides for budgetary reasons to reduce welfare payments (and incidentally support the self-help work ethic), it finds that some individuals will adopt the desired behavior pattern and others will not. Some people, faced with reduced benefits, will work very hard to find a job and become self-sufficient. Others, seeing few options, may adopt a life of crime as their avenue of escape. And the same individuals may react differently at different points in time.

The social sciences have developed ways to predict group behavior even though how individuals will behave is not known. For example, social scientists cannot predicate which particular individuals will be killed by handguns, or automobile accidents on a given weekend, but they can predict with surprising accuracy the total number who will be killed. Pollsters are likewise able, through sam-

---

[4] Russell Kirk, a critic of the scientific study of politics, has argued that "Human beings are the least controllable, verifiable, law-obeying and predictable of subjects." See Russell Kirk, "Is Social Science Scientific?" in Nelson W. Polsby, Robert Dentler, and Paul Smith (eds.), *Politics and Social Life* (Boston: Houghton Mifflin, 1963), p. 63.

[5] For example: Democratic society is based upon the assumption that rational people acting "freely" may decide to violate the law. The cost of such action is determined by the probability of being punished. The sanction of the law makes sense in part because it presumes that most people will "freely decide" to obey the law. In fact it is only because we can act freely that we can be held responsible. For example, deranged individuals are less accountable precisely because they do not "freely" choose their actions. These, then, are research problems, not unbeatable methodological barriers.

pling techniques, to learn the major concerns of voters. Political candidates can use this knowledge to place themselves in a favorable position to gain the support of potential voters. The ability to predict is of course crucial for makers of public policy who wish to know how people will react to a policy change in, for example, the capital gains tax. One's reaction to a capital gains tax cut will depend upon several factors, such as income level, expectations regarding how one's own position will be helped or hurt by the proposed tax change, and awareness of the law and its effect. Some individuals will react in surprising ways, but the overall response will be predictable within a small margin of error.

Public policy analysis bases its predictive efforts on the assumption that individuals act so consistently in their rational self-interest that they can be said to obey "laws" of behavior. Several such generalizations about human behavior provide a logical matrix for understanding human behavior similar to the laws used to account for events in the material world. Human beings bent on maximizing their self-interest may behave in a number of different ways, depending upon their understanding of their situation. All of this is in the way of saying that one must be aware of the limitations of social scientific generalizations.

Nevertheless, the unpredicted or random movements—the error—of individuals tend to offset each other. Knowledge of this fact makes possible *the statistical law of large numbers* that is based on the **normal curve of error**. It states that the average error of all individuals combined will approach zero. Since the irregularities (errors) of individual behavior will tend to cancel each other out, the regularities will tend to show up in replicated observations.

Normative Analysis

Not all policy analysts spend their time measuring hypotheses against historical events or proposing experimental case studies. Many, if not most, of them are also concerned with what is referred to as **normative policy analysis**. **Normative policy analysis** is directed toward studying what public policy **ought to be** to improve the general welfare. Normative analysis deals with statements involving value judgments about what **should be**. For example, the assertion that "The cost of health care in the United States is too high" is a normative statement. This statement cannot be confirmed by referring to data. Whether the cost is too high or is appropriate is based on a given criterion. Its validity depends upon one's values and ethical views. Individuals may agree on the facts of health care costs but disagree over their ethical judgments regarding the implications of "the cost of health care."

It is important to be aware of the distinction between positive and normative policy analysis, and not to substitute the goals or methods of one for those of the other. That is because the value of policy analysis is determined by the accurate observation of the critical variables in the external environment. Only an accurate rendering of factual relationships can indicate how best to achieve normative goals. For example, a normative view that we should improve the educational system in the United States does not indicate how to achieve that goal most effectively or most efficiently. If we have limited resources to add to the education budget, how should we spend the funds? Would higher salaries attract more capable teachers? Should we extend the school year? Should we improve the teacher-to-pupil ratio by hiring more teachers? Should we add alternative educational programs? Only a rigorous study of the costs and benefits of various alternatives can indicate a preferred solution. In a republican form of government such as our own, such questions are settled by voting and through decisions made by those elected to run the institutions of government.

Frequently, however, normative statements can be used to develop positive hypotheses. Generally, most people do not feel strongly about the value of a capital gains tax cut. Their support or opposition to such a change in the tax law depends on a prescriptive belief about a valued end state. George Bush as President pressed to reduce the federal tax on capital gains. He argued that a reduction in the capital gains tax would increase incentives to invest in the economy and thus fuel economic growth. However, computer estimates have shown that this change in the tax structure would reduce government revenues after several years and increase the federal deficit. Estimates also showed that upper-income groups would receive a larger per capita benefit by far than other income groups. The result of these estimates, when publicized, was an increased popular perception that the tax cut would be "unfair." Republicans have had difficulty in pressing the proposal for this reason.

In the decision to study public policy, there is an implicit ethical view that people and their welfare are important. We must try to learn about all the forces that affect the well-being of individuals and of society in the aggregate. The desire to improve the current system is the basis for public policy. To achieve that goal, students of public policy must first understand how the current system works.

PUBLIC POLICY AND THEORY

The scientific method was developed in the natural sciences as a way to help explain phenomena by developing theories,[6] to explain and predict how things happen; the same is true in the social sciences, of which public policy studies are a part.

Why Theory Development Requires Simplification

If we wished to provide policy makers with a complete description of "income distribution," we could go out and collect all the facts we could find and present the data to decision makers and "let the facts speak for themselves." But a complete description including information gathered from thousands of researchers gathering data from millions of households, thousands of separate federal, state,

---

[6] For our purposes we can use the terms "theory" and "model" interchangeably.

and local governments, and thousands of firms is unworkable and would be ineffective as a guide to public policy.

Theories help make sense of the millions of facts. Theories help explain how the political and economic aspects of society work by identifying how basic underlying causal relationships fit together. A **theory in a scientific sense is a set of logically related, empirically testable hypotheses**. Theories are a deliberate simplification of related generalizations used to describe and explain how certain facts are related. Their usefulness derives from their ability to simplify otherwise complex phenomena. Thus a theory is not a mirror image of reality.[7] A theory will usually contain at least one **hypothesis** about how a specific set of facts is related. The theory should explain the phenomena in an abstract manner. The inclination to abstract from nonessential details of the world around us is necessary because of the awesome complexity of reality. **Abstraction** is the process of disregarding needless details in order to focus on a limited number of factors to explain a phenomenon. As an abstraction, a theory is useful not because it is true or false, but because it helps analysts understand the interactions between variables and predict how change in one or more variables will affect other dependent variables.

Scientific theories have frequently been compared to road maps. Road maps are abstractions of the world. Different road maps will be useful for different purposes. A person wishing to drive around Washington, DC, en route to Alexandria, Virginia, would find the map shown in Fig. 2-2(a) more useful than the map shown in Fig. 2-2(b). The latter map contains too many details and is likely to be confusing for the purpose of going to Alexandria. However, the map shown in Fig. 2-2(a) would not be very useful for a tourist wishing to see the sights, or in locating a specific street in Washington, DC. Neither map is a complete representation of the world around Washington. But each provides the details necessary for those using it for the appropriate reasons. A theory like a model may be an oversimplification for one purpose and unnecessarily complicated for another.

Theories attempt to do the same thing—bring order and meaning to data which, without the theory, would remain unrelated and unintelligible. For example, a policy analyst might wish to explain why some people have very high incomes while others barely survive economically. To do so, the analyst must try to separate or abstract the meaningful variables from the data without significance. Thus, variables such as gender, age, education, and occupation may be considered critical. Other variables such as the educational level or parents' income may be considered important but less crucial. Still other variables such as eye color, height, or weight may be considered unimportant and not be included among the explanatory variables. The theory developed by the analyst is built on all these assumptions and makes up a simplified, logical account of income inequality and its causes.

A theory must be consistent with the facts that it draws together. And the facts, in turn, must lend themselves to the interpretation that the theory puts upon them.

---

[7] A model is a simplified representation of how the real world works. Its usefullness is judged by how well it represents reality. Models may be depicted by mathematical equations, charts, and graphs, or may be descriptively stated.

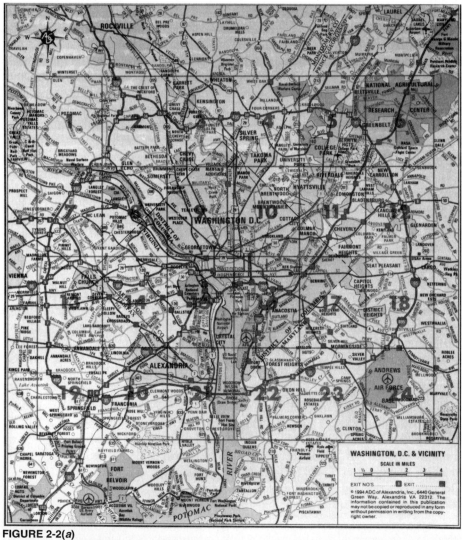

FIGURE 2-2(*a*)

Road map useful for going from Washington, DC, to Alexandria, Va. (*Source*: ADC'S Street Map of Washington, DC and Vicinity, *The Langenscheidt Publishing Group, Alexandria, VA*.).

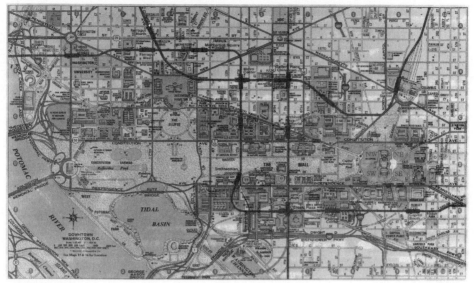

FIGURE 2-2(*b*)
Detailed map helpful in locating specific streets in Washington, DC.

Finally, the conclusions derived from the theory must flow logically from the theory's premises.

The policy analyst must determine which variables to include and which to ignore when conducting social analysis. Events and forces in a socioeconomic setting reflect all the intrinsic ambiguity of human nature in motion. But it should also be kept in mind that under comparable circumstances, events and forces will appear in a similar manner. As Michel de Montaigne said:

> As no event and no shape is entirely like another, so also is there none entirely different from another. . . . *If there were no similarity in our faces, we could not distinguish man from beast; if there were no dissimilarity, we could not distinguish one man from another.* All things hold together by some similarity; every example is halting, and the comparison that is derived from experience is always defective and imperfect.[8]

From the interpretations of variables (known as theories), we are able to formulate hypotheses. A **hypothesis is a tentative assumption or generalization that has not yet been tested**. Because hypotheses, like theories, are abstractions, it is necessary to test them. The hypothesis must be stated as an affirmative proposition (i.e, not as a question) that is capable of being tested against empirical evidence. Accordingly, a hypothesis is most useful when it relates two or more variables in terms of a comparison. In regard to health care, for example, we might develop a hypothesis like the following: "Cost-control incentives in health care proposed by

---

[8] Michel de Montaigne, *The Essays of Michel de Montaigne*, edited and translated by Jacob Zeitlin (New York: Alfred A. Knopf, 1936), Vol. III, p. 270 (emphasis by Montaigne).

the private sector are more effective than those imposed by government agencies." The analyst will include only those variables in the hypothesis that are critical in explaining the particular event.

Hypotheses contain variables that can take on different values. **Values refer to the measurable characteristics of a variable (such as strong, neutral, or weak)**. We might hypothesize: "Strong support (value) for a President will vary positively with low (value) inflation and low (value) unemployment." In this hypothesis, Presidential support is the dependent variable. Inflation and unemployment rates are independent variables. The variables or values selected depend on the questions being asked or the problems to be resolved. **Variables** are the most basic elements in theories. A **variable is a term in a hypothesis that can assume different values or characteristics**. In the hypothesis above we could have substituted the variables "support for a member of the Senate" or "support for a member of Congress" for "support for a President."

Suppose we were trying to generalize about housing problems in the United States; then income levels and housing costs would be two core variables to consider. We could use those variables to explain and predict failures in the housing market sector.

We used the term "assumptions" a few paragraphs above, and they also play their part in the development and testing of theories and hypotheses. **Assumptions** are statements that are made, usually without justification, to simplify a problem. For example, we may assume that visual acuity is unrelated to a decision to embark on a life of crime. We make this assumption to reduce the complexity of the problem. But to determine if our theory is valid, we must conduct tests to see not only if the overall theory but if its assumptions are consistent with the facts.

All this is part of the scientific method applied to the social sciences, as shown in Fig. 2-3.

The Scientific Method in Social Sciences

The scientific method as typically applied in the social sciences to develop theories progresses along the pathway of theory and observation suggested in Fig. 2-4. The variables are defined, assumptions noted, and hypotheses framed. Various implications and predictions are deduced from the hypotheses. This deductive process moves from the general to the particular, from a general theory to implications for a particular case. Predictions are then stated. These three steps comprise the building of a theory. In the fourth step, the theory is tested. The data either fail to reject the theory or do reject it. If the data fail to reject the theory,

FIGURE 2-3
Steps in the scientific method.

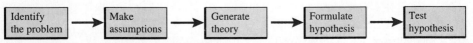

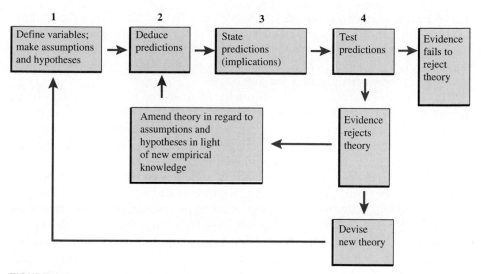

FIGURE 2-4
Deduction and measurement in theory building (theory and observation continuously interact).
(Adapted from Roger A. Arnold, Macroeconomics, *West Publishing, New York, 1989, p. 15.
Reprinted with permission of West Publishing Co.)*

this still does not prove it true. It merely fails to disprove it. This can increase one's confidence in the theory, but it must continue to be monitored by seeking additional tests. If, on the other hand, the evidence rejects the theory, there are two possibilities. Either the theory can be amended based on the evidence obtained from the test, or it can be abandoned altogether, in which case those who formulated the theory must return to step 1 and start developing a new one. Usually political scientists prefer simple theories to complicated ones. The preference for the simplest of competing theories over more complicated theories when both are consistent with the data is known as **Ockham's razor,** after a fourteenth century philosopher who urged its use to "shave away" superfluous theoretical complexities.

When a theory cannot predict the consequences of the actions being studied better than alternative explanations, it must be modified or replaced. The scientific method requires setting up a theory to explain some phenomenon and then ascertaining if that theory can be disproven by evidence. An alternative is to develop a theory and search for confirming evidence. The danger in this approach is that the world is so complicated that **some confirming evidence** can be found for almost any theory—which is why conspiracy theories abound in American politics.

The Role of Theory in Policy Science

One of the most humbling aspects of the study of public policy is how complex it actually is. Dividing the policy-making process into the stages of agenda setting, selection of an alternative, adoption, implementation, and evaluation simplifies it into workable segments for inquiry. However, most researchers feel forced to concentrate their efforts on just one stage of the process to reduce their studies to manageable size. In the last two decades those studies have contributed to understanding what goes on in policy making, but by themselves do not show the causal relationships between the policy-making stages.

There has been a considerable effort by those in the rational public choice school to develop a theory of policy making within that tradition.[9] Rational public choice theory can be applied across many of the social sciences. While it tries to focus on the most significant factors determining individual behavior, it does not lend itself well to the incorporation of institutional and social factors.

As noted earlier, it is important to bear in mind that theories are **abstractions**, based on assumptions. This means the resulting predictions are **theoretical** predictions, and will hold true only as long as the basic assumptions of the theory are valid. Public policy makers are not so much interested in theoretical predictions as they are in broader factual forecasts. That is, they are more likely to be interested in cosmopolitan views rather than narrower political or economic theories in a given situation. For example, theory can correctly claim that a competitive labor market erodes wage discrimination based upon gender. But that is clearly not an accurate prediction of events in the socioeconomic environment of the United States. Where it is institutionalized gender discrimination makes it difficult for the erosion of wage discrimination predicted by competitive labor theory to make itself felt. Policy research shows that gender discrimination acts as an intervening variable. For the maker of public policy, then, economic forces that are offset by social forces are only of **theoretical** and not of **actual** value in making predictions.[10] The policy maker must understand social reality as well as economic theory to develop appropriate policy. In the case of wage discrimination based on gender, the political entrepreneur must have a broad knowledge of the institutional arrangements and cultural aspects involved in order to find a viable solution.

We must distinguish between policy theory and public policy. **Policy theory** can develop rules and principles of policy that can serve as a guide for action in a given set of circumstances. **Public policy** refers to the actual action taken. In an ideal world public policy would always be consistent with policy theory. Policy problems and issues by definition have political ramifications. The result is that policy theory is modified by political realities. For instance, theory might indicate

---

[9] See for example, Larry Kiser and Elinor Ostrom, "The Three Worlds of Action," in E. Ostrom (ed.), *Strategies of Political Inquiry* (Beverly Hills: Sage, 1982), pp. 179–222.

[10] Theories require modification when masked variables are detected. A typical example of price discrimination that has been frequently used is doctors' pricing of health care services. A patient with fewer alternative providers, the theory postulates, can be charged a higher price for medical care. However, masked variables have caused trouble for this theory. Take the issue of race. Suppose that black patients have lower average incomes than whites. Some physicians might be less willing to accept black patients because of racism and/or a fear that black patients will be less able to pay for medical services. If that were true, according to the above theory, then those physicians willing to treat black patients could charge higher prices and be less likely to lose black patients to other physi-

that we should raise taxes to reduce inflation, but during an election year the theory may yield to political realities resulting in reduced taxes to win votes.

Policy theory has developed a disreputable public image—partly because of its inability to predict future outcomes with the same precision as the natural sciences, partly because of some theorizing that is irrelevant or trivial, and partly because many politicians have found it expedient to ridicule theory in policy analysis.

But it is exactly the importance of public policy that makes policy theory so critical. If there were no possibility of changing the general social welfare through public policy, political science and economics might both be disciplines asking merely historical questions such as "How did the U.S. government react to the stagnant economy during the Great Depression of the 1930s?" or "How have health or education policies changed since the mid-1970s?"

However, the general social welfare can be affected by public policy. In recognition of that fact, and in order to improve the effectiveness of public policy making, theories have been developed that go beyond historical questions and descriptive analyses. Public policy as a subfield of political science utilizes knowledge and theories from throughout the social sciences and weaves them into its own approach to theories about, and methodologies for understanding the social policies with which it is concerned.

The Role of Policy Analysts

The way in which scholars have influenced policy decisions is reflective of the policy-making environment. First, the fact that policy is dependent upon values suggests that the community of policy scholars is no more unified in outlook than is the political community. Policy scholars generally agree on various analytical aspects of policy, yet they hold different views about what is best for society. Since public policy analysts, like everyone else, come from across the political spectrum, they hold different opinions about the "best" or "right" solution to public policy problems. One example may illustrate why the analysis of public policy problems may not lead to agreement on a policy decision.

In the early 1980s, policy makers were determined to wring inflation out of the economy. Public policy analysts regardless of political persuasion agreed that there is a Hobson's choice in dealing with inflation and unemployment. Most poli-

---

cians. Some studies in the 1970s found support for that hypothesis. More recent studies using more extensive data have found no evidence of physician price discrimination on the basis of race. Earlier studies had not included region of the country, which masked cost of living and fee differentials, and misattributed those effects to the racial composition of a physician's patients. The point is that this example illustrates the importance of not ending analysis at the theoretical level. The question must be pursued in the real world to determine if the theoretical argument is an accurate explanation of what is really happening. Accordingly, basing our understanding of the world and public policy on empirically empty theory is dangerous. See Alvin E. Headen, Jr., "Price Discrimination in Physician Services Markets Based on Race: New Test of an Old Implicit Hypothesis," *The Review of Black Political Economy*, vol. 15, no. 4 (Spring 1987), pp. 5–20.

cies that reduce inflation cause an increase in unemployment. The government instituted policies to bring down the rate of inflation, and exacted a significant cost by putting many people out of work. Unemployment, which averaged 6.1 percent through the 1970s, rose to an 8.1 percent average during the first 5 years of the Reagan administration, and reached 10.4 percent in 1983. Was it worth the price of lost productivity and unemployment to reduce inflation? Public policy analysts are no better at answering this question than physicians in determining whether the right to abortion is justifiable. The judgment is based upon ethical beliefs about the tradeoffs between high unemployment and low inflation. Such judgments in the United States are determined by the people through the democratic process of voting those with specific policy goals into office.

The result is that much policy analysis research is used in the U.S. political process in an advocacy fashion. The research is not examined, by political entrepreneurs or special interest groups, for its utility in improving policy so much as it is used selectively to undercut an adversary's position or to strengthen one's own. Politicians and lobbyists often look for support for preformed political and ideological positions rather than information to help shape and guide policy. Administrations are distressed to find that the results of policy analyses hinder the pursuit of policies on which they have already embarked. The more ideologically motivated the administration or bureaucracy, the more policy is made on the basis of ideological inputs rather than policy analysis. In recent years conservatives backing conservative policy analyses to buttress their aims have funded conservative policy study groups to provide alternatives to institutes perceived as having a more liberal orientation.[11]

THE POLICY-MAKING PROCESS

Public policy did not appear as a subfield of political science until the mid-1960s. The effort to provide an abstract framework for the entire policy process, from the articulation of policy demands through the selection of alternative programs, to tactics of implementation and feedback was presented by David Easton.[12] Since that time effort has concentrated on the analysis of specific substantive areas of public policy research. Studies have focused on topics such as health care, education, the environment, welfare, and national security. Many of these studies have provided very detailed descriptive historical examinations of the development and evolution of policy in particular topic areas. More recently there have been greater

---

[11] In addition to institutes funded to conduct policy research such as the American Enterprise Institute or The Brookings Institute, the Congress employs thousands of staff members who also do such research. There are several thousand more analysts who work for other government support agencies, such as the General Accounting Office (GAO), the Office of Technology Assessment (OTA), the Congressional Research Service (CRS), and the Congressional Budget Office (CBO). These agencies generally respond to requests by Congressional representatives and their staffs for specific studies. They also may engage in studies on their own initiative. As such, they are a significant source of policy agenda items.

[12] David Easton, *A Systems Analysis of Political Life* (New York: John Wiley and Sons, 1965).

efforts to apply theoretical models to these case studies, focusing on the factors that affect policy formulation and implementation. Evaluation research judges the formulation of the policy proposal, the process of policy adoption, and the operation of the policy program.

Public policy analysis has not progressed in developing empirically testable theories. The current understanding of the policy process is really a heuristic model, not a theory that allows explanation and prediction. This model separates the policy-making process into five stages: problem identification, policy alternatives, adoption, implementation, and evaluation (see Fig. 2-5). The model contains no clear and consistent postulates about what drives the process from one stage to the next. Its primary value has been that it divides the policy-making process into manageable units of analysis. Thus the model has resulted in research projects each of which focuses almost exclusively on a single stage without tying its results into the results of other projects that have focused on other stages. So little theoretical coherence exists from one stage to the next.[13]

Problem Identification and Agenda Setting

Step 1 in Fig. 2-5 simply indicates that public policy begins when a problem is perceived and gets on the **policy agenda**. There are many problems in society that are not part of the policy agenda because they have not gotten the attention of the authoritative actors in the government and therefore do not cause any policy

[13] Paul A. Sabatier, "Political Science and Public Policy," *PS Political Science and Politics*, vol. 24 (June 1991), p. 145.

FIGURE 2-5
Five key elements in the policy-making process. *(Source: Grover Starling,* Strategies for Policy Making, *Dorsey Press, Chicago, 1988, pp. 8–10.)*

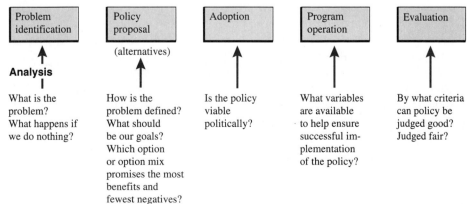

Action

Problem identification	Policy proposal	Adoption	Program operation	Evaluation
	(alternatives)			

Analysis

What is the problem? What happens if we do nothing?

How is the problem defined? What should be our goals? Which option or option mix promises the most benefits and fewest negatives?

Is the policy viable politically?

What variables are available to help ensure successful implementation of the policy?

By what criteria can policy be judged good? Judged fair?

response.[14] The desire for policies to provide for individual needs is insatiable, while room on the agenda is scarce. This raises the question as to why some issues get on the agenda while others do not. The dynamics of a changing political environment, new political players, policy entrepreneurs, and new windows of opportunity are major elements in new issues gaining a place on the agenda. For instance the Great Depression provided a window of opportunity for New Deal legislation which ushered in various policies such as Social Security and minimum wage laws. More recently, the conservative reaction that swept Ronald Reagan to the Presidency provided a window of opportunity for the reduction of social welfare legislation and the introduction of supply-side economics on the policy agenda.[15]

But in truth, success in getting on the policy agenda does not ensure a policy response. Some issues manage to get on the agenda yet drift along for years without getting beyond step 1. For example, health care reform has been accepted as a policy item because of the strength of voter attitudes on the issue. However, both political parties are in disarray as to how to proceed in implementing any reforms. The two major alternatives proposed are a universal plan administered by the government, or a plan that would require coverage but use existing structures of private insurance. Neither political party has coalesced around any firm proposals. Intense lobbying by special interest groups, ideological biases, and questions regarding costs have made it difficult to get beyond the agreement that something should be done. The lack of consensus on how to proceed has resulted mostly in considerable debate and posturing by political entrepreneurs.

Other items may get on the policy agenda only to disappear into a black hole by the crush of other issues, then resurface later in slightly modified forms. Thus the question as to whether the United States should develop an **industrial policy** to promote a resurgence of U.S. business growth was placed on the agenda in the early 1980s. The idea was brushed aside by the Reagan White House, which viewed industrial policy as inappropriate interference with an unfettered free market, one of the goals of his administration. More recently, the administration of Bill Clinton has quietly instituted an industrial policy designed to strengthen business and U.S. exports as part of his overall economic program.

The first step in the policy-making process is a prerequisite for all the steps that follow. So even though getting on the policy agenda provides no assurance that an issue will go any further, failure to get on the agenda guarantees it will not go anywhere at all. For that reason, getting on the policy agenda is the most critical step, and also the most nebulous and amorphous in the entire process.

Some researchers suggest that the policy agenda should be thought of as consisting of a **systemic** and an **institutional agenda**. The **systemic agenda** is made

---

[14] For a sophisticated and sound theoretical treatment of agenda setting, see John Kingdon, *Agendas, Alternatives, and Public Policies* (Boston: Little, Brown and Co., 1984). See also Barbara Nelson, *Making an Issue of Child Abuse* (Chicago: University of Chicago Press, 1984).

[15] See Kingdon, *Agendas, Alternatives, and Public Policies*, pp. 183–184.

up of those issues perceived by the political community as meriting public attention and resolution.[16] However, the systemic agendas of national and state governments are largely symbolic in nature. The issues they contain are often controversial, and some items may be on one systemic agenda but not another. For example,
some believe that the "right to bear arms" is guaranteed by the Constitution, and
that it should be beyond the authority of Congress or the states to regulate in any
way. Therefore, the issue of gun control has until very recently remained on the
systemic agendas of the federal government and most state governments, with
many gun control opponents urging its removal altogether.

Another subset of items on the systemic agenda are those subject to nothing
more than discussion; these are termed "pseudoagenda items."

The **institutional agenda** consists of those items that receive the powerful and
earnest attention of decision makers. These items are not always easily identified
or agreed upon either. They do include those issues that are actively pursued
through the various institutions of government.

Items may shift from the systemic to the institutional agenda as a result of a
variety of events. For example, Congress may prefer to keep an item such as a bill
on abortion on the systemic agenda because it may be perceived as a no-win situation for members to take a stand by voting. However, a decision by the Supreme
Court, such as *Roe v. Wade*, may force the issue back to the national legislature
and require some action. Policy issues typically move from private decision making to the public agenda when they progress from the systemic to the institutional
agenda.

Setting the Agenda: The Scope of the Conflict   If policy is not made through
public decisions by the government, it will be made through private decisions, primarily by businesses or financial elites. Traditionally the principle of laissez faire
meant that government should not interfere with business. As a practical matter, it
meant that government supported business decision making through legislation
and court decisions that legitimized and reinforced corporate interests. Thus corporations made policy that provided pervasive control over the lives of individuals
unhindered by government interference. Businesses were given a free hand to set
the terms of employment, wages, hours, and working conditions for employees,
and those terms were supported by government stipulations regarding the rights to
private property and freedom of contract.

Under laissez faire doctrine, business provided for individual economic needs
through free enterprise, and was loosely supervised by lower levels of government.
But with the rise of giant corporations in the late nineteenth century, the power of
business organizations over the lives of individuals grew correspondingly. The
result was an overwhelming popular demand for government action to correct the
perceived abuses of power by corporate interests.

---

[16] See Roger W. Cobb and Charles D. Elder, *Participation in American Politics: The Dynamics of Agenda Building*, 2nd ed. (Baltimore: Johns Hopkins University Press, 1983), p. 85.

This demand for reform expanded the scope of the conflict from the private arena of management versus labor to the public arena of government versus business. For example, the national government took the lead in legislating workmen's compensation and child labor laws. With the Great Depression came even more pressure for the government to take an active role in managing the economy and business.

Despite this expansion of governmental regulation, businesses still have a "privileged position" in American politics even today. They can often make major decisions with only a minimum of government control. In arguing for corporate autonomy from government regulation, executives point out that business must submit first of all to the discipline of the marketplace if it is to be successful. When an issue affecting business does get on the public policy agenda, business organizations are well represented in the public and governmental debates. Corporate leaders are effective proponents for their companies and for the interests of capitalism in general. They also provide many people for government positions, which encourages a probusiness bias in government policy making.

As long as decisions are made in the private sector, they are outside the realm of politics, even though those decisions may affect many people and the allocation of vast resources. Indeed (as noted in Chap. 4), private conflicts are taken into the public arena precisely because someone or some group wants to make certain that the power ratio among the private interests shall not prevail in the final decision making.[17] In fact **politics may be defined as the socialization of conflict**:

> The political process is a sequence: conflicts are initiated by highly motivated, high-tension groups so directly and immediately involved that it is difficult for them to see the justice of competing claims. As long as the conflicts remain **private** . . . no political process is initiated. Conflicts become political only when an attempt is made to involve the wider public. Pressure politics might be described as a stage in the socialization of conflict.[18]

Setting the Agenda: Enlarging the Scope   As noted earlier, democracies provide the political means for private controversies to spill over into the public arena. An issue or condition must attract sufficient attention and interested bystanders to expand the scope of the conflict over it into the public arena if there is to be any hope of changing its current disposition or status.

Some of those involved in the issue will prefer the status quo, and attempt to limit the scope of the conflict to keep it off the public policy agenda. And those with interests already on the public policy agenda will not welcome new items

[17] E. E. Schattschneider, *The Semi-Sovereign People: A Realist's View of Democracy in America* (New York: Holt, Rinehart and Winston, 1960) p. 38.

[18] Schattschneider, *The Semi-Sovereign People,* p. 39.

that threaten to displace their own. Since only a finite number of items can be considered at any given time, there is always tension when new issues erupt into public consciousness. Those items already on the agenda have a public legitimacy by virtue of having been accepted onto it. New items have not yet established their public legitimacy. For all of these reasons, **the political system has a bias in favor of the status quo and will resist the addition of new issues to the public policy agenda**.

Setting the Agenda: Who Sets the Public Policy Agenda?   Determining which issues move from the systemic to the institutional agenda is an extremely important part of the entire policy-making process. The policy agenda is overburdened with a wide assortment of foreign policy issues, national security affairs, economic questions, and domestic concerns. For a problem to become a salient agenda item, it is important that it have an influential advocate, most especially the President. Another route for an issue to move onto the institutional agenda is for it to be regarded as a crisis. The perception of a problem as being serious may even be more important than its actual seriousness. A triggering event, for example, the single act of a terrorist, may focus attention on an issue like terrorism even though the overall threat of terrorism is receding.

Increasingly, policy agendas are determined by tightly knit groups that dominate policy making in particular subject areas. **Iron triangles** refer to the reciprocal bonds that evolve between Congressional committees and their staffs, special-interest groups, and bureaucratic agencies in the executive branch.[19]

Members of Congress have incentives to serve on committees that deal with special-interest constituencies from their districts. Senators and representatives will bargain for such appointments. And over time, committees in Congress tend to be dominated by members who are highly motivated to provide generous support for the agencies they oversee. This translates into an expansion of the programs of those agencies in the districts of the members of Congress overseeing them. These congressional committees make up one side of the iron triangles; they tend to be insulated from many party pressures and to develop committee member alliances that cross party lines.

The special-interest groups form a second part of the triangle. These lobbyists and political action committees provide specialists, or experts in the special-interest area. They provide committees with resources for public relations and media coverage, and supply campaign financing to committee members. Finally, the bureaucracies of federal agencies in the executive branch are the third side of the triangle, with their own entrenched interests in particular issues or programs.

---

[19] See Jeffrey M. Berry, "Subgovernments, Issue Networks, and Political Conflict," in Richard Harris and Signey Milkis (eds.), *Remaking American Politics* (Boulder, CO: Westview Press, 1990), pp. 239–269.

Congressional hearings provide excellent opportunities for government agency representatives and lobbyists to build imposing cases for their positions.[20]

Iron triangles exemplify disturbing problems in public policy. Policy alternatives that challenge the established interests of the triangle may never receive serious attention. Also Congressional and bureaucratic agency oversight of a congenial special-interest group is not vigorously pursued.

Responses to the situation created by iron triangles have been based mainly on two different approaches to understanding the nature and functioning of government: elite theory and pluralism or group theory. Those espousing elite theory are critical of iron triangles, pointing to their power as proof of the victory of greedy special-interest groups over the general welfare. Pluralists, on the other hand, are more likely to conclude that such triangles simply reflect strategies developed to promote policies in a diverse nation whose subgroups have different interests.

We now turn to a discussion of elite and pluralist theory.

Elite Theory   **Every political system has inherent biases concerning who has access to it**. Chapter 4 develops the idea that the American Founding Fathers produced a system based on the notion that "all men are created equal." But according to elite theorists, the machinery of government was (and is) not open to all men (and certainly not to all women). There were built-in mechanisms designed to make it difficult for most groups to gain access to the government or to make changes in the way it functioned. Therefore, the idea that American government reflects "the will of the people," as popularly understood, is inaccurate in the view of elite theory.

Elite theory holds that most government decisions are made by a minority elite that has enormous power. Elites derive their power from the control of key financial, communications, industrial, and governmental institutions. Power flows not from the elite individuals themselves, but from the positions of authority they have in large institutions. Their power and "privileged positions" originate from the immense wealth of large corporations and the significance of those corporations for the overall national economy.[21]

Supporters of this view that elites and not the masses govern America make a strong case that it is the elites who have access to and largely determine the public policy agenda, because they have the real authority over the major institutions that

---

[20] The lobbying on behalf of the B-1 bomber is an excellent example of an iron triangle at work. Although various studies over 30 years recommended against its production, the U.S. Air Force formed an alliance with various defense contractors to build the B-1. They were able to rouse political support for the program, valued in excess of $28 billion, in part because of the jobs it was anticipated it would create across the country in 48 states. The Air Force and defense contractors lobbied many members of Congress not on any of the armed services committees, emphasizing the jobs and the money that would flow into each Congress member's state. See Nick Kotz, *Wild Blue Yonder: Money, Politics, and the B-1 Bomber* (Princeton, NJ: Princeton University Press, 1988).

[21] Elite theory has been developed in many works. C. Wright Mills, *The Power Elite* (New York: Oxford University Press, 1956), is certainly a classic work. See also, Michael Parenti, *Democracy for the Few*, 5th ed. (New York: St. Martin's Press, 1988). Also see Thomas R. Dye and Harmon Zeigler, *The Irony of Democracy*, 7th ed. (Monterey, CA: Brooks/Cole, 1987). Charles Lindblom, *Politics and Markets* (New York: Basic Books, 1977), is another who argues that business has a privileged position in the American political system (see especially pp. 170–185).

shape the lives of the masses. Elite theory holds that elites govern **all** societies, not just America. Alexander Hamilton explained the existence of elites in the following way:

> All communities divide themselves into the few and the many. The first are the rich and well-born, the other the masses of people. The voice of the people has been said to be the voice of God; and however generally this maxim has been quoted and believed, it is not true in fact. The people are turbulent and changing, they seldom judge or determine right.[22]

The privileged aristocracy in preindustrial Europe has been generally superceded by wealthy capitalists of the present time. Elites in every era tend to believe that what is good for themselves must be good for all.

Elite theory accepts upward social mobility that permits nonelites to become elites because this openness provides stability by reducing the potential of revolution from below. Individuals who might supply the revolutionary leadership become part of the elite, and in the process assimilate the values of the ruling class they are joining. Privileged elites have a vital interest in the perpetuation of the system upon which their entitlements rest. Upward social mobility means that even potential members of the elite share a consensus on the need to preserve the system by discouraging changes that would jeopardize the elite's position.[23] Competition thus occurs over a rather narrow range of issues and usually concerns **means** rather than **ends**.[24]

Consensus among American elites is built around the sanctity of private property, limitations on government authority, and the economic virtues of a capitalist culture. In this view, public policy does not result from the popular will so much as it mirrors the concerns and values of the elite. Public policy changes and innovations result from shifts in elite positions. Since elites tend to be very conservative because of their overriding interest in preserving the system, changes tend to be incremental rather than radical. Major changes take place only when the security of the basic system is jeopardized. Then elites may move swiftly to institute the reforms required to preserve the system and their privileged position within it. Elite theory does not argue that elites are unconcerned about the welfare of the

---

[22] Alexander Hamilton, *Records of the Federal Convention of 1787*, as quoted in Thomas R. Dye, *Who's Running America: The Bush Era* (Englewood Cliffs, NJ: Prentice-Hall, 1990), p. 3. This discussion of elite theory relies heavily on this book by Dye, and on Dye and Zeigler, *The Irony of Democracy*, pp. 3–11.

[23] Richard Hofferbert has developed a conceptual framework of public policy making that emphasizes elite influences. The policy process in his model is developed with governmental decisions being the dependent variable. The policy output is dependent upon historical-geographic conditions, socioeconomic conditions, mass political behavior, governmental institutions, and, most immediately, the behavior of the members of the elite itself. The model has been criticized for dealing in aggregate rather than individual choices. It also presumes that policy decisions are driven by socioeconomic conditions and mass political behavior filtered through governmental institutions and elite behavior. Other researchers noted above, however, suggest that it is the elites who drive the policy decisions rather than merely filtering them. See Richard Hofferbert, *The Study of Public Policy* (Indianapolis: Bobbs-Merrill, 1974).

[24] Dye and Zeigler, *The Irony of Democracy*, p. 6.

THE ISSUE ATTENTION CYCLE

Anthony Downs contends that many issues appear on the policy agenda in a standardized process that comprises an "issue-attention cycle." In his view, key domestic problems leap into prominence and remain the center of public attention for a short time, then fade from concern even though they remain largely unresolved. It is in part the length that public attention stays focused upon any given issue that determines whether enough political pressure will be brought to bear to effect a change. This cycle is rooted in the nature of many domestic problems and the way the communications media interact with the public. The cycle has five stages each of variable duration that usually occur in the following sequence:

1 *The preproblem stage.* Some major problem arises, and although policy experts and special-interest groups may be alarmed by the situation, the general public is generally not aware of the problem or its magnitude. The general press has given it prominent coverage. It is not unusual for problems, such as racism or malnutrition, to be worse during the preproblem stage than they are by the time the public's interest is aroused.

2 *Alarmed discovery and euphoric enthusiasm.* Often as a result of some dramatic events (like riots or demonstrations), the public becomes aware of the problem. Authoritative decision makers then make speeches, which are enthusiastically received by the public, regarding the politicians' determination to resolve the problem. This optimism is embedded in American culture, which tends to view any problem as *outside* the structure of society, and naively believes that every problem can be resolved *without any basic reordering of society itself.* American optimism in the past has clung to the view that we as a nation could accomplish anything. Since the late 1960s, a more realistic awareness that some problems may be beyond a complete "solution" has begun to develop.

3 *Realization of the cost of significant progress.* A realization that the cost of solving the problem is extremely high sets in. The solution would not only take a great deal of money, but would also require that some groups give up some economic security (through taxes or some other redistribution of resources) in favor of others. The public begins to realize the structural nature of the problem, and a human inconsistency regard

masses, only that the general welfare of the masses depends upon the actions of the elites. Thus public policy decision making is limited to issues that do not imperil the elites. They organize the policy agenda so that certain kinds of decisions are eliminated from it.[25]

The theory holds that the masses are largely submissive, and indifferent to and poorly informed regarding policy issues. Elites, having more at stake, and holding their positions of power, are more active and well informed. Elites generally control the communications process, which means that information generally flows

---

[25] Dye and Zeigler point out that it is critical to understand what elite theory is **not** as well as what it **is**. Elite theory does not assume that those in power are constantly at odds with the masses, or that they always achieve their goals at the expense of the public welfare. Nor does it hold that elites are involved in a conspiracy to suppress the masses. The theory does not suggest that members of the elite are always in agreement with each other, and it does not even hold that they always get their way. It also acknowledges that elites may well be influenced by the masses. It only claims that elites will more frequently influence the masses than the masses will influence the elites.

ing public policy makes itself felt: We favor collective coercion to raise our personal standard of living, and oppose it when it is used to limit our own actions and raise someone else's income.

Many social problems involve the exploitation, whether deliberately or unconsciously, of one group by another, or people being prevented from benefiting from something that others want to keep for themselves. For example, most upper-middle-income (usually white) people have a high regard for geographic separation from poor people (frequently nonwhite). Consequently equality of access to the advantages of suburban living for the poor cannot be achieved without some sacrifice by the upper middle class of the "benefits" of that separation. The recognition of the relationship between the problem and its "solution" is a key part of the third stage.

4 *Gradual decline of intense public interest.* As more people realize how difficult and costly to themselves a solution would be, their enthusiasm for finding a "solution" diminishes rapidly. Some come to feel that solving the problem threatens them; others merely get bored or discouraged with the perceived futility of grappling with the issue. Also by this time another issue has usually been discovered by the media and is entering stage 2, and it claims the public's attention.

5 *The postproblem stage.* Having been replaced by successive issues at the center of public interest, the issue moves into a stage of reduced attention, although there may be a recurrence of interest from time to time. This stage differs from the preproblem stage in that some programs and policies have been put in place to deal with the issue. A government bureaucracy may have been given the task of administering a program and monitoring the situation. Special-interest groups may have developed a symbiotic relationship with the bureaucracy and have had a successful impact even though the "action" has shifted to other issues.

Source: Anthony Downs, "The 'Issue-Attention Cycle,'" *The Public Interest*, no. 28 (1972), pp. 38–50; also, Anthony Downs, "Up and Down with Ecology: The Issue-Attention Cycle," *Public Interest*, no. 32 (1973): 38–50.

from the elites to the masses. The masses rarely decide issues but accept the symbolic "democratic" institutions of voting and party membership, which gives them a means to identify with the system.[26]

Elites find some issues more acceptable than others, based upon how the issues are perceived and presented to those with the real power. The net effect of this, according to two analysts, "is that new demands, particularly those of disadvantaged or deprived groups, are the least likely to receive attention on either the systemic agenda of controversy or the institutional agenda."[27]

Pluralism (Group) Theory   Pluralism is a theory of government that attempts to reaffirm the democratic character of American society by asserting that public policy is the product of competition and negotiation between groups in society.

[26] Dye and Zeigler, *The Irony of Democracy*, pp. 6–7.
[27] Roger W. Cobb and Charles D. Elder, "The Politics of Agenda Building," *Journal of Politics* vol. 33, no. 4 (November 1971), p. 910.

This model differs from the elite model by contending that mass demands (and power) flow from individuals united in interest groups to decision makers through the political process of elections and political parties. Pluralism accepts that there are shortcomings in traditional democratic theory, which emphasizes individual responsibility and control. Pluralism itself emphasizes the tendency of individuals with common interests ("factions" in James Madison's term) to form groups to push their demands upon government. Competing groups make demands upon government through political institutions. Individuals are important to the extent that they act on behalf of group interests.

Competition between interest groups helps to protect individual interests by placing checks on the power groups can accumulate and preventing them from abusing the power they do achieve. Public policy at any given time results from the equilibrium achieved among the competing groups. The legislature, in this theory, acts as a referee of the group competition and records the victories of different groups in the form of statutes.[28] If the competing interest groups are roughly balanced, the policy that results roughly approximates the preferences of society in general. Overlapping group membership helps maintain the balance by preventing any single group from moving too far from societal values. Public policy tends to move in the direction of groups whose influence is growing and away from those whose influence is waning.

Group theory does not deny that individuals by themselves have little power or influence: Individuals play only a limited role by voting, or working in interest groups. (The political parties are the largest agglomerations of interest groups.) Unlike elite theory, the fundamental point of this model is not that some groups have more power than others, but that a semblance of democracy exists despite the importance of groups, based upon decentralized institutions in which interest groups protect minority interests.

Setting the Agenda: Getting from the Systemic to the Institutional Agenda
Elites who are powerful in their own right have relatively little trouble getting their issues before the public. Those who own the media can publish stories or air television shows.[29] A member of Congress or the President, including their respective bureaucracies, can propose a policy. Special-interest groups also frequently approach the government with their perceptions of problems and proposed solutions.

Ordinarily an individual must enlarge the scope of the conflict by mobilizing public opinion. This might be done by enlisting the aid of experts who are knowledgeable about the issue and how to publicize it. Frequently, the simplest solution is to seek out an interest group that already deals with a related topic. For exam-

---

[28] Earl Latham, "The Group Basis of Politics," in Heinz Eulau, Samuel Eldersveld, and Morris Janowitz (eds.), *Political Behavior* (New York: Free Press, 1956), p. 239.

[29] A number of works make the point that the media, popular opinion to the contrary, tend to be conservative and supportive of the conservative bias of elites. See, for example, W. Lance Bennett, *News: The Politics of Illusion*, 2nd ed. (New York: Longman, 1988).

ple, if one is concerned that local public school students appear to be falling below national standards in testing, one might approach the local Parent Teachers Association (PTA) regarding remedial steps that might be taken. Getting the local newspaper to write an article might elicit support for new school policies designed to improve the quality of education in the local schools.

The number of people affected by an issue, the intensity of the effect an issue has on the community, and the degree to which everyone's self-interest can be aroused to confront the problems are all factors to be considered when trying to get an issue on the institutional agenda. An analysis of what will happen if nothing is done about a problem, in terms of who will be affected and in what ways, can be a powerful inducement to action.

Setting the Agenda: Symbols and Getting on the Agenda   Ultimately the need to attract broad support to get an issue on the political agenda, and to try to move it to the institutional agenda, encourages the use of symbols. Symbols legitimize issues and attract support for the proposed policy goals. Symbols help people to order and interpret their reality, and even create the reality to which they give their attention. A major attribute of successful symbols is ambiguity. A symbol may be a slogan, an event, a person, or anything to which people attach meaning or value. Symbols can mean different things to different people. They permit the translation of private and personal intentions into wider collective goals by appealing to people with diverse motivations and values.[30] Ambiguity permits maneuvering room to reduce opposition to a policy. For instance, in the 1980s "welfare" came under increasing attack in a period of tight budgets and declining support for egalitarian policies. Calling the programs "workfare" rather than "welfare" reduced some of the opposition to them since the new term implied welfare recipients would not be getting "a free ride."

Civil rights efforts in the 1960s were initially known primarily for their use of slogans and symbolic marches rather than for any solid achievements. When marchers appealing to "equal rights," the "Constitution," and "justice and equality" were shown on television being attacked by police using dogs and fire hoses, the news reports had a powerful impact on the nation. After a relatively brief period, several effective pieces of legislation passed Congress. It is doubtful that the legislation could have passed without the powerful symbols that preceded it.

Policy Formulation and Proposal

Success in getting a problem accepted onto the policy agenda may depend in part on the ability to convince others that it is amenable to some governmental solution. Once the problem is on the agenda, however, specific plans for attacking it must be addressed. The problem has been clearly identified, and the need to do something about it accepted; policy formulation is then concerned with the

---

[30] Charles D. Elder and Roger W. Cobb, *The Political Uses of Symbols* (New York: Longman, 1983), pp. 28–29.

"**what**" questions associated with generating alternatives. What is the plan for dealing with the problem? What are the goals and priorities? What options are available to achieve those goals? What are the costs and benefits of each of the options? What externalities, positive or negative, are associated with each alternative?

The first option after looking at the proposed solutions may well be **to do nothing**. Most, but not all, public policy proposals cost money. Currently there are severe economic constraints on new policy initiatives at the state level and particularly at the national level. The **economic costs** of new programs at the national level have made it extremely difficult to add any new programs.

The huge budget deficits that started in the 1980s have created a dilemma for policy makers. Some believe the solution is to slash government expenses to equal tax revenues. Others argue that the public demands the social programs already in existence and would like to see new ones, so they propose raising taxes to meet the demand. Those espousing this view believe that America, as a rich nation, has needs that government can and should meet, such as homelessness or health care. They see the huge deficits as a way to prevent proposals for any new spending program.[31]

Federal budget deficits resulted in the "Balanced Budget and Emergency Deficit Control Act"—better known as Gramm-Rudman after Senators Phil Gramm (R-TX) and Warren Rudman (R-NH), who along with Senator Ernest Hollings (D-SC), sponsored it in 1985 as a means of balancing the budget by fiscal 1991. The bill was revised in 1987, but the deficit reduction targets were never achieved. It left nearly 70 percent of the federal budget exempt from across-the-board cuts, even if Congress did not meet the reduction goals.[32]

A more recent version of the legislation, Gramm-Rudman III, stated that proposed new policies would have to be presented along with the means to pay for them either through reductions in spending elsewhere in the budget or new revenue sources. President Bush—who in the 1988 campaign had pledged "no new taxes"—was then forced to accept "tax revenue increases" as the price for getting a budget compromise with Congress.

The result of these huge federal deficits has been that, since the mid-1980s, budgetary problems have dwarfed all others as the President and Congress have wrestled with the gap between revenues and demand.

The result has been few new policies being added to the public agenda, and old

---

[31] In his book *Came the Revolution: Argument in the Reagan Era* (New York: Harcourt Brace Jovanovich, 1988), Senator Daniel Patrick Moynihan contends that the deficit was intended to limit government growth. He wrote, "By the close of 1983, I knew the early deficits had been deliberate, that there had been a hidden agenda." Senator Moynihan said that few accepted his theory regarding the deficit being deliberate because it was "beyond the reach of the American political imagination that a small group of people deliberately created a protracted crisis." See *The New York Times*, December 2, 1988.

[32] Interest on the national debt, Social Security benefits, and veteran's retirement payments, were among the exempted budget items. The savings-and-loan bailout, which may reach $500 billion (about $2000 per capita) and benefits the financial elite primarily, was left exempt, as was approximately $50 billion dollars for the military effort against Iraq.

programs being reauthorized at the same or even reduced spending levels. For example, George Bush indicated his desire to be known as "the education President," and arranged a "summit conference" on education between the White House and state governors in 1989. However, the conference did not produce any offer of significant financial resources from Washington to help fund the educational programs everyone agreed were needed.

Increasingly programs are expected to be financed by their recipients. For example, the Medicare Catastrophic Coverage Act that was passed with bipartisan support prior to the 1988 election provided insurance against catastrophic illnesses for those on Medicare by imposing a ceiling on medical bills and paying 100 percent of the costs through Medicare. The goal was to relieve worry among the elderly that they would be impoverished by the high costs of medical care, especially hospitalization. This insurance was to be paid through a surtax on the income taxes of the elderly. The wealthiest elderly would pay most—a maximum surtax of $800 per year in 1989, rising to $1050 in 1993. The poorest among the elderly would pay $4 per month. The theory was that the elderly as the program's beneficiaries should bear the cost.[33]

Another major concern for political entrepreneurs are the **political costs** associated with taking action. Since many policies will alter the distribution of income, it can be expected that those whose incomes will be adversely affected will generally oppose them, while those who will be helped will generally be favorably disposed toward them. Political entrepreneurs sometimes find themselves caught between doing what they think is right and choosing the alternative that is the least costly from a political perspective.

Selecting Alternatives   The formulation of a policy proposal ordinarily includes not only a statement of the goals of the policy, but various alternatives (or programs) for achieving the goals. How the problem is formulated will often suggest how the alternatives are proposed.

Some policy theorists promote **rational analysis** as a plan for achieving government efficiency through a comprehensive review of all the policy options and an examination of their consequences. Rational analysis selects the option that **maximizes utility**.

Much of the animosity surrounding the budgetary process is claimed to result from its *lack* of rationality. Everyone from the person-in-the-street, to bureaucrats, to special-interest groups, to Congress, to the President believes that he or she can

---

[33] It may be surprising to some that an administration committed to tax reduction would propose such a program. It was put forth in part to secure the support of the elderly, whose backing of the Republicans had been weak. The pay-as-you-go plan flopped, however. Retirees who had procured insurance benefits in the private sector led an effort to repeal the bill. The wealthier elderly did not want to trade some of their economic independence to help less-well-off retirees reach an equal plane regarding health care. They resented subsidizing the less wealthy. Those leading the opposition, however, appealed to the less wealthy retirees by arguing that the medical costs of the elderly should be the responsibility of younger Americans as well. They argued successfully that to make the elderly alone pay more, regardless of economic circumstances, was unfair, and the beginning of a reduction in benefits for all retirees was to be firmly resisted.

produce a better, more rational budget. However, rational analysis of the budgetary process implies that **each** option be considered, and no analyst can do this nor can any analysis of the budget be completely comprehensive.[34] Some things are inevitably left out of every analysis. There is not even a basis for constructing a satisfactory list of criteria to determine which goals or alternatives are the most reasonable and which could be left out.

A model of all social problems that included their ranking by importance would be very expensive and difficult to keep up to date. People's and society's concerns change constantly. For instance, until about 1980, most Americans outside the medical profession were unaware of Alzheimer's disease. It is now generally known to be a relatively common form of dementia that afflicts a significant percentage of the elderly population. It causes memory loss, personality disorders, and a decrease in other mental capabilities. After research helped to define Alzheimer's as a particular pathology, an organization was formed by people who had family members diagnosed with the disease. The Alzheimer's Association has since opened an office in Washington to lobby Congress to double the amount of federal funds currently dedicated to Alzheimer's research. However, a complete analysis of the appropriate amount of federal money to spend for Alzheimer's research would have to include an analysis of **all other possible ways to spend the money**. That is, every other item in the budget such as aid to education, the space program, cancer research, environmental protection, even deficit reduction and lowering taxes would have to be considered.[35]

Only the political process can do this. **Budgetary decision making is a political process regarding choices about values.** The suggestion that this process could be replaced with an apolitical rationality is ingenuous. Several Presidents have argued in favor of Congress giving the President a **line-item veto**, as though this would take politics out of the process. But nothing can take politics out of the budgetary process.[36]

Other policy theorists therefore contend that an incremental approach is actu-

---

[34] See Charles E. Lindblom, "The Science of 'Muddling Through,'" *Public Administration Review*, vol. 19 (1959), pp. 79–88.

[35] Other supporters of the rational model agree that it is impossible to find the best of all possible courses of action. They would instead reduce the number of courses of action to a reasonable set of contenders. Then statistical decision-making models might be used to decide on a final rational allocation of budgetary resources. However, critics point out that the initial selection of contenders is a political decision and arbitrary.

[36] The budgeting process in the federal government is known as **line-item budgeting**. Congress presents a budget to the President that is broken down by organizational units such as the Department of Energy, and then by subunits such as renewable energy, solar energy, etc. Within all the subcategories, spending is broken down by accounts to include salaries, research, grants, etc.

A President using a line-item veto would merely be substituting one individual's judgment for the collective will of Congress—and a judgment presumably based just as much upon ideology, special-interest-group pressure, partisan concerns, and personal views about the nature of the general welfare as that of any senator or Congressional representative.

To suggest taking politics out of the budgetary process is rather like saying one should take doctors out of medicine or pilots out of flying. That is, the budget is inherently a political document.

ally much more rational. **Incrementalism** is an approach to decision making in which policy makers change policy at the margins. That is, they begin with the current set of circumstances and consider changing things in only a small way. Particularly in budgeting, this is the typical approach. Just note that **the best predictor of what next year's federal budget allocations will be is this year's allocations.** Incrementalism assumes that public policy decisions will usually involve only modest changes to the status quo and not require a thorough inspection of all the available options.

Incrementalism assumes the rational self-interest approach of individuals and groups. Since individual and group interests usually conflict, compromise will be required in which everyone will have to settle for less than they hoped for. This results in relatively small changes in existing policy. The budgetary process is thus simplified into a task that assumes each existing program will continue to be funded at its existing level because this level is perceived as fair. If the budget is growing, each program gets approximately the same percentage increase, with those programs having unusually strong support getting a slightly larger increase and those whose support or visibility are waning receiving slightly less. These new funding levels become the bases for the next year's budget.

Aaron Wildavsky maintains that incrementalism is the best technique for reaching budgetary decisions, because it reduces the decision-making process to manageable size. It focuses only on the **changes** to existing programs rather than requiring a complete justification of the entire program annually. The result is also an allocation of money according to each program's political strength. Since the selection of programs is a normative decision, according to Wildavsky, it is about as good a measure as we have regarding which programs are most deserving.[37]

The result of incrementalism is **satisficing**, or adopting a policy acceptable from all viewpoints rather than seeking the best solution possible. The "best" solution might prove unacceptable to so many decision makers that it would be voted down if proposed. For example, many public policy experts have recommended a significant tax increase on gasoline at the pump as the "best" way to reduce gas consumption and U.S. reliance on imported oil. Fear of consumer reaction and Republican opposition forced President Clinton to reduce a proposed gasoline tax increase from 20 cents to 5 cents a gallon. When the tax kicked in during the fall of 1993, few even noticed. In the fall of 1994, after inflation, gasoline prices were actually lower than before the tax increase. Since politics is the art of the possible, a negotiated compromise that wins some, if not all, support is preferred to defeat.

Incrementalism works, then, because it is in some ways the most rational approach to policy making. Time and resources are too limited to permit an examination of all the alternatives. There is a legitimacy in previous policies and programs, while the feasibility of new ones is less predictable. Incrementalism also

[37] Aaron Wildavsky, *The Politics of the Budgetary Process* (Boston: Little, Brown, 1964; rev. 4th ed., 1984).

permits quicker political settlements, particularly when disputes are at the margins regarding the modification of programs.

Adoption

Getting a proposed policy from the institutional agenda through the adoption process is crucial to effecting a change. In the late 1960s many public policy scholars focused on the question of how a bill becomes a law and the many veto points in the process. The process of proposing a bill and getting it passed is very straightforward in that it must follow a standardized procedure. However, the pitfalls that can befall a bill in the process are well known.

The definition of an issue and its impact on different portions of the population usually changes in the debate during the policy process. It is at this point that political entrepreneurs try to redraw the dimensions of the dispute in an effort to reconfigure political coalitions to gain a winning edge. Party leaders and senior members of the Congressional committee considering the issue often bide their time, waiting for other members of the committee or of Congress to become familiar with the issue. They generally then move when they sense the time is ripe for action, based upon their experience in dealing with such matters.

The separation of powers in government allows each branch to judge the legitimacy, and if necessary to take action to check the moves, of the other branches. The actors involved here are clearly political elites and must be persuaded not of the wisdom of the proposed policy, but of its chances of success politically. For this reason the major concern at this point is the following: "Is the proposed policy politically viable?" The broadest support for the program must be in evidence here to convince political entrepreneurs that it is in their own interests to promote the policy through their votes.

Implementation and Operation

Implementation bears a striking resemblance to the endgame in chess. This is that part of the game where the number of forces in play have been significantly reduced. The game moves into its final phase of accomplishing the original goal of pressing the advantage until someone achieves victory. This is a very critical phase, however, because any carelessness can result in disastrous failure.

In the policy process, once a problem has been identified, alternatives examined, and a solution selected and legitimated through the adoption of legislation, one part of the policy-making process has been completed. But this is also the beginning of another part of the process—implementing the policy. **Implementation** means carrying out the policy or program operations. Or as Robert Lineberry asserts, implementation is "a continuation of policy making by other means."[38] Implementation has attracted a significant amount of research

---

[38] Robert Lineberry, *American Public Policy* (New York: Harper & Row, 1977), p. 71.

because policies often do not accomplish what they were designed to achieve.[39] There are a series of decisions and actions that are necessary to put a policy into effect, and as in chess, miscalculation in the original design strategy or in implementation may bring the entire effort to naught.

Policy advocates have come to realize that **the time to plan for the implementation phase is during the formulation and policy selection stage**. All the earlier phases, if done well, will reach this stage where the proposal is to be translated into action. Several factors in the design phase will facilitate the implementation stage. Perhaps most critical is the question of **policy design**. That is, has the problem been accurately defined? Only if the problem is accurately understood do the causal relationships become evident and allow the policy analyst to correctly perceive the connections between a particular policy's operation and its intent.

It is usually much easier to implement a policy if it is **clearly stated and consistent with other policy objectives**. Vague and ambiguous language will be received by the state officials handling the implementation quite differently than crisp lucid legislation. Vaguely worded laws may be subject to varying interpretations by bureaucrats or state officials tasked with implementing a program. Vagueness may even permit opponents to effectively sabotage the policy. On the other hand, there are times when vagueness may be preferred to clarity, if the alternative would be no program at all. An excellent example of this is the Constitution, which as the basic framework of the U.S. government is also a policy statement. When the Founding Fathers were unable to agree on clear statements on several issues, they compromised on vague, broad statements and agreed to let later practice determine the outcome. The "necessary and proper" clause is an obvious instance.

Another factor that facilitates the implementation of a policy is its perceived legitimacy. For instance, a program that passes both houses of Congress with large majorities or a decision by the Supreme Court that is unanimous or nearly so will generally also have the support of those tasked with its implementation. Even those who have misgivings will be more inclined to go along with the perceived mandate.

Implementation problems can arise when programs cut across the jurisdictions of different agencies at the national, state, and local levels. Unless precautions are taken, coordination difficulties among the levels of officials who must carry out programs in the field are not uncommon. Another design flaw that causes implementation problems is ignoring the limitations of agencies given the responsibility for the programs. For example, in an effort to reduce the costs of Social Security Disability Insurance (SSDI) benefits, the Reagan administration used administrative rules to dramatically increase the number of eligibility reviews needed to determine if people were still disabled and entitled to continued benefit payments.

---

[39] See Paul Sabatier, "Top-Down and Bottom-Up Models of Policy Implementation: A Critical Analysis and Suggested Synthesis," *Journal of Public Policy*, vol. 6 (January 1986), pp. 21–48. See also Laurence O'Toole, "Policy Recommendations for Multi-Actor Implementation: An Assessment of the Field," *Journal of Public Policy*, vol. 6 (April 1986), pp. 181–210.

Most state agencies had been performing an average of approximately 25,000 reviews a quarter. Under the new rules, they were required to review an average of about 125,000 cases a quarter, with the federal Social Security Administration ordered to review the state decisions. State agencies were not given any significant increases in resources to conduct these reviews and buckled under their expanded case loads. Backlogs increased, the termination rate increased, and legal appeals increased as people believed they had been removed unfairly from the roles. In the summer of 1983, Congress stepped in and imposed a 6-month moratorium on removing people from eligibility. In addition to illustrating the need to design carefully, this example also suggests the wisdom of making changes incrementally.[40]

Implementation is the most important part of the policy-making process for students of public administration. Much of the important work of implementing policy is done by the "street-level" bureaucrats, including judges, public health workers, school teachers, social workers, and other federal, state, and local government employees.

Evaluation

The last stage of the policy-making process is evaluation. Every stage involves a purposeful effort to bring about some change in the political environment. But in particular the process of formulating a proposal and choosing among alternatives to achieve the policy's objectives suggests the need for some criteria or standard to determine if the implemented policy has achieved its objectives.

Evaluation is the assessment of how a program achieves its intended goals. All the earlier stages of the policy process look toward a future goal to be achieved; evaluation looks backward. It is a tool whose primary purpose is to appraise the operation of a program and provide feedback to those involved in the earlier stages. This feedback permits modifications in the policy to improve its efficiency and effectiveness. Evaluation also pinpoints unintended effects of a policy and allows adjustment in the implementation process to avoid those that are undesirable. In addition, it can be used to monitor the expenditure of funds to see that they were spent according to the terms of the law or grant. Thus, such assessments focus on the implementation of a program and how it has met the goals and objectives spelled out in the selection and adoption phases of the policy process.

Evaluation of public policy programs came into its own during the 1960s. Under Great Society legislation, there was a surge in government programs to deal with a variety of social ills. At the same time critics charged that these programs resulted in many **government failures**, and at a significant cost to taxpayers. The media reported cases of waste and inefficiency, as well as programs that

---

[40] Martha Derrick *Agency Under Stress* (Washington, DC: Brookings Institution, 1990), pp. 33–45. See also Donald Chambers, "The Reagan Administration's Welfare Retrenchment Policy: Terminating Social Security Benefits for the Disabled," *Policy Studies Review*, vol. 5, no. 1 (November 1985).

were not achieving their intended goals. Congress began requiring more vigorous evaluations of programs by agencies like the General Accounting Office (GAO).

It is useful to make a distinction between policy making and policy analysis. This course is primarily concerned with the policy-making process. Policy analysts, however, emphasize the evaluation process and use a variety of different methods to assess policy. Those include laboratory studies, simulations, case studies, sample surveys, and cost-benefit analyses, to name just a few. The process often also involves the use of analytical techniques, such as applied statistical analysis, to measure program effectiveness in meeting goals.

CONCLUSION

1 Public policy has developed as a subfield within the discipline of political science since the mid-1960s. As a social science, it draws upon the humanities, and history in particular, for its data. It also utilizes the scientific method in an effort to explain and predict underlying causal relationships in policy making and uses empirical methodology to test the validity of causal relationships. Existing at the confluence of the social sciences, public policy draws upon theoretical developments in the various social sciences.

2 The complexity of the problems in policy analysis has made the development of public policy theory difficult. Predictions that may be valid solely in terms of the underlying assumptions of a discipline such as economics or political science are often not based on data broad enough in scope to assure their accuracy in the larger policy scheme. Such predictions fail to take into account all the significant phenomena that influence the politicoeconomic variables related to a problem. This means that any effective theory development must begin at the micro level and take into account individual rational actors and their decision-making preferences, then move toward the macro-level aspects of institutional constraints and the societal effects of policy.

3 Scholarship over the last 20 years has resulted in a significant accumulation of knowledge regarding the public policy-making process. Dividing the process into stages beginning with getting an issue on the public agenda, formulating the policy proposal, achieving its adoption, implementing the policy as a program, and evaluating the program's effectiveness in achieving the original policy goals has been the standard analytical approach. This has resulted in uncovering phenomena, such as "critical actors," that were previously overlooked.

QUESTIONS FOR DISCUSSION

1 Discuss the role of theory in understanding phenomena from the natural sciences. Does it differ from the role of theory in the social sciences? Why?

2 Why is the development of theory in the social sciences more difficult than in the natural sciences?

3 What are the special problems in developing theory in the policy sciences?

4 Why are the contributions of policy analysts not held in high regard by policy makers? What if anything can be done to strengthen the role of policy analysts?

5 Why is it so difficult to get a proposed policy adopted and implemented? How would you suggest streamlining the process?

KEY CONCEPTS

Abstraction	Normal curve of error
Adoption	Pluralism
Assumption	Policy agenda
Elite theory	Policy formulation
Evaluation	Rational analysis
Hypothesis	Satisficing
Implementation	Scope of conflict
Incrementalism	Symbols
Institutional agenda	Systemic agenda
Iron-triangle	Theory
Issue-attention cycle	Values
Line-item veto	Variables

SUGGESTED READINGS

Bruce Adams, "The Limitations of Muddling Through: Does Anyone in Washington Really Think Anymore?" *Public Administration Review*, vol. 39 (November/December 1979).

John J. Bailey and Robert J. O'Connor, "Operationalizing Incrementalism: Measuring the Muddles," *Public Administration Review*, 35 (January/February 1975).

William E. Connally (ed.), *The Bias of Pluralism* (New York: Atherton, 1971).

Robert Dahl, *Who Governs?* (New Haven, CT: Yale University Press, 1961). This is the classic pluralist work.

Thomas R. Dye, *Who's Running America? The Bush Era*, 5th ed. (Englewood Cliffs, NJ: Prentice-Hall, 1990).

John S. Furnival, *Colonial Policy and Practice* (New York: New York University Press, 1956).

John W. Kingdon, *Agendas, Alternatives, and Public Policies* (Boston: Little, Brown, 1984).

Charles E. Lindblom, "The Science of 'Muddling Through,'" *Public Administration Review*, vol. 19 (Spring 1959).

C. Wright Mills, *The Power Elite* (New York: Oxford University Press, 1956).

David B. Truman, *The Governmental Process* (New York: Knopf, 1971).

3

RATIONAL PUBLIC CHOICE

The supply of private goods is generally determined by market forces (as discussed in Chap. 1). There is some degree of government involvement in any market-oriented economy in the production of public goods. Government involvement in the economy includes indirect control of the macroeconomy through the mechanisms suggested by the fiscal and monetary policies of Keynesian theory.

Government intervention frequently does not achieve the goals its policies intended, nor does it achieve as efficient an allocation of goods as possible. This chapter is concerned with how decisions in government are made and why they do not always achieve government ideals. A widely accepted approach to this topic is **rational public choice theory**. This is an elaboration of an approach originally associated with microeconomic theory, which views the individual as a consumer of government goods and services. The model assumes that individuals are rational and respond to information regarding their own self-interest. Public choice theory can be applied across many of the social sciences, although there may be differences in emphasis among the disciplines. It attempts to focus on the most significant factors determining individual behavior, while recognizing that individual preferences may change depending upon the different positions they occupy in a decision-making spectrum. These abstractions make it possible to reach conclusions about many different circumstances and types of behavior in the policy-making process. There are several limitations to this approach. A major problem is that making individuals the focal point of the institutions being studied makes it awkward, if not impossible, to account for the variety of behaviors that occurs in different institutions and at different levels in the same institution. Public choice theorists also debate whether the political system under significant pressure from special-interest groups is institutionally capable of representing the needs of individual citizens. Finally, the model treats all policy goals and demands as equally valid.

INTRODUCTION

The discussion of public goods and externalities in Chap. 1 was based on the concept of market failure. It also explained why societies substitute collective action for individual endeavors in certain situations.

Whenever market performance is judged to be defective, we speak of **market failure**. Market failure does not mean that nothing good has happened, but only that the best attainable outcome has not been produced. There are two senses of "the best attainable outcome has not been produced." One relates to the inability of the market to achieve efficiency in the distribution of the community's resources. The other sense has to do with the failure of the market to further social goals, such as achieving the desired distribution of income or providing adequate health care for everyone. Consequently, a private market that functions without government intervention may lead to consequences a society is unwilling to accept.

When markets cannot achieve the best attainable outcome, governments intervene to improve the situation. We more or less assume that democratically elected governments must be responsive to promoting "the general welfare" of society and will therefore provide the necessary improvements upon and corrections to market failures. But just as there are discrepancies between the theory of market efficiency and the failure of the market to produce ideal outcomes, there are gaps between the theory of democracy and democracy's failure to preserve certain values such as equality or equity. Government's overall ability to counteract market failure has itself become an issue.

The U.S. government acts through a distinctive assortment of institutional arrangements to develop public policy. Our representative democracy is based upon majority voting, frequently focused through special-interest groups, and its policies and programs are implemented by a government bureaucracy. The theory of **rational public choice** was developed to explain how governments operate in developing policy. Rational public choice theory makes it clear that government policy making, like market allocation, may not result in the best attainable outcome. A society may be faced with the dilemma of choosing between a market solution that is imperfect and a government policy that is also not perfect. Simplistic notions demanding that we should return to basics and "let the market do it" or that we should abandon the market and "let government do it" must themselves be abandoned. Instead the costs and benefits of market solutions to social problems, government solutions, or a combination of the two must be examined in order to select policies that will be the most effective in meeting society's needs.

A basic premise of rational public choice is that "political man" or "woman" (political entrepreneurs, voters, and members of special-interest groups) an "economic man" or "woman" (producers and consumers) are one and the same person. The person who votes or runs for political office is also the consumer of economic goods and concerned with opportunity costs. In both roles people decide on their preferences based upon their rational self-interest and act purposefully to bring about outcomes that are desirable to them. This is not to deny that people may also have social consciences or value altruism. But it suggests why it may be difficult to develop a broad commitment in society to transfer benefits from contributors to noncontributors, i.e., from the privileged to the poor. It also suggests why the "haves" acquire more power with which to further their self-interest than the "have-nots."

Rational public choice provides an analysis and an explanation of the society **as it is** and not necessarily **as it should be**. That is, it explains actual social behavior. It explains why individuals with high incomes are more likely to vote than those with low incomes, and why they are more likely to be active members of special-interest groups. The theory also suggests why there are built-in social and political supports for the status quo.

We have already identified public policy as having a strong normative component. When people ask the government to intervene, to correct a failure, they are bringing to bear their moral judgments to determine how and where society has fallen short of an ideal. This involves the concepts of justice and fairness. Thus, when studying the public policy-making process we should concern ourselves with the way political institutions work with a view to making them work better.

John Maynard Keynes seems to have overestimated the ability of rational economic management by democratic governments. Governments are not neutral institutions that can correct market failures and implement a consensus of societal views regarding equity and fairness. While problems that often occur in private markets may justify government intervention using public policies, the conclusion is inescapable that public decision making by governments has imperfections of its own.

Still, we noted in Chap. 2 that governments everywhere play central roles in the economic and social lives of their populations. One useful procedure to get a good sense of the importance of government as discerned through its public policies is to examine tax revenues as a percentage of gross domestic product (GDP). In the group of Western countries included in Fig. 3-1, from 30 to over 50 percent of all output flows to the government sector.

The government is the major consumer and supplier of goods. Households supply labor to governmental bureaucracies in the form of military and civilian personnel. Households also supply money through taxes and loans to the government and receive back services such as national defense and assistance in education, health care, housing, communications, highways, unemployment compensation, retirement benefits, and a myriad of other government-influenced or -controlled goods and services.

Since government is central to our examination of public policy, we need to analyze government decision making. It is fairly easy to assume that individuals act on the basis of rational self-interest so that consumers maximize their utility (Chap. 1), and that business entrepreneurs act to maximize their profits (see Chap. 4). But such an assumption is not as obvious when one discusses government decision making. Nonetheless, rational public choice theory as applied to public policy

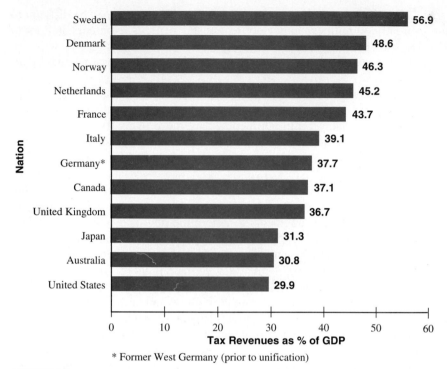

* Former West Germany (prior to unification)

FIGURE 3-1
Tax revenues as a percent of gross domestic product, 1990. *Source:* Statistical Abstract, *1993, p. 857.*

assumes that government decisions are made by individuals acting alone or in groups to serve their self-interest just as predictably as the economic decisions made by consumers and producers.

This chapter considers different theories about and players in government decision making and policy growth from this perspective, and why there are so many government failures in public interventions. **Government failure exists when government establishes public policies that fail to produce efficient or more equitable results as their outcomes**, and this involves the behavior of those who take part **in the political process**. Participants include politicians, special-interest groups, the media, voters, and bureaucrats.

PUBLIC INTEREST THEORY OF GOVERNMENT

According to the **public interest theory of government, the actions of the government are designed to optimize the welfare of the general public**. If the purpose of government is to maximize the public interest, then presumably when the U.S. government issues safety regulations regarding commercial aviation, or permits the Food and Drug Administration to require pharmaceutical firms to meet testing requirements, it does so with the aim of improving the general welfare of society. If interest rates are limited to protect people's ability to borrow money, or rent controls are instituted to protect the ability of low-income families to find housing, it is held to be in the public interest.

Yet we often hear of cases in which government appears to side with special-interest groups and against the interest of the general public. For example, in the United States, why does the government subsidize tobacco farmers to grow tobacco when it is clear that smoking is a threat to people's health? Why does the government not take action to reduce the emissions of sulfur dioxide into the atmosphere in the Ohio Valley when it has been clearly established that those emissions produce acid rain, which kills forests and streams in New England and Canada? Why are the prices of dairy products held above the levels demanded by competitive market forces through government policies, then low-income individuals subsidized to purchase those products by means of food stamps?

It is beyond question that many government endeavors are inconsistent in their effects and not in the public interest. Why and how does this happen? One response is that the regulatory agencies, and sometimes even the government as a whole, are "captured" by special-interest groups. When special-interest groups control the agencies or the government itself, the outcome is policies that are beneficial to those special interests rather than to the public as a whole.

THE CAPTURE THEORY OF GOVERNMENT

It often appears that the government acts inconsistently, making various public policy decisions that seem incompatible. To many this is taken as evidence of incompetence on the part of the bureaucracy. To others it is an illustration of how various political groups in society exercise political power. The view that **government policies serve special-interest groups that have captured particular regulatory agencies or the governing authority as a whole is the capture theory of government. This theory contends that government maximizes the welfare of special-interest groups.** The special-interest groups typically argue that support of their position is in the public interest. Generally they are reluctant to admit that they are the primary beneficiaries of policies developed by the agencies they have captured. For instance, the dairy lobby denies that dairy farmers are the primary beneficiaries of dairy price supports. Lobbyists insist that it is important for the dairy industry to remain profitable so that an adequate supply of milk will remain available, especially for America's children to aid in their growth into strong, healthy adults.

The capture theory of government is useful in explaining some effects of government intervention, but not all. Interest groups often conflict with other organized groups in the political arena, and are forced to compromise on some issues or lose entirely on others. Automobile manufacturers have long opposed mandatory pollution control devices, seatbelts, and higher mileage requirements on cars, but have had to compromise on these issues. Likewise, pharmaceutical companies have long opposed the expensive testing and long delays required to get new drugs onto the market, but have had to accept these constraints anyway in the interests of public safety.

PUBLIC CHOICE THEORY

A theory that incorporates some aspects of public interest theory and the capture theory of government is public choice theory. **Public choice theory is the study of the collective decisions made by groups of individuals through the political process to maximize their own self-interest**. It is based upon the premise that competition takes place in the political arena. Although the coercive power of government is imposing, it is still limited by several factors. It is constrained, first of all, by the resources that it can command. The government relies on its taxing and spending powers in many instances to conduct public policy. **The function of taxes is to transfer control over capital from the private sector to the public sector**. By using that purchasing power to buy goods and services for the public, the government is altering the mix of goods and services that would be demanded if everything were left to the private sector. This inevitably means a move to a different point on the production possibilities curve (see Chap. 1).

The government is also constrained by the political landscape. For example, there are only two major political parties in the United States, which constrains the selection of alternatives by the voters. In the private sector, if there were only two firms producing a good, we would define the market as a shared monopoly with no competition to give consumers a choice.

COST-BENEFIT ANALYSIS

Externalities and the need for public goods compels government intervention to provide a variety of goods and services. But to assume that government can obtain the required information about how to rectify negative externalities and provide public goods in the correct quantities may be unwarranted. Since consumers of public goods or services have incentives to not disclose their true preferences and to downplay their willingness to pay in the hopes that others will be taxed, how is the government to decide how much to provide? Moreover, when government moves to use resources to alter the mix of goods and services produced, there will inevitably be conflicting goals and constituencies between which political choices must be made. Government finds itself in the middle of the adversarial relationship between those private-sector forces that stand to lose as a result of government action and those that stand to gain.

In theory, determining the optimal mix of output is uncomplicated: More government-sector endeavors are advisable only if the gains from those activities exceed their opportunity costs. So **cost-benefit analysis (CBA) as applied to government activities is used to calculate and compare the difference between the costs and the benefits of a program or project**. Basically, the benefits of a proposed public project are compared to the value of the private goods given up (through taxes) to produce it. But while the notion that the benefits or utility of a project should exceed its costs is uncomplicated enough in principle, it is exceedingly complex to determine this ratio in practice.

In theory, all the costs and benefits of a program should be identified and converted into monetary units covering the life of the proposed project. Ideally an attempt is made to consider the negative externalities resulting from the program, such as the roadside businesses that will be lost due to the construction of a new limited-access highway. In theory also, with benefits and costs measured in the same units, the benefits and costs of alternative policies can be determined not just within a policy sector, but across diverse sectors. For example, cost-benefit analysis could be used to determine policy alternatives in health care such as whether funds would be more efficiently spent on prenatal care for pregnant women who are indigent, for AIDS research, or for a screening and preventive medicine program to reduce mortality from cardiovascular disease. Such analysis then could also be used to determine if the funds to be allocated to the highest benefit-to-cost ratio program in the health care sector would be more efficiently spent if allocated to the construction of a dam.[1]

The most efficient use of public resources would be to rank proposed programs from highest to the lowest in terms of their benefit-cost ratios, and proceed to implement those programs in priority order beginning with those having the highest ratios. This would meet one goal of cost-benefit analysis: determining the most efficient ways of using public funds.

But cost-benefit analysis has a second goal: determining the merit of specific government policies such as discouraging the use of disposable containers, encouraging higher average miles-per-gallon standards for use of gasoline by automobiles, promoting transportation safety, and establishing honesty in product labeling. "Merit" is different from "efficiency," but it also has economic consequences.

In dealing with private market goods, the demand for a particular good determines the benefits of its production. But in regard to some public goods, the benefits generated by its "output" are less clear. For example, government control over air quality usually involves political tradeoffs between a healthy and aesthetic environment and the loss of production of other economic goods. Reducing air pollution from automobiles increases the price of cars, which results in the decreased production of automobiles and therefore fewer jobs. In this case, the losers from this government policy are those whose jobs are lost or who cannot afford to buy a higher-priced car. The winners are those who advocate environmental protection, and those who will suffer fewer illnesses (or perhaps will not die) because of a cleaner atmosphere.

Cost-benefit analysis is thus typically forward-looking in that it tries to calculate the costs and benefits of proposed actions to help government policy makers decide on those programs that will best serve the public interest. However, such analysis has its defects. Two of them were mentioned in footnote 1. A third problem is that cost-benefit ratios do not supply the political dexterity needed to navigate legisla-

---

[1] A significant defect of cost-benefit analysis is that it does not consider the distributional question of "who" should pay the costs and "who" should receive the benefits, a decision presumably left to the political process. It may be that a new highway will exact a cost from those in a low-income housing project who will be displaced, while it will benefit well-heeled business investors who own commercially zoned land along the proposed highway route.

Another defect of cost-benefit analysis is associated with the difficulty of quantifying some factors in terms of dollars. An example would be attempting to estimate the cost in dollars of destroying the natural habitat of the spotted owl—the survival of which has little or no economic value—by permitting the lumber industry to continue harvesting trees in the state of Washington.

tors or government bureaucrats through the negotiations often needed to satisfy opposing interests on a given issue. And a fourth problem has to do with the nature of politics itself: Even when not captured by special-interest groups, the government often functions in ways that have to do more with getting politicians reelected than with serving the public interest.

The most serious defect of cost-benefit analysis, however, was already alluded to in footnote 1: It seeks to maximize only the value of efficiency when other values such as equity, justice, or even the environment might deserve inclusion in the consideration of public policy decisions. Since it is not possible to reduce moral or ethical concerns to the requirements of cost-benefit analysis, this means the analysts who use this approach must go beyond it in making their policy recommendations; not to do so will have the effect of **positively excluding normative concerns**. In a period of tight federal budgets, government officials often defend their reliance on CBA by claiming that they should not be involved in controversial "ideological" debates, but rather only with the most efficient policy. They may even assert a moral obligation to apply CBA in order to save taxpayers money. But issues such as reducing acid rain in the Northeast or reducing timber cutting in the Northwest have normative and environmental as well as efficiency dimensions, all of which should be addressed.

POLITICAL ENTREPRENEURS

Politicians play a role similar to business entrepreneurs when making collective political decisions. They are as essential to the political process as business leaders are to the operations of their firms. But there are also big differences. In business, entrepreneurs must bring together the right mix of the factors of production for productive efficiency. Consumers register their opinions about the value of a product by the simple decision of whether to buy it or not. A negative decision by consumers leads to business losses, and if corrective action is not taken quickly by the company producing the product, to business failure. Chrysler Corporation is an example of a corporation willing to admit its mistakes and take corrective action when the message of threatened bankruptcy became unmistakable. Lee Iacocca as the head of Chrysler was willing to admit personal mistakes in an effort to maintain his job. In business this kind of changing direction is seen as courageous.

But politicians often have strong incentives to avoid admitting errors. After all, the get elected by insisting they definitely have solutions to the problems facing the nation, not by claiming they might have solutions. In politics, to admit a policy is not working and to change direction is seen as a sign of weakness and being in disarray. The Reagan campaign in 1980 used President Carter's shifts in policy to defeat him in the election. Besides, in the end the politician does not personally have to pay for an expenditure, even if it turns out to have been a mistake.

An elected official also is expected to reflect the views of his or her constituents, not merely his or her own personal views. But unlike business where consumers clearly "vote" on products by buying or not buying them, in politics the voting mechanism is not well suited to determining how constituents want to be represented on any given issue. Take education as an example. In theory, one votes for more education by electing the candidate committed to initiating new programs or putting more resources into education. Nonetheless, in practice it is much more complicated than that since every candidate campaigns on a whole series of issues of which education is only one, and the winning candidate may have been elected on the basis of issues other than his or her position on education or even despite it. This makes constituent views on any issue difficult to discern, nor is there any reliable way to assign weights to the different views of voters.

Furthermore, fewer than half those eligible to vote usually participate in any given election. In 1988, George Bush was elected with 53.9 percent of the votes cast for President. Almost 90 million votes were cast, which means just over half of those eligible to vote actually did so. Thus he was elected by about 28 percent of the eligible voters. Presidential elections show the highest voter turnout. For off-year Congressional and state elections, the turnout rarely exceeds 40 percent of those registered to vote.[2]

Therefore, since the first task of political entrepreneurs is to get elected and the second to get reelected,[3] and since they are expected to reflect the views of their constituents, this means they are likely to reflect the views of constituents who actually vote or who make their views known to their political representatives in other ways (writing letters, lobbying, etc.).

As Table 3-1 suggests, the higher a person's socioeconomic status as measured by income, education, employment, and other demographic characteristics, the more likely the person will be to register and vote. The gaps between the lowest and highest in income and education approaches 40 percent, which is a point that a political entrepreneur cannot fail to consider.

The voting records of Congressional representatives, senators, and even Presidents reflect a heightened awareness of constituent interests as elections draw nearer. Conversely, their voting records show more independence immediately after they are safely voted back into office. Senators show the most independence after an election, since they are safely in office for 6 years. Members of the House of Representatives, who run for reelection every 2 years, are the most closely attuned to the views of the constituents who voted for them. Their high return rate to Congress may reflect that to some extent. Presidents also respond to the political

---

[2] Usually about two-thirds of those eligible to vote are registered in local elections. Thus a political entrepreneur may win an election with only about 20 percent of those eligible to vote, which reduces any legitimate claim to a mandate. See Norman R. Luttbeg, "Differential Voting Turnout in the American States, 1960–82," *Social Science Quarterly*, vol. 65 (March 1984), pp. 60–73.

[3] There is little disagreement with Richard Fenno's statement that candidate goals include reelection, influence within the Congress, and good public policy. See Richard Fenno, Jr., *Congressmen in Committees* (Boston: Little, Brown Co., 1973). This is not to suggest that politicians seeking election or reelection are motivated by greed. Politicians may seek power, not as an end in itself, but as the means for implementing their visions of good public policy. But election is a prerequisite to the achievement of good policy, and therefore must be an immediate goal.

TABLE 3-1
REGISTRATION AND VOTING ACCORDING TO SELECTED SOCIAL
CHARACTERISTICS, 1988

Characteristics	Were registered, %	Voted, %
Income		
Under $5,000	48	35
$5,000– $9,999	53	41
$10,000–$14,999	57	48
$15,000–$19,999	63	53
$20,000–$24,999	67	58
$25,000–$34,999	72	64
$35,000–$49,999	78	70
$50,000 and over	82	76
Education		
Elementary	47	37
High School, 1–3 yrs.	53	41
4 yrs.	65	55
College, 1–3 yrs.	73	65
4 years or more	83	78
Employment status		
Employed	67	58
Unemployed	50	39
Race		
White	68	59
Black	64	51
Hispanic	36	29
Age		
18–19	43	32
20–29	52	41
30–44	66	58
45–64	75	68
65 and older	78	69
Sex		
Male	65	56
Female	68	58

"market" pressures exerted by the not so invisible hands of voters at the ballot box. The late H. R. Haldeman, Richard Nixon's chief of staff, noted how political self-interest dominated that administration's policy making when he wrote the following in his diary dated December 15, 1970:

> K [Henry Kissinger] came in and the discussion covered some of the general thinking about Vietnam and the P's [President Nixon's] big peace plan for next year, which K later told me he does not favor. He thinks that any pullout next year would be a serious mis-

take because the adverse reaction to it could set in well before the '72 elections. He favors, instead, a continued winding down and then a pullout right at the fall of '72 so that if any bad results follow they will be too late to affect the election.[4]

President Nixon understood that the United States could not "win" in Vietnam and that after an American pullout, the South Vietnamese army would disintegrate. In the end he agreed with Kissinger, and delayed that outcome for political reasons. After the election in 1972, an agreement was signed in January 1973 on terms that led quickly to the inevitable North Vietnamese victory. In the private marketplace, communications between consumers and producers are much more direct and time-sensitive.

BALLOTS AND DECISION MAKING

Political discussions often make references to the "will of the people." But ascertaining what that will is when people make conflicting demands is not an easy task. Different voting rules have been suggested, including unanimity voting, simple majority voting, and two-thirds majority voting.

Unanimity

In an ideal world, there would be no conflict. Public choice would result from the unanimity of views from the population. The great advantage of the unanimity rule is that no one is misused, since every voter must approve each proposition. The difficulty with a unanimity rule is that each voter has a veto power. Anyone likely to be made worse off by the proposal would veto it. Thus, a government's public policies would have to meet the condition of a **Pareto improvement, which occurs when a reallocation of resources causes at least one person to be better off without making anyone else worse off.**[5] Unanimity is at the base of any policy agreement between two individuals in that, when two people agree on a policy, they do so because it makes both of them better off. That is, they are unanimous in

---

[4] H. R. Haldeman, *The Haldeman Diaries: Inside the Nixon White House* (New York: G. P. Putnam's Sons, 1994), p. 221.

Other Presidents have also made military decisions with an awareness of the political implications. President Lincoln was willing to shift troop deployments during the Civil War in a way that strengthened his chances for reelection. Troop units from states in which his reelection chances were close were either moved to the rear of battlefronts or out of the fighting altogether to reduce their casualties and the reasons that families and friends from those states would have to oppose Lincoln. Troops from states where his reelection chances were either very high or very low were moved to areas where the fighting was heaviest and the likelihood of casualties the greatest. See Gore Vidal, *Lincoln* (New York: Ballantine Books, 1984). Robert Tollison's research supports Gore Vidal's position. See Robert Tollison, "Dead Men Don't Vote" (Fairfax, VA: Public Choice Center, George Mason University, 1989).

[5] This is distinguished from a Pareto optimum, which is a situation in which it is impossible to make any Pareto improvement, that is, when it is impossible to make any person better off without making someone else worse off. Under unanimity rules, the individual being made worse off would veto any change.

agreeing to the exchange or they would not have agreed upon it. But in the real world of public policy matters, unanimity is not likely to lead to useful outcomes.

Suppose, for example, that a remote community is considering the construction of a community satellite dish to receive otherwise inaccessible television programming. Suppose also that the dish is to be financed by dividing the cost equally among the members of the community. Sensing how much the project means to everyone else, one villager who greatly desires access to satellite television may nevertheless profess a preference for keeping the intrusions of the outside world out of the community's peaceful valley. He or she may then demand a large bribe not to veto the project. A unanimity rule is an invitation to bribery because it offers individuals an incentive to hide their true preferences regarding public goods in order to reduce personal costs or to gain something at the expense of others. The costs of reaching a decision under such conditions are prohibitive, and government paralysis results with no practical decisions able to be made. Therefore it is necessary to accept some principle for public decision making short of unanimity.

Majority Voting

The excessively high costs of decision making associated with unanimity voting leads to a search for lower-cost alternatives. **The majority voting rule provides that in the choice between alternatives an action or decision is approved if it receives a majority of the votes**. Majority rule is a basic principle of decision making in democratic societies.

Unfortunately, majority rule also has serious problems. For example, under it, a bare majority may get some benefit no matter how slight, while a ponderous sacrifice is exacted from the minority. Thus majority rule may result in a situation in which a society is worse off in that the benefit to the majority may fall far short of the total costs imposed on the minority.

For example, suppose there are 100 villagers in the remote community we mentioned earlier considering the investment in the satellite dish. Each would require a line from the dish to their cottage to receive the benefit of the cost to the community. Suppose under majority rule 51 villagers vote to invest in the satellite dish and connect their cottages by cable to it, and also to assess every villager an equal amount to pay for the dish and the hookups. The minority 49 villagers who voted against the measure must pay the tax but will get no benefit and thus will suffer significantly, while the majority 51 villagers may well receive a benefit that barely exceeds their assessment. Consequently, there is an overall loss to this community because of majority rule.

Majority rule can be inefficient also because a policy that may benefit a minority a great deal may be defeated if it makes the majority slightly worse off. For instance, most people will not contract AIDS. But for the minority that do, the cost of treatment is extremely high. The majority may resist paying a relatively small tax to cover the cost of health care for those so afflicted however.

This last example points up the major weakness of majority rule, and one long recognized: It places minority rights at risk. Thus most democratic forms of government that employ majority rule try to protect the rights of minorities against "overbearing" majorities by Constitutional means.[6]

The Voting Paradox

Majority rule does not generate such manifestly unfair results if voters act rationally in their decisions. But for rational behavior to occur, transitivity is necessary.[7] **Majority rule, to be rational, should produce a transitive group decision. However, majority rule may not necessarily generate a transitive group decision, even though each individual chooses rationally.**

Table 3-2 shows an example of what happens when transitivity is violated that illustrates the problem. In this example, the figure is perfectly symmetrical in that all three voters rank their preferences for three different issues. Every policy is one person's first choice, another person's second choice, and another's third choice. But if two policy issues are voted on at a time, it will result in an intransitive ranking. Each person presumably ranks the issues in order of their importance to themselves. As shown in Table 3-3, if education is paired against health care, education wins as it is Colleen's first choice and Cassie prefers it to health care. If health care is opposed to housing, health care wins as it is Mike's first choice and Colleen's second choice. If housing is paired against education, housing wins because Mike prefers it to education and joins Cassie in a winning coalition. Here majority rule has resulted in incompatible results. It is this inconsistency that is **the voting paradox. The voting paradox is that majority rule can produce inconsistent social choices**. If the second and third choices of one of the voters were reversed in Table 3-2, the paradox would disappear. Nonetheless, majority rule may result in no clear winner.

When majority rule does not result in transitive preferences, any policy choice is somewhat arbitrary. The final choice will be determined by the politi-

---

[6] Another obvious dilemma that arises with majority rule is that minorities have an incentive to break majority coalitions in order to become a part of new majority coalitions. Accordingly, in the satellite dish example, the 49 villagers excluded from the winning coalition might try to reform the coalition by persuading at least two members of the majority to join them in return for a side payment. Under majority rule, the search for new coalitions always continues while existing coalitions try to firm up their support.

[7] The transitivity axiom states that if preferences are transitive, then all the alternatives can be placed in order whenever there are more than two choices. Therefore if **a** is preferred to **b**, and **b** is preferred to **c**, then **a** is preferred to **c**. This permits ranking alternatives from the most to the least preferred.

TABLE 3-2
VOTER'S PARADOX

Program	Colleen	Mike	Cassie
Education	1st choice	3rd choice	2nd choice
Health care	2nd choice	1st choice	3rd choice
Housing	3rd choice	2nd choice	1st choice

TABLE 3-3
OPPOSING CHOICES AND OUTCOMES

Opposing choices	Outcome
Education versus health care	Education
Health care versus housing	Health care
Housing versus education	Housing

cal process. The majority party in the legislature usually can determine the agenda and the order of voting, and thereby control the outcome. Regardless of the option selected, a political entrepreneur can argue that he or she followed the popular mandate. This inconsistency leads to incongruous policies in which the government provides agricultural subsidies that raise the prices of food items and then provides food stamps to assist poor people to purchase the higher-priced foodstuffs.

In the example shown in Tables 3-2 and 3-3, if limited funds mean only one or two programs can be funded, which is funded will depend entirely on the arbitrary order in which they are taken up. Although each program is as high in overall priority as the others and each voter has indicated a rational transitive priority of concerns, in the aggregate the result is intransitivity,[8] and thus no clear-cut mandate of importance overall is evident.

Logrolling—Rolling Along or Getting Rolled

When several issues are involved, **logrolling** can result in the adoption of policies that are opposed by a majority of the voters. This form of vote trading is often used to organize compromises that include several policy issues in one informal understanding. **Logrolling is vote trading by representatives who care more intensely about one issue with representatives who care more intensely about another issue**.

A major benefit of logrolling is that it permits legislators to indicate the intensity of their choices among different issues. Majority rule does not distinguish between the intensity of support or opposition when a vote is cast. The votes of those who are fervently in support of a bill count the same as the votes of those only mildly in favor. With single issues, the intensity of preference in voting is not important. However, in the political process the issues being considered are always multiple, and each involves varying degrees of support by minorities. Some people are very concerned about some issues, while other people are indifferent regarding those particular policies. By trading votes, representatives can register just how strongly they feel about various issues. Suppose Katherine and Chip tend to be slightly negatively inclined toward more defense spending. Christy, however,

---

[8] Kenneth Arrow, who won a Nobel Prize in economics in 1972, produced an exceptional proof of the impossibility of formulating a democratic process for reaching a majority decision that ensures transitive and nonarbitrary group choices in his work *Social Choice and Individual Values* (New York: John Wiley, 1951).

strongly feels the need for more defense spending. In a system that permits logrolling, Christy may be able to convince Katherine to vote for more defense spending if Christy promises to vote for a health care bill sponsored by Katherine.

Logrolling can increase or decrease government program efficiency depending upon the circumstances. But the practice has its defenders. They contend that logrolling can potentially lead to public policies benefiting society that otherwise would not be produced. Such vote trading also has the advantage of revealing the intensity of preferences. And finally, compromises, such as those implicit in logrolling, are necessary for a democratic system to function.

Table 3-4 illustrates the advantages of logrolling. If both policies—health care and defense—were put to a simple majority vote, both would lose. But passing them is a Pareto improvement in that everyone is better off relative to not passing them. In this case, logrolling can overcome the problem of an "oppressive major-ity."

Logrolling can just as easily lead to negative outcomes for society. Table 3-5 illustrates the same programs as those shown in Table 3-4. However, Chip opposes both more intensely. The sum of the preferences indicates that Chip's intense oppo-sition will count for more than the combined support by Christy and Katherine. Thus logrolling among the three will hurt the chances of both programs being passed. If neither program passes, there will be a net loss to society's welfare, even if Christy and Katherine logroll as before because the net benefit to them individu-ally is greater.

Tying two bills together can be very convenient for legislators, who can then claim they do not support policies opposed by their constituents even though they voted for them. They defend themselves by arguing that they did not want the health care bill, for example, but had to vote for it to get the defense bill they and their constituents do want.

In general, logrolling has a negative reputation. Called "pork-barrel" legislation, it may lead to policies that are not only inefficient, but also opposed by the major-ity of voters. For example, the United States maintains many military bases that do not contribute significantly to national security. Unneeded military bases are noto-riously difficult to close down, however, because Congressional representatives in effect become lobbyists for special-interest legislation to keep the bases in their dis-tricts open. Many military bases continue to exist because votes are traded to keep

TABLE 3-4
LOGROLLING—POSITIVE OUTCOME*

	Christy	Katherine	Chip	Net benefit to society's welfare
Health care	+20	−5	−3	+12
Defense	−5	+20	−3	+12

   * Logrolling can produce an efficient outcome when the benefits (+) exceed the costs (−) to each indi-vidual or society. Each project would lose with simple majority voting. Yet with logrolling each project can pass, improving the general welfare.

TABLE 3-5
LOGROLLING—INEFFICIENT RESULT*

	Christy	Katherine	Chip	Net loss to society's welfare
Health care	+20	−5	−17	−2
Defense	−5	+20	−17	−2

* If the costs (−) exceed the benefits (+), logrolling can lead to an inefficient outcome.

them in Congressional districts to maintain certain levels of economic activity and numbers of jobs in those districts. On the other hand, the Pentagon has lobbied occasionally **for** the closing of bases so that the savings could be used for higher military salaries and more weapons systems.[9]

It is apparent then that **logrolling may lead to an improvement in the results of simple majority voting, but it may as frequently lead to inefficient outcomes**.

The Median Voter—In the Eye of the Storm

We have noted that political entrepreneurs have a particular incentive to be responsive to voters rather than to nonvoters. One way to accomplish this is for them to determine and be attentive to the **median voter**. The **median voter is the voter whose preferences lie in the middle of an issue, with half the voters preferring more and half preferring less. The principle of the median voter states that under majority rule the median voter will determine the decision**.[10]

To illustrate the principle of the median voter, suppose that five people must vote on a tax increase to provide more police protection for their community, as shown in Table 3-6. Since each voter's preference has a single peak, the closer another

[9] It is not clear that the net benefit to society would be greater by transferring the funds from closed bases to higher salaries and weapons systems. See Richard Halloran, "Pentagon Fights for Budget Cut (Yes)," *The New York Times*, Apr. 30, 1989, Sec. E, p. 5.

[10] This assumes that the voters have single-peaked preferences, so that as they move away from their most preferred position in any direction their utility of outcome consistently falls.

TABLE 3-6
THE MEDIAN VOTER—IN MAJORITY RULE,
VOTING THE OUTCOME REFLECTS THE
PREFERENCES OF THE MEDIAN VOTER

Voter	Most preferred annual tax increase for added police, $
Christy	0.00
Collie	25.00
Cassie	75.00
Chip	125.00
Jim	300.00

voter's position is to one's own, the more the second voter prefers it. Christy does not perceive a need to increase expenditures for police protection at all and would prefer no tax increase for that purpose. A movement from zero expenditures to $25.00 would be approved by Collie, Cassie, Chip, and Jim, however. And an increase to $75.00 would be approved by Cassie, Chip, and Jim. A movement to $125.00 would be thwarted by a coalition consisting of Christy, Collie, and Cassie. A preference for either extreme will be outvoted by four votes, and a preference for the second or fourth position will be blocked by three votes. But a majority will vote for an assessment of $75.00, which is the median voter's preference. Notice that the median voter in this example does not prefer the average amount of the proposed expenditures, but is merely the voter in the middle.

Since each voter will vote for the candidate who is closest to his or her own position, the candidate who is closest to the median position will win the election. This is not lost upon candidates for public office.

Let us assume that political competition mobilizes public opinion along a political spectrum from the far left to the far right, as shown in Fig. 3-2. In a normal distribution of opinions, there is a split right down the middle by **M** indicating the "middle-of-the-roaders." The voter right at **M** is the **median** voter. Each candidate will try to get to the middle of the spectrum to increase his or her chances of winning. If either party's candidate moves away from the median and adopts an extreme such as the liberal (**L**) position, that office seeker will get less than half the vote. As voters will vote for political candidates closest to their own positions, less than half the voters will be closer to **L** than to a candidate positioned at **M**. If one candidate is at **L** and one is at **M**, the candidate at **L** will receive all votes to the left of **L**, while the candidate at **M** will receive all votes to the right of the median and

FIGURE 3-2
Single-peaked ideological spectrum.

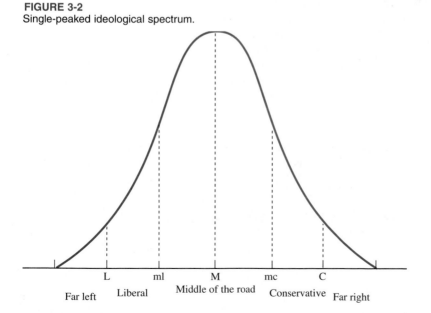

the larger percentage of the votes under the curve between **M** and **L**. Clearly, each candidate will move toward the center.

If a third candidate enters the race, the possibilities change dramatically. If the latest candidate adopts a position such as **C** and the other candidates are at **M**, he or she will get all the votes to the right of **C** and defeat the two centrist candidates. However, the entry of the third candidate will probably encourage the more liberal of the two centrist candidates to move toward **L**. The candidate still at **M** will be boxed in with a small portion of the vote between **L** and **C**. That candidate then has an incentive to move just outside the **LC** portion, thereby trapping one of the other candidates. In a three-party contest in which all three start at the center, there will be an incentive for one to move away. There are limits, however. As long as the voter distribution is single-peaked with its center at **M**, an office seeker can increase his or her portion of the vote by moving toward **M**. And with three candidates at **L, M,** and **C**, additional political contestants can increase their votes by shifting toward the center.

The threat of H. Ross Perot in the 1992 Presidential election encouraged George Bush to move from the centrist position. To strengthen his support on the right, he stressed opposition to abortion and gay rights, and support for "traditional family" values. This permitted Governor Bill Clinton to grab the strategic center, which is often difficult for a challenger to do. When Perot dropped out of the race, it became impossible for Bush to regain the center by credibly portraying Clinton as being out of the mainstream.

Median positions maximize the vote-getting potential. The disruptive potential of major third-party candidates to challenge the centrist political party's control of government provides the major parties with an incentive to make it difficult for third parties to get on the ballot either by erecting election-rule barriers, or by incorporating variations of the third parties' positions into a more moderate setting.

Now consider a situation in which there are just two candidates a Republican (R) and a Democrat (D). The Republican is concerned with keeping taxes low and wants to increase per capita expenditures by $25.00 a year. The Democrat wants to increase per capita spending by $125.00 per year. With an eye on public opinion polls and sensing the potential to gain the necessary majority, candidate D proposes a $120.00 per capita increase. Candidate R, not to be outdone proposes a $35.00 increase. In short, both candidates will try to move toward the middle in order to attract the median voter. In truth, they will try to move to the center sooner rather than later to preempt their opponents from seizing the middle ground. Fig. 3-3 illustrates how candidates move toward the middle as campaigns progress toward election day.

There are several conclusions that follow from the principle of the median voter.

1 Public choices selected may not reflect individual desires. The system will result in many frustrated voters who feel that their views are not being considered. Many, perhaps 49 percent, of the voters in the minority will not have their views accepted.

The principle of the median voter will permit, and perhaps even require, that the views of those on the extreme left or right be neglected at least to the extent that no political entrepreneurs can overtly court those views beyond listening to their pro-

(*a.*) **Campaign begins**

(*b.*) **Election day**

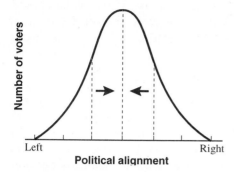

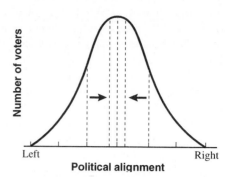

FIGURE 3-3
Political entrepreneurs move toward the middle.

ponents sympathetically then stating that they themselves are safer than their opponents who are "dangerously out of touch," i.e., further to the right or left.

Since the median voter determines the outcome, the intensity of the views of the other voters is irrelevant. Only the intensity of the median voter's view is significant. Thus, the most dissatisfied voters will likely be those of the far right or left. This is in distinct contrast to the market in private goods, where demand counted in terms of "dollar votes" clearly records the intensity of preferences.

2 Candidates for office will try to seize the middle ground first, and claim to be moderate, while labeling their opponents as "out of the mainstream" on the right or left. At the national level, the power of the President in having access to the media is a commanding position from which to label an opponent as being out of the mainstream and an "ultraliberal" or "ultraconservative." It also offers an explanation as to why the nonincumbent party is often put in the position of running a "me-too" campaign—"We can do the *same* job as the incumbents, only better."

This is not to suggest that all candidates are actually alike. Candidates as political activists usually do have political philosophies and positions that can be labeled as more or less conservative, more or less liberal. But as political entrepreneurs, they are forced to mask them during campaigns to seize the middle. Once elected, they may try to support their philosophical inclinations so long as they can still position themselves to maintain their majority support in the next election.

Some polls have suggested that President Clinton enrages voters on both extremes because they believe that his claims to be a "centrist" are phony. Those on the right believe his effort to allow gays in the military and his support for gun control reveal his core liberalism. Those on the left feel that his abandonment of gays in the military and his support of "three strikes and you're out" crime policy actually reveal a crypto-conservative.

3 Candidates will constantly monitor public opinion through polling. They will make slight modifications in the direction of their opponents' positions on those issues in which the opposing candidates are preferred in the polls. In order to successfully sell themselves in the political market, political entrepreneurs try to make position adjustments as subtly as possible to avoid the charge of "political opportunism." Political opponents are always quick to seize on shifts of position to question the integrity of each other. That is, they question whether those they are running against are just "waffling" or, in a more sinister fashion, are not being honest regarding their positions until after the election. Position adjustments also tend to blur the distinction between candidates, which no one wants.

The positions of parties will not be identical. In part this is because political entrepreneurs are not able to identify the median positions perfectly since public opinion, and the median voter, is a moving target. Also since there are many nonvoters, candidates may stake out positions that they believe will appeal to the median of the population he or she expects to vote. In some instances, a candidate may stake out a position to appeal to the median of a group including a set of nonvoters precisely because he or she hopes to increase voting turnout by appealing to that group.

4 Political candidates will prefer to speak in general rather than specific terms. Voters (and candidates for public office) are inclined to agree on the **ends** much more than on the **means** to achieve those ends, or in some cases the **feasibility** of reaching the ends. For instance, voters across the political spectrum agree that an expanding economy is preferable to a contracting economy. They agree that low unemployment rates are preferable to high unemployment. There is also a consensus that lower taxes are preferable to higher taxes, and that a good educational system is preferable to a bad educational system. However, there are great differences between how those we might label conservative and those we might label liberal think these goals might be accomplished. Conservatives tend to prefer pursuing them through less government intervention and private means, while liberals are more likely to perceive a positive role for government in seeking what they perceive as public goods.

VOTING AND THE POLITICAL MARKETPLACE

If politicians are the entrepreneurs of the political marketplace, voters are the consumers looking out for their best interests by voting for the candidates promising the most benefits to them.

As noted above, many people who are eligible to vote do not. The key question is: What motivates a person to vote? There is a cost to voting and the probability of a single voter determining the outcome of an election is extremely small. Therefore the marginal costs of learning about the issues and the candidates' positions, registering to vote, and going to the polls may exceed the marginal benefit of voting. If, however, the candidates have staked out contrasting positions on certain issues and there are indications the election will be close, the marginal benefit of voting increases and voter turnout also rises.[11] In essence, it appears that individuals do

---

[11] See Yoram Barzel and Eugene Silberberg, "Is the Act of Voting Rational?" *Public Choice*, vol. 16 (Fall 1973), pp. 51–58.

make a cost-benefit analysis of their interests in resolving to vote. And in addition to the benefits hoped for from a candidate's promises, voters also receive the psychological "benefit" of knowing they have performed their civic duty.

A concern in the formation of public policy is whether people make informed choices when they vote. We can expect voters to gather information about candidates that will influence their decisions about whom to vote for as long as the benefits of gathering additional information exceed the costs. Often, though, voters decide that it is not cost-effective to gather information. Anthony Downs labels the shortage of information gathered on the part of the public that does vote **"rational ignorance," which is the decision not to actively seek additional information because people find the marginal cost of its acquisition exceeds the marginal benefit of possessing it**. This feeling of excessive marginal cost in turn can arise because information gathering is more complicated for public choices than for private choices. There are several reasons for this.

In the political market, voters must evaluate and select a package deal. This is unlike the commercial marketplace, where in buying apples or shirts you can decide to buy one item more or one item less; that is, you can engage in making decisions at the margin. When you place an additional item in your shopping basket, you register a clear plebiscite for its production. However, when you vote in a political election your vote is registered not for a single item supported by the political entrepreneur, but for the entire package of issues the candidate or party supports. Like many voters, you may vote for a candidate because of his or her support for a particular issue that is of intense interest to you, such as defense spending. You are likely to find several other items in the candidate's bundle that you really do not want.

Voting occurs infrequently and irregularly, in contrast to the buying in the commercial marketplace where consumer choices are registered frequently and repetitively. In the commercial market, consumers communicate very effectively when they cast millions of votes every day to producers by deciding to buy or not to buy the products offered. But the electorate does not have the opportunity, or perhaps the inclination, to vote frequently enough to send a clear signal to political entrepreneurs regarding its political desires. Voters typically get to vote for candidates only every 2, 4, or 6 years. This makes it difficult to find candidates who will support public wants reliably for their entire term and over a range of issues that often emerge after the election. It is impossible to know in advance whether a candidate will support a particular position on issues that were not foreseen at the time of the election. It is also impossible to know the final shape of future bills to be voted on by representatives.

This means political entrepreneurs are relatively free of control by the electorate. The main control voters have is in elections in which an incumbent is running for reelection, where they can retrospectively sanction or reject the candidate's record in the voting booth. Voters can use indicators providing clues about how someone might vote on unanticipated issues such as claims by a candidate that he or she is "conservative," or "moderate," or "Republican." But picking someone based on a label is a very inexact system.

The infrequency of elections also requires that many different choices be made at the same time. The many candidates and the many different issues at the local, state, and national levels inevitably lead to great complexity for voters trying to make informed choices.

There is little incentive for voters to be informed. The political realities noted above make it difficult for the best intentioned voter to evaluate candidates and issues with confidence. The cost of acquiring useful information is very high. For example, suppose the government suggests it is necessary both to spend billions of dollars on the savings and loan bailout to protect confidence in the U.S. banking system and to provide aid to the Soviet government to provide assistance for Yeltsin's continued leadership there, and that those expenditures will require a cutback in unemployment compensation for U.S. workers laid off from their jobs. How can the average voter obtain information to make a rational choice in such a situation?

Some voters will decide to remain rationally uninformed because they decide that the costs exceed the benefits of being fully informed on these issues. Others may choose to become **free riders** not only by refusing to gather any information but by not even voting. If the choices of those who vote are beneficial to the nonvoters, the nonvoting free riders will benefit without incurring any costs. More likely, the political entrepreneurs will soon discover who the nonvoters are and ignore those items in the package that would most benefit them.

Many voters reduce the cost of gathering information for themselves by relying on the "brand names" in the political marketplace of Republican and Democrat. Brand names are at least as important in the political market as in private markets. They provide information regarding general public philosophies. The packaging of a candidate as well as factors like incumbency also provide brand-name information regarding quality. An incumbent has a track record that can be evaluated and has a brand-name identification usually not found among challengers. Voters tend to support incumbent reelection bids just as consumers tend to develop brand-name loyalty to products they buy in stores.

In conclusion, there are important differences between the political and the private marketplaces. Communicating demands in the political marketplace through the process of infrequent voting is more problematic than communicating them on a daily basis through the process of buying and selling. In this area the political marketplace is less efficient than the private marketplace, due in part to the way the political marketplace is designed.

INTEREST GROUPS—ADDED MUSCLE IN THE POLICY MARKET

Interest groups are collections of individuals with intensely held preferences who attempt to influence government policies to benefit their own members. Because their interests are strongly affected by public policies in a particular area, their members keep themselves well-informed regarding legislation in that area. This contrasts with the general voter, who is often uninformed on many issues because the cost of acquiring information is deemed too high relative to its benefit.

And if a proposed policy will confer benefits on one group while imposing costs on another, both affected groups will probably organize, one to support and the other to oppose the policy. For example, teachers will be well-informed about tax laws and programs that support public education or hurt it. Members of the teaching profession usually know much more about the laws affecting education then the general public, so as individuals they make informed voting decisions and through teachers' organizations they lobby for or against specific laws.

The existence and importance of special-interest groups have to do with the principle of rational ignorance. Individuals, and members of groups, are more likely to have incentives to seek information concerning candidates' stands on issues affecting them personally. They are more likely to try to influence other people to adopt their positions, to take an active part in campaigning for candidates supporting their interests, and to vote. Political entrepreneurs seeking election thus try to court special-interest groups, and not infrequently elected officials support special-interest groups at the expense of the general welfare. Thus special-interest groups are likely to have significant effects on policy decisions in areas where they think they have the most to gain or lose by the outcomes.

There are limits on the influence of special interests, though. Politicians seeking election or reelection typically take money from interest groups in return for supporting positions favorable to the groups. Although they need contributions to mount successful campaigns, however, they are wary of accepting money from groups whose positions may be unacceptable to **unorganized voters**. Interest groups themselves are aware that it may be best not to press legislators in causes to which the unorganized voters are hostile. Thus legislators often vote as the unorganized, but interested, voters want, and Congressional decision making often takes into account the wishes of voters who are not members of interest groups. This can even diminish the possible number of special-interest groups since by not antagonizing unorganized voters it encourages them to remain unorganized.[12]

Special-interest groups propose and support legislation they perceive as important to their interests; in general, voters who are not members of such groups are not likely to oppose such legislation or to lobby politicians against it if they do not think it will affect them adversely or at all. As an example, assume that a state proposes to reduce the budget for its state-supported university system because of a shortfall of tax receipts. The state may propose a reduction in the faculty and staff, to be accompanied by an increase in tuition for the students. Since the faculty, staff, and students will bear the brunt of this decision, they may form an interest group to propose an increase in taxes within the state to be used not just to avoid layoffs, but to maintain low tuition and even increase faculty and staff salaries. In other words, this interest group is petitioning the state to raise the wealth of its members at the expense of general taxpayers. They are demanders of a transfer of wealth from the state.

---

[12] See Arthur T. Denzau and Michael C. Munger, "Legislators and Interest Groups: How Unorganized Interests Get Represented," *American Political Science Review*, vol. 80 (March 1986), pp. 89–106.

The suppliers of this wealth transfer are the taxpayers, who probably will not find it worthwhile to organize to oppose having their wealth taken away by the state university system. General taxpayers probably will be less well-informed about this legislation than members of the special-interest group. But even if they are well-informed, they will have to calculate the costs and benefits of opposing the legislation. Say that if the tax increase passed, the average taxpayer would have to pay out approximately $2. But he or she might have to spend $10 to defeat the proposal. Thus even those knowing of the legislation and aware its passage would cost them money would probably conclude it was not worth the cost of opposing it.

The role of special-interest groups in the making of public policy cannot be overemphasized. In a large and complex economy such as that of the United States, a high number of interest groups is to be expected. Many of the interest groups overlap. There are, for example, woman's rights groups, minority rights groups, religious groups, physician groups, lawyer groups, farmer groups, and so forth. And special-interest groups are responsible for much of the misallocation of public resources. However, special-interest group legislation is not necessarily bad. Much of it may even benefit the general public. In the example used, education is a public good and the citizens of the state may be well served by having a good state university system for the general population. The point to be stressed is that **the costs and benefits of being informed on certain issues and the marginal costs and marginal benefits for lobbying for or against those issues are different for members of a special-interest group and the general public. It is this difference in the allocation of costs and benefits of being informed and taking an active political stance that usually influences the type of legislation proposed and implemented**.

James Madison denounced interest groups ("factions," he called them) as being the cause of instability, injustice, and confusion in democratic politics. He defined factions as "a number of citizens . . . who are united and actuated by some common impulse of passion, or of interest, adverse to the rights of other citizens, or to the permanent and aggregate interests of the community."[13] Since that time, every interest group has claimed to represent the national interest rather than a parochial interest. And each group has looked suspiciously at every other interest group as aggregations of conniving, self-seeking individuals.

Mancur Olson[14] accepts the Madisonian standard model of human nature that **individuals know their self-interests and act rationally to further them**. He concludes that **collective goals** are seldom rationally pursued. If, as we noted above, broadly dispersed interests find it difficult to organize for political action, then in all likelihood small narrow interest groups will engineer a redistribution of benefits toward themselves and away from the dispersed interests. However, since individuals discover the benefits of group organization for themselves, a stable society gradually accumulates an increasing number of special-interest groups. Each will have a disproportionate political influence on the areas of its needs. The implications for society are ominous, in that **special-interest groups redistribute**

---

[13] James Madison, *The Federalist*, #10.
[14] Mancur Olson, *The Rise and Decline of Nations* (New London: Yale University Press, 1982).

national wealth to themselves, which reduces society's overall efficiency. In other words, special-interest groups seek to preserve their benefits at the cost of general economic stagnation.[15]

For example, neither Herbert Hoover nor George Bush wanted a depressed economy, but there were many in their constituencies who were financially secure and not threatened with unemployment. Many in this more affluent element preferred those conditions to taxing and spending policies to reduce unemployment and stimulate economic activity, which they feared might reduce their status.

THE BUREAUCRATIZATION OF THE POLITY

The legislative branch of government passes laws and approves specific levels of public policy spending. The actual implementation of the laws and the actual distribution of funds is delegated to various agencies and bureaus of the executive branch. German sociologist Max Weber (1864–1920) held: "Bureaucracy is **the** way of translating social action into rationally organized action."[16] In Weber's view,

> Bureaucracy develops the more perfectly, the more it is 'dehumanized,' the more completely it succeeds in eliminating from official business love, hatred, and all personal irrational, and emotional elements which escape calculation.[17]

In other words, by developing professional experts with authority to act in a rational manner, bureaucracies promote policy implementation that is precise and reliable and provides equality of treatment for everyone.

Weber's sentences suggest the advantages of an **ideal type** of bureaucracy. Bureaucracies are justified in his model because they are **effective**. Bureaucratic authority is the successful application of power. In a bureaucracy, managers can require subordinates to share the same assumptions as their managers so as to produce agreement with management's prior conclusions. Members of a bureaucracy must accept and support the common goal. This is a critical requirement for the

---

[15] By intensifying distributional struggles and encouraging the primacy of political competition, special-interest groups siphon a society's talents and energies away from the production of goods and focus them instead on winning the distributional contest. Olson claims that the postwar economic miracles in Germany and Japan were due in part to the purging of all special-interest groups as a result of the war, which opened the way to rapid growth. Countries like the United States and England found their special-interest groups still viable at the end of the war and experienced slower growth in the postwar era as a result.

Olson's solution would be to save democracy from its own excesses by reducing special-interest group influence on the political process. He hopes that schools and mass media will create a widespread antipathy to special-interest groups and bring about a cultural change. Perhaps society could then achieve the ideal of a state devoid of special-interest politics and continually remain adaptive and innovative.

But the proposed system, lacking interest group mediation, would effectively cripple democratic institutions. Without interest groups, which are the breeding grounds for democratic opposition independent of state power, the strength of representative democracy would be weakened. Special-interest groups shape social values. Group morality is defined and refined through their workings.

[16] From the essay "Bureaucracy," in Max Weber, *Economy and Society: An Outline of Interpretive Sociology*, 3 vols., edited by Guenther Roth and Claus Wittech and translated by Ephraim Fischoff (New York: Bedminster Press, 1968), Vol. 3, p. 987.

[17] Weber, "Bureaucracy," Vol. 3, p. 975

bureaucrat to receive the rewards that flow from being "a team player." Bureaucracies then appear monolithic to the outside world.

In reality bureaucrats are often attacked for being unresponsive to the public they serve. Still other critics complain that politicians make their bureaucracies too responsive to special-interest groups instead of allowing them to impartially administer the programs for which they were created.

Although Weber's analysis refers to bureaucratic organizations in the private as well as the public domains, our concern is primarily with U.S. governmental bureaucracies. **Bureaucrats are the unselected U.S. government officials tasked with carrying out the program approved by Congress and the President**. Many laws are passed that are more symbolic than substantive insofar as they indicate the "intent" to ensure automotive safety, guarantee safe working conditions, or protect the environment without specifying exactly how to accomplish these goals. Bureaucrats must use their administrative authority to give meaning to vague platitudinous legislation and determine how the law will actually be applied.

Those working in bureaus tend to be supportive of the legislature's goals. They also prefer a growing budget, which usually correlates with opportunities for promotion and higher salaries for themselves. In private business organizations there is an incentive to minimize costs in the pursuit of profits. In public bureaucracies, though, there are no incentives to minimize budgets. Instead bureaucrats try to maximize the sizes of their agencies through high salaries and the perquisites of office, power, and patronage. Within these organizations, in fact, a person's prestige and authority is measured by the number of personnel under his or her authority. (Even if bureaucrats did operate very efficiently, the general voter would be unaware of that due to the principle of rational ignorance.) Therefore bureaucrats try to increase the sizes of their bureaus in many of the same ways that firms attempts to grow, except that firms obtain their capital from voluntary buying decisions made by the public. In contrast, bureaucrats secure the money they need from the legislative appropriation of tax revenues. They **compete** with other bureaucrats for a larger share of the available funds. Bureaus typically do not end each fiscal year with budget surpluses, but rather spend all their revenues before the end for fear of appearing not to need as much money in the future.

Another way of saying this is that one of the main differences between a private firm and a bureaucracy is the customers they serve. The business firm is dependent for its survival upon the continued patronage of a satisfied clientele buying its goods or services. Failure to please that clientele will quickly show up in terms of financial profits and losses. A bureaucracy, however, may deal with a certain clientele—those needing car licenses, for example, or building permits, social security checks, or unemployment compensation. But their true customers are members of the legislature, who must appropriate the funds to keep them operating. Thus the signals that bureaucracies are succeeding in satisfying their customers are different than the profit and loss statements businesses use. They may indeed be providing efficient services to the special-interest groups that were responsible for the legislation creating the bureaus, and they may even be serving the public that is their clientele efficiently. But they must also answer to the legislatures that fund and oversee them. It should be noted that in doing this, bureaucracies have significant information advantages over the typical legislator, who must be concerned with literally hundreds of different programs. And bureaucracies themselves provide the information the legislators need to oversee the bureaus. This provides a leverage business firms lack in dealing with their customers.

Those who criticize bureaucracies for being less efficient than private firms miss a fundamental point of the purpose of a bureaucracy. Typically its existence is the result of some market failure—of a situation in which market competition could not resolve some issue or issues. Consequently it cannot be measured by normal market criteria. Many government bureaucracies provide services for which there is no competition. For example, there is only one place to go to get a driver's license, or a zoning permit.

Public bureaucracies associated with high national purposes of the state such as the military, the Central Intelligence Agency, or the Federal Bureau of Investigation are generally held in high regard as patriotic public servants. Ironically, the members of the largest governmental bureaucracy, the military, often do not even consider themselves bureaucrats. Bureaucracies associated with domestic regulatory or redistributional programs adversely affecting the more privileged members of society are generally condemned as being wasteful and inefficient, while the individual bureaucrats tasked with enforcing those policies are usually held in contempt as incompetent bumblers.

CONCLUSION

1 Markets fail to produce ideal outcomes in the best attainable allocation of goods and services. Democratic governments are asked to intervene to correct the deficiencies of market outcomes, but must do so through the institutions of representative democracy, with voting procedures, political entrepreneurs, and interest groups serving as intermediaries.

2 The process is one in which individuals in politics act, as people are assumed to do in the marketplace, on the basis of their preferences based on their views of their rational self-interest. Rational public choice theory offers an explanation regarding how individuals act in the political marketplace. It should be seen as a view about how the system actually works and not how the system *should* work.

3 In some ways the government is even less efficient than the private marketplace. This is particularly true in limiting voters to infrequent elections and in requiring the political "package deals" achieved through logrolling.

4 The principle of the median voter results in the "middle ground" of the electorate being critical in any election. Since both candidates in a two-way race must compete for the median voter's position and portray their opponent as being an extremist and "out of touch with the mainstream," campaigns usually fail to produce any bold initiatives for change. Rather they eschew substance in favor of efforts by candidates to tar their opponents with negative symbols.

5 The voting paradox also allows political entrepreneurs to take almost any position on an issue and claim that this was supported by a majority. Consequently whoever controls the voting agenda on several related items will have a powerful influence on the voting outcome.

6 Special-interest groups are organized voters who see their self-interest bound up with a specific issue, are informed about it, and are therefore inclined to vote based upon that issue. The general population of potential voters, following the principle of rational ignorance, is likely to be uninformed about and indifferent to most political issues. Special-interest groups, then, have a political influence out of proportion to their numbers, although politicians are reluctant to antagonize the general voter needlessly because they too have the potential to mobilize and retaliate through their own interest groups.

7 The accumulation over time of special-interest group legislation redirects public resources toward those groups at the expense of the unorganized and less-likely-to-vote general public and particularly the poor. This may result in further movements away from the ideal of government correction for market failures.

QUESTIONS FOR DISCUSSION

1 What is public choice theory? How does it help in analyzing public behavior and policy?
2 How can democratic voting behavior lead to undemocratic results? How can that be squared with the idea of justice? Is there a solution to this problem?
3 Why do political candidates move to the center in a single-peaked two-party system? Why are parties more likely to have more fixed ideological points in multiparty systems?
4 Why do candidates prefer to campaign on general terms rather than specific issues? Conversely, why do candidates reduce an opponent's general stands into specific positions?
5 What is the idea of rational ignorance? How can this be squared with the democratic ideal of an informed citizenry?
6 The democratic ideal also contains the concept of each citizen having an equal voice in government. How then can special-interest legislation be justified?
7 Are there ways to make government bureaucracies more concerned about the efficiency of their programs?

KEY CONCEPTS

Bureaucracy	Political entrepreneur
Cost-benefit analysis	Public choice theory
Government failure	Rational ignorance
Interest groups	Rational public choice
Logrolling	Single-peaked preferences
Majority voting rule	Transitive preferences
Market failure	Unanimity rule
Median voter	Voting paradox
Pareto improvement	

SUGGESTED READINGS

Kenneth Arrow, *Social Choice and Individual Values* (New York: John Wiley, 1951).

David Austen-Smith and Jeffrey Banks, "Elections, Coalitions, and Legislative Outcomes," *American Political Science Review*, vol. 82 (June 1988), pp. 405–422.

Nicholas P. Lovrich and Max Neiman, *Public Choice Theory in Public Administration: An Annotated Bibliography* (New York: Garland, 1982).

Dennis C. Mueller, *Public Choice* (New York: Cambridge University Press, 1979).

Kenneth Shepsle and Barry R. Weingast, "Political Preferences for the Porkbarrel: A Generalization," *American Journal of Political Science,* vol. 25 (February 1981), pp. 96–111.

Kaare Strom, *Minority Government and Majority Rule* (Cambridge, England: Cambridge University Press, 1990).

Gordon Tullock, *Private Wants, Public Means: An Economic Analysis of the Desirable Scope of Government* (New York: Basic Books, 1970).

Louis F. Weschler, "Public Choice: Methodological Individualism in Politics," *Public Administration Review*, vol. 42 (May/June 1982), pp. 288–294.

Viktor Vanberg and James M. Buchanan, "Rational Choice and Moral Order," in James H. Nichols, Jr., and Colin Wright (eds.), *From Political Economy to Economics and Back?* (San Francisco, Institute for Contemporary Studies, 1990), pp. 175–191.

4

PUBLIC POLICY IN A STRANGE NEW WORLD

Public policy in the United States must be considered in the context of the peculiarities of its political institutions, its culture, and its enormous resources. If politics is the art of the possible, it is also a truism that the possibilities are circumscribed by the governmental institutions. The parameters of public policy in America are strongly influenced by the work of the framers of the Constitution, which established the rules within which political struggles over policy takes place. The government could enact public policy with more dispatch and efficiency if power were concentrated rather than fragmented. Instead the Founding Fathers, partly by choice and partly because of the political realities of the time, instituted numerous checks on the exercise of power by the national government. They also strengthened the role of the national government over the states, while they guaranteed that states would have a powerful role to play. The balance of power between the nation and states is often at the center of policy struggles involving whether policy will be adopted and how it will be implemented. By guaranteeing certain individual liberties, the framers also provided a channel through which public opinion may place boundaries on policy.

Major changes in the polity resulted from the Civil War and again from the Great Depression and the New Deal. Both eras strengthened the national government relative to state politics. The Presidency in particular benefited not only from the trend toward national government politics, but also from a shift of power from Congress to the President. The trend toward nationalization was also accompanied by the construction of a powerful bureaucracy as a separate governmental force. The struggle over the scope of the conflict continues.

Indeed, opinion is divided over whether the system can provide for effective government as we approach the twenty-first century. Changes are proposed to streamline institutions, and encourage a concentration of power. Others praise the work of the framers for its protection of minority rights. Its defenders also point out that most proposed remedies may well be, in Madison's words, "worse than the disease." This chapter examines the origins of this debate. It examines the conservative bias among the delegates to the Constitutional Convention, and how that bias was reflected in the Constitution. It examines the role of federalism and its impact on policy making. And last, it examines the complications resulting from divided government and the concern it raises regarding public policy formulation.

DECLINING FAITH IN GOVERNMENT

It is ironic that the United States was born in a revolution that provided a decided break from European monarchies and cast it in a progressive political direction based upon broad based institutions and active popular participation. Nevertheless, despite our great wealth and resources, unmatched throughout most of the world, the United States now lags behind many countries in "promoting the general welfare." Its citizens are not guaranteed a sufficient level of the basics of education, health care, housing, or income necessary to provide them with comfortable lives.

A major commitment of conservatives is to maintain the status quo and not involve the government in an effort to deal with areas of increasing concern to many Americans. For example, many argue the Bush administration did not have a domestic program. After passage of the Americans with Disabilities Act and some amendments to the Clean Air Act into law in 1990, John Sununu, then White House Chief of Staff, said that Congress could adjourn for the rest of the term because "there's not a single piece of legislation that needs to be passed in the two years remaining."[1]

Prior to the 1992 election, President Bush vetoed 35 bills. Appealing to voters in his reelection bid, he frequently cited how his record of vetoes kept the government from further meddling. Opponents argued his vetoes said more about his domestic agenda than his policy initiatives did. For example, he vetoed the Family Leave Bill, campaign finance and voter registration reform, mass transit authorization, civil rights bills, increases in the minimum wage, extension of unemployment benefits, and increased funding for programs in the Departments of Education, Health and Human Services, and Labor. The election outcome demonstrated that the slow economy stimulated a majority of voters to look elsewhere for positive policies on issues such as the economy, job creation, education, the environment, and national health care.

The political institutions responsible for the formulation and implementation of public policy are under indictment by an increasingly disillusioned public. While problems continue to mount, the government response is too often failed policies, paralysis, or stalemate. American attitudes toward the government and politics began to decline after 1964; at that time 78 percent of the public indicated that one

---

[1] Maureen Dowd, "Bush: As the Loss Sinks In, Some Begin Pointing Fingers," *The New York Times*, Nov. 5, 1992, p. B5.

could "trust the government in Washington to do what is right always or most of the time." By late 1991, only 36 percent said that the government could be trusted to do the right thing always or most of the time.[2] People who believe that the government wastes "a lot of money we pay in taxes" increased from about 46 percent in 1952 to 75 percent in 1991. Recent public opinion polls have consistently indicated that only about 25 percent of the population approves of the way Congress is handling its job.[3] Only 7 percent of the public indicates that it has a lot of confidence that when the government in Washington decides to solve a problem, the problem will actually be solved.

The traditional American idea that progress is inevitable and things will improve is being seriously challenged. Both economic and political indicators have been slipping in recent years. And American voters indicate a worrisome concern that the politicians they have elected to Congress and, increasingly, the White House, cannot be trusted to fix their problems. Just as the antitax movement has demonstrated a reduced public faith in the ability of the government to spend money wisely, so the term-limits movement has exhibited a shrinking faith in democratic processes. The antigovernment mood promotes a conservative agenda of reducing the role of the political and bureaucratic elite with negative consequences for policy effectiveness. That agenda would achieve its goal by limiting Congressional terms and pay, as well as limiting government taxes and spending.

Part of the blame for the growing cynicism can be laid at the door of negative campaigning that constantly attacks the character and integrity of political opponents. Despite a pervasive condemnation of negative advertising in campaigns, it is used increasingly, because it has been found to be very effective in influencing perceptions regarding the political opposition. Members of Congress are often portrayed and perceived as cynical, self-promoting, and concerned primarily with their own reelections rather than with the welfare of the polity. The lower the regard in which politicians and politics are held by the public, in part as a result of negative campaign ads, the more voters respond to attack themes in those ads. However, because of a backlash against negative campaigns, candidates try to disguise their attacks as issue-related campaign advertising. The backlash against politicians produced by a politics that depicts government as the root of the problem illustrates that such methods cannot help but damage faith in and the effectiveness of political institutions,[4] although in the 1992 campaign voters appeared to be increasingly resistant to negative campaigning and the media also began analyzing campaign ads for accuracy and distortions.

---

[2] *The Washington Post*, Nov. 3, 1991.

[3] *The Gallup Poll Monthly*, No. 301 (October 1990), pp. 34–42. In late October 1991, only 21 percent of Americans indicated that they had confidence in Congress as an institution, as reported in a *Washington Post*–ABC poll, *The Washington Post*, Nov. 3, 1991.

[4] Concern over the impact of negative campaigning does not mean candidates should not attack their opponents' positions on issues. Campaigns try to simplify politics to focus voters' minds and distinguish between candidates positions on such issues as health care, education, or energy and the environment. Consequently, they must be loud and raucous (and expensive) to capture the attention of voters and stimulate them to vote. Low-key, low-budget decorous campaigns do not arouse people out of their lethargy to vote.

The staging of politically inspired spectacles for photo opportunities or scripted interviews, especially by the President, may get air time on the evening news, but a lack of substance where it exists is not lost on the public. Symbolic politics rather than serious policy have become the standard fare of partisan politics. The growing perception that money from special-interest groups heavily influences political decisions has increased the gap between the politicians and the public. The declining numbers of those voting in Presidential elections from 64 percent of the adults in 1960 to 50.1 percent in 1988 is a reflection of this decline in confidence in government and its institutions including the political parties and the process that provides the basic foundation for democratic society in the United States. In 1992 voter turnout increased over 1988, rising to 55 percent, the highest level since 1972 and reversing the declines of the last three decades. That higher turnout was the result of increased voter registration drives by the Democratic party, and the effort of that party to refashion its image to appeal to a centrist coalition of Democrats that had voted for Reagan and Bush. Significant interest was also generated by a strong independent candidate in the person of Ross Perot, who promised to "clean up the mess in Washington."

The staging of photo opportunities by candidates and negative campaigning reflect the increasing importance of the media in American politics. Politicians have learned that the media are critical in getting elected, and in getting reelected. Endorsement by a political party is not as important as favorable press coverage for oneself and negative coverage of an opponent.

The rising importance of the mass media has an almost inverse relationship to the decline in the influence of political parties. By the use of investigative reporting, politicians have become more vulnerable to critical media coverage.

Political struggles are increasingly carried on outside the electoral process, which discourages popular participation in elections. Through the technique of investigations and leaks of potentially damaging information intended to negate election results, political power is splintered, denying elected officials a secure political base to effectively pursue policy initiatives. Those dissatisfied with the electoral results increasingly attempt to make public any negative information regarding elected or appointed government officials by leaks to the media, which then conduct their own investigation. The subsequent investigation often arouses hostile attitudes toward the individual or the political party investigated. Supporters become passive under the attack, lest they be viewed as favoring the alleged misconduct. Embattled supporters are strongly tempted to abandon a beleaguered politician, especially if the charges appear to be substantive. The result is weakened government.

The break-in at the Democratic national headquarters known as Watergate is sometimes pointed out as the first example of a steady leaking of revelations of misconduct leading to further investigations and the indictment of several federal officials, ultimately forcing Nixon's resignation. In this case, however, there was evidence of on-going criminal activity at the highest levels of government. Subsequently, the Iran-Contra conflict revealed violations of the Boland amendment which prohibited the selling of arms to Iran, and the diversion of the proceeds to fund the Nicaraguan Contras. Several high-ranking members of the Bush administration were the subject of criminal prosecutions for their role in Iran-Contra. President Bush pardoned several administration officials before leaving office, charging that the Democrats were trying to criminalize policy differences.

Members of both political parties subsequently attacked prominent members of the opposite party in an effort to weaken their opponents. Republicans drove House Speaker Jim Wright and Democratic Whip Tony Coehlo from office for financial misdeeds, and called upon Democratic Congressman Barney Frank to resign after allegations of sexual misconduct. One of President Clinton's nominees for Attorney General was attacked for failing to make Social Security payments for a household worker. Republican forces also scuttled the nomination of Lani Guiner as Assistant Attorney General for Civil Rights by characterizing her as a radical liberal. Those who orchestrated the attack readily acknowledged their effort and indicated that they had a score to settle with the Democrats for their opposition to the nomination of Robert Bork and Clarence Thomas to the Supreme Court. They claimed to be playing by the rules established by the Democrats starting with Watergate (see Michael Isikoff, "Power Behind the Thrown Nominee: Activist with Score to Settle," *The Washington Post*, June 6, 1993, p. A11). Republicans such as Senator Alphonse D'Amato of New York made clear their intention to embarass President Clinton by raising questions of possible wrongdoing over investments known as Whitewater, and questions of sexual improprieties.

There is no reason to believe that the level of political corruption is greater today than before 1970; however, the increasing use of planting stories in the press and demands for investigations as a tool to discredit opponents also reduces the effectiveness of government. The result is that the voter is increasingly alienated, which leads to less involvement and more hostility toward government.

A major reason for frustration in dealing effectively with society's problems is the basic design and evolution of the Constitution. The Founding Fathers designed the Constitution to make governing difficult by decentralizing power and authority. The result has left political leaders weak and unable to make binding decisions. Popular participation in the American system is encouraged by means of picking candidates through petition drives, primary elections, and party caucuses. Since money is essential to running campaigns, and political parties cannot provide it in significant amounts, candidates must develop independent fund-raising capabilities. In this system, "all politics is local" in that individuals must organize and run campaigns on local levels. This permits politicians to ignore or even oppose their party's positions on the national level.

In Europe the parliamentary democracies function much differently. The constitutional systems of Europe centralize power. In the United States, the judiciary is a powerful check on Presidential and Congressional actions. In Europe, courts cannot overturn acts of parliament. In Europe also, candidates for office are chosen by party leaders, which makes successful candidates accountable to their parties.

At the heart of the low esteem in which the government is held these days in the

United States is its inability to deal effectively with issues in which there is a clear national consensus that problems exist and that policies should be developed to deal with them. For example, public opinion polls have indicated for the last 20 years that a clear preponderance of public opinion is supportive of stricter gun control laws, but only recently has any progress been made in this area. Also, for the last decade a significant majority of the American people has felt that the government is not sufficiently supportive of affordable housing, health care, high-quality education, or protecting the environment, and want some immediate and drastic action to protect it,[5] which has not been forthcoming.

Polls consistently have shown American concern over the size of the federal deficit throughout the decade of the 1980s and into the 1990s. Yet the government seemed powerless to do more than the Gramm-Rudman-Hollings Act, which did little to deal with the problem, until President Clinton moved to reduce the deficit.[6]

Government failure to act in these and other areas of national concern reflects a failure of political institutions and suggests that government is anything but responsive to the needs of its citizens. How has a government born in the hope of being "of the people, by the people, and for the people" proven to be so impotent? What remedies are there to improve the performance of its institutions? What other noninstitutional barriers are there that inhibit effective governmental policy making?

This chapter addresses these problems, and also suggests possible remedies. At the same time, it is clear that political institutions are not the sole cause of the U.S. government's inability to deal effectively with all of society's problems. **Voters make many inconsistent demands upon their political representatives.** Candidates taking the pulse of the American electorate through polling assess what will have the greatest appeal and then offer a package deal of policies to the voters in which the inconsistencies are muted. And voters are inclined to respond without scrutinizing the incompatible nature of their demands. For example, polls indicate that in the early 1990s most Americans support increased government spending on health care, while they oppose any tax increase to pay for it; in fact, they are inclined to vote for candidates favoring tax cuts, while they simultaneously want to

---

[5] Regarding the environment, see *The Gallup Poll Monthly*, No. 295 (April 1990), pp. 5–12. On gun control see the same publication, No. 300 (September 1990), pp. 34–37.

[6] The Balanced Budget and Emergency Deficit Control Act, is better known as Gramm-Rudman-Hollings Act after its cosponsors, Senators Phil Gramm (R) of Texas, Warren Rudmen (R) of New Hampshire, and Ernest Hollings (D) of South Carolina. The legislation, with its amendments, mandated maximum allowable deficit levels for each year until 1993, when the budget was projected to be in balance. If Congress did not meet the deficit goals, automatic across-the-board spending cuts, half of which were to come from defense and half from domestic programs, were to be ordered by the President. Congress and the White House have been able to remain in compliance only as a result of sleight-of-hand accounting procedures. For example, it was decided not to include the cost of the savings-and-loan bailout as part of the budget deficit. The Social Security trust fund, which has been running a surplus, can only be used to pay Social Security recipients. However, the surplus, in the range of $50+ billion per year, is subtracted from the deficit, making it appear smaller than it is. These types of deceit in counting budget deficits prompted Senator Hollings to declare, "I want a divorce."

reduce or eliminate budget deficits.[7] The proposed solution they seem to accept is simple: eliminate government waste, mismanagement, and fraud. That eliminating waste and increasing bureaucratic efficiency cannot possibly achieve a balanced budget is conveniently overlooked. In a like manner, Americans have reacted enthusiastically to the declining price of gasoline by consuming more of it, while at the same time they indicate a desire for reduced dependence on oil from the Middle East. Yet they oppose any increase in taxes on gas consumption that would reduce demand for oil from Middle East and could be used for research on alternative fuels.

To the extent that political representatives are primarily political entrepreneurs, they are discouraged from considering the long-term consequences of exploiting the contradictions in voter preferences to win election. The Founding Fathers were not unaware of this problem and expressed their apprehension of dangers regarding the follies and excesses of democracy. On the other hand, they were also concerned to protect the citizenry from the arbitrariness of dictatorial authority, with which they were all too familiar from dealings with the British monarchy. **The Constitution was purposely designed to make governing difficult—not to simplify political choices but to complicate them. Rather than entrusting political leaders with sufficient control, it stymies them with insufficient authority.** The Constitution, both in its formal written provisions and in the way those provisions have been interpreted and carried out, provides a process for making public policy with predictable results. And among those results are numerous things that many Americans find unpleasant about public policy making.

THE CULTURAL-HISTORICAL HERITAGE

One explanation for the failure to produce a public policy supportive of basic human necessities is the nature of U.S. political culture. A **political culture** is a society's attitudes toward the merit, style, and vitality of its political processes and government affairs.[8]

It has been maintained that two contrasting societal values—equality and

---

[7] Ronald Reagan's campaign in 1980 was the first to put together on a national scale all these promises into a single package. He campaigned on a platform in which he promised to (a) reduce taxes, (b) increase spending, and (c) balance the budget. The reduced taxes, it was claimed, would increase economic activity, resulting in increased government tax receipts. Increased tax revenues would permit an increase in government spending, primarily for defense, while simultaneously balancing the budget. The critics, including George Bush who at the time ridiculed the proposal as "voodoo economics," pointed out the logical and algebraic impossibility of carrying out all three promises, but were dismissed as pessimists while Reagan was characterized as restoring optimism and having faith in America. The Reagan campaign's appeal was overwhelming, and the candidate won in a landslide.

[8] Daniel Elazar holds that American political culture can best be understood by dividing it into three major subcultures for analytical purposes: individualistic, moralistic, and traditional. Individualistic political culture espouses the view that politics is "just another means by which individuals may improve themselves socially and economically." Moralistic political culture conceives of politics "as a public activity centered on some notion of the public good and properly devoted to the advancement of the public interest." The traditionalist view perceives political culture as a "precommercial attitude that accepts a substantially hierarchical society as part of the ordered nature of things, authorizing and

achievement—distinguish American culture. The Declaration of Independence, written by Thomas Jefferson, states: "Governments are instituted among men, deriving their just powers from the consent of the governed." This statement was built upon the belief that "all men are created equal," and that each person has a right to live according to his or her own beliefs and to have an equal voice in the political decisions of the community.

The American Revolution was a revolt against the conservative, class-dominated societies of Europe based upon "natural inequalities" of heredity. The United States was conceived in eighteenth-century **liberalism**, which was based on the belief that everyone has certain rights simply because each person is a human being. This implies that the inequalities of rank, power, and wealth are **social** rather than **natural**, and reflects the view that each person has an inherent dignity and should be treated as an end and not merely as a means.[9] The rights granted to everyone by the Creator include, according to Jefferson in the Declaration of Independence, "life, liberty, and the pursuit of happiness." Government should be based on the consent of the governed. Power in a democracy should not only be shared, it should be **limited** in terms of the legitimate authority it can exercise.

These ideals of the American Revolutionary leadership looked to the eighteenth-century philosophers who proclaimed "the rights of man" and who believed that the central function of government was to protect those natural rights. These concepts were in stark contrast to the unlimited power of monarchical government. John Locke, as an example, had argued that everyone seeks life, liberty, and property. However, in a state of nature, the strong can use their liberty to divest the weak of theirs. The need for security to prevent this leads people to form a "social contract" in which they delegate the authority to government to protect these rights. Unless government is limited, however, it might itself deprive those it governs of their liberty. Thus the problem is to design a government strong enough

expecting those at the top of the social structure" to take a leading role in government. See Daniel Elazar, *American Federalism: A View from the States*, 2nd ed. (New York: Crowell, 1972).

[9] This is not a minor point regarding American culture. Much of the tradition of Western thought on the question of equality had been strongly influenced by the writings of Plato, who thought that society was naturally divided into classes. According to Plato, only a few philosophers, who were superior to everyone else, should have the right to rule. Likewise Aristotle ranked humankind in terms of reason, such that persons whose reasoning abilities fitted them only to be slaves or artisans were hardly to be considered human beings. Only the Stoics held that all people are equal based upon their individual relationship to the Divine Order.

The early Christians further developed the idea of human equality. Their most striking symbol of God's abrogation of human rank is the crucifixion, in which the Lord of all creation, accepted an ignoble death between two thieves. Theologically the idea that everyone is equal in the eyes of God means that everyone is equal in his or her humanness and equally valuable. All natural or contrived social distinctions such as intellectual or athletic abilities as well as opulence, status, and attractiveness pale into irrelevance. John Locke, who greatly influenced the framers of the Constitution, maintained this transcendent concept of equality in stating that people are equal only in the rights they receive from God. It was in this same vein that Thomas Jefferson declared that "all men are **created** equal" and are **"endowed by their Creator** with certain inalienable rights."

to preserve order, but not so strong as to threaten liberty.[10] The protection of these human rights and the right of the individual to enjoy them is "the first object of government," according to James Madison.[11] So the protection of these rights based on the notion of human equality encourages government policies that foster competition and self-advancement and discourage unity and universal social programs.

The American Revolution was also an attack on efficient, unified executive power as represented by the British monarchy. The Founding Fathers had experienced the impressive powers that could be brought to bear by a unified government under a monarch, whether benevolent or tyrannical. They had experienced the ill effects of abusive and arbitrary authority, and were determined to erect barriers to protect the citizenry from an all powerful and efficient government. Since the rallying cry of the revolutionaries was "give me liberty or give me death," it is hardly surprising that priority was given to providing protection from government rather than creating an efficient, vigorous government.

THE CONSTITUTIONAL CONVENTION AND THE GOVERNMENT IT CREATED

The members of the 1787 American Constitutional Convention agreed that the Continental Congress had erred in the direction of being weak and powerless when it wrote the Articles of Confederation, which unified the executive and legislative powers; individual liberty had not been threatened, but the national government was totally dependent on the states to validate and ratify all its actions, and could not control the competitive impulses of the states that worked against the common national interest. It had also become apparent that the European powers sought to exploit the competition between states regarding overlapping claims on western territories and trade and tariff policies in order to weaken the new nation.

The failure of government under the Articles of Confederation to meet these and other challenges was the reason for the 1787 convention, held in Philadelphia. The delegates agreed on the need to develop a new form of national government that could act with more vigor and dispatch. And while there were crucial disagreements on many features of the proposed government, there was no disagreement either on the principle of **separation of powers—the notion that the powers of government must be separated into legislative, judicial, and executive branches**. They believed that this separation—"fragmentation" is probably a better description—would make a tyrannical concentration of power inconceivable. The

---

[10] James Madison, stated the problem this way: "If men were angels, no government would be necessary. If angels were to govern men, neither external nor internal controls on government would be necessary. In framing a government which is to be administered by men over men, the great difficulty lies in this: you must first enable the government to control the governed; and in the next place oblige it to control itself." *The Federalist*, #51.

[11] Madison, *The Federalist*, #10.

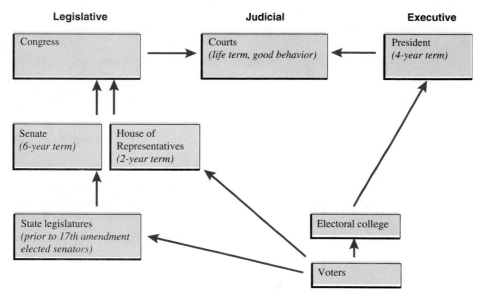

FIGURE 4-1
Separation of powers in the U.S. federal government.

separation of powers as eventually embodied in the U.S. Constitution is shown in Fig. 4-1.

The Bicameral Legislature

The success of the state assemblies and the Continental Congress in maintaining government authority during the American Revolution guaranteed that the legislature would be given a preeminent position in the new Constitution. The document details legislative functions, duties, and prerogatives in significant detail in Article I. But there was fear of giving too much authority to the legislature. James Madison also expressed the concern that a legislature could not be counted upon to act for the common good when competing issues were presented.[12] So, much consideration was given to the means of controlling the legislature's potential usurpation of power. Ultimately, **checks and balances (see Table 4-1) were introduced, designed to prevent any power from becoming the undisputed dominant force by being balanced against, or checked by, another power source within the**

---

[12] Madison maintained, "No man is allowed to be a judge in his own cause because his interest would certainly bias his judgment, and, not improbably, corrupt his integrity. With equal, nay with greater reason, a body of men are unfit to be both judges and parties at the same time; yet what are many of the most important acts of legislation but so many judicial determinations, not indeed concerning the rights of single persons, but concerning the rights of large bodies of citizens? And what are the different classes of legislators but advocates and parties to the causes which they determine? ... It is in vain to say that enlightened statesmen will be able to adjust these clashing interests and render them all subservient to the public good. Enlightened statesmen will not always be at the helm." *The Federalist*, #10.

TABLE 4-1

CHECKS AND BALANCES

	Congress	President	Courts
Legislative power	Enact legislation	Call special sessions of Congress Recommend/veto legislation Issue executive orders	Review Constitutionality of legislation
Executive power	Advise and consent (treaties and appointments) Authorize appropriations Declare war Authorize administrative organization Impeach and try President	Administer laws	Review Constitutionality of executive actions
Judicial power	Confirm appointments Prescribe appellate jurisdiction Establish inferior courts Impeach and try judges	Appoint judges	Interpret laws

government. Thus governmental power was divided among the three branches, and each branch was to be given authority to prevent encroachments on its power by the others. As Madison said in his famous maxim, "ambition must be made to counter ambition."[13]

However, this means of dividing power was itself a compromise between competing views. Initially the delegates to the Constitutional Convention were presented with a comprehensive plan for a new national government by the Virginia representatives. The delegation was led by Governor Edmund Randolph but the plan was largely the product of James Madison. As the Virginia proposal was presented first, it became the basis for discussion for several weeks. It proposed a strong national union composed of three separate branches, the legislative, executive, and judicial, of which the most powerful would be the legislature. Consistent with its emphasis on the preeminence of the Congress, the Virginia Plan provided that the chief executive should be designated by the legislature. This bicameral leg-

---

[13] James Madison, *The Federalist*, #51.

islature would have supreme legislative powers in areas where the states were not competent to act individually, and the power to veto state laws. The only check on its power would be its division into two houses: the House of Representatives, to be directly elected by the people, and the Senate, to be chosen by the House of Representatives from people nominated by the state legislatures.

After 2 weeks of debate the smaller states, concerned that they would be out-voted if both houses of the legislature were represented on the basis of population, countered with the New Jersey Plan. This proposal would have amended rather than scrapped the Articles of Confederation. It would have given more authority to the national government than existed under the Articles, but not as much as the Virginia Plan. It proposed a unicameral legislature based upon one vote per state, thus maintained the existing powerful role of the states.

A committee was appointed to reach a settlement on the question of representation. The eventual compromise provided for a national bicameral legislature consisting of:

• A House of Representatives, consisting originally of sixty-five members apportioned among the states on the basis of population and directly elected by the people every 2 years.
• A Senate, consisting of two senators from each state to be chosen by the state legislatures, each elected for 6 years but one-third of the total being up for reelection every 2 years.

At the time of the Constitutional Convention, every state with the exception of Pennsylvania had a bicameral legislature, so the compromise, although barely adopted, was a well-known concept throughout the states.[14]

The Senate was intended to be more independent of public control than the House, so members were given longer terms. Also Senators were to be appointed by the state governments rather than elected directly by the people to give the Senate a status similar to that of the House of Lords. As a compromise, to enhance the status of the House of Representatives, it was given exclusive power to originate revenue bills. The compromise conciliated the small states by allowing them to dominate in the Senate and the large states by allowing them to dominate in the House.

The President

The executive branch that was to administer and execute the laws adopted by the legislature was treated in a rather cursory manner, but there were fears here too. Benjamin Franklin worried that a unified executive had the potential to drift to

---

[14] The plan was adopted by a vote of 5 to 4. Connecticut, Maryland, Delaware, New Jersey, and North Carolina voted in favor, Pennsylvania, Georgia, South Carolina, and Virginia against. The Massachusetts delegation was evenly split. New Hampshire and Rhode Island delegates were not present. The New York delegates had left Philadelphia before the vote.

monarchy because of a natural human tendency to prefer strong government. Other Founding Fathers expressed concern over the danger that the President could become an elected monarch unless care was taken to circumscribe the executive's power. Thought was given to checking executive power by having the President elected by Congress, as proposed by the Virginia Plan. But it was ultimately decided that the selection of the President by the legislature would violate the principle of separation of powers and make the chief executive clearly dependent on the Congress, as is the case for prime ministers in most parliamentary governments. The final plan provided for the chief executive to be elected independently of the Congress through the cumbersome procedure of the Electoral College.

To limit the power of the Congress, the Constitutional Convention gave the President the power to veto legislation, which could be overridden only by a two-thirds vote in both houses of Congress. The Constitution also makes the President Commander-in-Chief of the national military, and gives Presidents the right to make treaties, to appoint ambassadors, and to grant pardons for offenses.

Other than these relatively brief sections, the Constitution says little about the powers of the Presidency. Chief Executives have relied upon the clause that declares "the executive power shall be vested in a president" to expand their authority. The Constitution does not even define "executive power" which has allowed Presidents to claim that their actions fell within the realm of inherent executive powers not precisely spelled out in the Constitution. Abraham Lincoln suspended the writ of habeas corpus during the Civil War, which was undoubtedly an illegal violation of individual rights. Lincoln defended his action by insisting that, in a time of crisis, the President may do whatever is necessary to preserve the nation. Subsequent Presidents have acted on this precedent to claim expanded authority. These attempts have in some cases received support from Congress or the courts, while in others they have been denied or the President's power strictly limited.[15]

Over time Presidential power has expanded. Congress has responded to a more assertive Presidency by defending and extending its own authority through more specific instructions on how public monies can be spent. Indeed, it is Congress that has created and authorized the funding of various important agencies of the gov-

---

[15] President Truman claimed powers inherent in the executive authority to seize the steel mills to maintain production during the U.S. military involvement in Korea.

Richard Nixon took the idea of Presidential prerogatives a disconcerting step further when he said that "there are certain inherently governmental activities which, if undertaken by the sovereign in protection of the interests of the nation's security, are lawful but which if undertaken by private persons, are not." After he was forced to resign as a result of Watergate, he was asked, in an interview with David Frost, to elaborate upon and justify that remark. Nixon responded by referring to the example of Lincoln and claiming that the situation was comparable because the country was torn apart ideologically by Vietnam as much as it was torn apart by the Civil War. He then said, "If the President does it, that makes it legal." See *The New York Times*, May 20, 1977. Nixon thus claimed that his situation was rather like Lincoln's—a national emergency that provided him with the inherent authority found in the Constitution's "executive power" clause to act beyond the rights of the President explicitly stated in that document.

ernment such as the Securities and Exchange Commission, the Federal Reserve Board, the Interstate Commerce Commission, and other regulatory bodies. Congress can require the administrators of these agencies to testify in oversight hearings regarding how appropriated monies are being or will be spent. And detailed Congressional committee reports routinely accompanying new legislation give specific instructions regarding how laws are to be interpreted. Presidents have consistently sought greater autonomy in dealing with these agencies created and overseen by Congress. But every grant of additional authority to the President has been accompanied with protections assuring Congressional ability to shape the actions of the agency involved.

The Courts: Refereeing the Political Struggle

Article III of the Constitution, the judicial article, outlines the power of the courts. Because the Founding Fathers wrote obscurely about the nature of the federal court system, some argue that they did not want a strong judicial branch. To support this argument they quote Alexander Hamilton's description of the judiciary as "the least dangerous branch" of government, the one least likely to endanger rights and liberties (*The Federalist*, #78). But others argue that the Constitution laid a solid foundation for a strong federal court system and that history supports this contention.

The Constitution makes explicit the authority of the judicial branch to resolve disputes between state and federal laws. The federal courts' responsibility is to determine which power is exclusive to the federal government, which is exclusive to the states, and which is shared by both. The Constitution also directs the federal courts to resolve disputes between citizens of different states. This authority grew over time because, as the U.S. national economy developed, citizens turned to the federal court system to resolve many disputes.

Most would agree that the power of judicial review and the application of the due process clause of the fourteenth amendment brought the courts into equal partnership with the other branches of government. Judicial review, or the authority to declare a law unconstitutional, is not directly mentioned in the Constitution but scholars agree that it is implied. Ironically, the Supreme Court assumed this power only after a famous political and personality struggle between Thomas Jefferson, John Adams, and Chief Justice John Marshall in the celebrated case of *Marbury v. Madison*. The due process clause of the fourteenth amendment was designed to protect the rights of blacks freed after the Civil War. The clause's assertion that no one should be denied life, liberty, or property without due process became the basis for significant judicial expansion. Most of this expansion occurred during the tenure of Supreme Court Justice Earl Warren (1953–1969), who applied the due process clause to bring about a major extension of civil rights and liberties. Since that time, court activity has been more restrained. The judicial system today serves as an important instrument for resolving political disputes (for example, abortion and civil rights) that divided government fails to settle.

Federalism and Fragmentation

The greatest obstacle faced by the framers of the Constitution was the knowledge that, regardless of the design of the document, they had to obtain ratification from the state legislatures for it to go into effect. Consequently, it was understood that the states would have to retain significant autonomy regardless of other governing arrangements. The difficulty then was to strengthen the national government so that it could carry out its will in certain necessary areas while reassuring the states that they would retain all their essential powers. The delegates crafted a federal system because that was the most they could hope to get accepted by the states.

Federalism is a system of governance in which a national government shares authority with constituent governments. Federal systems have been formed usually to combine the strength of constituent parts for mutual defense. To be a federal system, governmental powers must be divided between the central government and the subunits. Each must be sovereign in some area. Thus, a highly centralized federal system assigns most significant powers to the national government. Conversely, a decentralized system assigns fewer important powers to the central government and more to the subunits. This differs from a confederation in which the subunits have ultimate sovereignty, and from a unitary form of government in which the central government has the ultimate authority in every case. Modern federalism was thus invented in Philadelphia by combining some features of unitary government with aspects of a confederation. Both the national and state governments exercise authority over the same citizenry in the same territory.

As shown in Fig. 4-2, the Constitutional Convention divided government powers in the Constitution between the national government and the states, with each unit able to exercise power over its citizens in its own area of authority. Since each unit derives its authority directly from the same Constitution, the distribution of authority cannot be changed through legislation. It can only be changed through the amendment process, which requires the active involvement of the states.[16]

A major concern of the delegates in Philadelphia was to design a national government with enough power to protect private property and provide economic stability.[17] Although they accepted the principle that government has a responsibility

---

[16] The framers provided, in Article V, for a process in which two-thirds of both Houses can propose amendments, or two-thirds of the legislatures of the states can call a convention for proposing amendments. Amendments are adopted when ratified by the legislatures of three-fourths of the states, or by a three-fourths vote of the convention called for amending the Constitution (this latter process has never been used).

Members of the delegations from the small states began questioning whether the Constitution could be amended to reduce their membership in the Senate. Without debate the delegates agreed to add a final clause to Article V holding "that no State, without its Consent, shall be deprived of its equal Suffrage in the Senate." This guarantees that the Senate will always be based upon equal representation.

[17] The concern of the delegates to the convention about protecting private property has been well documented. See Calvin C. Jillson and Cecil L. Eubanks, "The Political Structure of Constitution Making: The Federal Convention of 1787," *American Journal of Political Science*, vol. 28, no. 3 (August 1984), pp. 435–458. The view that the delegates' economic self-interest was the basis for private property and economic concerns was popularized by Charles Beard, *An Economic Interpretation of the Constitution* (New York: Free Press, reprinted in 1965; originally published in 1913). See also

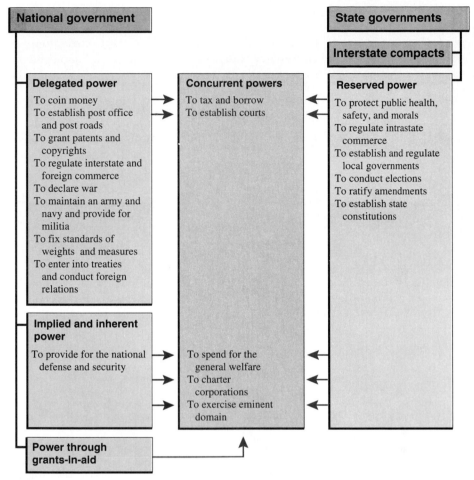

FIGURE 4-2
The Constitutional distribution of powers between the national and state governments in the United States.

to protect everyone's rights to life, liberty, and property, it is clear that property held a preferred position. On the one hand, they wanted to place the protection of property and commerce in the hands of the national government to protect them from state legislatures. But on the other, they wanted to ensure that the national government would not itself jeopardize commerce or private property. The delegates also specifically forbade the states to tax imports or exports, to coin money, to enter into treaties, or to impair obligations and contracts.

The Founding Fathers were also concerned about the possibility of power being

on economic stability, John P. Roche, "The Founding Fathers: A Reform Caucus in Action," *American Political Science Review*, vol. 55, no. 4 (December 1961), pp. 799–816.

fragmented between the national government and states in a **system of federalism** since they had observed the threats to property and to national unity that could occur when authority was too decentralized.[18] Article VI of the Constitution was added which contained the **supremacy clause** stating that the Constitution and the laws of the national government made in pursuance of its provisions are the supreme law of the land.

Both the national and state governments, then, can act only within their own proper spheres. Defining exactly what those appropriate spheres are has been a recurring tension between the states and the national government as well as ideologically between liberals and conservatives. One view argues that the United States was created by the people collectively, not by the individual states. Supporters of this view cite the document itself, which begins "We, the People of the United States" without any reference to a compact by the states. The other view, that the ultimate authority lies with the states, is referred to as the Compact Theory.[19]

Many of the framers were apprehensive regarding the states and would have preferred a much stronger central authority, but felt they had gone as far as would be acceptable by state legislatures. An example was Alexander Hamilton, who saw the promise of nationhood in the Constitution rather than in the identification of the authority of individual states. This view emphasized the community of interest as one nation, with the role of the national government being seen as essential for the task of nation building.[20]

---

[18] While they feared the tyrannical rule of despots, they had also experienced the difficulties of a government that lacked the ability to act because it had insufficient power under the Articles of Confederation. State governments ran up huge debts to finance the Revolutionary War. In the aftermath, the states raised taxes to repay the debt, which threatened many farmers with bankruptcy and farm foreclosures. Farmers frequently faced jail for their inability to pay their debts. The threat of armed rebellion over issues of debts and taxes led to Shays' Rebellion. This was a rebellion by Daniel Shays, a revolutionary war veteran, on behalf of beleaguered farmers that never seriously threatened the government but raised alarm over the inadequacy of the Articles of Confederation to maintain internal order. Madison expressed his concern over the threat from those who would nullify debts, contracts, or taxes in *The Federalist*, #10, when he decried "a rage for paper money, for an abolition of debts, for an equal division of property, or for any other improper or wicked project."

[19] Ronald Reagan's first inaugural address supported the general thrust of the Compact Theory when he proposed in his "New Federalism" to reduce or eliminate certain federal programs and transfer others to the states. He indicated his desire to do this to improve efficiency, and also stated they were improper for the federal government to undertake under the Constitution. They are improper, he asserted, not in the sense that they violate the law, but in the larger philosophical and historical sense that the current distribution of power between the national and state levels of government violates the "true meaning" and intent of the Constitution. In justification of that view, he pointed to the founding of the Republic, stating: "The federal government did not create the states; the states created the federal government." Reagan's view was immediately challenged by historians who alleged the President did not understand the Constitution, which begins with the words, "**We, the People** of the United States."

[20] Alexander Hamilton wanted to restore the public credit by full funding of the federal debt and the federal assumption of the debts that the states incurred during the Revolutionary War. This was aimed at encouraging the states to join the union and reducing the threat of the civil unrest that had sparked Shays' Rebellion. It favored the moneyed class who held the federal and state obligations. But it had the effect of strengthening the national government by attaching to it the interests of the more influential members of society. Hamilton believed that a central bank was necessary to support public

The framers distributed political power in the Constitution between the national government and the states to make it difficult for government at either level to threaten property rights. The fragmentation of authority would make it very difficult for any political interest to gain control of sufficient levers of power to produce any public policy adverse to the interests of the propertied class. By definition, a federal arrangement would make any unified policy very burdensome to achieve.

The separation of powers and checks and balances between branches of government at the federal level have prevailed at the state level as well, with subsequent states joining the union patterning themselves quite consciously after the national model. And federalism has not only protected property rights, but has stimulated economic competition among the nation's constituent parts. That competition began immediately, with each state attempting to attract business through a variety of policies that have ranged from antiunion laws, to tax exemptions for companies, to aids to commerce such as building harbors, canals, and roads. States were forced to compete to offer the most favorable terms to attract new businesses and financial interests. State politicians that failed to meet the lowest common denominators of economic attractiveness also risked the flight of businesses already within their borders to other states, as well as the wrath of voters. The major role of the states was fixed in the Constitution by the Tenth Amendment, which reserved to state governments those powers not delegated to the national government by the Constitution nor prohibited by the Constitution to the states.

Figure 4-3 shows how the Constitution fragmented power between the national and state governments and between the parts of government in such a way as to meet all these concerns. But the actual balance of power between the national government and the states has been determined by political realities rather than through law or political theory. For the first 70 years of government under the Constitution, the national government was very tentative in exerting its authority. There were sectional differences between the South, which opposed effective national government, and the industrial North, which wanted greater national control of trade and tariff policies. Nevertheless, there was a national movement toward industrialization, the building of railroads and canals, and the distribution of land that required national authority. This came to a head with the election of Lincoln in 1860, who favored a national government that would absorb the South into the national polity. Lincoln's election caused the union to break up. It was during the period of national emergency arising from the Civil War in 1861 to 1865 that the scope and authority of the national government grew as it responded to the crisis.

The Civil War paved the way for the expansion of political conflict from the local to the national level. National power was enlarged at the expense of state pow-

---

credit, promote economic welfare, and "cement the union." He believed a broad construction of the "necessary and proper" clause of Article I provided sufficient authorization for such a bank. Thomas Jefferson had expressed his concern for the national concept in the Declaration of Independence, but he disagreed with Hamilton over the claim of national authority in the "necessary and proper" clause.

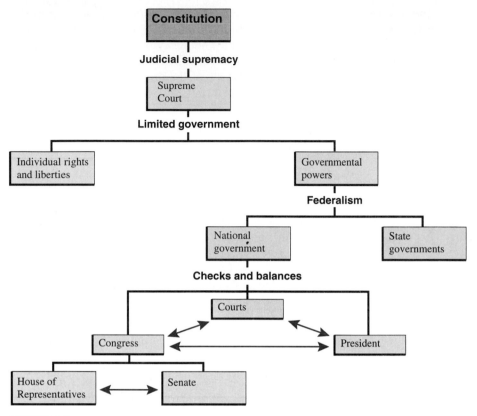

FIGURE 4-3
The fragmentation of power between different parts of the U.S. government.

ers due to several factors. In particular, the commercial power of the national government was expanded to accommodate the growth of the American economy on a national scale. Federal regulatory activity grew following the appearance of large corporations seeking national markets. National interest groups began to appear on the scene and made their influence felt in Congress. The Fourteenth Amendment increased Congressional power. The Sixteenth Amendment gave Congress the power to levy a federal income tax first utilized during the Civil War. The Supreme Court increasingly read Congressional taxing and spending powers broadly. The Seventeenth Amendment allowed the popular election of senators rather than their selection by state legislatures as originally provided. All three amendments expanded the authority of the national government and contributed to the shift to a national orientation of politics.

While the Civil War greatly enhanced national power vis-à-vis the states, it also resulted in a major increase in the role of the President as an integral part of the public policy framework. Over the decades since, the legislative and administrative roles of the office have grown tremendously as the result of Congressional delegation of legislative powers to the President. The increased legislative role of the President has required a larger White House staff and a bureaucracy shielded from partisan politics. Thus power has come to be increasingly centered in the executive.

It is important to be aware of the fact that it was the expansion of the economy on a national scale and the growth of large financial concerns that led to the nationalization of politics. In consequence, the concern over commerce, its support, its regulation, and its administration has meant that government has become increasingly concerned with economic issues. That is, increasingly economics has become the language of the state.[21] Economics is attractive as the language of policy makers and bureaucrats because it is, at least in part, a vehicle for the ruling ideology in this country. The use of economic analysis may close off debate, especially in public forums like Congress. Professor Theodore Lowi claims that the rise of economics as the language of the state parallels the decline of Congress as a creative legislature. Republicans have found that economics can be as useful for their political purposes as it is for the Democrats—by manipulating he cost, rather than the benefit, side of cost-benefit analysis they can limit conflicts over policies and programs as effectively as Democrats have expanded them.[22]

FEDERALISM AND THE SCOPE OF THE CONFLICT

Democratic governments are agents by which private conflicts are transferred to the political arena and are made into public conflicts.[23] In this theory, the political process is an agent of socialization of disputes between special interests. A conflict attracts curious bystanders who want to know what the quarrel is about. The outcome of any political dispute is determined by the reaction of the crowd, which has the ability to control the outcome if it gets involved. Consequently, the most important strategy of political disputes is concerned with defining the scope of the conflict.

In any conflict, those who are winning would like to limit its scope to the participants already involved to assure a favorable outcome. It is in the interest of those who are losing to enlarge its scope to involve bystanders on their behalf. Only the inclusion of bystanders can change the outcome. For that reason, the best time to limit the scope of the conflict is at the very beginning of the struggle, by mobilizing one's own forces to get a quick resolution before the opposition has time to mobilize new forces favoring its position.

---

[21] See Theodore J. Lowi, "The State in Political Science: How We Become What We Study," *American Political Science Review*, vol. 86, no. 1 (1992), p. 5. Lowi states that political scientists have failed to appreciate how the language has made political science a dismal discipline like economics.

[22] Also see Lowi, "The State in Political Science," p. 5.

[23] See E. E. Schattschneider, *The Semisovereign People* (New York: Holt, Rinehart and Winston, 1960), for a fuller explanation of the thesis regarding the significance of the scope of conflict for the outcome of political struggles.

Throughout American history there has been a continuing battle between the effort to privatize or limit, and the struggle to socialize or expand, the scope of political and social conflict. There are many concepts used to try limiting the scope of conflicts or even to keep them out of the political arena altogether: the right to privacy, individual freedom, private enterprise, limited government, and states' rights.

There are also many other ideas used to legitimate and encourage expanding the scope of political conflict: "whistleblowing," unions, political alliances, civil rights, equal protection under law, and justice. These tend to socialize conflict and invite outside intervention on behalf of those engaged in such struggles. A whistleblower by definition is someone who witnesses illegal or unethical behavior within a work situation, but is unable to effect any change by staying within the organizational hierarchy because his or her superiors are in fact the perpetrators of the acts in question and so finds it necessary to go outside the organization for support to stop the behavior.

Those involved on both sides of the civil rights struggle argued over whether the conflict should be limited to the state level or whether it was a national question. Those opposed to the expansion of the civil rights debate argued that it was a local issue, that it was up to the people of states like Alabama or Mississippi where the issue was most fiercely contested to decide it, and that the problems over civil rights in local areas were being caused by "outsiders." Martin Luther King, Jr., and other civil rights leaders argued that the scope of the issue was larger than any state or local community—that it encompassed all Americans because it involved rights granted under the Constitution.

James Madison was aware of the significance of the scope of the conflict for different political questions and referred to it rather extensively in his writings in favor of the new Constitution. He indicated that in the new federal system the states would retain their authority as the centers around which the ordinary concerns of citizens would be focused, while the national government would have authority over external affairs involving everyone, including "war, peace, negotiation, and foreign commerce."[24] He went so far as to argue that the Constitution achieved a happy balance in the handling of certain contentious issues and the protection of the rights of minorities:

> the great and aggregate interest being referred to the national, the local and particular to the State legislatures. . . . The smaller the society, the fewer probably will be the distinct parties and interests composing it; the fewer the distinct parties and interests, the more frequently will a majority be found of the same party; and the smaller the number of individuals composing a majority, and the smaller the compass within which they are placed, the more easily will they concert and execute their plans of oppression. Extend the sphere and you take in a greater variety of parties and interests; you make it less probable that a majority of the whole will have a common motive to invade the rights of other citizens; or if such a common motive exists, it will be more difficult for all who feel it to discover their own strength and to act in unison with each other.[25]

[24] James Madison, *The Federalist*, #45.
[25] James Madison, *The Federalist*, #10.

Throughout the nation's history, liberals and conservatives have often struggled over the scope of the conflict. Thomas Jefferson and his supporters, as liberals of their time, believed "that government which governs least governs best." They sought freedom from government, believing rational human beings could manage the majority of their own affairs without government intervention. Jefferson and his followers were supportive of states being the centers of political life.

Nevertheless, the increasing nationalization of politics over time has increased national government power at the expense of state power, and several factors have contributed to this result. For example, the role of the national chief executive has been changed by the unfolding expectation that the national government and the President in particular are responsible for ensuring a robust economy and providing jobs and a more secure future for everyone. Keynesian economic theory justifies executive intervention to achieve these goals, and as Keynesian policies have been adopted the American people have demanded more Presidential action.

What has ultimately developed is a power balance in which the national government can require state conformity with whatever conditions it deems appropriate as a condition to receive federal funds to pay for various programs. Nevertheless, the implementation and administration of the programs are usually left up to state or even local officials. In many cases this makes it extremely difficult for national officials to enforce federal guidelines for the administration of such programs although some, such as the policies aimed at encouraging states to adopt a uniform maximum speed, may be easier to enforce than others.

It should be noted that, in theory at least, state and local governments are more

---

NATIONAL FUNDS AND STATE LAWS

Under the Constitution, the federal government cannot pass a law that would directly regulate speeds on national highways to be enforced by state officials. Nor can the national government legislate a minimum legal drinking age. However, when MADD (Mothers Against Drunk Driving), a special-interest group, began lobbying state legislatures to raise the legal drinking age to 21, they were only partially successful. Between 1976 and 1983, 19 states raised their legal minimum drinking age. Several states successfully resisted the pressure from MADD.

A strategic decision was made to enlarge the scope of the conflict by going to the national level and try to pass one national law to achieve the same goal. In 1983 an amendment was offered to the Surface Transportation Act to withhold 10 percent of federal highway funds from those states that did not raise their legal age to purchase alcoholic beverages to 21 by 1988. The legislation passed Congress overwhelmingly. It was difficult for Congressional representatives and Senators to oppose the bill for fear that campaign challengers might portray a negative vote as the irresponsible supporting of teenage drinking and the resulting carnage on the highway. President Reagan, who preached the need not to encroach on state prerogatives, signed the legislation in a public ceremony in October 1984.

Several states protested the action, but all of them raised their drinking age to 21 by the end of 1989 to avoid losing federal highway funds.

responsive than the national government to people's needs. The autonomy of state governments was also, according to the Founding Fathers, supposed to provide a check against the emergence of an oppressive national government authority.[26]

It is true that states have frequently been major innovators in the formulation of public policy. In the last century, when the role of the national government was very limited, many progressive public policy initiatives came from state governments. States passed the first public education legislation, child labor laws, income tax laws, and minimum wage laws. And today, it would be surprising if 50 different states, each working on similar problems such as pollution, sewage treatment, crime, and health care, to name just a few, did not come up with innovative proposals, ideas, and policies. This is particularly so during a period when the national government has reduced its commitment to national standards in public policy making. Many states today have developed public policies to reduce pollution that are stricter than national government standards.

Republican Presidents from Nixon to Bush supported a reduced role for the national government on the premise that the national government has grown too powerful. The distrust of politicians and of the inability of government to deal successfully with domestic policy matters gave support to Republican initiatives seeking to cut taxes, reduce federal domestic spending, and deregulate industry. It gave life to Richard Nixon's proposed "new federalism" for public policy intended to decentralize government program responsibility by giving it to the states and reversing "a third of a century of power flowing from the people and the States to Washington" to a system in which "power, funds and responsibility will flow from Washington to the States."[27] Ronald Reagan was even more of an activist in reducing the policy role of the national as well as state governments; his policies were more radical than Nixon's, but he retained the Republic label "new federalism" for them.

Reagan's antigovernment views are supported by the tradition of public choice theorists. The reasoning is that national government in setting uniform standards acts much like a monopoly. And monopoly providers of services are not required to compete to provide goods and services efficiently. If states and local governments have more power in these areas, however, there will be a competitive "market" for police protection, health care, sanitation, fire protection, and garbage collection, as well as for tax levels and structures and a community's attractiveness to business.

---

[26] Thomas Jefferson wrote that states were the "true barriers of our liberty" against an authoritarian national government and an unfailing bulwark against antirepublican tendencies. See Saul K. Padover (ed.), *Thomas Jefferson on Democracy* (New York: Appleton-Century-Crofts, 1939), pp. 52–53.

[27] See Richard Nixon, "Address to the Nation on Domestic Programs," in *Public Papers of President Richard M. Nixon, 1969* (Washington, DC: Government Printing Office, 1971), pp. 637–645. It should be pointed out that, despite his rhetoric, Nixon expanded several federal programs and supported national standards to guide social policy. Gerald Ford, who replaced Nixon after his resignation, in 1976 ran on a platform that conceded some concerns were of a national character, such as pollution and civil liberties, but stressed that government action "should be taken first by the government that resides closest" to the people to be affected by it. See Donald Bunce Johnson (ed.), *National Platforms* (Champaign, Urbana: University of Illinois Press, 1978), Vol. II, p. 996.

Reagan's Domestic Policy Council urged state and local governments to compete to attract business investment to replace federal grants-in-aid to state and local governments which were being severely curtailed. It counseled:

> When the size of government is kept as localized as possible, there is the potential that jurisdictions will compete against one another in the kinds of public goods they provide, the kinds of regulation of private activity they permit, and the way they tax their citizens. . . . Ill-conceived public policy over the long-run leads to an exodus of business and talented individuals; the State's tax base erodes and its infrastructure deteriorates.[28]

State officials have engaged in economic competition to improve their business climates through promoting antiunion policies, encouraging low wages, and maintaining low taxes on businesses. The net effect is to pressure other states to reduce business regulations and cut back progressive labor and social welfare policies. Business threats to move to states with friendlier business climates will usually get quick results from politicians who do not want to have to respond to charges that their policies cost their states jobs and income (see Chap. 9 and the discussion there about the Tiebout model).

POLITICAL PARTIES

James Madison wrote in *The Federalist* about the dangers of "factions," which would include interest groups and political parties. Another Founding Father, Alexander Hamilton, wanted support for a **national bank** and tried to forge a coalition across the Constitutionally separated branches of the executive and Congress. The checks and balances between the branches of government made competition an inherent part of the Constitutional order. Hamilton's effort to join together what the Constitutional Convention had separated provided the foundation of the Federalist party, the first political party in America. The political party developed into an "indispensable instrument that brought cohesion and unity, and hence effectiveness, to the government as a whole by linking the executive and legislative branches in a bond of common interest."[29] A **unified national government**, in which the executive and the Congress are controlled by the same political party, has not always guaranteed cooperation, but it has given a strong impetus toward building a coalition to bridge the gap between those institutions and provide an effective vehicle for policy adoption and implementation.

The emergence of the Federalist party brought into being a countervailing coalition of political interests. Thomas Jefferson led this **coalition** composed primarily of agrarian interests to oppose the merchant/financial interests of Hamilton and the

---

[28] Domestic Policy Council, *The Status of Federalism in America* (Washington, DC: U.S. Government Printing Office, 1986), pp. 55–56. See Chap. 9 of this book for a discussion of the Tiebout model of neighborhood formation.

[29] James L. Sundquist, "Needed: A Political Theory for the New Era of Coalition Government in the United States," *Political Science Quarterly*, vol. 103 (Winter 1988–1989), p. 614.

Federalists.[30] After Jefferson was elected President in 1800, the Federalist party quickly faded. By 1820 its ability to compete for the Presidency came to an end.

The election of Andrew Jackson in 1828 actually ushered in the creation of the modern political party. He broadened the coalition to include southerners and westerners, as well as recent immigrants. The masses were mobilized to vote in the 1828 election, which helped to eradicate the last traces of the old elitism of the propertied class in American politics. Jackson's successor, Martin Van Buren, was the first to encourage the idea of the legitimacy of competing political parties. In Van Buren's view, one party could not represent all the segments of society and remain loyal to a set of principles. An opposition party could legitimately represent segments of society not adequately represented by the Democratic party. The idea of the loyal opposition and the appropriateness of ongoing political competition between parties finally gained acceptance. The initial opposition of the Whig party developed in reaction to the strong Presidency of Jackson. The Republican party grew out of the remnants of the Whig party in 1854 and Democratic-Republican competition became part of the structure of American politics.

DIVIDED GOVERNMENT

Divided National Government

Divided government exists when the executive branch and both houses of Congress are not controlled by the same party. While divided government occasionally has occurred at the national level in American history, unified government has been the rule. From Andrew Jackson's administration in 1828 until the reelection of Dwight Eisenhower in 1956, only three Presidents took office to find even one house of Congress controlled by the opposition party. All three occasions occurred in the nineteenth century.[31] Presidents faced opposition party control of one or both houses after midterm elections at least a dozen times between 1854 and 1954. Even in those unusual instances, however, the President had at least a 2-year period of undivided government.[32]

Since 1954 the norm of unified or undivided government has disintegrated.

---

[30] Jefferson became the champion of those opposed to a strong national government. They became known as the Jeffersonian-Republicans to indicate their opposition to the Federalists led by Alexander Hamilton, who supported the moneyed interests who wanted a strong national government to protect them from the "excesses of democracy." The Federalists referred to the emerging political party as the Democratic-Republicans in an effort to link the Jeffersonians pejoratively with the excesses of democracy. The Jeffersonians accepted the term as an indication of their faith in the ability of rational people to largely manage their own affairs without government intervention. They dropped the "Republican" part of the label and began calling themselves "Democrats." This is the oldest political party to continue in existence in the United States. The Federalists went out of existence in the early 1800s.

[31] Since the emergence of the Republican party, until 1956, only Rutherford B. Hayes, a Republican, faced a Democratic House of Representatives in 1876, and Grover Cleveland found the Senate controlled by the Republicans in his first term in 1884.

[32] The technical definition of divided government which occurs when the President's party does not control both houses of Congress is a clear indicator of partisan divisions that will likely obstruct coherent policy making. There are many cases where the President's party controlled one or both houses by such a thin margin that unified government was more apparent than real. For example, "conservative

Democratic Presidents have been in the White House for only 16 of the 44 years between 1952 and 1996. During the periods Democrats have been in the White House, the government has not been divided in that Democrats have also controlled both houses of Congress. The Kennedy-Johnson years are thought of as a period when the national government did take an active role in pursuing a variety of public policy goals ranging from the Peace Corps, to Keynesian tax cuts, to the War on Poverty, to increased aid to education, to the space program, to the Vietnam conflict.

Republican Presidents have been in the White House for 28 of the 44 years between 1952 and 1996, but Democrats have controlled the House of Representatives for the entire period. Democrats have been the majority party in the Senate for 18 of those years. In a government in which there is a division between party dominance in the executive and the legislature, the parties heighten the confrontation and encourage a stalemate. It is often presumed that Congress will be more likely to be obstructionist to administrations of the opposite party than of their own. However, the divided governments of Nixon and Ford dispel the notion that significant public policy legislation cannot be produced by divided government. The National Environmental Policy Act (NEPA) of 1969, the Occupational Safety and Health Act (OSHA) of 1970, the Equal Employment Opportunity Act of 1972, the Consumer Product Safety Act of 1972, and the Comprehensive Employment and Training Act of 1973 are examples of some of the more important pieces of legislation passed in the latter half of the century under divided government. Consequently, divided or unified government by itself cannot provide a complete explanation of legislative policy production.

The success of an administration in getting legislative initiatives approved in Congress rests on many factors, including the President's overall popularity, leadership skill, political ideology, and the strength and unity of the President's party in the Congress.[33] Thus, an explanation of President Carter's lack of success despite the unified national government at that time was his lack of leadership skill and his ideological differences with Congress, which left him without a working majority coalition.

The initiatives launched by the Reagan administration included some inconsistent elements. Only in defense policy was spending to be increased. In all other

---

coalitions" in which Democrats technically controlled Congress, but conservative Democrats defected to join Republicans frequently to veto programs of Roosevelt, Kennedy, and Johnson, meant that unified government existed in name only. James MacGregor Burns has argued that the "Presidential party" could not control the legislative program. See James MacGregor Burns, *The Deadlock of Democracy: Four-Party Politics in America* (Englewood Cliffs, NJ: Prentice-Hall, 1963). He postulated that both parties had national and Congressional wings. If we were to use this broader view, although it lacks the precision of our technical definition, then divided government has been much more common throughout this century and is not a phenomenon of the last 40 years. It also suggests an explanation for the lack of legislative initiative or success in some administrations that had a technically unified government, such as Kennedy and Carter.

[33] James A. Thurber, "Representation, Accountability, and Efficiency in Divided Party Control of Government," *PS Political Science and Politics*, vol. 24, no. 4 (December 1991), p. 653.

areas a reduction in government spending was proposed, especially in social welfare programs, to offset the higher military budgets. There was to be a tax reduction aimed primarily at upper-income groups. Government regulation of business was to be scaled back, and state governments were to be responsible for more social welfare spending. Tax cuts proved too irresistible to voters for even a Democratic House of Representatives to refuse. However, Congress was reluctant to cut back social services that people demanded, which exaggerated the budget deficit problem.

Historically, the Republican party has dominated the Presidency. Since 1860, Republicans have held the White House 84 years, and the Democrats just 52 years. Between 1860 and 1932 there were only two Democratic Presidents. Franklin Roosevelt and Harry Truman's 20-year occupancy of the office was occasioned by the Great Depression and World War II. In the years since 1952, Democrats have occupied the White House for only 16 years. The election of 1992 technically ended divided government. However, the divisions within the Democratic party between its more conservative members and its more liberal wing constrain President Clinton's options. Moreover, Republican prospects for winning a majority in the Senate in 1994 are very promising because of the small number of Republican Senators up for reelection compared with the number of Democrats who must run.

Long-term control of the executive by one political party and the dominance of the legislature by the opposite political party increases the tendency of the members of both parties to look out for their immediate interests rather than the long-term interest of the nation's welfare. There appears to be a growing consensus that neither party will find it easy to win control of the branch of government it does not traditionally control. George Bush and the Republican party have both supported term limits in Congress as a way of Republicans gaining control of that branch. But members of both parties are aware that they can be blocked by the opposition in their political aims and thus engage in risk-aversion strategies. Increasingly they practice the **politics of blame**. That is, they put forward issues to maintain their traditional support and try to avoid positions that would place them in position for a negative campaign to be run against them.

This means public vacillation between incompatible goals is reinforced. Republican Presidents play to their traditional constituency by proposing lower taxes and spending, and Democrats in Congress maintain social welfare programs. Both parties emphasize their strong points that are difficult to attack—lower taxes and social benefits—and the public is not required to reconcile its inconsistent public choices. Both political parties take positions that allow rational voters to support both preferences in the voting booth.

It may well be that **the content of electoral politics is the cornerstone of divided government**. Polls indicate that Democrats and Republicans have clearly differentiated profiles in the minds of the American electorate. The public perceives the Republicans as more likely to keep taxes and inflation down while maintaining a stronger national defense and possessing more skill in foreign relations than Democrats. Polls also indicate that Democrats are perceived as being more concerned about a wide range of civil rights issues and providing for social programs such as health care, education, and jobs than Republicans. The differences in party images provides a match in the different motivations people have when voting for President and for members of Congress.

Voters expect the President to maintain a strong defense as Commander-in-Chief, to be the nation's chief diplomat, and to keep taxes low. The collapse of the Soviet Union has deprived the Republican party of a major advantage in voter perception of its being better equipped to deal effectively with foreign policy. Congressional candidates get elected by defending the interests of their constituents at the local level. Thus the choice presented to the voters is framed differently in Presidential and Congressional elections, with the Presidency contested on the Republican party's natural turf, and Congressional elections contested on the natural turf of the Democrats.[34] Voting for different parties at different levels of government is called **ticket-splitting** and once it results in divided government, the practice is reinforced by the expectations of the voters. Voters may attempt to set up their own scheme of checks and balances. By voting for a Republican Presidential candidate who promises "no new taxes," they hope to support their own interest in low tax rates. That gives them all the more incentive to vote for Democratic majorities in Congress to protect themselves from a President who would cut their favorite programs, even while the Republican President would prevent Congress from raising their taxes.[35]

Republicans running for Congress under the antigovernment ideological banner of the "Reagan Revolution" faced a built-in contradiction when appealing to voters who wanted their programs protected. The result was that Republicans fielded mediocre candidates on the wrong side of issues important to voters in Congressional elections. For a Republican candidate who really believes in the antigovernment philosophy to succeed in getting elected is to become part of the problem one has railed against. In this sense, only those committed to the ideas that government can be a positive instrument for change and that a career in Congress is a principled way to pursue an honorable goal will not experience a conflict. This contributes to Democrats having more success in fielding attractive Congressional candidates.

Divided Government in the States

Divided government is not just a national phenomenon. Unified party control in the states, in which the same party wins the governorship and a majority control in both houses of the legislature, is also declining. After the introduction of the New Deal, levels of unified control in the states surpassed 80 percent. But since the mid-1940s

---

[34] Gary C. Jacobson, *The Electoral Origins of Divided Government: Competition in U.S. House Elections, 1946–1988* (Boulder, CO: Westview Press, 1990). Also see Jacobson, "Explaining Divided Government: Why Can't the Republicans Win the House?" *PS Political Science and Politics*, vol. 24, no. 4 (December 1991), p. 641.

[35] During the 1984 Presidential campaign, two Lou Harris polls showed that 55 and 60 percent of those polled believed that the country would be "worse off" if the voters elected "a Republican-controlled Congress that would pass nearly everything he [Reagan] wants." Harris Survey, news release no. 98, Nov. 2, 1984, reporting on polls taken Sept. 21–25 and Oct. 25–31, 1984.

unified government at this level has fallen. The tendency to look at state election results in terms of composites has given rise to the misperception that Democrats control state governments. Although Democrats unfailingly win over 60 percent of the governors' races and the same percentage of the legislatures, there is little correspondence between victories in the executive and legislative contests of individual states. Looking at election results state by state, Democrats have had overall control of a plurality of states for just 6 of the last 46 years.[36] They controlled a majority of state governments from 1964 to 1966, following Lyndon Johnson's landslide victory over Barry Goldwater at the national level. And after the Republican disaster because of Watergate in 1974, Democrats again gained control over a majority of the state governments until 1978.

The decline of unified control at the state level is shown in Fig. 4-4 and is fundamentally the result of a decrease in Republican control of state legislatures. The success of Democrats in the gubernatorial and legislative arenas has become disconnected. Thus the national pattern of a Republican Chief Executive faced with at least one legislative house controlled by the opposition party is increasingly mirrored at the state level, resulting in many cases of Republican governors faced with Democrats in control of the state legislature. Control over the governors' office alternates between the parties, but does not show any clear trend.[37]

---

[36] See Morris P. Fiorina, "Divided Government: The Story in the States," *The Public Perspective*, vol. 3, no. 1 (November/December 1991), p. 21.

[37] Professor Fiorina suggests that the decline of Republican legislative control may be related to the professionalization of the state legislatures. Today, there are few "amateur" state legislatures that sit for 1 or 2 months with minimal compensation and perks. He speculates that amateur legislatures

FIGURE 4-4
Percentage of states with unified party control (the same party holding the governor's office and majorities in both chambers of the legislature), 1946 to 1990. *(Source: Morris Fiorina,* The Public Perspective, *vol. 3, no. 1, November/December 1991, p. 24.)*

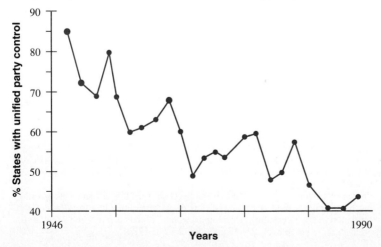

Time Horizons and Public Policy in a Divided Government

The purpose of public policy is to bring order and predictability into our world futures. It is based on the concept that we have the power to shape and control our destinies because we are rational beings. The framers of the Constitution were very clear on this when they wrote into its Preamble the purposes of forming a new government:

> We the People of the United States, in Order to form a more perfect Union, establish Justice, insure domestic Tranquility, provide for the common defence, promote the general Welfare, and secure the Blessings of Liberty to ourselves **and our Posterity**, do ordain and establish this Constitution for the United States of America. (emphasis added)

There was great concern among the Founding Fathers regarding how their actions would affect those who would come after them. George Washington, John Adams, and Thomas Jefferson constantly referred to the need to secure the conditions for a better future.[38]

In a divided government, where much of the struggle is over the scope of the conflict, political competition takes on the fascination of a game. As a consequence, media attention comes to focus on the spectacle rather than the effects of an election. Television and campaign coverage tends to focus on the strategy and tactics of a campaign, much in the same manner as reporting on a professional basketball or football game. Great attention is paid to the results of continual polling of the public's reaction to the candidates, and to who is gaining or losing in the polls. Considerable press attention is devoted to campaign managers written up as team coaches trying to select the winning strategy.

As indicated in Fig. 4-5, public policy planning occurs within a time continuum stretching from the known past into the guessed-at future. But when viewed as a game, politics and the resulting policy planning appear to have no purpose beyond the election. Politicians, too often, have shortened their planning horizons to winning the next election. Divided government has contributed to this shrinking of long-term policy planning. In public policy areas we cannot mobilize consensus planning for national investments whose payoffs appear to be more than a decade into the future. The future tends to be discounted in favor of the present. Deficits

---

might entice professionals and proprietors who can absent themselves from their primary occupations for significant periods without significant financial hardship. Their service is seen as a public service. Such backgrounds tend to correlate with Republican leanings. But successful professionals and proprietors would be less willing (or able) to leave their lucrative principal occupations for full-time legislative service. A professionalized legislature earning more substantial salaries would be more attractive to individuals earning midrange salaries.

Thus professionalized legislatures may favor Democrats in the long run by increasing the opportunity costs of serving in the state legislature for Republicans. Simultaneously it may increase the benefits of such service for Democrats. And since state legislatures are often the genesis of a path leading to Congress, declining Republican success in state legislatures may result in fewer experienced candidates for the national legislature.

[38] Historians have noted how George Washington could scarcely give a speech without talking about posterity. John Adams wrote to his wife Abigail after signing the Declaration of Independence, "I do not know what will be the outcome of this. We may pay a very high price. But it is certain that posterity will profit from our sacrifice." And Thomas Jefferson referred to the "thousandth and thousandth generation" in his first inaugural address.

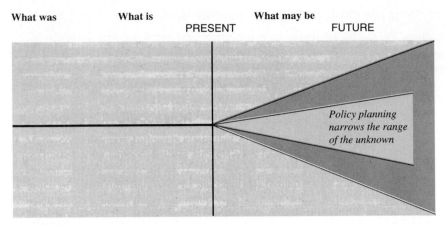

What was   **What is**   **What may be**
                    PRESENT   FUTURE

*Policy planning
narrows the range
of the unknown*

FIGURE 4-5
The public policy planning time continuum.

and their resulting long-term burden on economic growth are discounted. And government policy is geared more toward encouraging consumption than savings and investment. Excessive wrangling for partisan advantage over the scope of the conflict precludes long-term planning much as inflation does in business. In contrast to this situation in the United States, in Japan the Ministry of International Trade and Industry (MITI) has been drafting a 100-year plan to fight global warming. The significance of the plan is the determination to channel energies to reverse the global changes brought about by population and economic growth and by technological change. A 100-year plan reveals a society that understands its well-being lies in planning long-term policy, and that is self-confident it can meet the challenge.

The actions of the Founding Fathers in framing the Constitution had a major impact in influencing how the present contours of public policy have evolved. Just as their future is our present, our present will be the past for those who follow us.

Divided Government and Efficiency in Policy Making

Divided government has created considerable commentary about its being the root cause of the difficulty that prevents the U.S. government from producing coherent public policy. This failure, it is argued, leads to frustration among the public at large and the resulting low esteem in which governmental institutions are held. To be sure, political parties were developed to overcome the Constitutional design of the separation of powers and checks that the delegates to the Constitutional Convention designed. It is also true that an undivided government in which the President has a good "working majority" in Congress facilitates the passage of a legislative program and clearer party accountability for voters.

It is undeniable that frustration with government among the public at large is high and pressure to do "something" is growing. Various proposals have been put

SYMBOLIC GOAL SETTING

In the late 1980s, President George Bush set six ambitious national education goals to be achieved by the year 2000. Yet 2 years later, there had been no discernible progress toward achieving them. The President said he wanted to be "the education President," but he proposed to spend $27 million less in real dollars on education programs in fiscal year 1992 than was appropriated in 1991. The goals called for American students to leave grades 4, 8, and 12 only after having passed tests demonstrating competency in English, math, and science. Another goal was for American students to be first in the world in science and math. This improvement would take place with the goal of increasing the high school graduation rate from its current 76 percent to 90 percent or more. The President proposed that all American children should start school "ready to learn" by the year 2000. Yet another goal was eradicating illiteracy by the turn of the century. The final goal was that every school would be free of drugs and violence within the next 8 years. Declining SAT (Scholastic Assessment Test) and other test scores suggested that a majority of the elementary and high schools were not making progress. Setting such lofty goals while simultaneously reducing the national investment in education from preschool through graduate school did not instill confidence in public opinion that the goals were more than a rhetorical flourish.

A majority of parents in a survey done for the National Parent Teacher Association and the Chrysler Corporation believed that only one of Bush's goals—the ability of students to pass competency exams in math, English, science, history and geography—was attainable by the year 2000.

forward by serious scholars for Constitutional reform. Their claims are based on the proposition that the framers of the Constitution meeting during the summer of 1787 expected their work to be only a beginning. They did not believe their document was perfect and anticipated it would be amended as needed. However, few people questioned the wisdom of their work or suggested tampering with the basic governmental structures they created until approximately the last 25 years. Now it is asked whether the nation can afford a governmental system based on the compromises the framers found necessary to persuade the states to adopt the Constitution in the first place.

There is a circularity in cause and effect here. The built-in inefficiencies of American government make it difficult to get policies supported by a majority of the voters, such as national health care, adopted over opposition by a determined minority. The success of such veto groups encourages the view that the government is too inept to accomplish its policy goals. This leads to the conclusion that since the government is unable to effectively achieve its goals, its involvement in policy should be kept to a minimum. The result is to encourage ineffective or regressive policies.

Others argue that the system is working as intended by the Founding Fathers to protect the citizenry from an actively aggressive and efficient government. In their view the inefficiency of government is a small price to pay for personal freedom. In their view, "If it ain't broke, don't fix it."

TERM LIMITS AND THE POLITICAL MARKET

The idea of limiting terms of elected officials is older than the Republic. But public disdain for politicians has reached a level where proposals to limit Congressional terms to 12 years has been supported by 75 percent of those polled in some instances. In 1992 a new "anti-big-government" lobby named U.S. Term Limits provided large sums of money and was successful in getting referenda on term limits on the ballots of 14 states. Term limits were overwhelmingly supported in each of those cases. At the same time, most election districts voted to return incumbents to Washington even though they had served 12 years. Term limits are not a solution to most criticisms one hears of Congress.

In economics there is a presumption in favor of free market operations. There is a supposition that the free market will result in mutually advantageous agreements. The only exceptions to this are situations in which there are market failures, or where there is a compelling reason in which the society indicates its intention to override market forces with a politically imposed decision. The burden of proof is upon those who propose to interfere with the free market to show that the interference is necessary.

Proposals to limit Congresspeople to 12 years sounds to free marketeers suspiciously like an interference in the political market requiring a justification. Some strong supporters of free market solutions without needless government regulations, such as President George Bush, have been the most vigorous advocates of term limits. Why?

A major argument is that incumbents have unfair advantages over challengers because of their ability to amass a campaign war chest, their franking privileges, their access to the media, and their professional staffs, to name just a few. Thus, so the argument runs, inferior incumbents hoodwink the public into support for themselves, even when they face superior challengers. This argument, if true, means that a fundamental assumption of democracy is fatally flawed. Democracy assumes that people are rational and are capable of making preferred choices. The status quo permits the defeat of an incumbent for any reason whatsoever, while interference in the political market with an imposed term limit actually limits the freedom of a democratic majority in selecting its preferred candidate. It denies voters a basic freedom of choice. The primary argument for term limits is that people are misled by elected officials and, unable to discern their true best interests, reelect incumbents. In an effort to guarantee that we throw the rascals out, term limits requires that we throw the baby out with the bath water. It also requires the indiscriminate rejection of capable, conscientious, experienced leaders. It assures that Congressional leadership will be in the hands of amateurs. And it will strengthen the power of unelected Congressional staffers and lobbyists, whose tenure will not be restricted.

Similar arguments have been raised, but rejected, in economic markets. It has been argued that major corporations have sufficient knowledge of the market and access to

Still others have pointed out that the lack of direction in the national government is an accurate reflection of the lack of consensus among the population regarding the proper role of government in the policy-making process. The views of a large portion of the population encourage an antigovernment politics. The wealthier segment of society tends to be more conservative, and less in need of government policy to provide social services. This group is more likely to view government taxes to provide for education, health care, unemployment benefits, and direct housing

advertising funds to induce buyers to prefer their often inferior brand over superior products produced by smaller firms without the advantages of economies of scale. This view has been rejected in favor of the rational self-interest of consumers to discipline the market through their decisions. Proponents of term limits do not have the same confidence in the decision-making ability of self-interested voters to support the candidates they perceive to be in their best interests.

The high rate of reelection of incumbents might well signal the satisfaction of the voters with their performance. Reelection is a reward for meritorious performance. A low rate of reelection would signal greater voter dissatisfaction, not less. The risk of incurring the wrath of voters and not being reelected is important only if the political entrepreneur aspires to continue in political office. Mandated term limits reduces an important incentive to good behavior.

Proponents of term limits suggest that the injection of fresh blood in Congress would result in better legislation than is provided by representatives with long seniority. However, experience provided by seniority is an important aspect of effectiveness in Congress. With seniority comes better committee assignments and great knowledge and understanding of government institutions, individuals, and special-interest groups. This is not unlike the rewards from seniority conferred in corporations in terms of wages or promotions based largely on experience. The seniority system is one method that political parties use to encourage good behavior among their members. Term limits would reduce the importance of seniority and weaken party discipline. The net effect would be to strengthen the executive at the expense of the legislature.

To the degree to which seniority translates into more power wielded by a legislator on behalf of constituents, voters may rationally calculate that the rejection of an incumbent may weaken their district's ability to obtain government largesse. If some states adopt term limits, they consign their states to junior status in Congressional power. A Congressional district has all the attributes of a special-interest group.

It is intriguing that conservatives, who tend to be the most vigorous defenders of free markets, are some of the most ardent advocates of term limits for Congress. Since the Democratic party has dominated Congress since the 1930s, the proposal would initially aid Republicans more than Democrats. It would also shift power away from Congress toward a Republican-dominated executive branch. Thus the proposal has far more to do with competition between political parties and between the executive and legislative branches than with an abiding wish to improve public policy. A better policy solution would be campaign finance reform, which would reduce the financial advantages of incumbency and increase the importance of a candidate's record.

subsidies as unnecessary at best, destructive of motivation, and best left to private market forces. Government intervention to supply these goods leads inevitably to greater problems caused by higher tax rates, increased inflation, and a generally more intrusive government. Divided government has considerable difficulty in producing a vigorous legislative program and is therefore rather supportive of the conservative desire for a less meddlesome policy approach.

To the extent that government policy is seen to be gridlocked, it plays to the conservative charge that government is incompetent and wasteful. This permits con-servatives to widen the scope of the conflict to include groups who are less well off economically, but who have also concluded that government, particularly a Congress controlled by Democrats, is incompetent and servile to various **special-interest groups** including blacks and Hispanics, radical feminists, labor unions, homosexuals, welfare recipients, and liberal elites.

Those who are less well off financially, and more in need of social welfare pro-grams, are more inclined to support Democratic Congressional candidates who articulate the need for jobs and aid to education, housing, and health care.

Split-ticket voting, in which the individual votes for an executive from one party and legislators from another, now includes about one-third of all voters. This may be viewed as a very democratic outcome in which voters express their desire to have their cake and eat it too when they vote for low taxes and social welfare pro-grams simultaneously. If that view is correct, then divided government reflects the genuinely conflicted desires of the American voter rather than frustrating popular preferences. The 1992 elections may signify the view that, unlike in a parliamen-tary system, in our government Congress **should** be a check on the executive branch. Nevertheless, in 1992 the voters showed they wanted a responsive govern-ment by choosing a President and Congress of the same party which can be held accountable for their leadership.

A less optimistic view argues that, faced with government gridlock and indeci-sion, a large percentage of voters are declining to vote, further subverting any claim of legitimacy for the electoral results which have produced divided government. The dissatisfaction is shown by the fact that in 1992 Bill Clinton won his election by receiving only 44 percent of the votes cast for President. Third-party candidate Ross Perot, running on a platform that both political parties have failed to address the nation's problems, won 17 percent of the total vote. This, combined with George Bush's 36 percent, means that Bill Clinton received the smallest percentage of the popular vote of any recent President.

Proposals to reduce divided government range from mild reforms, such as strengthening political parties so that politicians would be more closely identified with party positions, to sanctioning or compelling straight-ticket voting at least in national elections.[39] Strengthening the parties is more difficult than it might first appear, given the independent nature of campaign financing. Increasing voter turnout might also produce clearer political mandates. A variety of proposals, such as moving election days to weekends—Saturday or Sunday—to make it easier for lower-income workers to get to the polls, have aimed at this. However, most of these suggestions would have the effect of expanding the power of the President at the expense of Congress.

---

[39] Other more radical proposals have been put forward to avert divided government. Such approaches include, but are not limited to, limiting Congressional terms in office, promoting a Presidential-Congressional team ticket, providing the President's party with bonus seats in Congress, and changing the terms of office to strengthen the relationship between the President's party and other candidates running for office.

CONCLUSION

1 Government failure to provide a clear direction in policy formulation and implementation has caused an increase in frustration and dissatisfaction among the electorate. Politicians have exploited the lack of direction by campaigning on antigovernment platforms, which further reduces the credibility of government institutions.

2 American political culture has been profoundly influenced by the views and actions of the framers at the Constitutional Convention. They were concerned to reduce the power of the executive and to place checks on each branch of government to reduce the likelihood of any branch being able to exert too much power. They were also concerned to curb the excesses of democracy and to place barriers between the citizenry and the government. The concern of the Federalists to protect property rights led them to also make it difficult to amend the Constitution. The separation of powers, checks and balances, federalism, and limited government are a testimonial to the framers' efforts to make government cumbersome and difficult to control. These barriers also contribute to the inefficiencies in policy making that many find so frustrating. The barriers to the formulation and implementation of new public policy options reflect a bias against change. They also give whatever existing public policy there is a certain legitimacy by its very existence.

3 Political parties were developed to overcome the separation of powers and checks and balances put in place by the framers. Parties also have to deal with the issue of whether most public policy issues should be controlled by the states or the national government. Recently, at both the state and national levels, divided government where different parties control different branches has been the norm.

4 Divided government is blamed as the cause of the inability of the government to deal effectively with the many problems facing society. Constitutional reform is put forward by some as the only way to change outmoded institutions that are irrelevant to the needs of society as the United States approaches the twenty-first century.

5 Close examination reveals, however, that divided government may, but does not necessarily, compound the difficulties in the policy process created by the framers. The current problems may well be, at the same time, an accurate reflection of the views of the voters and a failure of political leadership, particularly at the Presidential level, for the last two decades.

QUESTIONS FOR DISCUSSION

1 Can any reforms be designed to deal with the immobility of government brought about by the partisan wrangling between the President and Congress?

2 Would term limits, or longer terms for the President or Congress, permit a more thoughtful consideration of policy issues and a deliberate selection of policy alternatives? Why or why not?

3 Has the political and social environment so changed since 1789 that the inefficiencies that once seemed insignificant no longer can be tolerated?

4 Decentralization through federalism encourages a struggle over the scope and hence the legitimacy of the conflict, that is usually a minor issue in European politics. Is this the major cause of fragmented government in the United States?

5 If the two American political parties are unable to produce a set of policies to provide for the nation's economic future, should we seriously consider reforming the government, the parties, or both?

KEY CONCEPTS

Checks and balances
Coalition
Divided government
Eighteenth-century liberalism
Federalism
Limited government

Political culture
Political parties
Scope of the conflict
Separation of powers
Supremacy clause
Unified government

SUGGESTED READINGS

Peter Bachrach, *The Theory of Democratic Elitism: A Critique* (Boston: Little, Brown and Company, 1967).

John E. Chubb and Paul E. Peterson (eds.), *Can the Government Govern?* (Washington, DC: The Brookings Institution, 1989).

Alan Ehrenhalt, *The United States of Ambition* (New York: Random House, 1991).

Mark P. Petracca, "The Rational Choice Approach to Politics: A Challenge to Democratic Theory," *Review of Politics*, vol. 53 (Spring 1991), pp. 289–319.

David B. Robertson and Dennis R. Judd, *The Development of American Public Policy* (Glenview, IL: Scott, Foresman and Company, 1989).

E. E. Schattschneider, *The Semisovereign People* (New York: Holt, Rinehart and Winston, 1960).

James L. Sundquist, *Constitutional Reform and Effective Government* (Washington, DC: The Brookings Institution, 1986).

5

ECONOMIC THEORY AS A
BASIS OF PUBLIC POLICY

Some knowledge of the nature of economic forces and economic theory is a pre-requisite for thoughtful public policy analysis. So the purpose of this chapter is to address the implications of economic theory for public policy. It is impossible to comprehend the significance of policy choices without some understanding of the economic theory underlying market capitalism. Adam Smith's *Wealth of Nations* is based upon the concept that the nation-state is a collection of people bound together in a shared responsibility for each other's mutual well-being. But the idea of a "national purpose" to promote the general welfare has come under increasing strain in recent years.

Political and economic theories that seek to explain the conditions of social and economic existence have moral as well as explanatory implications, while those who have prospered within a given economic system usually look for explanations that will support the moral legitimacy of their success. Those favored by the status quo derive an ideology from such theories to justify the continuance of the policies that brought them their good fortune. Those favored by the system are also dominant in the political and economic life of their societies. Thus, it is important to be aware of how theories can be adapted to the service of policies not originally foreseen when those theories were developed.

INTRODUCTION

Though not every public policy of the government involves questions of resource allocation, most do. In Chap. 1 we saw that micro failures in the economy bring about situations which force government intervention to prevent free riders and to produce certain public goods. Individuals organize to distribute the costs of public goods among those people who receive the benefits. Cost sharing is necessary through government purchases to realize an ideal supply of a public good. Other failures, such as externalities, force government intervention to influence production or to determine who pays for certain goods. Members of society on occasion may decide that they are unhappy with the market determination of what, how, or for whom that society's goods are being produced. Government is also asked to intervene when real markets deviate from the ideal markets envisioned in classical economic theory.

The failures of the market provide specific justifications for government intervention through public policy. The trend of government growth and involvement in the public sector has increased dramatically in the United States since the 1930s. Until then the government was limited primarily to the basic functions of providing for defense, administering the system of justice, and providing a postal service. Since the Depression, and largely because of it, the federal government has become involved in a whole range of new activities including public works, environmental regulation, education, health care, income redistribution through income transfer programs like social security, and medicare. Significant growth in government does not just mean at the federal level. State and local governments are even more important than the federal government as sources of employment and production.

Does economic theory have anything to say about what role the government should have in policies that affect the public sector? Can economic theory suggest what effect public versus private spending will have on the economy, job creation, and social well-being? Is it supportive or negative? Can it suggest what kind of policies should be used in certain situations? This chapter will explore these questions.

ADAM SMITH AND CLASSICAL OPTIMISM

Adam Smith (1723–1790) in the eighteenth century recommended a system of natural liberty in which the individual would be free to pursue his or her own interests. By pursuing one's self-interest, each person maximizes benefits for herself or himself or for other individuals and for society as a whole. The supporters of **mercantilism**, with whom Smith took issue, advocated government regulation because they believed that the selfish pursuit of one's own self-interest would lead to less wealth for everyone. The mercantilists viewed competition as a zero-sum scenario where more for one by necessity meant less for others.

Smith challenged that notion. He maintained that if I want something from you that I cannot produce myself, I must make something you want and then agree upon an exchange. Both of us benefit because we agree to give up something that has less value to us personally than the products we receive. Thus the total welfare has been enhanced. As Smith stated in a famous passage: "It is not from the benevolence of the butcher, the brewer, or the baker, that we expect our dinner, but from their regard to their own interest."[1] According to his theory, self-interest and competition will eliminate two kinds of waste: unrealized trades and inefficient production. Conversely it will encourage mutually beneficial trades and efficient production.

Smith had none of the illusions of later classical economists that associated wealth with morality. He noted that people of the same trade seldom are in each other's company even on social occasions "but the conversation ends in a conspiracy against the public, or in some contrivance to raise prices."[2] He pointed out the concern of merchants only for their own self-interest:

> Our merchants and master-manufacturers complain much of the bad effects of high wages in raising the price, and thereby lessening the sale of their goods both at home and abroad. They say nothing concerning the bad effects of high profits. They are silent with regard to the pernicious effects of their own gains. They complain only of those of other people.

Smith said that greed and competition are the driving forces of production.[3] Further, all goods have two prices: a **natural price** (today referred to as normal price) and a **market price**. He defined a natural price as the price that would have to be realized to cover the costs of production, with a small amount left over for a profit. He defined the market price as the price the product actually brings in the marketplace. Whenever the market price deviates from the natural price, it will be driven back in the direction of the natural price as if by an invisible hand. Every

---

[1] Adam Smith, *An Inquiry into the Nature and Causes of the Wealth of Nations*, edited by Edwin Cannan (New York: G. P. Putnam's Sons, 1877; originally published in 1776), p. 27. Further on Smith said that there is an invisible hand which channels behavior to improve social welfare. He stated: "Every individual necessarily labours to render the annual revenue of the society as great as he can. He generally, indeed, neither intends to promote the public interest nor knows how much he is promoting it . . . he intends only his own gain, and he is in this, as in many other cases, led by an invisible hand to promote an end which was no part of his intention. Nor is it always the worse for the society that it was no part of it. By pursuing his own interest he frequently promotes that of the society more effectually than when he really intends to promote it. I have never known much good done by those who affected *to trade* for the public good. It is an affectation, indeed, not very common among merchants, and very few words need be employed in dissuading them from it" (p. 354; emphasis added).

[2] Adam Smith, *The Wealth of Nations*, 6th ed. (London: Metheun & Co., Ltd., 1950), Vol. 1, p. 144, p. 110.

[3] Smith was against the government meddling with the market mechanism. As Robert Heilbroner has pointed out: "Smith never faced the problem . . . of whether the government is weakening or strengthening the market mechanism when it steps in with welfare legislation. . . . There was virtually no welfare legislation in Smith's day—the government was the unabashed ally of the governing classes. . . . The question of whether the working class should have a voice in the direction of economic affairs simply did not enter any respectable person's mind . . . by a strange injustice the man who warned that the grasping eighteenth-century industrialists 'generally have an interest to deceive and even to oppress the public' came to be regarded as their economic patron saint. Even today—in blithe disregard of his actual philosophy—Smith is generally regarded as a *conservative* economist, whereas in fact, he was more avowedly hostile to the *motives* of businessmen than most New Deal economists." See Robert Heilbroner, *The Worldly Philosophers*, 3rd ed., rev. (New York: Simon and Schuster, 1967), pp. 63–64.

entrepreneur attempting to accumulate profits is held in check by other competitors who are also trying to attain a profit. This competition drives down the price of goods and reduces the revenue earned by each seller. In a market unrestrained by government, the competition between entrepreneurs erases excessive profits, employers are forced to compete for the best workers, workers compete for the best jobs (usually defined in terms of wages and working conditions), and consumers compete to consume products. Consequently, producers are forced to search for the lowest-cost production methods. Finally, resources are distributed to their most highly valued use, and economic efficiency prevails.

According to Smith, the owners of business tend to reinvest their profits, thereby consuming little more than the workers. The entrepreneurs inadvertently share the produce of all their improvements with the workers, though they intend only "the gratification of their own vain and insatiable desires."[4] He continued this thought with the following:

> [Business owners] . . . are led by an invisible hand to make nearly the same distribution of the necessaries of life which would have been made had the earth been divided into *equal portions among all its inhabitants*. . . . (emphasis added)

Because reality deviates from the market ideal, society experiences significant inequality and waste. Adam Smith conceived of the idea that order, stability, and growth are intrinsic characteristics of capitalism. **In the classical view, the economy will "self-adjust" to any departure from its long-term growth trend.** The market is self-regulating in that, if anyone's profits, prices, or wages depart from the levels set by market forces, competition will quickly force them back. Thus the market, which is the apex of economic freedom, is also an uncompromising taskmaster.[5]

Smith opposed government intervention as a hindrance to the unfettered workings of self-interest and competition. Therefore, he has become identified with a laissez-faire economic philosophy. This is the fundamental philosophy of conservative-minded individuals today. His commitment to freeing individuals from the heavy hand of monarchical rule through a commitment to liberty as benefiting the

---

[4] Adam Smith, *The Theory of Moral Sentiments*, edited by D. D. Raphael and A. L. Macfie (Oxford, England: Clarendon Press, 1976; originally published in 1759), p. 386.

[5] Smith's writings in *The Wealth of Nations* were at least in part an effort to refute the mercantilists' contention that the economy should be regulated by the monarchy to provide support for merchants, which would ultimately increase the nation's power.

In Smith's view, the English king felt free to intervene in the most arbitrary and capricious ways as an exercise of "sovereign right." Smith supported private rights when he wrote: "England, however, has never been blessed with a very parsimonious government, so parsimony has at no time been the characteristic virtue of its inhabitants. It is the highest impertinence and presumption, therefore, in kings and ministers, to pretend to watch over the economy of private people, and to restrain their expence, either by sumptuary laws, or by prohibiting the importation of foreign luxuries. They are themselves always, and without exception, the greatest spendthrifts in the society. Let them look well after their own expence, and they may safely trust private people with theirs. If their own extravagance does not ruin the state, that of their subjects never will." See Smith, *An Inquiry into the Nature and Causes of the Wealth of Nations*, 1877 ed., pp. 227–278.

general public was a very liberal position to take in his day.[6] Smith did see a significant although limited role for the state. He advocated three principal uses of government, including (1) the establishment and maintenance of national defense, (2) the administration of justice, and (3) the maintenance of public works and other institutions that private entrepreneurs cannot undertake profitably in a market economy.

Smith's classical economic view was optimistic. According to its principles, the economy would continue to expand through growing production based upon increased investment in machinery and the resulting division of labor. It considered machinery as the main way of strengthening the division of labor that was so beneficial in expanding economic output and as central to improving the productivity of the workers. It saw the market system as an enormous power for the buildup of capital primarily in the form of machinery and equipment, which would provide jobs and result in self-sufficiency for all. It predicted any slowdown in the economy would be only temporary and self-correcting.

Smith was confident that the system would generate economic growth. The purpose of this growth was to improve society's welfare by extending consumption opportunities "to the lowest ranks of people." Smith believed that free market forces would bring about an agreeable, mutually acceptable solution to the problem of individual self-interest within society as long as individuals were free to pursue their self-interest in a political and moral environment where everyone had equal basic rights that were acknowledged by all. This aspect of Smith's views is not usually emphasized, but in fact **he was explicit in his judgment that self-interest could be destructive if it was not moderated with justice.** He condemned capitalist "rapacity." **He noted that civil government "is in reality instituted for the defense of the rich against the poor, or of those who have some property against those who have none at all."**[7] He wrote: "All for ourselves, and nothing for other people, seems, in every age of the world, to have been the vile maxim of the masters of mankind."[8]

It should also be noted that Smith did not endorse the view that the unequal distribution of income was inherently just. He clearly indicated that coercion influences wages agreed upon between capitalists and workers. Capitalists want to pay as little as possible and possess a stronger bargaining position when dealing with

---

[6] Smith was opposed to many conservative views of his time and openly sympathized with the working class against the "manufacturing class." He opposed the low-wage doctrine of the time and wrote approvingly of the increase of wages that accompanied economic development: "Is this improvement in the circumstances of the lower ranks of the people to be regarded as an advantage or as an inconveniency to the society? The answer seems at first sign abundantly plain. Servants, labourers and workmen of different kinds, make up the far greater part of every great political society. But what improves the circumstances of the greater part can never be regarded as an inconveniency to the whole. No society can surely be flourishing and happy, of which the far greater part of the members are poor and miserable." See Adam Smith, *An Inquiry into the Nature and Causes of the Wealth of Nations*, edited by Edwin Cannan (New York: Modern Library, 1937), p. 79.

[7] See Smith, *An Inquiry into the Nature and Causes of the Wealth of Nations*, 1937 ed., p. 674.

[8] See Smith, *An Inquiry into the Nature and Causes of the Wealth of Nations*, 1937 ed., p. 389.

workers. The legal system during Smith's time also favored capitalists by permitting cooperation among manufacturers to hold wages down while prohibiting worker associations. Smith clearly broke with mercantilist views favoring a large working class that would be paid as little as possible to provide an incentive for hard work.

Smith also disagreed with the view that traits associated with individuals in different social classes were inherent in people's makeup but attributed them instead to their positions in society. He held that "the very different genius which appears to distinguish men of different professions, when grown to maturity, is not upon many occasions so much the cause as the effect of the division of labour."[9] He believed that the poor were victims of the capitalist economic system and argued that high wages would be more fair. He said:

> It is but equity, besides, that they who feed, cloathe and lodge the whole body of the people, should have such a share of the produce of their own labour as to be themselves tolerably well fed, cloathed and lodged.[10]

Smith argued against policies that worked against the poor. For instance, he criticized the Settlement Act, which prevented workers from moving from one parish to another to take advantage of employment opportunities. His writings support the conclusion that **he favored the workings of market forces and laissez faire policies as preferable to government support of mercantilist policies which oppressed the poor. He left the door open for government policies to reduce economic inequalities**.

CLASSICAL MALTHUSIAN MELANCHOLY

Despite Smith's vision of how the natural forces of a self-regulating market would lead to a constant improvement in the living conditions of the labor force, there was a nagging concern about the numbers of workers whose conditions were not improved by a market economy. The problem concerned the nature of what Smith termed "effectual demand" and its association with the distribution of income. In a nutshell, the problem is that since capitalists produce only for consumers with the money to buy, production will mirror their demand. Businesses will produce everything for those with money, and nothing for those without. It is one thing to argue that the market process is efficient. It is quite another to defend a system that produces nothing or almost nothing for the many, which after all make up the bulk of the population. The pure free market system ignored those in poverty, and indeed made it difficult for the poor to share in the benefits of an expanding market economy.

This anxiety was soon raised by the socialists, who perceived that things were not as universally rosy as Smith believed. Karl Marx was among the most famous

---

[9] Smith, *An Inquiry into the Nature and Causes of the Wealth of Nations*, 1937 ed., pp. 15–16.
[10] Smith, *An Inquiry into the Nature and Causes of the Wealth of Nations*, 1937 ed., p. 79.

of those to analyze the problem and offer a solution along socialist lines. But others tried to defend the market approach, with less than satisfactory results. Among these was Thomas Robert Malthus (1766–1834), who was the first to suggest a resolution within a market economy framework. A minister by vocation, the Reverend Malthus found the problem of poverty to be essentially moral in nature and therefore not susceptible to resolution by government policy. In his view, natural forces were at work and capitalists need not feel any pangs of conscience regarding wages that maintained their employees at subsistence levels of existence.

According to Malthus, there is a natural law of wages that tends toward the subsistence level. This occurs on the one hand because any increase in wages above subsistence results in workers procreating, and more mouths to feed means their wages in effect fall back to a subsistence level. On the other hand, say the price of food rises; workers then will force their wage rates up to pay for the necessities of their existence, thus maintaining a subsistence level. Either way, there is a natural wage rate that always tends toward the level of subsistence, which Malthus termed the "Iron Law of Wages."

The conclusion for Malthus was inescapable. Assisting the poor only transfers more resources to them and enables them to have more children. The resulting increase in population means there is no overall improvement of the living conditions of the population. Therefore it is futile to look for social causes and cures for poverty. In fact, giving assistance to the poor only transfers wealth from the productive wealthy to the poor, generating ever more poor people. According to Malthus, if the "lower classes" do not want to be poor, all they have to do is to have fewer children. The burdens associated with poverty are a natural punishment for the failure of the lower classes to restrain their urges to procreation. Their only salvation is literally dependent upon their moral reform, not government assistance.

A very important public policy implication of the Malthusian analysis is that no government assistance should be provided to the poor. On the contrary, a Malthusian view sees tragedies such as the miseries of poverty, famine, plague, and war as natural means of punishing and increasing the death rates of those who do not practice moral temperance. If it were not for these "natural" checks on population growth, the increasing numbers of poor would soon outstrip food production, which in turn would lead to their starvation. Malthus wrote that we should encourage the operations of nature in producing this mortality:

> . . . and if we dread the too frequent visitation of the horrid form of famine, we should sedulously encourage the other forms of destruction, which we compel nature to use. Instead of recommending cleanliness to the poor, we should encourage contrary habits. In our towns we should make the streets narrower, crowd more people into the houses, and court the return of the plague. In the country, we should build our villages near stagnant pools, and particularly encourage settlements in all marshy and unwholesome situations. But above all, we should reprobate specific remedies for ravaging diseases; and those benevolent, but much mistaken men, who have thought they were doing a service to mankind by projecting schemes for the total extirpation of particular disor-

ders. If by these and similar means the annual mortality were increased . . . we might probably every one of us marry at the age of puberty, and yet few be absolutely starved.[11]

Not surprisingly, Malthus recommended the abolition of the poor-laws that provided meager relief in England at the time. Thomas Carlyle, after reading Malthus' pessimistic analysis, called political economy "the dismal science!" He was only partially correct since Malthus' analysis was dismal—but only for the poor.

Malthusian analysis proved to be incredibly reassuring to the economically influential members of society. It calmed their doubts and fears by asserting that the chase after wealth primarily served the interests of society. Perhaps more importantly, it claimed that affluent, as well as business leaders, need not concern themselves with an undue sense of social responsibility for the conditions of the poor, since workers were the causes of their own miserable fates. By inference, the converse was also true—the affluent were morally superior to the poor. The doctrine of laissez faire holds that the free market system has within itself the capacity to best resolve economic problems on the basis of justice and fairness for all participants. By reinforcing the commitment to a doctrine of laissez faire, Malthus devised a superb justification for the affluent to deny any responsibility for a serious economic problem. The effects of this immensely reassuring and convenient theory on the affluent made Malthus one of the most influential economic thinkers of his century. The fact that his theory was based upon his personal pondering and was not subject to empirical verification did not cause any serious objections at the time. But subsequently it led to the scathing attack on market economics by Karl Marx.

THE HAUNTING SPECTER OF KARL MARX

The writings of **Karl Marx** (1818–1883) posed a different view of market economics than those of either Adam Smith or Thomas Malthus, and led to a radically different proposed solution for society's problems. Marx was impressed with the ability of a capitalist economy to automatically allocate resources efficiently with no direction from the government, and to be extraordinarily efficient in producing goods and services. As Marx and his colleague Friedrich Engels commented, "The bourgeoisie, during the rule of scarce 100 years, has created more massive and more colossal productive forces than have all preceding generations together."[12] Nonetheless, Marx viewed history as a continuing struggle between elites and the masses. He thought that the class struggle between capitalists and workers over profits and wages would ultimately lead to the end of capitalism. Marx, unlike

---

[11] Thomas Robert Malthus, *An Essay on the Principle of Population*, 6th ed., in E. A. Wrigley and D. Souden (eds.), *The Works of Thomas Robert Malthus* (London: William Pickering, 1986), Vol. 3, p. 493.

[12] Robert C. Tucker (ed.), *The Marx-Engels Reader*, 2nd ed. (New York: W. W. Norton & Company, 1978), p. 477.

Adam Smith, saw the potential for instability and chaos in the laissez faire market economy. His intricate analysis held that capitalists are able to increase their profits and wealth only at the expense of the workers. In his theory of **surplus value**, he argued that exploited labor generates profits which are squeezed out through the capitalist ownership of machinery.

The significance of Marx for our purpose is that he was among the most influential thinkers to focus upon the failures of the market system. He emphasized the importance of the economic and social instability resulting from the tension between the opposing demands of capital and labor. In his view, the rapaciousness of business results in ever larger business firms because small firms go under and their holdings are bought up by surviving firms. This trend toward a few large firms and the resulting concentration of wealth intensifies the struggle between labor and capital, and will eventually lead to a small group of wealthy capitalists and a mass of impoverished workers. In the end, the imbalance will be too great, resulting in the collapse of the market system. The means of production will then be centralized, that is, taken over by the government. Great inequalities and exploitation will cease.

Marxian theory has generated controversy regarding whether a pure market economy would collapse from its internal tensions. Critics of Karl Marx point out that, despite difficulties in market economies, they have not collapsed. On the contrary, those systems that ostensibly have tried to model themselves upon Marx's precepts have shown the most internal tension and in most instances have come unraveled.

Marx's contribution primarily rests on his pointing out the dynamic tensions in the market system. While market capitalism has not collapsed, it has survived in part because it has been willing to move away from a laissez faire model. In particular, government public policy programs have moved into many areas to ameliorate the living conditions of middle- and lower-income workers.

THE REALIST CRITIQUE OF KEYNES

The economist who did the most to challenge Karl Marx's pessimistic conclusions regarding the inevitable collapse of the market system was **John Maynard Keynes** (1883–1946). There is far more to the Keynesian analysis than the few points depicted here.[13] His contribution represents his effort to deal with the apprehension produced by the Great Depression of the 1930s. The severe disturbances of the economies throughout Europe and North America shook the very foundation of those economic and political organizations. It is difficult for anyone who did not live through the Great Depression to grasp the dimensions of the catastrophe. But the statistics are very impressive. The Depression wiped out one-half

---

[13] In addition to Keynes' own *General Theory of Employment, Interest, and Money* (New York: Harcourt, Brace & World, 1936), recommended works for further reading include: Dudley Dillard, *The Economics of John Maynard Keynes* (New York: Prentice-Hall, 1948); also G. C. Harcourt (ed.), *Keynes and His Contemporaries* (New York: St. Martin's Press, 1985).

of the value of all goods and services produced in the United States. Twenty-five percent of the labor force lost their jobs; another 25 percent had their jobs reduced from full to part time or had their wages reduced. Over 9 million savings accounts disappeared when banks failed and more than a million mortgages were fore-closed.

The level of despair and discontent raised doubts about whether the market system could survive. Many of the more affluent who had not been seriously hurt by the Depression viewed the crisis with calm detachment. They opposed the reforms proposed by Franklin Roosevelt in the New Deal as a threat to their favored status. Roosevelt linked the political machines of urban areas, organized labor, farmers, and ethnic minorities to the federal executive branch through programs which benefited these constituencies. The federal government entered the economic life of the nation through the New Deal to assume responsibility for the nation's economic well-being. There is a general consensus that the policies of the Roosevelt revolution not only changed the character of the national government, but also rescued the traditional capitalist economic system in America.

The classical school of economics offered no solution to the problems facing the nation during the 1930s. But obviously the optimistic view that the economic problems were temporary, requiring only belt-tightening and waiting for the economy to grow, was not acceptable to most of the population. Keynes asserted that classical economists

> were apparently unmoved by the lack of correspondence between the results of their theory and the facts of observation—a discrepancy which the ordinary man has not failed to observe. . . . The celebrated optimism of traditional economic theory . . . is . . . to be traced, I think, to their having neglected to take account of the drag on prosperity which can be exercised by an insufficiency of effective demand. For there would obviously be a natural tendency towards the optimum employment of resources in a Society which was functioning after the manner of the classical postulates. It may well be that the classical theory represents the way in which we should like our Economy to behave. But to assume that it actually does so is to assume our difficulties away.[14]

It was also no longer possible to contend that people out of work were simply too lazy to get a job, or that they could find work if they would only lower their wage demands. Marxists of the day felt vindicated, believing that the Depression was the death knell of the market system.

Keynes' *The General Theory of Employment, Interest, and Money*, published in 1936, was a much more complex analysis of the market economy than Adam Smith's.[15] **At the core of his disagreement with the classical view was his argu-**

---

[14] Keynes, *General Theory*, pp. 33–34.

[15] Keynes stated his profound disagreement with the classical tradition in his one-paragraph first chapter: "I have called this book the *General Theory of Employment, Interest, and Money*, placing the emphasis on the prefix *general*. The object of such a title is to contrast the character of my arguments and conclusions with those of the *classical* theory of the subject, upon which I was brought up and which dominates the economic thought, both practical and theoretical, of the governing and academic classes of this generation, as it has for a hundred years past. Moreover, the characteristics of the special case assumed by the classical theory happen not to be those of the economic society in which we actually live, with the result that its teaching is misleading and disastrous if we attempt to apply it to the facts of experience." See Keynes, *General Theory*, p. 3 (emphasis in original).

ment that a market economy is inherently unstable. The market system could reach a "position of under-employment equilibrium" in which the economy could have a high level of unemployment and idle industrial equipment.[16] The significance of his theory in relation to classical theory was that it claimed **there is no self-correcting property in the market system to return a stagnant economy to growth and full employment**. If his analysis was correct, the classical nostrum of tightening your belt and riding out the storm was disastrous. It meant that if demand was established at levels so low that unemployment would remain high and businesses would not be willing to invest in new capital investments the situation would remain indefinitely in that depressed state, unless some variable in the economic equation was changed. According to Keynes, political management of the economy was the solution. **Government spending might well be a necessary public policy to help a depressed market economy regain its vigor**.

Keynesian thinking was almost the opposite of Adam Smith's views. Disturbances in employment, output, or prices are likely to be magnified by the invisible hand of the marketplace. A catastrophe like the Great Depression is not a rare occurrence but rather a disaster that will return if we depend on the market to self-adjust. Thus when the economy stumbles we cannot wait for an invisible hand to provide the needed adjustments. The government must intervene to safeguard jobs and income. The total number of jobs in the economy is determined by macroeconomic variables including the levels of consumption, investment, and imports and exports. **Monetary and fiscal policies are the mechanisms by which the government can achieve the objective of economic growth**. **Monetary policy** involves influence over the money supply and credit controls to influence the economy. **Fiscal policy** is the use of government taxing and spending to stimulate or slow the economy. To increase the total number of jobs in the economy, the government makes more money available, lowers interest rates, buys more output, and even becomes the employer of last resort.

A critical factor in determining the total number of jobs in the economy, or the

---

[16] Keynes stressed the significance of aggregate demand as the immediate determinant of national income, output, and employment. Demand is the sum of consumption, investment, government expenditures, and net exports. Effective demand establishes the economy's equilibrium level of actual output. A problem frequently occurs when the equilibrium level of actual output is less than the level that would exist to maintain full employment.

Keynes held that investment spending is inconstant. Investment spending is determined by the rate of interest and the expected rate of return on investments. The interest rate, in turn, depends on people's preferences for liquidity and the quantity of money. Investments are made only on the expectation of future profits and the cost of capital.

He also challenged the classical notion that wages and prices are flexible downward. Implicit understandings between employers and workers that wages will not be cut in temporary downturns are common. Union contracts and minimum wage laws may also prevent employers from reducing costs by lowering wages. Employers tend to respond to lowered demand by reducing production and laying off workers. Businesses are also reluctant to reduce prices. Declining demand usually results in reductions in output and employment rather than reduced prices.

Keynes held that government should intervene through fiscal and monetary policies to promote full employment, stable prices, and economic growth. In a Depression, the government should increase the money supply to keep interest rates down. That policy might also be matched by reducing taxes for workers to increase demand and increasing government spending to stimulate business investments, employment, and demand.

"employment pie," is the relationship between employment and inflation, which constrains the number of jobs that decision makers can or should create. Liberal Keynesians are more concerned about high rates of unemployment than inflation, are opposed to high interest rates, and prefer fiscal—as opposed to monetary—policy to pursue broad economic goals. Conservative Keynesians are more concerned about inflation, and therefore accept higher unemployment to reduce it, and are less willing to use fiscal policy (especially deficits) to provide full employment.

From the mid-1930s on in the United States, a consensus emerged on government fiscal policies that accepted mild deficits. The principal goal was the achievement of "full employment," which was defined as an unemployment rate of about 4 percent. At 4 percent, existing unemployment was thought to be "frictional" or "structural" rather than "cyclical."[17]

Political leaders of both parties in the United States have long held an overwhelming presumption that in regard to election and reelection prospects few things are more foolhardy than a tax increase or more helpful than a tax cut. The temptation to run big deficits **when the economy is not** in recession was reined in by Keynesian theory, which held that large deficits would result in higher inflation, requiring high interest rates to stop rising prices, bringing about a recession, which would spell disaster in elections. The perceived close connection between short-term economic trends and politics produced an arrangement that permitted deficits but kept them within a narrow range.

Keynesian theory became the dominant way of thinking about economics by the 1950s, although among the more affluent it continued to be viewed with as much alarm as Roosevelt's policies since it was seen as interfering with the "natural processes" of the market economy.

Stagflation

In the early 1960s, John F. Kennedy became the first President to avowedly follow the Keynesian approach to shaping public policies. For nearly 8 years this interventionist approach to policy was so successful in producing an uninterrupted expansion of the economy that economics was declared to be a science. The decision to extend the Nobel Prize to include an annual award in the area of economics capped this new-found prestige. But ironically, Keynesian economics was about to suffer an erosion in confidence at the moment of its greatest triumph.

Keynes' theory suggested that unemployment and inflation could not occur simultaneously. Rather he saw an inverse relationship between the rate of unem-

---

[17] Frictional unemployment refers to the temporary unemployment of new entrants into the labor force or those who have quit one job while they look for a better one. It is not considered a serious problem. Structural unemployment refers to unemployment due to a mismatch between the skills of the labor force and the jobs available. Cyclical unemployment refers to unemployment caused by a lack of jobs in the economy due to a general economic downturn.

ployment and the rate of inflation. Lower unemployment would result in higher inflation. At full employment, inflation would be higher than at higher unemployment rates but not intolerably high. Inflation could be reduced by increasing the rate of unemployment since higher unemployment reduced demand and entrepreneurs could not raise prices in the face of falling demand. Conversely, unemployment could be reduced at the price of higher inflation. These alleged tradeoffs between unemployment and inflation were known as the Phillips curve, after the economist who developed it. (A. W. Phillips, 1914–1976).

This view of the relationship between unemployment and inflation broke down in the 1970s with the occurrence of **stagflation, or the concurrent increase in both unemployment and inflation**. And in the 1980s the opposite phenomenon occurred—simultaneous low **un**employment and low inflation. These unexpected combinations created a major policy dilemma for government. Economic stabilization policies had been based on the idea that high unemployment and low levels of inflation or low unemployment and high levels of inflation occur in a tradeoff relationship. Unemployment was thought to be caused by insufficient demand, necessitating expansionary government policies to increase demands.

This occurrence led to the development of the concept that there is a "natural rate of unemployment," referred to as the "non-accelerating-inflation rate of unemployment" (NAIRU).

This theory holds that there is a "natural" rate of unemployment which will result in a stable inflation rate. If unemployment falls below the natural rate, then inflation will rise. Unemployment levels above the natural rate will cause inflation to decline. The traditional notion of a tradeoff held that, if unemployment is kept at a constant low level, then inflation will be maintained at a high but constant level. By contrast the natural rate theory holds that unemployment below the natural rate will result in an **increasing** rate of inflation. In this theory the relationship between the unemployment **rate** and the **rate** of inflation is stable only at NAIRU.[18] The natural rate of unemployment is currently estimated to be between 5.5 and 6.0 percent.

In election year 1992, despite a stagnant economy, then President Bush and his economic advisers maintained that the current high rate of unemployment would gradually decline to the natural rate of unemployment on its own. Democratic challenger Bill Clinton and his advisers were of the view that the economy might not return to the natural rate of unemployment quickly enough, or in a way that was acceptable to society. The Bush administration hoped that unemployment would return to the NAIRU by itself, hopefully in time for a beneficial effect on voter attitudes. Therefore, it claimed nothing needed to done to stimulate the

---

[18] This theory does provide a good explanation of the observed relationship between unemployment and inflation since the 1950s. The natural rate of unemployment changes with the changing composition of the labor force and the changing economic structure of the society. Different models generally use slightly different assumptions, resulting in differing conclusions about the natural rate. See Robert J. Gordon, *The Phillips Curve Now and Then* (Working Paper No. 3393) (Washington, DC: National Bureau of Economic Research, June 1990), 18 pp.

economy, and that, in fact, efforts to do so run the risk of overshooting the mark and driving unemployment below the natural rate, thus stimulating inflation.

Inflationary fears are a very real concern to policy makers, whose choice of policy ultimately determines the course of the economy. Yet many observers feel that the risk of inflation inherent in an active monetary policy to stimulate economic growth and employment is worth taking since the costs of recessions are not shared equally throughout society. Lower- and middle-income workers are much more likely to become unemployed than the more affluent members of the labor force. Inflation, however, appears to impact the more affluent. As economist Alan Blinder of Princeton University wrote:

> Sometimes inflation is piously attacked as the "cruelest tax," meaning that it weighs most heavily on the poor. . . . On close examination, the "cruelest tax" battle cry is seen for what it is: a subterfuge for protecting inflation's real victims, the rich. . . . [E]very bit of evidence I know of points in the same direction: inflation does no special harm to the poor. . . . The meager costs that inflation poses on the poor are dwarfed by the heavy price the poor are forced to pay whenever the nation embarks on an anti-inflation campaign. . . .[19]

Activists believe that the small costs inflation inflicts on the poor are overshadowed by the high price paid by those in the lower-income brackets when policy makers begin an anti-inflation campaign.

Supply-Side Economics

In the late 1970s, a new approach to economic problems began to take shape. It did not displace the Keynesian emphasis on government intervention, but did suggest different ways for public policy to deal with economic stability and growth. This variation on classical economics was the **supply-side approach, which stresses the need to increase productivity by increasing incentives for working, saving, and investing.** Supply-side policies include a reduction in taxes, particularly for corporations and upper-income groups. Supply-side proponents see greater aftertax income as a key inducement to save and engage in economic investments. Another major supply-side lever is the deregulation of business to remove "impediments" to profits.

The suggestion that reducing marginal tax rates would result in economic growth prodigious enough to produce increased tax revenues was novel. If correct, it would permit government to cut taxes and spend more at the same time—the politicians' equivalent of the medieval alchemists' assertions that they could turn lead into gold.

The major difference between supply-side and classical economists is that the former supported an **activist** approach. Classical economists favor a laissez faire policy, fearing that government activism, however well intentioned, will usually

---

[19] Alan Blinder, *Hard Minds, Soft Hearts: Tough-Minded Economics for a Just Society* (Reading, MA: Addison-Wesley, 1987), p. 54.

EEK and MEEK reprinted by permission of NEA, Inc.

EEK & MEEK® by Howie Schneider

make things worse. Supply-siders differ from Keynesians in that they believe government should actively intervene only to promote a promarket agenda. Keynesians believe government should intervene to regulate as well as stimulate the market, and favor policies that focus on demand forces.

Paul Peterson argues forcefully that the Reagan-Bush deficits cannot be understood apart from the breakdown of the economic consensus that permitted only mild government budget shortfalls.[20] Reagan needed an economic theory that would provide an acceptable policy doctrine as the intellectual basis for a dramatic departure from previous practice. Supply-side theories along with monetarism (see below) provided those doctrines.

The supply-side approach, largely identified with the Reagan administration, reopened a debate many thought had been settled by the Great Depression when it boldly admitted its intention to widen the gap between economic "winners" and the "losers" as an incentive to work hard, save, and invest. Many observers felt that the distribution of income in the United States was already so unequal as to be unjust. And cynics labeled supply-side programs a return to the "trickle-down" economics of a bygone era. Nevertheless President Reagan was swept into office in a tremendous victory in 1980, partly on the basis of a "supply-side" campaign: He promised to cut income taxes, particularly for those in the upper-income brackets, pass investment tax credits for firms, and increase defense spending. He argued that the latter step would increase productivity growth and expand the tax base sufficiently to more than make up for revenues lost from the tax cuts.

Critics of this policy point out that productivity growth actually declined in the 1980s (to less than 2 percent per year) from levels in the 1970s (3.2 percent per year). Savings and investment rates also declined significantly in the 1980s despite the implementation of policies to encourage both. The tax cuts contributed to unprecedented budget deficits throughout the decade. Government spending more than offset any increase in private saving, resulting in high real rates of interest during this period. And finally, average wages failed to keep pace with the con-

[20] Paul E. Peterson, "The New Politics of Deficits," in John E. Chubb and Paul E. Peterson (eds.), *The New Direction in American Politics* (Washington, DC: The Brookings Institution, 1985), p. 393.

sumer price index for 6 of 8 years Reagan was President. Median weekly family earnings from wages and salaries, adjusted for inflation, went from $516 in 1979 to $501 in 1990 according to the U.S. Labor Department. Only those in the top 20 percent of the income scale finished the 1980s with real incomes well above their earnings in the late 1970s.

For all of these reasons, supply-side economics has been quietly dropped as an alternative theory to Keynesian economics. However, individual policies consistent with the approach, such as a cut in capital gains taxes, are still supported by special-interest groups.

Monetarism

Monetarism as a school of thought has its roots in the classical tradition of economic theory and, like the supply-side approach, rejects much of the Keynesian school. Just as the more affluent found a great appeal in the convenient logic of supply-side thinking, they also found an appeal in monetarism because it promises a way to achieve steady economic growth without inflation. For the affluent, inflation is a great economic evil because it redistributes income in an arbitrary manner. The usual way to halt inflation is to lower aggregate demand, either by raising taxes or raising interest rates. Among the more affluent, raising interest rates rather than taxes is the preferred method of curing inflation. Tax rates may not be reduced again once raised but higher interest rates reward those with money to lend even while they reduce inflation by reducing aggregate demand. But having to deal with inflation after it occurs is not ideal either, and monetarism proposes an alternative.

The central tenet of monetarism is simplicity itself. **Monetarism holds that the most important determinant of aggregate demand is the quantity of money in circulation. It claims that, if the quantity of money in circulation is allowed to expand at a steady rate based upon the long-term growth of the economy, prices will be stable and the economy will be encouraged to continue its growth.**[21] Monetarists believe, like the classical economists, that the economy is self-regulating and that it tends to equilibrium at full-employment output. Further, they argue, it is monetary—not fiscal—policy that has the greatest short-term effect on the business cycle. Given this view, monetarists support a limited "laissez faire" role for government. Actually, the wing of monetarism led by Milton Friedman proposes that the government limit its own activities so they will not interfere and prevent the economic system's self-regulating tendencies from asserting themselves.

Friedman argues that allowing the Federal Reserve System to exercise discretionary policy regarding the money supply, credit, and interest rates actually destabilizes the economy. He describes this approach as being like a driver alter-

---

[21] Monetarism must be distinguished from **monetary policy**, which refers to Federal Reserve policies directed at changing the money supply or changing interest rates or both.

nately hitting the brakes and flooring the accelerator. He argues that, if the money supply were increased at a steady, predictable rate of between 3 and 4 percent, the economy would grow at a constant rate and without inflation.[22]

The monetarist position is largely based upon the principle of rational expectations. It holds that inflation is fueled by expectations of future inflation and that it can be cured quickly if a commitment not to accommodate inflation by increasing the money supply can be made credible to the public. Monetarism has always been understood as more effective in pulling inflation down by tightening the money supply than in stimulating the economy by increasing it.

In late 1979, Paul Volker, then Chairman of the Federal Reserve, announced that the Fed would make the control of the growth of the money supply its chief priority. Somewhat over a year later, monetarist theory became the leading macroeconomic approach of many influential advisers in the Reagan administration. But already midway through Reagan's first four years the Fed announced it was abandoning the effort to achieve strict monetary growth targets. In several short years, monetary policy had been tried and was found to be incapable by itself of providing economic stability. Tightly controlling the money supply resulted in high interest rates, rising unemployment, and unused productive capacity. In fact, it contributed to the recession in 1982, the most severe economic downturn since the Great Depression.

Monetarism lost many of its supporters after this disastrous experiment. Those still devoted to the monetarist view seem to be survivors of an earlier age. Monetarism and supply-side economics share an unusual and dubious distinction. They have both been tried in practice and have failed.

President Reagan nonetheless remained faithful to the constituency of satisfied voters who supported him by employing economic theories supportive of laissez faire. Both supply-side economics and monetarism view the state as an unnecessary burden at best since according to their tenets the economy will return to full employment by itself if one is sufficiently patient. (Patience of course is much easier to feel in this case if one is fully employed.) President Bush continued in this tradition by insisting on the need to "get the government off the back of the American people." His supporters never faltered in their belief that a free market, which permits government support for but not regulation of business, offers the best hope for long-term economic growth. In their view, the low growth of the 1980s and 1990s has been part of the self-correcting adjustments necessary in the economy and should not result in a misguided panic response of intervention by the government. Bush abandoned a reliance on supply-side arguments in favor of a call for a "kinder gentler nation." In his inaugural address, however, he noted that "we have more will than wallet," indicating that he did not envision a larger role for government in securing that kindness and gentleness.

---

[22] This theory had acquired such intellectual respectability among conservatives that by the early 1980s there were serious discussions about whether to enforce a tight control over the money supply by returning the country to the gold standard.

THE ECONOMY: STABLE OR UNSTABLE?

The year 1776 was pivotal for the Declaration of Independence and also for the publication of Adam Smith's *Wealth of Nations*. Both were basic manifestations of the movement away from authoritarian monarchical forms of governmental control, and toward individual liberty. The American Revolution attacked not only the political control of the American colonies by England, but also the system of economic authority which made that control inevitable. The colonists—and English entrepreneurs—had already experienced what Adam Smith argued: State domination of the economy inhibited the new opportunities for increasing production and profits.

For more than a century following the political and economic revolutions represented by the American War for Independence and Smith's writings, the state shrank as the dominant and controlling force in the economy of the United States and much of Europe. Economies grew largely with government support, but without political interference, finally leading to a new theoretical approach to economics and politics that viewed them as separate fields. In fact, the word "economics" was firmly established as a term on its own only in 1890, when Alfred Marshall wrote his *Principles of Economics*. Before then the phrase used was "political economy," with the adjective serving as a reminder of the origin and effects of the "economy," and thinkers had found it impossible to consider the subject separately from specific political and social settings.

In spite of the diminishing role of government in economic matters, however, it was recognized that markets are dependent upon governments for their existence. Democratic societies are based upon a *social contract* in which the government is given monopoly power on the legitimate use of force in return for the state's agreement to use that power to protect people's lives and property, and to enforce contracts. Smith wrote about the mutual self-interest among parties to trades in a market system. However, such a system cannot function unless there is some instrument that is entrusted to interpret and protect individual and corporate property rights. Without such a guarantor, agreed-upon trades cannot be enforced and dishonest parties can steal back the items traded, or otherwise not live up to their parts of business bargains, with impunity. This would lead to mutual distrust, a radical reduction in trade, and the collapse of the system itself. Thus the need for government as economic guarantor to establish an environment in which markets can function was recognized.

The classical view just described, identified with Adam Smith, emphasized that individuals following their own self-interest lead to economic order, not chaos. Karl Marx, writing approximately three-quarters of a century later, saw economic trials and troubles everywhere and predicted the collapse of capitalism. John Maynard Keynes, writing still later, was also critical of the problems created by an unfettered market system, but aimed his theories not at the collapse of capitalism but its reform. Keynesian theory changed the conception of the market system and its intricacies. Undertaking a macroeconomic analysis which Smith had not concerned himself with, his analysis led him to conclude that laissez faire was not the appropriate policy for a stagnant economy like that of the 1930s. According to

Keynes, to the extent that there were market failures leading to insufficient demand, government should engage in public policies that would stimulate the economy as well as provide for increased productivity. The fiscal and monetary policies he suggested were designed to encourage demand and investment while simultaneously improving the general social welfare by improving the position of those who are the most vulnerable in periods of economic stagnation: the unemployed.

Conservative critics of Keynes charged that his views were too radical and threatened the very foundations of capitalism. Many denounced him as a socialist. Keynes, however, viewed himself as a conservative trying to defend capitalism against the growing attractions of communism. Even before the Depression, Keynes had observed that market capitalism had imperfections which, if corrected would strengthen capitalism. In a book titled *The End of Laissez-Faire*, he noted aspects of the unfettered market that lead to reduced efficiency and production and suggested how governments might exercise "directive intelligence" over the problem while leaving "private initiative unhindered." He wrote:

> Contrariwise, devotees of Capitalism are often unduly conservative, and reject reforms in its technique, **which might really strengthen and preserve it**, for fear that they may prove to be first steps away from Capitalism itself. . . . For my part, I think that Capitalism, wisely managed, can probably be made more efficient for attaining economic ends than any alternative system yet in sight, but that in itself it is in many ways extremely objectionable. Our problem is to work out a social organisation which shall be efficient as possible without offending our notions of a satisfactory way of life.[23] (emphasis added)

Keynes never faltered in his admiration of capitalism. Keynesian theory was dedicated to the preservation of the capitalist economic system and the position of those who were most favored by it. Yet his theory required some tinkering with the system by the government. The affluent were highly suspicious of any proposal that permitted government control over their interests. And they deeply resented the improved status he gave to the "working class" as an essential ingredient in the overall health of the economy. They found especially irritating his suggestion that their own privileges might actually contribute to economic instability.

If Keynes was right in his analysis and prescriptions for curing the ills of capitalism, then the attraction of a planned economy as represented by communism would atrophy because people prefer to be employed and self-sufficient rather than dependent upon the government for everything. His public policy solution was one in which business and government would act as partners in running the economy. The government would engage in public policies that would create a sufficient demand to maintain full employment, and profits would go to business as they had in the past. Government was the only party to this arrangement that could pull it off, however, since it alone could act in the role of a non-self-interested party. He

---

[23] John Maynard Keynes, *The End of Laissez-Faire* (London: Hogarth, 1926), pp. 52–53.

saw government acting as a positive instrument for individual freedom by, for example, funding programs such as education that would help individuals as well as society, and for economic freedom by protecting a system whose entrepreneurs could flourish, albeit in a regulated way.

Keynesian theory was a clear advancement in our understanding of market capitalism. Part of his success was also based upon the fact that he addressed not only pressing problems of the moment—economic depression and unemployment—but enduring policy concerns like growth and stability. And, like Adam Smith before him, he developed a theory that rationalized what was already being done out of necessity. Without the Great Depression, Keynes would never have written his *General Theory*; but already by the time of its publication Franklin D. Roosevelt had been elected and was implementing his New Deal, which was Keynesianism in practice.

Conservative critics of Franklin Roosevelt argue that his efforts to stimulate the economy by running deficits did not get the United States out of the Great Depression. Rather, they argue, that WWII ended the Depression. This misses the point however. Roosevelt's New Deal deficits did not offset the reduction in private expenditures by business, households, and state governments. It is true that it was not until the Second World War that the economy began to come out of the Depression. This expansion was caused by the vast increase in government purchases associated with the war. This actually reinforced Keynes' theory of the role of government as employer of last resort and purchaser of goods to stimulate the economy.

Keynesian theory supplanted the classical school not only because of its more penetrating analysis, but also because the essentials of the classical school supported a basic posture of passivity regarding government public policy. Especially in crisis situations such as depressions or wars, it is not a realistic option for governments to "do nothing." Part of the legacy of Keynes is an understanding that government does bear a major responsibility for the macroeconomic performance of the economy. The questions of economic stability, employment, growth, and inflation require government leadership and cannot be left to laissez faire inaction and faith that the system will resolve all economic problems in its own time.

Parts of Keynes' theories were inconvenient to the accepted orthodoxy of the affluent. Among other things his analysis suggested that the poor and the unemployed are not less moral than the affluent, but rather too frequently fall victims of economic forces beyond their control. In fact, he insisted that insufficient demand leading to unemployment can be caused by low wages as well as by a tendency of the affluent to save rather than to consume and invest. Such analysis legitimized policies that included increased government intervention and a progressive tax policy aimed at taking wealth from the affluent and returning it to the circular flow of the economy through, among other things, increased public expenditures that would benefit the poor. The anger of the affluent over both the analysis and the resulting policies is well known.

However, it is clear that Keynes, like Smith, was too optimistic in his economic views. He assumed that a better understanding of the relationship between economic variables would permit government to enter the market system to maximize social welfare. He implicitly accepted the notion that government would be neutral and benign and would intervene only to increase demand and provide employment, thus increasing output and improving income distribution. He assumed that an understanding of the shortcomings of market economics would lead to agreement about solutions. He seems not to have been aware of the degree to which governments are penetrated by self-interested groups who lobby for their own special interests rather than the general welfare of society.

Despite flaws in his analysis or in his optimism about the impartiality of government, in one sense Keynes has won the debate with the classical school regarding whether or not governments should intervene in the natural processes of the market to achieve societal goals in economic and other policy matters. Several factors that cannot be ignored compel government involvement in a wide range of public policy issues and will prevent its withdrawal in the future. Among these factors are the following:

1 Democratization. Around the world democratic forms of government are increasingly displacing authoritarian forms. One element of democracy is greater access to government by interest groups demanding that their needs be placed on the policy agenda.

2 Demands for economic security. As nations have become more prosperous, demands have increased for governments to provide protection form the vagaries of market forces. Tolerance of economic disruption declined at the very time when the expansion of industrialization and modernization was increasing competition. This trend began before the Great Depression, but was legitimized by that crisis of enormous proportions. More recently major businesses have demanded that government not let them fail, citing the potential damaging effects on the overall national economy (to say nothing of the effects on company executives). Government has been pressured to undertake measures ranging from protective legislation, to favorable tax treatment, to business loans, and to outright bailouts in the cases of Chrysler Corporation and the savings-and-loan industry.

It is not surprising that, if corporations can successfully plead their special right to subsidies to remain in business, ordinary citizens will plead their right for aid to alleviate the vicissitudes of poverty through assistance in unemployment compensation, health care, education, food stamps, and Aid to Families with Dependent Children among other programs.

3 Demands for social justice. The demand for equal treatment before the law in the United States and throughout the world reflects the demand that gender, ethnic, racial, and religious discrimination come to an end. There is an unwillingness to endure humiliating and degrading treatment at the hands of an elite. Not infrequently the discriminatory practices are protected by the state at the expense of victims and in favor of those not discriminated against.

4 Urbanization. Increased urbanization has enlarged the public sector of the economy in areas such as public health, police protection, sanitation, and education that in a more rural society were left to individuals or private groups.

THE APPEAL OF CONVENIENT LOGIC

The effort to understand the world through rigorous analysis is essential if we are to achieve social progress. Unfortunately, there is considerable evidence that what is passed off as objective analysis is often largely an exercise in seizing upon those parts of a theory most in harmony with our financial and political self-interest. Human beings have a remarkable tendency to believe those things most in accordance with their self-interest. We resist the intrusion of reality that might suggest otherwise. And we rationalize away inconsistencies in thought to eliminate any inconvenience of "cognitive dissonance."

Problem-solving techniques taught in academic settings usually move from cause to effect. A diagnosis of a problem leads us to appropriate corrective action. In real-life situations, though, what often happens when our interests are involved is that we choose the remedy in which we incur the least cost and which will require the least amount of reorganization of our other self-interested beliefs. We then reason back to a cause for which our lowest-cost remedy provides the greatest congruence. In some cases, this may require significant mental gymnastics.

By way of illustration, this chapter has pointed out the problem of poverty in a market economy. Adam Smith wrote hopefully that natural forces would lead to a nearly equal distribution of income between capitalists and workers in a market economy. And he approved of higher wages for workers.

The failure of this to occur was worrisome because it raised fundamental questions about the soundness of Smith's model. Malthus' view that the poor are immoral and responsible for their own fate was a most welcome and gratifying reasoning from the effect (poverty) back to the cause (immorality) for the affluent because it relieved them of any burden of conscience concerning subsistence wages. And it provided them with a basis for righteous indignation at any suggestion of an unwelcome obligation to transfer financial resources to the poor. Subsequently, "Social Darwinism" was invoked as a self-explanatory justification through adaptation of Darwin's law of the "survival of the fittest": Wealth should not be passed from the wealthy (or "fit") to the poor (or "unfit") as doing so would violate a natural law.

More recently Keynesian analysis showed that the causes of unemployment and poverty can be found in impersonal market forces such as inadequate demand, and in economic policies that tolerate unemployment to keep prices down. Other studies make it

5 **War**. Two world wars and a Cold War in this century have resulted in a quantum increase in government spending on national defense. Even with the collapse of the major military threat represented by the Soviet Union and Eastern Europe, military spending in the United States will still remain at levels high enough to be a pivotal influence on the national economy.

6 **Technology**. Governments have been forced to respond to problems created by new technologies that require national regulation in communications (radio, telephone, and television), aviation, legal and illicit drugs, and automobiles, just to name a few.

7 **Policies in other countries**. Governments in developing countries have resorted to economic planning in an effort to modernize and achieve living standards comparable with those of the Western World. Governments elsewhere

clear that economic deprivation in childhood, racial and gender discrimination, and inadequate education among other factors are also causes of poverty.

It can no longer be claimed that poverty is caused primarily by personal immorality (or that the wealthy are more moral than the poor—recall the recent savings-and-loan scandals). And one might reasonably expect solutions to be proposed related to the new diagnosis of the causes of poverty—for example, economic policies that do not rely on accepting high unemployment to reduce inflation, strict enforcement of equal opportunity laws, greater efforts to provide educational opportunities to the disadvantaged. Unfortunately all these remedies require the affluent to incur a cost, which they find deeply disturbing. So less painful alternatives are suggested, based on a view of the causes of poverty more in keeping with the solutions they wish to see implemented. Poverty can no longer be explained as the result of immorality, but instead is blamed on government policy: The poor are "victims" of the well-intentioned but misguided Great Society programs of the 1960s aimed at helping them. This view alleges that the poor have no incentive to work because they are the beneficiaries of the welfare programs that been lavished upon them. In other words, they have too much! So the true solution of poverty, according to this view, is a reduction in public expenditures for the poor so they will be motivated to work harder.

Obviously this is a most agreeable policy proposal for the more affluent. And its logic is carried a disconcerting step further: Just as the poor have too much and need to feel the misery of deprivation to spur them to work, the wealthy have not been working because they have too little. High taxes are identified as the reason for a lack of incentive for performance by the wealthy. A reduction in taxes, especially a cut in the capital gains tax (along with a corresponding increase in income) would be an excellent motivation for the wealthy. And, it is claimed, this proposal favoring the affluent is motivated by compassion for the poor. It is primarily in the interest of the poor because it is alleged to create useful employment for them.

Thus, in this logic, the poor have too much to be motivated. The wealthy have too little. Therefore benefits should be reduced for the poor and increased for the affluent.

This is loosely adapted from a graduation address by John Kenneth Galbraith titled "Reverse Logic" and reprinted in J. K. Galbraith, *A View from the Stands* (New York: Houghton Mifflin, 1987), pp. 34–38.

---

engage in a variety of policies such as education to improve the quality and productivity of their labor forces. Many countries such as Japan and Germany have industrial policies, in which the government acts as a partner with business firms in charting national economic development. These policies are designed to improve the economic competitiveness of the countries' firms internationally, thereby improving the national economic and social welfare. The U.S. government is, however reluctantly, being pushed in this direction just to compete with these countries in international trade.

For all of these reasons, government in the United States will continue to play an ever increasing role in the affairs of Americans. There is irony in the fact that Presidents Reagan and Bush came into office after having campaigned on pledges to reduce the role of government in the lives of the American people and to reduce the deficit. However, total federal expenditures increased from 22.3 percent of the gross domestic product (GDP) in 1980 to 23.5 percent in 1992, while the national debt as a percent of GDP shot up dramatically, from 26.8 percent in 1980 to 51.1 percent in 1992.

The effort to reduce the role of the government in public policy under Reagan was to be reinforced by a reduction in taxes that would presumably force a reduction in expenditures. But not only did no reduction in federal expenditures occur, state and local governments increased their spending during this period. So if federal and state spending are added together, total government expenditures as a percent of GDP were higher in the early 1990s than at any previous time in the nation's history.

Moreover, the view popularized during the 1980s that government intervention is unneeded and that it is actually likely to be harmful has come increasingly under question. Social problems such as homelessness, the need to improve education standards, and the need to deal with public health problems such as AIDS have contributed to this. At the same time, scandals in the banking and the securities industries have led to calls for greater government regulatory powers.

ADVANTAGES OF GOVERNMENT INTERVENTION TO CORRECT MARKET FAILURES

Government by definition has a universal membership made up of all its citizens; it also has the power to compel obedience to its laws. Together these give it distinct advantages in attempting to correct failures in the marketplace:

1 It can avoid **free rider problems** in providing a public good precisely because of its universal membership. Individuals may not easily opt out of the system.

2 It has the power to **prohibit** certain activities—what we might call public "bads." For example, by law or through regulatory processes it may prevent the opening of a bank, the selling of certain drugs, or the practice of medicine by particular individuals.

3 It has the power to **punish**. The government can exercise a range of punishments for violations of its laws far more severe than any that could be carried out through private arrangements.

4 It has the power to **tax**—perhaps its most important advantage. Individual insurance firms may recognize that certain behaviors increase the risks against which they provide insurance. Those firms would like to discourage smoking, for example, since it increases the incidence of health problems. Insurance companies can run ads against smoking, but the government can actively discourage the practice by raising the prices of tobacco products through taxes on them.

5 Government can improve **informationally imperfect markets**. Business can provide information on products in ways aimed at preventing consumers from comparing differences in quality and price. The government can require that such information be provided in a standardized, easy-to-understand manner.

CONCLUSION

1 The classical school of economics associated with Adam Smith promotes an economic model that claims full employment of workers and capital can be maintained without any government intervention. Deviations from the ideal resulting in economic slowdowns, reduced output, or unemployment will self-adjust as if an invisible hand intervened, thus eliminating the need for government involvement. This school concludes that government should not intervene in the economy because any economic problem is only temporary. From this perspective, government's role should be limited as much as possible. Although there is much in Smith's analysis supportive of government intervention into the economy, today's conservatives are inclined to ignore those aspects of his writings.

2 Thomas Robert Malthus focused on a problem noticed early on in market capitalism—the increasing economic disparity between the rich and the poor. His analysis led him to conclude that poverty is a moral problem: the poor lack moral restraints in reproduction. Any effort to improve their conditions through government relief or higher wages will result in their producing more offspring until they fall back to subsistence levels again. This is the "Iron Law of Wages." Any effort to improve their situation by higher wages, government policy, or charity is doomed to failure. This theory reinforced laissez faire thinking and justified opposition to any policy proposal on behalf of the lower classes by the more affluent. Conversely, it can be directly linked to arguments that tax rates on the wealthy should be kept as low as possible and that it is immoral and counterproductive to take wealth from productive individuals and transfer it to those who have contributed less to the social good.

3 Karl Marx pointed out failures in the laissez faire model due to market power and insufficient income for workers to maintain the demand for goods necessary to maintain full employment. Marx saw threats to the continuance of the capitalist system everywhere.

4 John Maynard Keynes revolutionized economic theory with his analysis holding that market economies are inherently unstable, and that they have no self-correcting properties. According to Keynes, government may be the only part of society capable of intervening in the economy to create the demand necessary to maintain full employment. His analysis showed the economy to be much more complex than anything suggested by the classical school. His conclusion was that there are several different areas of monetary and fiscal policy in which the government may successfully intervene. These interventions may also be geared to achieve social goals of the society other than those purely economic in nature.

5 Since the Great Depression, government involvement in public policies has grown for a variety of reasons. Government expenditures, both national and state, now account for 30 percent of GDP in the United States.

6 The supply-side approach brought back many of the arguments of the classical school in a slightly different form. The decade of the 1980s saw a concerted effort to return to earlier policy prescriptions of reducing government involvement in social and economic issues. The policies were not successful in achieving the macroeconomic goals claimed. Although the supply-side school as an approach has receded in importance, a conservative perspective with the goal of reducing government influence is still very much alive.

7 Government does have some advantages over private efforts to correct failures in the economy or to influence what, how, or to whom goods will be distributed.

QUESTIONS FOR DISCUSSION

1 Many contemporary followers claim that Adam Smith was above all a supporter of laissez faire. What support is there for this view? On what basis could that view be challenged?
2 Much of the Malthusian analysis has been discredited today. Yet he was onto something when he focused on the relationship of population and a nation's economic well-being. How would you revise his theory to apply it to developing nations today?
3 The Malthusian analysis had instant appeal to the affluent of his time, while the Marxian analysis had more appeal to the working class. Discuss the psychological appeal of each theory to the self-interest of each group. Is there a way to determine which theory is more in accordance with the facts? How?
4 Contrast the major tenets of the classical school as discussed in this chapter with those of Keynes.

KEY CONCEPTS

Adam Smith	Natural price
John Maynard Keynes	Phillips curve
Karl Marx	Self-adjusting market
Laissez faire	Stagflation
Market price	Supply-side theory
Monetarism	Thomas Robert Malthus

SUGGESTED READINGS

John Kenneth Galbraith, *The Culture of Contentment* (New York: Houghton Mifflin Company, 1992).

Robert Heilbroner, *The Worldly Philosophers: The Lives, Times, and Ideas of the Great Economic Thinkers*, 4th ed. (New York: Simon and Schuster, 1972).

Robert Heilbroner and Lester Thurow, *Economics Explained* (Englewood Cliffs, NJ: Prentice-Hall, 1982).

John Maynard Keynes, *The General Theory of Employment, Interest, and Money* (New York: Harcourt Brace Jovanovich, 1964; originally published in 1936).

Thomas Robert Malthus, *An Essay on the Principle of Population*, edited by Philip Appleman (New York: W. W. Norton & Company, 1976).

Robert B. Reich, *The Work of Nations* (New York: Vintage Books, 1992).

Adam Smith, *An Inquiry into the Nature and Causes of the Wealth of Nations*, edited by Edwin Cannan (New York: G. P. Putnam's Sons, 1877; originally published in 1776). There are many more recent annotated editions available.

Adam Smith, *The Theory of Moral Sentiments*, edited by D. D. Raphael and A. L. Macfie (Oxford, England: Clarendon Press, 1976; originally published in 1759).

6

ECONOMIC POLICY: CRUNCH TIME: STRATEGIES FOR TIGHT BUDGETS AND NEW SOCIAL NEEDS

As Chap. 5 indicated, prior to the 1930s most policy analysts believed that a market economy would achieve the macroeconomic goals of full employment, price stability, and productivity growth without government intervention. The Great Depression, which was a period of high unemployment, declining incomes, and considerable political unrest, shattered such complacent beliefs. John Maynard Keynes' theories demonstrated how achieving macroeconomic goals required government intervention through monetary and fiscal policies. This was officially endorsed in the United States by the Employment Act of 1946 which committed the federal government to policy goals of achieving maximum employment, production, and purchasing power.

INTRODUCTION

Several economic policy goals are generally accepted by all governments. They include **full employment, price stability** (low levels of inflation), and **economic growth**. The role of the policy analyst is to design policies that will best achieve these goals. In the United States the Congress and the President, along with a host of policy advisers, try to formulate policies to achieve the goals through the political process.

POLICY INSTRUMENTS

Problems

The principal policy tools available to Presidential administrations for influencing the economy are monetary policy, regulatory policy, and fiscal policy (including taxing and spending).

There are at least two major problems with using these instruments effectively. The first is that, even if the goals are accepted, there is considerable debate about the best way to achieve them. **Nowhere is the disagreement regarding how to achieve noncontroversial goals more apparent than the schools of thought regarding market failure**. If unregulated markets generated full employment, price stability, economic growth, and an equitable distribution of income as classical economic theory suggests, there would be no need for government intervention. But as already pointed out, markets do fail and governments are called upon to intervene. Does government intervention accomplish its goal of economic growth, reduced unemployment, and inflation? If not, government interventions also fail. In the real world, of course, nothing is perfect, so the real choice is between imperfect markets and imperfect policy interventions.

A second major problem for economic policy is that governments may be unable to achieve full employment, prevent inflation, or stimulate economic expansion because those responsible for economic policy are either *unable, or unwilling*, to take the action required. The separation of governmental powers in the United States fragments the responsibility for economic policy and weakens the government's ability to control the economy. While the President is by far the single most important player in economic policy, Presidential ability to control events or policy is often overestimated. Since Presidents submit a proposed budget to the Congress annually, and use all the powers of the office to persuade the rest of the government to accept their approach, they appear to be more of a leader than they actually are. But **fiscal policy**, i.e., taxing and spending, is largely determined by the performance of the economy at the time the budget is introduced to Congress, and economic forecasts during the period of the budget. And much of the budget includes programs over which a President has little control such as debt refinancing and various entitlements.

The President

The executive branch itself contains different departments at the cabinet level such as Commerce, the Treasury, and Labor, each with goals that differ from the others. In addition, the Office of Management and Budget (OMB) assists the President in preparing the budget and submitting it to Congress. The OMB tries to submit a budget that reflects the priorities of the President. But federal agencies submitting their budget requests usually believe in the value of their own programs and press for expanded funding. If the OMB lowers those requests, the agencies may appeal directly to the President or seek informal support from the Congress.

Since Article I of the Constitution provides that Congress alone has the power to "appropriate" money, the budgetary process inevitably involves partisan maneuvering for political advantage between the executive and legislative branches of government, sometimes with dubious results. For example and not surprisingly, politicians often color budget projections to win support for their agendas. The most flagrant examples of predicting unrealistically low projections of inflation and optimistic projections of economic performance occurred during the first 2 years of the Reagan administration. Ronald Reagan ran his Presidential campaign and began his Presidency promising to eliminate the deficit, increase defense spending, cut taxes, and reduce what he perceived to be the excesses of the welfare state. He held that this agenda would stimulate such economic growth that enough tax revenues would be created to balance the budget by 1984. There were critics of this notion. For example, George Bush, as a Presidential candidate in 1980, called the proposal "voodoo economics." But once Reagan was elected, it was put into practice. Starting with Reagan's assumption and working backward, OMB director David Stockman hastily put together a 5-year plan openly referred to as the "Rosy Scenario." Secret calculations by Stockman and his colleagues showed the deficit rising dramatically. But in public Stockman denied any such outcome and insisted the "Rosy Scenario" projecting falling deficits was valid. In his memoirs, David Stockman stated that he "out-and-out cooked the books. . . ," inventing spurious cuts to make the deficit appear smaller.[1] Congressional Democrats verbally sparred with Republicans over the Reagan budgets, but in the end enough Democratic votes were found to pass the needed legislation. This was not just because of Reagan's popularity among the American people, but because the political maneuvering between Congress and the White House resulted in a compromise acceptable to both sides: lower taxes, more jobs because of increased defense spending, and few or no cuts in entitlement programs that would affect important voting constituencies.

Sometimes the partisan nature of the budget process produces confusion. Republicans in Congress in 1993, without a member of their party in the White House for the first time in 12 years, have been unsure whether they should propose an alternative fiscal plan, or merely oppose President Clinton's proposals. During a Presidential election, challengers are anxious to place the blame for any economic failures on the incumbent when offering their own solutions to economic problems.

Presidential influence on **monetary policy**, or the use of money and credit to influence the economy, is based upon the President's power to appoint individuals to the Federal Reserve's Board of Governors. The President's influence beyond such appointments is largely informal, although the relationship is often much closer than press accounts indicate. The President often works the good cop/bad cop routine with the Fed for public consumption when the latter makes a politically difficult decision. The President complains to the press that soft economic conditions are caused by a recalcitrant Fed that refuses to lower interest rates sufficiently, or, conversely, that inflation could be brought under control if the Fed would only tighten the money supply. Blaming the Fed is convenient since its members do not run for election and doing so allows the President to appear to be a nice guy without sufficient clout to implement the administration's more compassionate goals.

[1] David Stockman, *The Triumph of Politics* (New York: Harper & Row, 1986), p. 383.

The President's influence over **regulatory policy** is also limited since most reg-ulation is based upon legislative backing. Presidents may be constrained to support regulatory legislation against their own wishes.

The major focus in this chapter is on **fiscal policy**, which is under the more direct control of Congress and the President.

The Policy Makers

Policy makers do not prefer high unemployment to full employment, inflation to price stability, or recessions to economic growth. But political entrepreneurs have short time horizons and may not find it in their interest to take the action required to reduce inflation or get a vigorous economic expansion underway. They may agree with the notion that there is no free lunch, but they are also aware that **the price of lunch may be deferred**. Elected officials prefer policies that provide short-term benefits before election day and bills that will not come due until after voters have cast their retrospective votes. Thus, in the American political process, there is a bias in favor of policies with short-term benefits and long-term costs. That fact has profound implications for the conduct of long-term economic growth and stabilization policies as opposed to near-term policies.

In practical terms, suppose that the government increases its expenditures by borrowing rather than raising taxes. The result will be an increase in aggregate demand. **Aggregate demand is the total demand for an economy's goods and services**. The distributional benefits of increased output and employment will be felt almost immediately. The costs of this expansion reflected in higher prices will manifest themselves only months later, hopefully after an election. So from a politician's perspective, the political "goods" arrive first: an increase in employ-ment and a rise in real gross domestic product (GDP). **GDP is the total money value of all final goods and services produced by workers within the nation over a period of a year**. The political "bads"—higher debt servicing and higher inflation—arrive later. Every member of the House of Representatives is never more than 2 years away from election and averages only a year away from the next election. Every President is never more than 4 years from an election and averages only 2 years. Politicians have a very strong incentive to pursue the near-term polit-ical "goods" and put off worrying about the "bads" as long as they are in office.

To the extent that Presidents do engage in economic tightening, they have a strong incentive to pursue such policies early in their terms and pursue expansion-ist policies as elections draw near. And to the degree that voters have short memo-ries and limited sophistication about economic policies, they are likely to reward the political entrepreneur who engaged in economic expansion just before an elec-tion.[2] Survival being a basic instinct among all politicians, these facts of political life also lead to short-term thinking.

Many recent economic problems require the spending of more money by the

---

[2] Thomas D. Willett and King Banaian, "Models of the Political Process and their Implications for Stagflation: A Public Choice Perspective," in Thomas D. Willett (ed.), *Political Business Cycles: The Political Economy of Money, Inflation, and Unemployment* (Durham, NC: Duke University Press, 1988).

government to solve, but the string of massive federal deficits in recent years precludes increased spending. A conspicuous solution to increased spending needs and huge deficits would be large tax increases. But such increases would cause pain to taxpayers and threaten a reduction in consumer demand that could lead to greater unemployment long before a reduction in the deficit would reduce inflation or free up new government monies. In this case the political "bads" would arrive rather promptly, while the "goods" would likely arrive much later and be felt only gradually. Not surprisingly, the three Presidential elections in the 1980s were won by the candidate who took the hardest line against raising taxes. In 1992, Presidential candidate Clinton was able to neutralize the appeal of President Bush, who had broken a 1988 campaign pledge of "no new taxes," by claiming that he himself was a "new kind of Democrat" committed to reducing the deficit by reducing expenditures and also to cutting taxes for middle-income taxpayers. Once in office, though, President Clinton faced pressure to initiate spending cuts but increase taxes, and to do both quickly. If the process was delayed, it was feared, it would be impossible to do either as the midterm 1994 elections approached. Clinton was actually able to achieve tax increases, but just barely and only by limiting the increases to wealthier Americans who had seen steep tax decreases during the Reagan-Bush years. The effects of these tax increases on his reelection chances in 1996 have yet to be seen.

Political entrepreneurs thus have a bias toward expansionary fiscal and monetary policies since lower taxes and increased expenditures for special-interest groups provide strong support for an incumbent's bid for reelection. Policies to reduce spending and increase taxes cause unrest among voters. Even though the optimal policy often requires long-term strategies, the political incentives for incumbents may not jibe with the long-term economic interests of the nation. Political entrepreneurs find it extremely difficult to continue unpleasant policies as the exigencies of elections threaten their futures.

There is considerable irony in the fact that voters deplore the federal deficits and rail against the inability of government to act decisively to end them, yet threaten to retaliate against candidates who support the painful economic measures needed to do so. But cutting government spending inevitably means reducing benefits to someone who is currently receiving them, and raising taxes means someone must pay more. Voters who are hurt by government policies are thought to have long memories at election time, a notion that definitely has long-term effects on politicians' voting behavior.

THE POLITICAL ECONOMY OF DEFICITS

Democratic governments, which must consider public opinion, tend to make only **incremental** budgetary changes from one year to the next. In the United States the President and Congress usually accept the previous year's spending priorities as the starting point for the current year's budgetary calculations. Congressional appropriations committees make only minor changes by adding an "increment" to each agency's previous year's budget. It is typically more than the previous year's appropriation, but less than the increase requested by the agency.

But the current explosion of deficits and the national debt have gone far beyond any concept of incrementalism, and have caused considerable alarm among voters as well as politicians. The seeming inability to control the national debt has come to symbolize the ineffectiveness of government. Several questions have to be considered. Why is there concern over the deficit, and over the national debt? Do deficits really matter? Should we be more concerned with the overall health of the economy than with the size of the deficit? What are the alternative views about the deficit? Is a large federal debt a threat to economic stability? Aside from the concern about the effect of the national debt on the economic health of the nation, are there ethical issues involved in deficits? Should we have a balanced budget amendment?

Before turning to the larger questions, let us briefly consider some definitions. What is the federal deficit? The **deficit is the amount by which government spending exceeds tax receipts during a fiscal year**. A government deficit occurs whenever government expenditures exceed revenues, and a surplus occurs when government receipts exceed revenues. If the government spends $1.2 trillion but takes in just $800 billion, as it did in fiscal 1992, it must borrow the difference, or $400 billion. The difference is borrowed from the pool of private savings available, from the Social Security trust fund (what is paid into the fund currently exceeds Social Security payments by about $50 billion annually), and from foreign lenders.

What is the federal debt? The **debt is the accumulation of all past deficits**, or stated differently, **it equals the accumulated deficits minus the accumulated surpluses**. The deficit is a flow concept, while debt is a stock concept. Debt and deficits are closely related since the government accumulates debt by running deficits. The relationship has been illustrated by using an analogy of running water in a tub. By running water in a tub (running a deficit) the volume of water (the debt) rises. When you let water out of the tub (run a surplus), the debt falls. Similarly, budget deficits increase the national debt and surpluses lower it.

Deficit spending is not new. Recall that the U.S. government began back in the eighteenth century by taking on the debt burden of the states incurred during the Revolutionary War. In the nineteenth century, the government would typically run surpluses during peaceful years to pay down the debt incurred during wars. Before World War II, the Federal budget had a surplus about as often as a deficit. Since 1945 the federal budget has run a surplus in only 8 years, the last being 1969.

As Fig. 6-1 shows, the current national debt is enormous. At the start of the Reagan administration, the accumulated debt was $908 billion. The accumulated federal debt at the end of 1992 was over $4 trillion, and is currently growing at over half a million dollars per minute. The Reagan-Bush years set a record for the highest deficits ever in peace time. The new debt taken on during the 12-year period was more than four times as large as all the debt incurred between 1789 and 1980.

The dollar value of the national debt is not the only thing to be considered in assessing its meaning. Debt is backed by assets. Assets backing the federal debt

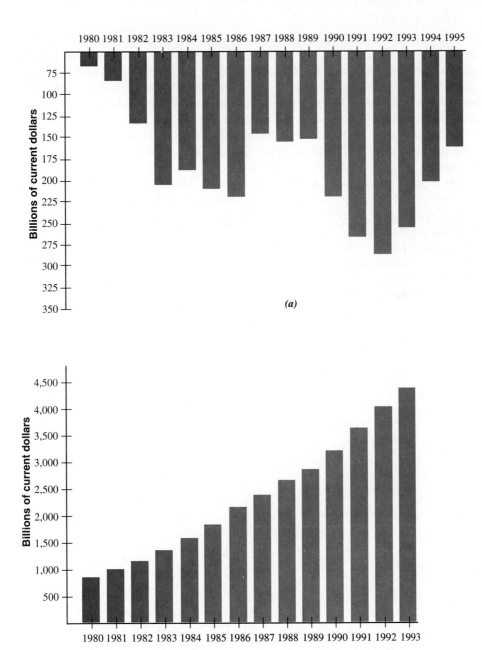

FIGURE 6-1
(a) Accumulating deficits. *(Source: The Economic and Budget Outlook: Fiscal Years 1994–1998, Congressional Budget Office, Washington, DC.)* (b) Accumulating debt. *(Source: Statistical Abstract, 1993, p. 328.)*

include federally owned lands and resources like coal, oil, and gas reserves; they also include structures like office buildings, as well as military and other government equipment. The American economy is also an asset that includes its skilled and educated workforce, along with corporate factories and buildings and even the assets of individuals since the government gets a portion of the worth of every company and individual through tax revenues.

As the economy grows, we would expect debt to grow also. An appraisal of the national debt must take into account the size of the economy from which the economy can derive its revenues to meet its obligations. An individual with a larger income can afford to carry a larger debt burden through mortgages or loans than someone with a smaller income. Similarly, in considering whether the federal debt is too big, we must compare it to the overall size of the economy. To illustrate the point, consider two individuals: One has a debt of $250,000 and assets of $3 million; the other has a debt of $50,000 and total assets of $50,000. Who is in the better financial position? The individual with more debt is, because her debt is significantly exceeded by assets.

Figure 6-2 compares the ratio of gross federal debt outstanding to GDP from 1945 to 1993. This illustrates that the debt grew less rapidly than the GDP until about 1980, but has reversed that trend by growing more rapidly than GDP since 1980. Figure 6-2 shows that the current high ratio of debt to GDP is not unprece-

FIGURE 6-2
National debt as a percent of GDP, 1945 TO 1993. *(Source: Statistical Abstract, 1993, p. 328.)*

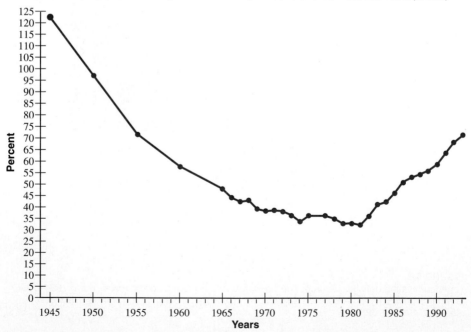

dented (see the years immediately following World War II). But by 1992 the debt had more than doubled its percentage of GDP over the 1979 level. This is one reason why policy analysts are concerned by the continuing huge budget deficits.

Prior to 1983, almost all of the national debt arose from financing wars, and from economic slowdowns and the resulting loss of tax revenues and increased expenditures that accompany recessions. When the economy falters, the deficit increases even if there are no changes in tax rates or spending programs. As earnings fall and unemployment rises, government tax revenues, which rely heavily on the personal income, payroll, and corporate taxes, fall because people and corporations pay fewer taxes. At the same time, government expenditures for unemployment and welfare benefits rise. Similarly, when the economy expands, tax revenues rise and unemployment and welfare benefits fall. Changes in tax collections and expenditures that arise from changing economic conditions are **automatic stabilizing mechanisms** that reduce the impact of economic fluctuations. Automatic stabilizers are important because they adjust immediately to a rising or falling economy, and do not require any policy debate to begin working. Therefore, the deficit will rise during a recession and shrink during a robust economy even if there is no change in fiscal policy. So the same fiscal policy could result in a budget surplus, a balanced budget, or a deficit.

Public policy analysts consider the **structural budget deficit** as a better measure of the thrust of fiscal policy than the actual dollar deficit recorded from year to year.[3] The **structural budget deficit** is defined as **the theoretical deficit that would exist if the economy were operating at full employment**.

What distinguishes the deficits and the resulting debt incurred since the early 1980s is that they were a direct result of tax cuts primarily for the affluent, without a corresponding decrease in spending. (See Table 6-1.) The Reagan administration cut taxes while it simultaneously began an enormous defense buildup.[4] Tax cuts reduced the government revenues necessary to support the gen-

---

[3] The structural deficit is sometimes referred to as the **standardized employment deficit**. Another reason for referring to the structural deficit rather than the actual deficit is that a cyclical fall in output increases the deficit by reducing tax revenues and raising transfer payments for unemployment, but such an increase **reflects the influence of the economy on the deficit and not the influence of the deficit on the economy**. By estimating what the deficit would be at full employment, it removes cyclical influences and allows us to focus on the effects of fiscal policy on the deficit.

The structural deficit can change for reasons other than a policy change. For example, Medicare spending could rise faster than GDP because of an increase in the number of recipients or an increase in the price of medical care rather than because of a change in Medicare policy.

[4] The administration did propose cutbacks in nondefense spending to offset a significant portion of the defense buildup. And reforms of the Social Security system enacted in 1977 and 1983 increased Social Security payroll taxes to cover increased spending and to build up surpluses in the Social Security trust fund. This Social Security tax increase **more than offset the losses in income tax revenues caused by the tax cuts under Reagan**. Thus, **the Reagan administration did not reduce overall tax revenues**. It shifted taxes from individual income tax returns to employers and employees through payroll, i.e., Social Security, taxes. Taxpayers who made up to the maximum level of income for Social Security taxes found their overall federal taxes significantly higher. In fact, during the years of the Reagan and Bush administrations, total tax revenues as a percentage of GDP were slightly higher than during the previous decade. Spending rose from 20.6 percent of GDP in 1979, the last high-employment year before the surge in deficit spending, to 23.5 percent in 1991.

TABLE 6-1
THE STRUCTURAL DEFICIT

| Fiscal year | Standardized employment* | | |
	Revenues ($ billion)	− Outlays ($ billion)	= Structural Deficit ($ billion)
1981	633.0	670.4	−37.4
1982	683.5	730.3	−46.7
1983	677.8	783.1	−105.2
1984	704.9	837.9	−133.1
1985	760.5	938.0	−177.4
1986	794.2	978.9	−184.7
1987	875.6	994.5	−118.9
1988	902.7	1053.9	−151.2
1989	979.5	1125.2	−145.7
1990	1035.1	1196.0	−161.0
1991	111.8	1291.6	−179.8
1992	1163.9	1365.4	−201.5

* Standardized employment *revenues* are the federal revenues that would be collected if the economy were operating at full employment. Standardized *outlays* are those outlays that would be recorded if the economy were at an employment rate consistent with stable inflation.

Source: Congressional Budget Office, *The Economic and Budget Outlook: Fiscal Years 1994–1998* (January 1993), App. E.

eral operating budget. Increases in Social Security taxes were aimed at offsetting the deficit in the general operating budget. But expenditures increased so greatly, especially in defense spending, health care (Medicare and Medicaid), and interest payments on the national debt, that the result was an increase in the full-employment or structural deficit.

Conservative critics blamed Keynesian economics for these huge deficits. They argued that Keynesian theory had removed the stigma associated with deficits by suggesting that in times of insufficient demand deficit spending to bring about theoretical levels of full employment was good and that the deficits accumulated in periods of a slowdown could be balanced by budget surpluses in times of prosperity.

But holding Keynesian theory responsible was seriously undermined by the Reagan and Bush administrations' disavowal of Keynesian economics and substitution of supply-side policies. Supply-side thinking focused on tax cuts as the key to economic prosperity. The tax cuts of 1981 were hailed as supply-side incentives that would unbridle the energies of the American people and encourage them to seek opportunity, work harder, and to save and invest more. The new productive capacities unleashed would lead to rapid economic growth. However, the "**Laffer curve**" theory that **tax cuts would actually increase revenues** proved to be the "no brainer" its critics had claimed it was. Deficits did not decline, they grew. So this new doctrine was used to argue that, in any event, deficits were of little concern. And as many people were willing to be convinced of something they wanted to be true, they went along with it. Nevertheless, as James Tobin, a Nobel

Laureate in economics, concluded, supply-side claims were "proven false by experience."[5]

It was the Keynesians who argued that the **size** of the deficits and the rapidly mounting public debt in the 1980s and early 1990s was a ticking time bomb that would ultimately cause serious harm to the economy. They began advocating higher taxes to close part of the gap. In 1988, George Bush argued that tolerating a deficit was better than raising taxes. In fact, Bush's "read my lips" pledge not to raise taxes was a major part of his successful 1988 campaign. In 1992 he again promised an across-the-board tax cut if reelected. But public opinion polls consistently show that the public wants smaller deficits. This concern played a large role in the 1992 election (think of Ross Perot), and most politicians profess to agree.

POLICY IMPLICATIONS OF THE DEFICIT

The foregoing discussion of some of the "facts" regarding budget deficits provides a perspective from which we can consider the arguments about them one frequently hears. The current large federal deficit is a very real problem that deserves serious attention. But many notions put forward reveal a panic based upon very tenuous connections between theory and the evidence available.

False Arguments

One argument advanced is that the nation, like any household, will go bankrupt if it continues to live beyond its means by borrowing. But while it is certainly possible to amass a national debt that might result in economic chaos, there is nothing in the current situation to justify such fears of imminent danger.

It is true that any household can quickly find itself so heavily in debt that it must default on it financial obligations. But the U.S. government is nowhere near being unable to pay its bills. The federal government's ratio of debt to GDP is approximately 60 percent, which is lower than it was since about 10 years after World War II. This is not very different from the ratios of several of our major economic competitors including Japan, although it is worrisome that our debt is growing while most other nations' debt is holding steady.

The government, unlike a family, can raise taxes to meet its obligations. Also the national government's debt is an obligation to pay the bearer of bonds in U.S. dollars. The government can pay off its debt by creating money. In a worst-case scenario, the government could print the money necessary to pay bondholders. Individuals, sadly, do not have this as a legal option. Many countries do not have this option either, because their debts must be **paid in U.S. dollars.**[6]

---

[5] James Tobin, "Voodoo Curse: Exorcising the Legacy of Reaganomics," *Harvard International Review,* vol. 14, no. 3 (Summer 1992), pp. 10–13.

[6] It should be noted that some who argue for a balanced budget have suggested that the government **should** default on its obligations. Then no one would buy U.S. government securities in the future, thereby forcing Congress and the President to pass only balanced budgets.

A second argument is that the deficit is a drag on our well-being. The answer is: It all depends. Why was the deficit incurred? Sometimes a deficit can stimulate the economy when there is insufficient demand to maintain full employment. Or a deficit may permit the undertaking of important projects like defending the nation during a war. Here the analogy of the family is more apt. It may be worthwhile for a family to take on debt in buying a house or in paying for a daughter's or son's college tuition. It may not be wise to go into debt to take a world tour. Likewise, it may not be wise to increase the national debt by reducing taxes on those most able to pay. The cause of the debt is pertinent to the question of whether or not it should be incurred, and whether it is an acceptable burden or not.

A third argument is that the nation will never be able to pay off such a huge debt, or doing so would ruin the nation. This argument is often based on the analogy to a family, but is not apt. A family cannot be extended credit indefinitely, because individuals have a limited life expectancy. When an individual dies, all outstanding obligations must be paid before his or her assets can be passed on to heirs. We hope the government never has to make such a final accounting. A better analogy is that governments are like corporations, in that they do not have limited life expectancies. When the principal comes due on corporate or government bonds, they simply "roll it over" and continue paying the interest.

WHO DOES BEAR THE BURDEN OF THE NATIONAL DEBT?

As in most policy matters, there are a number of questions about the distributional effects of budget deficits: Is government debt borne exclusively or only partly by the present or by future generations? That is, are we burdening our children and grandchildren with the obligation of paying the debt? Do deficits tend to help the more affluent, or the less affluent?

There is no complete agreement on the answers to these questions, because there are several facets to each.

Bear in mind that deficits occur when government expenditures exceed tax revenues. The government must pay for everything it buys, and must borrow when its funds are insufficient to cover its expenses. The burden of the debt is created at the time the debt-financed activity takes place, and the government borrows by selling bonds on the open market to pay for the goods and services demanded. Bonds are a *liability* for the federal government but they are an *asset* for the people who buy them.

Older Americans may prefer government borrowing to current taxation. When the government issues bonds rather than raising taxes for its purchases, the elderly avoid much of the cost. For them taxing and borrowing are not equivalent forms of financing. Borrowing shifts significant costs to future generations. The elderly make up the fastest-growing sector of the population, and as America ages, therefore, we might expect more Americans to be supportive of borrowing rather than taxing.

Deficits also have significant distributional effects over time for different income segments of society. Deficit financing provides more benefits to the affluent than to the less affluent. In theory, when debt is undertaken, buyers and sellers engage in a voluntary exchange and so no one is worse off. Borrowing is less of a threat than raising taxes espe-

Reasons for Concern about Budget Deficits

There are generally three arguments advanced by policy analysts who believe that current budget deficits cannot be sustained for very long into the future.

The first focuses on the connection between the growth of the economy and the growth of the debt. A society with a growing economy is becoming wealthier and can manage more debt. However, if the debt grows faster than the overall economy, then interest payments will make up an ever larger part of the federal budget. The fastest-growing item in the federal budget for the last 12 years has been the interest payments on the federal debt. But total debt cannot grow faster than GDP forever. Reducing the debt ratio to a healthier level would allow the national debt to grow more slowly than GDP for an extended period of time. Real growth in the American economy in recent years has averaged close to 2.5 percent per year, which means that the debt could grow at that same rate without increasing the debt/GDP ratio. In 1993 the debt was just over $4 trillion and the GDP was just over $6 trillion. Thus the government debt/GDP ratio was just over 60 percent. A growth rate of 2.5 percent suggests that real GDP was growing at about $150 billion (2.5 percent × $6 trillion = $150 billion). At those levels, therefore, the government could run a deficit of about $90 billion without increasing the debt/GDP ratio (0.60 × $150 billion = $90 billion). Contrast this to the more than $200 bil-

cially for the wealthy. In the short run, it is attractive to all taxpayers whose tax receipts merely service the debt, since actually reducing the deficit would mean higher taxes immediately. Bonds are typically bought by the more affluent members of the society. They are purchased because they are perceived as a good investment and because they contribute to the purchaser's net wealth. But the interest on the bonds is paid through taxes which are borne by all income groups. So bond-holders will receive payment for their loans by receiving checks from the government. Those who must pay their taxes, but do not receive offsetting checks because they do not hold bonds, will be less well off. This payment of interest involves a redistribution of wealth from the less affluent to the more affluent in society. It is a basic principle of finance that lenders are in a stronger position than borrowers.

To the extent that future generations must finance the debt incurred at the present time, the burden of that debt will be borne by all future taxpayers. Some will have inherited bonds from their parents and grandparents, while others will not.

A part of the U.S. national debt requires more than merely transferring money from one group of Americans to another. An increasing portion of it (about 20 percent currently) is held by foreigners. Paying interest on bonds held by those outside the country means that an increasing portion of American GDP will have to be sent abroad to pay interest on the debts incurred in the 1980s and 1990s. These payments will result in reduced domestic income. American taxpayers will be poorer while foreign holders of U.S. bonds will be richer.

Source: Robert Heilbroner and Peter Bernstein, *The Debt and the Deficit: False Alarms/Real Possibilities* (New York: W. W. Norton & Co., 1989).

lion in interest charges alone the government was required to pay in 1992 on the $4 trillion debt. Such charges are an "uncontrollable" element of the federal budget. **Because of the obligation to service such debt, less money is available to the government to fund other public programs.** As a service charge for past expenditures, it constrains today's choices regarding the funding of programs. Past debts represent future opportunities squandered.

The second argument, which probably commands the largest following among policy makers who think the national debt should be lowered, believes that deficits erode the prospects for the nation's long-term growth. In this view, deficits are not seen as threatening imminent catastrophe, but rather as quietly gnawing away at the health of the economy in the long run, rather like termites in the basement. Policy makers point out that government borrowing to finance the deficit comes at the expense of private borrowing that would increase the nation's productive wealth. They focus on the connection between monetary and fiscal policy. Recall that an **expansionary fiscal policy** stimulates the economy by increasing spending or cutting taxes, or both, i.e., by running a deficit. However, to finance the deficit, the government must turn to **monetary policy.** The Treasury must sell bonds at high enough interest rates to make people want to buy and hold them. The government can do this because of its ability to tax and create money. And when government borrowing is added to and competes with private borrowing, especially in periods of full employment, interest rates in general are driven up. High interest rates then **crowd out** the ability of **private borrowers**, whether business firms or households, to borrow because it is too expensive for them to do so.[7] But this crowding out reduces the expansionary effect of the fiscal stimulus represented by deficit spending. **The deficits absorb savings that would ordinarily flow to private investment.** A decrease in investment results in a decrease of income and lowers the trajectory of economic growth.[8]

The United States in the last decade or so has become a massive net importer of capital by selling foreign investors government bonds and selling interests in American businesses. Approximately 20 percent of the U.S. national debt is currently owned by foreign lenders. By 1992 the United States was paying foreign

---

[7] Crowding out does not occur when there are unused resources. Government deficits in periods of high unemployment stimulate economic activity by "crowding in." Only at full employment will a dollar spent on a public project crowd out a dollar for a private one. In a democracy, the government, exercising the collective will of society, must have priority over private decisions regardless of employment levels. Society could not function without public health services, police protection, the court system, and national defense to name just a few. We delegate collective decisions to the government through the democratic process. The government then funds public services through taxing and/or borrowing.

[8] Robert Heilbroner and Peter Bernstein found the evidence for crowding out to be unclear. In the early 1980s, several countries that ran the largest deficits had lower interest rates than others that had lower rates of increased indebtedness. However, several factors were not examined, such as how accommodating those countries' monetary policies were in increasing the money supply. See Robert Heilbroner and Peter Bernstein, *The Debt and the Deficit: False Alarms/Real Possibilities* (New York: W. W. Norton, 1989), pp. 101–111.

lenders over $100 billion on foreign-held U.S. government securities. This cost the average family about $1000 in 1992. By the late 1980s our excessive borrowing has resulted in the United States, which was the world's largest creditor nation as recently as 1982, becoming a net debtor nation for the first time since the nineteenth century. **Large deficits have increased our dependency on foreign investors, and have resulted in a net outflow of capital**.

A third argument for lowering the national debt is closely related to the first two, but emphasizes the troubling **ethical** implications of the deficit. As Benjamin Friedman aptly stated it:

> . . . [T]he radical course upon which U.S. economic policy was launched in the 1980s violated the basic moral principle that had bound each generation of Americans to the next since the founding of the republic: that men and women should work and eat, earn and spend, both privately and collectively, so that their children and their children's children would inherit a better world. Since 1980 we have broken with that tradition by pursuing a policy that amounts to living not just in but for the present. America has thrown itself a party and billed the tab to the future. . . . With no common agreement or even much public discussion, we are determining as a nation that today should be the high point of American economic advancement compared not just to the past but to the future as well.[9]

In conclusion, politicians and the public have become aware that budgets do not have to be balanced every year, but only over the course of a business cycle, in which deficits in a stagnant economy can be balanced by surpluses in periods of prosperity. The problem is that in recent times the surplus is always projected for a next year that never arrives.

THE POLITICS OF THE DEFICIT

What Can or Should Be Done about the Deficit?

From what we have already said, it should be clear that there are three ways to reduce the burden of the debt. Two of these methods work by a **contractionary fiscal policy**: that is, by **raising taxes** or by **reducing spending**. This requires a delicate balancing act. If government spending is reduced and taxes are raised, then monetary policy must be expansionary to offset the smaller government demand. The goal would be to shrink the deficit without reducing economic activity. Many analysts advocate a shift toward tighter budgets and easier monetary policy.

The third way to reduce the burden of the deficit is to stimulate the economy to grow at a faster rate than the growth rate of the deficit. Most "discretionary" domestic programs have been sharply reduced since the early 1980s. At the same time demands for new spending for everything from environmental protection to

---

[9] Benjamin Friedman, *Day of Reckoning: The Consequences of American Economic Policy Under Reagan and After* (New York: Random House, 1988), pp. 4–5.

aid for Russia to rebuilding the nation's infrastructure have been accumulating. It is politically impossible to significantly reduce defense or other entitlement spending. But even a radical slashing of these programs would not eliminate the deficit. So merely cutting spending will not close the gap. **The deficit may be reduced but it will not be eliminated by a reduction in spending**. One policy goal with this approach **would be to keep the rate of growth of spending below the rate of growth of the economy**. The ratio of federal debt to GDP would then begin to decline. Robust economic growth would reduce the relative size and importance of the deficit without requiring either sharp spending cuts or tax increases.

PROPOSED CONSTITUTIONAL AMENDMENT TO BALANCE THE BUDGET

Several Presidents and Congress have gone on record supporting deficit reduction as a policy goal. Nevertheless, despite explicit commitments to that objective, no President has proposed, and Congress has not passed, a balanced budget in over two decades. The lack of political will is directly related to the requirement for current sacrifices in exchange for hoped-for long-term benefits. Efforts to restrict decision-making options through legislation like Gramm-Rudman-Hollings have not been effective. This has resulted in growing support for a Constitutional amendment requiring a balanced federal budget.

Supporters claim an amendment would require more self-control. But the apparent lack of political will to balance the budget thus far might suggest that it would work no better than prohibiting the sale of alcohol amendment. Typical proposals for a balanced budget amendment require that total outlays not exceed total receipts for a given fiscal year unless Congress approves a specific excess amount by three-fifths of the members of each house on rollcall votes. Proposed amendments also permit the limit to be waived for any national emergency such as war. But once the door is opened for unforeseen emergencies, it is very hard to limit them.

The proposed Constitutional amendments would actually allow a 41 percent minority in either house to block adoption of a budget with a deficit. And they do not provide for waiving the balanced budget requirement if the economy goes into a recession. To set aside the balanced budget requirement in a recession would also require a three-fifths vote in each house.

Political scientists and policy analysts generally point out the following consequences of a balanced budget amendment:

Such an amendment is based on the premise that, except for rare occasions, the only appropriate fiscal policy is a budget in balance or surplus each year. This raises the following question: Should the budget be balanced every year? A balanced budget amendment would largely nullify the automatic stabilizers in the budget that expand outlays and reduce tax collections in economic slowdowns. Since the budget would not moderate business cycles, it would result in greater reliance upon monetary policy. Lack of automatic increases in unemployment compensation while tax revenues were declining would likely result in more severe recessions.

There is a mistaken notion that a balanced budget amendment will require the federal government to do what is already being done by the states. Forty-nine states have either

Outlawing Deficits: Gramm-Rudman-Hollings and the Budget Enforcement Act

Frustrated by its inability to cut growing deficits, Congress in 1985 passed the Balanced Budget Act, better known as the Gramm-Rudman-Hollings Act after its Senate sponsors. The bill originally established declining fixed annual deficit targets, and required a balanced budget in fiscal 1991. Most importantly it established a mechanism to assure that the spending targets would not be exceeded, by a formula providing for automatic across-the-board cuts in the event that Congress failed to make the necessary reductions by specific dates. These cuts, called

Constitutional or legislative provisions requiring balanced budgets. But states *do not*, in fact, balance their budgets. They balance their operating (general) budgets, not their capital budgets. In some states only about 46 percent of the budget must be in balance. Most state projects like road construction, sewerage, education, housing, urban renewal, and pension benefits are not covered by balanced budget requirements. States have also resorted to "gimmicks" such as creating "off-budget" agencies. And increasingly states have turned to *nonguaranteed* bonds to avoid debt ceilings.

A Constitutional amendment to balance the federal budget would likely lead to increased Presidential powers over the budget at the expense of Congress. Governors have strengthened their control over spending at the state level by arguing that balanced budget imperatives necessitate their having greater power over spending through line-item veto authority, impounding funds, or shifting expenditures to the next fiscal year. A federal balanced budget amendment would strengthen the claim of the President to the same authority. Every recent President has publicly pressured Congress to provide him with a line-item veto "like many state governors have."

The President can currently win a struggle with Congress by maintaining support from one-third plus one of the members in either house. The legislative process works on any bill. But the amendment would require a faceoff every year on a general revenue number that would be new. In regard to tax increases, it would give the President preponderant power. Congress would be at a political disadvantage, since it would have to go on record every year as wanting higher taxes or cutting social programs. The President would escape both burdens since proposed amendments do not require the President to submit a balanced budget.

Deficits can be reduced without amending the Constitution. But this can happen only if the President takes a more responsible role in the budget process than has occurred in the recent past. The President must submit budgets that realistically reduce the deficit while trying to encourage cooperation with Congress.

Sources: Testimony by Louis Fisher of the Congressional Research Service on the balanced budget amendment before the House Committee on the Budget, May 11, 1992; Louis Fisher, "Federal Budget Doldrums: The Vacuum in Presidential Leadership," *Public Administration Review*, vol. 50 (1990), p. 693; Donald W. Kiefer, William A. Cox, and Dennis Zimmerman, *A Balanced Budget Constitutional Amendment: Economic Issues* (Washington, DC: Congressional Research Service, May 26, 1992).

sequestration, would reduce the deficit to the agreed-upon target. After lengthy negotiations, several programs were exempted from the automatic cuts, including veterans' pensions, Social Security, food stamps, Aid to Families with Dependent Children, Medicaid, and interest on the national debt. Budget cuts would be concentrated on nonexempted programs. In 1987 President Reagan and Congress, not wanting to cut $45 billion from defense, concluded the time schedule was too severe and the goal of a balanced budget was postponed to 1993. Both Congress and Presidents Reagan and Bush showed considerable skill in employing gimmicks that technically adhered to the law but defied its intent. The administrations used "rosy budget forecasts" to cynically underestimate the size of the budget deficit, and the Congress accepted them. Or a federal payday was shifted to the next fiscal year. In 1990, the last year the Gramm-Rudman-Hollings procedures were in place, the revised deficit target established in 1987 was $100 billion, up from the original $36 billion, but the actual deficit was $221 billion. Of course it can be argued that Gramm-Rudman-Hollings succeeded in the sense that deficits may have been even higher without the act.

The Budget Enforcement Act (BEA) largely replaced the Gramm-Rudman-Hollings procedures in 1990. The BEA set up a plan for a deficit reduction of almost $500 billion over 5 years. The first enforcement mechanism of the BEA was the establishment of annual appropriation and outlay ceilings for discretionary spending in the defense, international, and domestic categories in fiscal years 1991 through 1993. For fiscal 1994 and 1995, budget authority and outlay caps exist for the total of discretionary spending. The second enforcement mechanism was a pay-as-you-go (PAYGO) process that applies to mandatory spending (such as Medicare and farm price support programs). The PAYGO rules require that legislative actions after 1990 affecting entitlements and other mandatory spending may not increase the combined deficit of the current and next fiscal year. If that condition is not met, funds are withheld from programs not specifically exempted, such as Social Security.

The BEA was successful in its first 2 years in enforcing the deficit reduction actions mandated by the 1990 budget agreement. The discretionary spending caps held and Congress lived within its limits for 1991 and 1992. Shortly after his election, President Clinton's budget passed the House by two votes and the Senate by one. His deficit reduction plan included spending cuts as well as tax increases on those in the top 2 percent in income, along with efforts to stimulate economic growth. As a result, budget deficits have declined to $202 billion in fiscal 1994 and are projected to decline to $162 billion in fiscal 1995 (see Fig. 6-1, p. 157).

The Election of 1992 and Economic Policy

In the early spring of 1992 it appeared that both political parties wanted to avoid the topic of the deficits in the coming election. Democrats were reluctant to take it on since they had been branded as "**tax and spend liberals**." Republicans avoided

JOB CREATION AND THE BEA

Proposals to change some part of federal economic policy are frequently justified by the argument that they will create jobs. The clear implication is that creating jobs will expand the economic pie. However the Budget Enforcement Act of 1990 established budget control procedures which impose limits on spending within overall budget totals. Budget totals are established by a Congressional budget resolution based upon a judgment of the appropriate economic policy considering the state of the economy. **Once budget totals have been agreed to, subsequent proposals to expand any program or to cut a tax must be offset by an equivalent change elsewhere in the budget to stay within the requirements of the budget control procedures of the BEA**. Spending a given budgetary dollar amount will have very nearly the same effect on aggregate employment. Therefore, regardless of where equal amounts of tax dollars are spent within the budget, **it will not add to total employment**.

A specific budget change is important because it determines who will get a slice of the economic pie and the size of the slice. For instance, an ongoing debate has been whether funding for the National Guard should be drastically reduced. Some argue that the proposed cuts would result in a loss of military jobs along with private-sector jobs dependent on the National Guard payroll in hundreds of towns across the country. But if the National Guard is not downsized, others argue, programs somewhere else will have to be sliced thinner to meet the budgetary requirements. If the choice is not to downsize the National Guard, then an equivalent cut in appropriations for Medicaid and Aid to Families with Dependent Children will be needed, resulting in a similar loss of jobs, most acutely by the providers of health and welfare services for the poor instead of the military.

Thus the argument that funding for a program will create jobs is not helpful in choosing among policy alternatives given current budgetary constraints. If job creation is the major criteria for selecting a policy alternative, then the decision may well be determined by voter appeal. It may be easier to support the National Guard based upon "patriotism" than funding for "welfare mothers."

Other criteria such as economic efficiency or distributional equity offer a more promising set of standards for policy selection. Uncompensated private costs to the community such as industrial pollution will result in too much of certain goods being produced because some costs can be passed on to the community at large. And uncompensated external benefits such as a more highly skilled workforce produced by more education may result in an underproduction of other goods. Government tax policies frequently try to adjust production and consumption decisions by taking into account these uncompensated benefits and costs transferred to society. Policy is also motivated by distributional equity in which government tax and transfer policies redistribute income usually from the more affluent to the less affluent.

Source: Jane Gravelle, Donald Kiefer, and Dennis Zimmerman, *Is Job Creation a Meaningful Policy Justification?* (Washington, DC: Congressional Research Service, September 8, 1992).

it because federal deficits had soared out of control during the administrations of Republican Presidents. Since the economy was in a recession, however, it inevitably became the focus of the campaign. The Bush administration tried to blame the economic ills of the nation on Congress with its Democratic majority. But this attack was neutralized by Democratic charges that Republicans were irresponsible "**borrow and spend conservatives**." The deficit issue was thus in the back wings, and when Ross Perot entered the race, he concentrated on it because, as an outsider, he could not be blamed for it. He repeatedly criticized Congress, and particularly the President, for their unwillingness to confront the issue.

George Bush, reluctant to call for sacrifice from voters in an election year and burned politically over breaking his "read my lips" pledge of 1988, pledged once more that he would never "ever, ever" raise taxes again, and promised to cut taxes if reelected. He said he would eliminate the deficit mainly by cutting nondefense spending, but promised to keep Social Security off-limits for cuts. He proposed allowing taxpayers to check off 10 percent of their income taxes to reduce the federal debt. For every dollar taxpayers elected to cut the debt, he promised to find an equal amount of spending to cut from the budget. Democrats were more inclined to close the gap by raising taxes, but were unwilling to take the lead in calling for increases, especially with Bush declaring he would never again raise taxes.

Dealing with the deficit thus became a hostage to political considerations in 1992 and may remain so in future elections. But the idea that the gap between tax receipts and expenditures can be **eliminated** by cutting nondefense spending is not a realistic policy option in the short run. Figure 6-3 shows why. The national gov-

FIGURE 6-3
National government expenditures, 1993.*(Source: Budget of the U.S. Government, Fiscal Year 1995, Washington, DC, 1994.)*

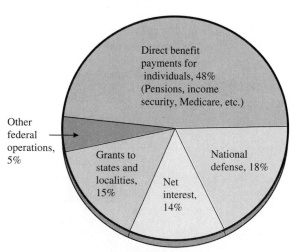

ernment spends most of its money on national defense, social insurance programs (primarily Social Security), and interest on the national debt. Everything else—education, antipoverty programs, foreign assistance, AIDS research, and even the cost of running the government—accounts for only 6 percent.

Reducing Expenditures: Entitlements

Government budgeting consists of two types of spending programs. Discretionary programs are that portion of spending which Congress must reapprove through the appropriations process each year.[10] By 1990, it was clear that domestic discretionary programs had been cut to such an extent that there were no longer any significant savings, with the exception of spending for defense, to be found in this area. This meant that **entitlements** were the only other area of potential savings. **Entitlements are government programs that pay benefits to individuals or other governments that meet eligibility requirements set by law having to do with age, income, or occupation.** An individual who meets the eligibility requirements is "entitled" to the benefits. Entitlements are not discretionary spending, but mandatory. The money must be provided unless the basic law that authorizes the program is changed.[11] But Congress has the power to change or modify entitlements, although ordinarily is reluctant to do more than make minor adjustments like tightening eligibility requirements.

The major entitlement programs, their outlays for 1991, and their expected increases in outlays from 1991 through 1997 are shown in Table 6-2. Many of these programs were begun during the Great Depression or during the Kennedy-Johnson years. Collectively, the purpose of entitlements is to provide a safety net for those who are most vulnerable in society—the unemployed, the poor, the sick, and the elderly.

Recall that public choice theory explains why government finds it more difficult to decrease spending than to increase it. Voters support income increases and oppose decreases. A reduction in an entitlement program is a decrease in income for its beneficiaries, which those beneficiaries will vigorously resist. However, with Congress and the President looking for ways to reduce budget deficits, entitlements are the only remaining area of the budget to look to for cuts. Entitle-

---

[10] This section on entitlements relies heavily on George Hager, "Entitlements: The Untouchable May Become Unavoidable," *Congressional Quarterly* (January 2, 1993), pp. 22–30.

[11] Some of the biggest entitlements, like Social Security, have permanent appropriations and provide money outside the usual appropriations process, while others like Medicaid and food stamps are funded by Congress on an annual basis. Such "appropriated entitlements" are like permanently appropriated entitlements in that Congress must provide funding to meet the entitled needs.

Entitlements involve mandatory spending. But mandatory spending also includes nonentitlement programs such as salaries for judges. The Constitution states that Congress may not reduce a judge's salary.

TABLE 6-2
MAJOR ENTITLEMENT PROGRAMS

The size of mandatory spending programs makes them obvious areas to look to for savings in the federal budget. Shown in the table are the top 10 entitlements, ranked by size.

Rank and program	Outlays in 1991, $ billion	Annual average % change, 1991–1997
1. Social Security	267	5.8
2. Medicare	114	11.6
3. Medicaid	53	15.8
4. Federal civilian retirement*	37	6.9
5. Unemployment†	25	0.7
6. Military retirement	23	5.7
7. Food stamps**	20	4.0
8. Supplemental Security Income	15	9.4
9. Family support	14	5.3
10. Veterans' benefits	14	4.6

* Includes civil service, foreign service, Coast Guard, and other retirement programs, including annuitants' health benefits.

† Unemployment insurance and food stamps are "automatic stabilizer" programs. Their year-to-year growth rates and total spending are dictated by the health of the economy.

Source: Adapted from George Hager, "Entitlements: The Untouchable May Become Unavoidable," *Congressional Quarterly* (January 2, 1993), p. 26.

ments and other mandatory spending programs (sometimes referred to as "uncontrollables") have grown from about 25 percent of the budget in the Kennedy administration to almost two-thirds of the budget today, and are still expanding rapidly.

Defenders of entitlements note that the programs do exactly what they were intended to do. Although critics complain about their growth, some entitlements are designed to be automatic stabilizers and grow especially when the economy enters a downturn. In such periods, programs such as food stamps and unemployment compensation are automatically available rather than depending on Congress to provide benefits through the discretionary budget process. Other entitlements such as Social Security, Medicare, or military pensions are not automatic economic stabilizers, but protect vulnerable groups and should not be held hostage to budget appropriation struggles.

Defenders also point out that entitlements doubled from 5 to 10 percent of GDP in the 10-year period between 1966 and 1976 following the creation of Medicare and Medicaid, but have merely kept pace with the growth of the economy since that time. They note that the growing deficits of the 1980s were caused not by increases in spending for entitlements, but by large tax cuts unaccompanied by cuts in government spending, a prolonged economic slowdown, and the savings-and-loan-bailout among other factors. To this critics reply that future projections show Medicare and Medicaid costs now beginning to spiral upward. And in the longer term, retirement programs will spiral up after 2010 when baby boomers begin to retire.

Entitlements are iron triangles, and the political price of tackling the deficit through scaling them back may be very high. But if Congress decides to go this route, there are three basic ways to do so. The first is to go through such programs looking for ways to trim benefits on a program-by-program basis. A second approach is to limit the growth of entitlements by some formula involving the rate of inflation and increases in the overall number of those eligible for benefits. And a third approach involves attempting to match level of benefits to level of need. This would be accomplished by **means tests, which would determine eligibility based upon recipients' incomes**. Currently, most entitlements are not means-tested. Recipients of programs accounting for only about 20 percent of all entitlement benefits such as Medicaid, food stamps, and Aid to Families with Dependent Children are subject to such rules. However, it has been proposed that recipients of other programs such as Social Security, Medicare, and federal military and civilian retirement also be subject to means testing in the form of taxes on benefits for recipients whose overall incomes are above a specified limit.

TAX POLICY AS A PARTIAL SOLUTION

Tax Increases

According to virtually all serious policy analysts, **tax increases are unavoidable** in taming the debt monster. But new taxes along with the spending cuts in federal programs needed to reduce the debt threaten to set the young against the old, the healthy against the sick, suburbs against the cities, and the rich against the poor. The risks of this are so great that almost every measure that would confront the deficit is politically unpalatable. Most voters do not see a close association between deficit reduction and job growth. Many believe that most of the money collected in taxes is wasted and are skeptical of politicians who say that deficit reduction requires either cutting popular federal programs or raising taxes, or both. In the final analysis deficit reduction will result in some people becoming winners and others losers.

Most public attention riveted upon tax policy at the present time is concerned with its role in reducing the deficit. Although the government borrows money to finance its operations, taxes collected from a variety of sources are the main reservoir of government expenditures.

But the question of **"who pays?"** is inextricably linked to several other questions regarding tax policy: What is a fair distribution of income? What are the major issues involved in deciding who should bear the burden of taxes? What do political scientists and policy analysts take into consideration when they talk about a fair tax system? Does the American tax system meet the criteria for fairness?

Government intervention is a conscious decision not to leave the provision of certain goods or services to the marketplace. It is a determination that political, not economic, considerations will prescribe which services the government will provide. Taxes are required to finance these goods and services. **Therefore, the main purpose of taxation is to move purchasing power from the private to the pub-**

lic sector. But in order to understand and judge these economic policies, their distributional consequences must be understood.

Antitax sentiment has always run high in America. Recall that the American Revolution began as a tax revolt with the dumping of tea in the Boston Harbor, because the colonists objected to the taxes levied by the British upon the tea. After the adoption of the Constitution, the government relied primarily upon customs duties to fund the limited national budget. Congress enacted an income tax during the Civil War, but it expired at that war's end. In 1894 Congress passed another income tax bill. That tax was declared unconstitutional a year later in *Pollock v. Farmers' Loan and Trust Co.*, 158 U.S. 601 (1895). As a result, the Sixteenth Amendment to the Constitution was passed in 1916, which gave Congress the power "to lay and collect taxes on incomes, from whatever source derived."

Although the personal income tax soon became the primary source of revenue for the government, the portion of income paid in taxes in the United States is still well below the percentage of income paid by workers as taxes in other countries. Table 6-3 illustrates this fact. The data in the second column support the evidence that Americans are not overtaxed. Taxes from all levels of government are expressed as a percentage of each country's GDP in the third column. This is the best measure of relative taxation because it indicates the ability to pay the taxes

TABLE 6-3
THE TAX BURDEN IN SELECTED COUNTRIES, 1989
(Per Capita and as a Percentage of GDP)

	Per capita in U.S. $	As a % of GDP
Turkey	416	29.0
United States	**6,119**	**30.1**
Australia	5,269	30.1
Japan	7.260	30.6
Spain	3,343	34.4
Canada	7,501	35.3
United Kingdom	5,349	36.5
Ireland	3,629	37.6
Italy	5,716	37.8
Finland	8,867	37.8
West Germany	7,304	38.1
Austria	6,805	41.0
France	7,503	43.8
Belgium	6,813	44.3
Netherlands	6,936	46.0
Norway	9,790	45.5
Denmark	10,314	49.9
Sweden	12,537	56.1

Sources: Statistical Abstract of the United States, 1993, p. 857, No. 1381; data from *Revenue Statistics of OECD Member Countries* (Paris: OECD, annual).

levied. Despite Americans being among the least taxed people in the industrialized world, however, the aversion to taxes runs so high that politicians are usually rewarded for a vigorous and righteous defense of constituents against rapacious tax collectors. This is often accompanied by an indignant opposition to any increase in social welfare spending, since any increase in public expenditures would entail higher taxes.

The reality is that, when compared to most industrialized nations, the United States is a tax haven. Overall government expenditures as a share of GDP were at historical highs in the Reagan-Bush years even though in actual dollar amounts the United States had lower public spending than any other Organization for Economic Cooperation and Development (OECD) country except Turkey. If all levels of government are counted, only Turkey **spent** less as a share of GDP than the United States. And looking again at Table 6-3, citizens in only six of the eighteen countries listed there paid **fewer taxes** than people in the United States, whose tax burden was just over 30 percent of GDP in 1989. The OECD report indicates that the United States "would remain among the least taxed even if taxes were raised sufficiently to balance the Federal budget."[12] **The American tax burden is very light by any international comparison**.

Taxation and Income Distribution

The government gets the revenues to finance its programs from a variety of tax sources. Figure 6-4 presents a breakdown of the sources of revenue for the national government. The largest single source is **personal income taxes**, followed by **social insurance taxes** and **corporate income taxes**. Insurance taxes are levied in the form of company **payroll taxes**, half of which are paid by the company and half of which are deducted from employee paychecks to finance the Social Security and Medicare programs. The Social Security payroll tax is now the second major source of federal revenue. Workers transfer part of their earnings to retired workers through mandatory payroll deductions, amounting to 7.65 percent of wages on income up to $55,500 in 1993. Employers contribute an equal amount.

Excise taxes, which are taxes on specific products, are a source of revenues for state and local governments, as well as the national government. Politicians find that raising taxes usually costs some voter support. Therefore they prefer that taxes be borne by as small a group as possible, or by such a large group that it is a minimal burden on each payer. Politicians find it easier to impose excise taxes than any other form of tax because they can raise significant amounts of revenue while

---

[12] *OECD Economic Surveys: United States, 1992* (Paris: OECD, 1992), p. 52. The same study pointed out that one reason the U.S. government per capita expenditures are low relative to other OECD countries is the comparatively low public-sector share of health expenditures. If a more typical portion of health-care costs was borne by the U.S. government (80 percent), the 1989 share of government spending in GDP would have risen to 38 percent, still below the OECD average of 41 percent.

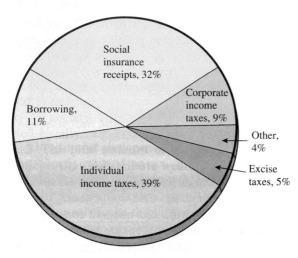

FIGURE 6-4
Federal government receipts, 1992. *(Source: Budget of the United States Government, Fiscal Year 1995, Washington, DC, 1994.)*

affecting a relatively small number of voters. Nevertheless, excise taxes have declined in importance as a source of federal revenues over the years, falling from 13 percent of federal revenues in 1960 to just over 4 percent in 1992. Taxes levied on the sale of tobacco or alcohol are often referred to as **sin taxes** because the use of these products imposes externalities on nonsmokers or nondrinkers in the form of air pollution, litter, driving accidents, health hazards, and increases in medical care. Most such taxes are levied on goods with a relatively **inelastic demand**. If the demand were highly elastic, the tax would push sales down significantly, resulting in only small government revenues.[13]

Some excise taxes are targeted at purchasers of goods who will eventually benefit when the money is spent by the government. Gasoline taxes, for example, are used to finance highway construction. Others such as **luxury taxes** are levied on buyers of expensive nonessential items such as yachts or jewelry whose incomes are assumed to be high enough to absorb the costs easily.

Most states raise revenues from a combination of income taxes and **sales taxes** imposed on the purchase of a wide variety of goods and services (although many states exclude some essential items such as food from their sales taxes). **Property taxes** have traditionally been the main source of revenue for local governments, but income and sales taxes are increasingly important for them also.

---

[13] The decline in sales resulting from a tax that is not offset by the tax revenue generated is referred to as a "deadweight loss" in that no one gets the money. Since a small number of voters buy cigarettes and alcohol but demand is steady, a price increase will not significantly affect sales. A much larger number of voters buy gas, but the political cost to an elected official of a tax on petroleum is acceptable because the deadweight losses are minimal and because the tax burden on each voter is relatively small.

Principles of Taxation: Efficiency and Fairness

Although no one likes to transfer control over part of their income to the government, most people grudgingly comply. The primary purpose of taxation is to raise revenues to carry out government policy goals, although there are other purposes as well such as discouraging the consumption of certain goods. Voluntary compliance is related to the perceived **efficiency** (or neutrality) and **fairness** of the system.

Efficiency   Efficiency, or neutrality, suggests that, unless there is adequate justification, there should be as little interference as possible with the market allocation. Unfortunately every tax influences economic activity and the allocation of resources, even in cases where the market process works well and needs no outside regulation. For example, the preferential treatment that allows individuals to deduct the cost of mortgage interest and property taxes on their homes from income taxes distorts the market by increasing the demand for homownership over that for rental units. Similarly tax laws allow child care payments to be deducted from taxes owed. Such preferential treatment referred to as **tax expenditures**, represents a loss in government revenues just as though the government wrote checks for the amounts of the deductions.

Special-interest groups receiving preferential treatment are vigorous defenders

---

TAX EXPENDITURES

Policy analysts consider tax expenditures and entitlements in an effort to reduce mandatory spending and cut the deficit. Tax expenditures are as big, automatic, and hard to control as many entitlement programs. And the benefits of the major tax expenditures tend to go to more affluent Americans to an even greater degree than do entitlements.

The Joint Committee on Taxation estimated the top 10 tax expenditures in fiscal 1992 in billions of dollars as follows:

1 Net exclusion of pension contributions and earnings, $54.0
2 Home mortgage interest deduction, $38.8
3 Employer-paid health benefits exclusion, $37.7
4 Social Security and railroad retirement benefits exclusion, $25.6
5 State and local income and personal property tax exclusion, $23.8
6 Charitable contribution deduction, $12.5
7 Deferral of capital gains on sale of home, $11.5
8 Real property tax deduction, $11.0
9 Exclusion of capital gains at death, $10.5
10 Exclusion of interest on state and local debt, $10.0

Source: George Hager, "Entitlements: The Untouchable May Become Unavoidable," *Congressional Quarterly* (January 2, 1993), p. 27.

of their tax subsidies, and thus subsidies are very difficult to eliminate. However, they were significantly reduced by the 1986 Tax Reform Act.

While there is a bias in favor of allowing the market to resolve many issues, there are many cases where it is thought to be appropriate to intervene. This brings up the issue of fairness.

Fairness Political scientists, economists, and philosophers have wrestled for hundreds of years with the concept of what constitutes a just and equitable tax system. If the system is perceived as unfair, people are more likely to try evading taxes or to pressure political entrepreneurs more aggressively to reduce their tax burden.

There are two main principles of fairness.

The Benefit Principle **The benefit principle holds that those who benefit from government expenditures should pay taxes in proportion to the benefits they receive**. This may work in instances like a toll bridge ,where only those who use the bridge pay the toll. The more they use the bridge, the more they pay. Those who do not use it need not pay and those who do not pay can be excluded from using it. The major disadvantage of this principle is that it does not work for public goods where nonpayers cannot be excluded from their use or where it is difficult to determine who benefits or by what amount. For example, who benefits most from law enforcement and the judicial system, the rich or the poor? Whose interests are best served by the Securities and Exchange Commission, the Federal Reserve System, the national defense establishment, or environmental protection? Who would be best served by a national health care system? If there were agreement on **who benefits** and **by how much** from each government program, taxes could be allocated accordingly and there would be no income redistribution. But the difficulties just enumerated mean this principle instead provides an incentive for complaining that someone else is the main beneficiary of public goods and for feeling resentful about taxes.

The Ability-to-Pay Principle **The ability-to-pay principle claims that fairness requires taxes be allocated according to the incomes and/or wealth of taxpayers, regardless of who benefits more from government expenditures**. According to this principle, the wealthy may benefit more than the poor from some government expenditures and less than the poor from others. But since they are better able to pay than the poor, they should pay more in taxes. Fairness according to this principle requires both **horizontal equity** and **vertical equity**. **Horizontal equity means that individuals who have nearly equal incomes should have nearly equal tax burdens**. This is the concept Plato had in mind when he wrote in Book 1 of *The Republic*, "When there is an income tax, the just man will pay more and the unjust less **on the same amount of income**." Horizontal equity is lacking when those with equal abilities to pay are treated differently because of tax deductions, credits, or preferences not available to all taxpayers on equal terms.

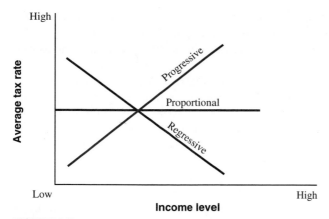

FIGURE 6-5
Tax incidence: Progressive, proportional, and regressive.

Vertical equity states that those with a greater ability to pay taxes should pay more than those with a less ability. In fact, taxes are generally classified according to their **incidence**. **Tax incidence is the actual distribution of the tax burden on different levels of income**. Tax systems are classified as **progressive, proportional** (sometimes referred to as a **flat tax**), or **regressive**, as illustrated in Fig. 6-5.

A **progressive tax** is one in which the tax rate rises as income rises. A progressive tax redistributes wealth from the more affluent to the less affluent. Most Americans support progressive taxes on the ground that ability to pay rises more than proportionately with income. A **proportional tax** is one in which the tax is the same through all income levels. A proportional tax is **neutral** in regard to income distribution. A **regressive tax** is one where the average tax rate declines as income rises. A regressive tax redistributes income from the poor to the wealthy. Regressive tax systems are so manifestly unfair that few *openly* advocate them. A notable exception is George Gilder, a conservative writer with refreshing frankness but doubtful logic who wrote, "Regressive taxes help the poor."[14] Gilder's work, which was widely and approvingly read by supply-siders of the early 1980s, also declared: "To help the poor and middle classes, one must cut the taxes on the rich."[15]

In the early 1940s the federal income tax rate was highly progressive, with a top tax rate of 90 percent on high incomes. The top rate had been lowered to 70 percent by 1980. In reality, of course, because of many loopholes no one paid the top rate. The reduction in the progressivity of income tax rates and the increase in regressive taxes during the 1980s were among the most dramatic changes of the Reagan-Bush administrations. The Reagan administration reduced the top tax rate

[14] George Gilder, *Wealth and Poverty* (New York: Basic Books, 1981), p. 188.
[15] George Gilder, *Wealth and Poverty*, p. 188.

form 70 to 50 percent, and reduced the lowest rate from 14 to 11 percent. It also lowered the rate on capital gains, an additional help to the wealthy. Changes in the tax system in the 1980s are often cited as a major factor in the current trend toward greater income inequality.

The Tax Reform Act of 1986 raised the bottom rate to 15 percent while it further reduced the top rate to 33 percent in return for closing **tax loopholes** (including capital gains). The resulting robust increase in aftertax income among the more affluent was gratefully accepted. **Tax loopholes consist primarily of tax deductions and exemptions that may be subtracted from personal income to determine the taxable income. This effectively reduces the tax rate if certain conditions are met**. One tax loophole left open after the 1986 cut was the **tax-exempt** status of state and municipal bonds, meaning the interest on those bonds is exempt from federal taxes.[16] **Income is tax-exempt if it comes from sources not subject to taxes**.

The **tax deduction** for the interest on mortgage payments and property taxes constitutes preferential treatment of home owners compared to renters. **A tax deduction is money that may be subtracted from total income to determine one's taxable income**. The mortgage deduction encourages home ownership. Since home owners on average have a higher income than renters, this erodes the progressivity of the income tax (see Chap. 9). To make matters worse, home owners are tempted by lenders urging them to consolidate their debts at lower rates of deductible interest through "home equity" loans. Renters do not have this opportunity and must pay higher nondeductible interest rates.

All tax loopholes encourage taxpayers to engage in certain types of behavior to avoid paying taxes. Most loopholes primarily benefit the more affluent and therefore erode the progressivity of the income tax structure. Tax reform did not reduce the actual progressivity as drastically as the percentages would indicate, however, because it eliminated many loopholes that allowed the wealthy to legally reduce their **taxable incomes** and pay taxes at the lower rates. **Taxable income is the income that remains after all the exemptions and deductions have been subtracted from personal income. Taxable income is the income that is subject to taxation**.

The 1986 act increased Social Security taxes. This levy is proportional at first, in that it requires all employees and employers to pay the same rate (7.65 percent) on wages up to $55,500. After that the **marginal tax** rate is zero. Rather than exempting low incomes it exempts high incomes. Once the ceiling is reached no more payments are made for the year.[17] Also, since only salaries are subject to the

---

[16] Tax-exempt bonds are a curiosity peculiar to the United States. It is a remnant of the doctrine of state sovereignty that originally held that the salaries of state employees must be free from federal tax. States fiercely resist any hint of eliminating the tax-free status of their bonds because of the increase in the cost of their borrowing that would result.

[17] Robert Reich pointed out that Michael Milken, who earned $550 million in 1987, fulfilled his 1987 Social Security payment obligations at about 12:42 A.M. on January 1. See Robert B. Reich, *The Work of Nations* (New York: Vintage Books, 1992), pp. 198–199.

Social Security tax, not income from interest or other investments, it is ultimately regressive.

Because of a shift in federal expenditures during the 1980s toward the military and away from assisting states in various social programs, states raised their taxes to offset the loss of federal revenues. It is important to be aware that state and local taxes tend to be regressive. State and local sales taxes increased during the 1980s along with local property taxes. Sales and property taxes are regressive because poorer people must spend a higher percentage of their incomes for goods and services and for housing costs than the affluent. User fees for state colleges, highways, and public hospitals also increased rapidly during this period.

LOTTERIES AS A REGRESSIVE TAX

Gambling generates enormous amounts of revenue for governments and the gaming industry. But its enchanting promises of significant benefits for the general welfare frequently do not live up to expectations, because of mismanagement or corruption.

The average voter does not consider the lottery to be a tax. Instead, lotteries are thought to be a form of entertainment that may make the ticket purchaser rich. Political entrepreneurs have discovered that this perspective removes a major barrier to increasing government revenues. The transfer of lottery revenues to state treasuries is an implicit tax on lottery bettors. There is a consensus among researchers regarding who bears the burden of state lotteries. It is a decidedly regressive form of taxation in that average lottery sales are highest in low-income areas and are lower in areas of higher economic and educational levels.

This tax is *popular* and avoids the aggressive reaction of the more affluent to any tax increases, especially when the benefits accrue to the affluent themselves. The result is that states have increasingly resorted to lotteries to increase revenues as a way of sidestepping opposition to tax increases. New Hampshire started the first modern state lottery in 1964. By 1992, 35 states and the District of Columbia sponsored lotteries.

Per capita lottery ticket sales were three times higher in inner-city Detroit than in Detroit's suburbs. Of $104 million contributed to Michigan's school aid fund in 1988 by Detroit lottery ticket purchasers, they received back only $80 million. The remaining $24 million was transferred to more affluent suburban school districts. A study of the Florida lottery, which also earmarks profits to go into the general education fund, found that when one includes the tax incidence (who pays) and the benefit incidence (who receives the funds), the tax was regressive for those with incomes below $40,000. The benefits of the net tax were proportionally distributed at incomes between $40,000 and $70,000 and became progressive at incomes above $70,000.

As a result, lotteries violate the tax principles of both neutrality and equity. There is also a question of the ethics of exploiting the human desire for wealth by extracting a regressive tax from the poor.

Sources: Mary Borg, Paul Mason, and Stephen Shapiro, *The Economic Consequences of State Lotteries* (New York: Praeger, 1991); Charles Clotfelter and Philip Cook, *Selling Hope: State Lotteries in America* (Cambridge, MA: Harvard University Press, 1989).

In theory, the federal income tax supports the principle of vertical equity by being very mildly progressive. Although many critics believe that it **should** be more progressive, there is no agreement on how much more, or even on how the ability to pay should be measured. For example should adjustments be made for catastrophic medical expenses? Or what of families that may have several children in college at once?

Federal tax progressivity has been declining for over two decades. When taxes paid by individuals to federal, state, and local levels of government are combined, the mildly progressive features at the national level are offset by regressive taxes at the local level resulting in a roughly proportional tax system. The trend toward inequality is attributable to the increased influence of those who argue in favor of tax neutrality (proportional). The avowed purpose of the 1986 tax reform was to make the federal tax system more "neutral." By primarily reducing the taxes of those in the highest brackets and cutting government funding for social welfare programs, it aimed at reducing the redistributive effect of transferring wealth to the poor.

Many who support the neutrality of the tax system argue that efforts to redistribute wealth through tax transfers are not very effective. They maintain that a pro-

THE PROPOSED CAPITAL GAINS TAX CUT

Proposals to cut the capital gains tax rate would increase income inequality in America since only the affluent receive substantial amounts of their income from this source. Adoption of a capital gains tax cut would aggravate the trend since the early 1980s of using the tax system to *increase inequality*. Increases in *aftertax* income during the 1980s became more unequally distributed than increases in *pretax* income.

Tax law prior to 1986 exempted 60 percent of net long-term capital gains income (assets held for 6 months or longer) from tax. The Tax Reform Act of 1986 repealed this preferential treatment. This bill, embraced by then President Reagan and by Congress, was an attempt to lower overall tax rates by broadening the base of taxable income. The goal was to provide horizontal equity in each tax bracket. This would improve the efficiency of the tax system by not favoring one form of income over another. The drop in marginal rates at the top bracket went from 50 to 28 percent.

Almost immediately after the bill was passed, however, the Republican party proposed scrapping the capital gains part of the agreement, but keeping the lower overall tax rate on upper-income tax brackets.

As Henry Aaron of the Brookings Institution has pointed out, the question of whether tax rates on income from realized capital gains should be set below rates on other income is an academic question: "More than half of all capital gains are never taxed. Either they are held until the owner dies, after which they are exempt from tax to subsequent owners. Or they accrue to tax-exempt U.S. entities, such as pension funds, or to foreign owners not subject to U.S. tax." Most capital gains are realized several years after they accumulate, which significantly reduces effective tax rates. In actual practice, Aaron concludes, *"the tax rate on capital gains is less than 10 percent."*

Since capital gains are concentrated in upper-income groups, a cut in capital gains

gressive income tax reduces the incentives for the more affluent to work and save. They believe in the **trickle-down theory**, which holds that allowing the affluent to keep their wealth will result in greater investment and ultimately greater economic output, thus improving the welfare of the poor. By encouraging the affluent to invest their wealth, the size of the total economic pie will be increased so that the benefits that trickle down to the poor will exceed any benefits they might receive from the redistribution of wealth through tax transfers. They insist that the fact that some entrepreneurs become extraordinarily wealthy is irrelevant because their actions have improved society.

Research on the effects of the progressive income tax on incentives to work and save is inconclusive. The effect of taxes on saving is even more contradictory. Joseph Pechman, a late authority on tax systems, wrote that "the strongest conclusion one can draw from the available evidence is that the incentive effects of taxation have been relatively small."[18]

[18] Joseph A. Pechman, "Why We Should Stick with the Income Tax," *The Brookings Review* (Spring 1990), p. 10.

---

taxes would produce a significant reduction in the tax burden for upper-income families. Between 1977 and 1988, aftertax real incomes of the bottom 80 percent of the U.S. population rose by 0.1 percent while incomes of the top 1 percent rose a whopping 96 percent. The tax rate of the bottom 80 percent held steady, while taxes on the top 1 percent fell by 25 percent. The capital gains tax cut proposed by President Bush would have given the top 1 percent of taxpayers more than 50 percent of the benefits, for an average of $3730 annually. The bottom 80 percent would have received only 10 percent of the benefits, or an average of $8 annually. A capital gains tax cut would mean abandoning the goal of distributional neutrality agreed to in the 1986 tax act unless regular tax rates on upper-income individuals were increased to offset capital gains losses.

Nevertheless, the Bush administration defended the proposal by claiming that it would stimulate growth. For example, Bush stated "I am sick and tired of the demagogues who call this a tax cut for the rich. It means jobs, it means savings, and it is good for all Americans" (*The Washington Post*, p. A5, January 9, 1990). Research indicates that a reduction in the tax on capital gains would result in fewer government revenues. Supporters insist that a lower tax would create jobs but others insist that claim is based upon unrealistic assumptions about the response of investers to increases in the rate of return. Most researchers agree that cutting capital gains would lower investment and the GDP.

Sources: Henry J. Aaron, "The Capital Gains Tax Cut," *The Brookings Review* (Summer 1992), pp. 30–33; *The Washington Post*, January 9, 1990; Kevin Quinn, *False Promises: Why the Bush Capital Gains Tax Cuts Would Not Result in More Savings, Investment, Economic Growth or Jobs* (Washington, DC: Economic Policy Institute, 1990); Gregg Esenwein, "Taxation of Capital Gains," *CRS Issue Brief,* 12 pages (1990).

In the view of the authors of this book, a progressive income tax is perhaps the most effective fiscal tool for reducing extreme inequalities in the distribution of income and wealth inherent in capitalism. Asymmetric income distribution gives rise to great variations in personal welfare, opportunity, and economic power.

Trends in Tax Progressivity

Nothing has contributed to the current growing inequality in the distribution of income more than the reduction of taxes on the affluent in the last decade. The distribution of pretax income since 1981, after decades of relative stability, has become much more unequal. At the same time, the income tax has become less equalizing, so the trend toward inequality has become even greater after taxes than before taxes.

Changes in the tax law have led to a different tax structure than the one in effect before 1981. But despite the changes in tax structure, there was little change in the overall tax burden between 1979 and 1993. In 1993 the effective tax rate (ETR)—the percentage of income paid in federal taxes—was just over 23 percent, which is about the same as in 1979. And the tax burden is distributed today much like it was in 1979, except that the highest-income quintile has a slightly lower ETR. The top 1 percent of U.S. families received the largest tax cuts (about 5 percent lower in 1993 than in 1979). The total ETR did not change because the highest-income groups had a larger share of total income in 1993. During this period, the share of revenues from income taxes had shrunk and the share from social insurance taxes has grown, which made the tax system less progressive.[19]

Voter Turnout and the Power of the Poor

Although many analysts conclude that income should be more equally distributed, it is not easy to institute policies that redistribute income through taxes or any other method. The **political struggle** over who gets what and not the analysis of economists like Keynes, or the philosophy of thinkers like John Rawls, determines tax policy. In the political realm, economic and social inequalities are thought to be eradicated by the mechanism of one person, one vote. But it is still true that those with the most influence in electing political candidates see to it that the tax policies enacted benefit themselves at the expense of those with less influence. Some people by virtue of their affluence, education, or position have more power than others.

The egalitarian logic of political equality would appear to favor the redistribution of wealth toward those who are less well off, especially since by definition there are fewer who have been treated well by the economic system than those who

---

[19] *The Economic and Budget Outlook: Fiscal Years 1994–1998* (Washington, DC: Congressional Budget Office, January 1993), pp. 66–68.

have not. The poor could use their larger number of votes to force the passage of tax laws that would redistribute wealth to them from the wealthy. This was, in fact, one of the main fears of the Founding Fathers when the Constitution was being hammered out in 1787. Property qualifications were a device used by many states to keep the voting electorate down to about 5 percent of the adults in the late eighteenth century. However, Populist demands for "universal suffrage" were successful by the Jacksonian era and property qualifications were abolished (although suffrage back then was for men only). Voter participation rose dramatically. Women and minorities now vote. But the poor still have not forced a redistribution of income. Why not? There are several reasons.

First, the political market for votes is very imperfect. About three-fourths of the wealthiest 20 percent of eligible voters turn out to vote in Presidential elections. But among the bottom 20 percent of eligible voters only about 40 percent vote. Political entrepreneurs are not as concerned about the overall level of political participation as they are about getting their supporters to the polls. Also, candidates need money to hire staff, build their campaign organizations, and get their messages to the voters.[20] That financing primarily comes, not surprisingly, from wealthy contributors and special-interest political action committees (PACs). These donors with deep pockets contribute money to candidates who respond to their interests. That response in campaigns takes the form of advertising suggesting that policies supporting the wealthy are also in the interests of the poor. Often explanations of policies by candidates of their campaign literature—such as the redistributive effects of lowering capital gains taxes—are biased or misleading, which can lead to those who are economically naive to vote against their own interest. Both Reagan and Bush took advantage of the general opposition to taxes to advance policies to cap government social spending. In so doing they were faithful to their wealthy constituents but also able to appeal to a broader base. Bush's pledge of "No new taxes!" in 1988 played favorably with many segments of the voting populace, not just the Republican faithful. However, his agreement later to a small tax increase forced on him by a spiraling budget deficit resulted in a sense of betrayal by his upper-income constituency, which helped cost him the 1992 election.

Low turnout among the less well off occurs in part because neither party actively campaigns for the poor vote in terms of economic issues. To do so would mean coming out in favor of larger government spending programs, which would run the risk of losing votes to opposition candidates promising "fiscal restraint." A

---

[20] In the 1992 election, more money was spent by Presidential candidates (almost $400 million) and Congressional candidates (almost $500 million) than ever before. The Federal Election Campaign Act allows unrestricted contributions (called "soft money") for party-building activities, while it tries to restrict the influence of wealthy individuals who can bankroll political candidates with large contributions. But obviously soft money plays its part in campaign financing, and the Bush-Clinton election set a record for soft-money contributions. The Republican party raised more federally limited funds (called "hard money") than the Democrats in 1992 just as it has in previous election years. See Candice J. Nelson, "Money and Its Role in the Election," in *America's Choice: The Election of 1992* (Guilford, CT: The Dushkin Publishing Group, 1993), pp. 101–110.

political candidate who ran on a platform promising to increase taxes to provide social programs for the poor would find few large donors willing to contribute generously to his or her campaign. Such a campaign would be regarded as an act of political suicide. But to vote when no one is actively soliciting your support can seem futile. The less affluent conclude that they do not make a difference and become cynical about the usefulness of electoral politics making a difference in their lives.

The correlation between income status and political parties still persists, as shown in Table 6-4 for the 1992 Presidential election. But low-income workers are frequently conservative on social issues, even if willing to support candidates who are liberal on economic issues. As a result, the poor do not constitute a solid voting bloc since politicians who are conservative in the economic sense frequently can gain their support by emphasizing conservative social issues.

Support for a progressive candidate rises as incomes decline, but the likelihood of voting at all also declines as one moves down the income ladder. Thus, despite the egalitarian nature of one person, one vote, nonvoting reduces the political influence of the less well off. What the affluent lack in numbers, they more than make up for in voter turnout, money, and organization to ensure that their views are publicized and candidates supporting their positions are elected. And since political entrepreneurs respond to the demands of voters rather than nonvoters, the effect of this imperfect political market is to provide a weighted voting system in favor of the affluent. Thus there is a clear link between the low turnout of lower-income voters and a conservative bias in American politics.

Registration restrictions based on residency requirements, and periodic purges of voter rolls to remove people who have moved or who failed to vote in a previous election, among other practices, also discourage electoral participation among lower-income voters. There have, however, been attempts to reverse this situation. The Department of Transportation estimates that 87 percent of the voting age population has a driver's license. So a nationwide "motor-voter" bill that would make voter registration easier by requiring states to permit people to register when they apply for driver's licenses could assist millions of unregistered voters to participate

TABLE 6-4
INCOME AND VOTING PATTERNS IN THE 1992 PRESIDENTIAL ELECTION*

Income	Candidate voted for, %		
	Clinton	Bush	Perot
< $15,000	58	23	19
$15,000–29,999	45	35	20
$30,000–49,999	41	38	21
$50,000–74,999	40	41	18
$75,000 +	36	48	16

* Sample: 15,490 voters as they left voting booths.
Source: Survey conducted November 3, 1992, by Voter Research & Surveys, a consortium of ABC News, CNN, and NBC News.

in the political process. In an effort to sweep away barriers to voting by lower-income persons, Congress passed the motor-voter bill which was vetoed by President Bush who stated that it was in essence a Democratic registration bill. After the election of President Clinton, the motor-voter bill was reintroduced into Congress. Clinton signed the National Voter Registration Act of 1993 into law. The law, effective January 1, 1995, requires states to arrange for voter registration by mail at driver's license facilities and at state agencies.

The bill was criticized by some state officials who objected to yet another example of an "unfunded mandate," which is a federal law that requires states to carry out certain legal obligations without providing funds for the costs of compliance. The cost of such mandates has become burdensome for state governments that are then required to raise taxes to comply with the federal statute. Before the large deficits of the 1980s, Congress usually voted money for mandated programs. But since the deficit squeeze, Congress has continued mandating but has cut the money. Governors oppose unfunded mandates which force them to spend and tax more. But governors and state legislatures are often just as guilty of burdening local governments with state mandates.

CONCLUSION

1 Macroeconomic policy is made up primarily of fiscal and monetary policy. Fiscal policy is determined by the federal government's taxing and spending totals in the national budget.

2 The deficit is the gap between tax revenues and government expenditures. The national debt is the accumulated federal deficits. All previous deficits were incurred primarily as the result of wars or recessions. The quadrupling of the national debt in the Reagan-Bush years was the direct result of a decision to cut taxes without cutting spending. Those administrations engaged in a "borrow and spend" policy when the economic growth that would have eliminated the deficit did not occur as their supply-side theories promised. "Borrow and spend" is politically more palatable to the public than "tax and spend."

3 The current federal deficit would be less of a concern if the government had invested the borrowed funds to strengthen the economy. For example, by investing in research and development, or in the nation's infrastructure such as roads and bridges, or in education, American productivity could be expected to be more robust in the future. However, the money was not been spent on these public goods, but largely to maintain living standards. In fact, federal investment aimed at strengthening the economy declined by about one-third during this period.

4 The alternative scenario would have resulted in higher taxes primarily for the affluent, and federal borrowing would have been lower. The economy would have grown more slowly, but would be healthier today. The interest on the deficit is one of the fastest growing parts of the "uncontrollable" portion of the budget.

5 Slower economic growth today means higher government expenses through automatic stabilizers such as unemployment compensation. It also means lower tax receipts, which in turn means entitlements for Medicare and Social Security will come from a smaller economic pie so that these benefits too will consume larger portions of tax dollars.

6 Huge deficits are primarily beneficial to the affluent and represent a transfer of wealth from the less affluent to the more affluent. Interest payments on the money the government borrows today will also be paid to primarily affluent recipients in the future, as well.

7 Any serious effort to deal with the deficit will require a combination of policies. Tax increases, however unpopular, are required. This may be accomplished by a variety of means, including closing tax loopholes and raising marginal tax rates. A reduction in government expenditures and entitlements must be implemented. In some cases this may be accomplished by taxing benefits as well as by reducing payments. And finally, the deficit as a percentage of GDP can be reduced if the economy can be stimulated to grow more rapidly while government expenditures are held constant, or at least are not allowed to grow at the same rate.

QUESTIONS FOR DISCUSSION

1 What kinds of problems do large budget deficits pose for the nation's economy? What are the different problems in the short run as opposed to the long run?

2 Budget deficits are a serious problem. What additional information does a policy analyst need to make a policy assessment of that statement?

3 Is a balanced budget amendment a wise policy? Why or why not?

4 The causes of the current debt problems are different from those for all earlier increases in the national debt. Why is this so? What are the implications for resolving the problem?

5 What alternative tax policies are available to the government? What are the positives and negatives associated with each?

6 What are the characteristics of a "good" tax system? Why is vertical and horizontal equity important?

KEY CONCEPTS

Automatic stabilizers
Benefit principle
Budget enforcement act
Crowding out
Debt
Deficit
Discretionary expenditures
Effective tax rate
Entitlements
Excise taxes
Fiscal policy
Gramm-Rudman-Hollings
Horizontal equity
Marginal tax rate
Means-tested program

Monetary policy
Progressive tax rate
Property taxes
Proportional tax rate
Regressive tax
Structural deficit
Tax efficiency
Tax exemption
Tax expenditure
Tax fairness
Tax incidence
Tax loophole
Trickle-down theory
Vertical equity

SUGGESTED READINGS

Martin Neil Baily, Gary Burtless, and Robert E. Litan, *Growth with Equity: Economic Policymaking for the Next Century* (Washington, DC: The Brookings Institution, 1993).

Congressional Budget Office, *The Economic and Budget Outlook: An Update* (Washington, DC: U.S. Government Printing Office, 1993).

John Cranford, *Budgeting for America*, 2nd ed. (Washington, DC: Congressional Quarterly, 1989).

Louis A. Ferleger and Jay Mandle, *No Pain, No Gain: Taxes, Productivity, and Economic Growth* (New York: The Twentieth Century Fund Press, 1992).

Robert Heilbroner and Peter Bernstein, *The Debt and the Deficit: False Alarms/Real Possibilities* (New York: W. W. Norton & Company, 1989).

Paul Heyne, *The Economic Way of Thinking*, 5th ed. (Chicago: Science Research Associates, 1987).

Kevin Phillips, *The Politics of Rich and Poor* (New York: Random House, 1990).

James M. Rock, *Debt and the Twin Deficits Debate* (Mountain View, CA: Mayfield, 1991).

7

THE POLITICS AND ECONOMICS OF INEQUALITY

The concept of egalitarianism has been a cornerstone of American social and political culture. Thomas Jefferson embedded that idea in the Declaration of Independence when he stated: "We hold these truths to be self evident, that all men are created equal, that they are endowed by their Creator with certain inalienable rights, among them are life, liberty, and the pursuit of happiness." This liberty, to be protected by government, was aimed at permitting people to acquire material goods according to their abilities. But the result has been an inequality of outcomes.

During the 1930s, President Franklin D. Roosevelt inaugurated the New Deal. The Depression caused a crisis in the country which resulted in "one-third of the nation ill-fed, ill-housed, and ill-clothed." Government responsibility to narrow the gap between rich and poor was largely accepted by liberals and conservatives alike after the New Deal. It was seriously challenged only in the 1980s by a resurgence of extreme conservatism under Ronald Reagan. Supply-side economic thinking defended economic inequality as a source of productivity and economic growth. International circumstances, including the collapse of communism, put many who support more egalitarian attitudes on the defensive.

We hear a great deal about political equality, which typically means that individuals are equal before the law and that regardless of ability or income, each person has the right to vote. There appears to be an assumption that this technical political equality is **the** significant equality in the United States, and we disregard or minimize the fact of economic inequality. Most countries of the Western World have policies designed to **reduce** the economic differences between rich and poor. In those countries most people concede that the role of government should not be to widen the gap between rich and poor, but rather to reduce it.

190

INTRODUCTION

As earlier chapters have examined other public policies, this chapter will examine why policies that promote greater equality in the distribution of income **may reduce** economic efficiency. We will look at why this happens and what can be done about it. This chapter describes the inequalities of wealth and income in the United States, and whether they have increased or decreased in recent years. Finally, we look at how society can decide **rationally** how much (in)equality it wants, and once it does decide on this what policies are available to pursue its goals.

EQUITY AND EQUALITY

Although the current intellectual climate is not as supportive of the egalitarian position as it was a decade or two ago, it is still true that in most Western countries significant majorities continue to believe that it is the responsibility of government to reduce differences in economic inequality between people with high incomes and those with low incomes[1] (see Table 7-1). A bias in favor of equality also accords with the democratic approach.

However, while people may declare their sympathy for policies favoring equality, most would support inequality if it resulted from certain conditions:

1 People would agree that inequality is justified if everyone had a fair (not necessarily equal) chance to get ahead.[2] Not only would most people not object to inequality in the distribution of wealth or income if the economic "race" was run under fair conditions with no one handicapped at the start, but they would actively support it.

However, the situation becomes murky quickly. Many people do try to compete for scarce highly paid jobs by attending college so their future incomes will be

---

[1] No poll has asked if it is the responsibility of the government to increase the gap between rich and poor. Presumably few would support such an idea. Yet many proposed policies do just that.
[2] See especially in this regard Robert Heilbroner and Lester Thurow, *Economics Explained* (Englewood Cliffs, NJ: Prentice-Hall, 1982), pp. 199–202. This discussion on the bias in favor of equality relies heavily on that source.

TABLE 7-1
ATTITUDES TOWARD GOVERNMENT RESPONSIBILITY
TO REDUCE INCOME INEQUALITY BETWEEN PEOPLE

Country	% Agree government responsible
Italy	81
Hungary	77
Netherlands	64
Britain	62.9
Germany (All)	58.6
United States	27.9

Source: U.S. News & World Report, August 7, 1989, p. 29. From Gallup International Research Institute.

higher. Some may **choose** not to attend college, so that their economic handicaps are voluntary. Yet others may have grown up in families that could not afford to send them to or provide a background conducive to preparation for college. For those people, the resulting handicaps and lower incomes are not voluntary.

What parameters make conditions fair? Of particular concern is the fairness of various kinds of inheritance. For example, there is the genetic inheritance of talent. Much of our most important "human capital" is carried in our genes, with the ownership of these "productive resources" just an accident of birth. Is it fair that some individuals through their genetic endowment—a factor beyond the control of the people so equipped—have high innate intelligence, the ability to become professional athletes, or the attractiveness to become highly paid models while others have a genetic inheritance leaving them mentally or physically limited or even both? We usually do not worry too much over this kind of inheritance, but its effects are very real.

What of the inheritance of gender? Studies make it plain that females born in the United States doing the same job as men receive approximately 70 percent of the pay received by males. Is that fair? What about the inheritance of those who did not "pick" their parents wisely and grew up as members of an ethnic minority in a culturally deprived family in a ghetto neighborhood as opposed to being born into a white, privileged family able to afford the richest cultural environment and best schools available for their children?

Then there is the income differential resulting from inherited wealth. Many of the superrich in America got that way merely through inheriting large sums of money. That it should be possible to pass some wealth on from one generation to another is generally conceded, but the ability to pass on large fortunes virtually intact from generation to generation is frequently challenged.[3]

Any discussion of inherited wealth brings up the **role of chance** in income distribution. Chance operates not only in inheritances, but in the wider region of income differentials. One individual hits a lottery jackpot, another finds a superhighway built adjacent to her farm increasing its value several times over, another unexpectedly finds oil on his land. On the other hand, a worker may find himself out of work for a prolonged period due to a recession beyond his control or may be the victim of an expensive debilitating illness; yet another may find that a highly paid position she was trained for disappears.

2 No one objects to inequalities if they reflect individual choice. If an individual decides to turn his back on the secular world, become a Franciscan monk, and take a vow of poverty, no one objects. If someone else decides to take a job that offers financial incentives because of unpleasant or inconvenient working conditions, or because it is dangerous, no one objects to her higher wages. The problem

---

[3] Paradoxically, conservatives are often the most supportive of the theory of "Social Darwinism," which suggests that society is a place of competition based upon the principle of "survival of the fittest" in which those most fit win in the competition for material goods. However, Social Darwinists tend to be most opposed to the passing on of large inheritances from one generation to the next, because it nullifies the fairness of the social and economic condition. Someone who inherits $10 million does not have to "compete" and prove his or her ability to succeed through that competition.

is that frequently these decisions do not result from free choices but are brought about by uncontrollable circumstances. A person born in a ghetto whose economic situation is desperate may have no opportunity to sacrifice **current** income to improve his skills through education so that his **future** income will be higher, and thus may not have the option of choosing to work in a highly paid profession.[4]

3 People accept inequality when it reflects merit. Nearly everyone believes in the correctness of higher pay when it can be shown that it is justified by a higher or more valuable contribution to output.[5] Some people work longer hours than others, or work harder when they are on the job. This may result in income differences that are largely voluntary. Other workers acquire experience over time, which may result in their earning higher wages. This is part of the justification for wage differentials based on seniority.

4 People accept, and even support inequality, when they are persuaded that the inequality will benefit everyone. Often the common good is thought to include an increase in the gross domestic product (GDP), since greater productivity typically means a brisk demand for labor, higher wages, and greater economic activity. Therefore, the argument is often made by some politicians and some economists that policies encouraging inequalities that benefit those with higher incomes are justified because they will lead to higher savings for the wealthy that will ultimately

---

[4] Why is it that jobs with greater educational requirements usually offer higher wages? The conviction that educated people are more productive is not accepted by everyone. Some claim that the educational system primarily **sorts** individuals by ability. Skills like self-discipline and intelligence that lead to success in college are the same abilities that lead to success in the job market. Therefore, individuals with these skills stay in school longer and achieve academic success. Employers try to hire those productive workers. Education is partly an investment in human capital and partly consumption. Education is one way to acquire human capital, and while success in it may also signal innate abilities, it is usually some combination of the two. Highly educated people do earn higher wages than less highly educated people. Education may indeed be a cause of the higher wages, but the higher wages may also be a cause of education. Many people enjoy going to college and view it as a consumption good (and not only an investment good). Thus we would expect people with greater wealth to consume more of the education good: Just as wealthier people buy more luxurious mansions, so they also buy more education. Yet it would not be suggested that because rich people live in posh mansions, buying a mansion will make one rich.

A more radical view holds that the wealthy are better positioned to buy the best education available and keep their children in school regardless of ability. In this view, education sorts people according to social class, not according to ability. The more privileged members of society consequently pass their economic positions on to their children while making it appear that there is a legitimate reason for businesses to give them higher earnings. See Chap. 8 for a fuller distinction.

[5] **Economic discrimination** is defined to occur when duplicate factors of production receive different payments for equivalent contributions to output. This definition is difficult to test because of the difficulty of measuring all the relevant market characteristics. For example, the average black person earns less than the average white person, and the average woman earns less than the average man. Some of the differentials are easily accounted for. The average black worker is about 6 1/2 years younger than the average white worker. Younger workers earn less than older workers based upon work experience. Proportionately more black workers live in the South, where wages still lag behind levels in other areas of the country. Women are less likely to have majored in technical subjects than men. It might not be "discrimination" if a woman with a high school diploma receives a lower salary than a man with a college degree (although discrimination might help in explaining their educational achievements). It is clearly too simplistic to try to measure discrimination by merely comparing the typical incomes of different groups. In regard to race, the question is not "Do blacks, earn less than whites?" but "Do blacks earn less than whites *with like market characteristics* (work experience, age, education, etc.)?"

be translated into investments, which will create the jobs enriching the economic prospects of everyone else. The proposal for a lower capital gains tax was justified along these lines by both the Reagan and Bush administrations. This is the "trickle-down" theory of economic prospects which claims that, if the well-to-do only had more money, they would be more highly motivated to invest more of it in the hope of making a profit,[6] and these investments would create more jobs, thus helping society in general.

The above four general principles describe how the unequal distribution of income and wealth *is* defended. There is no suggestion that this is the way everyone *should* think about inequality.

THE FUNCTIONALIST THEORY

There is a theory that maintains inequality is **functionally imperative** because no stable system can long survive without it.[7] According to its arguments, society must first distribute its members into the various jobs or roles defined by the society and then motivate them to perform their tasks efficiently. Some jobs are more important than others in the sense that the successful performance of them is crucial to the welfare of the whole society.[8] Additionally, some tasks require skills that are difficult to acquire or scarce because they require special training. To ensure that the most important jobs are performed competently, every society provides a system of unequal rewards to produce incentives to channel the most competent people into the most important and difficult jobs. This ensures the greatest efficiency in the performance of these jobs.

It should be emphasized that, according to this theory, "a position does not bring power and prestige because it draws a high income. Rather it draws a high income because it is functionally important and the available personnel is for one reason or another scarce."[9] **The population comes to understand that inequality is functional**. The system of unequal rewards works to the advantage of the whole system

---

[6] We could achieve the same goal without yielding to inequality by financing investment through taxation and government purchases (public investment) rather than through private investment through savings.

[7] The functional theory of inequality is a variation on the marginal productivity theory of distribution (MPT), which holds that the income of any factor will be determined by the contribution that each factor makes to the revenue of the endeavor. Its income will be higher or lower depending on the ability and willingness of the suppliers of the factors of land, labor, and capital to enter the market at different prices. But at each price, factors will earn amounts equal to the marginal revenues they produce. The result in theory is that there cannot be exploitation of any factor in a perfect market.

The functional theory challenges the assumption of the marginal productivity theory that a perfect market exists. If it does not, then the earnings of each factor may not reflect its contribution to output. The MPT cannot explain the variation of incomes due to nonmarket factors such as discrimination, imperfect markets, and other factors.

[8] Kingsley Davis and Wilbert Moore, *Some Principles of Stratification* (Reprint Series in Social Science) (New York: Columbia University Press, 1993).

[9] Davis and Moore, *Some Principles of Stratification*.

by guaranteeing that jobs essential to society's welfare are performed efficiently and competently.[10]

Milton Friedman believes that the market is the most efficient way of filling the most important positions with the most capable people. Equality of opportunity is the principle that allows the market to select the most competent individuals:

> No society can be stable unless there is a basic core of value judgments that are unthinkingly accepted by the great bulk of its members. I believe that payment in accordance with product has been, and in large measure still is, one of these accepted value judgments or institutions.[11]

Functionalist theory is intuitively appealing. But it immediately raises several problems.

The Tradeoffs between Equity, Equality, and Efficiency

Equality and **equity** of income are not the same. Equality deals with income in terms of "the same amount," while equity refers to "fairness." Equality deals with what incomes **are** while equity is the normative question of what incomes **should be**. There are arguments both against and in favor of greater equality of income, associated with liberal and conservative economic positions, respectively.

The main argument against the equal distribution of income is based upon efficiency: An unequal distribution provides incentives to work, to save, to invest. To illustrate the point, imagine the consequences of an extreme situation where a society decided to achieve equality by taxing away all individual income and dividing the taxes collected equally among the entire population. The realization that harder work would no longer lead to a higher income would eliminate an important work incentive. It would also abolish any incentives to forgo current consumption in favor of purchasing capital goods (i.e., investing in future economic growth), since there would be no chance of future additional income. Since all the rewards associated with hard work, investing, taking risks by developing capital and land, and entrepreneurship would disappear, the gross domestic product would decline dramatically. This suggests that policies aimed at increasing the amount of economic equality (or reducing inequality) may reduce economic efficiency—that is, may lower the incentives to produce, which would thus lower the GDP.

A second argument against the equal distribution of income or wealth is based on the concept of equity. As noted earlier, it seems unfair that people with different natural abilities who make unequal contributions to output should receive the same

---

[10] James Madison, in *The Federalist*, #10, clearly states that it is a primary function of governments to protect individual freedom, which will lead to inequalities in income based upon differing abilities and interests. He notes that this is the basis for factions, which he laments. The most common and enduring source of factions is the unequal distribution of property. This poses a major dilemma for governmental administration.

[11] Milton Friedman, *Capitalism and Freedom* (Chicago: University of Chicago Press, 1962), p. 167.

incomes. An equal distribution is not equitable if individual contributions are unequal.

The case in favor of the equal distribution of income must include the argument that an unequal distribution leads to unequal opportunities. Some income differences arise because of differences in **wealth**. Many people with income-producing assets such as stocks and bonds receive sizable incomes from them. Not only are these individuals able to acquire additional income-producing assets such as land or capital investments (i.e., more stocks and bonds), but they are also more able to invest in human capital through training and education to increase even further the amount of income they can earn in the future. A person with less or no wealth is, by contrast, less able to invest in productive factors such as land and capital, or in education. Therefore an unequal distribution tends to be perpetuated and even increased because of the unequal market power of those who already have wealth, unless the government intervenes through taxes and transfers of income.

A second argument made by those in favor of a more equal income distribution is that a highly unequal distribution providing a great deal for the few and little or nothing for the many creates political unrest and threatens the stability of society. When 25 percent of the population lives at the subsistence level and the top 10 percent receiving most of the income also dominates the political and economic levers of power, the poor may be driven to rebel against the economic and political elites.

Third, it may be argued that a highly unequal distribution of income can, contrary to the conservative view, inhibit the investment in capital that is crucial to economic growth. While it is true that investment usually comes from people with higher incomes, if relatively few members of a society have most of its income, the rest of the population cannot put significant demand into the economy to stimulate growth. This means a lack of investment incentives, and the wealthy may opt to use their incomes for personal consumption instead.

Liberals sometimes undermine their case for more equality of income by denying that their proposals will have any harmful effects on economic incentives. Conservatives, on the other hand, undermine their case against greater equality by making greatly exaggerated claims about the loss of efficiency that would arise.

Qualifications to the Theory

The functional theory of inequality is therefore open to some criticisms which do not demolish it, but which significantly narrow the range of inequalities that can be justified as functionally imperative.

To begin with, it is relatively easy to determine which skills are in scarce supply, but difficult to tell which jobs are the most important to the welfare of a particular society. Questions of comparable worth are notoriously complex problems. After agreement is reached regarding the extremes—for example the importance of a cardiovascular surgeon compared with a street-sweeper—it becomes very difficult to determine the relative importance of jobs more at the "center"—managing a corporation versus teaching young children, for instance, or working as an accountant versus being a dentist. How does one decide?

Those supporting the functionalist approach usually shift from assessing the relative **importance** of any particular position to assessing its relative **skill** level and the **scarcity** of that skill in the society.

Scarcity of needed skills becomes the primary test, then. But this runs into another set of problems: Some professions, like physicians can affect the supply of skilled personnel in that occupation. The profession tries to promote the economic interests of its members by increasing their incomes. Under competitive conditions, this would attract more members and potentially develop a surplus and drive incomes down. So the profession typically tries to limit its membership through occupational licensure creating a contrived scarcity. Licensure is often state-regulated. But just as frequently it is very strongly influenced by the professionals already in the field who claim that they alone are competent to judge the criteria necessary for training and certification. The members of the profession justify their control by citing the need to exclude "quacks." But the certification, whether for architects, accountants, lawyers, or physicians, has substantial economic value. Frequently the license acts to raise wages in a particular profession by limiting competition. Typically licenses are granted by a panel of practitioners in the field who determine how many are to be granted and to whom. The potential for conflicts of interest is apparent.[12]

The point is that once the first criterion of the functionalists—the importance of a particular kind of job—recedes into the background, the functionalist interpretation of the second criterion—the scarcity of needed skills—becomes doubtful.

Functionalists emphasize the positive side of their theory and ignore its negative aspects. The "theory" does identify the value of talent and shows how rewarding various talents motivates those who possess them to work efficiently. However, it ignores the demotivating effects on those with fewer talents. Those at the higher end of the income stream can be motivated by bonuses, higher wages, life and health insurance benefits, promotions, and pension programs. But workers at the lower end of the income stream cannot be motivated by higher pay, for at least two main reasons: (1) Low income at this end of the pay scale must provide the differential to fill the higher positions with competent and conscientious workers. (2) The money needed to pay some people more must be taken from those who are paid less. Thus, in functionalist theory, the workers on garbage trucks who are quick and efficient cannot be rewarded by higher pay or bonuses, although they may be valued employees. As these individuals get older and slower, they must continue to work because of the need to provide for their families even under the most adverse conditions. Consequently low income, unemployment, and the threat of unemployment are concentrated among those jobs where the skill levels are the lowest and the supply of people having the skills the greatest. In sum, the carrot motivating

---

[12] See, in this regard, Doug Bandow, "Doctors Operate to Cut Out Competition," *Business and Society Review* (Summer 1986). Bandow illustrates that entry into the medical profession is essentially controlled through the use of licensing arrangements, which increase health care costs and decrease the options available to patients.

THE INCOME PARADE

We might dramatize the problem of inequality and poverty by lining up America's roughly 65 million families according to size of income in 1991, starting with the smallest, along an imaginary road around the world at the equator, 25,000 miles long. That would mean that a family averaging 3.8 people would be found every 2 feet. Assume that the height of the middle family is 5 feet 10 inches (70 inches), representing the median income of $30,126 in 1991 dollars. Let us assume that our height is also 5 feet 10 inches so we can look the middle family directly in the eye. What would this parade look like?

For over the first 1000 miles we would see families of tiny dwarfs beginning from a few inches high to just under 1 foot tall as we approached 1100 miles. For the next 2000 miles or so these grotesque creatures would grow from about 1 foot tall to just over 23 inches in height, representing all those families whose income is less than $10,000. They would be generally poorly educated. We would notice that they are about three times as likely to be black, twice as likely to be Hispanic, and three times as likely to be female heads of households and sickly children.

For the next 2250 miles, or more than one-fifth of the parade, we would see these dwarfs increase in size to almost 3 feet tall. They would still be more likely to be young, poorly educated, members of minorities, and female. During the next 5000 miles, their height would grow from 3 feet to about 4 feet 10 inches.

At the half-way point in the parade, we would see people whose faces are at our level. When the parade was about three-fifths over, we could begin to appreciate what it is like to have others tower over us as we towered over the dwarfs. Here people would go from 6 feet 8 inches to almost 10 feet tall. Now the individuals would begin to get gigantic. During the next 5000 miles, the height in the parade would reach 15 feet. Then as we reached the last 2000 miles we would find those with incomes over $75,000 whose heights went from 15 feet on up. These people would have the dimensions of King Kong. At $150,000 a year, family members would tower 30 feet in the air. Those with incomes of $1,000,000 per year and above would be taller than skyscrapers beginning at 200 feet high. The superwealthy, those with incomes over $10 million annually, would be half a mile tall.

Source: Adapted from Jan Pen, *Income Distribution*, translated by Trevor S. Preston (New York: Praeger, 1971), pp. 48–59.

those at the upper-income levels necessitates the stick to motivate those at the lower levels of income. Functionalist theory rarely mentions this.

Finally, for the functionalist system of inequality to operate smoothly, the society as a whole must see it as working to benefit the entire population. Most of the population must also believe that their tasks and their income levels reflect their skills and their relative contributions to the society. The stratified system will then rest upon a consensus in which even those at the lower end of the income stream understand that their low wages and the threat of unemployment are necessary motivators to keep them working. Not surprisingly, those who wholeheartedly believe in the system tend to be found at the upper end of the income stream. Those at the lower levels cannot both believe in the system *and* have a sense of self-esteem.

TRENDS IN INEQUALITIES OF INCOME AND WEALTH

Anyone interested in studying the social structure of America must begin by examining the disparities of income and wealth. **Income is defined as the total monetary return to a household over a set period, usually a year, consisting of wages, rent, interest, and gifts**. Income tends not to be as unequally distributed as wealth. **Wealth refers to the monetary value of the assets of a household minus its liabilities, which is its net worth**.

Wealth

An examination of wealth provides a more complete picture of family economic well-being than an examination of income. Wealth can provide the security to guarantee a family's well-being by providing the resources necessary to endure major illness and economic downturns, or to purchase goods that cost more than one could afford based on income alone.

Through the first three-quarters of this century, distinctions based upon class became progressively less important, and opportunities for upward mobility expanded. That stopped during the 1970s, and since then American society has been moving in two directions. Wealth and income in the United States have become much more concentrated since 1980. Both poverty and wealth are increasing together, indicating that the distance between the rich and poor is widening.

The most recent study completed by the Federal Reserve based on data compiled at the end of 1989 (see Table 7-2) found that the top ½ percent of the population held 24.1 percent of the total net worth in 1983, which grew to 29.1 percent of net worth in 1989. Members of the same top ½ percent increased their average wealth from $8.5 million in 1983 to $10.7 million in 1989, an impressive 26 percent rise. The net worth of the wealthiest 1 percent of American households increased from 31.3 percent of the country's wealth in 1983 to 36.2 percent in 1989. The top 1 percent, consisting of 834,000 households, had more wealth than all the assets held by the bottom 90 percent of 84 million households. Approximately 70 percent of the growth in wealth came from the appreciation of existing wealth, while about 30 percent resulted from personal savings. The increased share of wealth held by the rich was offset by a decline in the share of net worth held by the bottom 90 percent from 33.3 to 30.7 percent, and a decline for the 90 to 98.9 percentile group from 35.3 percent to 33.1 percent. The largest part of the shift toward the top ½ percent came from a decline in the proportion of net worth held by the remainder of the top 10 percent. In fact, every group **except** the top ½ of 1 percent lost ground in this 6-year period. This shift was the direct result of changes in government fiscal policies. The top 1 percent has more wealth (36.2 percent) than either the next 9 percent (33.1 percent), or the remaining 90 percent of the population (30.7 percent). In real terms this means that the richest 1 percent of the population has 36 percent of the nation's wealth to divide among its members, while 90 percent of the society has 30 percent to divide among its members.

The bottom fifth of the population actually has no wealth at all because for its members debts exceed assets. That is, the poorest fifth owes more than it owns. If

TABLE 7-2
CHANGES IN CONCENTRATION OF WEALTH BETWEEN 1983 AND 1989 (AMOUNTS IN BILLIONS OF 1992 DOLLARS)

	Top 0.5%		Next 0.5%		Next 9%		Remaining 90%		All households	
	1983	1989	1983	1989	1983	1989	1983	1989	1983	1989
Assets	22.1	26.4	6.8	6.4	33.3	31.6	37.9	35.5	11,708.9	20,092.7
Principal residence	4.6	5.0	3.8	3.4	26.2	29.3	65.5	62.2	3,738.5	6,415.5
Other real estate	29.5	34.1	6.9	8.9	39.6	39.1	24.0	17.9	1,687.5	2,907.2
Stocks	49.6	37.1	8.0	7.5	32.2	38.1	10.2	17.4	1,041.1	1,062.9
Bonds	42.9	59.4	8.1	5.8	42.8	28.3	6.2	6.6	367.0	994.6
Trusts	60.7	24.8	5.7	28.8	25.5	33.2	8.1	13.2	309.4	413.9
Life insurance	12.0	8.0	4.3	5.9	21.9	28.7	61.7	57.4	284.8	359.8
Checking accounts	8.5	14.9	5.4	4.1	30.9	27.7	55.3	53.2	119.4	210.0
Thrift accounts	10.0	10.3	11.1	7.0	48.1	46.1	30.7	36.6	154.3	452.5
Other accounts	9.6	13.8	4.4	6.9	36.6	38.4	49.3	41.0	1,049.1	1,968.8
Business	37.2	60.0	12.9	7.7	40.5	25.3	9.4	7.1	2,284.3	3,718.9
Automobiles	1.8	5.8	1.4	1.8	17.5	20.3	79.2	72.1	373.3	773.5
Other assets	12.5	32.0	8.2	7.2	43.4	36.0	35.8	24.9	300.1	815.0
Liabilities	8.2	12.1	3.9	2.7	19.6	23.8	68.3	61.5	1,507.6	3,129.2
Principal residence	1.6	2.2	2.4	1.6	15.9	20.0	80.0	76.1	864.6	1,749.1
Other real estate	25.6	36.3	4.9	5.8	33.2	39.5	36.3	18.3	324.1	764.4
Other debt	8.3	10.1	6.9	1.6	15.5	15.0	69.3	73.3	318.9	615.7
Net worth	24.1	29.1	7.2	7.1	35.3	33.1	33.3	30.7	10,201.3	16,963.5
Total family income	5.8	10.3	2.7	3.6	19.1	20.2	72.3	65.9	2,254.1	3,623.2

Source: Arthur B. Kennickell and R. Louise Woodburn, *Estimation of Household Net Worth Using Model-Based and Design-Based Weights: Evidence from the 1989 Survey of Consumer Finances* (Washington, DC: Federal Reserve System, April 1992), pp. 38–39.

we went into the bottom 20 percent of all households and sold all its members' possessions including wedding rings, furniture, clothing, cars, and anything else we could find, then used the money to pay their bills, they would still be in debt. The second fifth only has about 3 percent of total wealth, the third fifth about 5 percent, and the fourth fifth 15 percent.

The great inequality in the distribution of wealth not only indicates radical differences in lifestyles—but leads to profound political and social consequences. **Power flows from wealth**. The affluent can use their wealth to exert political power through political action committees, campaign contributions, lobbying, and other forms of influence. The result is a government that accommodates and reflects the views of the affluent. The public philosophy of the affluent has been accepted by the many. Great concentrations of wealth are also great concentrations of power. Such concentrations place in the hands of a few the decision-making power in public and private matters that affects the lives of all Americans.

Income

Wealth is less equally distributed than is income. The wealthiest 1 percent of families has 36.2 percent of net worth, while the top 1 percent of families in income receive about 12 percent of all pretax income. In 1991, the median family income was $35,939, with half the households receiving more and half less. Table 7-3 illustrates the distribution of money income of families in the United States in 1980 and 1991.

Overall, the **wealthiest one-fifth** of American households **received 44.2 percent** of all income in 1991 (up 41.5 percent in 1980), while the **poorest one-fifth received just 4.5 percent** of all income (down from 5.2 percent in 1980). The growing inequality in the distribution of wealth and income over the past 15 years is clearly apparent. The share of all income earned by the wealthiest 20 percent of households in the United States today is significantly higher than in 1970 and 1980, while the share earned by middle-income and low-income households is somewhat lower.

TABLE 7-3
MONEY AND PERCENT DISTRIBUTION OF MONEY INCOME AMONG AMERICAN FAMILIES, 1980 AND 1991*

Quintile	1980 Money income,† $	% Aggregate income	1991 Money income, $	% Aggregate income
Lowest	17,023	5.2	17,000	4.5
Second	28,779	11.5	29,111	10.7
Third	40,761	17.5	43,000	16.6
Fourth	57,151	24.3	62,991	24.1
Highest	57,152+	41.5	162,992+	44.2
Top 5 percent	89,465	15.3	102,824	17.1

* Amounts in constant 1991 dollars.
† Upper limits for lowest, second, third, and fourth quintiles; lower limits for highest quintile and top 5 percent.
Source: U.S. Census Bureau, *Statistical Abstract, 1993*, p. 463.

TABLE 7-4
INCOME DISTRIBUTION IN U.S. HOUSEHOLDS, 1991

Quintile	1991, %	Upper limits of quintiles,* $
Lowest	4.5	17,000
Second	10.7	29,111
Third	16.6	43,000
Fourth	24.1	62,991
Highest	44.2	
Top 5 percent	17.1	>102,824

* Except the top 5 percent, for which the lower limit is shown.
Source: U.S. Census Bureau, *Statistical Abstract, 1993*, p. 463.

This unequal distribution is portrayed in a slightly different manner in Table 7-4. These figures can then be displayed in the form of a graph, designated as a **Lorenz curve**, by arranging the data cumulatively (Fig. 7-1). The curve shows the degree of inequality in the distribution of income for a certain year. The percentage of households in different groups is depicted on the horizontal axis, and the percentage of income received by those families is shown on the vertical axis. By adding the lowest, or poorest, quintile to the second lowest quintile along with the remaining points, we can produce the Lorenz curve. The Lorenz curve then portrays the cumulative percentage of income earned by the cumulative percentage of households.

Incomes vary over an individual's life cycle, so the degree of inequality will be somewhat overstated by a Lorenz curve. Families with either young or old major wage earners will ordinarily have lower incomes than those with middle-aged (people in their thirties, forties, or fifties) major wage earners, although the lifetime earnings of those individuals may be identical.[13]

By itself, the Lorenz curve is of limited value. Its usefulness is greatly strengthened if we know what such a curve would look like for similar data from other countries. Or, if we wanted to know the direction in which the United States is headed, we would want to know what the Lorenz curve looked like in previous years. At any given time there will be pressures pushing the curve inward and others pushing it out. In earlier years, government policy helped press the curve inward, or at least helped to keep it from expanding.

Between 1935 and 1945 there was a clear trend toward a more equal distribution of income in the United States, primarily because of the following reasons: (1) The

[13] One author has suggested the lifetime Lorenz curve with income adjusted for age in the United States would show about 50 percent less inequality. See Morton Paglin, "The Measurement and Trend of Inequality: A Basic Revision," *American Economic Review*, vol. 65, no. 4 (September 1975), pp. 598–609.

That conclusion has been sharply disputed by Sheldon Danziger, Robert Haveman, and Eugene Smolensky in "The Measurement and Trend of Inequality: Comment," *American Economic Review*, vol. 67, no. 3 (June 1977), pp. 502–513. See also Laurence Lynn, Jr., "A Decade of Policy Developments in the Income Maintenance System," in Robert Haveman (ed.), *A Decade of Federal Antipoverty Programs* (New York: Academic Press, 1977), pp. 94–95.

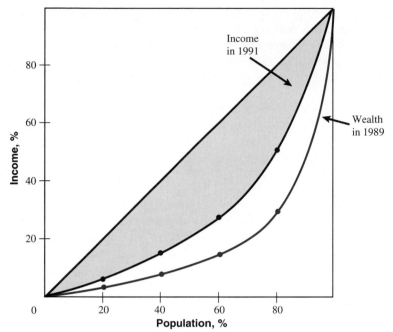

FIGURE 7-1
Lorenz curve showing cumulative percentage of income in 1991 and wealth in 1989 received by
the cumulative percentage of U.S. households. If everyone had the same income, the distribution
would follow the 45 degree complete equality line. The shaded area shows the amount of 1991
income inequality. The larger this area, the more unequal is the distribution of income.

end of the Depression and a wartime economy provided full employment, and significantly raised the wages of labor. (2) During the war, a more progressive income
tax and excess-profits taxes reduced the aftertax incomes of the rich more than
those of the poor. (3) Labor scarcity during the war reduced discrimination against
minorities and increased economic opportunities for them. (4) Union membership
quadrupled and increased the relative overall income of labor.[14]

In the decade between 1945 and 1955, the trend toward greater equality continued but at a much slower pace as unions began meeting more resistance after the
war; however, continued prosperity meant continued employment and educational
opportunities for minorities. Between the mid-1950s and the end of the 1970s,
inequality rose slightly. The year 1973 is noteworthy in studying earnings trends
because it marked the end of rapid growth in real earnings and the beginning of a
period marked by much slower growth.[15] In 1979 an abrupt increase in earnings
inequality began, which is still under way. Since 1979 earnings by males have

[14] See James Willis, Martin Primack, and Richard Baltz, *Explorations in Economics*, 3rd ed.
(Redding, CA: CAT Publishing, 1990), p. 43.

[15] Disposable income per full-time equivalent (FTE) worker rose by an average of 2.45 percent per
year from 1947 to 1973. From 1973 through 1988, it increased only by an average of 0.67 percent a
year.

become more polarized, with the proportion of men earning less than $20,000 and more than $40,000 (in 1988 dollars) increasing while the average income has remained stagnant.[16] When the average wage is stagnant and workers fall into lower-income groups at twice the rate as those who climb to higher-income groups, it means the rich are getting richer and the poor are getting poorer, while the middle class is shrinking.

Middle-class jobs can refer to those with pay somewhere near the middle of the distribution of income. Or they can mean those that pay from about $30,000 to $37,000, which would put them in the range for a lifestyle usually thought of as middle class. Such a lifestyle permits the purchase of goods such as a car and a modest home, among other items usually thought of as part of the "American Dream."

The loss of jobs in the midrange of wages has been attributed to several factors. Changes in the economy such as a reduction in tax rates particularly for those in the top brackets were championed by supply-side theorists who claimed that a tax reduction for the affluent was necessary to increase savings and investment.[17] When enacted during the 1980s, this scaling back of progressivity in the federal income tax led to a reduction in the federal funding of a variety of social welfare programs which in turn resulted in increased regressive taxes at the state and local levels. A second cause that has been cited is the decline in the number of middle-class jobs in manufacturing and the accompanying rise in the proportion of jobs in the service sector, which has few high-paying but many low-wage jobs.[18]

After 1979 incomes began rising much faster at the top end of the distribution and actually declining at the bottom. Seventy percent of the rise in average family income during the 1980s went to the top 1 percent of families. The share of income received by the top one-fifth of families grew by 3.8 percentage points from 1967 to 1991 (Table 7-5), while the shares of the bottom 60 percent declined by 4.2 percent. The percentage of income lost by the bottom 60 percent of families was gained by the top 20 percent.

Comparing changes in income levels in the United States with those in other countries is much more difficult. It may be argued that in underdeveloped countries the major problem is to attract sufficient capital for investment which will increase economic growth (expand the production possibilities frontier). Since the rich save a larger percentage of their incomes than the poor, who must consume their incomes for survival, an unequal distribution of income might help provide the cap-

---

[16] Robert Lawrence analyzed the decline in middle-class jobs in 1984 and found that they shrank from 56 percent to 47 percent, with two-thirds falling into the lower class and one-third moving up in terms of pay scales. See Robert Lawrence, "Sectoral Shifts and the Size of the Middle Class," *Brookings Review*, vol. 3 (Fall 1984), pp. 3–11.

[17] See George Gilder, *Wealth and Poverty* (New York: Basic Books, 1981).

[18] For a time, there was debate among scholars over whether wage inequality was increasing, and whether real wages have declined in absolute terms. The meaning of the data are now clear, though, and there is general agreement that both trends are occurring. See especially Bennett Harrison, Barry Bluestone, and Chris Tilly, "Wage Inequality Takes a Great U-Turn," *Challenge*, vol. 29 (March–April 1986), pp. 26–32. Also see Bennett Harrison and Barry Bluestone, *The Great U-Turn: Corporate Restructuring and the Polarizing of America* (New York: Basic Books, 1988).

TABLE 7-5
PERCENTAGE SHARE OF AGGREGATE INCOME RECEIVED BY EACH FIFTH OF
AMERICAN FAMILIES

Year	Quintile				
	Lowest	Second	Third	Fourth	Highest
1957	5.1	12.7	18.1	23.8	40.4
1967	5.5	12.4	17.9	23.9	40.4
1977	5.2	11.6	17.5	24.2	41.5
1987	4.6	10.8	16.9	24.1	43.7
1991	4.5	10.7	16.6	24.1	44.2

Sources: U.S. Census Bureau, *Money Income of Households, Families, and Persons in the United States, 1987* (Series P-60, No. 162) (Washington, DC: U.S. Government Printing Office, February 1989), p. 42; *Statistical Abstract, 1993*, p. 463.

ital necessary for investment. And indeed the share of income going to the wealthy is usually greater than that going to the poor in less developed countries. The greater inequality between rich and poor is an obvious indicator of the absence of a strong middle-income group.[19] But whether the wealthy use their money to invest in economic development within their own countries is another question.

In a developed country like the United States, on the other hand, the major economic concern is to maintain full employment and economic growth. To accomplish this, consumers must demand all the goods and services that business can produce. Thus, in a developed country, income should be more equally distributed with the rich receiving a proportionately smaller share than in an underdeveloped country and the rest of the population receiving slightly more to put out as consumer demand. This view, which was generally accepted in the United States after the New Deal era of the 1930s, was challenged in the late 1970s and 1980s by supply-side thinking, which held that more income should be given to the wealthy to provide incentives and savings for continued economic expansion.

Currently, the gap separating the upper from the bottom quintile of income earners is greater in the United States than in any other major industrialized nation.[20] Between 1980 and 1988 the pay gap between chief executive officers and typical factory workers increased from about 30:1 to almost 100:1. While comparisons with other developed countries are difficult to make, the Organization for Economic Cooperation and Development has found that Japan stands out as the industrialized nation having the most equal distribution of income, with Germany, the Netherlands, Sweden, and Taiwan contesting for second place.[21] In developed higher-income countries, the government is often involved in equalizing income through taxes. Thus governments limit the rights of the privileged to accumulate

[19] See *National Account Statistics: Compendium of Income Distribution Statistics* (New York: The United Nations, 1985).
[20] Kevin Phillips, *The Politics of Rich and Poor* (New York: Random House, 1990), p. 9.
[21] Malcolm Sawyer, "Income Distribution in OECD Countries," *OECD Occasional Studies* (July 1976), pp. 3–36. See also Gir Gupta and Ram Singh, "Income Inequality across Nations over Time: How Much and Why," *Southern Economic Journal*, vol. 51 (July 1984), pp. 250–257.

wealth without limit. In America, the insistence that government's role should be further reduced "to encourage economic incentives for entrepreneurs" is an argument for encouraging even greater inequality. It ignores the need to provide incentives to workers whose incomes have been stagnant for the last decade.

ETHICS AND DISTRIBUTIVE JUSTICE

Philosophers of various types—moral, political, economic—along with practical politicians have debated the distribution of income and justice throughout history. Thomas Hobbes, a conservative political philosopher in the seventeenth century, wrote:

> And whereas many men, by accident become unable to maintain themselves by their labour; they ought not to be left to the charity of private persons; but to be provided for, as far forth as the necessities of nature require, by the laws of the Commonwealth.[22]

More recently, Thomas Carlyle, a nineteenth-century economist and philosopher, wrote:

> It is not to die, or even to die of hunger, that makes a man wretched . . . all men must die. . . . But it is to live miserable we know not why; to work sore and yet gain nothing; to be heart-worn, weary yet isolated, unrelated, girt in with a cold, universal Laissez Faire.[23]

John F. Kennedy lamented the practical problem for public policy when he said, "If a free society cannot help the many who are poor, it cannot save the few who are rich."[24] **Distributive justice** is basically an ethical problem. Political scientists and economists may discuss the political and economic difficulties and consequences of certain policy choices, but they have no special claim to moral insights. That is for philosophy. Yet the dominant philosophies of distributive justice vary significantly in their views on equity in the distribution of income.

Natural Law

Natural law theorists generally hold that each person has the right to the product of his or her own labor. This view concedes that there will be an inequality of income since each factor of production should receive a return proportional to its contribution to output. Those who own factors of production or who are more productive because of special skills or intense effort should receive a return equal to that factor's portion, or the marginal revenue product in economic terms. However, many natural law philosophers have suggested that an unequal power relationship fre-

---

[22] Thomas Hobbes, *Leviathan* (Meridian ed.) (New York: World Publishing Company, 1963), p. 304.

[23] *International Encyclopedia of the Social Sciences*, #19 (quotations volume) (New York: Macmillan, 1972); taken from Thomas Carlyle, *Past and Present*, 2nd ed. (London: Chapman and Hall, 1903; originally published in 1845), pp. 201–211.

[24] John F. Kennedy, "Inaugural Address, January 20, 1961," *Vital Speeches of the Day*, vol. XXVII, no. 8 (February 1, 1961), p. 226.

quently results in labor not receiving its fair share. Thus the "**just wage**" theory was developed, which reinforces the contention that employers have an obligation not to use their greater market power to enrich themselves unjustly at labor's expense.

This philosophy recognizes that the major advantage of distribution according to marginal productivities is that everyone has a vested interest in raising the marginal productivity of factors which would result in an ever increasing productivity and total income. Its proponents also recognize the difficulty of measuring the contribution of each factor precisely, and generally accept the validity of the "trickle-down" theory of prosperity. They perceive the tradeoff between equality and efficiency.

The late Arthur Okun, an economist who favored a more equal distribution of income out of ethical considerations, described the equity versus efficiency argument in terms of a "leaky bucket" analogy: Redistributing income from the successful to the unsuccessful is like using a leaky bucket to transfer water from one barrel to another. In the process of making the transfer, some water will leak away and is lost for good. Okun's point was not that the redistribution should be stopped, but that undertaking such a program involved substantial costs, including those for administration as well as reduced incentives to work for recipients. This does not mean that welfare expenditures, for example, should be cut back. No one would object to providing a starving child with a nutritious meal even though it might cost $4.00 to provide the child with a $2.00 meal. But it does suggest that solving the problem of poverty may be more costly than often presumed. Therefore, an important goal of income redistribution programs should be to reduce the "leaks" in the "bucket" as much as possible.

Utilitarianism

The utilitarian theory as espoused by Jeremy Bentham challenged the justification for inequality. Bentham saw all humankind as seeking to avoid pain and to increase happiness. Different pains and pleasures can be compared, which in the political arena provides legislators with a "calculus" of pain and pleasure for determining policy. In Bentham's view, policies should be calculated to bring about the greatest good for the greatest number. Therefore, since people are fundamentally alike, the total utility of society will be greatest when income is distributed equally.

The utilitarian analysis has been used to determine a "correct" distribution of income, as follows[25]: An **additive social welfare function** may be defined as the total of all individuals' utilities living in the society. The basic rationale for the utilitarian view of income distribution rests upon the law of diminishing marginal utility. It assumes the following:

1 Individuals have identical utility functions. Two individuals would therefore receive the same number of **utils** from a given amount (say $1000) of consumption.

---

[25] See Michael Katz and Harvey Rosen, *Microeconomics* (Boston: Richard D. Irwin, 1991), pp. 670–672, for a more complete treatment of this model.

2 Everyone is subject to the law of decreasing marginal utility of consumption. The marginal utility of an extra dollar is less for someone who is rich than for someone who is poor. Increasing an individual's level of consumption will make that person better off, but at an ever decreasing rate. Consequently, the loss in utility of a dollar taken from a rich person is less than the gain in utils received by the poorer recipient. Accordingly, the reduction in inequality will increase the total utility for society. The total utility of society will be greatest when income is distributed equally.

3 The total amount of consumption available is fixed and unaffected by policies that redistribute wealth. Consider a United States with only two people, Jim and Christy, and suppose we want to divide $1000 between them in a way that would yield the most *total utility*. If we assume that Jim and Christy enjoy money equally, that is, that their *marginal utility* schedules are the same as shown in Fig. 7-2, we can prove the following conclusion: The optimal distribution of income is to give $500 to Jim and $500 to Christy, which is point E in Fig. 7-2. That is, if the income distribution is unequal, we can improve things by moving closer to equality. We prove this as follows: If Christy and Jim have identical marginal utility schedules (MU), the optimal way to distribute $1000 is to give $500 to each. A redistribution toward equality will maximize society's total utility. If Jim has $750 (point J) and Christy has $250 (point C), the law of diminishing marginal utility states that Jim's MU (which is J) is less than Christy's (which is C). If we take $50 from Jim, he *loses* the low MU of $50 to him. When it is transferred to Christy, she gains the higher MU of $50 to her. Total utility rises by $C - J$ because Christy's gain exceeds Jim's loss. This will be true until they reach equality (point E). Thus if we want to maximize total utility, the best way to distribute a *fixed* amount of money among people with identical MU schedules would be to divide it equally.

FIGURE 7-2
Optimal distribution of income.

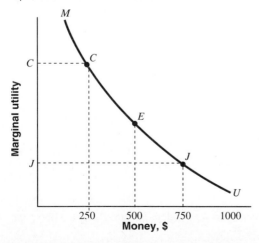

The utilitarian conclusions suggest a policy of complete equality. One criticism of this approach is, as has already been suggested, that people may have different marginal utility schedules. Some individuals may be more concerned with material goods than others. Nor is it proven that people with high incomes get less utility from their last dollars than do poor people. It is not possible to objectively measure satisfaction. Nonetheless, it seems reasonable for a government to assume the validity of the first two assumptions since different intensities of the psychological satisfaction for consumption by various individuals cannot be known or definitively measured. This means the government should act, when designing policy, as if everyone does have an identical marginal utility function.

The main weakness in the above analysis appears to be the third assumption. In order to improve everyone's utils, those making the economic decisions must aim at economic growth allowing for increased consumption by all. The dilemma is that the total amount of wealth is *not* independent of its distribution since complete equality destroys the incentives to be more productive. Equal distribution would clearly provide a disincentive for individual work decisions, thereby reducing total income.

Social Contract Theories

Social contract theorists conceive morality as a set of rules directing how members of society are to deal with each other. These rules are derived from rational self-interest and are based on the requirement that they are reciprocally binding. Several social contract theorists like John Locke (1632–1704) and Jean Jacques Rousseau (1712–1788) influenced the American Founding Fathers.

John Rawls, a contemporary philosopher, has proposed a modern variant on the theory of the social contract that he puts forward as an appealing alternative to utilitarianism. Rawls maintains that rational self-interested people would choose equitable principles of justice to govern a society in which they were going to live, **if** when choosing the standard they did not know what their own place in that society would be.[26] Rawls' argument is based upon the notion that an objective view would emerge if everyone operated behind a "veil of ignorance" in which they had no knowledge of what their places in society would be. In this "original position," people would be motivated to choose principles that are impartial and fair to everyone because if one chose principles that favored some people over others one might find oneself placed in a disadvantaged position when the "veil of ignorance" was lifted.

Rawls argues that inequality and injustice result from the fact that people know too much about their endowments of assets and skills when they enter into "bargaining" about their political, social, and economic rewards. Those who are already better endowed with political, social, and economic resources refuse to agree to any arrangement (such as a seriously redistributive tax system) that would give away

---

[26] John Rawls, *A Theory of Justice* (Cambridge, MA: Harvard University Press, 1971). Also see John Rawls, "Some Reasons for the Maximin Criterion," *American Economic Review*, vol. 64, no. 2 (May 1974), pp. 141–146.

these benefits. The rational self-interest of those so privileged not only does **not** allow a social consensus for a more equal distribution to emerge, it favors a system supporting inequality to allow the privileged to keep their higher incomes.

In fact, according to Rawls, everyone has a vested interest in a particular position. Those with high incomes favor a system of inequality to protect their privileges, while those with low incomes advocate a system of equality since it would improve their position.

Behind the "veil of ignorance," on the other hand, people would be motivated to adopt the **maximin criterion** which maximizes the utility of the person in the minimum position. Rawls argues that rational self-interested individuals would act as risk avoiders since they would realize that they could end up at the bottom of the income distribution, and therefore they would want the minimum income to be as high as possible. They would generally agree that social, economic, and political opportunities must be distributed equally. Since everyone would be equally situated in the original position, and not know how they would fare in advance, they would opt for risk aversion. They would be concerned for the welfare of the poor, since they could not be sure they would not end up being poor themselves. Consequently a consensus would develop in favor of an equal distribution of income, unless some other distribution could leave everyone better off.

Rawls recognizes that even in society as it exists there may be changes that improve the lot of the worst-off person a little while improving the positions of richer people a great deal. Even though this increases inequality, Rawls would approve of the change because the poorest individual would still be better off. However, some egalitarians would oppose such a change since they oppose any increase in inequality.

The implications of this theory for public policy are clear. Government should champion policies that move society in the direction that would be supported by everyone if they found themselves in the "original position," that is, it should promote policies that move society toward more equality. A criticism of this theory is that even in the "original position" there might be some people more willing to take risks than others. There might even be situations where taking greater risks would be rational—say where the choice involves a risk of losing $100 but the possibility of gaining $500. A second criticism is, once again, the tradeoff between equality and efficiency. Equality would be gained at the expense of efficiency in that there would be no incentives to be more productive if the rewards were taken away.

MEASURES AND DEFINITIONS OF POVERTY

One goal of organized society is to eliminate poverty. The government "promotes the general welfare" through its public policies, while the society's economy allocates goods and services to satisfy people's needs and wants. In many societies the larger part of the population is equally poor, while in others income is distributed unequally between middle- and upper-income groups. Equity and inequality are relative concepts, while typically poverty is an absolute. **Poverty exists when people lack an income sufficient to provide themselves and their families with the**

necessities of life. Overall the American economy has performed rather well in producing and distributing goods and services; nonetheless approximately 14 percent of the U.S. population lives below the poverty level defined by the government.

Poverty has the same causes as inequalities in the distribution of income: discrimination, inadequate human capital, and chance.

Absolute and Relative Poverty

The U.S. government attempts to define a **poverty line** below which a person's or family's annual income level is not adequate to provide the basic necessities of life. Food is one such necessity, so the minimum cost for a nutritious diet is calculated. And since the average family spends about one-third of its income on food, the cost of that diet is multiplied by 3 to ascertain the established poverty line.[27] The figure is then adjusted for family size. This provides an **absolute poverty level**, which is defined as the income level below which a household cannot afford the basic necessities. If a household falls below the minimum standard of living, it is classified as poor. If its income passes above that criterion, it is, by definition, not poor.

The use of an absolute level to measure poverty in the United States is criticized by some who argue the standard is arbitrary. People living in countries like Haiti or Ethiopia might feel elated to live at the poverty line in America, and even consider themselves fortunate. Still, members of a poor family in the United States would find little comfort in knowing their income was greater than the average income of a family in Ethiopia. Any measure of poverty must be gauged by income levels within the country being measured.

Today many poor people have a standard of living that includes modern utilities such as central heating, electricity, refrigeration, radios, and televisions unattainable by the wealthiest individual in 1800. For example, the refrigerator was once a convenience enjoyed only by the middle and upper classes. However, it revolutionized the food distribution system in the United States so that even a poor person now finds having one a necessity. But the cost of a refrigerator is a significant economic burden on a poor family. In some other countries where most of the population lives on farms, and the technology is structured differently, a refrigerator may still be considered a luxury. In one sense it takes more money even to be poor in America today.

---

[27] Conservatives are troubled by this measurement, which after 1968 was adjusted periodically to reflect changes in the overall Consumer Price Index (CPI). They contend that increases in the price of housing was driving the CPI up faster than increases in the price of food. Hence, the poverty rate was approximately 2 percentage points (and 4 million people) higher than it should be. See John Weicher, "How Poverty Is Mismeasured," *The Wall Street Journal*, January 23, 1986, p. 32. Since 1986, the cost of housing has in fact lagged behind increases in the price of food in the CPI.

Liberals criticize the measure for defining poverty at too low a level. It allowed less than $3.00 per day per person for food in 1990. At current food prices, that is insufficient for long-term nutrition and health needs. Liberals also argue that poor people have to spend a larger percentage of their incomes for housing than individuals who are better off. Thus, the definition is distorted in a manner that keeps the official poverty line lower than is realistic.

Clearly the concept of poverty will vary with the time and place where it is being examined. Therefore, a second approach to measuring poverty applies a relative standard. A **relative poverty level** designates the poor as those who fall too far below the average income. This definition makes it more difficult to reduce poverty, since the poverty line will ratchet upward as a nation's economy grows. If the incomes of the poor grow, allowing them a greater control over economic goods, they are better off. But what if everyone else's income has grown by the same percentage? The poor will not have improved their relative position. Although they have more income, they may not feel more content.

The relative standard defining poverty erodes the distinction between the poor and the nonpoor. Rather than a sharp line dividing them, it suggests a continuum—think of a line of people stretching from the most impoverished to the most fabulously wealthy. This illuminates the problem of poverty as one of the magnitude of disparities between levels of income. As Alan Blinder has written, "The poor are so poor because the rich are so rich."[28] According to this standard, poverty can be eliminated by moving toward an equal distribution of income.

The definition used by the government is the absolute poverty standard developed by the Social Security Administration in 1964 and based upon the Department of Agriculture's "economy food plan." It reflects the different consumption requirements of differing sizes of households. Using this definition, the "poverty income threshold" is attained when an individual's income is lower than three times the annual cost of a diet that is minimally acceptable. The **poverty rate** is the percentage of families whose incomes fall below the poverty line. The poverty threshold is updated annually to reflect changes in the Consumer Price Index. Figure 7-3 shows poverty levels in the United States from 1959 to 1991.

---

[28] William J. Baumol and Alan S. Blinder, *Microeconomics: Principles and Policy*, 4th ed. (New York: Harcourt Brace Jovanovich, 1988), p. 441.

FIGURE 7-3
U.S. poverty levels, 1960 to 1991. (*Source: Statistical Abstract, 1993, p. 469.*)

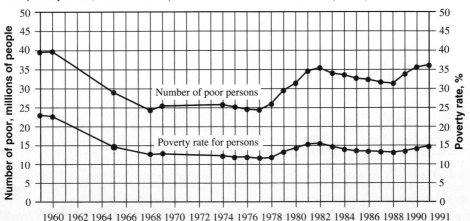

The poverty index is based solely on money income and does not reflect the fact that many low-income persons receive noncash benefits. If one takes into account the value of subsidized housing, health care, and food stamps, the percentage of the American population remaining in poverty is about 9 percent. There is irony in the declaration by President Reagan that "We declared war on poverty and poverty won" when the data conclusively show that poverty was reduced significantly by 1960s and 1970s "War on Poverty" government programs.

Who Are the Poor in America?

Poverty does not affect different races, sexes, or age groups equally. Someone with less than a high school education is much more likely to be poor than someone who has finished high school. Someone who is black or Hispanic is almost three times as likely to be poor as someone who is white. A family is more likely to be poor if the head of the household is under 25 than if the main breadwinner is older. Members of single-parent families are more likely to be poor than those living in families where two parents are present.

The chief characteristic shared by those who fall below the poverty line is they lack a job. However, most of the poor are poor because of their limited earning capacity. Approximately three-quarters of the families in poverty have breadwinners that work full time. Their jobs simply do not earn enough to pull them out of poverty.

Some studies suggest that approximately one-fourth of all Americans fall below the poverty line at some point in their lives. For almost half of those individuals, the period they live below the poverty line is temporary, lasting less than a year.[29] But over one-half of those in poverty remain beneath the poverty line for at least 10 years.

Nonworking students, or those with part-time jobs, often fall below the poverty line. Far more serious are the instances of people in long-term poverty due to lack of an education. It is also important to note that a growing economy helps all groups, but tends to help males more than females, and whites more than blacks and Hispanics.

Table 7-6 shows some statistics on poverty in the United States for the years 1979, 1989, and 1991.

POLICIES TO FIGHT POVERTY

The War on Poverty

President Lyndon Johnson declared a "War on Poverty" in 1964. Several anti-poverty programs were created or expanded during his administration. The most contentious of these was the **Aid to Families with Dependent Children (AFDC)** program, originally started in 1935 under the provisions of the Social Security Act as a measure to assist widows not covered by Social Security. It was expanded as

---

[29] See Mary Jo Bane and David Ellwood, "Slipping into and out of Poverty," *Journal of Human Resources*, vol. 21, no. 1 (Winter 1986), pp. 1–23.

TABLE 7-6
INCIDENCE OF POVERTY FOR THE YEARS 1979, 1989, AND 1991

	1979	1989	1991
All persons	11.7	12.8	14.2
White	9.0	10.0	11.3
Black	31.0	30.7	32.7
White female head of household	22.3	25.4	26.8*
Black female head of household	49.4	46.5	48.1*

*1990 data
Sources: U.S. Census Bureau, *Current Population Reports, 1991*; U.S. Census Bureau, *Statistical Abstract, 1993*, p. 469.

THE FEMINIZATION OF POVERTY IN AMERICA

The profile of the typical person in poverty has changed significantly in the last 30 years. In the 1950s and 1960s, the typical victim of poverty was elderly and living in a rural area. Since that time, expanded Social Security has helped raise the incomes of the elderly above the poverty level.

In the decade between 1965 and 1975 the number of families in poverty headed by women climbed from one-fourth to almost one-half of all poor families. This was at the very time that "affirmative action" policies endeavored to improve employment opportunities and wages for women. Attitudes regarding "women's liberation" encouraged more women to enter areas of the labor market that had previously been closed to them. Female participation in the labor force climbed from 42.6 percent of the female population in 1970 to 56.4 percent in 1989.

The feminization of poverty has resulted from several factors. First, there are far more female-headed households now as a result of an increase in divorce rates. The divorce rate, which is defined as the number of divorces relative to 1000 married couples, rose from 9.6 in 1965 to 20.7 in 1988 (Bureau of the Census, 1990, p. 87). The remarriage rate rose only modestly during this period. A mother who retains custody of her children creates a female-headed family, while the husband who lives alone is defined by the Census Bureau as an "unrelated individual" and is not counted as a family. The rate of poverty for these female-headed families has remained very consistent at around one-third of poor families. Today, more than one in five children live in a female-headed family. In 90 percent of the cases, the children have a living father.

The number of male-headed households in poverty has declined to a significant degree, because wives have joined the work force and reduced the poverty rate for male-headed households. Between 1960 and 1990, married wives in the labor force went from 30 to 57 percent. Census Bureau data indicate that median family income in households with two parents present was $43,578. In one-parent families where the mother has never been married, the median income was $9,272.

Another related factor is that extended families are an increasing rarity in American society. Divorced women are less likely than in the past to move in with their parents upon the breakup of their marriages. When that occurred in the past no additional family was

part of the War on Poverty to provide help to female heads of households below the poverty line. Families with unemployed males in the house were disqualified. This proviso was meant to make it difficult for men to receive any benefits. It targeted aid to assist the children of the poor on the premise that they were not responsible for their poverty. The federal government provides over half the funding, with state and local governments supplying the rest. The states establish the eligibility guidelines and the benefit levels. Accordingly, eligibility criteria and benefits can and do vary from state to state.

AFDC gives money to families in which there are children but no breadwinners. Typically no father is present and the children are too young to permit the mother to seek outside employment. In 1964, 29 percent of the nation's unwed mothers received AFDC, which increased to 63 percent by 1972. The proportion had dropped to 45 percent by 1988.

created. Likewise, single teenagers who give birth are more likely to move out of their parents' homes and set up their own households.

Interestingly, the data show that female-headed households are growing smaller, in line with general population trends. And female educational levels are also climbing. Consequently, the increasing feminization of poverty is concentrated among younger and minority female-headed families. The poverty of families headed by young women correlates with lower educational achievement. Young black female-headed households have almost twice the poverty rate as female-headed families overall.

The nature of the causes of this poverty makes public policy remedies in the United States difficult to adopt and implement since they are not acceptable to many. Requiring welfare recipients to work is increasingly favored by legislators. This may be more feasible now through government provision of child care, job training through such programs as the Job Corps, and subsequent assistance in job placement. But frequently these policies are not very effective because the jobs available to their beneficiaries pay too little to lift them out of poverty. Government income supports such as Aid to Families with Dependent Children, despite the criticisms regarding their disincentives to work, are still necessary.

The current government policy in which families receive a tax exemption for each child through an income tax deduction reduces taxes for more affluent families. But the poor— among them the poor female-headed households under discussion—do not pay income taxes and therefore receive nothing for their children. One proposal is to actively subsidize the efforts of poor families to raise their children. This could be accomplished by paying a direct "family allowance" stipend, as many European nations do, and limiting it to families below a certain income level. By eliminating the tax deduction, this stipend could be revenue neutral and not increase government debt. A payment for children would not be a work disincentive. And it could be limited to three or four children if that were thought wise. Such a system would provide support for children who are not responsible for their poverty as well as helping those most in need.

Sources: This relies heavily upon Steve Pressman's "The Feminization of Poverty: Causes and Remedies" in *Challenge* (March/April 1988), pp. 57–61. Some data are from *Statistical Abstract, 1993*, p. 100.

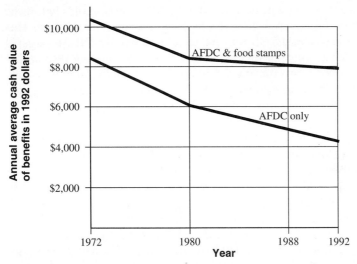

FIGURE 7-4
The declining welfare check, 1972–1992.

The value of benefits under AFDC has declined over the last two decades by about 40 percent when adjusted for inflation (see Fig. 7-4). The value of food stamps offsets this decrease by about 15 percent, resulting in about a 25 percent decline in the value of welfare. Real spending for AFDC and food stamps has therefore grown only slightly (although spending for Medicaid, a related program, has skyrocketed; see Chap. 11). The program sends smaller checks to larger numbers of people. A mother with two children now receives, on average, $380 per month.

Since the availability of welfare payments is thought to be a strong disincentive for the poor to seek work, the declining value of welfare support payments over the last two decades was intended to minimize that effect. It was hoped that by reducing the size of the payments, many able-bodied poor would have a greater incentive to find work and leave the welfare roles. However, the recession that began in 1989 increased the number of welfare recipients by over 30 percent to a record 14.3 million people. Despite the growing numbers receiving AFDC, real spending has remained flat because of the smaller benefits. As already noted, the program sends smaller checks to more people.

A major criticism of AFDC was that, as originally set up, a family with a father who could work but was unemployed or underemployed was not eligible for AFDC benefits. As a consequence, the children would get more money if the father left. Many fathers did leave so their families could obtain assistance, and others felt forced to ostensibly leave and then return surreptitiously. In 1988, the Family Support Act acknowledged the weaknesses in the bill that encouraged the breakup of families and made eligibility standards slightly more generous. It tied benefits to work, permitting two parents in the home as long as one of them worked. If employment could not be found, then community service or other unpaid work was acceptable. The Family Support Act makes the AFDC-UP program mandatory throughout the country (the UP refers to unemployed parent). Programs that require welfare recipients to accept public service jobs or participate in job training are called **workfare**. Through the Family Support Act, states can make participation in training or employment programs mandatory and can enact penalties on recipients who refuse to accept jobs offered them.

AFDC became the classic form of "welfare" derided by many. Many states now have programs that allow payments to families with unemployed fathers. AFDC is also criticized for providing no incentives for mothers to earn incomes since, after a grace period upon finding a job, the woman's welfare payments are reduced by an amount equal to the family's wages. In effect, the earnings are taxed at 100 percent through the reduction of AFDC payments. Not surprisingly, recipients are poorly motivated to look for work, especially if their skills command only low wages. The sharpest attacks on AFDC, however, come from critics who claim welfare rewards immorality and laziness and even encourages them as lifestyles instead of hard work and self-improvement. These critics also claim the system encourages "welfare mothers" to have more children to boost their "welfare checks." These attitudes, it should be noted, indicate more than a hint of racism in that black families constitute a disproportionate portion of AFDC recipients.

A final problem with AFDC arises from the fact that the federal funding portion varies between states, based upon the per capita income within each state. Federal money as a percent of the program's total funding is highest in states with the lowest per capita incomes. Federal funding averages approximately one-third of the total throughout the United States. Consequently, benefit levels and eligibility requirements show wide variations, as each state determines for itself the poverty-level requirements for food, clothing, and shelter within its borders. It then calculates AFDC payment levels for its citizens according to its own definition of those requirements. Ironically, the federal funding matching formula reimburses states at a declining rate: The amount is higher for the first $50 than for the second $50 paid to a family. Thus states have an incentive to minimize their own spending and maximize federal funds by providing small payments to their recipients (see the appendix at the end of this chapter). Several states, especially in the South, such as Alabama and Mississippi, which have some of the nation's poorest families set very low levels of funding, which has had the effect of encouraging needy families there to migrate to higher-paying states. Other states, particularly in the North, started enforcing residency requirements more strictly to discourage needy individuals from migrating to their state. But residency requirements were declared unconstitutional in 1969,[30] and since that time no state can any longer bar citizens of other

---

[30] *Shapiro v. Thompson*, 394 U.S. 618 (1969). The case involved a Massachusetts resident named Thompson who moved to Connecticut and applied for AFDC after 2 months residency. She was turned down based on a 1-year residency requirement in the state. The lower court noted the "chilling effect on the right to travel" caused by the requirement and held that it denied Thompson the equal protection of the law as guaranteed by the fourteenth amendment. The Supreme Court noted that the law created two classes of residents, those who had lived in the state 1 year or more and those there for less than a year. The Court held that it was a "device well suited to discourage the influx of poor families in need of assistance."

states from moving in and receiving the public services available to others already living within its jurisdiction.

Without residency restrictions, the mobility of those receiving welfare increased markedly, so that by the mid-1970s their long-distance mobility was greater than that of nonrecipients.[31] This situation held whether the poor consisted of a married couple or a family headed by a single woman. A state with more generous welfare benefits provides incentives for their resident poor to continue on in the state and for the poor from other states to move there. The net immigration has resulted in an increased poverty level in some states that has caused policy makers to be concerned about how their progressive policies attract and retain the poor from other areas and overburden their public service.

President Reagan used administrative rule changes as a means of cutting half a million AFDC recipients from the program during his first 4 years in office. And between 1980 and 1990, the median state AFDC benefits for families with no other income were approximately 40 percent lower in purchasing power than they were in 1970. Evidence shows that programs like AFDC which target nonworking, nonelderly adults do not receive the political support that programs covering low-income workers or the elderly generate.[32]

A second program associated with the War on Poverty is **food stamps**. Actually a food stamp program existed between 1939 and 1943. However, the current program was established in 1961. Under it, a poor family is eligible to receive food stamps to buy food, the dollar amount being based on family income. Spending for this program increased rapidly until 1981 when President Reagan eliminated 1 million recipients by tightening eligibility requirements through an administrative limit on allowable income and by cutting funding. The program was expanded again in 1985, 1987, and 1988, when some of the cuts were restored and the basic benefit levels were raised. Unlike AFDC, the food stamp program is fully financed by the federal government. In 1992 about 25.7 million people received food stamps (about 10 percent of the population), and federal spending on the program was over $20 billion.

The food stamp program is available nationwide, and everyone who qualifies is guaranteed benefits. In federal expenditures for benefits, the food stamp program ranks second among the means-tested programs, behind Medicaid. More than 82 percent of all food stamp benefits go to households with children.[33] The Food and Nutrition Service (FNS) is the largest element of the U.S. Department of Agriculture (USDA), which spends 41 percent of its budget (or $34 billion) on a

---

[31] See Paul E. Peterson and Mark C. Rom, *Welfare Magnets: A New Case for a National Standard* (Washington, DC: The Brookings Institution, 1990), p. 17. Between 1976 and 1980, 13 percent of the poor moved across state lines versus 11 percent of the nonpoor. Between 1981 and 1985, 15 percent of the poor moved across state lines versus 10 percent of the nonpoor. Between 1986 and 1987 5 percent of poor and 3 percent of nonpoor households moved to another state (data given by Peterson and Rom on p. 16 of their book).

[32] Robert Greenstein, "Relieving Poverty," *The Brookings Review*, vol. 9, no. 3 (Summer 1991), pp. 34–35.

[33] *Food and Nutrition*, vol. 21, no. 3–4 (March 1992), p. 5.

variety of food assistance programs, including food stamps, breakfast and lunch programs at elementary and high schools, and a supplemental food program for low-income mothers and their children.

To reduce fraud, FNS is encouraging states to pass laws against trafficking in food stamps. Another program seeks to replace paper food stamps with electronic "debit" cards. This would reduce the potential for food stamp fraud since individuals would no longer be able to barter the paper variety for money.

Since the late 1980s, over 30 states have received federal funds to build information systems to process applications for AFDC, Medicaid, food stamps, and child-support programs. Computer terminals linked to mainframe databases integrate the information for all programs. These systems can prompt checks or food stamps to be cut and mailed within 24 hours. Maryland and Texas have gone even further, by developing electronic benefits transfer (EBT) systems that use plastic identification cards to access benefits from two or more assistance programs with a single debit card. The accounts can be accessed through automated teller machines and in supermarkets to replace the exchange of food stamps at checkout counters.[34] These automated welfare programs have resulted in lower error rates, lower costs by eliminating the need for paper and postage, and a reduction of much of the paperwork for caseworkers, freeing them to spend more time finding jobs for recipients.

Criticisms of the War on Poverty

AFDC and food stamps are the two government programs that have been most prominent in the effort to fight poverty in this country. There has been widespread criticism of various aspects of these programs by both liberals and conservatives. But conservatives have been more critical of their fundamental nature. They often argue that these programs attack the **symptoms** of poverty in the short run, while leaving the **causes** of poverty undisturbed. Providing families with food stamps or AFDC improves their financial situation and makes their poverty more bearable, but does nothing to end their dependence on welfare. The poor are even given incentives **not** to increase their work efforts.

As conservatives claim, incentives for the rich and poor to strive to increase their productivity may be reduced by programs that transfer wealth from the rich to the poor. However, the major disincentive is not for the wealthy to work less, but for those just above the poverty level who do not qualify for benefits to stop working. Those with low earning capacities may have little incentive to improve their situation through work. Why should someone take a job earning $7500 per year in difficult working conditions where the stick is used for motivation, if he or she could be unemployed and receive almost the same income? It is particularly bothersome to people who earn around $12,000 a year and work 40 hours a week, but do not

---

[34] See Chuck Appleby, "The Welfare State of Confusion," *Information Week*, October 12, 1992, p. 40.

qualify for many welfare programs, to see someone who is unemployed receive two-thirds of their income.

But if the incentive to work is undermined, then total income is reduced, which means more people living in poverty. Consequently, conservatives are likely to suggest that the programs causing this undermining be reduced or eliminated, especially at the federal level. In their view the states are better situated to decide appropriate levels of funding for such programs, if indeed any government intervention is called for at all.

Both liberals and conservatives agree that it is preferable to attack the **causes** of poverty by, for example, providing opportunities to increase human capital through more support for education and training. This would help level the playing field between the affluent and the poor. However, conservatives tend to suggest that the responsibility for education should also be at the state and local levels.

Liberals contend that in many cases individuals who are poor have such personal limitations that no amount of training will permit them to earn a decent living. In such instances, direct maintenance programs may be the most practical form of aid. This may also be the case for many who need short-term help due to temporary economic conditions. Liberals also point out that disincentives to work could be alleviated by permitting welfare recipients to keep a larger percentage of their benefits as they move into the work force and start to earn a living. They are also inclined to argue that only the federal government can establish national welfare standards so that states do not compete to export their poor.

The Clinton Welfare Reform Proposals

Welfare programs have been widely criticized both by taxpayers and recipients. During the 1992 campaign, then candidate Bill Clinton seized on this unhappiness to move toward the center of the political spectrum on the issue and promised to "end welfare as we know it." He maintained that the welfare system is intended to provide a temporary cushion following a crisis such as a job loss or a divorce. Although approximately 70 percent of mothers first receiving benefits are off them within 2 years, however, only 37 percent stay off. Many return after losing another job, or when fathers stop making child support payments, or when other problems arise, frequently having to do with child care.

Clinton has proposed to change this pattern by placing a 2-year limit on benefits. He wants to increase training programs for those receiving AFDC. If a recipient was still on the rolls at the end of 2 years, he or she would be required to join a work program subsidized through tax credits that offered the minimum wage working for a private corporation, a nonprofit organization, or a government program. The training and work requirements would be aimed at discouraging additional pregnancies. Clinton's plan allows states to deny increased payments to recipients who have additional children while they are receiving AFDC payments. The average welfare family has, in fact, declined in size from four persons in 1969 to 1.9 persons in 1994. The President's plan would also attempt to collect child support payments from absent fathers.

The Republican party has traditionally used AFDC as an effective issue to label the Democratic party as being wasteful of taxpayer dollars and encouraging welfare dependency. By moving toward the center of the political spectrum, Clinton threatened to nullify the significance of that issue for the Republicans. So in an effort to prevent Clinton from seizing the initiative on welfare reform, some conservatives in the Republican party, notably William Bennett and Jack Kemp, have proposed that AFDC be eliminated. This, they argue, would force mothers on welfare to have fewer children and to seek help from their families or private charities. If those sources proved insufficient, the children could be placed for adoption or raised in orphanages. Supporters of this view contend it would be fairer to the children than the present system, which subjects them to environments where crime, drug abuse, and poverty abound. Others hear echoes of the Reverend Malthus in the proposal.

The Negative Income Tax

Since programs designed to relieve the **symptoms** of poverty by providing the resources necessary for survival have been criticized for their **disincentives** to work, various proposals have been put forward to overhaul welfare so that those disincentives are replaced by positive incentives to work.

The proposal that has received the most interest by public policy analysts is the **negative income tax (NIT)**, which is a tax system that would decrease welfare payments by some fraction of additional income earned. The term "negative income tax" is used because it resembles the regular income tax system, but works in reverse. It would permit people receiving government assistance to keep part of any money they earned from working rather than taking (taxing) it all away.

The proposal would have the government establish a minimum income level below which no one could fall. As shown in Table 7-7, for example, if the government established $7000 as the minimum for a family of four, then each family would receive at least $7000. The government would also establish a negative

TABLE 7-7
ILLUSTRATION OF A NEGATIVE INCOME TAX PLAN
This Example Has a Guaranteed Income of $7000 and a
Negative Tax Rate of 50 Percent

Income earned, $	Benefit payments, $	Total income, $
0	7,000	7,000
2,000	6,000	8,000
4,000	5,000	9,000
6,000	4,000	10,000
8,000	3,000	11,000
10,000	2,000	12,000
12,000	1,000	13,000
14,000	0	14,000

income tax rate (say 50 percent). If the family had no earned income, the government would provide the entire $7000. If the family earned $2000, the government payments would be reduced by $1000. At the 50 percent tax rate, the increase in total family income would be one-half of the increase in earnings.

Thus as family income increased, the total amount paid by the government would decline. However, there would always be an incentive for the breadwinner in the family to earn more since despite a reduction in government payments the total income received would continue to increase. The breakeven point (in this case $14,000) at which government benefits would fall to zero would be determined by the minimum-income guarantee level and the negative tax rate. In this example, the breakeven point is close to the poverty line determined for 1991. Note that a high tax rate reduces the incentive to work, but a lower tax rate (say of 25 percent, which is closer to what upper-income families pay) would raise the breakeven level to $28,000. Thus families with incomes as high as four times the guarantee level would receive payments.

This plan is designed to **replace** all other existing programs such as AFDC and food stamps, because combining those programs with the NIT would permit some recipients to receive higher incomes than others. Its supporters maintain it is an improvement over the current alternatives because it provides a minimum income for everyone while supplanting an assortment of existing programs with one policy that treats everyone equally. It would not vary from state to state. Nor would states have an incentive to compete to export their "welfare problems." It might also permit government funds to be transferred in a less "leaky bucket" since families would have an incentive to earn more, not less, and the cost of financing and administering several other programs would be closed down. Finally, those who worked would receive higher incomes than those who did not, an obvious incentive to work rather than not work.

Although NIT was supported by both Presidents Nixon and Carter, it never received sufficient Congressional support to be seriously considered.[35] Nonetheless, it promised to satisfy the needs for more economic efficiency and more equality at the same time.

CONCLUSION

1 The commitment to egalitarian ideals has declined in the United States in the last decade or so. That commitment has always accepted some inequality if it resulted from merit, different contributions, or choice, or if it benefited everyone.

---

[35] There have been four experiments supported by the federal government to explore the effects of NIT. The results of the experiments were not as positive as had been hoped. For example, there were modest reductions in work effort by NIT recipients, although several traded their work effort for an investment in education, which improved their human capital and their ability to earn a living later. Second, the cost was significantly higher than expected. The experiments suggest that a nationwide program to provide income at the poverty level would cost **at minimum** $20 billion dollars annually. See Alicia H. Munnell (ed.), *Lessons From the Income Maintenance Experiments* (Boston and Washington, DC: Federal Reserve Bank of Boston and The Brookings Institution, 1987), chap. 1.

Functionalist theory suggests that inequality in fact provides a positive incentive for individuals to produce more. The theory that the market system produces a fair distribution, however, must be qualified by the fact that some individuals and groups have more market power than others, whether because of inherited wealth, luck, choice, or other factors.

2 Inequality in the distribution in income has been increasing within the United States particularly within the last two decades. For many, the trend is cause for concern, especially when it results from conscious government policy. Poverty is the inability to buy the basic necessities of life. The poverty line is calculated by multiplying the costs of a minimally adequate diet by 3. In 1989 the poverty level was $6310 for an individual and $12,674 for a family of four. The number of Americans living below the poverty line has begun to increase in the last decade. The poor are not distributed evenly across age, gender, ethnic, or educational groups. Blacks, Hispanics, children, female heads of households, and the less educated are far more likely to be poor in America than other groups.

3 Most philosophical schools, including natural law, utilitarian, and social contract theories, suggest government has a responsibility to reduce inequality. Short-term programs designed to reduce the symptoms of poverty are often criticized because of the disincentives to work that they generate. Current programs are also criticized as being inefficient and inequitable. In the late 1980s Congress moved toward a program of workfare, which requires that people accept work in order to qualify for welfare. The negative income tax appears to address many of the criticisms of some welfare programs. However, the cost of implementing such a program appears to be prohibitive.

APPENDIX

MONTHLY AID TO FAMILIES WITH DEPENDENT CHILDREN BY STATE, FISCAL 1990*

State	Average number of recipients	Average number of children	Average Payment, $	
			Per family	Per person
Alabama	129,998	92,631	113.64	39.62
Alaska	20,234	13,191	646.57	244.90
Arizona	124,040	86,735	269.11	93.57
Arkansas	71,540	51,082	190.64	65.96
California	1,902,048	1,293,804	636.79	218.31
Colorado	102,157	68,768	321.24	111.20
Connecticut	120,086	81,324	567.67	205.86
Delaware	21,165	14,468	290.73	113.66
District of Columbia	48,872	34,403	378.40	143.50
Florida	369,907	264,152	261.83	95.43
Georgia	293,366	205,991	263.01	91.31
Hawaii	43,917	29,293	575.03	187.71
Idaho	16,577	11,302	264.45	97.93
Illinois	635,839	435,516	342.54	112.28
Indiana	153,709	104,768	263.44	92.43
Iowa	98,040	63,607	366.12	129.58

State	Average number of recipients	Average number of children	Average Payment, $	
			Per family	Per person
Kansas	77,046	52,373	340.08	113.88
Kentucky	175,421	117,309	225.17	85.21
Louisiana	281,501	199,001	167.36	55.81
Maine	50,009	35,254	422.68	150.12
Maryland	185,507	124,413	368.31	132.86
Massachusetts	263,371	167,992	558.28	200.99
Michigan	655,101	426,871	464.73	154.75
Minnesota	170,575	110,283	515.37	171.75
Mississippi	178,588	128,690	119.66	40.22
Missouri	210,772	139,414	273.15	91.93
Montana	28,963	186,735	342.37	114.95
Nebraska	42,636	29,218	335.64	115.15
Nevada	22,594	15,879	278.03	100.25
New Hampshire	16,329	10,688	428.23	164.20
New Jersey	309,036	212,827	352.30	121.99
New Mexico	61,445	42,585	236.00	81.87
New York	981,153	657,765	550.86	193.48
North Carolina	223,442	151,806	237.61	91.65
North Dakota	15,534	10,334	364.25	130.49
Ohio	632,283	414,381	322.64	115.26
Oklahoma	111,867	76,924	279.54	96.98
Oregon	89,016	59,892	369.76	135.99
Pennsylvania	520,683	345,192	374.22	127.70
Rhode Island	46,150	30,358	496.96	179.37
South Carolina	110,931	79,619	205.11	71.91
South Dakota	18,991	13,340	270.84	95.52
Tennessee	211,185	143,897	182.03	65.93
Texas	611,281	427,701	166.17	56.79
Utah	45,134	30,548	344.16	118.36
Vermont	21,934	13,661	519.41	183.36
Virginia	150,858	103,972	263.22	97.98
Washington	228,191	147,587	450.18	160.41
West Virginia	111,084	68,498	249.77	82.94
Wisconsin	237,430	158,030	463.86	155.04
Wyoming	14,135	9,462	304.71	113.84
U.S. total[†]	11,464,500	7,760,510	390.44	135.42

* Payments include AFDC-Basic, AFDC-Unemployed Parent, Title IV-A Payments under JOBS, Home Repair, and Payments to Indian Tribes.
† U.S. total includes Guam, Puerto Rico, and the Virgin Islands in averages.

Source: Family Support Administration Office of Family Assistance, U.S. Dept. of Health. Adapted from *World Almanac 1992 and Book of Facts* (New York: St. Martin's Press, 1992), p. 562.

QUESTIONS FOR DISCUSSION

1 Some people suggest that the government should levy an income tax of about 20 percent on all citizens with no allowable deductions. Would this be equitable? Why, or why not?

2 Describe how the welfare trap works to discourage recipients from working. How does an increase in benefits affect the working poor not receiving payments?

3 Discuss the "leaky bucket" analogy. Is it apt? How much leakage in income would you be willing to permit in transferring money from the middle- and upper-income individuals to aid the poor? Why do people differ in their responses to this question?

4 How much inequality of wealth is fair? Is there an optimal amount of inequality? How could it be determined?

5 How can public policy fight poverty in ways that do the least to reduce incentives for everyone?

KEY CONCEPTS

Absolute poverty	Natural law
AFDC	Negative income tax
Efficiency	Relative poverty
Equality	Social contract
Equity	Utilitarianism
Functionalist theory	Wealth
Income	Workfare
Lorenz curve	

SUGGESTED READINGS

McKinley Blackburn, "What Can Explain the Increase in Earnings Inequality Among Males?" *Industrial Relations*, vol. 29, no. 3 (Fall 1990), pp. 441–456.

Barry Bluestone and Bennett Harrison, *The Deindustrialization of America* (New York: Basic Books, 1982).

Gary Burtless (ed.), *A Future of Lousy Jobs*? (Washington, DC: The Brookings Institution, 1990.

Robert B. Carson, *Microeconomic Issues Today: Alternative Approaches,* 5th ed. (New York: St. Martin's Press, 1991).

George Gilder, *Wealth and Poverty* (New York: Basic Books, 1981).

Morley Gunderson, "Male-Female Wage Differentials and Policy Responses," *Journal of Economic Literature*, vol. 27, no. 1 (March 1989), pp. 46–72.

Bennett Harrison and Barry Bluestone, *The Great U-Turn: Corporate Restructuring and the Polarizing of America* (New York: Basic Books, 1988).

Robert Lekachman, *Greed Is Not Enough: Reaganomics* (New York: Pantheon Press, 1982).

Frank Levy, *Dollars and Dreams: The Changing American Income Distribution* (New York: Russell Sage Foundation, 1987).

U.S. Bureau of the Census, "Money Income and Poverty Status in the United States: 1988," *Current Population Reports* (Series P-60) (October 1989).

8

CRIME: THE POLICY QUAGMIRE

In 1992, the FBI reported nearly 14.5 million criminal offenses. Crime has risen steadily throughout the United States despite efforts to curb it. As citizens read daily newspaper accounts of car theft, muggings, child abuse, robberies, murders, drug sales, and vandalism, they clamor for public policies to thwart this rising "crime wave." Ironically, while everyone agrees that there is a serious problem, few have much perspective on it. Most public reaction to crime reflects anecdotal experience springing from fear, not reasoned thinking. In this chapter we explore the crime problem by asking **how much crime is out there, what are its causes, and how can policies be created that prevent crime, punish criminals, and protect the innocent from becoming victims.**

HOW MUCH CRIME?

FBI director J. Edgar Hoover conceived of the "Ten Most Wanted" list of criminals in the 1930s as a way to build public awareness about the extent of crime. Now some 50 years later, this list of 10 serves as a weak harbinger of the magnitude of crime. The FBI also continues to publish an annual report on crime entitled the *Uniform Crime Report* (UCR).[1] This statistical summary, compiled from data supplied by state and local agencies, presents a detailed breakdown of criminal activity in the United States. The most commonly cited UCR statistic is the **crime index**, a highly aggregated measure of the volume and rate of reported crime.[2] Table 8-1

---

[1] Federal Bureau of Investigation, *Crime in the United States 1992* (Washington, DC: U.S. Government Printing Office, 1993).
[2] The crime index includes murder, nonnegligent manslaughter, forcible rape, robbery, aggravated assault, burglary, larceny-theft, motor vehicle theft, and arson.

TABLE 8-1
INDEX OF CRIME, UNITED STATES, 1973–1992, PER 100,000 INHABITANTS

Year	Crime Index total[1]	Violent crime[2]	Property crime[2]	Murder and non-negligent manslaughter	Forcible rape	Robbery	Aggra-vated assault	Burglary	Larceny-theft	Motor vehicle theft	Arson[3]
1973	4154.4	417.4	3737.0	9.4	24.5	183.1	200.5	1222.5	2071.9	442.6	
1974	4850.4	461.1	4389.3	9.8	26.2	209.3	215.8	1437.7	2489.5	462.2	
1975	5298.5	487.8	4810.7	9.6	26.3	220.8	231.1	1532.1	2804.8	473.7	
1976	5287.3	467.8	4819.5	8.8	26.6	199.3	233.2	1448.2	2921.3	450.0	
1977	5077.6	475.9	4601.7	8.8	29.4	190.7	247.0	1419.8	2729.9	451.9	
1978	5140.3	497.8	4642.5	9.0	31.0	195.8	262.1	1434.6	2747.4	460.5	
1979	5565.5	548.9	5016.6	9.7	34.7	218.4	286.0	1511.9	2999.1	505.6	
1980	5950.0	596.6	5353.3	10.2	36.8	251.1	298.5	1684.1	3167.0	502.2	
1981	5858.2	594.3	5263.9	9.8	36.0	258.7	289.7	1649.5	3139.7	474.7	
1982	5603.6	571.1	5032.5	9.1	34.0	238.9	289.2	1488.8	3084.8	458.8	
1983	5175.0	537.7	4637.4	8.3	33.7	216.5	279.2	1337.7	2868.9	430.8	
1984	5031.3	539.2	4492.1	7.9	35.7	205.4	290.2	1263.7	2791.3	437.1	
1985	5207.1	556.6	4650.5	7.9	37.1	208.5	302.9	1287.3	2901.2	462.0	
1986	5480.4	617.7	4862.6	8.6	37.9	225.1	346.1	1344.6	3010.3	507.8	
1987	5550.0	609.7	4940.3	8.3	37.4	212.7	351.3	1329.6	3081.3	529.4	
1988	5664.2	637.2	5027.1	8.4	37.6	220.9	370.2	1309.2	3134.9	582.9	
1989	5741.0	663.1	5077.9	8.7	38.1	233.0	383.4	1276.3	3171.3	630.4	
1990	5820.3	731.8	5088.5	9.4	41.2	257.0	424.1	1235.9	3194.8	657.8	
1991	5897.8	758.1	5139.7	9.8	42.3	272.7	433.3	1252.0	3228.8	659.0	
1992	5660.2	757.5	4902.7	9.3	42.8	263.6	441.8	1168.2	3103.0	631.5	

Percent change: rate per 100,000 inhabitants:

1992/1991	−4.0	−.1	−4.6	−5.1	+1.2	−3.3	+2.0	−6.7	−3.9	−4.2	
1992/1988	−.1	+18.9	−2.5	+10.7	+13.8	+19.3	+19.3	−10.8	−1.0	+8.3	
1992/1983	+9.4	+40.9	+5.7	+12.0	+27.0	+21.8	+58.2	−12.7	+8.2	+46.6	

[1] Because of rounding, the offenses may not add to totals.
[2] Violent crimes are offenses of murder, forcible rape, robbery, and aggravated assault. Property crimes are offenses of burglary, larceny-theft, and motor vehicle theft. Data are not included for the property crime of arson. All rates were calculated on the offenses before rounding.
[3] Although arson data are included in the trend and clearance tables, sufficient data are not available to estimate totals for this offense.
Source: Federal Bureau of Investigation, Uniform Crime Reports for the United States, 1992 (Washington, DC: U.S. Government Printing Office, 1993), Table 1.

shows a data trend which demonstrates the rise in the crime index over the 20 years from 1973 to 1992. Other UCR data give a yearly snapshot of the level of criminal activity. UCR data for 1992 (the latest available) tell us that geographically the largest volume of crime occurred in the South (38 percent of the total) followed by the West, the Midwest, and Northeast.[3] Table 8-2 shows this regional distribution more accurately by breaking out the incidence of crime according to population distribution. All regions of the country have experienced rising crime rates over the years, despite occasional modest declines. Not surprisingly most offenses occur during the heat of August while the least occur in February.

Thirteen percent of reported crime is violent in nature. Violent crime includes murder, nonnegligent manslaughter, forcible rape, robbery, and aggravated assault. All violent crimes involve force or the threat of force. Firearms were used in 31 percent of assaults, robberies and murders; knives in 15 percent. The UCR reports that ". . . the proportion of violent crimes committed with firearms has increased in recent years."[4]

Murder nationwide reached an all time high in 1991, with 24,703 murders reported.[5] The volume was down by 4 percent in 1992, which translates to a rate of nine murders for every 100,000 people. This represents a 12 percent rise nationally since 1983. Most murder victims, like offenders, were male (78 percent) between 20 and 34 years old (47 percent). Seven out of 10 murders involved the use of firearms. Most murder victims knew or were related to their assailants. Nearly one-third of the murders resulted from arguments. Most murders occurred in large cities. Washington, DC, the nation's capital, has also become its murder capital with 443 murders recorded for the year 1992.[6]

The number of rapes was up 2 percent from 1991 and up 15 percent from 1988. In 1992 eighty-four out of every 100,000 women were raped. **Over one-third of violent crimes were robberies**. The 1992 UCR reported that 565 million dollars were lost to robberies. Table 8-3 gives a percentage breakdown of data on robbery for that year.

Nonviolent, property crime, which includes larceny theft, burglary, and motor vehicle theft, equaled 12.5 million reported offenses in 1992. The total dollar loss of property was estimated at about $15.2 billion, with the average loss per offense being about $1,217.00. Thirteen percent was motor vehicle theft; a little over one-third of stolen cars are recovered (38 percent).

As part of these UCR summary statistics, the FBI also reports "**clearance rates**." These are offenses cleared by arrest or "other exceptional means."[7] The 1992 clearance rate was 21 percent or about 3 million arrests. Clearance rates have remained stable over the past 10 years, though there were 13 percent more arrests in 1987

---

[3] It is important to note that the South consists of the largest number of states and includes populous ones like Maryland, Virginia, Florida, and Texas, along with the District of Columbia. This may explain why the crime index there is higher than in other regions.

[4] *UCR, 1992*, p. 8.

[5] *UCR, 1992*, p. 11.

[6] *UCR, 1992*, p. 117.

[7] Examples of "exceptional means" include death of the offender or denial of extradition.

TABLE 8-2
INDEX OF CRIME, REGIONAL OFFENSE AND POPULATION DISTRIBUTION, 1992

Region	Population	Crime Index total[3]	Violent crime[1]	Property crime[1]	Murder and nonnegligent manslaughter	Forcible rape	Robbery	Aggravated assault	Burglary	Larceny-theft	Motor vehicle theft	Arson[2]
United States total[3]	100.0	100.0	100.0	100.0	100.0	100.0	100.0	100.0	100.0	100.0	100.0	
Northeastern states	20.0	17.1	19.4	16.8	16.9	13.8	25.5	16.2	16.0	15.8	23.1	
Midwestern states	23.8	20.9	19.1	21.2	19.5	25.3	18.7	18.7	19.6	22.5	18.0	
Southern states	34.6	37.6	36.9	37.6	41.1	37.3	31.6	40.0	40.8	37.7	31.6	
Western states	21.6	24.4	24.6	24.3	22.5	23.6	24.2	25.1	23.5	24.0	27.3	

[1] Violent crimes are offenses of murder, forcible rape, robbery, and aggravated assault. Property crimes are offenses of burglary, larceny-theft, and motor vehicle theft. Data are not included for the property crime of arson.
[2] Although arson data are included in the trend and clearance tables, sufficient data are not available to estimate totals for this offense.
[3] Because of rounding, percentages may not add to totals.
Source: UCR, 1992, Table 3.

TABLE 8-3
ROBBERY, PERCENT DISTRIBUTION, 1992

	United States total	North- eastern states	Midwestern states	Southern states	Western states
Total[1]	100.0	100.0	100.0	100.0	100.0
Street/highway	55.6	62.7	60.0	50.4	51.8
Commercial house	11.9	10.3	10.1	12.0	14.5
Gas or service station	2.5	2.1	3.1	2.5	2.6
Convenience store	5.3	2.4	3.2	8.6	5.6
Residence	10.1	10.3	9.4	12.0	7.9
Bank	1.7	1.0	1.1	1.3	3.2
Miscellaneous	13.1	11.4	13.2	13.3	14.4

[1] Because of rounding, percentages may not add to totals.
Source: UCR, 1992, p. 27.

HOW ACCURATE ARE THE NUMBERS?

Conventional wisdom says, "No data are better than bad data." Just how accurate are crime statistics? The most commonly reported numbers are those collected by the FBI in its *Uniform Crime Report* (UCR) and the Census Bureau in its *National Crime Victimization Survey* (NCV). Both data collections are made annually; both report on similar crimes, though the NCV surveys do not include arson and homicide. Both collections also suffer from errors of measurement and bias, and both **underreport** crime.

The UCR data are based on police reports. Underreporting is largely due to unwillingness on the part of citizens to call the police. Not surprisingly, much petty theft (like someone stealing your wallet) goes unreported. Most people wager the police cannot do much about the loss, so why bother. A second source of inaccuracy comes from the reporting methods used. Some police departments do a better job reporting crime than others. Perhaps their collection techniques are better. Sometimes it is in a department's best interest to report crime; it reflects a job well done. It might even help the department's budget allocation. On the other hand, sometimes a police department would rather not report as much crime. It raises questions about the competence of the police force. If the FBI discovers intentional underreporting, it refuses to publish the statistics of the offending agency until the discrepancies are corrected. Further, when the UCR data are collected the police report all crimes committed in a given locality. Consequently, big cities, like New York, which experience lots of commuters and visitors report high crime rates.

Police reports also emphasize certain types of crimes and not others. Selling drugs, for example, is not included. And if several crimes are committed by a criminal at once, only the most serious is counted.

Victimization studies are equally flawed. The Bureau of the Census randomly selects households for inclusion in the study. In 1991, about 83,000 people age 12 or older participated in the NCV survey. **NCV too underreports crime**, but for different reasons. NCV studies only count personal and household crimes, not crimes against business. Consequently, they are not as sensitive to crime rates overall, nor are the rates they report

than in 1990. Typically, property crimes represent the lowest clearance rates. The violent crime clearance rate was 45 percent in 1992.

Juvenile crime (committed by young people 10 to 17 years old) registered its highest rate in 1991 (latest available data). Out of each 100,000 juveniles, 430 were involved in criminal activity. Black juvenile criminal activity was nearly five times that of white juvenile criminal activity, though crime among white juveniles rose 44 percent from 1980.

Crime data show increases across all categories over time. The disturbance and cost to American society are tremendous. Looking at these data, many people observe that, despite the best efforts of the law enforcement community, along with significant public expenditures, no success in the "war on crime" has been realized. Analysts nevertheless claim that we have made progress. Data alone fail to give the full picture. To fully understand what has been accomplished in fighting crime, we

---

as volatile, as UCR statistics. On the other hand, NCV studies report up to three times the number of crime victims that police reports do. It makes sense that if five people are robbed at gunpoint, the victim study presents a different tally than the police report.

Other factors also skew the data collected in each report. Victims are likely to report some kinds of crime to the police and others, like rape, to interviewers. Women are more likely to report to interviewers that they have been robbed than that they were assaulted (possibly by a relative). Over time people also forget or grow confused about when a crime occurred, so human error tends to creep into NCV data since the information is collected longer after the crime than most police reports. Further NCV interviews include data from the previous year. All this makes data from the two sources difficult to compare. Moreover, **any comparison should keep in mind that UCR data reports perpetrators while NCV data reports victims**.

So, are no data better than bad data? It depends. Certainly if crime statistics are used for political convenience, the public is not well served. But if policy makers use the data with an awareness of their inaccuracies and a sense of appropriateness to the crime issue, then they serve a valuable purpose.

Generally, it is wise to consider these aggregated data as providing a good sense of **long-term trends**. The data from year to year probably do not indicate much. Locality comparisons are suspect too. Minor differences should be disregarded. **Large differences** probably do indicate something. These widely cited studies give researchers some sense of the amount of crime occurring throughout the country. As noted by James Q. Wilson, they do not specify the **prevalence** of crime or the **incidence** of crime. In other words, they do not indicate what proportion of a given population consists of criminals or the number of crimes committed per year by the average criminal, indicators that would give a more valid measure of crime in the United States. Wilson warns that the best statements about crime are those supported by as many different measures as possible.

Sources: James Q. Wilson (ed.), *Crime and Public Policy* (San Francisco: ICS Press, 1983); U.S. Department of Justice, *Criminal Victimization in the United States, 1992* (Rockville, MD: Bureau of Justice Statistics, March 1994), p. 9.

need to take a more careful look at the causes of crime and the criminal justice system.

CRIME: A DEFINITION

When we speak of the crime problem, what do we mean? How is crime defined? In their book *Crime and Human Nature*, Harvard University scholars James Q. Wilson and Richard J. Herrnstein explore the meaning of crime.[8] Wilson and Herrnstein tell us that crime is not easily defined or measured. Yet it is very common. In fact, the authors explain, "Using interviews and questionnaires, scholars have discovered that the majority of all young males have broken the law at least once by a relatively early age."[9]

As a concept, crime is vague and hard to categorize. Categories of crime like property crime and crimes against persons, white collar crime, victimless crime, or public corruption fall short because they are not mutually exclusive. Moreover crimes have different social costs. For example, most people fear property loss from street crime yet the financial loss from white collar crime is far greater.[10]

Obviously, some crimes are more abhorrent and more destructive of the social fabric than others. Wilson and Herrnstein argue, then, that **"a crime is any act committed in violation of the law that prohibits it and authorizes punishment for its commission."**[11] A serious crime is aggressive, violent behavior categorized as murder, rape, assault, and theft.

One way to gain an understanding about crime is to look at the **causes of criminal behavior**. This approach focuses attention on the criminal and his or her relationship to the rest of society. A second approach explores the processes and characteristics of the **criminal justice system** established to deal with crime. Here one asks how effectively the system protects the innocent and punishes offenders. This perspective concentrates largely on the legal system. When looking at the criminal justice system, one also asks how well it operates in reducing the level of crime. Specifically, one wonders if our current decentralized (even if highly federalized) system of criminal justice can work constructively to lower the level of crime.

CAUSES OF CRIME: WHAT DO WE KNOW?

Judging from the amount of crime reported, many observers feel very little is known about causes of criminal behavior. Wilson and Herrnstein argue overall that "crime is as broad a category as disease, and perhaps as useless. To explain why one person has ever committed a crime and another has not may be as pointless as

---

[8] James Q. Wilson and Richard J. Herrnstein, *Crime and Human Nature* (New York: Simon & Schuster, 1986).

[9] Wilson and Herrnstein, *Crime and Human Nature*, p. 21.

[10] An article in the *St. Petersburg Times*, November 1, 1993, p. 1A, entitled "Not All Fruit Juice Is Pure as Label Says," describes the widespread consumer fraud of watering down fruit juice. The article estimates loss to consumers at $1.2 billion a year.

[11] Wilson and Herrnstein, *Crime and Human Nature*, p. 22.

explaining why one person has ever gotten sick and another has not."[12] But, in fact, scholars who study the determinants of criminal behavior know quite a bit about its etiology or origin. This scholarly endeavor forms the field of criminology.

Criminologists have proposed many scientific, empirically testable theories of criminal behavior. George B. Vold and Thomas B. Bernard in their book *Theoretical Criminology* assign criminologists as social scientists to one of three essentially different ways of thinking about crime.[13] They describe these three frames of reference as follows:

> Two of the frames of reference focus on the behavior of criminals. The first argues that behavior is freely chosen, while the second argues that it is caused by forces beyond the control of the individual. The third frame of reference views crime primarily as a function of the way criminal law is written and enforced.[14]

Given these different points of departure, it is no wonder there is a great deal of scholarly disagreement among criminologists over the causes of crime. Those who see a life of **crime as one freely chosen** describe people as rational. A criminal act is considered like any other act—as a rational purposeful choice whose aim is to promote one's best self-interest, much as choice is described by public choice theory. This "classical" view is highly legalistic and emphasizes ways society can maximize the cost and minimize the benefits of criminal behavior.

The second perspective, **criminal behavior as caused**, is deterministic. In other words, it proposes that people behave as they have been determined to behave. This "positivist" school of criminal behavior looks for causes in biology, psychology, and social settings. Some of the criminologists holding this view question the efficacy of punishment in dealing with criminal behavior. This perspective has dominated the field of criminology.

The last perspective, the **behavior of criminal law**, emerged in the 1960s when, as Vold and Bernard explain, ". . . some criminologists [began] to address a very different question: why some individuals and behaviors are officially defined as criminal and others not."[15] These scholars ask why, given a place and time, certain people and behaviors are defined as criminal.

Thus, the field of criminology offers compelling theoretical arguments and divergent explanations. Some criminologists argue crime relates to intelligence, hyperactivity, or chromosomal characteristics. Others assert that poverty and economic inequality lead people to criminal behavior.

Sociologist Emile Durkheim (1858–1917) presented an analysis of the process of social change in which he argued that in the process of modernization societies became highly differentiated. A consequence of differentiation was "anomie" or a breakdown in social norms and rules. Crime is one normal consequence of anomic

---

[12] Wilson and Herrnstein, *Crime and Human Nature*, p. 21.

[13] George B. Vold and Thomas J. Bernard, *Theoretical Criminology* (New York: Oxford University Press, 1986).

[14] Vold and Bernard, *Theoretical Criminology*, p. 9.

[15] Vold and Bernard, *Theoretical Criminology*, p. 13.

society. It is a price society pays for progress. Many criminologists and sociologists in the tradition of Durkheim look to society as a whole to explain criminal behavior.

More recent explanations, like strain theory, offer the intuitive appeal of a causal relationship between social inequality, lack of economic opportunity, and crime.[16] Some see crime as learned behavior. Others offer a Marxist interpretation. All theories of criminal behavior have been extensively criticized. They are afflicted with a large number of theoretical and empirical problems and offer limited guidance to the policy-making community.

In the introductory chapter to their book on crime, Wilson and Herrnstein summarize the facts we do know. They write:

> Predatory street crimes are most commonly committed by young males. Violent crimes are more common in big cities than in small ones. High rates of criminality tend to run in families. The persons who frequently commit the most serious crimes typically begin their criminal careers at a quite young age. Persons who turn out to be criminals usually do not do very well in school. Young men who drive recklessly and have many accidents tend to be similar to those who commit crimes. Programs designed to rehabilitate high-rate offenders have not been shown to have much success, and those programs that do manage to reduce criminality among certain kinds of offenders often increase it among others.[17]

For the policy maker, individual indicators of crime like age, gender, or intelligence do not translate easily into practical policy. Even policies emphasizing the deterrence of **criminogenic factors** like drugs, alcohol, and guns are hotly debated (see later sections of this chapter).[18] As a result, policy attention shifts to an area more easily identified and controlled, the criminal justice system. Here, consideration is given to the relative costs of legal protection and punishment and the efficient delivery of criminal justice services.

CHARACTERISTICS OF THE CRIMINAL JUSTICE SYSTEM

There is no single criminal justice system. What exists is a conglomeration of legal avenues. Mapped out, these legal avenues look more like a very poorly designed interstate road system and far less like a carefully constructed legal structure.

The American criminal justice system is **decentralized**. It consists of local, state, and federal jurisdictions. Again, this reflects the American historical experience. When drafting the Constitution, the Founding Fathers left most criminal law to the states. They wanted criminal law to reflect community standards and enforcement to be localized.

---

[16] For an excellent discussion of strain theories see Vold and Bernard, *Theoretical Criminology*, pp. 185–204.

[17] Wilson and Herrnstein, *Crime and Human Nature*, p. 19.

[18] Mark H. Moore, "Controlling Criminogenic Commodities: Drugs, Guns and Alcohol," in James Q. Wilson (ed.), *Crime and Public Policy* (San Francisco: Institute for Contemporary Problems, 1983), pp. 125–143.

The Courts

Different state and local criminal jurisdictions follow somewhat similar organizational patterns, although they often use different names to describe similar functions. The design and size of jurisdictions vary. To fully understand all the systems, each jurisdiction would need a separate look. Nevertheless they all share **basic similarities in organization and process**. Generally, at the bottom of each state system are courts of **limited** or special jurisdiction. They hear civil cases and criminal misdemeanors.[19] The next level of courts have **general jurisdiction**. Here **the state prosecutes individuals accused of serious crimes**—felonies and certain types of important civil cases. **The appeals courts** review and rule on the legality of decisions made by the lower courts. State supreme courts are the top appellate courts within these judicial systems.

The organization of the federal court system is simpler. It is divided into 97 federal district courts and 10 courts of appeal. Again, cases originate in federal district court and move upward in the appeals process to the U.S. Supreme Court. The Supreme Court hears only those cases with far-reaching policy implications.

Many people take part in the administration of justice. Key participants include police officers, prosecutors, public defenders, judges, wardens, psychiatrists, and parole officers. Often they have competing goals. Some seek to protect citizens' rights under the law, others see that punishment is effectively carried out. **Ultimately there is always a struggle between speed and due process of law, between protection and punishment**.

Our criminal justice system seeks to **investigate and arrest, prosecute, determine guilt or innocence, and punish and/or rehabilitate**. The process from arrest to sentencing has changed little from colonial times. A crime is investigated and an arrest made by the police. The prosecutor seeks an indictment and an arraignment follows. A trial consists of the admission of evidence and questioning of witnesses till a final verdict is reached. If guilt is determined, a judge or jury establishes the appropriate sentencing. From there the penal system takes over.

Understand too that most criminal cases never follow this process; rather a **plea bargain** is forged. Here a defendant pleads guilty to a certain charge in exchange for the court dropping more serious charges or the promise of a lighter sentence. In the United States, if a defendant pleads guilty, there is no trial. By reducing court loads and avoiding long and costly trials, plea bargaining expedites the judicial process. Critics argue that the plea bargain works against those who insist on the Constitutional right to trial by jury. But trials too can work against defendants. As noted by one author, "If defendants exercise this right, they risk a harsher sentence."[20]

---

[19] In a civil case individuals bring action against one another hoping to recover financial damages. A misdemeanor is a crime less serious than a felony punishable by less than a year of jail.

[20] Marianne LeVert, *Crime in America* (New York: Facts of File, 1991), p. 116.

The Role of the Police

Because the police are the most visible part of the criminal justice system, much attention focuses on their effectiveness. Writes one author: The police represent ". . . that 'thin blue line' between order and anarchy."[21]

The United States has no national police force, and state and local police agencies operate autonomously. Local autonomy has its roots in America's historic opposition to any type of standing army. Today the FBI catalogs 13,032 police agencies or 2.3 law enforcement officers per 1000 inhabitants.[22]

The chief function of the police is keeping the peace, not enforcing the law. Police officers share a subculture not unlike the military subculture. Police departments are organized to follow a chain of command, and regulations and discipline govern police behavior. As peacekeepers, the police use patrolling techniques to protect public safety and enforce the law.

Many argue that the police have been restricted in their ability to exercise their **investigative and arrest powers**. These powers to stop, question, detain, use force, and to search have been constrained by Supreme Court decisions. Much public policy debate about the criminal justice system centers on legal decisions critics claim have tied the hands of law enforcement agencies.

During the tenure of Supreme Court Chief Justice Earl Warren (1953–1969), a revolution in **procedural rights** occurred. Because the rights of the accused are the same as the rights of the innocent, Constitutional protections against unjustified searches, admission of hearsay as evidence, and inadequate legal defense apply. Since the 1960s, the rights of the accused have been expanded. This expansion may have stopped with the appointment of more conservative justices to the Supreme Court during the Reagan-Bush years.

The Exclusionary Rule   One such expansion involved the exclusionary rule, which prohibits illegally obtained evidence from being introduced in a court of law. Despite the arguments by critics that the rule protects only the guilty, the Supreme Court fully extended the principle to the state justice systems in *Mapp v. Ohio* (1961).[23] *Mapp* produced immediate reactions from enraged police departments throughout the country, which felt it seriously diminished their legal investigative powers. Conservatives feared that criminals would now be able to walk away due to mere legal technicalities.

The exclusionary rule was eventually set back by the "good faith" exception enunciated in *U.S. v. Leon* (1984). Here the Supreme Court ruled that, though a search was determined to be technically illegal, if the police acted in good faith, the evidence obtained could be introduced in court.

---

[21] James A. Inciardi, *Criminal Justice*, 3rd ed. (New York: Harcourt Brace Jovanovich, 1990), p. 168.

[22] *UCR, 1992*, p. 289.

[23] In 1957, Cleveland police officers sought entrance to the home of Mrs. Dollree Mapp, in search of a man suspected of an earlier bombing and of gambling paraphernalia. The police forced their way into Mrs. Mapp's home, forcibly arrested her, and conducted what was later established to be an illegal search. The Supreme Court ruled that evidence seized from Mrs. Mapp's home was illegally obtained and therefore not admissible in any courtroom in the country.

Custodial Interrogation   The Supreme Court extended the right to counsel at state expense to all felony cases with *Gideon v. Wainwright* (1963). Shortly afterward the Court moved even further to protect defendants by addressing police conduct during arrest and interrogation in *Escobedo v. Illinois* (1964), when it decided suspects have the right to counsel back to the point of arrest. And two years later, in *Miranda v. Arizona* (1966), it required police to inform every suspect of his or her Constitutional rights upon arrest. These cases and others represented the belief that convictions often resulted from confessions obtained through inappropriate interrogations by the police—in other words, from defendants who were unaware of their Constitutional rights in regard to criminal matters. Since most convictions result from confessions, once again bitter reactions followed. New York City's police commissioner argued that "if suspects are told of their rights they will not confess."[24]

Many argue the *Miranda* decision has reduced the effectiveness of confessions as a crime-fighting tool and symbolizes an obsessive concern for the rights of the accused. However, the original strength of the *Miranda* rule has been diluted through decisions reached in cases beginning with the 1970 Burger Court.[25] Chief Justice Warren Burger, a Nixon appointee, espoused a "law and order" position. More recently, concern with custodial rights has centered on the use of plea bargaining, as discussed earlier. Today the number of defendants deciding to "cop a plea" far exceeds those opting for jury trials. Some critics maintain the practice subverts justice by violating the Constitutional protection against self-incrimination and the guarantee of a fair jury trial. But its widespread use also lessens pressure on the criminal justice system.

Often manipulated, blamed, or even hated, police departments are caught in the cross-fire of criminal justice policy debates. The police find it difficult to balance the demands for more aggressive anticrime measures, which require more expenditures and greater intrusiveness on people's lives, with demands that they adhere to Constitutional protections ensuring proper investigative and arrest procedures. Increasingly the police are forced to use **discretion**, or selective enforcement of the law, in doing their job.

Prisons: Perspectives on Punishment and Correction

By the 1960s not only had the orientation of the courts changed, but so had public attitudes about crime. The decade was in many ways a turning point in criminal justice policy. Citizens had come to fear crime as never before, in part due to increasing street crime, drug use, and civil rights protests. Consequently President Lyndon Johnson declared a "war on crime" and established a Presidential commission to

[24] Robert F. Cushman, *Cases in Constitutional Law* (Englewood Cliffs, NJ: Prentice-Hall, 1979), p. 400.

[25] For example, in 1975 the Supreme Court ruled that, even if a suspect asserts the right to remain silent during interrogation, the police can commence questioning him or her about **another** crime (*Michigan v. Mosley*). Beginning in the 1980s, a series of cases were heard which dealt with issues of public safety. In *Berkemer v. McCarthy* (1984) the Court held that roadside questioning of suspected drunken drivers does not require *Miranda* warnings.

study the psychology, sociology, and appropriate policy responses to crime in America. Commission recommendations led to passage of the Omnibus Crime Control and Safe Streets Act in 1968. This act was viewed by some as a way to offset criticism that the country had "gone soft" on crime.

The emphasis on "law and order" continued through the 1970s. President Richard Nixon supported increased funding to local governments via the Law Enforcement Assistance Administration to conduct research into and carry on programs directed at crime abatement.[26] By the 1980s, both President Reagan and President Bush fought hard for strict law enforcement policies along with protection for victims' rights and stricter drug laws. And the emphasis has not been just at the federal level. A recent study reports:

> Criminal justice is the fastest growing area of state and local spending. In constant dollars, expenditures grew 232% between 1970 and 1990. In comparison, public expenditures on hospitals and health care increased 71%; public welfare, 79%; and education, 32%.[27]

Per capita U.S. prison population is also the highest in the world. See Table 8-4.

Despite recent trends, no explicit philosophy serves as an underlying rationale for American criminal justice policy. Traditionally such policy has been based on one of four competing philosophical attitudes about punishment—**retribution, deterrence, incapacitation, or rehabilitation**—the emphasis on which particular attitude reigns at any given time depending on shifting national values, as described above, and growing or waning fears about crime.

---

[26] The Law Enforcement Assistance Administration (LEAA), now defunct, grew out of the earlier Office of Law Enforcement Assistance set up within the Department of Justice. The LEAA was set up to financially assist local government efforts to fight crime.

[27] U.S. Advisory Commission on Intergovernmental Relations, *Guide to the Criminal Justice System for General Government Elected Officials* (Washington, DC: U.S. Government Printing Office, 1993), p. 11.

TABLE 8-4
PRISON POPULATIONS, 1989: INTERNATIONAL COMPARISONS

Country	Prisoners per 100,000 population
United States	426
South Africa	333
Soviet Union	268
•	•
•	•
•	•
United Kingdom	97
France	81
Denmark	68
Japan	45

Source: Marc Mauer, *Americans behind Bars: A Comparison of International Rates of Incarceration* (Washington, DC: The Sentencing Project, 1991).

Retribution is the age-old philosophy of "an eye for an eye." Now often referred to as a policy of "just deserts," it emphasizes punitive sanctions: Criminals must pay their debts to society through punishment which "fits the crime."

Somewhat related is the philosophy of incapacitation. This postulates that, through restraint or incapacitation, criminals are **removed from society so that they can no longer endanger others**. Incapacitation emphasizes citizen protection and crime prevention.

Rehabilitation seeks to reintegrate criminals into society through corrections programs and services. More humanitarian in its outlook, this philosophy looks to social causes to explain crime. As noted earlier, humanistic philosophy has dominated twentieth century thinking and policy making about crime.

In recent years deterrence philosophy has come to the fore. Here, some argue that **the effective use of sentencing will function as an example to deter would-be offenders (general deterrence) or to convince criminals not to commit another crime (specific deterrence)**.

Often the appeal of a particular philosophy is tied to our assumptions about human nature. In an effort to sort through competing policy approaches, David Gordon has laid out the logical flow of conventional criminal justice policy.[28] He notes that liberal and conservative philosophies about crime correspond to liberal and conservative positions on other social issues. Both liberals and conservatives share the assumption that criminal behavior is irrational. To a conservative, the problem and the solution are for the most part straightforward. Social order as reflected in the law is rational. Because criminal behavior is irrational, it must be met with a response that protects public safety. Policies to combat crime must emphasize forces which deter crime. This translates into more police, more equipment, and more prisons.

On the other hand, liberals, although they agree that criminal behavior is irrational, also see imperfections in the social order. And because the system is imperfect, they note, some people are more likely to be driven toward a life of crime. As Gordon states this point of view: "Criminality should be regarded as irrationality, but we should nonetheless avoid *blaming* criminals for their irrational acts."[29] Liberals postulate relationships between poverty or racism and crime. Consequently, their answer to crime is found in more research, more technology, more professional help for criminals. Liberals argue that societies will never rid themselves of crime till the root causes are discovered and eliminated.

The conservative emphasis upon order and protection leads to policies promoting incapacitation and deterrence. The liberal emphasis on justice and equality has a stronger connection to rehabilitative techniques.

This dichotomy prevailed until a more recent economic analysis of crime began to question traditional liberal and conservative assumptions.[30] These scholars chal-

---

[28] David M. Gordon, "Capitalism, Class and Crime in America," in Ralph Andreano and John J. Siegfried, *The Economics of Crime* (New York: John Wiley and Sons, 1980).

[29] Gordon, "Capitalism, Class and Crime in America," p. 98.

[30] See in particular the work of, Gary S. Becker, "Crime and Punishment: An Economic Approach," *Journal of Political Economy*, vol. 76, no. 2 (April 1968), and Gordon Tullock, "An Economic Approach to Crime," in Andreano and Siegfried, *The Economics of Crime*.

lenge the assumption that criminal behavior is irrational. Building upon nineteenth century utilitarian thinking, they argue that criminal behavior is a rational choice, as follows:

> A person commits an offense if the expected utility to him exceeds the utility he could get by using his time and other resources at other activities. Some persons become "criminals," therefore, not because their basic motivation differs from that of other persons, but because their benefits and costs differ.[31]

This rational choice model of crime claims that criminals rationally calculate the cost/benefit ratio of an act. In doing this, they consider the likelihood of being caught, the probability of punishment, and the length and nature of their possible punishment. Solutions to crime from this perspective can be found in an analysis of why criminals make the choice they do and in the development of cost- (punishment-) optimizing policies to deter people from making that choice. Public policy should thus aim at raising the cost of crime disproportionately to its potential benefits.

Notions of deterrence pervade current policy for combatting crime. One example of this is the renewed practice and enthusiasm for **definite and determinate sentencing policies**. A definite sentence sets a fixed period of confinement that allows no reduction by parole. A determinate sentence is a fixed confinement, set by the legislature, with parole eligibility. These contrast with the more customary **indeterminate sentence**, which offers more court discretion and is based on a correctional (not deterrent) model of punishment.

The Implications of Punishment and Reform of Criminals

Although crime-fighting policies have moved increasingly toward deterrence, many find fault with this logic. They question the assumption of criminal rationality, arguing that **even if individuals knew that the risk** of being caught for committing a crime was low, **most people would not commit that crime**. This is particularly true of violent crime. Further, critics point out that the assumption that criminals understand and weigh the possible costs/punishments for their criminal acts lacks empirical support. Many analysts argue that it takes more than the threat of punishment to keep people in line.[32]

Those who defend deterrence argue that, while **particular deterrence**, or the effect of deterrence on criminals, may be hard to prove, it is likely to have a great **general** effect. They claim the average citizen is less likely to commit a criminal act because of the "demonstration effect" of punishment. However, critics argue that such an effect is nearly impossible to prove or disprove.

---

[31] Quoted from Gordon, "Capitalism, Class and Crime in America," in Andreano and Siegfried, *Economics of Crime*, p. 100.

[32] See the recent work by James Q. Wilson, *The Moral Sense* (New York: Free Press, 1993), which argues that to combat crime societies need to nurture more private virtue.

Some refine deterrence policy by asserting a relationship between **the certainty and severity of punishment and the level of crime**.[33] In other words, they claim criminal behavior is deterred if the punishment is swift, certain, and severe. This proposition reinforces arguments used against the more traditional rehabilitative policies. Research has found that traditional rehabilitation has achieved only limited success. Alfred Blumstein explains that by the mid-1970s studies showed that "rehab" programs had a "null effect."[34] In other words, corrections programs broke even on reducing recidivism.[35] Recidivism seems more closely associated with personal characteristics of the criminal and to the outside environment to which the prisoner returns upon release. As Robert Blecker explains, this led policy makers to pass laws like the Sentencing Reform Act of 1984, in which Congress[36]

. . . rejected rehabilitation as an outmoded philosophy, abolished parole, and established the United States Sentencing Commission to fix sentences for a vast array of federal crimes based largely on a philosophy of giving each criminal his just deserts.[37]

The resulting "get tough" policies on crime led to longer sentencing. A recent National Research Council study states that **average prison time served per violent crime approximately tripled between 1975 and 1989, returning to the levels of the 1950s**. But this does not seem to have had the desired deterrent effect either. Crime data since 1975 show longer sentences have not reduced the level of crime. As noted in the National Research Council study,

. . . if tripling the average length of incarceration per crime had a strong deterrent effect, then violent crime rates should have declined in the absence of other relevant changes. While rates declined during the early 1980s, they generally rose after 1985, suggesting that changes in other factors . . . may have been causing an increase in potential crimes.[38]

Some even argue that longer sentences may have aggravated the crime problem. Certainly longer sentences put more pressure on prison resources (see Fig. 8-1 for growth in prison population) and raise costs. A recent study reports that "the United States has more of its population behind bars than any other country in the world."[39] The annual operating expenditures per inmate is estimated today at about

---

[33] See studies noted in Albert J. Reiss, Jr., and Jeffrey A. Roth (eds.), *Understanding and Preventing Violence* (Washington, DC: National Academy Press, 1993), 291–294.

[34] Alfred Blumstein, "Prisons, Populations, Capacity and Alternatives," in *Crime and Public Policy* (San Francisco: ICS Press, 1983), p. 232.

[35] Recidivism is recurring criminal behavior.

[36] *Sentencing Reform Act of 1984*, Pub. L. 98-473, 98 Stat. 1987 (1984).

[37] Robert Blecker, *Haven or Hell? Inside Lorton Central Prison: Experiences of Punishment Justified* (unpublished internal study of Lorton Prison conducted in 1990 by Robert Blecker, Professor of Law, New York University Law School).

[38] National Research Council, *Understanding and Preventing Violence* (Washington, DC: National Academy Press, 1993), p. 292.

[39] U.S. Advisory Commission on Intergovernmental Relations, *Guide to the Criminal Justice System for General Government Elected Officials* (Washington, DC: U.S. Government Printing Office, 1993), p. 11.

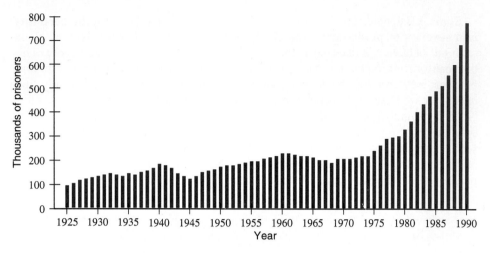

FIGURE 8-1
Sentenced prisoners in state and U.S. federal institutions, 1925 to 1990. (*Source of data: Sourcebook of Criminal Justice Statistics, 1989, U.S. Department of Justice, Bureau of Justice Statistics, Washington, DC, 1991.*)

$15,000. But a number of experts fear that jail houses and prisons have become "schools for crime." Blumstein points out how some critics argue that ". . . prison is harmful because it socializes prisoners, especially younger ones, into a hardened criminal culture."[40] Box 8-1 describes the current prison population.[41]

How society finds a suitable mix of retribution, deterrence, incapacitation, and rehabilitation to fight crime is a practical issue, but it also has important moral dimensions. Robert Blecker makes the following trenchant critique: "What actually happens to prisoners—their daily pain and suffering inside prison—is the only true measure of whether the traditional concepts have meaning, the traditional goals are fulfilled, the traditional definitions apply."[42]

INGREDIENTS OF VIOLENCE: DRUGS, GUNS, AND POVERTY

Crime abatement has been linked with policies aimed at lowering levels of drug and gun use, along with policies designed to lift people out of poverty. The relationship between these factors and crime is controversial. Politicians often proclaim such policies because they appeal to voters. But prudent analysis shows that the connection between drugs, guns, poverty, and crime is not obviously direct or causal.

---

[40] Alfred Blumstein, "Prisons: Population, Capacity and Alternatives," *Crime and Public Policy* (San Francisco: ICS, 1983), p. 232.
[41] U.S. Advisory Commission, *Guide to Criminal Justice System*, p. 30.
[42] Blecker, *Haven or Hell?* p. 1152.

BOX 8-1

WHO IS IN PRISON?

Age—Half are over 28.
Race—47 percent are black, 38 percent white, 12 percent Hispanic, and 3 percent other.
Education—Only 38 percent have completed high school.
Marital status—20 percent are married and 54 percent were never married; 80 percent of the females have at least one child, and over 40 percent of them had their first child before age 18.
Drug and alcohol use—54 percent admitted to being under the influence of drugs and/or alcohol at the time of the crime; drug testing surveys show a higher percentage.
Family crime—About 40 percent had an immediate family member with a prior incarceration record.
Prior criminal record—82 percent had a prior felony conviction. Almost half of inmates with nonviolent records were in prison for at least the third time. Only 7 percent were nonviolent first offenders, and over 25 percent of these were convicted of drug trafficking.

Source: U.S. Advisory Commission, Guide to Criminal Justice System, p. 30.

The War on Drugs

The shattering effects of drug dependency lead citizens to endorse just about any program directed at eliminating illegal drug use. Public drug policies are based on medical, commercial, and moral concerns, and increasingly they are connected with crime policy. Most Americans support a "war on drugs" and believe any efforts to decriminalize drug use are morally bankrupt. But the links between drugs and crime are often unclear, and the empirical evidence demonstrating their relationship weak.

Supply and demand considerations govern current drug policies. Reducing drug supplies through interdiction and the punishment of drug traffickers and reducing demand through the education, incarceration, and rehabilitation of drug users form the basis of the government's antidrug strategy. This strategy relies heavily on the criminal justice system for its effective implementation. Most Americans buy into the argument that drugs and crime are closely related. Consequently, they support employing the resources of the criminal justice system to fight the war on drugs. But is doing so justified?

Illegal drugs today include a wide range of psychoactive products such as opiates, cocaine (and its derivative, crack), amphetamines, PCP, and hallucinogens. Medical research reveals that the behavioral response—in other words, the biological, pharmacological, and neurological reactions—to these various drugs differ significantly from one person to the next and one drug to another. But setting up good scientific research on drug use and behavior to learn more is difficult. Reactions to drugs are highly individualistic and depend on factors like how much and how often a drug is taken.

THE ENDURING DEBATE: CAPITAL PUNISHMENT

In October 1993, the state of Maryland began preparing for its first criminal execution in over 25 years. Despite the legal and moral debate that has threatened the use of capital punishment, most Americans still support it. But the death penalty raises a number of problems, including proportionality of punishment, consistency of state statutes, and the vagaries of sentencing.

When the Bill of Rights was added to the Constitution, few intended the eighth amendment's restriction against "cruel and unusual punishment" to preclude capital punishment. The concern was to assure that punishment was proportional to the offense. Flagrant acts of punishment like burning at the stake were outlawed. The use of capital punishment continued historically. It peaked in the 1930s and began to decline precipitously in the 1960s. Critics denounced the variability in state statutes and pointed out that the poor, blacks, and other underrepresented groups were more likely to be executed. By the 1960s the NAACP and the ACLU had mounted a campaign against the use of capital punishment, making the issue one of public policy debate.

Beyond the question of arbitrary use, others raised the larger question of "evolving standards of decency." They argued that, though our colonial ancestors found no moral distaste in imposing the death penalty, perhaps contemporary standards of decency had changed. These two concerns, combined with growing worry that juries lacked sufficient direction in imposing the death penalty, led to a virtual moratorium on its use by the late 1960s.

Perhaps inevitably the question came before the Supreme Court. The first challenges to the death penalty addressed questions like the legality of "death qualified juries," that is, jurists selected for their willingness to impose the death penalty. The court rules such juries unconstitutional. The Court also invalidated the death penalty mandated under the Federal Kidnapping Act.

The major challenge to the death penalty occurred in the 1972 case *Furman v. Georgia*. The Supreme Court in its decision temporarily struck down the death penalty because of the "arbitrary, capricious and racist manner" in which it had been applied. Essentially the Court reacted to how the death penalty had been used, not to the death penalty per se. Though the decision was complex, it did leave two legal avenues open to the states. States could pass laws which established a bifurcated procedure for the death penalty. Here

Scientists do know that different drugs elicit different reactions.[44] For example, heroine and opiates tend to inhibit behavior, though it is not at all clear what happens during periods of withdrawal. The chronic use of these drugs may affect the central nervous system and lead to aberrant social behavior. Drugs like cocaine, LSD and PCP, and amphetamines produce effects not unlike alcohol. In small

---

[44] For a detailed summary of the leading scientific research on drugs and their effects, see the study prepared by the National Research Council already cited, Reiss and Roth (eds.), *Understanding and Preventing Violence*.

defendants would face a trial to establish culpability. If found guilty then a second proceeding would follow to establish grounds for the death penalty. The other legal avenue available to states was to make the death penalty mandatory for certain crimes.

The Supreme Court ruled on the legality of the two-step procedure in *Gregg v. Georgia* (1976). In this case, the Court ruled that the death penalty for murder did not necessarily constitute cruel and unusual punishment. Further, it declared the bifurcated system Constitutional. However, the Court ruled in *Woodson v. North Carolina* (1976) that the death penalty may not be made mandatory.

Despite the fact that the Gregg case upheld the Constitutionality of the death penalty, a series of rulings have eroded jury discretion in applying the statutory guidelines. In addition to these fundamental legal questions, other objections have been voiced regarding the cost and effectiveness of the death penalty. While some are persuaded that it is a cost-effective form of punishment, others point out that given the need to guarantee procedural safeguards its costs are much higher than other forms of punishment. In other words, the death penalty results in unavoidable legal appeals and this costs taxpayers more money. Studies show that the deterrent effect of the death penalty is far from proven. Comparisons show few differences in crime rates for those states with the death penalty and those without it. And in states with the death penalty, comparisons of the crime rate before and after an execution show no differences. Many conclude that the death penalty is popularly supported by Americans and politically useful. Some elected officials, however—among them the Governor of New York, Mario M. Cuomo—have argued forcefully for life in prison without parole as a preferable sentence. As noted by Cuomo in a *New York Times* editorial, "That alternative is just as permanent, at least as great a deterrent and—for those who are so inclined—far less expensive than the exhaustive legal appeals required in capital cases."[43]

[43] Mario M. Cuomo, "New York State Shouldn't Kill People," *The New York Times,* June 17, 1989, p. 23.

Sources: Donald D. Hook and Lothar Kahn, *Death in the Balance: The Debate over Capital Punishment* (Lexington, MA: D.C. Heath, 1989); Bonnie Szumski, Lynn Hall, and Susan Bursell (eds.), *The Death Penalty: Opposing Viewpoints* (St. Paul, MN: Greenhaven Press, 1986); *Gregg v. Georgia*, 428 U.S. 153 (1976); *Woodson v. North Carolina*, 428 U.S. 280 (1976).

doses, individuals tend to act out in a disruptive fashion, while higher doses lead to more disorganized, clumsy behavior that may have an inhibiting effect on social interaction. Crack cocaine may lead to a psychotic state, though no direct relationship has been established. **Essentially, the analysis of individual drug use and crime levels shows no consistent relationship**. Data in Fig. 8-2 illustrate this comparison for cocaine use in five major American cities. As explained by researcher James Inciardi,

New York, with the highest cocaine prevalence of the five cities, and Los Angeles, with the second lowest, have the lowest homicide rates. The New York, Miami, and D.C. data

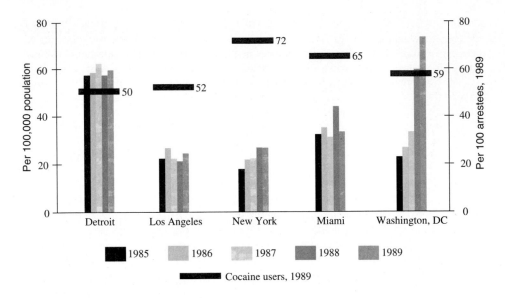

FIGURE 8-2
Homicide rates, 1985 to 1989, and cocaine users among male arrestees, 1989, for several major U.S. cities. (*Sources: National Research Council, Understanding and Preventing Violence, p. 188; J. A. Inciardi, The Crack/Violence Connection within a Population of Hard-Core Adolescent Offenders, paper presented at the National Institute on Drug Abuse, Technical Review on Drugs and Violence, September 26, 1989, Rockville, MD.*)

resemble, if anything, an inverse relationship between homicide rates and arrestees' cocaine use.[45]

While the physiological connection between drugs and crime is not verifiable, **economic arguments** are persuasive. Do drug addicts steal or kill to feed a drug habit? Again good data to confirm this proposition are hard to come by. One study found the empirical support for economic violence to be very inconclusive. But the report's first author, P. J. Goldstein, further concludes from a study done of the New York City Police Department that drug-related violence can be categorized as "systemic" rather than just "economic."[46] That is, it can be understood as the result of factors having to do with the overall drug "market place," in line with the following analysis: Current public policy aims at **minimizing the supply of drugs**. An artificial drug scarcity results, which drives up the price of drugs. Dealers capture these **excess profits**, and drug users are forced to find ways to pay the contrived high prices. Among the reactions to this "systemic" condition is violence resulting from territorial disputes, gang warfare, battles with police and informers, the cre-

[45] Reiss and Roth (eds.), *Understanding and Preventing Violence*, p. 188.
[46] P. J. Goldstein et al., "Drug Related Involvement in Violent Episodes, Final Report" (National Institute on Drug Abuse) (New York: Narcotic and Drug Research, Inc., 1987). See also P. J. Goldstein "Drugs and Violent Crime," in N. A. Weiner and M. E. Wolfgangs (eds.), *Pathways to Violent Crime* (Newbury Park, CA: Sage, 1989).

ation of black markets, and the lure of corruption. Prostitution increases, and drug dealers enter the school yards. A logical extension of this argument is the "iron law of prohibition." If all drugs are prohibited, dealers have a greater incentive to traffic in the more profitable and more dangerous drugs. In other words, if the punishment for dealing marijuana is the same as that for dealing cocaine, then logically it is preferable to deal cocaine, which is more profitable.[47] Analysts point to the rising use of expensive "designer drugs" as an indication of this trend.

One public policy direction consistent with this reasoning is decriminalization of drugs. Not surprisingly, some elected officials have concluded that, given the costs of combating drug use, decriminalizing them makes the most sense. Proponents of this position argue that studies fail to confirm drug use causes crime, and that maybe coincidentally criminals just use drugs. In addition, some worry that effective drug programs will infringe on civil liberties.

Decriminalization has only a small following. Most Americans simply will not accept the risk. It is estimated that as many as six million people already use drugs, and legalizing them could lead to even greater numbers. Yet the costs of treating drug use as a crime are also great. Prison overcrowding, caseload pressure, and ballooning police and military budgets raise practical questions about the policy (see Fig. 8-3). Some argue that deemphasizing the crime connection and reemphasizing the public health aspects of drug use is a more viable and appropriate course.[48] This approach would target education and rehabilitation rather than interdiction and prosecution as its main goals.

Gun Control

Like drugs, guns represent something tangible policy makers can control in the fight against crime. Policy makers point to the experience of other countries, like England, which have far lower crime rates and tough gun control policies. But the relationship between guns and crime is very complex. While analysts concede that tough gun laws could mitigate crime, they argue that those laws would not work unless all the states agreed to the same standards.

Gun control policies affecting the **availability, use, distribution, and deadliness** of guns are already in place in the United States. Congress passed the Federal Gun Control Act in 1968 in reaction to public outcries over the assassinations of Senator Robert Kennedy and the Reverend Martin Luther King. The act emphasized restrictions on the availability and distribution of guns. It **banned** mail order

---

[47] This argument is presented by David Boaz, "The Case of Legalizing Drugs," in Herbert Levine (ed.), *Point Counter Point Readings in American Government*, 4th ed. (New York: St. Martin's Press, 1992).

[48] In October 1993, Attorney General Janet Reno agreed to a new approach to fighting the war on drugs. Drug offenders arrested in Washington, DC, would come before a "drug court" rather than the DC Superior Court. The drug court would supervise intensive treatment for nonviolent drug offenders. The goal, as expressed by Attorney General Reno, is to deal with the underlying problems of drugs rather than adjudicate for criminal charges. Other drug court experiments have been set up in Florida's Dade and Broward counties.

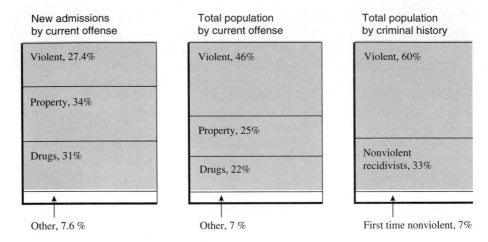

FIGURE 8-3
1991 State prison populations; the category of Other includes gambling, weapons offenses, driving under the influence of alcohol, nonviolent sex crimes, commercial vice, etc. (*Source of data: Prisons and Prisoners in the United States, U.S. Department of Justice, Bureau of Justice Statistics, Washington, DC, 1992.*)

sales of guns and outlawed sales to convicted felons, fugitives, and individuals with certain mental illnesses. It restricted private ownership of automatic and military weapons. The law required that gun dealers be **licensed** by the Bureau of Alcohol, Tobacco and Firearms (AFT) and that the serial numbers on all guns sold by licensed dealers be recorded. It also required that individuals buying guns from licensed dealers must show proofs of identification and residency and certify their eligibility to own guns.

Despite this effort to control the distribution and availability of guns, gun ownership today is widespread. The AFT estimates 150 to 200 million firearms are privately owned. Most are used for hunting, sport, or self-protection. Twenty-four percent of privately owned guns are easily concealed handguns, which are used disproportionately in homicides. Estimates provided by the FBI indicate that in 1989 about 60 percent of all homicides resulted from gun attacks and that the cost of gun injuries was about $14 billion.[49]

These frightening statistics have led to a ground swell of support for more effective gun control. Many states have tightened their gun ordinances by insisting on waiting periods before purchase, licensing of purchasers, and laws against carrying concealed weapons. But these stricter requirements are often undercut by the less demanding regulations of neighboring states. Frustration has mounted sufficiently

[49] Dorothy P. Rice et al., *Cost of Injury in the United States: A Report to Congress 1989* (San Francisco and Baltimore: Institute for Health and Aging, University of California, and Injury Prevention Center, The Johns Hopkins University, 1989).

that Congress finally passed the popular "Brady Bill." The bill, named after Presidential press secretary James Brady, who was seriously wounded in the 1981 assassination attempt on President Ronald Reagan, requires a background check and a 5-day "cooling off" period prior to purchasing a gun. Despite widespread popular support, the Brady Bill met with ongoing Congressional opposition. Its passage came only after a threatened filibuster attempt by Senate members and an aggressive advertising campaign mounted by the National Rifle Association (NRA). Both failed to sway public sentiment. In an emotional ceremony, President Clinton signed the Brady Bill shortly after Thanksgiving 1993.

However, many gun enthusiasts complain that legislation like the Brady Bill misses the point. Their common refrain, "Guns don't kill people, people kill people," reflects their belief that gun control will not solve the crime problem. Further, they argue that gun control violates individual rights. Supported by the aggressive lobbying of the National Rifle Association (NRA), gun control opponents challenge any attempts to curtail their right to own and use weapons. They base their opposition on the right to bear arms protected by the Constitution's second amendment and on what they perceive as a commonsense judgment that ownership of guns is uncontrollable. They find efforts to control certain types of guns—for example, the ban on imported assault rifles imposed by President Bush—to be illogical, particularly when no such ban was placed on similar domestic-made weapons. Opponents also point to studies that show no difference in crime patterns between jurisdictions with strict gun laws and those without.[50]

Despite this opposition, though, increasingly the public opinion has coalesced around the demand to do something to counteract gun availability.[51] Some scholars argue that gun use tends to be **an instrumental act much more than an intentional act**. They point to the fact that firearms are rarely used by serial killers. Tragically gun availability has changed victimization patterns. Empirical evidence supports the conclusion that, **while guns do not increase the overall levels of crime, they seem to increase the seriousness of criminal attacks**.[52] One study concludes:

> Where guns are available, commercial targets are robbed more than individual citizens, and young men more frequently than elderly women. Similarly, in domestic assaults husbands are more frequently the victims. Thus the most important effects of guns on crime are that they increase the seriousness of criminal attacks and affect the distribution of victimization; they do not seem to markedly increase the overall levels of criminal attack.[53]

[50] The National Research Council reports estimates showing that only one out of six firearms used in crimes was legally obtained.

[51] A recent study of children's hospitals reported in *The Washington Post* (November 26, 1993) estimates the average cost of treating a child for a gunshot wound at more than $14,000. One study reports that gunshot wounds are the fifth leading cause of death for children under 14.

[52] Mark H. Moore, "Controlling Criminogenic Commodities: Drugs, Guns and Alcohol," in *Crime and Public Policy* (San Francisco: ICS Press, 1983), p. 130.

[53] As noted in Moore, "Controlling Criminogenic Commodities," p. 130.

Poverty and Crime

Does poverty cause crime? The connection between these two societal illnesses is far from simple. Yet many propose that the antidote to crime is the elimination of poverty. Unfortunately what research tells us about the relationship between poverty and crime is inconclusive and sometimes misleading.

Much of the research about crime and poverty takes as its starting point assumptions about criminal behavior. In this model, individuals choose crime over employment when crime seems a more expedient course of action. They do this particularly **if the risk of being caught is low and the utility (money) to be gained is high. It follows, then, that the appropriate reaction to this rational choice is to increase the deterrent (punishment) for prospective criminals**. A further implication is that poor people are more likely to make this rational calculus than members of other segments of society. They have less to lose than those who have sufficient income sources.

Empirical research advanced to confirm this rationale is common but methodologically weak. Many studies use unemployment statistics to measure poverty, but these have proven to be very unrefined measures, neither reliable nor valid. Time series studies comparing crime rates and unemployment statistics fail to explain mounting crime rates, nor do they show that unemployment causes crime. Cross-sectional studies comparing crime rates and unemployment trends across different geographic areas are even more difficult to interpret. States and cities differ widely in the nature and extent of the crimes committed within their jurisdictions. Fluctuations in differing labor markets make unemployment figures difficult to compare. Nonetheless, the intuitive sense that if individuals have jobs they are less likely to commit crimes has resulted in the government promoting jobs programs. Yet the effects of this approach too have been unclear, leading some to wonder if the causes of unemployment and crime are the same, if some people simply cannot succeed economically no matter what help they receive, or if the problem is not simply that criminals choose a life of crime (a return to rational choice notions). Analysts continue to struggle with these questions. Though unable to explain **how crime factors relate, researchers continue to point to correlations between delinquency, homicides, and the socioeconomic characteristics of communities**.

Indicators like population density of households, residential mobility, family disruption, the presence of gangs, gun density, and drug distribution typically characterize low-income communities. All correlate with high crime rates. Studies point out that the three factors of population density of households, residential mobility, and disrupted family structures are particularly significant indicators of crime.[54] They are all typical of communities with high numbers of teenagers and single-parent households.

Research concludes that poverty today goes hand in hand with significant social disorganization. In his study, *The Truly Disadvantaged: The Inner City, the*

---

[54] National Research Council, Reiss & Roth (eds.) *Understanding and Preventing Violence*, p. 133.

Underclass, and Public Policy, William Julius Wilson writes of the social isolation of the inner city.[55] Beyond the extreme racial segregation of inner cities in relation to other parts of the larger social fabric, there is a further breakdown within these communities themselves. People live side by side but do not know one another. Great mistrust exists among neighbors. In these communities, unlike poor communities of the past, parenting becomes highly individualistic. Everyone is a stranger. Intergenerational relationships fall apart. There are no positive identifications with a neighborhood, no explicit community norms, and no sanctions against delinquent behavior. A street culture develops with its own set of norms and symbols. Embedded in this is a deep distrust for established institutions such as the police, schools, and businesses. Furthermore, given the current ongoing structural economic change toward service production and away from traditional industrial production, little opportunity exists in these communities to find good jobs and move out of the inner city culture. Crime is convenient, pervasive, and attractive.

The crisis for public policy makers is where and how to break into this cycle. In the 1970s theories took hold proposing the concept of a "defensible space."[56] Here the objective was to create a more livable and more easily protected environment. City planners took hold of these ideas and experimented with better architectural design, improved lighting, more green space. Twenty years later, these experiments have met with mixed success. While still aware of the need to make communities more hospitable, studies now recommend the use of more informal social controls. Community watch programs, beat police patrols, and exact change requirements for public transportation are all examples of the changing emphasis. Increasingly policy makers have come to consider crime and poverty as social illnesses that need not just deterrence, but improvements in areas such as public health. The complex relationship between crime and poverty defies any simple solution. Better studies, improved social and anticrime programs, and better economic opportunities may help shed light on the issue.

WHITE COLLAR CRIME

White collar crime is defined as illegal activity conducted in the course of one's occupation. This differs from **organized crime**, which is economic gain through illegal business practices like gambling, loan sharking, prostitution, and narcotics. Organized crime *is* one's occupation; white collar crime is perhaps more insidious. The activities of white collar criminals cut across business and politics, the professions, and labor organizations.

Too often white collar offenders hide behind corporate or professional sanctuaries. This leads to claims that white collar criminals experience more lenient penalties. Critics say white collar crime is just a "better racket."

---

[55] William Julius Wilson, *The Truly Disadvantaged: The Inner City, the Underclass, and Public Policy* (Chicago: University of Chicago Press, 1987).
[56] Oscar Newman, *Defensible Space: Crime Prevention through Urban Design* (New York: Macmillan, 1973).

Classifications of white collar crime include "theft after trust" such as financial manipulations, fraud, and acceptance of bribes, or "restraint of trade" like phony limited partnerships and pyramid schemes. Some argue that these types of crimes reflect the dark side of the business subculture of competition and profit maximization. Crimes like false advertising, misuse of campaign funds, and occupational and environmental violations are further examples of betrayals of the public trust by business and political leaders. Ironically, most citizens worry little about or are unaware of the effects of this activity. In fact, the systematic study of white collar crime did not take hold until recently.[57]

The general lack of documentation and prosecutorial activity regarding this kind of activity is not surprising. White collar crime is hard to investigate and often very complicated. One investigator complained that it was like "doing someone else's checkbook."[58] Paper trails are papered over, increasingly with the help of computers and other sophisticated forms of technology. Nevertheless the FBI has established a special branch of forensic accountants and lawyers to investigate and prosecute white collar criminals. This, combined with new and tougher sentencing guidelines, means the criminal justice system is starting to focus on these illegal operations.

With the white collar crime price tag estimated at approximately $200 billion per year, society can no longer afford to allow professional and business standards alone to regulate the workplace.[59] In the aftermath of the savings-and-loan crisis, which cost the American taxpayer about $180 billion, the heavy artillery of criminal law is increasingly being used.[60] Many Americans have yet to learn that there is a much greater property loss associated with white collar criminal activities than with street crime. Paradoxically, crime prevention funds are allocated in just the opposite way.

CONCLUSION

1 While Americans are united, often passionately, over the need to fight crime, no public policy problem is more elusive. Science offers advances in medical treatment and environmental protection, but tells us little about how to keep peace in our streets.

---

[57] "White collar crime" as a term was first used by Edward Sutherland in an address to the American Sociological Society in 1939.

[58] Comment quoted by a reporter for "Sheriff's Investigation Follows More Paper Trails," *St. Petersburg Times*, August 30, 1993, p. 1.

[59] See Chantico Publ. Co., *Combating Computer Crime: Prevention, Detection, Investigation* (New York: McGraw-Hill, 1992). Also see Francis T. Cullen, William J. Maakestad, and Gray Cavender, "The Ford Pinto Case and Beyond: Assessing Blame," in *Justice, Crime and Ethics* (Cincinnati: Anderson Publishing, 1991).

[60] See Congressional Budget Office, *Resolving the Thrift Crisis* (Washington, DC: U.S. Government Printing Office, April 1993). See also F. Stevens Redburn, "The Deeper Structure of the Savings and Loan Crisis," *PS: Political Science and Politics*, vol. 24, no. 3 (September 1991), p. 436.

2 How much crime is there? Newspaper accounts give the impression that crime-free, safe neighborhoods no longer exist. The days of unlocked cars and houses are of another era. Systematic studies of crime like FBI and police reports along with academic studies confirm this impression and tell us that violent crime in particular has reached record levels. The associated physical, emotional, and financial costs have forced policy makers at all levels to put crime at the top of their agendas.

3 What are the causes of crime? Efforts to answer this question have so far offered minimal direction to policy makers. Diverse theories point to a range of possible origins, but none explain conclusively why some individuals commit criminal acts and others do not. More is known about specific conditions associated with crime, like the use of drugs, the availability of guns, and poverty. Unfortunately, policy recommendations based on this knowledge are controversial and too often aimed at achieving political aims rather than true solutions.

4 How can the American criminal justice system create effective policies to control crime, punish offenders, and protect the innocent? The criminal justice system is the crossroads for testing our resolve to protect the rights of victims and of the accused before conviction yet to punish offenders. Often bogged down by its own size and complexity, the system is characterized by the right to legal appeals, pervasive plea bargaining, and complex sentencing requirements. The police, the front line in fighting crime, typically suffer "whiplash" from the need to observe procedural safeguards, protect victims, and respond to society's demand that they catch the criminals.

5 Consequently, crime abatement creates a policy quagmire. There is no consensus and there are no viable remedies. A rough starting point is the healthy uneasiness about current crime control practices voiced by individuals like Attorney General Janet Reno. Reno calls for a redirection in fighting crime to emphasize prevention and the welfare of children, rather than tougher punishment. Despite this, President Clinton's $30.2 billion crime bill passed after an aggressive partisan battle over what some representatives saw as social "pork." The resulting biggest crime bill in history suggests few of the suggested links between crime, public health, and education. It calls for $13.4 billion in grants to localities to hire more police, $9.9 billion to build more prisons, and just $5.5 billion for crime prevention programs—the pork. The bill also bans 19 more assault weapons, increases to 60 the number of federal crimes punishable by death, and introduces the so-called three strikes penalty for repeat offenders. It appears that the future portends stronger gun control laws, more prisons, new antidrug campaigns, and increased police visibility as the plan of action.

6 This chapter's discussion calls for a warning: Finding the answer to crime has proven as intractable as eradicating any of humanity's most deadly diseases. Like disease, crime rots the social system. Analysts know that until the true root causes of this social illness are determined, money spent and prisons built will only treat the symptoms.

QUESTIONS FOR DISCUSSION

1 What factors contribute to America's rising crime rate? Is there a relationship between public expenditure and crime abatement?
2 How accurate are crime statistics? Why is crime underreported?
3 Compare and contrast leading theories of criminal behavior. What policy guidance have they offered?
4 Describe the competing philosophies of criminal justice. How does deterrence differ from other philosophies?
5 What are the implications of a decentralized criminal justice system?
6 Is the "war on drugs" winnable? What is the theory underlying decriminalization?
7 Do "guns kill people" or do "people kill people?" Discuss.
8 Why are Americans less concerned about white collar crime? How important is the "fear factor" in our criminal justice policy?

KEY CONCEPTS

Brady Bill	Due process
Clearance rates	Incapacitation
Crime index	Mandatory sentencing
Criminal justice system	Plea bargain
Criminogenic factors	Procedural rights
Criminology	Rehabilitation
Decriminalization	Retribution
Deterrence	White collar crime

SUGGESTED READINGS

Ralph Andreano and John J. Siegfried (eds.), *The Economics of Crime* (New York: John Wiley & Sons, 1980).

Hugh Adam Bedau, *The Death Penalty in America*, 3rd ed. (New York: Oxford University Press, 1982).

James A. Inciardi, *Criminal Justice*, 3rd ed. (New York: Harcourt Brace Janovich, 1990).

Joseph E. Jacoby (ed.), *Classics of Criminology* (Prospect Heights, IL: Waveland Press, 1988).

Marianne LeVert, *Crime in America* (New York: Facts on File, 1991).

Albert J. Reiss, Jr., and Jeffrey A. Roth (eds.), *Understanding and Preventing Violence* (Washington, DC: National Academy Press, 1993).

Tom R. Tyler, *Why People Obey the Law* (New Haven: Yale University Press, 1990).

George B. Vold and Thomas J. Bernard, *Theoretical Criminology*, 3rd ed. (New York: Oxford University Press, 1986).

James Q. Wilson (ed.), *Crime and Public Policy* (San Francisco: ICS Press, 1983).

James Q. Wilson and Richard J. Herrnstein, *Crime and Human Nature* (New York: Simon and Schuster, 1985).

9

CRISIS IN HOUSING AFFORDABILITY

This chapter examines housing, the land use that very directly affects the welfare of families. During the Great Depression, millions of Americans lost their homes to bank foreclosures. Housing starts came to a virtual halt. A majority of those in the home building industry were unemployed due to lack of demand. Builders, banks, and those needing shelter looked to the national government for help. The response of the Roosevelt Administration was the National Housing Act of 1934 that declared: "The general welfare and security of the Nation and the health and living standards of its people require . . . the realization . . . of the goal of a decent home and suitable living environment for every American Family." This chapter examines the difficulty in reaching that goal. While real advances have been made, problems in the area of housing have been increasing, especially in the last 15 years. Housing policy is intimately associated with the changing patterns of urban and suburban living.

HOUSING POLICY AND THE "AMERICAN DREAM"

Housing is of special importance in the U.S. economy and public policy. A house is the largest single consumer purchase for the majority of Americans. Owning a home has become part of the "American Dream." Thus, there is a belief that a strong relationship exists between the quality of housing and the quality of life.

Housing is a **merit good**. A **merit good is a good or service that the government considers desirable and therefore encourages by subsidies or regulation**. Some argue that an unsubsidized market can do a sufficient job of allocating housing resources in the quantities desired for those with money. In their view, there is little need for government financial support in the housing market except for low-income housing assistance. Nevertheless, housing is also viewed as having so much influence on individual well-being and the character of a community that government intervention to enhance housing conditions is generally considered economically appropriate and politically necessary.

Arguments in Favor of Homeownership

Substandard housing has been held responsible for disease and crime. Physically unsuitable housing has been likened to a bad apple: If left alone, it causes the deterioration of nearby housing.[1] Homebuilding creates jobs and provides housing stock in communities, which in turn attracts other kinds of employment. The foregoing factors provide the ingredients for powerful bipartisan, political constituencies in housing, especially in regard to homeownership. Indeed, encouragement for the idea of homeownership has come from the leadership of both political parties. In 1968, President Lyndon Johnson said that "owning a home can increase responsibility and stake out a man's place in his community. . . . The man who owns a home has something to be proud of and reason to protect and preserve it."[2] President Ronald Reagan said that homeownership "supplies stability and rootedness."[3] Both political parties have pledged to work for a decent home for every citizen.

It has long been held that homeownership promotes social stability because the individuals owning homes have a stake in the system. Recall that voting was originally limited to male property holders on the theory that they would vote more responsibly than those without property. Consequently, government at all levels has provided housing assistance for households at all income levels.[4]

For most individuals homeownership provides a psychological and financial confidence not typically identified with rental occupancy. Purchase of a home severs the dependency relationship between tenant and landlord. It also allows families to accumulate wealth through the equity they have in their homes. **Equity in homes is the main source of wealth for most families.**

---

[1] Wallace Smith, "Housing America," *The Annals of the American Academy of Political and Social Science* (Beverly Hills, CA: Sage Publications, 1983), p. 9.

[2] Lyndon B. Johnson, "The Crisis of the Cities," the President's Message to the Congress on Urban Problems, February 12, 1968.

[3] Ann Mariano, "Action Urged to Keep Public Housing Units Available to Poor," *The Washington Post*, July 13, 1985. Support for the idea of homeownership appears to be almost universal. The leaders of the least privileged groups have also expressed their support. Dr. Mason Wright, Jr., Chairman of the National Housing Conference on Black Power, testified, "Fulfillment can never come through housing efforts which afford people no sense of investment, nor ownership with control of, their immediate environment. Renters tend to be far less responsible than home-owners. Black people in our urban ghettos, are a renter class, and hence the system tends inevitably to make them into irresponsible people." See *Housing Legislation of 1967: Hearings before the Subcommittee on Housing and Urban Affairs of the Committee on Banking and Currency* (Washington, DC: U.S. Government Printing Office, 1967), p. 865.

[4] The government has, in fact supported homeownership beginning with the Homestead Act in 1860, and extending through the federal income tax in 1913 right up to the tax policies in effect currently. However, it is debatable that homeowners are more responsible than renters in all respects: There is some evidence that free-rider behavior leaving neighborhood improvements to others extends across both groups.

TABLE 9-1
POSITIVE EFFECTS OF HOMEOWNERSHIP

Positive effects	% Americans agreeing
Economy in area	57
Young people obtaining college degrees	54
Families getting ahead financially	54
Neighborhood safety	49
People voting in elections	49
Positive overall effects on community	49

Source: Fannie Mae, *Fannie Mae National Housing Survey 1994* (Washington, DC: U.S. Government Printing Office, 1994), pp. 3–4.

In April 1994 survey research firms conducted the Fannie Mae National Housing Survey to determine American attitudes toward homeownership. Just over 86 percent of those surveyed believed that people are "better off owning," while 74 percent said the best time to buy a home is "as soon as you can afford it." By an overwhelming majority both owners (86 percent) and renters (84 percent) agreed that a home is a good investment. As shown in Table 9-1, the survey found that Americans do associate homeownership with a host of positive effects on the economy and their neighborhoods.

In addition to these personal gains, some analysts argue, there are broader societal gains related to homeownership. In their view, homeowners are able to save at a higher rate than renters. This occurs through the portion of their mortgage payments paid directly on the principal that builds up home equity, the appreciation of the worth of their homes over the years, and the tax advantages homeowners enjoy. These savings make funds available for national investment, which stimulates greater overall economic growth. Also, homeowners are more likely to maintain and improve their property than renters, and maintenance and renovation extends the life of the housing stock. Moreover, studies confirm that homeowners are more likely to vote in local and federal elections than are renters.[5]

Negative Views of Homeownership

Some critics have argued that the customary case made on behalf of homeownership regarding independence, family pride, security, and social responsibility is not necessarily valid today. Present circumstances are very different from the frontier conditions that existed when those values were first thought to emanate from ownership. Putting together a homestead on a prairie is quite different from buying a

---

[5] Raymond J. Struyk, *Should Government Encourage Homeownership?* (Washington, DC: The Urban Institute, 1977). Homeowners' greater propensity to vote at present may well reflect their economic status relative to the average renter, rather than being related to homeownership per se.

house on a small urban or suburban lot with little likelihood of the owners remaining there for more than a few years.[6]

Other critics have argued that the social costs of homeownership are understated because they do not take into account

the devaluation of many inner cities; the increasing length of the journey between work and home, with accompanying traffic congestion and pollution problems; the reduction of employment accountability, as between cities and regions; and, of course, the social isolation of typical suburban life, tied to the shopping center, but cut off from the rest of the world by lawns and freeways.[7]

Still others criticize the American fixation with the higher level of investment in housing as having largely occurred through governmental taxing and spending policies that have directed investment funds into real estate at the expense of new plants and equipment. In this view, overinvestment in facilities that provide instant gratification for some, such as new houses, is encouraged, while the necessary investment in factories that provides long-term benefits for everyone is discouraged.[8]

HOUSING AND POLITICAL TRENDS

From Farms, to Cities, to Suburbs

Thomas Jefferson believed that the ideal society would be composed of farmers with enough property to provide support for the social order. He believed that an equitable distribution of property would help prevent excessive concentrations of wealth and power. Therefore, he thought property ownership was useful in deterring civil disorder and revolution.

Nineteenth century America was primarily agrarian, and reflected the Jeffersonian ideal of the yeoman farmer. However, social patterns in much of twentieth century America have reflected an excitement for cities as the centers of culture and

---

[6] Catherine Bauer, "Social Questions in Housing and Community Planning," *Journal of Social Issues,* vol. 7, no. 1/2 (1951), p. 13, cited in Michael A. Stegman, *More Housing, More Fairly: Report of the Twentieth Century Fund Task Force on Affordable Housing* (New York: The Twentieth Century Fund, 1991), p. 31.

[7] Eric Carlson, "Policy Implications of Housing Ownership: A Background Paper," *Only One Earth Forum* (New York: Rene Dubois Society, May 1989), p. 8. Also quoted in Stegman, *More Housing, More Fairly*, p. 31.

[8] Alfred L. Malabre, Jr., *Beyond Our Means* (New York: Vintage Books, 1987), pp. 42–43. Malabre also claims that housing policy has encouraged excessive indebtedness and overspending as more and more Americans have been going into deeper debt by borrowing against equity in their homes (p. 44). Albert Crenshaw reported in "Borrowing Surge Erodes Americans' Home Equity," *The Washington Post*, May 28, 1991, p. 1, that the equity Americans had in their homes dropped sharply in 1990 as homeowners borrowed on their properties in large part to finance vacations, medical bills, cars, and a host of other consumer purchases. Equity in homes dropped 16 percent (by over $300 billion). This trend runs counter to a public policy goal of the 1986 Tax Reform Act, when Congress cut back tax deductions for consumer credit payments in an effort to reduce Americans' indebtedness.

Critics also contend that home equity loans give undue advantage to homeowners—who tend to be more affluent than renters—because they are cheaper than other consumer loans—the critics contend, in other words, that these loans help "the rich get richer."

the very heart of industrial production and national prosperity. Throughout the nineteenth and well into the twentieth century, most American cities were manufacturing centers. They contained neighborhoods of different socioeconomic classes in which people lived and worked in close proximity, with everyone under the same political administrations.

But manufacturing firms eventually found that skyrocketing land prices within the cities made it difficult for them to expand. More affluent families began considering moves to outlying regions to escape the unpleasantness of crowded city life.[9] And the automobile also expanded opportunities for middle-class workers to move to the suburbs, where housing was cheaper and residential environments, as noted, are more pleasant than in cities.[10] The absence of buildable land for new homes in cities and an increase in real incomes from the 1950s through the 1970s also exacerbated the decline of central cities by expediting the exodus to the suburbs. The realities of the housing market ultimately determined that the "less affluent" would live in the older, deteriorated housing inventory in the central cities.

Nevertheless, central cities retain many facilities that cannot be reproduced in the suburbs, such as large hospitals and medical facilities, museums, and art galleries. These have attracted suburbanites back into the city. Moreover, the "central" locations of central cities sustain central business districts (CBDs) that employ suburbanites. Jobs utilizing primarily communication skills rather than manual labor thrive in cities, so that suburbs become "bedroom" communities with many of their residents commuting daily to work in nearby big cities. Ironically, many of the urban dwellers living closest to the CBDs offering highly paid jobs find themselves excluded from such employment.

This split between poorer urban areas and affluent suburbs is reflected not just in private finances and levels of personal income, but in the realm of public finances. Those living in the suburbs often benefit from the amenities cities have to offer while largely avoiding their costs. Urban facilities such as roads, public sanitation, and mass transportation are used by everyone, but paid for out of the declining tax bases of lower-income city residents since cities cannot levy taxes on richer sources such as suburban real estate. On the other hand, suburban communities benefit from their more affluent property tax bases, which assure them of superior

---

[9] The movement to the suburbs is not a recent phenomenon in reaction to the decay and deterioration of inner cities. The movement toward less densely populated areas began by the turn of the century and actually preceded the automobile. It was not apparent at first because growth at the fringes was still largely inside city limits. See William G. Grigsby and Thomas C. Corl, "Declining Neighborhoods: Problem or Opportunity," *Annals of the American Academy of Political and Social Science*, vol. 465 (January 1983), p. 90.

[10] A survey conducted by Louis Harris in 1978 found that people living in cities were less satisfied with city living than people in suburbs or rural areas with life in those areas. Approximately half of the city dwellers would have preferred to live in the suburbs, while suburban and rural dwellers both preferred rural areas. Regardless of **where** they preferred to live, 75 percent of all those surveyed preferred to **own** a single-family house. This was true for all income levels and racial and ethnic backgrounds. See Louis Harris Associates, *The 1978 Survey of the Quality of Community Life: A Data Book* (Washington, DC: U.S. Department of Housing and Urban Development, 1978).

HOUSING LOCATION AND NEIGHBORHOOD CHANGE

What factors shape a family's choice of where to live? Families in similar situations often engage in parallel decision-making processes that have the cumulative effect of forming identifiable neighborhoods. Several models have been developed to explain neighborhood change. The filtering-down theory is one such model.

The Filtering-Down Theory

This model holds that as the incomes of families rise, the families will be able to satisfy their increased demand for housing by buying newly built housing. Newly constructed housing will usually be built away from the central city because urban lots are too small to satisfy the preference of upper-income families, and the cost of buying sufficient land and demolishing existing construction is prohibitive. Suitable vacant land at lower opportunity cost is usually available outside the city.

This means an empty house, and there are two likely scenarios for the home that has been vacated. First, it may be purchased by a family having socioeconomic characteristics similar to the previous owners. In this case, the neighborhood remains unchanged, and no filtering occurs.

A second possibility is that families of similar economic backgrounds are not interested in buying the property at the price paid by the original owners, even though the quality of the housing has not declined. The equilibrium price of housing in the neighborhood thus falls and becomes affordable to households with incomes lower than those who moved away. Families with incomes below those of the families that have moved will clearly benefit from this filtering operation.

As lower-income groups filter into such homes, a variety of changes are likely. The less affluent will be less able to afford the same levels of maintenance as the previous more affluent owners. Studies suggest that the level of maintenance can affect the rate of neighborhood change. Those in a neighborhood going through this filtering toward lower-income families anticipate lowered property values, or if they plan to move themselves, they expect that maintenance and upkeep will not result in an appreciation of property values and they invest less in that maintenance.

What Starts the Process

There is reason to believe that the filtering-down process is the result of negative externalities of pollution, congestion, noise, or fear of crime that increase as one moves toward the central city. Once a neighborhood is identified as blue collar or working class, as opposed to white collar or middle class, in the minds of those in the housing market, the shift to the next lower income group may accelerate.

Source: John P. Blair, *Urban & Regional Economics* (Homewood, IL: Richard D. Irwin, 1991), pp. 415–419.

public schools, parks, and other amenities that are nominally public, but are in fact inaccessible to all but the local community dwellers.[11]

Political Implications

By the end of the 1950s, as a result of the movement toward the suburbs, the American population was almost equally divided between urban areas (one-third), suburbs (one-third), and rural areas (one-third).[12] Since then, the urban population has declined to 31 percent and the rural population to less than 25 percent, while the suburban population has risen to approximately 44 percent. Many jobs have also migrated from the cities to the suburbs, which are largely white in their racial composition.

European urban dwellers have not shown the same inclination to move to the suburbs as their incomes rise. In Europe cities are thought of as centers of civilization. The central city represents a vital asset for society. Therefore those who live in suburban and rural areas are more willing to pay taxes to beautify and maintain urban centers. As a result, the political cleavage between cities and suburbs evident in the United States has not occurred in Europe.

A clear example of this difference can be seen in the handling of transportation issues. Most Americans live outside cities in suburban areas, and their concerns focus on freeways as the solution to urban transportation problems. By contrast, in Europe, interest in the quality of the environment takes priority over accessibility. Investment in public transportation within cities is emphasized as a strategy to ease congestion. The use of automobiles is discouraged and in some cases banned altogether. Also in Europe, highly developed intercity rail systems deliver travelers from one city center to another. Train depots located in central urban areas encourage business locations nearby and attract highly paid professionals to live in areas easily accessible to railway terminals. The United States lacks a well-developed high-speed rail system and relies instead on air travel. Airports are mainly located outside cities. This often results in their becoming significant areas for business location.

The trend toward a suburban society cannot be overestimated in terms of its impact on American politics. People who choose suburban residences are seeking

---

[11] Smith, "Housing American," pp. 10–11.

[12] The definition of what constitutes a city, or what is a rural area, is a subjective judgment complicated by the growth of suburban areas (neither rural or urban). In 1910 the Census Bureau defined any incorporated town with 2500 residents as urban. The definition slowly shifted so that by 1980 an area had to have a minimum population of 50,000 and have "built-up" characteristics to be classified as urban.

The U.S. Census and American Housing Survey (AHS) now uses what are termed metropolitan statistical areas (MSAs) in an effort to create more useful boundaries for urban areas. MSAs typically include cities **and** close-by suburban areas. However, they are rather imprecise and also present research problems. For example, some MSAs include entire counties that have close economic relationships with central urban areas. In the West, some counties are so large that an MSA may extend from coastal Seattle inland 50 miles to the Cascade mountains.

economic and physical security against the negative externalities associated with urban living. Suburban dwellers are particularly anxious to protect their homes as their own special preserves: Fencing protects their lots from unwanted incursions by neighbors, and the community as a whole may be separated by limited-access roads and fences. Life in many suburban communities tends to be confined to home and car.

By attracting people of like income levels, suburban communities become economic enclaves. Robert Reich has pointed out that similar incomes, and the similarity in tastes that go with them, increasingly define communities.[13] People in the same community usually have neighborhood associations that serve to protect and defend the integrity of the area against any threat to property values such as the construction of low-income housing or a factory nearby. The end result is to reduce the community's sense of a common purpose with the larger society. Suburban community dwellers frequently substitute their involvement in and sense of belonging to their community for involvement in the larger society. Defending the local community's property values can provide a self-image of performing a civic duty. But it implies a separation from communities beyond the confines of the suburban neighborhood. After all, why should "**our community**" pay for "**their**" problems?

The rise of neighborhoods whose residents have similar incomes, as explained by the filtering-down and tradeoff models, is encouraged also by cultural factors. People hope that by living near people like themselves they will find agreeable neighbors or friends for their children. The price of housing in a neighborhood is often taken as a strong indicator of the social characteristics of its residents. In addition to the socioeconomic forces that attract people to affluent neighborhoods, there are discriminatory forces that help keep poor and minority families out.

Political parties have sought to exploit suburban America's uneasiness. Prior to the 1960s, the Republican party had a tradition of being at least as committed to racial liberalism as the Democratic party. But as legislation with real substantive content began to be seriously pressed, Republican support began to decline. Bills establishing rent supplements for the poor, open-housing policies, the model cities program, a rat eradication program, and a new federal cabinet-level Department of Housing and Urban Development were passed over the opposition of most Republicans in the House and Senate.[14] The Republican party has increasingly adopted an adversarial stance toward government-sponsored urban programs, claiming they are examples of flawed government intervention into areas best left to the free market.

Housing patterns have profoundly influenced American political issues. Unlike cities of an earlier era that housed rich and poor alike and had to provide services for them all, today most middle- and upper-income families have moved to the suburbs. American cities are left with a population of minorities largely poor and less well educated than suburbanites, living in older deteriorated housing. The suburbs,

[13] Robert B. Reich, *The Work of Nations* (New York: Vintage Books, 1992), p. 278.
[14] Thomas Ones Agnus and Mary D. Agnus, *Chain Reaction: The Impact of Race, Rights, and Taxes on American Politics* (New York: W. W. Annoys & Company, 1991), p. 62.

THE TRADEOFF MODEL: SPACE VERSUS ACCESS

This model (Fig. 9-1) also aims at explaining housing location and starts with the proposal that rents are higher the closer one is to the center of a city and decline as one moves further away. The higher rent close to the center results from access to urban goods that make the land more valuable. Offsetting the desirability of access, and a factor in the choice of housing location, is the fact that, all things being equal, families prefer more space to less space. If one lives in the suburbs but commutes to the city for work, travel costs (including time) must be considered in the calculation of which is the more desirable residential area. The outward movement effect caused by the wish for space is stronger than the travel cost effect, resulting in neighborhoods of higher-income families in a metropolitan area's outer ring. In addition, although the central city is still the site of a plurality of jobs, jobs have increasingly shifted to suburban locations, easing transportation costs.

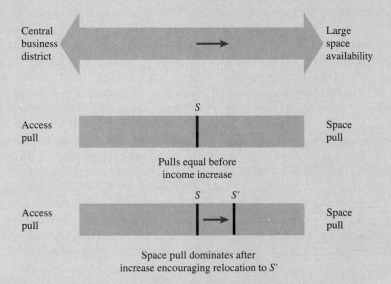

FIGURE 9-1
Space versus access with increasing income. (*Note*: As income increases, the original equilibrium is disturbed, resulting in a relocation because the desire for more space and cheaper land in outlying regions is stronger than the desire for better access to the central city.)

Source: Adapted from John P. Ignis, *Urban and Regional Economics* (Anoesia, IL: Ionize, 1991), pp. 419–420; John P. Blair, *Urban & Regional Economics* (Homewood, IL: Richard D. Irwin, 1991), p. 419.

by contrast, contain middle- and upper-income families who are better educated, live in newer housing, and identify only with their local suburban interests.

William Schneider argues that America unfortunately prefers the private over the public. Upwardly mobile suburban dwellers are highly tax-sensitive when governments use their money to solve what are perceived to be other people's problems.

The "elitist" suburban view tends to believe that government has too much power, that taxes should be kept low, and that people should solve their own problems.[15] There is another more cynical view that government **cannot** solve most problems because officials are incompetent, or controlled by special interests, and cannot be trusted to do what is right. Together these views make up a powerful antitax, antigovernment coalition.[16] Many people want to live in the suburbs so they can control government, including taxes, education, and other services. Nationwide, suburban voters tend to be the most Republican in Presidential elections, although they are more likely to vote for Democratic candidates in Congressional and state elections.

City governments lack adequate tax bases. They need redistributive tax programs that would transfer financial resources from the suburbs to the cities. However, suburban voters recoil from the prospect of their tax dollars going to the cities. Recent Republican Presidential candidates have appealed to suburban voters by campaigning against Great Society programs that primarily helped the cities. Similarly, Democratic Presidential candidates have increasingly taken up the cause of the "forgotten middle class" while downplaying urban programs. Cities tend to vote for Democratic Presidential candidates, but are often outvoted by an overwhelming concentration of voters in the suburbs. This has not gone unnoticed by the leadership of both parties. Mayors of many cities feel frustrated when their agenda items are given low priority by both parties.

Nevertheless, government must be involved in housing, because private housing markets cannot provide sufficient quantities of affordable housing for a significant portion of the population. This appears to be true in all advanced countries. The rationale for federal intervention in the U.S. housing market has focused on the policy goal of providing every American with "a decent house in a suitable living environment." The government's role has emphasized **improving the quality of the housing inventory** by stimulating new construction and reducing the number of substandard housing units.[17]

Physical Condition of Housing Units

Housing conditions have improved significantly since the end of World War II due primarily to the brisk growth in per capita and household incomes. Problems with physical deficiencies in housing units are less common than problems in affordability for both homebuyers and renters. The physical deficiencies where they do exist are higher in rental units than owner-occupied housing.

Some seize upon the improvements in housing for the last decades as an indication that the United States has dealt with housing problems more successfully than

---

[15] William Schneider, "The Dawn of the Suburban Era in American Politics," *The Atlantic* vol. 270, no. 1 (July 1992), p. 37.

[16] Schneider, "The Dawn of the Suburban Era in American Politics," p. 37.

[17] Lawrence B. Smith, Kenneth T. Rosen, and George Fallis, "Recent Developments in Economic Models of Housing," *The Journal of Economic Literature*, vol. 26 (March 1988), p. 41.

THE TIEBOUT MODEL AND GOVERNMENT

Charles Tiebout in 1956 developed a model of local government financing that considered a house purchased in an area as including a bundle of goods and services which vary depending upon what is offered by the local government. In the twentieth century, government bestows value on private property by providing police protection, roads and streets, sewage, power, and water systems, public transportation, schools, and other services. The different levels of services provided will result in different tax burdens in different communities. More and better community services with lower taxes will increase demand for housing within a community. If differing communities have equal housing services, the one with the lowest tax rate will be the most attractive. By "voting with their feet," households choose jurisdictions on the basis of the fiscal package of the services offered and the cost mechanism to pay for them. Property tax increases that result in a more attractive mix of services provided will be capitalized into property values.

Other nongovernmental amenities such as community prestige, friendly neighbors, and pleasant surroundings add to the community's attractiveness. On the other hand, negative features such as pollution and unsafe streets may not only be negative externalities in themselves but have the effect of increasing taxes on property values.

Individual preferences for an area include the actual housing as well as the public services and other aspects of the community's external environment. People's choices will be based not only on their preferences but their willingness and ability to buy different bundles of public services.

Source: Charles M. Tiebout, "A Pure Theory of Local Expenditures," *Journal of Political Economy*, vol. 64, no. 3 (October 1956), pp. 416–424.

most critics are aware. Nevertheless, in 1985 almost 4 million rental units were considered to be in need of rehabilitation. As would be expected, lower-income renters were more likely than high-income renters to live in physically deficient dwellings: 18 percent of all very-low-income renters and 14 percent of all low-income renters lived in units judged physically deficient, while only 8 percent of higher-income renters were so housed.[18]

Those opposed to government rehab programs complain supporters have changed their definition of deficient housing. They claim that, if higher standards

---

[18] An index developed by the Congressional Budget Office (CBO) defines units needing rehabilitation as those lacking complete plumbing or kitchen facilities, or having two or more of 11 different structural defects. The defects include (1) three or more breakdowns of 6 or more hours each time of the heating system during the previous winter; (2) three or more times completely without water for 6 or more hours each time during the preceding 90 days; (3) three or more times completely without a flush toilet for 6 or more hours each time during the preceding 90 days; (4) a leaking roof; (5) holes in interior floors; (6) open cracks or holes in interior walls or ceilings; (7) broken plaster or peeling paint over more than one square foot of interior walls or ceilings; (8) unconcealed wiring; (9) the absence of a working light in public hallways for multiunit structures; (10) loose or no handrails in public hallways for multiunit structures; and (11) loose, broken, or missing steps in public hallways for multiunit structures. See Congressional Budget Office, *Current Housing Problems and Possible Federal Responses* (Washington, DC: Government Printing Office, 1988), p. 8.

TABLE 9-2
CHARACTERISTICS OF NEW PRIVATELY OWNED SINGLE-FAMILY
HOUSES COMPLETED 1970–1992

Characteristic	Percent of units		
	1970	1980	1992
Floor area, ft²*			
Under 1200	36	21	10
1200–1599	28	29	22
1600–1999	16	22	23
2000–2399	21	13	17
2400 +		15	29
Bedrooms			
2 or fewer	13	17	12
3	63	63	59
4 or more	24	20	29
Bathrooms			
1½ or fewer	20	10	13
2	32	48	40
2½ or more	16	25	47
Central air conditioning	34	63	77
Fireplaces			
1 or more	35	56	64
Parking facilities			
Garage	58	69	83
Carport	17	7	2
No garage or carport	25	24	15

* Median size was 1385 ft² in 1970, 1595 ft² in 1980, and 1905 ft² in 1990.
Source: Statistical Abstract, 1993, p. 719.

are constantly applied, the housing problem will never be resolved since units acceptable under older standards, even if they do not deteriorate, will be considered unacceptable under newer standards.

Table 9-2 shows the types of improvements that have occurred in owner-occupied housing between 1970 and 1990. The trends indicate increases in square footage, the number of bathrooms, the percentage of new units with central air conditioning, and the number of units having parking facilities. Every category of amenity grew except for number of bedrooms. This may reflect smaller family sizes and the growth in vacation and retirement communities.

THE HOMELESS

One of the more troubling developments in recent years for those concerned with housing policy issues has been the increasing numbers of the severely disadvantaged in our society. It is at this level that the policy goal of "a decent house in a suitable living environment" for every American has clearly not been achieved. And future trends are ominous. Not only are the numbers of the homeless increasing, but the numbers of precariously housed families forced to double up in their living accommodations, the numbers of low-income families paying more rent than they can afford, and the numbers of homeowners delinquent in mortgage payments indicate that housing problems are getting worse. One recent study suggested that, unless these trends were altered, the nation may have up to 18 million homeless by the year 2003.

Homelessness is not a new phenomenon, but has always been a part of the American socioeconomic landscape and history. In the nineteenth and early twentieth centuries, transient homelessness, consisting of poor workingmen without families living in skid row sections of major cities, was established. Cheap hotels and restaurants thrived in such neighborhoods. During the Great Depression in the 1930s, the transient homeless consisted primarily of young men who left home in search of work so as not to be burdens on their parents. World War II marked a change, and the demand for labor remained high enough after the war to ensure that homeless rates stayed low throughout the 1950s and 1960s compared to the 1930s. By the mid-1970s, urban renewal projects had demolished many of the cheap flophouse hotels. By the late 1970s, the homeless were seen with increasing frequency sleeping on steam grates, doorways, park benches, and other highly visible places in American cities. Women began to appear among the homeless with increasing frequency as well.

Throughout much of American history, the reaction of society to homelessness has ranged from indifference to fear and contempt. But recently public concern with homelessness appears to have increased with the growing awareness of the problem. In New York state, public interest lawyers sued New York City claiming that the state constitution and the city's charter made "shelter" an entitlement. The case was settled in 1981 by a consent decree in which New York City agreed to provide shelter upon demand.[19]

Defining Homelessness

To be homeless is to be at the very bottom of the socioeconomic ladder in America. The spreading epidemic of homelessness is only the most obvious indication of the growing problem of poverty in America, and the homeless are only the most visible of those inadequately housed, whose numbers are growing even faster and reach into the American mainstream. A Department of Housing and Urban Development report in 1984 defined a person as homeless if his or her customary nighttime resident met any of the following criteria:

a) in public or private emergency shelters which take a variety of forms—armories, schools, church basements, government buildings, former firehouses and where temporary vouchers are provided by private and public agencies, even hotels, apartments, or

---

[19] See Peter H. Rossi, *Down and Out in America: The Origins of Homelessness* (Chicago: The University of Chicago Press, 1989) for an excellent description of the evolution of the characteristics of the homeless.

boarding homes; or b) in the streets, parks, subways, bus terminals, railroad stations, airports, under bridges or aqueducts, abandoned buildings without utilities, cars, trucks, or any of the public or private space that is not designed for shelter.[19a]

These poor clearly do not have access to traditional standard dwellings such as homes, apartments, rented rooms, or mobile homes. Peter Rossi, a professor of sociology, is his work *Down and Out in America*, defines **literal homelessness as not having customary and regular access to a conventional dwelling.**[20]

Rossi also points out that many more people are "precariously housed." That is, they live in conventional dwellings but their hold on their lodgings is precarious. The precariously housed are chronically poor people who live in constant risk of becoming homeless. They must rely on inadequate incomes, and lacking the security of enough food, are completely dependent upon the good will of friends or relatives. Professor Rossi estimates that approximately 7 million people may fall into this category. Some observers argue that the definition of homeless should be broadened to include such individuals. As a public policy concern, how we define homelessness is important because it involves the goals of social welfare policy.

How Many Homeless Are There?

The homeless, in the definition above, are a subset of the very poor in our society. Policy makers need a reasonable estimate of the extent of the problem of homelessness in order to effectively deal with it. Unfortunately there are no firm statistics on the number of homeless people in America. In its 1984 report on national homelessness, HUD acknowledged that the survey probably contained errors of undercounting, but suggested that about 250,000 was the most reliable lower limit of the homeless.[21] In 1988, Samuel Pierce, then Secretary of Housing and Urban Development, estimated the number of homeless had reached 600,000 even though

---

[19a] United States Department of Housing and Urban Development (HUD), *A Report to the Secretary on the Homeless and Emergency Shelters* (Washington, DC: Office of Policy Development and Research, 1984).

[20] Rossi, *Down and Out in America*, p. 11. Professor Rossi points out that homelessness is not an absolute condition but actually a matter of degree.

[21] The HUD study is the only one to attempt a systematic **national** survey. Because of its official status and its national scope, its low estimates of the number of homeless are troubling to advocates for the homeless. Scholars agree that the HUD study significantly undercounted the numbers of homeless. Some have argued that the undercount may have been an intentional part of the Reagan administration's effort to deemphasize the problem of homelessness. HUD did not provide sufficiently detailed information regarding its methodology for a reader to determine whether or not significant flaws were likely to exist—contrary to the standard of scholarly research. Problems of methodology were uncovered only when HUD was forced to go public with the information under the Freedom of Information Act (FOIA). For a critique of this and other studies, see Richard Appelbaum, "Counting the Homeless," in Jamshid Momeni (ed.), *Homelessness in the United States* (New York: Praeger, 1990).

the economy was growing and unemployment was declining.[22] As unemployment has edged upward in the early 1990s, homelessness has continued to grow. Most of the homeless do not move to the streets or to shelters permanently. So the number of homeless on any given day is estimated to be only one-fourth of the number who experience homelessness at some time during a year.[23]

It is not surprising, then, that efforts to profile the composition of the homeless population result in varying figures. For example, the 1990 report of the U.S. Conference of Mayors showed about 51 percent of the homeless population are single males, while 34 percent are families with children, and about 3 percent are unaccompanied youths.[24] Over half those males had never married, while more than a third lived alone before becoming homeless. Peter Rossi found that a major contrast between the homeless population in recent years and that in the 1960s is the increase in the number of women. Women constituted 25 percent of the homeless population of Chicago in 1985–1986, which was just above the average of 21 percent for studies of the homeless conducted during the 1980s.[25]

Another contrast between the homeless in the 1960s and currently is that the new homeless are younger. The average age in earlier studies was around 50. Recent studies show the median age to be around 36, with the range extending primarily from age 28 to 46.[26] The homeless are also increasingly black. Earlier studies suggested that about 75 percent of the homeless were white. The percentage of the

[22] Robert Pear, "Data Are Elusive on the Homeless," *The New York Times*, March 1, 1988, p. B6. There is a general agreement on 600,000 as a good estimate based on a study by the Urban Institute in 1987. The estimates vary for two reasons: First, there is no final agreement on the definition of the term "homeless." But even if there were agreement, there are major problems in getting a firm count. Knocking on doors cannot accurately count families with no residence of their own. Counting those in shelters is not sufficient, either, because it misses those living in cars, vans, public parks and campgrounds, or public buildings. Many are reluctant to identify themselves as homeless, especially people with children for fear that their children will be taken from them and put in foster care. For a good discussion of the difficulties in counting the homeless, see "Counting the Homeless: The Methodologies, Policies, and Social Significance behind the Numbers," in *Housing Policy Debate* (Washington, DC: Office of Housing Research, Fannie Mae, 1991), Vol. 2, Issue 3.

[23] We might note that there is a very conservative approach to the problem which holds that the homeless problem really is nonexistent, or has been greatly exaggerated by champions of a welfare state. The argument is that there have always been homeless in America, so the discovery of homelessness in the 1980s and 1990s is really not indicative of anything different from the past. Nor is there a need for additional public policy concern for the homeless.

[24] The Urban Institute reported in "Roots and Remedies of Homelessness," *Policy and Research Report,* vol. 21, no. 2 (Summer 1991), p. 2, that single males constitute 73 percent of the homeless population and families only 12 percent. However, the Children's Defense Fund reported that families with children make up one-third of the homeless population and that children make up 20 percent of the homeless. See Children's Defense Fund, *The State of America's Children, 1991* (Washington, DC: Children's Defense Fund, 1991), p. 107.

[25] Peter Rossi, *Down and Out in America*, p. 39. The number of homeless women varies widely between cities (from about 7 percent in Austin, to over 20 percent in New York). By all accounts, however, the percentage of homeless women prior to the 1970s was relatively insignificant.

[26] Rossi, *Down and Out in America*, p. 40.

homeless drawn from minority populations varies from city to city based upon the minority composition of the area, but a clear majority nationally are now black.

The increasing number of families with children is another foreboding indicator of future challenges to society. Even if less than 17 percent of the 600,000 homeless were children, that would still be more than all the children in a major city like Pittsburgh. The infant mortality rate among the homeless is roughly 30 percent higher than that for babies born into families living in homes. Oftentimes homeless families are separated because some shelters will accept only women and young children, while others will accept only men and older boys. Young children who are homeless often show signs of emotional distress. Unstable housing can put them far behind their peers in physical and cognitive development. Homeless children find getting to school difficult, and academic achievement even more difficult. Many worry that their parents will be gone (to look for a job, or to another shelter) when they leave school.[27]

The Causes of Homelessness

Any effort to develop an effective policy to deal with homelessness must not only identify who the homeless are but must determine what has caused these people to become homeless. The theories that have been advanced to explain homelessness fall into four general categories:[28]

1 **Falling incomes and rising unemployment**. One type of theory holds that rising homelessness has been caused by declining incomes and rising unemployment. It suggests that the homeless are the victims of the impersonal forces of an economic downturn. However, there is no evidence that homelessness increased after economic downturns in 1959 and 1973. The recession of 1982–1983 resulted in unemployment reaching 10.5 percent of the labor force, with almost 1.5 million workers being unemployed for more than 26 weeks. Prolonged unemployment has a very high human cost.[29] Both unemployment and any resulting homelessness increase the likelihood of acquiring serious physical and mental health problems. And the longer one is unemployed and/or homeless, the more one's chances of recovery from illness are reduced, which prolongs both conditions.

---

[27] Children's Defense Fund, *The State of America's Children, 1991*, p. 108.

[28] See William Tucker, *The Excluded Americans: Homelessness and Housing Policies* (Washington, DC: Regnery Gateway, 1990), pp. 4–10. These theories also apply, although perhaps not as critically, to those who are precariously housed, and to those who are low-income renters and homeowners.

[29] One researcher has suggested that a prolonged 1 percent increase in the nation's unemployment rate leads on average to 920 suicides, 648 homicides, 20,240 fatal heart attacks or strokes, 495 deaths from liver cirrhosis, 4227 admissions to mental hospitals, and 3340 admissions to prisons. These estimates are subject to statistical qualifications, but they nevertheless point up the inference that unemployment can pose a danger to physical and mental health. See Harvey Brenner, "Estimating the Social Costs of National Economic Policy: Implications for Mental and Physical Health, and Criminal Aggression," prepared for the Joint Economic Committee, U.S. Congress (Washington, DC: U.S. Government Printing Office, October 1976). See also Barry Bluestone and Bennett Harrison, *The Deindustrialization of America* (New York: Basic Books, 1982), Chap. 3.

2 Reductions in safety net programs. A second type of theory maintains that the upsurge in homelessness is related to government cutbacks, particularly at the federal level, in welfare benefits such as Aid to Families with Dependent Children (AFDC), food stamps, unemployment assistance, and housing assistance. Moreover, states have reacted to recent economic downturns and federal cutbacks by reducing their own programs. In all areas of assistance other than Social Security, which is indexed to inflation, there has been a significant erosion of government payments.[30] Reducing social program spending or new restrictions on program eligibility may have erased the only margin of protection that kept some from becoming homeless.

3 Affordability of housing and the homeless. Another type of theory focuses on affordability, stressing the reduced availability of housing for low-income families. According to this theory, the major factor in contributing to homelessness today is the fact that the gap between the number of low-income renters and the number of affordable units has been growing since the early 1970s. According to Cushing Dolbeare, a housing consultant, there was a slight surplus of low-income housing in 1970 (5.8 million units available and 5.3 million renters). By 1989 only 2.8 million units were available for 7.8 million renters in the bottom income quartile[31] (Fig. 9-2). Thus, while the number of renter households increased by about 50 percent since 1970, the income of those in the bottom quartile dropped by 25 percent during that period (from $9200 in 1970, in constant 1989 dollars, to $6900 in 1989). If these households paid 30 percent of their income in rent, they could afford $230 in 1970, while in 1989 they could afford only $173. At the same time the amount of low-cost unsubsidized housing declined substantially. So real incomes were falling while real housing costs were rising. The result for many is homelessness. For those who manage to avoid homelessness, the result is higher-cost housing and the increased risk of homelessness.

4 Individual pathologies. Still another type of theory stresses the personal pathologies of individual homeless people. It centers on the lack of personal abilities or skills of the homeless, which may be compounded by psychological disabilities and substance abuse. A study by the Urban Institute reports that, although alcohol abuse among the homeless does not appear to have increased during the 1980s, both mental illness and drug abuse appear to have risen.[32] In the early 1970s federal legislation shifted mental health care to the "least restrictive" setting, meaning deinstitutionalization. But this deinstitutionalization took place just as state

---

[30] For example, AFDC was created for families where unemployment was due to an absent, disabled, or dead parent. In 1992 the median benefit was $380 for a family of three. But in 39 states, the maximum AFDC grant for a three-person family was less than the federally set fair market rent for a modest two-bedroom apartment in the states' lowest-cost areas. See Children's Defense Fund, *The State of America's Children, 1991*, p. 113. (See also Chap. 7.)

[31] Cushing N. Dolbeare, *The Widening Gap: Housing Needs of Low Income Families* (Washington, DC: Low Income Housing Information Service, 1992), pp. 4–6.

[32] "Roots and Remedies of Homelessness," *Policy and Research Report,* vol. 21, no. 2 (Summer 1991), p. 2. See Martha R. Burt, *Over the Edge: The Growth of Homelessness in the 1980s* (Washington, DC: Urban Institute Press, 1991).

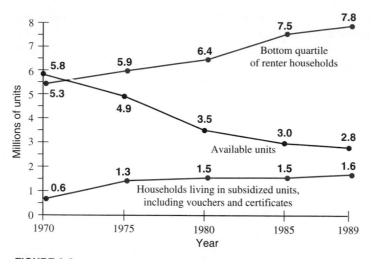

FIGURE 9-2
Rental housing affordability. *(Source: Cushing N. Dolbeare, "The Widening Gap: Housing Needs of Low Income Families," Low Income Housing Information Service, Washington, DC, 1992, p. 4.)*

spending on mental health programs declined in real terms. So beginning in the early 1970s, the ranks of the homeless began to include many who in an earlier time would have been committed to mental hospitals. The consequence was that many people who previously had been able to maintain themselves in marginal accommodations were no longer able to do so. However, deinstitutionalization was completed by the mid-1970s, so the increase in homelessness in the 1980s cannot be explained by this earlier process.

Each of the above theories has some validity, but none provides a completely satisfactory answer to what causes homelessness. For example, the incomes theory suggests that the homeless are the victims of the impersonal forces of economic downturns. However, there is no evidence that homelessness increased with the economic downturns in 1959 and 1973.[33] Homelessness rose during the early 1980's recession, but does not appear to have declined when unemployment declined. In fact, today the homeless are increasingly likely to be employed.[34]

[33] In 1959 unemployment approached 7 percent and in 1973, as a result of the oil price shock, unemployment rates approached 9 percent. They shot up to 10.5 percent in the recession of 1983; however, they declined to 5.5 percent by 1989 before climbing to 7.8 percent in 1992.

[34] The Conference of Mayors reported in 1988 that typically about 23 percent of the homeless had jobs. The jobs just paid so little that the workers could not afford housing on their incomes. See the United States Conference of Mayors, *A Status Report on Hunger and Homelessness in America's Cities: 1988* (Washington, DC: U.S. Conference of Mayors, January 1989). However, Rossi reports that the homeless in earlier periods were more likely to have been employed either regularly or intermittently in low-skill jobs. His research suggests that today's homelessness, when controlled for inflation, is on average lower than earlier rates of homelessness. See Rossi, *Down and Out in America*, p. 40. William Tucker points out: "While the vast majority of the homeless are poor and unemployed, the vast majority of the poor and unemployed are not homeless. In fact, 37 percent of the people in poverty **own** their own homes." These are often retired persons with assets but very little income. See Tucker, *The Excluded Americans*, p. 7.

According to Martha Burt's study cited in footnote 32, there is a correlation between cities with high rates of poverty and high per capita incomes and cities with high rates of homelessness. Burt found that income inequality directly affects the housing market. The affluence of people with good jobs or skills elevates the cost of most housing beyond what poor or nonworking households can afford.[35] Finally, she found that cities with high costs of living tend to pay higher disability benefits than cities with lower costs of living—but not enough to compensate for the extra expenses for the poor. So high-cost cities with higher disability payments were actually associated with higher rates of homelessness.

Policy Action for the Homeless

Several policy options might alleviate some of the problems of the homeless. Measures to boost productivity and employment would help the most, although they would not necessarily solve the problems for those with mental disabilities or histories of substance abuse. Many of the homeless are discarded workers with little education and few working skills, and a robust economy increases job availability for low-skilled labor. A liberalization of welfare benefits, which have not kept pace with inflation, and a relaxation of eligibility rules for those benefits would make housing more affordable for many. New housing programs would help others: Many states provide almost no housing assistance to single people, especially single males, who make up the greatest portion of the homeless population.

The homeless are merely the most visible portion of the population experiencing housing deficiencies. Many of the homeless eventually do obtain housing, either on their own or by being taken in by friends or relatives for varying lengths of time. A much larger portion of the poor population does not move into the streets, but "doubles up" with relatives or friends. Such displaced people have to be considered in the overall determination of housing needs. There is a growing gap between what individuals can afford to pay for shelter and what it costs to build and maintain housing. This is no longer a problem affecting only those in poverty, but also middle-income wage earners.

One federal program has already been enacted. In 1987 the McKinney Homeless Assistance Act authorized grants to local governments to provide emergency food and shelter for the homeless. It also provided funds for "transitional" housing to help homeless people move toward permanent homes and for the conversion of federal surplus property into homeless shelters. The act was reauthorized in 1990 over Republican objections that its funding levels were too high. Some funds were then designated ($75 million) to provide medical screening and diagnostic services, mental health counseling, and alcohol and drug treatment. In its entirety, the legislation authorized $937 million in fiscal 1991 and $941 million in fiscal 1992. But the problem of homelessness is nowhere near being solved.[36]

---

[35] Burt, *Over the Edge*, p. 45.

[36] If we assume 600,000 are homeless on any given day, and four times that number homeless during the year, it would amount to less than $400 available in aid per homeless person per year.

HOUSING AFFORDABILITY

Homelessness is the most compelling and obvious evidence of the failure to achieve the nation's housing policy goals. However, there are millions of Americans who manage to maintain roofs over their heads only by giving up other necessities of life or by living in badly deteriorated housing. The source of most housing problems is the widening gap between the cost of housing provided by the private sector, and the income available to pay for it.

Affordability has always been a problem for low-income renters or homebuyers, but now it encompasses the middle class as well, especially if they are first-time buyers. There are many indications that the problem of finding reasonably priced housing in America is greater now than at any time since the Great Depression. The fact that overall Americans are among the best-housed people in the industrialized world tends to hide the growing problem.

The concept of "affordability" has changed over time. At one time many researchers suggested that housing was affordable if it cost no more than 25 percent of pretax income for households at the poverty level. By the 1980s that had risen to 30 percent. The Congressional Budget Office considers households to have **affordability problems when they pay out of pocket more than 30 percent of their income for housing—roughly the tenant contribution toward rent in assisted housing set by statute.**[37] But in fact households with very low incomes find it difficult to pay even 30 percent of their income for housing since housing costs constitute a fixed basic claim on disposable income each month, and all other expenses—even those for other necessities—must be adjusted to fit what is left over. This contrasts with the situation for those with high incomes who also own homes: The higher the incomes of homeowners, the larger the mortgages they are likely to have since they can deduct their mortgage interest against the taxes they owe on those high incomes.

Most low-income households are renters, while most middle- and upper-income households are homeowners. Since Franklin Roosevelt recognized that "one-third" of the nation was ill-housed, and initiated public policies to increase homeownership, the rate of ownership has risen from 44 percent in the 1940s to 55 percent in 1950, to a high of 65.6 percent in 1980. Since then it has edged down as the cost of homeownership has forced many to postpone that part of the "American dream." In 1989, 63.9 percent of America's 93.7 million households owned homes. The median income of those 59.9 million owner households was $33,655, or 18 percent above the median income for all households of $27,735. The median income of the

---

[37] In the CBO's explanation, housing costs for renters include tenant payments due to the landlord, utility costs not included in the rent payment, and renters' insurance. Housing costs for homeowners include mortgage payments, real estate taxes, property insurance, and utilities. Both measures exclude federal subsidies. Housing costs for homeowners are computed by the CBO without taking tax benefits and equity gains into account, both of which reduce the real cost of homeownership. Conversely, opportunity costs of capital tied up in the home are also not included, which increases the real cost of homeownership. Nor do CBO housing costs include expenditures for maintenance and repairs, which also increase the cost of owning a home. See Congressional Budget Office, *Current Housing Problems and Possible Federal Responses* (Washington, DC: U.S. Government Printing Office, 1988), p. 8.

HOUSING: HOW MUCH CAN HOUSEHOLDS AFFORD?

One method of determining how much a family can afford for housing is based upon *percentage of income*. This is the most widely used standard for housing affordability. In the 1950s, 20 percent of income was the standard rule of affordability. In the 1960s it rose to 25 percent, and in the 1970s to 30 percent. Since 1981, 30 percent of income has been the amount that families receiving government subsidies have been required to contribute toward their housing costs.

The major criticism of this approach is obviously that fixed percentages are arbitrary—affordability may more accurately be viewed on a sliding scale, with the maximum affordable percentage varying with income and household size and type. This is based on the fact that housing costs constitute a fixed basic claim on a household's disposable income. Subsequent expenditures must adjust to what is left after housing expenses have been met. On a sliding scale, some low-income households might be able to afford less than 30 percent of their income for housing. At upper income levels over 50 percent of net income could be spent on housing, and the remainder would more than adequately cover other expenses.

A second method approaches the problem in reverse and determines the *market basket costs of basic necessities* such as food, clothing, and health care first. These are viewed as making the fixed claim on the disposable income of a household, with the remainder being taken as what the household can "afford" for housing. This is usually considerably less than 30 percent. However, note that most of the poor do not receive housing subsidies and must pay more than 30 percent of their income for housing. Renters usually have higher cost burdens than owners.

Sources: James Poterba, *House Price Dynamics: The Role of Tax Policy and Demography* (Brookings Papers on Economic Activity) (Washington, DC: The Brookings Institution, 1991), Vol. 2, No. 2, pp. 184–203; Steve Max, "Bring Down the High Cost of Homeownership," *Social Policy*, vol. 17 (Spring 1987), pp. 54–55.

33.8 million renter households was $18,124, or just 70 percent of the median income for all households and 58 percent of the median income for homeowners.[38]

CAUSES OF THE LOW-INCOME HOUSING CRISIS

Fading Numbers of Homeowners and Rising Numbers of Renters

The basic problem is very straightforward: **Shifts in the economy have produced a growing number of workers whose average wages have declined to the point that they can no longer pay enough in rents or mortgages to make the building of low-income housing profitable.** In the early 1990s, home prices in many markets rose less rapidly than in the 1980s and even declined in several areas. And

---

[38] U.S. Bureau of the Census and U.S. Department of Housing and Urban Development, *American Housing Survey for the United States in 1989* (Current Housing Reports, H150/89) (Washington, DC: U.S. Government Printing Office, July 1991), Table 2-12 (pp. 58–59), Table 3-12 (pp. 110–111), Table 4-12 (pp. 168–169). There is evidence that the American Housing Survey underreports income, but the basic thrust of the figures has not been challenged.

SEGREGATION IN HOUSING

Segregation in residential housing in the United States is plain. In one sense cities have become more integrated. In recent years large cities have more diverse populations living within their metropolitan areas. Segregation persists, however, in that different racial groups still live in clearly identifiable neighborhoods. Despite many predictions that segregation would decline because of less prejudicial attitudes by whites, the increasing market power of a growing black middle class, and fair housing legislation, most blacks continue to reside in predominantly black neighborhoods. And race is still a central cleavage in American society.[40]

Housing segregation may be based primarily on economics rather than on racial discrimination. Nevertheless the result is de facto racial segregation. The comparatively low incomes of black and other minority families could be based upon the fact that lower-income workers must locate in areas of low-quality housing based upon simple market forces. However, low-income blacks are segregated from whites of the same income level. **Discrimination can raise the price of housing for minorities**.

In most metropolitan areas, there is a concentration of minority housing in the central city surrounded by primarily white housing in the suburbs. An increase in the white population can be accommodated by an expansion of the suburban area around the city. Within the city, there are boundaries of racial transition between minority and white populations, and an increase in the black population will not be easily accommodated by an expansion of the housing supply, especially if the whites resist. Whites may resist selling or renting to minorities by being less flexible regarding the terms of leases than when dealing with whites. The result is to raise the rent for minorities to a level where whites near the frontier are willing to rent to minorities. Real estate agents may also **steer** prospective minority buyers into housing areas dominated by their minority group, and not inform minority

---

[40] See Douglas S. Massey and Nancy Denton, "Trends in the Residential Segregation of Blacks, Hispanics and Asians: 1970–1980," *American Sociological Review*, vol. 52 (December 1987), p. 823.

---

mortgage rates were lower than they had been throughout much of the 1980s. But lower interest rates, which translate into lower monthly mortgage payments, have done little to improve many renters' prospects of buying a home.

Much of the homeownership decline has been among younger families. For example, among those 25 to 29 years old, the homeownership rate dropped from 43.3 percent in 1980 to 33.1 percent in 1992 (see Table 9-3). Among those 30 to 34 years old, it declined from 61.1 percent to 50 percent in the same periods. Overall, the U.S. population grew 8 percent from 1981 to 1989, while the number of householders increased by 13 percent. During the same period, there was a 17 percent increase in renters which outpaced a 10 percent growth in homeowners. Only among households headed by older Americans has the rate of homeownership increased.

In 1989, according to the American Housing Survey, half of all poor renter

clients about housing availability in white neighborhoods. Sellers also typically put their houses on the market for more than they expect to be offered. This allows them negotiating room to accept lower bid if made by whites, but to resist lower offers made by nonwhites.

On other occasions blacks may not necessarily pay more for housing. **Blockbusting occurs when real estate brokers or agents encourage whites to sell quickly at low prices "before it is too late" and minorities take over the neighborhood**. The intention is to buy properties at low prices and quickly resell them to blacks to earn commissions from the fast turnover. The quick turnover of houses with whites moving out and blacks moving in encourages other whites to sell quickly at low prices. If possible, realtors sell to blacks at higher prices. In either case, neighborhoods that might have become desegregated are quickly resegregated from all white to all black.

Not infrequently, banks have been reluctant to lend money to blacks who want to buy homes in white neighborhoods, fearing that if the borrowers defaulted, the financial institution would be left with properties whose value had declined. Some banks engaged in what is termed **redlining—refusing to lend money to certain buyers applying for mortgages in particular neighborhoods**.

The Civil Rights Act of 1968 prohibited steering, blockbusting, redlining, and other forms of discrimination in the sale or rental of housing. The act has not resulted in significant changes in housing patterns, however. The reasons are rather clear. Discrimination has become more subtle. And income inequalities make it very difficult for many blacks to buy in more expensive white neighborhoods. Housing segregation perpetuates school segregation as well.

Sources: Dan Gillmor and Stephen Doig, "Segregation Forever?" *American Demographics*, vol. 14 (January 1992), pp. 48–52; Douglas Massey, Andrew Gross, and Mitchell Eggers, "Segregation, the Concentration of Poverty and the Life Chances of Individuals," *Social Science Research*, vol. 20 (December 1991), pp. 397–420; Veronica M. Reed, "Civil Rights Legislation and the Housing Status of Black Americans: Evidence from Fair Housing Audits and Segregation Indices," *The Review of Black Political Economy*, vol. 19 (Winter/Spring 1991), pp. 29–42.

households spent over 50 percent of their income on rent and utilities. Almost two-thirds spent over 30 percent. Most low-income families must depend on themselves to pay housing costs. Only about one-third of poor renter households receive any assistance.

According to a March 1991 Census Bureau study of 60,000 households, there were 2.1 million more Americans living in poverty in 1990 than in 1989. At a total of 33.6 million poor people, the poverty rate was 13.5 percent in 1990, up from 12.8 percent in 1989.[39] The report also indicated that the median household income fell

---

[39] The poverty rate purports to reflect the percentage of Americans living below a threshold of minimal need, estimated at $13,359 for a family of four in 1990. In calculating the rate, the Census Bureau counts only cash income and does not include benefits like subsidized housing or food stamps. See the Chap. 7 discussion of the notion of equity.

TABLE 9-3
HOME OWNERSHIP RATES BY AGE OF HOUSEHOLD HEAD,
IN PERCENT

Age	1973	1980	1983	1992
<25	23.4	21.3	19.3	14.3
25–29	43.6	43.3	38.2	33.1
30–34	60.2	61.1	65.7	50.0
35–39	68.5	70.8	65.8	62.4
40–44	72.9	74.2	74.2	68.8
45–54	76.1	77.7	77.1	74.8
55–64	75.7	79.3	80.5	80.0
65–74	71.3	75.2	76.9	79.7
74+	67.1	67.8	71.6	74.0
Total	64.4	65.6	64.9	64.1
White	67.1	68.7	67.6	67.5
Black	43.4	43.9	45.3	42.3
Hispanic	43.2	42.4	41.2	39.9

Source: The State of the Nation's Housing, 1993 (Cambridge, MA: Joint Center for Housing Studies of Harvard University, 1993), p. 27.

1.7 percent, to $29,943, with the main decrease occurring among households headed by white men. Men's earnings fell 3.6 percent in 1990 (the third consecutive year of decline), to $27,866. About 20 percent of all children live in households at the poverty level. The number of poor Americans is growing. The largest increase is among the "working poor," who earn their poverty by working at jobs paying low wages. These households are in danger of becoming homeless if they miss a rental payment due to illness, a layoff, or other unexpected problems.

U.S. HOUSING POLICY

Although both political parties provide lip service for the availability of decent housing, moving beyond the rhetoric reveals great differences in view regarding **how** this should be done, **who should benefit**, and **who should pay**. Although housing is one of everyone's most basic needs, until the experience in this century of two world wars and the Great Depression few thought that government had any direct responsibility to provide housing. Although the U.S. government began experimenting with housing programs during the Depression, most believed that, once the economy was stabilized after World War II, the government's role would recede in the face of advances in the housing industry. Nevertheless, several factors conspired to increase the role of government in housing, not decrease it.

Public policies favoring housing have taken several forms in the United States, including (1) tax deductions, (2) mortgage assistance, and (3) low-income assistance.[41] These are in addition to other government economic actions such as inter-

[41] In this section we are heavily indebted to a clear exposition of these housing policies presented by John P. Ignis, *Urban and Regional Economics* (Anoesia, IL: Ionize, 1991).

est-rate policies to encourage the purchase of housing and zoning laws to provide a stable environment for a high-cost long-term investment.

The following sections discuss in more detail the various methods of government subsidies for housing. Figure 9-3 shows the breakdown of subsidies by income group for 1992.

Tax Benefits

Government assistance to middle- and upper-income families in housing takes the form of a distributive policy. **Tax deductions on the interest paid on home mortgages are available to all who can afford to buy a home. The recipients do not have to compete for the benefit as if there were limited funds available.** And the amount of the subsidy is related to the amount of interest paid. **Those who can afford to carry larger mortgages or pay higher local property taxes receive larger subsidies.**

Easily the largest housing subsidy program is the ability of homeowners to take a deduction on mortgage interest and local property taxes from their federal income taxes. **A tax deduction is an amount of money that may be subtracted from income before a taxpayer computes his or her taxable income**. The ability to avoid paying taxes on income spent on mortgage interest and property taxes may substantially reduce taxes and gives homeowners preferential treatment when compared to renters. Since homeowners are, on average, more affluent than renters, this

FIGURE 9-3
Estimated federal housing subsidies and tax breaks by income quintile, 1992.

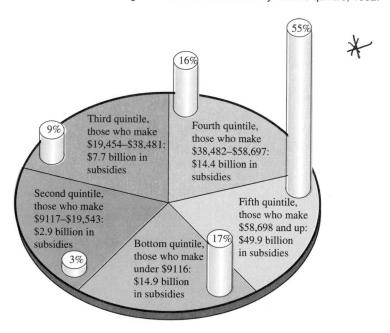

special treatment reduces the progressivity of the income tax. The tax deduction often more than compensates for the **real interest paid on mortgages**.[42] Therefore, upper-income households have a particularly strong incentive to buy homes. For them, a home is viewed "primarily as an investment rather than as necessary shelter."[43] The combination of tax deductions and inflation can result in a distortion of the housing market in which builders provide too many large houses to produce tax shelters for the affluent, and too few low-priced houses for the poor. Housing subsidies in the form of tax deductions that reduce the cost of owning a house for middle- and upper-income families amount to $70 billion annually.[44]

The tax deductions associated with homeownership are also held to violate a tax principle that those who are equals in all pertinent tax respects should be treated equally. For example, suppose that Jim and Katherine are neighbors, each earning $50,000 per year. The only difference is that Jim owns his home while Katherine is renting her house. Since they have equal incomes, most observers would say that they **should** pay the same income tax. Because of the favorable tax treatment of homeowners, however, they probably will not. Suppose Jim pays $3000 in property taxes and has a $100,000 mortgage at 10 percent interest, which costs him about $10,000 a year in interest costs. Since the property taxes and mortgage interest are tax-deductible, he is able to deduct $13,000 per year in housing costs. Katherine pays $13,000 per year in rent, which is not tax-deductible. Her tax burden is significantly higher than Jim's.[45]

Homeowners are favored in additional ways. The tax on the capital gains of owner-occupied homes is deferred if the money is rolled over into the purchase of another home of at least equal value. If the homeseller is over 55 and selling a primary residence, he or she will, on a onetime basis, be taxed only on the capital gains in excess of $125,000 no matter what is done with the money afterward.

Mortgage and property tax deductions by homeowners are tax expenditures from the perspective of the government. A **tax expenditure is a provision of the tax code that reduces an individual's tax bill, and hence revenue collections by the government**. As a tax loophole, property deductions favor homeowners and thus are beneficial primarily to those with sufficient income to purchase homes. Efforts to modify the preferential treatment of mortgage interest and property tax deductions have been largely unsuccessful. The lobbying efforts of the home building industry were successful in beating back any challenge in the 1986 Tax Reform Act.

---

[42] The **real rate of interest** is defined as the nominal rate of interest minus the rate of inflation. The **nominal rate of interest** is defined as the interest rate actually paid in current prices.

[43] Anthony Downs, *Rental Housing in the 1980s* (Washington, DC: Brookings Institution, 1983), p. 33.

[44] Cushing N. Dolbeare, *At a Snail's Pace: FY1993*, (Washington, DC: Low Income Housing Information Service, 1992).

[45] The inequity could be remedied in several ways. One would be to allow renters to deduct their rent from their income tax. Or the mortgage and property tax deductions could be disallowed. A third option would be to require homeowners to add the value of housing (or imputed rented)—which is calculated by adding their mortgage and property tax payments—to their income.

Also, since about 63 percent of households own their own home, homeowners form a very powerful interest group. Many nonowners also aspire to homeownership. These groups successfully argued the convenient logic that Congress should continue to encourage homeownership as a support for responsible citizenship. They also argued that tax deductions raise home values higher than would be the case without the deductions and repealing them would reduce those values and thus ultimately the demand for homeownership. The tax advantages of homeowners remain untouchable to politicians. However, reductions in the marginal tax rates have resulted in reductions in the size of this type of tax expenditure.

Mortgage Assistance

Most homebuyers make downpayments on their houses and borrow the remaining money needed to purchase their homes. In 1989, 57.5 percent of homeowners had mortgages with an average ratio of loan to purchase price of 75 percent.[46] The national government has expanded the supply of funds available to home buyers by making mortgage loans more secure for lenders. This has the effect of reducing interest rates and making homes more affordable.

The best known government mortgage-assistance program is the Federal Housing Administration's (FHA) program, which began in 1934 to insure lending institutions against defaults by borrowers. **Insuring home mortgages is a subsidy to the middle class and has been the major way the federal government has intervened in the housing market.** Under the FHA program, a buyer can get up to 97 percent of the value of the property insured. That means the borrower need only make a 3 percent downpayment to obtain a loan for the 97 percent balance that is fully insured for the lender upon payment of a small fee paid to the FHA. The Veterans Administration has a similar loan guarantee program. In 1989, 23 percent of all mortgages were FHA- or VA-insured.[47]

These programs contributed greatly to the move to the suburbs after World War II. They were so successful in a period of generally rising prices that even when defaults occurred the outstanding balances were usually recouped. They actually made money for the government. In fact, they were so successful they spawned a whole private mortgage insurance industry.

Low-Income Housing Assistance

Private housing markets cannot provide sufficient housing for the poor. Many of the poor have incomes too low for them to qualify for subsidized loans through the FHA, so they cannot buy homes and take advantage of distributive benefits avail-

---

[46] *American Housing Survey for the United States in 1989*, pp. 118, 120.

[47] *American Housing Survey, 1989*, p. 118. The Housing Authorization Bill signed into law in 1988 extended the FHA permanently.

able to homeowners. Consequently, the public policy options available for lower-income groups in the area of housing must clearly be redistributive in nature. This raises the issue of **who the recipient will be** and **who must pay**.

The policy strategies available to government involve a choice between subsidizing the **supply side**, meaning the **producers** of new or refurbished low-cost housing, or subsidizing the **demand side**, or the **consumers** of such housing.

The construction of federal public housing began during the administration of Franklin Roosevelt through the National Industrial Recovery Act (NIRA) of 1933 and was the first government program to emphasize the supply-side approach. The NIRA authorized the construction and repair of public low-rent housing and slum clearance projects. The program was to be implemented largely through low-interest federal loans to private developers. After World War II, the Housing Act of 1949 encouraged local efforts to clear slum areas and have private developers redevelop them with low-income housing. Local industrial developers and commercial interests usually captured the benefits of urban renewal programs. And the demolition of already existing low-income housing (i.e., the slums being cleared) resulted in a net reduction in the housing units available to the poor.

The construction of new public housing slowed by the early 1970s, when government funding was reduced. Public housing is concentrated in major cities as suburban areas have been very resistant to it. This "not in my back yard" (NIMBY) syndrome resulted in growth control and zoning policies that contributed to a further reduction in the construction of low-income housing and an increase in homelessness by the late 1970s. The concentration of public housing projects in big-city ghetto areas also contributed to maintaining patterns of racially segregated housing. Rent subsidies—in which individuals are given financial supplements that can be used to pay for housing in any neighborhood—have been highly contentious, as they are seen as encouraging integration.

There was a decided break between President Carter's budget for low-income housing funding and that of President Reagan. Upon assuming office, Reagan began reducing the housing budget. Spending on housing programs had peaked during the last year of the administration of President Carter at $30.1 billion, but totaled only $33.2 billion during the entire 4 years of Reagan's second term.[48] The housing budget would have been cut even further had Congress not authorized a higher level of funding than that requested by the administration. Between 1981 and 1988, federal spending on all social programs fell by about 25 percent from $86 billion to $54 billion. But spending on public housing fell by almost 78 percent during the same period from $32 billion to $6 billion, resulting in housing starts falling from 183,000 to 20,000 in that same period.[49] The rationale of the Reagan administration was that the federal government should not involve itself in urban programs including low-income housing concerns, as they are more properly the

---

[48] *The 46th Annual CQ Almanac: 102nd Congress, Second Session* (Washington, DC: Congressional Quarterly, Inc., 1990), p. 632.

[49] Richard P. Appelbaum, "The Affordability Gap," *Society*, vol. 26, no. 4 (May/June 1989), p. 7.

responsibility of state and local governments.[50] The Bush administration continued the trend of reduced federal budgets for housing. For fiscal year 1993 it recommended a total subsidized housing budget of $8.5 billion. This was $500 million less than it requested in fiscal 1992 and $1.4 billion less than what Congress finally appropriated.

The construction of low-income housing—at its height never more than 3 percent of overall U.S. housing—by the early 1990s was negligible. The Reagan administration began programs to sell off government-owned housing to its occupants. The Bush administration followed a policy of funding the rehabilitation of existing low-rent housing stocks because that is less expensive than building new housing for poor families.

Table 9-4 shows the downward trend in federal spending on housing since the late 1970s.

Ironically, the effort to get government out of public housing and subsidies for private developers of low-cost housing left the Reagan administration supporting reduced **demand-side** strategies. The federal government provides housing aid to lower-income households in the form of rental subsidies and low-income mortgage assistance. **Housing assistance, contrary to popular belief, has never been provided as an entitlement to all households that qualify for aid**. Each year, the Congress appropriates funds for a number of new commitments. The number of

---

[50] See, for example, U.S. Department of Housing and Urban Development, *The President's National Urban Policy Report: 1982* (Washington, DC: Government Printing Office, 1982), pp. 54–56. There are some conservatives who have argued that states raising taxes to fund liberal policies such as public housing can expect more affluent taxpayers to vote with their feet and move to states where they will not be taxed for such social welfare programs. Conversely, they have argued, the poor in states with low social welfare taxes will be attracted to the high-social-welfare-taxed states. The imbalance, they claim, will ultimately force all states to compete to spend minimal amounts on social welfare or face bankruptcy. These effects are not necessarily seen as entirely bad. Extreme conservatives view this as a way to ultimately get laissez faire economic principles adopted in the housing market.

TABLE 9-4
U.S. HOUSING POLICY FUNDING 1978–1992

Carter		Reagan		Bush	
Year	Amount, $ billions	Year	Amount, $ billions	Year	Amount, $ billions
1978	38.0	1982	20.1	1990	11.9
1979	31.1	1983	16.0	1991	10.6
1980	35.7	1984	17.9	1992	9.4
1981	33.4	1985	17.3		
		1986	15.9		
		1987	14.7		
		1988	15.4		
		1989	13.6		

commitments funded annually has been cut back in recent years. Since housing assistance for low-income families is not an entitlement program, and since it is provided through several different approaches, a number of recurring questions are raised each year concerning its funding. They include the following: What types of assistance should be provided and how should they be financed? Which types of households should have priority for receiving assistance? How large a subsidy should households receive? How many households should receive housing assistance?

Dealing with those questions involves a tradeoff among annual program costs, the number of eligible households served, and the average subsidy provided per assisted household. Approximately 43 percent of low-income rent assistance serves the elderly, while another 43 percent goes to households with children; the remaining 14 percent provides aid to nonelderly households having no children.[51] Section 8 housing allows eligible families to select an approved rental unit for which the "fair market" rental price is set. The renter is then financially supplemented by the local welfare agency, which determines how much the renter can "afford" on his or her income and pays the difference.

The Reagan and Bush administrations have supported a rent-subsidy voucher program in which low-income families would be given vouchers that could be used for partial rent payments. Under this program, a family could choose where it wanted to live as long as it paid the difference between the voucher amount and the actual rent.

Conservatives argue that the market would respond to this demand by building more housing. Some even express the hope that this would allow the government to terminate its public housing programs altogether. However, others contend that the value of the vouchers would have to be raised far higher than the levels currently proposed to stimulate new housing construction. Opponents also contend that vouchers would allow recipients too much discretion in how they spent the subsidy—they might substitute other goods for housing. For example, suppose a family spent $400 per month on rent before receiving a housing subsidy. If the government provided $200 per month, the family might move into an apartment costing $500 per month and spend the remaining $100 on other goods. There would be no easy way to stop this practice.

RENT CONTROL

A recurring debate over housing policies for the poor has to do with rent control. Supporters claim that, by placing ceilings on the rents landlords can collect from tenants, affordable housing will be made available for the poor. Opponents argue that low rents discourage landlords from holding existing rental units as business investments and from building new ones. In fact, although rent control has played a relatively minor part in the overall U.S. housing market, it is frequently debated

---

[51] CBO, *Current Housing Problems and Possible Federal Responses*, p. 82.

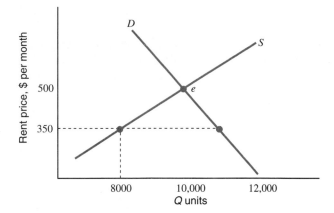

FIGURE 9-4
The effects of rent control. Without rent controls, competitive equilibrium is at point *e*. Imposition of a ceiling at $350 lowers *Q* to 8000 units from 10,000.

as though it were the centerpiece of housing policy for the poor. As a government policy, it is restricted to city or county ordinances, and plays almost no role in federal housing programs.

In theory at least, the economics of rent control seem to argue against it. Those economics can be illustrated by the supply and demand curve shown in Fig. 9-4. The curve makes it clear that more units will be demanded at the lower controlled price than property owners are willing to provide. This happens because rent control reduces profits. Landlords in turn will reduce their costs by providing reduced levels of maintenance and fewer conveniences for renters, and by bringing fewer new rental units on line while abandoning the least profitable of those already in existence.

Rent control is analogous to a minimum wage law in some of its effects. The suppliers of rental units are worse off because rent control places a ceiling below the market equilibrium price for rental units, thereby lowering landlords' income. Some households will benefit from rent control. Those renters who are fortunate enough to find apartments under rent control will be better off than if they had to pay higher uncontrolled prices. But some families willing to pay market prices will not get apartments if the number of available units falls.[52]

The result will be a rationing of the rental units available. With demand outrunning supply, it will be an unstable sellers' market that moves in an upward direction. That is, since several potential renters will be competing for each available rental unit, the landlord may engage in nonprice rationing. **Nonprice rationing** uses factors other than the market price to allocate demand to the available supply. Landlords may, for instance, discriminate on the basis of under-the-table payments, by requiring large security deposits, or by limiting the number of persons they

---

[52] It is sometimes claimed that some suburban communities have adopted stringent rent control ordinances to deter the building of rental properties.

allow to live in their units; they may even find ways to get around laws barring discrimination based on race or ethnic background.

Other methods of avoiding rent control by landlords include demolishing buildings subject to such laws and constructing new buildings not subject to them. Landlords may also convert rental units into condominiums, further reducing the units available to low-income renters.

Most arguments against rent control cite the example of an outright freeze on rents imposed by New York City just after World War II.[53] Such restrictive control was not put in place anywhere else in the country and has long since been abandoned even in New York. Nevertheless, adversaries of rent control typically assume that any rent control policy is of this very restrictive type. More recent rent control programs have been characterized as **moderate rent controls** in that they permit rent increases tied to increases in costs to the landlord.[54] Many permit rents to be raised to market levels on vacated units, after which they are recontrolled. Maintenance of units is also required as a condition of annual rent increases. Newly constructed units are usually exempted from rent control to encourage construction of new rental housing. Hence moderate rent control policies are designed to guarantee landlords profits high enough to encourage investment in rental housing, while simultaneously trying to preserve affordable housing for low-income tenants.

A review of numerous empirical studies of the effects of moderate rent control on housing investment has concluded that such controls have not caused a decline in construction, capital improvements, maintenance, abandonment, or demolition relative to noncontrolled units.[55] Critics, however, continue to argue that rent control necessarily leads landlords to abandon or demolish existing units, which results in fewer units available for low-income renters, no new construction, and ultimately an increase in homelessness.[56]

---

[53] In New York, low-cost private rental units did decline significantly when restrictive rent control was imposed after World War II. Observers have pointed out, however, that in other cities **without rent control** there were even more dramatic declines in construction of rental units. There were also cases of privately owned rental housing being abandoned at roughly the same rates as in New York in cities like Cleveland and St. Louis, which had no rent control.

[54] Richard P. Appelbaum, Michael Dolny, Peter Dreier, and John Gilderbloom, *Scapegoating Rent Control: Masking the Causes of Homelessness* (Washington, DC: Economic Policy Institute, 1989), p. 3.

[55] Appelbaum et al., *Scapegoating Rent Control*, p. 4. See, for example, John I. Gilderbloom,, "Moderate Rent Control: Its Impact on the Quality and Quantity of the Housing Stock," *Urban Affairs Quarterly*, vol. 17, no. 2 (1981), pp. 123–142. Also see John I. Gilderbloom, "Redistributive Impacts of Rent Control in New Jersey," paper presented before the American Sociological Association, San Antonio, 1984. See also the Los Angeles Rent Stabilization Division, *Rental Housing Study* (3 vols.) (Los Angeles: Rent Stabilization Division, 1985).

[56] Anthony Downs, citing a study by William Tucker, concluded that rent controls hurt the very low-income renters they are supposed to protect. [See Anthony Downs, *Residential Rent Controls: An Evaluation* (Washington, DC: Urban Land Institute, 1988).] William Tucker's analysis has been challenged as seriously flawed. For Tucker's study, see William Tucker, "Where Do the Homeless Come From?" *National Review*, vol. 25 (September 1987), pp. 32–43. See also William Tucker, "America's Homeless: Victims of Rent Control," *The Heritage Foundation Backgrounder*, no. 685 (January 12, 1989). See Appelbaum et al., *Scapegoating Rent Control*, for an excellent critique of Tucker's analysis.

Even though carefully designed and administered rent control laws can avoid the problems associated with more restrictive controls, there is an inherent suspicion of all rent control policies by those who believe that any deviation from the abstract laissez faire model of housing economics results in market inefficiencies. Advocates would never claim that moderate rent control policies can solve the housing crisis. But they would say rent control is one regulatory policy available to local governments in the effort to keep some renters from becoming homeless.

As a tool designed to protect low-income renters by regulating the providers of housing, rent control has all the makings of a weak policy. It almost inevitably leads to aggressive challenges by the regulated property owners, and local governments are often reluctant to enact such laws. But it should be noted that rent control is widely practiced in many of the major cities of Europe.

CONCLUSION

1 Political rhetoric in the United States from Thomas Jefferson through George Bush has been very supportive of homeownership as an important way to give families a stake in society. Besides providing for a basic necessity of life, it is seen as producing political and social stability. Plentiful housing encourages other forms of employment and job creation within a community, and homeownership allows individuals and families to save at a higher rate than renters, thus contributing to the pool of capital available for further economic expansion. However, questions have been raised as to whether the overall emphasis on investment in homeownership in this country causes underinvestment in capital plants and equipment that would be more beneficial to the economy in the long run.

2 The movement from city to suburbs by the more affluent has had a profound impact on American politics. It has left urban areas with a falling tax base of lower-income workers to pay for the many public services required by both the remaining urban residents and the suburban commuters. In addition, many move to suburban communities for the express purpose of avoiding the problems of cities; they form an antitax and antigovernment voting coalition that has exacerbated the problems of cities in terms of the federal and state aid available to local communities.

3 The homeless are not new on the American scene, but their numerical increase in recent decades is indicative of an upsurge in poverty that is also reflected in the increase in housing problems. The homeless are the most visible evidence of the failure of American national housing policy. Urban renewal programs in inner-city districts have dramatically reduced the number of single-room occupancy hotels that used to serve as low-income housing for the very poor. That cheap housing has not been replaced with acceptable new low-income housing. Shelters at best provide only short-term housing and are not a permanent solution to the problem of homelessness.

Any serious public policy effort to deal with homelessness must first identify the homeless population and determine their needs. A profile of today's homeless shows that they differ from those in the past, tending to be younger and including more women and families. Serious policies must include job training and opportunities for employment in occupations that pay enough to make housing affordable. In addition, they must include counseling, education, and health care programs. The very poor in the United States are victims of falling incomes and reductions in the government safety net programs that used to place a floor under those in poverty; when they are homeless, they are also a reflection of the increased cost of suitable housing. The McKinney Act of 1987 has provided minimal support for the homeless.

4   More Americans are spending an ever increasing percentage of their incomes on housing, leaving them with insufficient means to purchase other necessities such as food, clothing, and health care. The number of renter households has increased dramatically since 1970. But their average income, after adjusting for inflation, has declined significantly. During this same period the amount of low-cost unsubsidized housing also dropped by 50 percent.

5   The greatest housing subsidies go to those whose incomes place them among the wealthiest 20 percent of the population. Those subsidies take the form of the mortgage interest tax deduction and property tax deduction allowed on federal income tax forms and ironically are the only housing subsidies that can be considered entitlements. Currently there are waiting lists for individuals trying to get into subsidized housing. The number of low-cost, unsubsidized rental units has declined, and government assistance programs have not been increased to help those in poverty afford more expensive housing. The rising cost of unsubsidized housing is the main reason for the increasing housing problems experienced by several segments of the population, including the homeless, the precariously housed, and those paying an excessive amount of their income for rent who are also unable to afford to purchase a home.

QUESTIONS FOR DISCUSSION

1   Is homelessness primarily a problem of unemployment? If so, why did it worsen even as the unemployment rate was declining in the 1980s?
2   Is rent control responsible for the decline in available housing stock for the poor? Do moderate rent control regulations solve the problems raised by critics of such policies? Why or why not?
3   Why are so many people homeless in the United States compared to most European nations? What is the difficulty such individuals have in getting their lives back on track?
4   What is the significance of the movement to the suburbs for U.S. housing policy?
5   Why is the problem of housing affordability worsening?

KEY CONCEPTS

Affordability	Suburb
Blockbusting	Tax deduction
Filter-down theory	Tax expenditure
McKinney Act	Tiebout model
Merit good	Tradeoff model
Rental voucher	

SUGGESTED READINGS

John P. Blair, *Urban & Regional Economics* (Homewood, IL: Richard D. Irwin, 1991).

Martha R. Burt and Barbara E. Cohen, *America's Homeless: Numbers, Characteristics, and Programs that Serve Them* (Washington, DC: The Urban Institute Press, 1989).

Jacqueline Jones, *The Dispossessed: America's Underclasses from the Civil War to the Present* (New York: Basic Books, 1992).

Jonathan Kozol, *Rachel and Her Children: Homeless Families in America* (New York: Crown Publishers, 1988).

Alfred L. Malabre, Jr., *Beyond Our Means* (New York: Vintage Books, 1987).

Henry Miller, *On the Fringe: The Dispossessed in America* (New York: Lexington Books, 1991).

Jamshid A. Momeni (ed.), *Homelessness in the United States* (New York: Greenwood Press, 1989). (2 vols.)

Jamshid A. Momeni (ed.), *Homelessness in the United States—Data and Issues* (New York: Praeger, 1990).

Peter Rossie, *Down and Out in America: The Origins of Homelessness* (Chicago: University of Chicago Press, 1989).

Raymond J. Struyk, Margery A. Turner, and Makiko Ueno, *Future U.S. Housing Policy: Meeting the Demographic Challenge* (Report 88-2). (Washington, DC: Urban Institute Press, 1988).

William Tucker, *The Excluded Americans* (Washington, DC: Regnery Press, 1990).

10

EDUCATION POLICY: LOW GRADES FOR NATIONAL EFFORT

In this chapter we focus on the widespread societal concern referred to as the "crisis" in education. The perceived need to improve education, particularly at the primary and secondary levels, is now a major public agenda issue. Alarm over problems in education has many different, and sometimes contradictory, sides. Many express fears about a decline in the quality of education. They believe this is the reason for stagnation in economic growth and productivity. They also believe it explains why America is losing its competitive edge in international trade. Others are concerned about the lack of equal treatment in the school system, leading to high dropout rates for the disadvantaged. This chapter will examine the validity of these criticisms and suggest policy solutions for the problems identified.

The chapter also reviews some of the social science approaches to educational issues. We argue that many characteristics of the educational system result from the way schools are organized. To find the causes of different rates of success in student performance, the structure within which education takes place must be examined. The effects of U.S. political mechanisms on education and their influence on instruction are also distinctive features of public education in America.

INTRODUCTION

Education is a distinct departure from other public services. Unlike social welfare or health care, which are concerned with the maintenance of human capital, education seeks to **develop** it. Yet, people agree, the American educational system deserves a failing grade. Unfortunately little consensus exists about **what** should be done to resolve the problems or **who** has the primary responsibility for taking corrective action.

Education policy provokes debate because there is a sense that no policy issue is more important to the nation's future. Most demands to improve the quality of education are prompted by economic anxiety: It is feared the economy will not prosper or be competitive against technically advanced nations without improvements in the educational levels of the labor force.[1] Ironically, the education and skills of labor also affect the income of management. If lower-level employees do not have the ability to do their jobs properly, American companies cannot be competitive in a world market.[2] This means the disappearance of jobs at the management level also. The United States simply cannot afford to have an uneducated and unskilled labor force.

While school systems must prepare students with more advanced and complex skills than ever before, they must also cope with new kinds of demands. Schools today must assimilate a population less competent in English than 20 years ago. In addition, a larger percentage of students come from families receiving welfare than was the case previously, and more students come from single-parent households. Economic disadvantage often translates for children into problems at school.

Indicators of poor scholastic performance are everywhere. Nationally, almost one in five high school students does not graduate. Drugs and violence are persistent problems in many American schools. Scholastic Assessment Test (SAT) scores have been declining for years, though part of the decline is due to the increasing numbers of students taking the test[3] (see Table 10-1).

These failures were documented in a series of critical reports in the 1980s that urged immediate remedial steps be taken.[4] Several studies have suggested that problems in education are a significant factor in the decline of U.S. productivity growth and faltering American international economic competitiveness.

Critics have challenged the accuracy of these studies and argued that some of the generally proposed reforms such as a longer school year, smaller class sizes, and larger financial investments in teachers, books, and computers will not necessarily produce the desired effects.

FEDERAL SPENDING ON EDUCATION

Some research suggests that spending more money on the current American educational system will not necessarily result in improved academic achievement. President Bush, who yearned to be known as the "education President," declared that financial resources are not a central issue for improving educational output. At his "Education Summit" in 1989, Bush stated that the American government "lav-

---

[1] Pearl M. Kamer, *The U.S. Economy in Crisis* (New York: Praeger, 1988), p. 108.

[2] Lester Thurow, *Head to Head: The Coming Economic Battle Among Japan, Europe, and America* (New York: William Morrow, 1992), p. 55.

[3] College Entrance Examination Board, *On Further Examination: Report of the Advisory Panel on the Scholastic Aptitude Test Score Decline* (New York: College Board, 1977).

[4] The National Commission on Excellence in Education, *A Nation At Risk: The Imperative for Educational Reform*, April 1983.

TABLE 10-1
SCHOLASTIC ASSESSMENT TEST SCORES, 1967–1993

	1967	1975	1980	1985	1990	1993
Verbal	466	434	424	431	424	424
Math	492	472	466	475	476	478

Source: 1967–1991 data, *Statistical Abstract, 1993*, p. 170, and the College Board; 1992–1993 data, *The New York Times*, August 19, 1993.

ishes" more on education than the governments of most industrialized nations.[5] Policy makers at all levels seized upon this as a rationale for not providing more revenues to education in a period of tight budgets. However, most research suggests that to improve educational output a higher level of financial support is needed.

U.S. spending on **all levels of education** from kindergarten through college in 1985 was 6.8 percent of national income.[6] By this measure the United States is in a three-way tie for second place among 16 nations recently studied. This high expenditure is largely due to the significant amount the nation directs toward **higher education**. A higher percentage of students is enrolled in more expensive, postsecondary education (i.e., college) in the United States than in any other country.

Criticism of American education has not been aimed primarily at higher education, but rather at elementary and secondary school levels. As Table 10-2 shows, when spending on education in kindergarten through twelfth grade (grades K–12) is correlated to the size of the school-age population in 16 industrialized countries, **the United States spends less than all but two of those nations**. A comparison of funding for **all levels of education combined** is misleading and diverts attention from the main area of concern in the U.S. educational system. The United States actually devotes a smaller share of its resources to K–12 education than most industrialized countries. Certain features of American society suggest that a greater effort is required to provide an adequate education here than elsewhere—American society is more culturally diverse, a significant number of students do not speak English, and a higher number of students live in poverty.

[5] Speech at the Educational Summit, University of Virginia, September, 28, 1989 (White House transcript).

[6] International comparisons of education expenditures are usually expressed as a percentage of the national income (gross domestic product or GDP) rather than in money amounts because it avoids the distortions caused by shifting exchange rates. This measure signifying the percentage of national income also gives us a gauge of the national effort each country devotes to education. See M. Edith Rasell and Lawrence Mishel, *Shortchanging Education: How U.S. Spending on Grades K–12 Lags behind Other Industrial Nations* (Washington, DC: Economic Policy Institute, 1989), p. 3.

TABLE 10-2
SPENDING ON ELEMENTARY AND SECONDARY EDUCATION,
AS A PERCENT OF GROSS DOMESTIC PRODUCT, 1985

Rank	Country	Percent of GDP
1	Sweden	7.0
2	Austria	5.9
3	Switzerland	5.8
4	Norway	5.3
5	Belgium	4.8
	Denmark	4.8
	Japan	4.8
8	Canada	4.7
9	West Germany	4.6
	France	4.6
11	Netherlands	4.5
	United Kingdom	4.5
13	Italy	4.2
14	**United States**	**4.1**
15	Australia	3.9
16	Ireland	3.8

Source: M. Edith Rassell and Laurence Mitchell, *Shortchanging Education: How the U.S. Spends on Grades K–12* (Washington, DC: Economic Policy Institute, 1990). Also reproduced in Children's Defense Fund, *The State of America's Children, 1991* (Washington, DC: Children's Defense Fund, 1991), p. 141.

THE STRUCTURE OF AMERICAN EDUCATION: AN OVERVIEW

Through education, a society transmits attitudes, beliefs, values, knowledge, and skills to its members. In the past, much of education was the responsibility of the family. This **informal education** took place primarily in the home, with relatives and friends serving as the teachers. Learning in this context took place largely through the socialization process and imitating the behavior of elders. This was because in an economy based on tradition, production techniques changed at a glacial pace, and the needed knowledge and skills would be passed from one generation to the next through apprenticeships and work experience.

In more advanced market economies, however, production techniques change more rapidly, requiring greater adaptability to the new skills needed by workers. Productivity growth is fostered by workers with more education who can more easily adapt to new work requirements than workers with less education. Modern societies have developed **formal education** systems in which professional teachers guide the learning process. The state has become largely responsible for transmitting culture, literacy, and technical knowledge.

Many modern countries spell out the right to education in their Constitutions. However, education is not mentioned in the U.S. Constitution, which was drafted in 1787, when formal education was a rarity and not perceived as critical to society or its citizens. As a result public elementary and secondary education was begun by the individual states in the early 1800s, funded by tuition payments from the parents. Private schools educated the children of the affluent.

Most U.S. business leaders of the early nineteenth century opposed efforts to require compulsory school attendance or taxation to support public education. The struggle to create publicly funded school systems in the various states was taken up as a crusade by educational reformers in the 1830s. Paradoxically, the drive to provide public schools, financed by property taxes, was given a boost by immigration. Successive waves of immigration generated the fear that unless the new arrivals were "Anglicized" the "American character" would be destroyed. In fact, the "Know-Nothing" party of the 1840s developed from fear of a Catholic takeover. Catholic and other religiously affiliated schools were founded not only to reinforce religious values, but also to escape societal religious discrimination.

Providing schools where poor immigrants learned American customs and morals along with the English language meant the system had to be tuition-free. Public school education was justified as a public good that reduced the distinctions between people and created a unified citizenry.

There is still uneasiness in the United States about parochial schools. These institutions maintain religious and cultural identities different from mass culture.[7] Still, the United States has the largest number of religious and private elementary secondary schools and universities in the world. Private and parochial schools enroll 13.4 percent of all elementary school children, 10 percent of all secondary school students, and 26 percent of all college students.[8]

In the United States, unlike most other industrialized societies, **education is a state and local responsibility rather than a national one. And it has traditionally been egalitarian**. The public educational system historically provided one school per neighborhood or community for children from all its social levels (segregation by race was a glaring anomaly). Limitations in transportation kept residents, their workplaces, and their schools in close proximity. Since World War II, the automobile has fostered the separation of workplace from residence and the development of large, socially homogeneous school districts. This coincided with an erosion of the egalitarian principle that underlay the notion of public education. It has also led to an erosion in the traditional local control of education. As school

---

[7] In *Everson v. Board of Education of Ewing Township*, 330 U.S. 1 (1947), the Supreme court reinterpreted the establishment clause to require an "absolute wall of separation between church and state" but then did not require it in that case. Critics charge that the "absolute wall" has little basis in Constitutional law or practice. Many Constitutional scholars argue that the Constitution contemplates local resolution of this issue. See Eileen Gardner, *A New Agenda for Education* (Washington, DC: Heritage Foundation, 1985), pp. 79–83. See also William A. Carroll, "The Constitution, the Supreme Court, and Religion," *The American Political Science Review*, vol. 61 (September 1967), pp. 657–674. Western democracies encourage or discourage such nonpublic private or parochial schools primarily through their governments' willingness to provide financial assistance or not.

[8] Figures are for 1991. Source: *Statistical Abstract, 1993*, p. 150. There are also a number of elite prep schools that began with a religious purpose, but have dropped any formal religious affiliations. These boarding schools (such as Phillips Exeter, Groton, Choate) provide the children of mostly affluent families with advantaged access to the more prestigious universities and from there to corporate and political leadership.

districts became larger and state and even federal governments increased their financial contributions, those levels of government began to exercise more control over school policy while the influence of parents and sometimes local school boards declined.

Local property taxes within a district, whose boundaries often are identical with local political boundaries, typically provide close to half of public school finances. But dependence on local property taxes has resulted in highly unequal funding available per student between property-rich and property-poor districts. Lawsuits challenging the fairness of relying on local property taxes for funding have resulted in states steadily increasing their financial contributions to local school districts.[9] Today states overall provide more funding than local districts. In 1990 states contributed 43.4 percent of the money needed for public elementary and secondary education and local districts contributed 42.9 percent. The federal government's contribution was only 5.6 percent, down from 9.1 percent in 1980.[10] States now establish standards for education within their boundaries, while local control is exercised within the constraints permitted by state governments.

EDUCATION: A QUASI-PUBLIC GOOD

Recall that in Chap. 1 we pointed out how competitive markets are very efficient mechanisms for meeting consumer demand. Why, then, should government be involved in providing education when a competitive market is such an efficient mechanism? The answer lies in the idea that education is a good for which private decisions about how much to buy do not lead to a socially optimal level of output. In other words, private "interests" lack incentives to provide an education for everyone. This is an instance we referred to earlier as **market failure**. Defenders of public education point to the important external effects on the welfare of others associated with having an education. Such goods are termed **quasi-public goods**.[11]

Functionalism

Public support of education has long been touted because of its positive impact on society. **Functionalism** holds the view that society can exist in harmony because its institutions spring from a shared culture. Consequently, the family, the educational system, and the economy among other institutions perform specific "functions"

---

[9] See John Augenblick, "The Current Status of School Financing Reform," in Van D. Mueller and Mary P. McKeown (eds.), *The Fiscal, Legal, and Political Aspects of State Reform of Elementary and Secondary Education* (Cambridge, MA: Ballinger, 1986).

[10] U.S. Bureau of the Census, *Statistical Abstract of the United States, 1993* (Washington, DC: Department of Commerce, 1993), p. 150. Business and private contributions contributed another 8.1 percent.

[11] Recall our earlier definition of a **pure private** good is characterized by excludability and depletability. A **pure public good**, in contrast, is **not depleted** (**nonrivalness**) by an additional user. Second, it is extremely difficult **to exclude** (**nonexcludability**) people from such a benefit if they do not pay for it. If the community "buys" national security, a newborn child in the community is also protected at no additional cost. The marginal cost approaches zero. And the new child does not interfere with the protection afforded to the rest of the community.

necessary for the survival of society. The function of education is to (a) transfer societal values, (b) produce a more informed citizenry, (c) produce workers with more productive skills, and (d) provide for "equal opportunity" by providing everyone, regardless of circumstance, with basic education skills. School serves as a "halfway house" to assist a child's passage between the familiar world of his or her family and the impersonal world of adult careers and community life.[12]

The belief that formal education correlates with good citizenship has passed into American culture. Thomas Jefferson supported the idea that education was necessary for democracy when he wrote, "If a nation expects to be ignorant and free, in a state of civilization, it expects what never was and never will be."[13] Considerable research supports the contention that the more education one has, the more likely one is to be knowledgeable and active in the democratic process and familiar with its current events.[14]

Functionalism supports the notion that all members of society should have an equal chance for educational and economic success. This meritocratic ideal strongly supports equality of **opportunity**, but not equality of **outcomes**.

A public education system fosters greater equality because it provides the opportunity for everyone to acquire the knowledge and skills necessary to perform those jobs that society rewards highly. Thus, wealthier members of society are not able to monopolize access to highly paid jobs. By broadening equality of opportunity, education encourages social mobility.

Critics of functionalism accuse it of disregarding the social class divisions in society perpetuated by the educational system. They charge that students are separated into vocational, general education, and college prep programs along the general class lines of their families. Earlier research suggested a similar sorting mechanism took place in the way curriculums were presented in different communities.[15]

---

[12] Kevin J. Dougherty and Floyd M. Hammack, *Education & Society* (New York: Harcourt Brace Jovanovich, 1990), pp. 13–14.

[13] Quoted in Clarke E. Cochran et al., *An Introduction to American Public Policy*, 3rd ed. (New York: St. Martin's Press, 1990), p. 307.

[14] See, for example, William, H. Flanigan and Nancy H. Zingale, *Political Behavior of the American Electorate*, 6th ed. (Boston: Allyn and Bacon, 1987), p. 18. They state that one of the factors in voting is a sense of civic duty reflected in the attitude that a good citizen has an obligation to vote. "Since such feelings are usually a prime focus of the political socialization carried on in the American educational system, turnout is highest among those with the longest exposure to this system: Length of education is one of the best predictors of an individual's likelihood of voting" (p. 18). They go on to state that because education is associated with relative affluence, people who vote are usually somewhat better off in socioeconomic terms than the aggregate population. "This bias is likely to increase in low-stimulus elections, as greater numbers of occasional voters drop out of the electorate, leaving the field to the better educated and more affluent who rarely miss an election" (p. 18).

[15] For example, one study of three communities, (a) an affluent community with politically active adults, (b) a lower-middle-class community with reduced levels of political involvement, and (c) a working-class neighborhood with primarily apolitical adults, concluded that the students in each community were being taught to play "different" political roles. Only in the affluent community were they taught the subtleties and nuances of decision making and given the expectation that they should be a part of the process. The lower-middle-class group was taught the "responsibilities" of citizens in a democracy. The school curriculum in the working-class neighborhood covered mechanics and procedures without stressing the utility of participation. See Edgar Litt, "Civic Education, Community Norms, and Political Indoctrination," *American Sociological Review*, vol. 28 (February 1963). Also reprinted in Richard Flacks (ed.), *Conformity, Resistance, and Self-Determination* (Boston: Little, Brown, 1973), pp. 136–141.

Many hoped that as education became more available and equally distributed, children from disadvantaged families would get as much education as those from advantaged families. But over recent decades it has become apparent that this has not happened. Therefore, the critics claim, while education can provide social mobility, it tends to "transmit inequality from one generation to another."[16] One recent study has shown that high school graduates from the top quartile in socioeconomic status are almost twice as likely to go on to college as those in the bottom quartile.[17] The gaps in educational achievement are a major factor in the transmission of inequality. Another study of male students by Christopher Jencks and his colleagues found that about 40 percent of the association between childhood family background and adult occupational status was due to the students' educational attainments, after controlling for the effects of IQ test scores. In other words, upperclass graduates received higher-status jobs than working-class graduates because they got more education.[18]

Pierre Bourdieu, a French sociologist and leading critic of higher education, has focused on the glaring inequalities in the distribution of wealth and status that persist despite the expansion of educational opportunities for everyone.[19] He is concerned with how inequalities of position endure over generations. Bourdieu argues that individuals use education to maintain their positions of privilege. The educational system has displaced the family, church, or work place as the determinant variable for the transmission of **social stratification**. Since democratic societies originated in a rebellion against privilege and therefore affirm a belief in the essential equality of individuals, privileged groups cannot openly claim a right to dominating positions. Modern democracies rely on indirect and symbolic forms of power rather than physical coercion to maintain authority. Dominant groups have found that institutions of higher education can transmit social inequalities by being converted into academic hierarchies.[20] Several points are stressed in Bourdieu's research. His investigation supports other findings that the academic performance of students is highly correlated with their parents' cultural background. This further relates to degree of success in the labor market, which hinges on both the **amount**

---

[16] Dougherty and Hammack, *Education & Society*, p. 248. It should be noted that there is evidence of social mobility in America. One survey taken among American men in 1973 found that 51 percent had a higher job status than their fathers, while only 17 percent had a lower status. See David L. Featherman and Robert M. Hauser, *Opportunity and Change* (New York: Academic Press, 1978), p. 93.

Education does have a powerful impact on income and occupational prestige, with about two-thirds of this effect being unconnected to family background. See Christopher S. Jencks et al., *Who Gets Ahead?* (New York: Basic Books, 1979), pp. 224–227.

[17] Dougherty and Hammack, *Education & Society*, p. 248. If the comparison is restricted to high school graduates who score in the top quarter in academic ability, the gap widens. Socioeconomic status was measured by a composite of parents' education, fathers' occupation, and family income.

[18] Jencks et al., *Who Gets Ahead?* pp. 214–218. Also reported in Dougherty and Hammack, *Education & Society*.

[19] See Pierre Bourdieu, "The School as a Conservative Force: Scholastic and Cultural Inequalities," in John Eggleston (ed.), *Contemporary Research in the Sociology of Education* (London: Methuen, 1974), pp. 32–46. Also see Pierre Bourdieu, "Cultural Reproduction and Social Reproduction," in Jerome Karabel and A. H. Halsey (eds.), *Power and Ideology in Education* (New York: Oxford University Press, 1977), pp. 487–511, and Pierre Bourdieu, and Jean-Claude Passeron, *The Inheritors: French Students and Their Relation to Culture* (Chicago: University of Chicago Press, 1979).

[20] Bourdieu and Passeron, *The Inheritors*, p. 153.

of education received and the academic **prestige** of the institution attended. Ultimately, many educational institutions develop their own academic interests and agendas. These may differ significantly from those proclaimed by the existing social order.

Class Conflict Model

Another explanation for the expansion of public education in the United States argues that education grows to meet the rising technical skill requirements of jobs. Given this premise, the **class conflict model** claims that employers use education to screen workers although no demonstrable connection exists in most cases between education and job performance. According to this model, formal education was developed to meet the growing problems created by industrialization and urbanization in the United States. Rather than meeting objectives like supplying workers with more complex technical skills or reducing social inequality, public education has provided social control by instilling behavior attributes like obedience, discipline, and respect for and compliance with authority.[21] In this view, educational credentials rank workers rather than measure skills.[22] Employers are willing to give a preference to more educated workers in hiring and salary because those workers are more willing to accept traditional corporate values.[23] Thus, education serves to legitimize inequalities rooted in the economic structure of society.

Research by Gregory Squires has concluded that the upgrading of the educa-

---

[21] Gregory D. Squires, "Education, Jobs, and Inequality: Functional and Conflict Models of Social Stratification in the United States," *Social Problems*, vol. 24, no. 4 (April 1977), pp. 436–437. Also reprinted in Dougherty and Hamrnack, *Education & Society*, p. 549.

[22] Lester C. Thurow, *Generating Inequality* (New York: Basic Books, 1975).

[23] Squires, "Education, Jobs, and Inequality," pp. 436–450. Reproduced in Dougherty and Hammack, *Education & Society*, pp. 548–560.

[24] Squires, "Education, Jobs, and Inequality," p. 445. The Department of Labor estimates increases in the amount of formal education required as a result of the increased technical skill requirements of jobs, and the Census Bureau reports on the increasing educational achievements of workers. Both show that educational accomplishments have risen faster than technical skill requirements (Squires, p. 550). In fact, when technological change affects skill requirements, workers typically learn the additional skills on the job. The effect of applying the principles of Adam Smith's division of labor with Frederick Taylor's principles of scientific management has, in fact, resulted in fragmenting many skilled occupations into several unskilled jobs, thereby reducing the skill requirements for many clerical, service, craft, and even some professional and technical careers (Squires, p. 551).

Interestingly, Adam Smith supported free public education financed by taxes especially to counter the reduced mental stimulation of those individuals performing jobs requiring no mental exertion. He wrote: "The man whose whole life is spent in performing a few simple operations, of which the effects too are, perhaps, always the same, or very nearly the same, has no occasion to exert his understanding, or to exercise his invention in finding out expedients for removing difficulties which never occur. He naturally loses, therefore, the habit of such exertion, and generally becomes as stupid and ignorant as it is possible for a human creature to become. . . . His dexterity at his own particular trade seems, in this manner, to be acquired at the expence of his intellectual, social, and martial virtues. But in every improved and civilized society this is the state into which the labouring poor, that is, the great body of the people, must necessarily fall, unless government takes some pains to prevent it" (Adam Smith, *The Wealth of Nations,* edited by Edwin Cannon [New York: G. P. Putnam's Sons, 1877], pp. 616–617).

There is a misconception that a change from farm laborer to assembly line worker or from blue-collar to white-collar job represents an increase in skill requirements. Although an assembly line worker may use more sophisticated machinery than the farmer, the former is not necessarily a more highly skilled worker (Squires, p. 551).

tional requirements related to work cannot be explained in terms of the increasing technical skill requirements of jobs.[24] He points to the growing **underemployment** particularly among college graduates. Employers frequently raise the educational specifications of jobs in reaction to an increase in the supply of better educated workers. And better educated workers receive the preferred positions within the job structure. With the expansion of schooling, both employers and occupational groups increasingly require formal education as an entry requirement.[25] One result is that individuals have responded by acquiring higher levels of educational achievement to improve their competitive position within the job market, thereby continuing the ever higher spiral of educational credentials and requirements.

Several studies have noted that the problem of underemployment is increasing.[26] As the gap between the supply and the demand for college graduates continues to increase, competition between them extends further down in the labor market, leaving those with less education with even fewer job opportunities. Thus, the wage gap between those with high school degrees or less and those with college degrees increases, while both groups experience underemployment. More highly educated workers receive higher pay, but it is based upon the amount of education rather than the content of learning or the skills required for the job.

This important point suggests implications for the popular belief that the primary reason the United States has lost ground to Germany and Japan in economic competition is that the American labor force is not highly skilled. According to the Department of Labor, salespersons, cashiers, clerical help, janitors, waiters and waitresses, receptionists, and truck drivers are among the fastest growing occupations in the American economy.[27] Most of the jobs created in the last decade of this century will be in low-skilled occupations, and only about one-fourth of them will require a college education.[28] The high-wage jobs in manufacturing that used to give high school graduates, especially males, relatively high-paying jobs have been replaced by low-paying jobs in the service sector. These low-wage jobs not only make it difficult for workers to purchase more education for their children, but provide few benefits like health insurance or a pension program. This raises the

---

[25] Floyd M. Hammack, "The Changing Relationship between Education and Occupation: The Case of Nursing," in Dougherty and Hammack, *Education & Society*, p. 561. Hammack points out that requiring greater educational achievements and "credentials" increases the prestige of a profession while encouraging higher pay and control over access to the profession. Thus efforts to abolish the apprenticeship system of "reading the law" and requiring the attendance of law school after obtaining a bachelor's degree and then passage of the bar exam has reduced the access of lower-class individuals to the legal profession.

There have been similar efforts by leaders of the nursing profession to improve the prestige and power of their occupation by increasing educational requirements. They propose that all registered nurses hold at least a bachelor's degree, thereby abolishing entrance into the profession through 3-year hospital "diploma" programs, or 2-year associate degree programs. Hammack concludes that this efffort is not required by the technical skill requirements of the health care nurses provide, but by the desire to counter the greater authority and prestige of the doctors with whom nurses work (pp. 561–573).

[26] See, for example, Denis F. Johnston, "Education of Workers: Projections to 1990," *Monthly Labor Review*, vol. 96 (November 1973), pp. 22–31. Also see James O'Toole, "The Reserve Army of the Underemployed," *Change*, vol. 7 (May 1976), pp. 26–33.

[27] *Statistical Abstract, 1991*, p. 398.

[28] See Henry M. Levin, "Jobs: A Changing Workforce, a Changing Education?" Reprinted in Dougherty and Hammack, *Education & Society*, pp. 574–582.

EDUCATION AS MARKET SIGNALING

The concept that education is an investment in **human capital** is widely known. Your decision to go to college rather than enter the labor force is costing you significant amounts of money in foregone current job opportunities as well as tuition payments and other costs associated with a college education. Although there are many reasons to attend college, including the joy of learning, social development, and other benefits, human capital theory analyzes the education decision as if it were purely a business decision. From this perspective the optimal investment in education is to stay in school until the marginal revenue (expected in higher future income) equals the marginal cost of additional schooling.

Human capital theory suggests that college graduates should receive an increased income that at least compensates them for their extra investment in education. Can you reasonably expect your investment to pay off? (Figures 10.1 and 10.2 below indicate that on average, the income differential earned by college graduates shows that the investment is a sound one). The theory implies that those with a college education can demand higher pay as a return on their investment. It assumes that students acquire skills as they successfully complete high school; and gain even more skills improving their productivity as they invest in a college education.

Other social scientists challenge this view of how education raises income. One view claims that the educational process teaches students little in the way of relevant knowledge or skills for subsequent job performance. Rather the educational system *sorts* people according to ability. Supporters of this view claim that competencies like perseverance, intelligence, and self-discipline are needed to succeed in college and also correlate with success in the labor force. A college degree indicates to employers that the individual is a high-quality worker who can be trained easily thus lowering productivity costs. Employers are therefore willing to pay a differential to more highly educated workers because they will be more productive on average.

Academic credentials thus provide a mechanism by which better educated workers separate themselves from those with less education. Suppose the labor force is divided

following questions: Should access to a college education be a right rather than a privilege? And should government policy concentrate on producing better jobs rather than low-wage jobs?[29]

Human Capital Theory

Closely related to the functionalist view of education in sociology is the **human capital theory** in economics. Human capital theory argues that education makes individuals inherently more productive and therefore more highly valued workers. Adam Smith included education with national defense and justice as essential poli-

---

[29] See for example, Gary Burtless (ed.), *A Future of Lousy Jobs? The Changing Structure of U.S. Wages* (Washington, DC: The Brookings Institution, 1990).

equally between low- and high-skilled workers: A low-skilled worker has a marginal revenue product (MRP) (the additional revenue generated by an additional unit of input) of $300 per week, and a high-skilled worker has a MRP of $500 per week.

If an employer cannot be sure whether a new worker has the qualities of a high- or low-quality worker when first hired, the wage will be based upon the *anticipated* MRP. Thus, the firm will calculate that a new hire has a 50 percent chance of being a high-quality worker and a 50 percent chance of being a low-quality worker, and pay a wage based upon the expected MRP of $400 (.50 × $300 + .50 × $500 = $400).

Since firms pay the average MRP, low-quality workers are better off since they receive $400 rather than $300, while high-quality workers are worse off since they receive $400 rather than $500. High-quality workers would like to signal the firm that they possess the characteristics associated with high productivity in the labor force. The educational system provides the means for them to signal the firm in a way that low-skilled workers would be *unable* to do. Employers are aware of the correlation and screen workers based on their education. Although education by itself does not increase a worker's productivity, it signals to the employer the probable possession of other qualities that improve productivity.

Signaling does not change the *average* wage, only its distribution. It has a positive effect on the incomes of more highly educated workers, and a negative effect on the incomes of those less educated.

A more radical view holds that the wealthy are able to buy the best education regardless of ability. Education thus sorts people according to social class, not ability. In this way, education is a device by which the privileged members of society are able to pass on their favored positions to their already privileged successors while providing the appearance of legitimacy for higher wages. In this model, education does not enhance ability, but does cultivate noncognitive traits like discipline, respect, obedience, and acceptance of the values of the business culture.

Source: A. Michael Spence, "Market Signaling: Informational Transfer in Hiring and Related Screening Processes," *Harvard Economic Studies* (Cambridge: Harvard University Press, 1974), Vol. 143.

cies of the government. He said that the capital stock of a nation includes the

useful abilities of all the inhabitants or members of the society. The acquisition of such talents, by the maintenance of the acquirer during his education, study, or apprenticeship, always costing a real expense, which is a capital fixed and realized, as it were, in his person. Those talents, as they make a part of his fortune, so do they likewise of that of the society to which he belongs. The improved dexterity of a workman may be considered in the same light as a machine or instrument of trade which facilitates and abridges labour, and which, though it costs a certain expense, repays that expense with a profit.[30]

[30] Smith, *Wealth of Nations*, Book 2, Chap. 1. Smith did not develop this idea beyond the statement quoted. Theodore Schultz and Gary Becker are usually given credit for developing human capital theory. See Theodore W. Schultz, "Investment in Human Capital," *American Economic Review*, vol. 51 (March 1961), pp. 1–17. See also Gary Becker, *Human Capital* (New York: National Bureau of Economic Research, 1964).

During preindustrial periods the value of individuals to society was measured primarily in physical productivity rather than mental ability. The size of a nation's population was a strong indicator of the nation's power. With the advent of the industrial and commercial revolutions, though, it became apparent that a nation's power was less dependent on physical labor and more dependent on brain power. A country with the largest population was not necessarily the most productive or powerful. The ability of colonial England and France to control far more populous colonial territories illustrated this.[31]

Education can be thought of as an **investment in human capital** much like a firm invests in physical capital. Just as a corporation commits some of its profits to buying new equipment to generate more profits at a later date, the individual may reduce current income (and consumption) by investing in education in the hope of increasing future income. By obtaining a college degree, you anticipate that your diploma will help you earn more money or result in a more pleasant job than a high school friend who did not continue on with his or her education.

Measuring the Returns to Human Capital: What is Education Worth?

Ordinarily, there is a positive relationship between education and lifetime earnings. High school graduates ordinarily have higher lifetime earnings than those without their high school degrees, and college graduates usually earn more during their lifetimes than high school graduates[32] (see Figs. 10-1 and 10-2). This leads to the conclusion that one is better off with more rather than less education, although this correlation does not by itself prove that higher education **causes** the higher earnings.

Further, estimates of educational benefits may be too low because of the difficulty of distinguishing between consumption and investment benefits.[33] Education is not only an investment, but also a consumption good. Many enjoy learning while the process is going on.

---

[31] Roe J. Johns, Edgar L. Morphet, and Kern Alexander, "Human Capital and the Economic Benefits of Education," in Dougherty and Hammack, *Education & Society*, pp. 534–535.

[32] Theodore Schultz in an address to the American Economic Association in 1960 first recognized education as an investment in human capital. He suggested that education should be examined in the same way that economic theory examines investments in machinery and equipment. Whenever greater amounts of reproducible capital are added to a fixed supply of land and labor, it should result in diminishing returns. However, when the returns do not diminish, it seems possible that improvements in the quality of human resources might be the cause. See Theodore W. Schultz, "Investment in Human Capital," *American Economic Review,* vol. 51, no. 1 (March 1961), pp. 1–17.

[33] Many look upon their school days, especially their period in college, as the most rewarding years of their lives. Therefore, if half the costs of education are assigned to consumption, then the benefits derived later compared to initial investment, are doubled. The share of costs assigned to consumption and investment might vary with the focus of the education. Vocational training, on-the-job apprenticeships, work-study programs, or other studies or training designed for particular jobs may involve less consumption and more investment aspects. On the other hand, the study of art, drama, music, and the humanities may have a higher consumption portion than the study of some of the sciences. In any case, the difficulty of assigning portions of educational costs to consumption and investment has resulted in most studies attributing all costs to investment, thus underestimating education's rate of return.

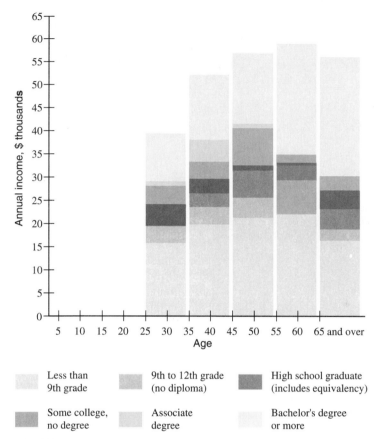

FIGURE 10-1
Mean male earnings by educational attainment and age, 1991. (*Source: Statistical Abstract, 1993, p. 467.*)

Costs and Benefits of Human Capital Investment

Who pays for the costs of education? In regard to public school systems, governments at the federal, state, and local levels underwrite the costs of education in their entirety. Those costs are **subsidized** through taxes, especially at the elementary and high school levels where compulsory attendance is required at least through age 16. Individuals during the years of their elementary and high school education forgo minimal income since the law precludes significant employment below the age of 16. Parents and other adults pay through their taxes, but not usually exorbitant amounts since the costs are absorbed by many people.

A college education is far more expensive since the government does not fully subsidize its costs. The students, or their parents, must pay directly for room, board, tuition, books, and other assorted fees. In addition, the individual receiving the education can forgo significant income during the typical 4-year period it takes to com-

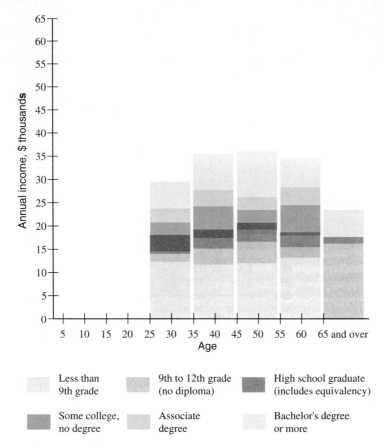

FIGURE 10-2
Mean female earnings by educational attainment and age, 1991. (*Source: Statistical Abstract, 1993, p. 467.*)

plete a college degree. And after the college education is completed, it may take time before a college graduate surpasses high school graduates in income levels since the latter have already acquired 4 years of seniority and experience on the job.

Government subsidies of college-level education are often justified because of the expansion of national output arising from the college-educated worker's increased productivity. For example, a highly educated researcher may invent new processes to save the ozone layer. This research rewards the inventor, but also brings tremendous benefits to society. Increasing the number of trained scientists promotes increased research and development (R&D), a major factor in stimulating productivity. Ultimately highly educated and skilled managers add to the output of any firm where they work by creating an environment conducive to improved efficiency and productivity. One study found that highly educated workers (defined as those with more than a high school education whether they have a college degree

UNEQUAL PAYOFFS FOR CAPITAL INVESTMENT

Investing in education has been considered a guarantee of a good job and upward mobility. Increasingly, however, relatively high-paying manufacturing jobs for high school graduates have been replaced with low-paying jobs in the service sector. The shrinking job market for well-paying male-dominated jobs in the manufacturing sector for high school graduates resulted in a decline in median male earnings of 9 percent in real terms in the decade from 1978 to 1988. While male high school graduates were the biggest losers, It was in large measure due to this decline that women's wages appear to have increased from 46 percent to 54 percent of the average men's wages in recent decades, although wages for all high school graduates have declined since the mid-1970s.

Investing in a high school education today provides fewer returns than in the past. Investing in a college education may provide greater job security although it may not result in an increase of income over college-level wages of the 1960s and 1970s.

Moreover, gender, racial, and ethnic discrimination still plays a significant role in determining the jobs and wages available to different individuals, often overriding the individual's own investment in education. A comparison of Fig. 10-1 with Fig. 10-2 shows that males get a greater return on their investment in education than do females at every level. While a comparison of age and education may not include other factors, such as continuous years in the labor force, the implications are too apparent to be ignored. These results challenge the theory of human capital investment that claims wages are based upon productivity which in turn is dependent upon an investment in education that improves the quality of labor. According to the theory, the wage gap should disappear as women and minorities invest more in education. This clearly has not happened.

Human capital theorists contend that people choose between investing in education or entering the job market after calculating the costs of an education and the income that will be lost during the period of education, as well as whether their lifetime earnings will exceed those of people with less education or their working conditions will be better. According to the theory, women and especially minorities choose to invest in less education because they place a greater value in current earnings than future earnings. This of course ignores other factors such as their current economic status, which may not permit a greater investment in education, or growing up in a neighborhood with poor schools and a poorer preparation for college. It also ignores the fact that investment in a college education for minorities is not as sound an investment as for white males in terms of the expected long-term payoffs. Human capital theory holds that the wages received are determined by the amount of education and skills invested in by the individual, but it overlooks the factors of cost, access, and discrimination in public education and in the job market. Thus it is a view supportive of conservative policy positions that see low educational achievement as a purely personal problem (or decision) and not a political problem.

or not) have an advantage over less educated workers in the implementation of new technologies in manufacturing.[34] This supports the hypothesis that growth in productivity growth is aided by a more highly educated work force.

[34] See Ann P. Bartel and Frank R. Lichtenberg, "The Comparative Advantage of Educated Workers in Implementing New Technology: Some Empirical Evidence," *Review of Economics and Statistics,* vol. 69 (February 1987), pp. 1–11.

Education and Productivity

One purpose of education is to increase worker productivity. Improved productivity is necessary to maintain and improve living standards in the United States, and is particularly important when one considers the increasing economic competition from abroad. It is of fundamental importance, then, to determine what types of educational skills have the greatest impact on worker productivity. There is considerable evidence that literacy and problem-solving skills in specific contexts are of primary importance.[35] A key to worker productivity is the ability to identify problems that occur in a work-related context and to synthesize new information and develop problem-solving strategies. This includes the ability to understand directions and to formulate appropriate questions. Other studies have found that workers' scores on tests of mathematical skills are significantly correlated with their supervisors' evaluations of their productivity. Mathematical ability may be particularly related to worker productivity because it typically requires a step-by-step approach to problem solving.

Some argue education policy should emphasize instruction in the skills of practical problem solving as opposed to instruction by means of lower-order skills such as recall and drill often used to teach arithmetic computation. There is concern that schools provide the former primarily to college-bound students.[36] Students from lower-income backgrounds are traditionally less likely to have developed these skills.

TRENDS IN AMERICAN EDUCATION

American education, especially when compared to education in European nations, reflects the nation's revolutionary origins. The Founding Fathers rejected the idea of a hereditary aristocracy and emphasized the equality of all citizens. Alexis de Tocqueville, in the early nineteenth century, noted that equality was the dominant value in American society, along with a culture of individualism that supported personal freedom to pursue interests without hindrance by the government. In this view, social conditions should enable individuals, whatever their pedigrees, to compete for positions on the basis of merit alone (though in the nineteenth century gender and race were sufficient grounds for exclusion from consideration for all higher-level positions).

One **goal** of the educational system in the United States **is to equalize differences in wealth and circumstances so that individuals can progress according**

[35] See Richard L. Venezky, Carl F. Kaestle, and Andrew M. Sum, *The Subtle Danger: Reflections on the Literacy Abilities of America's Young Adults* (Princeton, NJ: Educational Testing Service, 1987).

[36] For example, Venezky, Kaestle, and Sum (*The Subtle Danger*, p. 22) found that over 90 percent of young adults could follow simple directions and make inferences when all the necessary information was in one sentence. However 30 percent of the same group encountered difficulties in problem solving when they had to gather data from several sentences to solve multistep problems. The expanded use of computers as instructional aids in the classroom is often advocated as one way to improve student learning. Unfortunately, most educational programs emphasize drill and do not significantly improve problem-solving techniques.

to their abilities. Unfortunately, according to critics of that system, the results of American public education in the past reflected differences in the wealth of students' parents, and often do so today also:

> For despite the promise of American education, it was organized in such a way that it acted as an overwhelmingly powerful mechanism for preserving and promoting racial and social class segregation. Today its effects are so pervasive that probably no other public policies or government actions are as important in preserving inequality from one generation to the next.[37]

The mechanism for perpetuating inequality was and is the American method of financing public schools primarily through property taxes. Since property taxes reflect the value of the property within local school districts, the amount of money raised to support education on a per capita basis varies immensely from district to district.

School district boundaries reflect societal divisions between affluent and poor, and among white, black, and Hispanic students. Central city school systems tend to receive fewer funds and have disproportionate numbers of poor and minority students. Children attending these schools typically exhibit poorer academic performance than students attending suburban schools. "White flight" to suburban school districts, the result in part of efforts to escape the mandated desegregation of inner-city schools, has introduced a racial and ethnic factor into these educational problems. Concern over the strong association between family background and success in scholastic performance has led to much research and a number of theories.

ASSESSING FACTORS IN LEARNING

Researchers have developed two general approaches for analyzing educational achievement: student-centered and school-centered explanations.

Student-Centered Focus

Ordinarily, student-centered explanations are put forward by functionalists. These "elitist" theories emphasize the qualities students bring into a learning environment. They view these qualities as the primary reasons for success or failure in school.

Many of these arguments suggest a **cultural deficit** works to provide poor and working-class students with behavior patterns and attitudes different from the white middle- or upper-class culture reflected in the public educational curricula.[38] The

---

[37] David B. Robertson and Dennis R. Judd, *The Development of American Public Policy: The Structure of Policy Restraint* (Boston: Scott, Foresman, 1989), p. 246.

[38] Arthur Jenson, "Factors Influencing Academic Learning," in Dougherty and Hammack, *Education & Society*, Chap. 6, p. 340.

Jensen, an educational psychologist, argues the student-centered view that, since remedial education frequently fails, scholars must take seriously the argument that working-class and minority students do less well educationally because they have less intelligence due to an inferior genetic makeup. The genetic argument has been attacked as being based on culturally biased testing and ignoring social factors including family upbringing and schooling (see Dougherty and Hammack, pp. 340–341).

cultural deprivation theory holds that working-class and nonwhite students perform poorly because they are not raised in a manner that develops the skills needed for school success. Such children come to school without adequate language and auditory discrimination skills. This view holds that the effectiveness of the elementary and secondary educational systems depends on the quality of the home environment, which becomes increasingly important in secondary school. The lack of learning resources attending impoverishment has the effect of reducing the cognitive skills of poor children.

This student-centered theory has been attacked for letting schools escape criticism by focusing blame on the deprived children. Critics argue that "blaming the victim" allows policy makers to avoid facing the need for fundamental changes in the educational system.[39] They contend that, if society is sincerely interested in improving the work-related skills of the labor force of the future, it must improve the quality of the lives children lead outside of school. This is of particular concern since one child in five in the United States lives in poverty.

Cultural difference theory rejects cultural deprivation theory. It claims that the lack of educationally important skills is not due to any inadequacy in working-class or minority households, but results from children being raised in oppressed subcultures. It sees the low educational aspirations and achievements of working-class and minority students as reflecting the inequalities inherent in the American class structure.[40]

Some student-centered critics see school failure as a long-term effect of elitist and meritocratic school procedures which lead to different educational conditions for the advantaged and the disadvantaged. This view accounts for low student achievement by attributing it to individual inadequacies rather than to schools that do not serve their students well. It should be noted that, whatever their weaknesses, student-centered interpretations do delineate the differences between the skills and characteristics that students bring to school and those that lead to success in classroom settings.

School-Centered Focus

School-centered explanations shift the focus from students to the educational process. Until the mid-1960s, this approach started from the premise that a major reason disadvantaged students get less education is because they go to inferior schools, while, in contrast, middle- and upper-income students attend schools having substantially more resources and more experienced teachers. This explanation has an appealing inherent logic.

However, in 1966 a study by James Coleman and a team of social scientists analyzed the educational issues surrounding school desegregation and challenged the

---

[39] Dougherty and Hammack, *Education & Society*, p. 341.
[40] Dougherty and Hammack, *Education & Society*, p. 342.

HEAD START

One initiative that has been warmly received as providing significant improvement in educational quality is the Head Start program begun in 1965 as part of President Johnson's War on Poverty. It provides economically deprived children beginning at age 3 with a variety of educational and social services in an effort to put them on an equal footing with more affluent children as they enter school. At least 90 percent of the enrollees must be from families with incomes below the federal poverty level. It is designed to provide a comprehensive program to prepare children to learn to read and write. It also provides them with certain nutritional, health, and social services.

The program involves parents in the process by providing housing aid and legal assistance. Some parents even receive job training to become teachers within the Head Start program.

Several evaluations of Head Start have produced encouraging results which show that the program has improved the chances of success in school among its participants. However, in 1990, Head Start served only about 20 percent of those eligible. Although Congress authorized funding to serve all eligible preschoolers by 1994, budget realities make it highly doubtful that the necessary appropriations will be forthcoming. A major concern is that funds will be spread so thin that more participants will be included but the program will provide far fewer expenditures per pupil and thus see its quality lowered.

Source: The State of America's Children 1991 (Washington, DC: Children's Defense Fund, 1991), pp. 44–45.

"school resources" explanation.[41] A second study by Christopher Jencks and his colleagues a few years later supported the conclusions of the Coleman study.[42] The findings of both, based upon extensive empirical research, led to the conclusion that **academic performance is determined almost entirely by the background characteristics of the students** and their peers while the characteristics of the schools they attended have only minimal influence. The greatest gap in academic achievement in the schools they studied occurred "within" schools rather than "between" schools.

These findings were politically very controversial. They implied that changing school institutions or directing more resources toward disadvantaged students or schools—the sort of public policy most easily accomplished—would not significantly affect the educational achievement of students.

The harsh implication was that differences between schools do not matter very much. This seemed to destroy the school resources argument, and also seemed to

[41] James S. Coleman, Ernest Q. Campbell, Carol J. Hobson, James McPartland, Alexander M. Mood, Frederic D. Weinfeld, and Robert L. York, *Equality of Educational Opportunity* (Washington, DC: Government Printing Office, 1966).

[42] Christopher Jencks, Marshall S. Smith, Henry Acland, Mary Jo Bane, David Cohen, Herbert Gintis, Barbara Heyns, and Stephan Michelson, *Inequality* (New York: Basic Books, 1972).

refute the liberal rationale for educational reform. For the next several years studies relying on quantitative measures of educational inputs, such as teacher salaries, teaching credentials, level of funding, or the number of holdings in the school library, supported this conclusion.

Then critics began to appear who pointed out that such studies measured only those "inputs" that could be easily quantified. They ignored facets of school organization like the quality of teaching, or administrative leadership. For example, higher salaries may well result in an improved pool of teachers in terms of "credentials" or years of experience, but it would be wrong to conclude that this would automatically lead to improvements in the quality of teaching. Such improvements require selecting and retaining the best people in the enlarged pool of teachers. Another example: Enriching a school's resources does not guarantee improved aca-

JUSTICE AND EDUCATIONAL EQUALITY

John Rawls and Robert Nozick offer two conflicting philosophical approaches for considering the problem of inequality in education. Rawls holds that only those inequalities are justified which are to the benefit of the least advantaged. Only inequalities of position or resources that result in greater productivity and thereby provide greater benefits to all, may be justified. The implication is that Rawls would attempt to delete the "accidents of birth" wherever possible, thus creating a full equalization of opportunity for each child. By moving toward equality, individual liberty is lost to the central authority that imposes that equality.

Robert Nozick's position is based upon the entitlement of the individual to whatever property he or she has legitimately acquired. Accordingly, for him the imposition of equality in benefits signifies a loss of rights for the affluent as well as the poor. The extreme position of Nozick would suggest no public education. Public education is by definition redistributive. But according to Nozick, in regard to education each child is entitled to the untaxed benefits of his or her family's resources to the extent that the family chooses to apply those resources to the child's education. This would make all education private and paid for by each family according to its ability and desires. By moving in the direction of individual liberty, equality is lost to the variations in market power enjoyed by different individuals.

Because of the issue of school financing, parental choice of schools based upon residence conflicts with the attempts by states and federal agencies to reduce inequality. This problem arose as schools were no longer primarily financed from independent towns and cities. The schools reflected the social diversity within their communities so the poor and affluent had access to the same program of studies, which encouraged Rawlsian equality. But each school district was thought to be entitled to its own resources even if there was inequality between districts, which accorded with Nozick's position. Note that the policy decision to levy taxes for public schools so long ago early on resulted in surrendering control over resources for schooling to government authority.

demic achievement. Even if an improvement does result, there is not proof it could be replicated at another school or school in a different district.

This was not just a criticism of Coleman and Jencks et al.'s conclusions, but of the assumptions of many traditional proposals aimed at school "reform." The critics suggested that rather than focusing on aggregate data such as per capita school spending and average teacher salaries, or average years of teaching experience, studies should focus on the specific factors that foster high student achievement, and on how schools with a record of success in producing academically achieving students, especially those from high-risk backgrounds, are organized. Researchers began to investigate schools commonly considered effective and compared them, where possible, with schools commonly regarded as ineffective. This approach provided insight into the critical performance factors within the larger population of

With the shift in recent decades of the responsibility for financing public education away from local government to the state and federal levels, the issue of liberty versus equality has become more prominent. But now it involves the liberty of the local school district (not the individual) to freely allocate its own resources, versus equity among school districts (not individuals) restricting district liberty. The basic conflict is between those who appeal for financing by the state based on principles of equity, versus those who protest that resources should not be redistributed to other districts. In this issue there are policy alternatives that tend toward the positions of Rawls or Nozick, and a third that is somewhat of a compromise. The first would emphasize equality by providing full funding by the states. The extreme position precludes the liberty of individual districts to spend more on education by taxing themselves more heavily, insisting complete equality of funding for all children. A second option, more closely in tune with Nozick's views, would maintain local funding and local decisions regarding the level of expenditure. State and national funds would supplement local financing, but without regard to the level of the local tax burden for education.

A third alternative would encourage some aspects of both Rawls' and Nozick's principles. Rather than taking away rights from those who feel entitled by their economic power to opt for the school of their choice through residence, those rights might be expanded to include others who do not have that choice. Permitting choice would increase equality rather than inequality by allowing individuals otherwise effectively excluded by economics from the residential area of the school to choose a school other than that of closest residence. By exercising that right inequality is reduced. Full equality is not realized, however, the liberty of the affluent to maintain socially homogeneous schools is restricted. Importantly, however, a new liberty (option) is provided for the less privileged who previously were without it.

Source: This section draws heavily upon James Coleman, "Rawls, Nozick, and Educational Equality," *The Public Interest,* vol. 43 (1976), pp. 121–128.

schools. The validity of critiquing school organization as a source of educational success or failure could not be established until the proper investigative measures were developed.[43] But by the late 1970s and early 1980s, a number of studies reached the inescapable conclusion that **school organization does have an important impact on learning**.

Interestingly, one of the more weighty arguments in favor of the significance of school organization on the learning process came from James Coleman. In a study whose results were published in the early 1980s,[44] Coleman and two colleagues used the *High School and Beyond* (HSB) data set to conduct a comparative study of public, parochial, and private schools. They concluded that parochial school students generally received the highest scores on achievement tests, followed by private school students; in third place were public school students. This finding remained constant even when background characteristics of the students, such as family income or level of parental education, were controlled. The study also found that parochial schools, primarily those serving inner-city racial minorities, were more integrated than public schools.[45] Parochial and private schools consistently did a better job of educating the typical student than public schools, and much of the superior performance originated in important organizational differences.

Like Coleman's earlier study, this one also created political controversy. This time the controversy was stimulated by the finding that parochial and private schools are more effective in educating their students than public schools. Many in the public educational community rejected the study out of hand. But Coleman and his colleagues established an important theoretical point that **schools matter**. "Effective schools research," as studies of school organization have come to be called, suggest that it should be possible to identify how structural features of schools can condition teacher behavior and expectations and influence student success. Using this approach, schools are identified whose students perform much better than typical for comparable students elsewhere. Researchers then try to isolate those factors that differentiate such atypically effective schools. Comparing "effective schools" with those commonly regarded as "ineffective" also provides insight into the general elements of effectiveness within the educational system.

---

[43] John E. Chubb and Terry M. Moe, *Politics, Markets, and America's Schools* (Washington, DC: The Brookings Institution, 1990), p. 15.

[44] James S. Coleman, Thomas Hoffer, and Sally Kilgore, *High School Achievement: Public, Catholic, and Private Schools Compared* (New York: Basic Books, 1982).

[45] A Rand Corporation study in 1990 concluded that parochial schools have particular success with disadvantaged and minority students. Although minority students score lower than their white classmates in both Catholic and public schools, the gap decreases significantly by the eleventh grade. Children from single-parent families attending public schools drop out at twice the rate of those with both parents in the home. Children in single-parent homes drop out only at the same rate as those with both parents in Catholic schools, however. Although the educational level of parents of parochial school students exceeds that of parents of public school children, Catholic schools' achievement advantage over public schools is the greatest for children whose parents have the least education. Reported by Tim Baker, "Successful Schools are Right under Our Noses," *The Baltimore Sun*, June 3, 1991.

No single factor makes a school exceptional. Effective schools, these studies have concluded, are characterized by several ingredients that conventional wisdom has all along suggested are important:

• **Clear school goals**, and strong principal, or school-based, leadership. (Schools should have a mission rather than operate from force of habit.)

• **School autonomy**. Effective schools are free from extensive outside bureaucratic controls.

• **High expectations on the part of teachers** and principals for student performance.

• **Vigorous leadership and involvement by the principal** in the instructional program.

• **Rigorous academic standards** with high teacher expectations regarding students graduating from high school, going to college, becoming good readers, and being good citizens.

• **Professionalism among the teachers**. Teachers spend their time actually teaching and monitoring their students, and providing feedback to them. Teachers rely on tests they themselves have developed in judging student achievement.

• **Principals and teachers are able to experiment and adapt techniques and procedures in response to the circumstances encountered.**[46]

The research on effective schools has come at a time when dissatisfaction with the American public educational system has reached a critical level. It is consistent with the views of those who suggest a "back-to-basics" approach that accentuates order and discipline and emphasizes basic skills and more testing to measure progress. Coleman and others found in their research that Catholic parochial schools tend to be more effective and provide a significantly better education than public schools, due to their focus on just such aspects of education.[47]

In the private education sector the formal right to control a school is vested with a church, a corporation, or a nonprofit agency that has the legal right to make all the educational decisions. In the public education sector, different interests struggle over educational decisions. Ironically, though, a basic market or "choice" principle gives parents and students a more influential role in private-sector schools than in the public education system. Those who run private or parochial schools have a strong motivation to please their clientele because they know that if people do not like the educational services they are receiving they can switch. This is invariably

---

[46] See Stewart C. Purkey and Marshall S. Smith, "Effective Schools: A Review," *Elementary School Journal*, vol. 83 (March 1983), pp. 427–452, for a good review of the characteristics of effective schools research.

[47] See, for example, James S. Coleman, "Families and Schools," *Educational Researcher*, vol. 16 (August-September 1987), pp. 32–38. See also, particularly for research comparing public and private schools, Coleman, Hoffer, and Kilgore, *High School Achievement*; also see James S. Coleman and Thomas Hoffer, *Public and Private High Schools* (New York: Basic Books, 1987).

The findings of effective schools research have been challenged along with their policy implications by several scholars. Full issues of *Sociology of Education*, vol. 55 (April-July 1982), and the *Harvard Educational Review*, vol. 51 (November 1981), pp. 481–545, were devoted to a critique of the Coleman, Hoffer, and Kilgore study.

a strong possibility since the low-cost public school system is always an alternative. Moreover, private-sector schools that cannot attract a clientele of sufficient size must pass along the higher per pupil charges to the families of the students they are able to attract or to their sponsoring organizations. Otherwise they will go out of business.[48] This is a strong financial motivator to provide a good education.

Research findings suggest factors are at work in the public educational system that directly conflict with several of the indicators which make for effective schools. For example, John Chubb and Terry Moe have concluded that a public education system with low or declining quality may not keep parents from moving into a school district, and it is even less likely to cause existing residents to leave. Rather it might prod them to consider a private school. If they choose that option, it reduces the number of disgruntled parents in the public school system and reduces the average dissatisfaction of those left in the public sector.[49] The major disincentive to leaving is that **public education has a very low cost**. Therefore, the worth of private or parochial schools must be far superior to public schools to attract students. Or, stated differently, the low cost of public schools permits them to attract students without needing to be particularly good at teaching them.

Once **parents make a choice** in favor of a public school despite their apprehensions, they may try to correct perceived problems in methods or performance through the democratic process. The political struggle for control over the public schools involves parents, student advocacy groups, teachers, teachers' unions, administrators, business groups, local school boards, state governments, and the federal government. Victory comes in the form of tenuous compromises regarding goals that could vanish with a shift in political power. Thus schools will be directed to

> . . . pursue academic excellence, but without making courses too difficult; they will be directed to teach history, but without making any value judgments; they will be directed to teach sex education, but without taking a stand on contraception or abortion. They must make everyone happy by being all things to all people—just as politicians try to do.[50]

The winning coalition inevitably sets up a bureaucratic arrangement to force compliance upon the losers and to ensure against the risks of future defeat by opponents who would like to impose their own rules. Bureaucratic control means that teacher behavior will be regulated in minute detail and enforcement procedures will be set up by the winners that permit verifying teacher compliance with the rules and standards.

Thus, the tendency to blame the public education bureaucracy for educational problems is to misunderstand the nature of those problems. It is true that bureaucrats are rewarded for devising rules and regulations and sometimes set standards

[48] John E. Chubb and Terry M. Moe, *Politics, Markets & America's Schools* (Washington, DC: The Brookings Institution, 1990), pp. 32–33.

[49] Chubb and Moe, *Politics, Markets & America's Schools*, p. 33. This is the best analysis to date of the problems of public education in America and alternative approaches to resolving them.

[50] Chubb and Moe, *Politics, Markets & America's Schools*, p. 54.

based on policies and programs defined in the past. But the bureaucrats are put into place by the victors of the political struggles over public education in order to enforce compliance with their vision of what education should be.[51] Not to put bureaucrats in place would result in an uncertain political victory and an inability by the victors to enforce their terms.

Nor are teachers necessarily to blame for problems in public education. Good teaching consists of skilled operations that are extremely difficult to measure in formal bureaucratic assessments. Educational output results from the interaction between a teacher and a student. That is the primary relationship in education. Professionalism requires that teachers have the freedom to exercise their judgment in applying their knowledge and teaching skills to the specific students and circumstances they encounter. When administrators require uniformity and equal treatment of people, it limits the autonomy of all the school staffs and principals within a district. When the system is bureaucratized, the most important relationship for a teacher is with his or her supervisor, not with students. Increasing bureaucratic regulations and reporting standards guarantee that teacher discretion will be reduced and initiative stifled.[52] A school not controlled by an administrative bureaucracy responsible to political factions will be autonomous and its staff will interact more with its primary clients, the students.

Market-Oriented Reforms and "Effective Schools"

The obvious implication of the effective schools type of research is that policy alternatives need to be implemented which will move the educational system in the direction of decentralized educational "markets." Advocates argue this would give parents more choice in selecting schools for their children. It would also force

---

[51] *The Baltimore Sun*, June 3, 1991, reported that the parochial school system in Baltimore costs about $2000 per student or less than half the cost of the Baltimore public schools. Bureaucracy accounts for a major portion of the difference. Parochial schools educate 31,002 students in 101 schools in Baltimore and the surrounding counties with a central staff of 16 people. By comparison, the Baltimore public school system employs 570 people in its headquarters to run a system of 108,000 students in 180 schools. Comparable per-student staff levels would drop the public school bureaucracy from 570 to 56 people.

The parochial schools have some advantages in that they do not try to educate children with severe learning disabilities, handicaps, or discipline problems. But that does not entirely account for the superior results.

[52] The problems related to the bureaucratic control of education have increased as responsibility for funding has moved from local communities to the states and federal regulation has grown. Court decisions on funding equity and racial integration have also contributed to the trend. Increased regulation has also contributed to instruction taking a smaller portion of educational expenditures, declining from 68 percent in 1960 to 61 percent in 1980. Also between 1960 and 1984 the number of nonclassroom personnel grew 400 percent, approximately seven times the growth rate of classroom teachers. See John E. Chubb and Eric A. Hanushek, "Reforming Educational Reform," in Henry J. Aaron (ed.), *Setting National Priorities: Policy for the Nineties* (Washington, DC: The Brookings Institution, 1990), pp. 223–224.

Teachers' unions, in supporting greater autonomy for teachers, promote a formalization of teacher authority by imposing strict procedural rules for decision making on both principals and teaching staffs. This also reduces the principals' ability to take effective action to obtain teachers with the greatest teaching skills. The result is that principals and the staff members are stuck with each other, whether they get along with or approve of each other or not.

schools to compete for the financial support that would come through parental choice of schools. As a necessary component of choice, proponents point out, schools must be given greater autonomy in deciding their academic programs, in choosing their principals and staffs, and in determining how to compete for students. Thus they must come to resemble private and parochial schools more closely. The projected benefits would be public education systems guided more by market considerations and less by politics, and therefore less prone to the debilitating effects of excessive bureaucratic controls. Subjecting schools to fewer bureaucratic requirements, but to more competition, the market mechanism would reward clear goals and efficiency. Finally, proponents argue, the choice exercised by the consumers of education—parents and students—should foster more positive and cooperative affiliations between parents, students, and schools.[53]

The Debate over Market Mechanisms

The firestorm of controversy generated by the 1982 Coleman et al. study on education in America demonstrates that education is not an issue neatly dividing liberals and conservatives. Typically conservatives have supported the student-centered analysis of educational problems. They have stressed the abilities and attitudes students bring to school, not what schools do to educate their students. Student-centered arguments range from "geneticist" views at one end of the spectrum ascribing the lower educational attainment of disadvantaged students largely to an inferior gene pool, to "cultural difference" views imputing working-class or minority students' educational distress to their rebellion against school discipline or the intolerance of middle- and upper-class school culture regarding disadvantaged subcultures. In between is the "cultural deprivation" view attributing academic inadequacies to a deficient home life that fails to develop the skills and attitudes necessary for academic success. Conservatives tend to see these problems as being outside the purview of educational policy.

Liberals, on the other hand, have usually focused on school-centered explanations. Many liberals are very troubled by the impossible conditions teachers frequently confront when trying to carry out their educational tasks in public schools—the lack of a clear sense by many school systems of their education purpose, and their refusal to involve teachers in the process of curriculum design. Liberals tend to favor smaller and more focused schools that are permitted the freedom to adapt to local conditions.

The implications of the Coleman study and the subsequent research regarding what constitutes effective schools are threatening to many of the groups that helped install the bureaucracies which implement and defend educational policies opposed to effective schools research conclusions, whether those groups are in other respects conservative or liberal in their views. For example, both the National Educational Association and the American Federation of Teachers disagree with

---

[53] Chubb and Hanushek, "Reforming Educational Reform," p. 230.

the notion of school choice. Albert Shanker, president of the American Federation of Teachers, objects to the findings of private and parochial school superiority. While acknowledging the superiority of the test scores for students at private and parochial schools, he stresses that (a) the differences in the scores are not large enough to provide convincing evidence of private and parochial school superiority, (b) public schools accept **all** students and provide a wider choice of academic curriculums, and (c) all three school systems perform poorly when compared to schools in other countries.[54]

Shanker's proposed solution is to copy the advantages of private and parochial schools not by giving students (or their parents) a choice of which schools they may attend but by insisting students take "more academically challenging courses as they do in Catholic and other private schools."[55] Public schools should also heed the message of parents who send their children to private schools. Teachers cannot teach and students cannot learn if pupils are permitted to hold learning hostage to disruptive behavior. Private schools do not tolerate that, he claims, and neither should public schools.[56]

On the other hand, some critics who are very concerned to improve educational opportunities for the poor, such as John Chubb and Terry Moe, support the notion of school choice. In their view, consumer choice would spark needed competition to establish better public school systems, which would especially benefit those poor children most in need of good public education.[57] As they see it, this would give the disadvantaged more of the same choices in regard to their education that the affluent already enjoy. Affluence gives families the ability to buy homes in preferred public school districts or to opt for a private school education for their children. The affluent are also able to press for the best principals, teachers, and facilities available for their schools. According to Chubb and Moe, it is only equitable to provide disadvantaged families with an open-enrollment market-oriented plan so they can enjoy the market power to choose schools for their children that the affluent have always had. Currently, the poor have no choice.

Some opponents of choice argue from what are at least in part conservative principles. They point out that markets are inclined to "failure." Only rarely are there "perfectly competitive" markets. The environment is more often oligopolistically competitive or outright oligopolistic. For a choice program to work correctly, there would have to be a sufficient number of schools to choose from, yet many school districts are so small that they can offer little or no choice. Moreover, disadvantaged families would need the same market ability to choose as more affluent families, and because of income inequalities it would be necessary for the government to guarantee all children the same financial resources to shop for an appropriate

[54] See Albert Shanker, "Private versus Public Schools: What Education Gap?" *The Washington Post*, February 2, 1992, p. C3.

[55] Shanker, "Private versus Public Schools," p. C3.

[56] Shanker, "Private versus Public Schools," p. C3.

[57] As quoted in Linda Chion-Kenney, "The Choice Debate," *The Washington Post*, February 10, 1992, p. B5. Also see Chubb and Moe, *Politics, Markets, & America's Schools*.

CHOICE AND MARKET OPTIONS

A range of plans exist that allow parents some choice and introduce elements of market competition into the public education system.

Magnet Schools

Magnet schools usually build an advanced academic curricula around interested faculty, parents, and students. This concept permits students to attend the magnet school from anywhere in the district (intradistrict choice). Students usually choose between the magnet school and the normal high school. A frequently voiced criticism is that magnet schools tend to attract the best teachers and students from the district, resulting in a net loss in quality to other schools. The benefits to the magnet school may be offset by the losses suffered by the traditional schools in the district. Typically the organizational constraints of the large school system remain in force.

School Choice Plans (Open Enrollment)

Intradistrict open enrollment allows students to choose any public school within their school district. *Interdistrict* choice plans permit families to send their children to public schools in other districts. The overall results have been favorable. In East Harlem, a school district in New York, test scores in reading and math went from the bottom of 32 school districts to sixteenth.[58] The greatest drawback is that public authorities allow students who cross district lines to transfer only the share of educational costs contributed by the state. When costs exceed the amount guaranteed by the state, the district the students leave actually receive the local contributions as a benefit, while the district they enter must make up the difference. This inflicts a penalty on host schools attracting the pupils which is the very opposite of what free-flowing market forces would do.[59]

Although Albert Shanker does not like school choice, teachers' unions are supportive if the alternative is for parents to send their children to private or parochial schools.

[58] See Edward B. Fiske, "Letting Parents Choose a Public School: The Idea Now Has Champions in the White House," *The New York Times*, January 11, 1989. See also Raymond Ja Domanico, *A Model for Choice: A Report on Manhattan's District 4* (Education Policy Paper 1) (New York: Center for Education Innovation, Manhattan Institute for Policy Research, June 1989).
[59] See Chubb and Hanushek, "Reforming Educational Reform," pp. 237–238.

school. Another major concern about choice plans has to do with issues of discrimination. Federal law and Supreme Court decisions outlaw discrimination based on race, ethnicity, sex, or disciplinary problems in public schools, except perhaps to improve racial balances. But many parents send their children to private schools or move to particular suburban areas so their children can be educated with other children whose ethnic and economic backgrounds are similar to their own. Under choice programs, the government could require all schools to desegregate to prevent parents and students from selecting schools based upon ethnic or racial considerations. Education is a quasi-public good precisely because private funding does not provide a sufficient supply of education or necessarily lead to meeting

Tuition Tax Credits

These move beyond magnet schools and open-enrollment plans toward market forces by abolishing the monopoly that public school districts exercise over the supply of publicly supported education. Giving parents a credit against their federal or state income taxes for some portion of private or parochial school payments makes such schools more affordable and increases the pressure on all schools, whether public or private, to become more competitive. The Supreme Court's decision in *Mueller v. Allen*, 463 U.S. 388 (1983), established the legality of a Minnesota law allowing parents of children in elementary and secondary schools to deduct tuition from their income taxes.

A limitation of tax credits is that they reimburse only a small portion of the typical private school tuition. Thus they are of only small benefit to parents with low incomes. So while credits encourage some competition, their total impact is limited.

Voucher Plans

These moves beyond tuition tax credits by providing parents of school-age children with vouchers that can be used only to pay for school. The goal of vouchers would be to provide full payment for any student's education at any public or publicly approved private school. The school receiving the voucher would turn the certificate in to the issuing government for reimbursement. Such vouchers would provide all families with the market power now exercised only by the affluent. One variation on the proposal would provide the educationally disadvantaged with a voucher of greater value, which would make those students more attractive to schools that otherwise might not want them. Government would retain its right to set requirements regarding eligibility, admission, graduation, teacher certification, and any other societal goals it found warranted for participating public and private schools. Providing such broad educational choice would encourage all schools to improve their educational output to stay ahead of the competition.

Voucher plans originally received the support of such economic conservatives as Milton Friedman, and political conservatives such as Ronald Reagan. They have broadened their appeal to economic and political liberals as well.

Source: This section was broadly adapted from Chubb and Hanushek, "Reforming Educational Reform," pp. 235–240.

---

other public policy goals such as equality of opportunity. But public financial support for education also means government regulation.

Some liberals fear that school choice would be rigged against the poor. They wonder how choice programs could guarantee that the disadvantaged would receive information regarding all the available options and how they could best choose in their rational self-interest. Some believe that poor people would receive **inadequate information** and therefore not make optimum choices. Rational self-interest alone does not guarantee that everyone will make the best choice if they lack the correct information. Supporters of choice programs counter that parents would have a greater motivation to obtain accurate information from the schools and from other parents, although the government would need to be especially vigilant in ensuring truth in advertising and prohibiting false claims.

A final concern is whether choice would attract the better teachers, students, and resources to "effective schools," leaving the more poorly performing schools without the ability to improve. If so, would these ineffective schools shut down, or would they continue in operation, serving students who are unable to go elsewhere?

THE BRITISH EFFORT AT SCHOOL REFORM

The British school system has performed only modestly better than school systems in the United States, according to international achievement tests. As a result, reform of the educational system in Britain has been an issue since the early 1980s. The government passed the Education Reform Act of 1988, which created a new institutional framework for the British educational system similar to the types of reform suggested for American school systems. The intent was to provide for local management of schools and permit parents to choose among schools for their children. This open-enrollment program requires local education authorities to admit students to popular schools beyond their usual numbers even though it means less attractive schools have unfilled student slots. Many parents who were at first uneasy with the school selection process now are relaxed with it and have come to expect it as a right.[60]

The act also provided some funding for the building of approximately 15 city technology colleges (CTCs) as alternatives that combine academics with vocational training for students who do not intend to continue on to college. CTCs have curriculums devised to keep students in school, providing them with employable talents and stemming a serious dropout problem in Britain. The CTCs are oversubscribed and must turn away many economically and academically disadvantaged students.

Finally, the act permits schools to **opt out** of their local education authorities (LEAs) and become independent grant-maintained schools based upon per-child allowances. Such schools operate rather independently in regard to students and money; they also enjoy a much greater ability to control their own decision making than schools within the LEA structure. Schools that have opted out show signs of developing an entrepreneurial spirit in how they decide to spend funds. They do not receive a range of services from the LEAs for curriculum development, counseling, or teacher training. Some have purchased computers, musical instruments, and industrial arts equipment.[61] They have developed their own sense of mission. Opting out appears to be at least as popular in poorer districts as in wealthier ones. Parochial Anglican and Catholic schools are also permitted state funding if they accept some controls by their LEAs.

Finally, there is a certain irony in how the issue of school choice has played itself out in Great Britain. Intuitively one would not expect the Conservative Party to

[60] John E. Chubb and Terry M. Moe, *A Lesson in School Reform from Great Britain* (Washington, DC: The Brookings Institution, 1992), p. 19.

[61] Chubb and Moe, *A Lesson in School Reform from Great Britain*, p. 37.

favor such a program. Ideologically it has a tendency to support traditional social institutions, including the traditional elitist British school system. The Conservative Party's support for markets springs from a mindset that believes business affairs are best managed from the top down. It is less supportive of market and choice approaches when they are not controlled from the top. However, choice in education leads away from a concentration of power and authority to decentralization and a leveling of power. The Conservative Party's stance requires it to support market choice in regard to education, but without a commitment to a full-blown system of choice because its members sense that such an approach would confer disproportionate advantages to the poor and minorities in urban areas. In this, the Conservative Party in Great Britain is like the Republican Party in the United States.

However, in the spring of 1992 and with an election looming, the Labour Party found itself supporting the workers in the British educational bureaucracy and other employees fearful of the recent reforms because it did not want to alienate a constituency that gave it important support. But choice is very popular with British working class voters, who recognize that the traditional educational system has served the elites quite well and who see school choice as a way of achieving advantages already enjoyed by those elites. In the campaign, the Labour Party promised to reverse the choice options of the educational reform act. This provided the Conservatives with a golden opportunity to attract many voters from the Labour constituency, resulting in the Conservatives retaining control of the government despite the long and deep recession in Britain that made them unpopular otherwise.

Likewise in the United States, the Democratic Party, which has long felt that education is its issue, finds itself torn between its desire to defend the educational establishment and the political need to support the wishes of its working class constituency who wants choice, particularly for parochial schools. Republicans, not particularly noted for their support of public education, have eroded the Democrats' advantages in this area by supporting school choice. Nor have they alienated their traditional constituency by this stance: The more affluent would like to be reimbursed the equivalent of the taxes they pay for public education by vouchers to be used at the private schools of their choice. This would help them escape the burden of expensive higher educations for their children.[62]

DROPOUT PROBLEMS

High school dropout rates, which have declined steadily throughout this century, appear to have leveled off and may be actually increasing.[63] Students who drop out

[62] It should be noted that many of the less privileged resent private education, feeling that if it did not exist, many influential people would make sure that public education improved.

[63] Deborah B. Strother, *Phi Delta Kappan*, vol. 68 (December 1986), pp. 325–328. Reprinted in Dougherty and Hammack, *Education & Society*, p. 256. The dropout rate from high school which was 90 percent in 1900, fell to 80 percent by the 1920s, to 50 percent by the early 1950s, and to the low 20 percents by the mid-1970s. Other studies suggest that overall the dropout rates are not getting worse, but have actually improved marginally since the 1970s. However, the problem is still increasing in certain urban areas. See *Dropouts in America* (Washington, DC: The Institute for Educational Leadership, 1987), pp. 11–12.

are severely disadvantaged throughout their lives both socially and economically. This is more than just a personal failure; dropouts cost the economy billions of dollars in a variety of ways including welfare benefits and lost output.[64] Dropouts are a national tragedy. The goal of motivating at-risk teenagers to complete secondary school and acquire the skills necessary to work productively in the labor market must be given a high priority.

Defining the Dropout Problem

Nationally about 20 percent of potential high school graduates quit before graduation.[65] By contrast, in Japan only about 7 percent drop out, while in Germany only about 9 percent do so. In both Japan and Germany, dropouts are placed in apprenticeship systems to develop technical skills.

In Germany non-college-bound students begin their apprenticeships at age 15 or 16. They go into a 3-year school-industry program which concludes with comprehensive written and practical exams. Upon passing those examinations, they become journeymen. They may continue for another 3 years to become masters, which is a requirement if they wish to open their own businesses. German economic success is often attributed to this educational approach, which provides an excellent broad range of midlevel, noncollege skills.[66] In the United States, high school dropouts receive whatever training is available on their jobs. This sort of training tends to be job-specific and does not lead to broad technical skills.

Available data on the dropout problem clearly indicates that it is serious, but unfortunately there is no agreement on the definition of a **dropout**. Nor is there a standard system in this country for calculating the dropout rate. School districts frequently feel pressure to make dropout rates appear as small as possible. Since high dropout rates can erode public confidence in the quality of the local public educa-

---

[64] The societal costs of dropping out are incredibly high. According to research by Henry Levin at Stanford University, the cost of high school dropouts, ages 25 to 34, conservatively amounts to $77 billion every year: $71 billion in lost tax revenues, $3 billion for welfare and unemployment benefits, and $3 billion for crime prevention. See *School Dropouts: Everybody's Problem* (Washington, DC: The Institute for Educational Leadership, 1986), p. 2. Sixty percent of all prison inmates in the United States are high school dropouts, according to Mary Hatwood Futrell in "It's a Tragedy We Cannot Afford," *USA Today*, April 29, 1986, p. 8.

A 1985 study put the loss in adjusted lifetime earnings for a male dropout at $187,000 and for a female dropout at $122,000. Another study estimated that the losses for the nation ranged from a low of $60 billion to a high of $228 billion. The lower estimate amounted to approximately $60,000 for each dropout. See James S. Catterall, *On the Social Costs of Dropping Out of School* (Stanford, CA: Stanford University, 1985).

[65] *School Dropouts: Everybody's Problem*, p. 1.

Some estimates claim that the dropout rate could be as high as 25 percent. In inner cities, the average is twice as high where one in every two students drops out of high school. For some groups the rate is even higher. Race is a key factor. Overcoming hurdles is difficult if you are poor and white. It is even more difficult if you are poor and a member of a minority group. Approximately 40 percent of all Hispanic students drop out. Native Americans experience approximately a 48 percent dropout rate, and Puerto Ricans about 75 percent. See *School Dropouts: Everybody's Problem*, p. 1, and *Dropouts in America*, p. 3.

[66] Lester Thurow, *Head to Head: The Coming Economic Battle among Japan, Europe, and America* (New York: William Morrow, 1992), pp. 54–55.

tion system, some districts do not include students who leave school because of pregnancy or to join the military. Many count only high school dropouts and do not keep information on those who leave elementary, junior high, or special education schools or programs.[67] Central to the dropout problem is the unsurprising fact that poor children are more likely to leave school than their more affluent peers.

Growing up in poverty does not determine school failure. But when the difficulties of deprivation are not alleviated by the dedication of substantial resources and the commitment of concerned adults, it is extremely difficult to succeed. There is little help in many poor rural communities or in many inner-city schools. As Theodore Sizer, a former dean of the Harvard School of Education, wrote:

> The hard fact is that if you are the child of low-income parents the chances are good that you will receive limited and often careless attention from adults in your high school. Most of this is realism that many Americans prefer to keep under the rug, of course; it is no easy task for the poor in America to break out . . . of their economic condition.[68]

Because the dropout problem is concentrated in certain urban centers and rural pockets, it is practically invisible to most of society. Therefore it has been ignored in the effort to upgrade the nation's educational system and raise academic standards. In fact, there is reason for concern that, while upgrading standards may encourage many students to work harder, the higher standards will contribute to higher dropout rates for minority and disadvantaged students.[69]

Higher standards usually do not include funding for remedial programs. Increasing the number of required courses and upgrading course content may actu-

---

[67] The Census Bureau defines dropouts as "persons who are not enrolled in school and who are not high school graduates (or the equivalent)." A major problem with that definition is it includes groups beyond high school attendance age. Also, Census Bureau data are self-reported, and individuals may be reluctant to admit that they or other family members are dropouts.

The Department of Education uses state-generated data collected by the National Center for Education Statistics (NCES) and based upon the percentage of students who complete high school during the same year as their original ninth-grade class. States have no common reporting system, however. This measure may overstate the problem because those who earn equivalency degrees are still counted as dropouts.

Yet another major measure, High School and Beyond carried out by NCES, began tracking students *after* their sophomore year when many had already dropped out; it therefore underestimated the problem. Many school districts carry "perpetual truants" on their rolls even though they have actually dropped out.

Using different criteria leads to different estimates. The High School and Beyond analysis produced a 14 percent dropout rate, which is clearly too low; the Department of Education arrives at 28 percent, which probably overstates the problem; the Census Bureau comes up with 18 percent, also too low. Many researchers, taking the inherent problems of the collection methodologies into account, suggest 23 or 24 percent is a reasonable estimate of the dropout rate nationwide.

[68] Theodore B. Sizer, *Horace's Compromise: The Dilemma of the American High School* (Boston: Houghton Mifflin, 1984), pp. 36–37. Quoted in *Dropouts in America*, p. 3.

[69] A study completed in 1985, examined 32 state initiatives in education and found just 10 programs focusing on disadvantaged or underachieving students. See MDC, Inc., *The States' Excellence in Education Commissions: Who's Looking Out for At-Risk Youth* (Chapel Hill, NC: MDC, Inc., 1985). Since that time, at least 15 other states have initiated such programs, although new funding for them has been difficult to secure.

ally result in less time for teachers to aid students who are falling behind.[70] There are many programs with substantial funding to promote "excellence" in education, but few that take "equity" into account, which may be essential in helping potential dropouts to remain in school.

Who Drops Out and Why

Students drop out of school for reasons that have remained largely unchanged over several decades. In the study already noted in footnote 67, High School and Beyond, carried out by the National Center for Education Statistics, researchers found the most often cited reason for leaving school was poor academic performance. High-risk students frequently find school a hostile environment where they are confirmed as failures daily. School agendas prize uniformity, harmony, regulation, and intellectual competition. Success in these behaviors is often especially difficult for high-risk students. Their rebellion against them leads to truancy, suspension, or other forms of misconduct within school. In the High School and Beyond study, such students were likely to report that they were not popular with their classmates, were less likely than their not-at-risk peers to take part in extracurricular activities, and felt estranged from school life. Males who were older than average for their grade (because they had been held back at least once) and racial and ethnic minorities other than Asian Americans were more likely to experience disciplinary problems and become dropouts. Dropouts by and large are capable of doing the academic work. They are just inclined to be underachievers, as indicated in the High School and Beyond survey which found that their tested achievement was 7 to 12 percentiles higher than their school year grades.

Family and economic factors outside of the school situation itself usually have a major bearing on the decision to drop out. The dropout phenomenon is not new. However, the predicament of those who drop out of school is exacerbated by a stagnant economy. There are few if any jobs available to them that will pay a living wage, so that unlike in the early part of this century, high school dropouts today are very likely to become burdens on society. At the same time, the **lack of jobs** may actually serve as the reason for dropping out of school. Potential dropouts may be familiar only with low-wage, low-status jobs and not accept the widely held belief that more education is likely to lead to higher status and higher-paid employment.

A disproportionate number of dropouts come from single-parent homes. Children in single-parent homes are twice as likely to drop out as students living with both parents. Among females, approximately one-third report marital plans as the reason for leaving school, while one-fourth say they are leaving because of pregnancy (although many leave school and then become pregnant). Many dropouts

---

[70] There is some concern that raising scholastic performance requirements to be eligible to participate in extracurricular activities, such as sports, drama, or a band, may take away an important incentive for some students to stay in school. Most observers agree that no one benefits from watered-down courses or an emphasis on extracurricular activities. Yet it must be recognized that at-risk students may need additional assistance to be encouraged to stay in school and meet the higher requirements.

particularly males, leave school to support their families of origin, or the families they themselves have started.

Public Policy and the Dropout Problems

These findings have important implications for policy analysts. So far few efforts have been made to address the problem of high dropout rates and integrate solutions into regular school policy. Since students drop out for a variety of reasons, no single policy can meet the needs of all at-risk students. Nevertheless, different programs can be developed for different types of problems.

Any program aimed at lessening the dropout rate should address these school practices that discourage high-risk students by proposing substitute practices and arrangements to encourage them to remain in school until graduation. Recommendations from several studies include the following:

1 **Assistance for low achievers**. Higher requirements should be accompanied with support for low-achieving students. Setting higher standards without providing additional assistance for those with lower aptitudes and rates of achievement will reinforce their sense of failure and their negative views of school.

2 **Promotion policies**. The dropout rate among students who have repeated a grade is more than double those who have not been held back. This connection begins as early as the first grade. Research shows that holding a child back a grade in elementary school is less cost-effective than providing the special services the student needs to perform at his or her normal grade level. Several states are instituting standardized tests to determine competence for promotion and graduation. If such tests are implemented without remedial programs, they may simply divide "winners" and "losers" without identifying where help is needed. Holding back students without offering them remedial help is a form of punishment.

3 **School and class size**. The larger the school and its classes, the more problems reported by both teachers and students with the quality of teaching. Overcrowded classrooms increase teacher workloads, making it difficult to provide individual attention or provide remedial help for those with learning difficulties. Students experiencing problems find teachers less accessible, increasing the student's feelings of frustration and alienation at school. The greatest overcrowding occurs in poorer school districts, where there is insufficient funding to provide extra classroom space or hire the additional teachers needed.

4 **Lack of support for minorities**. Many ethnic minority students, primarily Hispanic, suffer from attending schools that do not provide sufficient bilingual education. Few Hispanic children with limited English proficiency, even in areas where they make up the majority of the class, are placed in a bilingual program. Help in this area is essential.

5 **Work-study programs**. Schools should develop programs to provide relevant work experience for students who are faced with the necessity of helping to provide a family income. One demonstration program titled STEP (Summer Training and Education Program) combines academic instruction and work opportunities over

two consecutive summers to high-risk youths. The participants receive 90 hours of remedial instruction in reading and math and they work for 80 hours and have an additional 18 hours' instruction in "life skills." The students receive the minimum wage for their activities in the classroom and at work. The results of the program have been encouraging.[71]

FEDERAL POLICY IN ELEMENTARY AND SECONDARY EDUCATION

Unlike the governments of many other countries, the U.S. government does not operate a national school system. Since the federal government's role in education is subordinate to those of state and local governments, its ability to initiate education policy is constrained. State and local governments alone have the Constitutional authority to decide whether teachers will receive merit pay, or to authorize school choice plans.

The policy-making problem for the federal government is not insurmountable, however. It merely means that federal policies cannot be directly mandated. If sticks are not available, carrots are probably more effective policy tools anyway. By offering financial grants to states or school districts that adopt certain reforms, the national government can encourage progressive policies.

The federal government could also establish national educational standards for achievement and offer financial assistance to local school systems wishing to implement them. National standards could not only raise the achievement levels of all students, but also encourage equity by requiring the least effective schools to provide their students with more skills. This would also help prevent an increase in the dropout rate, or perhaps even lower the number of students who leave school early.

Other proposals for school improvement may be more questionable. For example, lengthening the school day or the school year is frequently put forward. Fifty-one percent of those responding to a 1991 Gallup poll supported extending the 180-day U.S. school year to 210 days.[72] But mounting evidence indicates that this is not usually cost-effective because teachers tend to cover the same amount of material at a more leisurely pace, rather than adding new material.[73] Any initiative imple-

---

[71] See Cynthia L. Sipe, Jean B. Grossman, and Julita A. Milliner, *Summer Training and Education Program (STEP): Report on the 1986 Summer Experience* (Philadelphia: Public/Private Ventures, 1987).

[72] Forty-two percent opposed an extension of the school year and 7 percent had no opinion. The 210-day year would still fall short of the school year in Japan, which is 243 days, and in Korea, which is 220 days. In the same poll 48 percent opposed a longer school day, while 48 percent were in favor. There was strong opposition to making a longer school year optional and requiring parents choosing that option to pay the extra cost (56 percent opposed and 36 percent in favor). Various estimates put the cost of increasing the school year to 200 days somewhere between $11 billion and $20 billion. See Kenneth Cooper, "Longer School Year Gains Majority Backing," *The Washington Post*, August 23, 1991.

[73] One study found that a 10 percent increase in the amount of time spent in school only results in a 1.5 to 2 percent improvement in achievement tests. See Henry M. Levin and Mun C. Tsang, "The Economics of Student Time," *Economics of Education Review*, vol. 6, no. 4 (1987), pp. 357–364.

menting a longer period of instruction must include a commitment to cover additional material.

Another type of plan often put forward to improve educational performance is merit pay for good teaching. However, there is little evidence that such plans have been effective in raising the quality of instruction. Critics charge that merit pay is usually awarded on the basis of increased workloads rather than any measurable improvement in student achievement or clear superiority in teaching ability.[74]

At the very least, the federal government should make the results of successful education programs public. Doing so would encourage the adoption of effective programs elsewhere.

POSTSECONDARY EDUCATION

The United States differs from most industrial nations in that it lacks an organized postsecondary educational system for students not intending to go to college. As Lester Thurow points out, other nations invest much more heavily in the postsecondary skills of the non-college-bound. Britain, France, and Spain spend more than twice as much as the United States in this area; Germany spends over three times as much, and Sweden almost six times as much.[75]

In the United States, firms do not want to spend significant sums to educate their workers. They fear that employees will take their skills to other companies without training programs that can pay higher wages since they have avoided the costs of those programs. Local governments avoid postsecondary vocational training for the same reason: Students may take their skills to a different region of the country. Moreover, the higher taxes necessary to pay for such educational programs might encourage industry to relocate beyond the tax region and become a free rider on the better-trained work force the locality is producing. Community colleges come closest to providing the technical intermediate-level training for the technicians and semiprofessionals needed by a complex industrial society.[76]

According to Thurow, the problem in the United States is that there are too many people in college and not enough qualified workers. With high school graduation rates below those of major international competitors (approximately 80 percent in the United States versus 94 percent in Japan and 91 percent in Germany), the American labor force is undereducated and less competent than the labor forces of Japan and Germany.[77]

Those who graduate from American colleges make up the gap in education. However, first-rate economies require not only first-rate college graduates, but also very competent and skilled technical workers. If workers cannot staff the produc-

---

[74] Richard J. Murnane and David K. Cohen, "Merit Pay and the Evaluation Problem: Why Most Merit Pay Plans Fail and a Few Survive," *Harvard Educational Review*, vol. 56 (February 1986), pp. 1–17.

[75] Lester Thurow, *Head to Head*, p. 275.

[76] See Arthur M. Cohen and Florence B. Brawer, *The American Community College* (San Francisco: Jossey-Bass, 1982).

[77] Thurow, *Head to Head*, p. 159.

tion and service processes competently to operate an efficiently producing society, the management and professional jobs that go with those processes also disappear.[78]

CONCLUSION

1 There is widespread concern in the United States that the educational system is not performing adequately in terms of educational output as measured through student achievement, especially when compared to the educational systems of other countries. While there is evidence of deficiencies, international comparisons using standardized tests must be used very cautiously.

2 The United States is atypical in that education is primarily a state and local policy issue. Constitutionally states are responsible for educational systems. The federal government's ability to influence policy is primarily through the carrot of financial assistance. The result is that education has never been a major aspect of national policy. It is frequently a matter of symbolic politics. As recently as 1980, Ronald Reagan campaigned for the Presidency on a platform that called for abolishing the Department of Education based on the claim that education is not a question for national policy.

3 There are several theories regarding the benefits of education. Functionalism stresses that education prepares individuals for various positions in the job market; other theories contend that education should promote equality and that the current system should be changed since it reinforces social stratification. Human capital theory is one of the major arguments for government intervention in education and for treating education as a quasi-public good.

4 Recent studies have focused on the factors that affect learning. Student-centered and school-centered factors are both involved in the learning process. School-centered factors are the primary interest of effective schools research. The results of this research suggest that decentralized systems which encourage market competition are strongly correlated with effectiveness in educational achievement.

5 No one proposal can be expected to resolve all the problems connected with American education. The evolution of the educational system in the United States occurred long after the drafting of the Constitution. As a result, it has been primarily a state and local responsibility. This is decidedly unlike many other countries where education is a function of the national government based upon their more recently drafted constitutions. Countries noted for educational excellence, such as Japan, have strongly centralized ministries of education that set national standards. [West Germany and Britain are exceptions. West Germany vests its Lander (or states) with educational authority in a manner similar to the arrangement in the United States, while Britain gives its local educational authorities considerable autonomy.] A strongly centralized system will not work in the United States since states and local governments are jealous of their authority over education.

---

[78] Thurow, *Head to Head*, p. 55.

6 There are over 15,000 school districts in the United States, none of which uniformly turns out students that outperform foreign students in standardized tests. The system of school choice might introduce an element of market competition among American schools that would make them more effective. But choice programs should be accompanied by federal quality standards to be met by students on achievement tests. Every school graduate should be required to meet these standards. As an inducement, the federal government should contribute a large portion of the total funding for elementary and secondary school education. States whose students fail to meet minimum standards overall should be required to improve their performance in order to maintain federal funding.

7 High school dropout rates reflect serious social stratification problems in American society and the need for remedial assistance to encourage greater equality of educational opportunity. Meaningful vocational education should also be added to many school programs.

QUESTIONS FOR DISCUSSION

1 Do you think the economy grows because of its investment in human resources, or does it invest in education because it is growing and can afford to do so?

2 Explain the concept of "human capital investment." In what ways can education and training be considered investment? In what ways can they be considered consumption?

3 How can we measure the economic return on human capital investment?

4 Is there any reason to believe that Americans are becoming overeducated? What criteria would you use to decide?

5 What aspects of education seem to be more consistent with the market signaling view of education than with the human capital view?

6 Discuss school choice versus equal opportunity. Should parents be allowed to use government vouchers to pay for any type of education they wish to choose for their children?

KEY CONCEPTS

Choice	Pure public good
Class conflict model	Quasi-public good
Coleman report	School-centered theories
Effective schools	Social benefits
Functionalism	Student-centered theories
Human capital theory	Tuition tax credits
Magnet schools	Underemployment
Market signaling	Voucher plans
Meritocracy	

SUGGESTED READINGS

Clifford Adelman (ed.), *Assessment in American Higher Education: Issues and Contexts* (Washington, DC: Government Printing Office, 1986).

K. L. Alexander and A. M. Pallas, "Curriculum Reform and School Performance: An Evaluation of the 'New Basics,'" *American Journal of Education*, vol. 92 (1984), pp. 391–420.

Arthur N. Applebee, Judith A. Langer, and Ina V. Mullis, *Crossroads in American Education: A Summary of Findings* (Princeton, NJ: Educational Testing Service, 1989).

S. Bowles and H. Gintis, *Schooling in Capitalist America* (New York: Basic Books, 1976).

Ernest L. Boyer, *High School: A Report on Secondary Education in America* (Washington, DC: Carnegie Foundation, 1983).

John E. Chubb, "Why the Current Wave of School Reform Will Fail," *The Public Interest*, vol. 90 (Winter 1988), pp. 28–49.

John E. Chubb and Terry M. Moe, *Politics, Markets & America's Schools* (Washington, DC: The Brookings Institution, 1990).

John E. Chubb and Terry M. Moe, "Politics, Markets, and the Organization of Schools," *The American Political Science Review*, vol. 82 (December 1988), 1065–1087.

David K. Cohen and Eleanor Farrar, "Power to the Parents? The Story of Education Vouchers," in Nathan Glazer (ed.), *The Public Interest on Education* (Cambridge, MA: Abt Associates, 1984).

James S. Coleman, "Rawls, Nozick, and Educational Equality," *Public Interest*, vol. 43 (1976), pp. 121–128.

James S. Coleman, Ernest Q. Campbell, Carol J. Hobson, James McPartland, Frederic D. Weinfeld, and Robert L. York, *Equality of Educational Opportunity* (Washington, DC: Government Printing Office, 1966).

James S. Coleman, Thomas Hoffer, and Sally Kilgore, *High School Achievement: Public, Catholic, and Private Schools Compared* (New York: Basic Books, 1982).

James S. Coleman, Thomas Hoffer, and Sally Kilgore, *Public and Private Schools* (Washington, DC: National Center for Education Statistics, 1981).

Randall Collins, "Some Comparative Principles of Educational Stratification." *Harvard Educational Review*, vol. 47 (1977), pp. 1–27.

Richard Freeman, *The Overeducated American* (New York: Academic Press, 1976).

Eileen Gardner (ed.), *A New Agenda for Education* (Washington, DC: Heritage Foundation, 1985).

Arthur R. Jensen, "How Much Can We Boost I.Q. and Scholastic Achievement?" *Harvard Educational Review*, vol. 39 (1969), pp. 1–123.

David C. Paris, "Moral Education and the 'Tie That Binds' in Liberal Political Theory," *APSR*, vol. 85, no. 3 (September 1991), pp. 875–901.

Caroline H. Persell, *Education and Inequality* (New York: Free Press, 1977).

James Rosenbaum, *Making Inequality* (New York: Wiley, 1976).

Lester Thurow, *Investment in Human Capital* (Belmont, CA: Wadsworth, 1970).

Paul Willis, *Learning to Labour* (New York: Schocken, 1977).

11

HEALTH CARE: DIAGNOSING A CHRONIC PROBLEM

Health expenditures in the United States are growing at an alarming rate. They have risen from less than 6 percent of GDP in 1960 to 14 percent today, and could reach 17 percent by the year 2000 at current growth rates. Policy analysts believe that these expenditures are rising at a rate that is unsustainable. Health care in the United States has been absorbing an ever larger share of its Gross Domestic Product. However, while many Americans have comprehensive health insurance coverage ensuring access to the best medical care in the world, over 38 million, about 16 percent, have no health insurance coverage. Millions more have such limited coverage that a serious illness would leave them economically impoverished. Many are afraid to seek proper health care for fear of losing their coverage. The rising cost of health care has made affordability, once a concern primarily of lower-income households, an increasing middle-class worry. The rising cost of medical care has been cited by various pollsters as of greater concern to the public than any other issue. Two major problems in health care confronting policy makers are: the excessive **increase in costs** and the growing gap in **access** to health care. Not surprisingly a very high percentage of the population believes the American health care system is in need of fundamental reform.

INTRODUCTION: THE GROWING CONSENSUS ON THE NEED FOR CHANGE

In the United States, access to basic medical care is neither a right nor, for some, a reality.[1] There are many reasons for this, including our ideological commitment to

---

[1] Curiously, the only individuals with a Constitutional right to health care are the inmates of America's prisons. In *Estelle v. Gamble*, 429 U.S. 97 (1976) the Supreme Court held that deliberate indifference to a prisoner's medical needs is in violation of the Eighth Amendment's prohibition of "cruel and unusual" punishment.

free market forces and misgivings about the government's ability to manage a health care system. Nor is it coincidental that the disparities of access to health fall heaviest on blacks and Hispanics, who are more likely to be unemployed or employed in low-level jobs without health insurance protection. Many special-interest groups including employers, insurance companies, physicians, hospitals, and politicians have failed to compromise to bring about meaningful health care reform and regulation. Guaranteed access to health care has long been accepted in all other industrialized nations, with the exception of South Africa.

Several events have occurred to place national health care reform on the U.S. policy agenda. The stagnant economy of the late 1980s fell into a lingering recession in 1990, resulting in a crises of access to health care that extended well beyond those in poverty. This expanded the scope of the conflict when many politically active voters without adequate health insurance coverage began to demand reform. There are increasing numbers of articulate and seemingly financially secure families who have become economic paupers as a result of being underinsured for catastrophic medical events. A "lingering illness" before death as a result of cancer, AIDS, Alzheimer's disease, or an accident can wipe out an underinsured family's lifetime savings with breathtaking speed.

The disintegration of the Soviet Union has ended, at least for a time, the nation's preoccupation with massive defense spending. This has shifted voters' attention to competing issues like health care.

Moreover, the once solid opposition of the medical establishment to health care reform has also begun to break down. In 1992 the American Academy of Family Physicians (with a membership of 74,000) supported a limit on physicians fees. In the middle of the Presidential election campaign later that year, the nation's largest society of medical specialists, the American College of Physicians (with a membership of 77,000), also called for a national cap on health care spending, enforced by "limits on doctor and hospital fees." The group announced its support for a national health care budget with reasonable limits on fees that would be set in negotiations with doctor and hospital groups. Even the American Medical Association (AMA), which has strongly opposed any direct government cost controls, as did President Bush, began publishing a series of articles detailing shortcomings in the current system and acknowledging the need for significant health care reform.

The shift in the national political mood was made apparent in the Pennsylvania Senate race in 1991. After Senator John Heinz died in an airplane crash, Attorney General Richard Thornburgh, a popular former Governor of Pennsylvania, was picked by then President George Bush to keep the seat in the Republican column. Harris Wofford, a little known Democratic candidate who had never held elective office, won an upset victory, largely on his outspoken promotion of a national health care plan. Then during the 1992 Presidential campaign, candidate Bill Clinton advocated major reforms that would provide "universal coverage" for all Americans. President Bush put forward a modest proposal based largely upon market alternatives. He spent a considerable portion of the campaign denouncing Clinton's plan as too expensive with too much government involvement. In the election itself, 20 percent of the voters said health care mattered most in deciding how they voted. Of those people, fully 67 percent voted for Clinton, while only 19 percent voted for George Bush and 14 percent for Perot.[2]

President Clinton's electoral victory was based upon a call for change in several public policy areas, including the American health care system. The changes in American attitudes noted above along with Clinton's election have brought together a coalition of interests that is sufficient to assure reform. The major policy questions now are what changes will be made, how significant they will be, how incremental or drastic their implementation will be, and how effective they will be once they are in place.

HEALTH CARE EXPENDITURES: THE HEART OF THE PROBLEM

The health care system of the United States is a mixture of apparent inconsistencies. America, which spent just 3.5 percent of its GDP on health care in 1930, and 6 percent in 1960, spent 14 percent of GDP on health care in 1992. That is an increase from $2.8 billion ($23 per person) in 1930 to $836 billion ($3200 per person) in 1992. The latter amount was about 38 percent more than was spent in Canada or Sweden, which are the closest to the United States in health care spending. However, both of those countries have a national health care program that covers the entire population. As noted above, only the United States and South Africa lack some form of national health care. So even though the United States spends a greater portion of its wealth on health care, approximately 38 million Americans have no health coverage at all. We spend more and get less coverage.

Health care costs are also rising because the life expectancy is increasing. Between 1970 and 1990, the life expectancy in the United States increased from 70.8 years to 75.4 years.[3] Those over 65 currently account for one-eighth of the population. But they are responsible for about a third of the national health care costs. As the baby boom generation reaches retirement age, national health care costs will rise even further. Moreover, many of the elderly are just above the poverty level, making them ineligible for some public assistance programs.

Further, medical care costs have been far outpacing the rate of inflation. Rising costs mean that the crisis of access to health care extends far beyond the poor. Not only is the cost of health care rising too rapidly, but the burden of the increasing costs is not shared equally. Middle-income Americans increasingly bear the impact of increased costs, finding that health insurance is becoming unaffordable or unavailable, either because they work for small businesses that do not provide health insurance or because they have preexisting medical conditions which are not covered by their policies.

---

[2] William Schneider, "A Loud Vote for Change," *National Journal*, November 7, 1992, p. 2544. In 1988, health care was not even included on a list of 11 different items of major factors in voting. See *National Journal*, November 12, 1988, p. 2854.

[3] Life expectancy at birth for females went from 74.7 years in 1970 to 79.1 years in 1990. Life expectancy for males went from 67.1 to 72.2 years. Source: *Statistical Abstract 1993*, p. 85.

Critics also claim that much of the cost is due to inefficiencies in the health care delivery system. For example, hospitals in close proximity to each other are often pressured by physicians to compete with each other. Doctors demand state-of-the-art technology before they will refer patients to a particular hospital. The result is often expensive duplication of services and equipment and an excess of available hospital beds. Underutilized equipment and surplus hospital beds drive up hospital costs, which are passed on to insurers and patients. A form of Parkinson's law takes over in encouraging the use of high-tech equipment because it is available. This growth in the cost of health care occurs in spite of efforts by the government to utilize market forces to limit cost increases, and by corporations to pressure health care providers to keep costs down. Americans pay insurance premiums, copayments, and deductibles to help cover the costs of others who cannot pay for their own medical care. Even the prices of nonmedical goods are pushed up to cover the high costs of insurance. The price of an average American car, for example, includes about $1100 to cover health insurance costs.

It should not be surprising, then, that there is a general dissatisfaction with health care service in this country. Eighty-nine percent of Americans say they believe the health care system needs fundamental change. More Americans than Canadians or British say that financial barriers keep them from getting needed health care. Only 10 percent of Americans surveyed said their health system functioned "pretty well," while 56 percent in Canada and 27 percent in Britain said so. In the United States, 7 percent of those surveyed said that they had not received needed medical care during the past year because of prohibitive costs, while less than 1 percent in Canada or the United Kingdom said they found themselves in that situation. Americans were the most critical of their health care system, with 89 percent saying that the system is in need of fundamental change, compared to 43 percent of Canadians and 69 percent of the British who said the same regarding their systems.

Figure 11-1 and Table 11-1 show per capita rises in health care expenditures for a number of countries during the years 1960 to 1990 in graph and tabular forms.

The U.S. health care system is generally regarded as providing the highest quality care in the world, for those who can afford it. The problem is that an increasing number of people can no longer afford any form of health care, let alone the levels guaranteed to the residents of all other industrialized countries of Europe as well as Canada and Japan. American health care is unique in its display of lavish state-of-the-art medicine existing along with a surprising shortage of basic services. Critics of the current system note that it is no coincidence that the United States and South Africa are also "the only two such countries that have within their borders substantial numbers of underserved people who are different ethnically from the controlling group."[4]

---

[4] See George D. Lundberg, "National Health Care Reform: An Aura of Inevitability Is Upon Us," *JAMA: The Journal of the American Medical Association*, vol. 265, no. 19 (May 15, 1991), p. 2566.

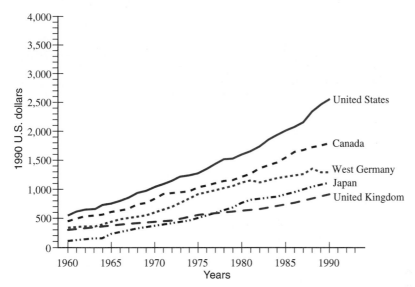

FIGURE 11-1
Real health expenditures per capita, United States and selected countries. (*Source: Trends in Health Spending: An Update, Congressional Budget Office, Washington, DC, June 1993, p. 28.*)

Beginning in the 1920s in Europe, governments began involving themselves in guaranteeing health care to their citizens. The major avenues have been either through a **corporatized** system in which the government regulates an insurance system that provides coverage, or more recently through **nationalized** systems in which the government assumes responsibility for health care. In the United States there have been legislative decisions to assure certain groups of citizens health care, resulting in a **segmented** health care system. For example the indigent are provided limited health care through Medicaid, the elderly through Medicare, the military and veterans through U.S. military health services.

Health care, like other policy issues, involves choice. The basic question becomes: **Should health care be a right or a privilege**? As long as health care is not a right, but a privilege for those who can afford it, there will be those who "fall between the cracks." Those who have health care coverage often believe that a safety net is in place that will provide care for all Americans, especially the poorest, and even the uninsured working poor, when it is urgent. But when almost one out of five Americans has no coverage, and millions more are inadequately insured, the "crack" has become a yawning chasm.

President Clinton has changed the nature of the debate, as the first Chief Executive to openly support the right to health care. He has proposed to provide "every American with comprehensive health benefits that can never be taken away

TABLE 11-1
REAL HEALTH EXPENDITURES PER CAPITA, UNITED STATES AND SELECTED
COUNTRIES, 1960–1990 (in 1990 U.S. dollars)

Year	United States	Canada	West Germany	Japan	United Kingdom
1960	592	468	345	104	303
1961	614	505	364	132	327
1962	646	530	389	151	330
1963	684	557	388	174	338
1964	740	579	411	174	352
1965	781	616	448	230	363
1966	815	646	491	258	386
1967	880	688	503	291	414
1968	941	741	542	325	421
1969	997	784	574	359	420
1970	1,059	840	608	383	445
1971	1,102	916	627	406	456
1972	1,172	937	709	440	485
1973	1,212	951	779	456	510
1974	1,247	963	845	488	569
1975	1,291	1,036	918	546	590
1976	1,378	1,084	964	566	607
1977	1,446	1,105	995	605	602
1978	1,503	1,150	1,027	652	624
1979	1,532	1,163	1,077	694	634
1980	1,601	1,215	1,120	772	665
1981	1,681	1,271	1,165	808	687
1982	1,757	1,351	1,129	849	685
1983	1,850	1,413	1,144	881	734
1984	1,921	1,477	1,203	892	743
1985	2,010	1,546	1,232	917	753
1986	2,095	1,643	1,259	946	786
1987	2,190	1,680	1,271	1,007	818
1988	2,319	1,712	1,346	1,049	844
1989	2,443	1,748	1,276	1,073	867
1990	2,566	1,794	1,287	1,113	909

Notes: Expenditures in different countries are expressed in a common currency (U.S. dollars) using OECD estimates of a "purchasing power parity" (PPP) rate of exchange among national currencies. PPP is an estimate of the exchange rate at which a dollar can buy the same basket of goods in each country.

The word "real" is used here to mean adjusted for general inflation rather than for inflation in the prices of health services, which is almost certainly different. Nominal currency values have been converted to 1990 currencies using the gross domestic product implicit deflator.

Source: Congressional Budget Office calculations based on data from the Health Data File of the Organization for Economic Cooperation and Development (OECD), 1991.

. . . and make care available to all Americans, no matter where they live or how old or sick they are."[5]

IMPERFECT MARKETS: IMPACT ON HEALTH CARE PRICE, SUPPLY, AND DEMAND

Health care in the United States is primarily a **private** matter. We treat it as a market commodity. Advocates of a competitive "health care marketplace" claim that such initiatives as rate regulation, health planning, and utilization review to control costs are compromised by political interference. In the early 1980s, this view became the adopted policy of the Reagan administration. The Reagan, and subsequently the Bush, administrations used the theoretical ideal of competition to raise warning signals against further government involvement in health care. These warnings were joined illogically with the reassurance that reducing the role of the government in health care and encouraging competition would take care of the cost problem. Others argue that health care is a social good that all citizens **require** at different times in their lives. Health care does not meet the ideal requirements of free market competition. The need for medical resources is potentially unlimited, but the supply of those resources is not. In a market-driven system there are not enough providers or money to give care to everyone.

For example, the model of pure competition requires that there must be **free entry into the market**. However the American Medical Association, backed by state regulation, allocates the right to perform health care services among a variety of medical professionals, reserving the most important and well-paying responsibilities for physicians. In the name of protecting the public, but not coincidentally with the outcome of protecting the privileged position of its own members, the AMA has restricted access to medical accreditation through the regulation of the medical education process, testing and licensing procedures, and other requirements it itself mandates and oversees.

A second requirement for a perfect market is that **consumers must have perfect knowledge about the quality of the product**. This condition is very difficult to achieve in the area of medicine because of the complexity of health care as a product. Most people are not inclined to search for the least expensive standard package of benefits when they are in good health, and when they are ill they may be unable to do so. A market search and the weighing of different recommendations and

[5] President Clinton, *Health Security: The President's Report to the American People* (Washington, DC: U.S. Government Printing Office, October 27, 1993).

In addition to the moral argument that health care should be a right for all citizens, Clinton's "New Democrats" offer economic reasons for universal coverage. They argue that the uninsured use our health care system in an uneconomic way. They receive little or no preventive health care which is relatively inexpensive. Further when they have a medical problem, they are more likely to receive more expensive emergency room care. When hospitals fail to receive payment from the uninsured, they shift costs to those with insurance. Estimates indicate this raises insurance premiums between 10 to 30 percent. Government contributes to this cost shifting by undercompensating hospital costs for Medicaid and Medicare. Finally, if all were covered, insurance companies would not spend large sums trying to distinguish between high- and low-risk individuals.

advice is difficult especially if a patient is ill at the time and is anxiously seeking relief.

This points to another condition for the working of the free market: **Consumers must have adequate time to search the market to exercise their judgment as sovereign consumers**. Unfortunately a patient because of illness or ignorance may be unable to fully evaluate the performance of a health care provider. Several studies have found that physicians even have the power to induce demand for their services.[6]

Ultimately few people can afford the costs of the care required for a major illness, so most of the consumer's money is spent on insurance, not on the actual medical care itself. This is true, despite deductibles and copayment requirements, because most health care expenses are incurred by a relatively small number of high-cost cases. Therefore, **most aspects of price competition really occur between insurers, and only indirectly among providers**. There would be little price competition if insurance firms were merely passive bill payers for claims made by their policyholders. Competition would then turn on such nonprice factors as the insurers' ability to screen out high-risk individuals. Competition among insurance firms will result in real cost savings only if they can affect the cost of health care itself. In theory, insurers compete to offer lower prices not by selling just insurance but by selling "insured health care."[7] In this model, the insurers adopt basic cost control measures, with the highest profits going to the companies that are the most efficient in doing this.

Financial incentives are a central concern in any market system. However, **competition in an imperfect market does not lead to lower costs**. In fact, competition between hospitals actually drives costs **up** because doctors who refer patients to a hospital do not pay for the services. As a result, hospitals compete by having the most advanced medical technology that is well reimbursed by insurance companies. Several hospitals in close proximity may have cardiac care or neonatal intensive care units when one such unit of each type would be adequate for the community's patient population. And since insured patients often do not experience out-of-pocket expenses at the time of care, they tend to request any medical service

---

[6] See Charles E. Phelps, "Induced Demand—Can We Ever Know Its Extent?" *Journal of Health Economics*, vol. 5 (December 1986), pp. 355–365.

[7] Mark Merlis, *Controlling Health Care Costs* (Washington, DC: Congressional Research Service, January 26, 1990), p. 21. Merlis points out that if consumers were fully informed about the relative price and quality of competing health plans, it would not mean that the health care market would consist of a single class of providers trying to achieve the same goals. Rather the health care market would remain as it has become, segmented in much the same way as the markets for other goods and services. Currently there are economy and luxury health plans just as there are low-income housing and luxurious housing. Insurance companies provide limited coverage with high deductibles and copayments for some, and comprehensive coverage for others. Improving the information available to consumers would mean only that purchasers could better distinguish what was available to them, not that the differences between what is offered would cease to exist.

that provides any benefit whatsoever. Physicians and hospitals typically receive payments retrospectively after submitting bills based upon the treatment provided to an insurer known as a **third-party payer**. Such charges are paid as long as they are considered "customary, prevailing, and reasonable" by the insurance company. Physicians are rewarded in a **fee-for-service** system for doing more rather than less. The more treatment that utilizes sophisticated diagnostic techniques—magnetic resonance imaging (MRI), for example—or new methods of treatment, the higher usually are the payments to the providers. Patients and physicians both have incentives to demand health care that provides any aid at all without regard to the cost to any third-party payer. Many studies have supported the conclusion that a significant number of procedures prescribed by physicians are unnecessary.[8] There are no cost controls on physicians and hospitals. Without such spending limits, patients do not face **budget constraints** when consuming health care, as they do when purchasing other goods.[9] To the contrary, we have cost-increasing incentives. Thus medical expenses continue to rise. A major concern in any public health care policy is how to create arrangements that provide mechanisms and incentives for budget constraints. Without such incentives, health care spending continues to climb. And technical advances that enable medical miracles do not usually come with a cheap price tag.

Critics of the free market approach point out the error in believing that free market forces are the best way to limit the costs of health care. They argue that when computer manufacturers compete with each it may well result in a lower price for each personal computer. But the aim of manufacturers is to increase their share of the market, that is, to sell more computers. If a company is successful, the result will be to expand the industry. But the same is not true when physicians and hospitals compete with each other. Market-based competition cannot control the growth of health care spending. American reliance on Adam Smith's invisible hand in the imperfect marketplace of health care has contributed significantly to problems in the American health care system.

---

[8] See John Wennberg, "Outcomes Research, Cost Containment, and the Fear of Health Care Rationing," *New England Journal of Medicine*, vol. 323 (October 25, 1990), pp. 1202–1204.

There is often disagreement among physicians about the appropriate use of a variety of medical treatments. Some procedures are merely "overused." For example, about 25 percent of all births in the United States are cesarean. That rate may be twice as often as is necessary. Hysterectomy is the second most common major surgery after cesareans. Some policy analysts say that over 25 percent of hysterectomies are unnecessary. Or take magnetic resonance imaging, where scanners use radio waves and magnets to produce detailed images of internal organs. MRI is particularly useful in detecting brain tumors and spinal cord injuries and in determining whether heart tissue is dead or alive without exposing patients to radiation. Although MRI equipment is very expensive (it ranges between $1 to $2 million dollars), both doctors and patients want it used because they find it reassuring. An MRI procedure usually costs about $1000. Since its use is risk-free, critics contend it is often utilized defensively, say to protect against any possible malpractice suit, when it would not otherwise be justified.

[9] Henry J. Aaron, "Health Care Financing," in Henry J. Aaron and Charles L. Schultze (eds.), *Setting Domestic Priorities* (Washington, DC: The Brookings Institution, 1992), p. 25.

PAYMENT PROBLEMS AND MORAL HAZARDS

A **moral hazard** refers to the reduced incentive of policyholders to protect themselves from what they are insured against. It is yet another example of a market imperfection.

A moral hazard is the increased probability for an insured party to change their behavior after a contract is made at the expense of the insuring party because that behavior is now protected.

An individual uninsured against the hazard of theft would personally sustain any financial loss resulting from burglary. Since the individual bears the financial risk, she has a significant incentive to take precautions against theft (for example, by installing and using window and door locks, or by installing burglar alarms). When an individual buys an insurance policy that protects against theft, the incentive to take precautions is significantly reduced. The fewer precautions the homeowner takes to prevent theft, the greater the chance of theft, and ultimately the liability of the insurance company.

Insurance companies try to reduce the problem of moral hazard by requiring a policyholder to share some costs of any claim. Cost sharing generally takes two forms. *Deductibles* in health insurance generally require the purchaser to pay the initial medical charges up to some predetermined limit. So a health policy might not cover the first $250 of health care in a year. Many health insurance policies also provide for *coinsurance* or *copayments*. Under a copayment arrangement, the insurance company pays for 75 or 80 percent of a physician's bills, and the policyholder pays the remaining 20 or 25 percent.

Moral hazards encourage higher health care expenditures than is medically warranted. Individuals have incentives to seek more care, including high-cost low-benefit care, when there is a third-party payer. Retrospective billing which cannot be determined until after a hospital and physician have provided the services and have reported the costs to the patient, the insurance company, or Medicare encourages the utilization of more services than medically indicated.

Part of what is claimed to be a moral-hazard contribution to rising health care costs is a subjective judgment, however. A jogger, with insurance, who falls and twists an ankle while running may have x-rays taken to determine if there is a fracture. Without insurance, the person may hope it is just a sprain that will heal in a few days by giving the ankle rest. Whether seeking medical attention in such a situation is excessive or not is unclear. It is also unlikely that possessing health insurance would increase one's incentive to take risks that might lead to cancer. Also, a cancer patient who receives large insurance payments is still less fortunate than healthy people who do not. Consider an individual spending a week at a resort hotel, and another spending a week in a hospital recovering from surgery. The patient will have more resources devoted to his or her well-being; however, we would all prefer to spend a week at the resort hotel and forgo the need to have the same medical services devoted to our welfare.

Finally, the concern with the insured patient as the focal point of a moral hazard is misplaced. The major choice made by the patient is typically that of the physician. After that choice, the physician acts as the patient's agent and decides what diagnostic tests to run, which medical procedures are appropriate, which hospital to use, and what the followup procedures will be.

A CLOSER LOOK AT THE MALADIES OF AMERICAN HEALTH CARE

Rising Costs

Curiously, health care is one area where there is general agreement that the problem is not that as a society we do not spend enough, but rather that we spend too much and get too little in return for what we spend. Rising costs in health care may be regarded as a problem because health care expenditures often purchase modest benefits at needlessly high costs.[10] In the United States, most health care is financed privately, through employer insurance plans. As shown in Fig. 11-2, those plans often involve exorbitantly high administrative costs.

Skyrocketing health care costs, which are growing faster than the general rate of inflation, claim an ever increasing larger share of national economic output. National spending on health care is approaching 15 percent of the U.S. gross domestic product (GDP), or about $800 billion in 1992, more than in any other industrialized nation. By contrast, Canada and Germany pay less than 9.0 percent of their GNP (or about 36 percent less than the United States) for their health care.

[10] Henry J. Aaron, *Serious and Unstable Condition: Financing America's Health Care* (Washington, DC: The Brookings Institution, 1991), pp. 8–9.

FIGURE 11-2
Administrative costs as a percentage of benefits for various health care programs, 1987. (*Source: Congressional Research Service analysis of data from Health Care Financing Administration, Hay/Huggins Co., and Health and Welfare Canada.*)

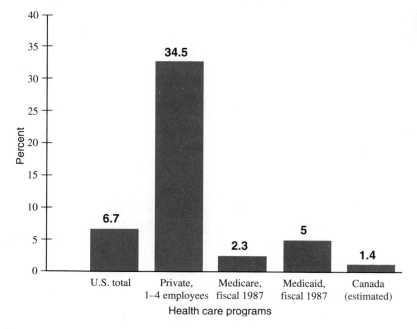

Japan and the United Kingdom spend just over 6 percent of their GNP on health care. But that amount provides for a system of universal national health care. The United States not only spends more, but has 37 million Americans (about 15 percent of the population) who are uninsured at any given moment. An additional 30 million people are without medical insurance for part of each year. Another 20 million Americans (8 percent of the population) are so minimally insured that any serious accident or illness would be financially devastating. Because of rising costs, the federal government has reduced its contributions to the joint federal-state Medicaid program, forcing many states to tighten the income eligibility rules for potential recipients. This has reduced the percentage of poor who are covered from 64 percent to less than 40 percent.

The United States spends more than twice as much per capita on health care than the average spent by the 24 industrialized countries that make up the Organization for Economic Cooperation and Development (OECD). The high cost might almost be tolerable if everyone was covered, or if it appeared that Americans were healthier than people in other countries. But of the 24 OECD countries, the United States lags behind most others in several categories: It is 21st in infant mortality, 16th in female life expectancy, and 17th in male life expectancy.

Soaring medical costs divert resources that could be used to address other social needs. Most other countries have placed an overall ceiling on health care expenditures. As a result, no other developed country spends over 10 percent of its GDP on health care. Soaring costs lead to a second negative aspect of the U.S. system.

Loss of Coverage

Rising health insurance costs lead to a loss of coverage for those who need it most. One reason the United States might enact a program of universal coverage is the **lack of access** to medical care suffered by the uninsured. In the early part of the twentieth century, private insurance was introduced. Proposals for a publicly financed universal health care system in America were made prior to World War I but garnered little support. President Franklin D. Roosevelt considered adding medical care to the Social Security legislation in 1935 but decided doing so might jeopardize the chances for passage of the program by Congress. In the 1940s the lack of medical insurance coverage was seen as a problem primarily of the poor and the elderly. President Truman made coverage of those groups and workers without employment-related health insurance a national health insurance (NHI) goal of his administration. His program was defeated, largely because of opposition by the American Medical Association. However, Truman's efforts did get health care on the public policy agenda. Finally, with the passage of Medicaid and Medicare in 1965, the Kennedy-Johnson administrations formally accepted the government's responsibility for paying the health care costs of the poor and the elderly. Since then, the national and state governments have retreated from their commitment to the poor and the elderly by failing to see that eligibility standards keep pace with inflation. The result of this incremental retreat is visible in the data showing that, while Medicaid covered 76 percent of the poor in 1965, it covered fewer than 38

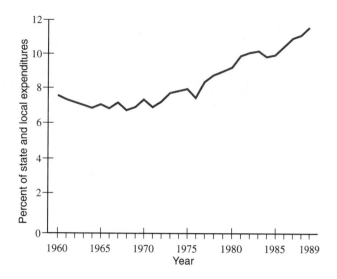

FIGURE 11-3
State and local health spending as a share of overall state and local expenditures, 1960 to 1989. (*Source: Analysis of National Health Expenditure Data, Congressional Research Service, Washington, DC.*)

percent in 1991.[11] The retreat of some states was dictated by the rising costs of health care as a part of their total budget.

The upward trend in state and local health care spending is similar to that in federal health spending, but not as pronounced since states have the ability to tighten their Medicaid eligibility requirements. As Fig. 11-3 shows, in 1960, state and local government health expenditures were under 8 percent of their total expenditures, which was actually more than the percentage of the federal budget spent on health care at the time. By 1991, they totaled 12 percent of all state and local expenditures, most of which went to Medicaid.

In 1960, federal health expenditures were $2.9 billion, or just 3.1 percent of all federal expenditures. With the introduction of the Medicare and Medicaid programs in 1965, large increases occurred (44 percent). Again, between 1980 and 1985 there were sharp increases (29 percent). In 1980, federal spending for health care was $72 billion, or 11.7 percent of total federal spending. By 1990, federal health expenditures accounted for 14.7 percent of all federal spending.

The Medicare benefits received by the elderly in excess of deductions and premiums are not counted as taxable income. Also, working-age individuals who itemize deductions may deduct the portion of their medical expenses not covered by insurance from their taxable income when that portion exceeds 7.5 percent of their

[11] Carl J. Schramm, "Health Care Financing for All Americans," *JAMA*, vol. 265, no. 24 (June 26, 1991), p. 3296.

MALPRACTICE

Conventional proposals to control rising health care costs usually include reform of malpractice law. Unfortunately the costs and the savings to be gained by such tort reform are often exaggerated. It is true that malpractice insurance costs are higher in the United States than in other countries. Under current law, a patient who suffers injury because of negligence on the part of a physician may sue for compensation for his or her losses. Various studies have concluded that medical malpractice insurance and litigation adds only marginally to health care costs. One study done for the state of New York using 1984 data found that 3.7 percent of patients suffered adverse events from medical procedures, and just over 25 percent of those instances could be attributed to actual negligence. Only about one-eighth of those who suffered negligent injuries ever filed a malpractice claim. And only one-sixteenth ever recovered damages. The researchers also found many instances in which patients filed malpractice litigation when there was no clear evidence of malpractice.

Malpractice insurance premiums for physicians in 1989 totaled about 3.4 percent of physician income and 0.8 percent of personal medical spending.

A more difficult question to answer is how much is added to the cost of health care by physicians who practice "defensive medicine" as a protection against potential lawsuits. There are difficulties with defining defensive medicine and distinguishing it from health care provided for other reasons. For example, is a physician performing additional tests that are not necessary because she or he is very thorough, or because the health care culture values aggressive diagnosis and treatment, or to avoid a lawsuit? Just under 25 percent of infants are born by cesarian delivery, although many experts suggest that only about 13 percent of pregnancies require the procedure. Is an unnecessary cesarian performed because physician fees average $500 more under those circumstances than for a normal delivery? Is it performed for defensive legal purposes, or for scheduling convenience? Tests performed for defensive purposes sometimes supply valuable information and lead to improved diagnosis and treatment.

Reforming the malpractice system would provide only modest savings. It would reduce the economic incentive of physicians to go along with the tort system's current tendency for overtreatment. It might also force the relatively few physicians involved in a disproportionate share of negligence to improve or cease practicing medicine.

Sources: Philip Corboy, "Medical Malpractice Insurance and Defensive Medicine," *National Forum,* vol. 73, no. 3, (Summer 1993); Kenneth Jost, "Healthcare Law: Warring Over Medical Malpractice," *ABA Journal, vol. 79 (*May 1, 1993).

adjusted gross income (AGI).[12] These tax law provisions obviously impact on federal tax revenues and must be counted as part of the government's medical cost burden.

[12] Medical expenses eligible for such deduction include payments for (1) health insurance (including aftertax employee contributions to employer health plans; (2) diagnosis, treatment, or prevention of disease; (3) transportation primarily for and essential to medical care; (4) lodging away from home primarily for and essential to medical care, up to $50 per night. Prescription drugs and insulin are also eligible for deduction.

TYPES OF MEDICAL INSURANCE COVERAGE

In theory health care coverage is available to almost everyone through either **(a) Medicare for the elderly and disabled, (b) Medicaid for low-income women and children and those with certain disabilities, (c) employer-subsidized insurance in the work place, or (d) private insurance plans purchased by individuals ineligible for the first three options**. We now look at these and their complexities.

Medicare

Medicare is the largest federal health program, serving over 30 million elderly and 3 million disabled Americans. The major requirement for access to Medicare is to have reached the age of 65, and to have worked in employment covered by Social Security or railroad retirement. It has relieved the fear of financial ruin because of illness for those it covers, although there are significant gaps in its coverage.

Actually Medicare consists of two separate programs, Parts A and B. It has three separate funding sources: general revenues, premiums paid by beneficiaries, and a payroll tax paid by workers and their employers. Part A, officially known as the Hospital Insurance (HI) program, pays for the full cost of hospital care for up to 60 days per illness and three-fourths of the cost of the next 30 days after the patient has paid a first-day deductible.[13] Part A also provides limited coverage for nursing home stays of up to 100 days. The patient is responsible for coinsurance payments of $74 per day after the first 20 days. It also provides for home health and hospice care.

In 1991, Part A was financed by the HI portion of the Social Security payroll tax, which was 1.45 percent paid by employees and matched by employers on earnings up to $125,000. The ceiling is increased each year by the percentage growth in earnings subject to Social Security.

Everyone eligible for Part A and all Americans 65 or older even if not qualified for Part A can enroll in Part B, technically known as the Supplemental Insurance program. Part B pays 80 percent of allowed physician's charges over an annual $100 deductible.[14] This portion also covers outpatient laboratory and other diag-

---

[13] The deductible was $204 in 1981, but has been growing rapidly. It was $560 in 1989, $628 in 1991, and $652 in 1992. Medicare will also pay for half the cost of an additional 60 days of hospitalization that can be used at any time, and pays for kidney dialysis for patients with end-stage renal (kidney) failure.

[14] Physicians may bill patients for the remaining 20 percent of the charges deemed "customary, prevailing, and reasonable" by Medicare. Roughly three-quarters of American physicians agree not to bill patients beyond the amounts reimbursed by Medicare. In return, physicians who agree to "take assignment," i.e., to not bill patients beyond the Medicare reimbursement levels, receive larger payments from Medicare, faster reimbursements, and free advertising in directories of participating physicians. See *Overview of Entitlement Programs, 1990 Green Book, Background Material and Data on Programs within the Jurisdiction of the Committee on Ways and Means: 1990 Edition* (Committee Print, House Committee on Ways and Means, 101 Cong. 2nd Session) (Washington, DC: U.S. Government Printing Office, 1990), p. 137. Also see Aaron, *Serious and Unstable Condition*, p. 62.

nostic tests, along with certain medical equipment used in the home, and home health care services.

This coverage was available to individuals at a monthly premium of $36.60 in 1993. The premium is adjusted annually; it rose to $41.10 in 1994, and will reach $46.10 in 1995. The premium actually pays for only about 25 percent of the program costs—budget appropriations from general revenues pay for the remainder. Part B provides a great return for recipients, so about 98.3 percent of those eligible for Part A elected coverage under Part B in fiscal 1991.[15] Social Security recipients can have the premiums deducted from their monthly checks.

Medicare beneficiaries' out-of-pocket expenses remain high because of coinsurance requirements and coverage exclusions such as prescription drugs. Nor does Medicare cover long-term nursing home care. As a result of these exclusions and rising costs, the elderly now spend on average about 18 percent of their income (about $2500) per year on out-of-pocket expenses for health care, about the same percent as before Medicare was enacted.[16] These costs are a hindrance for the less affluent elderly in obtaining medical care.

High out-of-pocket expenses and gaps in Medicare coverage are alleviated for many by the purchase of "**medigap**" private insurance policies. These policies generally pay the hospital and physician deductibles plus the coinsurance of 20 percent of physician and outpatient charges, and the increasing percentage for hospital stays longer than 60 days. The 1988 Medicare Catastrophic Coverage Act placed a cap on the amount Medicare beneficiaries could be required to pay for out-of-pocket expenses. But the law was repealed in 1989 when affluent Medicare beneficiaries protested the surtax on middle- and upper-income retirees that would have financed the new benefits. The repeal of the law makes a medigap policy almost a necessity for many of the elderly. About 40 percent of the Medicare population also have medigap policies. An additional 40 percent have other policies that have limited coverage of different types that are technically not medigap in nature.[17] Congress has tightened regulations on medigap insurance, requiring that policies be renewable and prohibiting agents from selling more than one medigap policy to a person.

[15] It was estimated that in fiscal 1991 about 7 million Medicare recipients would receive reimbursements for services under part A and 26 million would receive reimbursements for services under Part B. See *Overview of Entitlement Programs*, p. 129. The average annual benefit per elderly and disabled person enrolled in 1991 was estimated at $1915 and $2115, respectively, under Part A and $1420 and $1579 under Part B. See *Overview on Entitlement Programs*, p. 128.

[16] Michael D. Reagan, *Curing the Crisis: Options for America's Health Care* (San Francisco: Westview Press, 1992), p. 45.

[17] A Congressional investigation uncovered numerous abuses in the marketing of medigap policies. For example, about 8 percent of Medicare beneficiaries are also eligible for Medicaid coverage. Medicaid covers all health care not covered by Medicare. Nevertheless over 2 million medigap policies were sold to these "dual eligibles." The average medigap policy carries an annual premium of around $800.

Medicaid

Medicaid was designed, when enacted in 1965, to be a health insurance program for the poor. In fact it currently serves only a minority of those whose incomes fall below the federally defined poverty level ($10,419 for a family of three and $13,359 for a family of four in 1991). It does not cover all of the poor because in addition to being poor one has to meet other criteria such as welfare dependence, receipt of Supplemental Security Income (SSI) benefits, or being elderly; nor does Medicaid pay for costs of nursing-home care unless those needing such care have spent down their savings to a specified level. The elderly poor who are eligible for Medicaid are covered by Medicare since most states "buy in" to the program by paying the patient's premiums and deductibles.

Medicaid coverage has always varied from one state to the next because each state determines its own income levels for eligibility. Federal government spending for Medicaid, which must be matched by states on a sliding scale, ranges from 50 percent in states with the highest per capita incomes to 80 percent for low-income states. Typically, the poorer states not only contribute less, but also have lower cutoff levels, thus limiting the eligibility for Medicaid within their jurisdiction. For example, in 1987 family income had to be less than 38 percent of the federally defined poverty level to qualify for Medicaid in West Virginia, 55 percent in Maryland, and 82 percent in New York; in Alabama, a family of four was ineligible if its income was over $1860 per year.[18]

Participating states in the program are obligated to provide certain health care benefits to those who qualify for AFDC payments and also for those who qualify for supplemental security income, which is an assistance program for the elderly poor, blind, and disabled.[19] The federal guidelines require states to pay for a minimum package of services including acute care, rural health clinics, laboratory work, and long-term care for low-income households. Congress has, throughout the past decade, mandated new state coverage requirements. Congress directed a phased expansion of Medicaid to provide coverage for all children born after September 30, 1983, in families below the federal poverty threshold. This will provide Medicaid coverage for all children up to the age of 19 by the year 2002. Congress has also required states to pay the premiums of Medicaid beneficiaries eligible for private health insurance, if it will result in a net savings for Medicaid financing. States are required to extend Medicaid coverage to pregnant women whose incomes are below the federal poverty threshold and to use Medicaid funds to pay

[18] Reagan, *Curing the Crisis*, p. 21.
[19] Aaron, *Serious and Unstable Condition*, p. 64.
Beginning in 1990, Congress required that states provide coverage for pregnant women and young children in families below the federal poverty threshold.

Medicare premiums, deductibles, and coinsurance charges for those living below the federal poverty threshold.[20]

Other types of health care such as preventive medicine, optometry, and physical therapy are beyond the services mandated by the national government and are up to each state. Therefore, coverage varies between states. Northeastern and midwestern states ordinarily offer more generous benefits than southern and southwestern states. Some states reimburse health care providers at rates significantly below the customary charges in the area, so many physicians within their jurisdictions refuse to see Medicaid patients.[21]

Bear in mind that, in order to qualify for Medicaid assistance, one must first become eligible for welfare support in the **state** of residence. **States** determine who is eligible to participate in this program created by the **national** government. In the 1980s federal tax cuts and growing budget deficits began to strain the availability of resources for Medicaid. As the number of privately insured Americans has declined, state and federal governments have been forced to expand Medicaid. In 1991, state and federally funded Medicaid provided health coverage to 26.9 million low-income people, an increase of 5.7 million over 1989.[22] Despite these massive enrollment increases, Medicaid could not offset the decline in private coverage and population growth. This situation was further aggravated by a weaker economy and higher levels of unemployment. State governments have a major stake in financing health care. States currently spend an average of 20 percent of their total budgets on health-related programs, which places real constraints on their ability to deal with other issues. So states have begun to tighten their eligibility requirements and lower the maximum income allowed to maintain eligibility. Nonetheless Medicaid spending increased in all 50 states in fiscal 1992. The result basically was to restrain the number of beneficiaries nationally by reducing the proportion of the needy who can qualify for the program, even though the poverty rate was climbing to new highs. The net effect currently is that only about 40 percent of those in poverty are covered by Medicaid. The majority of the poor are not provided any health care protection by the program. Figure 11-4 shows the number of people covered by Medicaid for several years from 1973 to 1991.

---

[20] A major problem for Medicaid is that about three-fourths of its expenditures go to the aged, blind, and disabled, and especially to patients in nursing homes. Medicaid has become, in fact, the long-term care reinsurance plan for Medicare patients when they have used up their personal savings. For example, in 1989, 29 percent of Medicaid recipients who were aged, blind, or disabled received $39.4 billion in services, or $5868 per person. By comparison, AFDC adults and children, or 68 percent of Medicaid recipients, received $13.8 billion in services or $860 per person. Thus the benefits for the aged, blind, and disabled have risen about 40 percent since 1975, while the value of services for AFDC recipients has fallen about 20 percent. See Aaron, *Serious and Unstable Condition*, p. 65.

[21] Eligibility for Medicaid only provides the patient with a license to search for a physician because many either do not accept Medicaid patients or limit that segment of their practice. The effort to control Medicaid expenditures by capping payments has resulted in a decline of physicians accepting Medicaid patients.

[22] Federal and state Medicaid expenditures increased 56 percent from 1989 to 1991 (from $58 billion in fiscal 1989 to $90.5 billion in fiscal 1991). It increased an additional 29 percent to $117.1 billion in fiscal 1992.

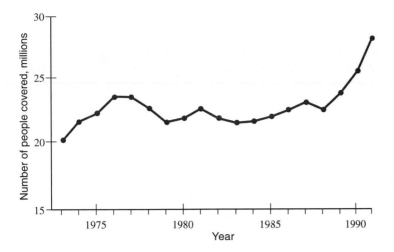

FIGURE 11-4
Number of people covered by Medicaid, 1973 to 1991. (*Source: David Himmelstein, Steffie Woolhandler, James Lewontin, Terry Tang, and Sidney Wolfe, The Growing Epidemic of Uninsurance: New Data on the Health Insurance Coverage of Americans, Center for National Health Program Studies, Cambridge, MA, December 16, 1992.*)

Government Regulation of Medicare and Medicaid Costs

The federal and state governments provide such a large percentage of hospital and physician revenues, that both hospitals and doctors must be sensitive to the bureaucratic rules of payment or risk reimbursements being withheld. The federal government has begun to use its regulatory powers to control medical costs. Until 1984 the Medicare program reimbursed hospitals for Part A expenses according to the "reasonable costs" incurred in providing services to beneficiaries. Since the actual reasonable costs were not determined until after a hospital had provided the services and submitted its bill to the government, this method of payment was known as **retrospective** cost-based reimbursement. The Health Care Financing Administration (HCFA) introduced a **prospective** payment system. Payments are made at predetermined rates that represent the average cost nationwide of treating a patient according to the medical diagnosis. The classification system used to categorize hospital patients according to their diagnoses is referred to as **diagnosis-related groups (DRGs)**.

Under a retrospective cost-based reimbursement, a hospital had little incentive to economize on the care provided. However, since a DRG payment is basically set, a hospital that treats a patient for less than the payment amount keeps the savings. If the treatment costs more than the payment, the hospital must absorb the loss. The prospective payment rates are updated each year based on government calculations of the market basket index of the goods and services hospitals must buy. The government update factor is slightly less than the expected average increase of hospital costs. This encourages hospitals to become very cost-conscious.

The immediate response of hospitals to the prospective payment system was to shorten the average length of hospital stay for each Medicare patient. This has led critics to contend that patients are being discharged "quicker and sicker," to nursing homes or to their own homes at periods in their recoveries when they still require hospital care. These critics argue that the prospective payment system has resulted in a decline in the quality of health care for Medicare patients since its implementation.

Physician Payment Reform

In the United States, physicians, like lawyers, are viewed as a high-income group. Certainly physicians' incomes in the United States are high compared to the incomes of doctors in other industrialized countries such as Germany, Canada, and the United Kingdom (see Fig. 11-5 for this comparison on a 5-year basis and Table 11-2 for the comparison on a 1-year basis for the years 1960 to 1989). Currently

FIGURE 11-5

Average real income of physicians, United States and selected countries, 1960 to 1989. (*Source: Trends in Health Spending: An Update, Congressional Budget Office, Washington, DC, June 1993, p. 36.*)

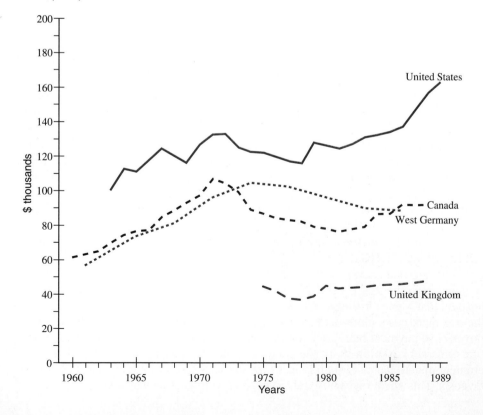

TABLE 11-2
AVERAGE REAL INCOME OF PHYSICIANS, UNITED STATES AND SELECTED COUNTRIES, 1960–1989 (in 1990 U.S. dollars)

Year	United States	Canada	West Germany	United Kingdom
1960	n.a.	61,379	n.a.	n.a.
1961	n.a.	63,995	54,926	n.a.
1962	n.a.	65,141	n.a.	n.a.
1963	99,104	70,335	n.a.	n.a.
1964	111,155	75,042	n.a.	n.a.
1965	110,840	78,156	70,235	n.a.
1966	n.a.	78,641	n.a.	n.a.
1967	123,322	84,648	n.a.	n.a.
1968	n.a.	89,514	88,201	n.a.
1969	116,532	92,343	n.a.	n.a.
1970	125,762	98,529	n.a.	n.a.
1971	131,751	108,852	95,490	n.a.
1972	131,700	104,952	n.a.	n.a.
1973	124,289	99,537	n.a.	n.a.
1974	121,808	89,160	103,513	n.a.
1975	120,552	87,060	n.a.	43,743
1976	n.a.	84,133	n.a.	40,184
1977	115,964	83,060	100,763	36,161
1978	115,709	82,917	n.a.	35,631
1979	127,196	79,826	n.a.	38,873
1980	n.a.	78,702	100,719	43,035
1981	123,691	77,788	n.a.	41,534
1982	126,290	78,748	n.a.	41,369
1983	130,125	79,017	88,948	42,468
1984	130,770	87,347	n.a.	43,377
1985	131,835	87,581	n.a.	43,701
1986	137,390	91,828	88,411	45,428
1987	147,769	91,496	n.a.	46,742
1988	156,414	91,720	n.a.	47,148
1989	162,292	n.a.	n.a.	n.a.

Notes: Average income of physicians equals the average earnings of physicians before taxes and net of deductible professional expenses. Reliable data on the incomes of physicians in Japan are not available.

Incomes in different countries were expressed in a common currency (U.S. dollars) using OECD estimates of a "purchasing power parity" (PPP) rate of exchange among national currencies. PPP is an estimate of the exchange rate at which a dollar can buy the same basket of goods in each country. Nominal currency values have been converted to 1990 currencies using the gross domestic product implicit deflator.

n.a. = not available. Data for the following years were missing, and values were imputed by CBO: 1966, 1968, 1976, and 1980 for the United States; and 1962, 1963, 1964, 1966, 1967, 1969, 1970, 1972, 1973, 1975, 1976, 1978, 1979, 1981, 1982, 1984, and 1985 for West Germany. Missing data at the beginning and end of the time period were not imputed.

Source: Congressional Budget Office (CBO) calculations based on data from the Health Data File of the Organization for Economic Cooperation and Development, 1991.

the ratio of doctors' incomes to the incomes of the general population is also higher in the United States than in Germany, Canada, or the United Kingdom (see Fig. 11-6 and Table 11-3 for those ratios from 1960 to 1989 on a 5-year and 1-year basis, respectively).

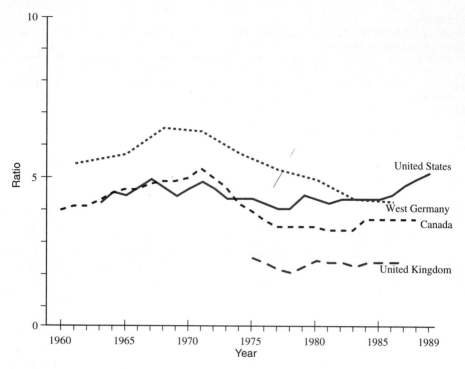

FIGURE 11-6
Ratio of average income of physicians and average earnings of all workers, United States and selected countries, 1960 to 1989. (*Source: Trends in Health Spending: An Update, Congressional Budget Office, Washington, DC, June 1993, p. 37.*)

This perception of high incomes, along with the rapidly escalating costs of physicians' charges to Medicare, has made doctors a major target for health care cost-containment efforts in general, but especially in regard to Medicare since between 1965 and 1989 Medicare spending for the services of physicians increased at an annual rate of 11.7 percent, faster than the average annual rate of general inflation and the rate of growth of Medicare enrollees.[23] A second problem of growing concern in regard to Medicare costs has been that the "reasonable charge" payment method led to payments which frequently were not related to the costs of the resources or services used.

The 1989 Omnibus Budget Reconciliation Act (OBRA 1989) provided for a three-part physician payment reform package. This new plan replaced the "reasonable" charge payment system with a "fee schedule" based on a "resource-based relative value scale" (RBRVS, usually shortened to RVS for "relative value scale") to be phased in over a 4-year period beginning January 1, 1992. The new system provides an incentive to physicians to get involved in efforts to reduce the growth in

[23] Committee on Ways and Means, *1992 Green Book*, p. 417.

TABLE 11-3
RATIO OF THE AVERAGE INCOME OF PHYSICIANS TO THE AVERAGE EARNINGS OF ALL
WORKERS, UNITED STATES AND SELECTED COUNTRIES, 1960–1989

Year	United States	Canada	West Germany	United Kingdom
1960	n.a.	4.0	n.a.	n.a.
1961	n.a.	4.1	5.5	n.a.
1962	n.a.	4.1	n.a.	n.a.
1963	4.3	4.3	n.a.	n.a.
1964	4.6	4.5	n.a.	n.a.
1965	4.5	4.6	5.8	n.a.
1966	n.a.	4.6	n.a.	n.a.
1967	5.0	4.8	n.a.	n.a.
1968	n.a.	4.9	6.6	n.a.
1969	4.5	4.9	n.a.	n.a.
1970	4.7	5.0	n.a.	n.a.
1971	4.9	5.3	6.5	n.a.
1972	4.7	5.0	n.a.	n.a.
1973	4.4	4.7	n.a.	n.a.
1974	4.4	4.2	5.8	n.a.
1975	4.4	4.0	n.a.	2.6
1976	n.a.	3.7	n.a.	2.4
1977	4.1	3.5	5.3	2.2
1978	4.1	3.5	n.a.	2.1
1979	4.5	3.5	n.a.	2.3
1980	n.a.	3.5	5.0	2.5
1981	4.3	3.4	n.a.	2.4
1982	4.4	3.4	n.a.	2.4
1983	4.4	3.4	4.4	2.3
1984	4.4	3.7	n.a.	2.4
1985	4.4	3.7	n.a.	2.4
1986	4.5	3.7	4.3	2.4
1987	4.8	3.7	n.a.	2.4
1988	5.0	3.7	n.a.	n.a.
1989	5.2	n.a.	n.a.	n.a.

Notes: Average income of physicians equals the average earnings of physicians before taxes and net of deductible professional expenses. Reliable data on the incomes of physicians in Japan are not available.

The concepts and estimating methodologies used to compile average earnings per worker are neither the same among countries nor necessarily the same within each country over time. Among the issues that cannot be taken fully into account are the regional or national basis of the estimates, whether both salaries and self-employed professionals are included in the figures, the exact nature of the professional groups covered, the treatment of part-time and female workers, and whether the income definitions used reflect income tax, census, or national accounts concepts.

n.a. = not available. Data for the following years were missing, and values were imputed by CBO: 1966, 1968, 1976, and 1980 for the United States; and 1962, 1963, 1964, 1966, 1967, 1969, 1970, 1972, 1973, 1975, 1976, 1978, 1979, 1981, 1982, 1984, and 1985 for West Germany. Missing data at the beginning and end of the time period were not imputed.

Source: Congressional Budget Office (CBO) calculations based on data from the Health Data File of the Organization for Economic Cooperation and Development, 1991.

cost increases. OBRA has also placed stricter limits on the amounts that physicians can charge Medicare patients in excess of the approved payments.

The Department of Health and Human Services' new payment-per-service regulations have the goal of reducing overall payments per service for all specialities by 6 percent. Generally primary care physicians will receive higher payments per service, while specialty physicians will receive lower payments per service (see Table 11-4). Because past experience suggested that a decrease in payments could be expected to be offset by physicians who would increase the number of patient visits or the "intensity of services," Congress provided that, if costs exceeded the targets for total spending, fees are to be reduced in subsequent years to keep total payments from rising.

Since the trend is toward higher payments for primary care practitioners and lower payments for specialists, payments are expected to decline by 20 percent or more for radiologists, anesthesiologists, pathologists, and ophthalmologists.[24] The experience of Canada with this approach to cost control provides a basis for optimism. However the Canadian fee schedule covers almost all physician services to all patients, not a small fraction of the whole as does Medicare. The RVS fee schedule may encourage insurance firms to adopt a similar physician payment schedule in an effort to manage costs. The changing fee schedule may also influence the appeal of certain areas of medicine to medical students.

---

[24] Payments per service are expected to increase for limited licensed practitioners such as optometrists (41 percent), chiropractors (26 percent), and podiatrists (14 percent). See Committee on Ways and Means, *1992 Green Book*, p. 427.

TABLE 11-4
MEDICARE PHYSICIAN FEE SCHEDULE: IMPACT BY SPECIALTY

Specialty	1992		1996	
	Payments per service, %	Total payments, %	Payments per service, %	Total payments, %
Family practice	15	16	28	30
General practice	17	18	27	29
Cardiology	−9	−3	−17	−8
Internal medicine	0	1	5	7
Gastroenterology	−10	−4	−18	−9
Radiology	−10	−4	−22	−11
Anesthesiology	−11	−4	−27	−14
General surgery	−8	−3	−13	−7
Pathology	−10	−4	−20	−10
Ophthalmology	−11	−4	−21	−11

Source: Committee on Ways and Means, *1992 Green Book*, p. 427.

The Need to Reform Medicare and Medicaid

Medicare provides for universal access to health care for those falling under its provisions and is an extremely popular program. Since it is financed and administered by the federal government, its benefits and management are uniform and stable. Cost containment programs initiated by the government are having an impact on the delivery of health care. It is protected by a strong middle-class constituency of the elderly.

Medicaid, in contrast, has a number of serious difficulties. Its costs are growing rapidly, contributing to the federal deficit. By definition its beneficiaries are poor. Not surprisingly they are also unorganized. The adage that programs for the poor make poor programs is appropriate here. Middle-class support for programs directed toward the poor is low in a period when most family incomes are stagnating. Reagan-Bush social policies actually encouraged resentment toward the poor by "blaming the victim" when many families were struggling to maintain their middle-class standard of living. That resentment has been compounded by means testing that excludes many uninsured or underinsured low-wage workers who desperately want health care coverage.

For states which pay between 20 and 50 percent of Medicaid costs and live under balanced-budget constraints, the program is their fastest growing expense. Since each state determines Medicaid eligibility standards, the services to be provided, and how to administer the program, the percentage of poor people served by Medicaid has actually dropped below 50 percent, compared to the 98 percent of those eligible served by Medicare. In several states, physicians are dropping out of Medicaid because of long delays being paid and low payments.

Medicaid would be improved and strengthened if it were combined with Medicare to form a national health care system with uniform eligibility standards accessible to the poor in any state. It would then be subject to the national government's cost control programs and provide coverage for workers who now have no health coverage. Broader access would encourage more middle-class support and permit greater mobility for the working poor, who could relocate without fear that they might lose health coverage.

Employee Health Insurance

For most Americans under 65, the cornerstone of health care coverage is employer-subsidized insurance for workers and dependents, supplied as an employment benefit. During World War II there were freezes on wages and prices to control inflation. However, companies were encouraged to make health insurance available as an employee benefit. Employers would provide health insurance for a worker, and deduct the cost from their tax obligation. This approach allowed companies to increase workers' incomes without raising wages per se. Workers increasingly came to expect health insurance benefits subsidized by their employers, or at least subsidized at group prices lower than the cost of individual policies. The trend toward increasing health care coverage through work-related insurance continued until the 1980s.

Tax Incentives and Health Costs

The government provides indirect payments to individuals through specific income tax deductions, exclusions, and credits related to health policy objectives. These are referred to as "tax expenditures" because the goals of these favorable tax incentives could be achieved by replacing them with direct government spending programs. Tax law also includes incentives for employers to provide health coverage for their employees. The Internal Revenue Service (IRS) has held that employer contributions to group health insurance policies are not subject to income taxes for employees or to payroll taxes for the employer. Since wages are subject to payroll taxes, an employer has an incentive to provide increased compensation through health insurance since such coverage is not currently subject to taxation.[25] Employees also have an incentive to substitute employer-subsidized health insurance premiums for part of their salaries. For example, an employee in the 28 percent federal income tax bracket will generally take home less than $60 of a $100 salary increase after Social Security taxes and federal and state income tax deductions. However, if the employer provides $100 in health insurance for the employee, there are no taxes due. The employee, consequently, receives $100 worth of health insurance for about $60 in net wages. Some commentators argue this is just one more government subsidy that provides the greatest benefits to the most affluent.[26] It has been suggested that one way to reduce the inequity in this subsidy would be to limit the amount that can be excluded from taxable income to the average employer subsidy for a "standard" health care policy.

The purpose of excluding health benefits from payroll and income taxes is to encourage employers to promote private health insurance. However, rising health care costs have resulted in many leaders of American business claiming that the cost of providing insurance benefits is reducing their companies' ability to compete in international markets. Moreover, small businesses claim that requiring all employers to provide insurance coverage would put them out of business.

---

[25] Wages are subject to a payroll tax of 7.65 percent to be paid by both employers and employees. Additionally, employees must pay federal taxes on income at 15, 28, or 33 percent rates. Most employees are also subject to state taxes on income as well. Income received as a health care benefit avoids those taxes. For the employer, every $1 paid in health benefits avoids the 7.65 payroll tax as well as state taxes that would be deductible from federal taxes. This means generally that every dollar an employer pays in higher wages would only cost the company between 55 and 70 cents in health insurance costs.

[26] The cost of buying employer-paid insurance is inversely related to income. The higher the income, the lower the net cost of buying insurance. For instance, the same $100 salary increase for a worker in the next lower tax bracket would result in a net increase of about $73 dollars after a deduction of 15 percent for federal income taxes, and an additional 7.65 percent for Social Security taxes, and about a 5 percent state tax. Therefore higher-income employees (in the 31 or 33 percent tax bracket) and perhaps in a higher state tax bracket, get a larger tax break for employer provided health insurance. The most highly paid employees tend to have more expensive and more comprehensive employer-provided health care benefits, so the tax expenditure applies to a larger total amount.

Employees of large companies, especially if unionized, with above average wages are most likely to have employer-sponsored health coverage. But employers which because of their small size or the nature of their business must pay their workers low average wages increasingly find the cost of health insurance an unaffordable fringe benefit. Those workers with the lowest-paying and least secure jobs are most likely to be without any coverage. The typical premium costs to a company run about $3.00 per hour per worker. This insurance can be provided only by lowering workers' wages. Workers with low incomes, if given the choice between earning $5.00 per hour with insurance, or $7.50 without insurance, will usually opt for larger paychecks without health coverage. Money compensation will have a greater marginal utility for them than insurance even if the insurance is not actually unaffordable. And for lower-income workers, the tax incentives to purchase insurance are not significant because they pay few or no taxes anyway. Figure 11-7 shows the rate of employer-sponsored insurance by type of industry in 1989.

FIGURE 11-7
Rate of health insurance coverage by type of industry, 1989. (*Source: Analysis of March 1990 Current Population Survey, Congressional Research Service, Washington, DC, 1990.*)

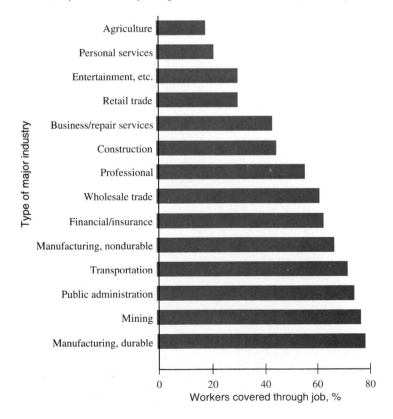

Recent Changes in Employer-Subsidized Insurance

Although 15 percent of the population is uninsured and ineligible for Medicare or Medicaid, critics of the current system claim that exempting health insurance premiums paid by employers from taxable income creates an incentive for many individuals to be overinsured. If employer-paid health insurance premiums were taxed like regular income, their argument goes, the government would take in about $43 billion additional tax dollars each year. In the view of these critics, since insurance pays most medical bills, many individuals have no incentive to ask questions about the cost of their health care or to compare the costs of different alternatives. And insured patients rarely pressure doctors to consider costs when ordering tests or providing treatments.

The tax incentives are not likely to be eliminated. But there have been moves on the part of employers to promote an awareness of the cost of health care among their employees, and even to promote cost containment. Large companies can offer a range of plans for their workers. Workers can select the insurance plans that offer the coverage most suited to their families' needs. Also, as health care costs have risen, employers have shifted more of those costs to employees by requiring them to pay a larger portion of the premiums, larger deductibles, and employee copayments; companies have also reduced coverage.[27] Increasingly, employers are reducing their health care cost burdens by subsidizing only their employees' insurance and requiring the workers to pay the entire premiums for dependents if they want insurance for them. This **cost sharing** is often justified as a **cost containment** effort by companies on the theory that, by making employees bear a larger portion of medical costs, they will demand less low-benefit health care. This reduction in demand in turn is supposed to put a downward pressure on health care prices. In reality such **cost shifting** has had the effect of reducing access to health care for **underinsured** employees.

Some companies have dropped health care coverage altogether for their workers. A *New York Times*/CBS News poll conducted in the late summer of 1991 found that 48 percent of respondents indicated their employers had cut health benefits or were requiring employees to contribute more toward paying medical costs. An additional 20 percent said that their households had been seriously hurt financially by medical bills, while 26 percent indicated that a member of their household had taken one job rather than another mainly for reasons relating to health benefits.[28] Figure 11-8 shows the ways in which companies plan to trim their health programs to hold down their costs.

There are over 1500 health insurance companies in the United States, each of which offers several distinct plans. Many companies offer their employees several

---

[27] One study found that the number of employers who paid the full premiums for their workers dropped from 61 percent in 1985 to 45 percent in 1991. For family coverage, the number dropped from 36 percent in 1985 to 23 percent in 1991. See *Hay/Huggins Benefit Report: Annual Survey of 1000 or More Employers* (Philadelphia: Hay Huggins, 1985, 1991). Cited in Aaron, "Health Care Financing," in Aaron and Schultze (eds.), *Setting Domestic Priorities*, p. 29.

[28] *The New York Times*, September 26, 1991, p. B12.

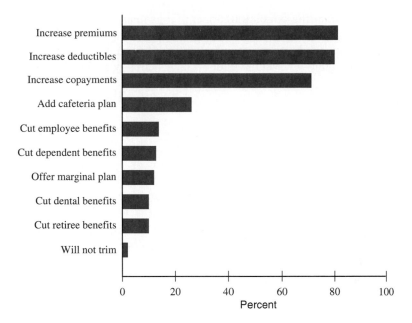

FIGURE 11-8
How companies plan to trim health programs to hold down costs. (*Source: Business and Health, vol. 9 of the Business Strategy Series, Georgia State University, Atlanta, 1990.*)

insurance plans and require them to choose among those offered. These plans vary enormously in the limits of their coverage, in the sizes of their deductibles, in the amounts that patients can be billed by physicians for copayments, as to whether or not mental health care or treatment for drug or alcohol abuse is included, and other family members besides the workers are covered.

In addition to all the health insurance companies, each of the 50 states and several federal agencies also pay health care bills. The costs of conforming to the different reimbursement procedures and filling out the diversity of forms involved contributes significantly to the growing administrative portion of total health care expenditures. Physicians and hospitals must hire workers to respond to each insurer's unique set of claims forms, procedures, and billing codes. It is estimated that close to 20 percent of total U.S. health care spending goes to pay for administrative overhead.

One reform that would reduce administrative costs would be to require all insurance firms and corporate payers to agree on a standardized set of claims forms and billing codes. Although estimates vary regarding precisely how much could be saved in this way, there is general agreement that billions of dollars could be saved from the well over $100 billion now spent on administrative costs.

Insurers increasingly require waiting periods for new employees before they are eligible for health care benefits. And new employees are usually not covered for preexisting medical problems such as cardiovascular diseases, cancer, diabetes, asthma, or any condition requiring ongoing treatment. Thus many workers who are "insured" are in fact "uninsured" for conditions known to require health care expenditures. Also, many insured workers face the problem of employers and insurers altering the type or amount of coverage under policies already in force.

Community and Experience Rating

Blue Cross and Blue Shield plans, reflecting their origins as nonprofit entities, originally offered insurance based upon "community rating." This meant that different employee groups were charged the same rates, based on the average cost of health care for broad groups of people, regardless of the age or the health experience of a particular firm's work force. Profit-oriented insurance firms confronting intense competitive pressure to lower costs and boost profits, began to offer policies at lower costs than Blue Cross and Blue Shield, based upon **"experience rating." Experience rating provides for different insurance rates based upon the predicted average health care costs of a particular company's labor force**. This saves money for employers with younger workers and for workers in certain occupations and industries. However it raises premiums and cost sharing for workers in higher-risk occupations and for companies with older workers and more retirees.

The market implications are clear. Every insurance company, including Blue Cross and Blue Shield programs, must offer insurance based upon experience rating or be driven out of business. The impact on those who seek insurance is equally unavoidable. Workers in certain high-risk industries or occupations can obtain insurance, if at all, only by paying rates several times higher than those paid by workers in low-risk industries or jobs.

Insurance companies prefer to insure those who are the least likely to have health care claims. Many insurance companies have resorted to occupational blacklisting in an effort to avoid high-risk employees. Among blacklisted occupations, for example, are gas station attendants, taxi drivers, security guards, and those working for liquor stores and grocery stores because of the increased likelihood of injuries due to robberies. Florists and hair dressers are often blacklisted because insurers insist the higher proportions of gays working in these job categories means an increased likelihood of AIDS. Health care workers including doctors, dentists, and nurses are sometimes blacklisted because it is claimed that they have a high rate of health care utilization because of their special medical knowledge.[29] Other occupations such as logging, commercial fishing, and construction are sometimes excluded because of the high risk of injury associated with them.

Experience rating is now moving from the work group to the individual level. Especially for small companies, insurers may exclude certain categories of individuals from coverage—for example, newborns with medical problems such as heart murmurs. However, some state laws prevent certain types of exclusions.

In response to the rising costs of health insurance or its unavailability, many companies have become **self-insured**, which also relieves them of state insurance

[29] Reagan, *Curing the Crisis*, p. 49.

ADVERSE SELECTION PROBLEM

Recall that the moral-hazard problem occurs when one party to a contract engages in opportunistic behavior *after* a contract is made. In contrast, the adverse-selection problem arises *prior* to entering the contract. The adverse-selection problem occurs when a party enters a disadvantageous contract on the basis of incomplete or inaccurate information. This happens generally because the cost of obtaining the information makes it difficult to determine if the agreement is truly mutually beneficial. For example, an insurance company may not know the real intention or risk involved in the contract. In that case, the party with superior information may entice the other party into an inequitable contract. A contract is inequitable if either one of contracting parties would not have entered into it if it had the same information as the other party.

One market response by insurers is to devise contracts to reveal the true risks of the parties involved. Insurers, especially of small companies, may refuse to insure a company until it supplies a health status profile of all its employees. If any of the employees or their dependents have a potentially costly illness, such as severe arthritis, those employees or their dependents may be excluded from the plan if state law permits. Or the insurer may raise rates to take any such conditions into account. The insurer may even deny a company insurance. Insurance companies include clauses that permit them to raise rates or cancel a company's insurance as experience indicates, usually on an annual basis. Deductibles, caps, and copayments are efforts by insurance companies to prevent "excessive" demand for health care.

Sources: Mark J. Browne, "Evidence of Adverse Selection in the Individual Health Insurance Market," *The Journal of Risk & Insurance*, vol. 59, no. 1 (March 1, 1992), p. 13; M.S. Marquis, "Adverse Selection with a Multiple Choice Among Health Insurance Plans: A Simulation Analysis," *Journal of Health Economics*, vol. 11, no. 2 (August 1, 1992), p. 129.

regulations. Under the federal Employee Retirement Income Security Act (ERISA) of 1974, passed to encourage the development of employer pension programs, companies may structure their own health plans if they act as their own insurers rather than using an insurance company.[30] ERISA preempts the authority of the states to regulate self-insured employer health plans. Its impact has grown as more firms have self-insured for health benefits. Currently over half of all U.S. workers are employed in companies that self-insure, and states cannot mandate specific health

---

[30] The law states that if employers act as their own insurers—pay premiums into a company fund and pay out benefits themselves rather than using an insurance company—they are exempt from all state taxes and regulations governing health insurance. The original purpose of the health section exemption was to allow companies with employees in several states to offer uniform health care coverage throughout those states. But companies soon discovered self-insuring was a way to avoid state laws mandating certain minimal coverage and to allow them to restructure health plans to reduce costs. In the early 1970s, prior to ERISA, only 5 percent of American workers were covered by self-insured plans. That number grew to 20 percent in 1980 and to 66 percent in 1988. See General Accounting Office, *Health Insurance: Cost Increases Lead to Coverage Limitations and Cost Shifting* (GAO/HRD 90-68) (Washington, DC: Government Printing Office, May 1990), p. 21.

SELF-INSURANCE AND EMPLOYEE VULNERABILITY

A case that made the national news concerned Joe McGann, an employee of the H & H Music Company of Houston for 5 years. In 1987 Joe developed AIDS. As the first of his medical bills began to trickle in, his employer decided to take advantage of ERISA and drop its commercial medical coverage and become self-insured. The company's self-insurance plan limited its coverage for AIDS—and only for AIDS—to a lifetime limit for each employee of $5000. Joe McGann reached that limit in a few months. McGann died in 1991 at the age of 47. He was dependent for the last 3 years of his life on Medicaid and the charity of physicians. A lawsuit was filed to prohibit employers from singling out one disease or individual employees in cost-reduction moves. The broader concern was that any disease such as cancer could be singled out if an employee was stricken. H & H argued that it had the right to structure its benefits any way it chose in its self-interest.

Legal arguments on behalf of McGann did not challenge the right of a company to change its benefits in response to work force conditions or economic circumstances, but claimed that, by focusing its cost-saving efforts on one individual, it had violated the antidiscrimination clause in the ERISA legislation. Neither the District court nor a federal appeals court found any violation by H & H. On further appeal, the Supreme Court asked the Solicitor General for an opinion on whether it should hear the case. The Bush administration instructed the Solicitor General to urge the Court not to hear the case, arguing that H & H was acting within its rights. In the end the lower court ruling was allowed to stand.

Source: Malcolm Gladwell, *The Washington Post*, August 20, 1992.

plan provisions for those employers or require them to pay state-imposed premium taxes.[31]

Competitive health insurance markets inevitably lead to efforts to shift costs to consumers (patients). The result may be positive when, for example, private insurers use the incentive of experience rating to reward positive behavior such as offering nonsmokers lower insurance rates. But incentives for reducing costs overall are reducing the ability of insurance to provide as broad a coverage in the future as it has in the past.

The problems of uncertainty in health insurance coverage produced by competition were in the past limited to small numbers of people, but are now reaching into

---

[31] Since ERISA preempts state authority to regulate all employer-provided insurance, states that have tried to get minimal coverage for all their citizens have had to work within those constraints. Hawaii was the first state to try to provide coverage for **all** its residents, and its uninsured rate is the lowest of all the states. A 1974 state law requires virtually every employer to provide health insurance for its full-time workers. Hawaii can enforce this requirement because its law went into effect before ERISA and is exempt from its provisions. The state requirement that virtually all employers provide insurance and that insurers cover all employees reduces uncompensated care and cost shifting. Residents not covered by their employers or Medicaid are eligible for a state-subsidized insurance program offering fewer benefits.

large groups of insured people as well. One tactic used by insurance companies is to significantly raise their rates each year for current subscribers. At the same time, the companies invite all their policy holders to reapply for a low rate offered to new subscribers. Those discovered during the previous period of coverage to have significant illnesses or preexisting conditions are turned down for the new insurance when they apply. They are forced to stay with their old policies and their rapidly escalating rates. Those with preexisting conditions cannot shop around for insurance because no other company will insure them. This allows insurers to escalate premiums for those who have illnesses to unaffordable levels within a few years. Such underwriting procedures sort out the healthier clients from those with health problems. Many insurance companies now exclude people for conditions that do not even appear to be terribly risky, such as mild hypertension or the need for family and marital counseling.[32]

People fear that if they disclose every little medical occurrence, they will be refused coverage. However, they also fear that if they do not disclose a medical problem and subsequently make a substantial claim, they may be denied coverage for failing to provide a full disclosure of their medical history. Some employees are reluctant to go to doctors, fearing that documenting something on their company health care records may make it difficult for them to get coverage if the company changes insurers or if they want to change jobs.[33] Nor are these fears unrealistic. Employers feel their own pressures in regard to medical insurance. In small firms, one or two expensive conditions could bankrupt the premium pool.

The form of discrimination just described is legal. That is, if there is evidence that a medical condition is going to cost an insurance company money, it does not have to provide coverage for it. The insurance industry defends high premiums, waiting periods, condition-specific payment denials, and denial of coverage to people with preexisting conditions as necessary to protect companies from the moral hazard of people who only want to pay for insurance when they need it. The practices are actuarially sound and permit more affordable rates for other employers and employees. Many workers agree, and contend that they cannot afford to subsidize others. This approach by definition, however, is at variance with the concept of

---

[32] Paul Cotton, "Preexisting Conditions 'Hold Americans Hostage' to Employers and Insurance," *JAMA*, vol. 265 (1991), p. 2451. The article pointed out that a survey of 2000 employers who offered insurance in 1987 found 57 percent had preexisting condition clauses in the health policies they offered to workers. Although such clauses were more common with small employers (64 percent of firms with less than 500 employees), they were also common in large firms (45 percent of companies with more than 10,000 employees).

[33] Small firms, those with fewer than 50 employees, are often denied coverage for their entire group unless those with preexisting conditions are excluded. Small businesses that provide health care for their employees may actually provide little coverage. For example, a federal employee covered by Blue Cross Blue Shield may have a routine but expensive health problem such as arthritis. Were that employee to leave her or his job with the federal government and join a small firm offering the same Blue Cross Blue Shield health coverage, she or he would probably be given a lifetime exclusion for all future coverage for anything related to the arthritic condition. The insurance company and policy would be the same, but the coverage would in effect be lost because of the job change.

insurance as a way to spread risk. Competition in the small-group insurance market now means insurance companies search for ways to avoid risks rather than for ways to share them. Employer-based coverage has become insecure and insured workers face the threat that their coverage will dissolve when they need it most. This has led to efforts to cap premiums so that those with health problems cannot be excluded or charged more than 50 percent more for coverage.

ORGANIZATIONAL CHANGE

The search for lower-cost coverage also has led to increasing pressures to change the nature of health care organization. Traditionally, health care has been delivered by a physician practicing alone or in partnership with others sharing office and equipment space and charging a **fee for service**. But pressures to control costs have resulted in "alternative delivery systems." Increasingly, insurance companies compete to offer plans which may lead to improved services, although the patient's free choice of medical providers may be reduced. For example, insurance companies have tried to contain costs by encouraging physicians to move away from individual partnerships of physicians sharing equipment at a common office location toward **preferred provider organizations (PPOs)**. These are groups of health care providers who agree to provide certain health care services to an insured population at rates lower than they would ordinarily charge. In return, the "preferred providers" have an increased number of patients referred to them by the insurer (or employer) reduced insurance form paperwork, and receive quicker payments. Patients are reimbursed at higher rates for using these preferred providers.

Health maintenance organizations (HMOs) are groups of doctors and hospitals who provide subscribers with a range of medical services. The health care providers of the HMO receive a **capitation fee**, which is an agreed-upon fixed monthly income based on the number of insured members enrolled. A variation on the HMO idea is the **independent practice association (IPA)**, which provides stipulated services to patients for fixed fees. However, physicians in an IPA continue to practice separately and bill the insurer on a fee-for-service basis unlike those in an HMO, in which the medical providers are paid salaries. Any excess of premiums is shared among the providers at the end of the year, while deficits are handled by reserve funds, or reduced payments to providers.[34]

The effort to hold down medical costs by the greater use of negotiated payment methods, particularly through PPOs, HMOs, and DRGs (mentioned earlier in the chapter), has reduced the ability of hospitals to shift the costs of treating the unin-

---

[34] The record of IPAs in curtailing health care costs is no better than fee-for-service providers. See Aaron, *Serious and Unstable Condition*, pp. 28–29. This is to be expected, however, when one considers that IPAs originated in response to the Reagan administration's encouragement of competition among HMOs as a way to hold down costs for Medicare in particular, but also health care generally. IPAs are actually "for profit" HMOs. A majority of HMOs are actually IPAs, although they cover approximately one-third of the subscribers.

sured to those with insurance. As cost shifting becomes more difficult, there is less access to care for the uninsured.[35]

THE UNINSURED

Size of the Uninsured Population

In 1978, about 12.3 percent of the population below the age of 65 did not have any health insurance. The rate increased to 14.8 percent by 1986. By 1991 the rate had risen to 16 percent.[36] Since the early 1980s an average of 100,000 Americans have joined the ranks of the uninsured each month.[37] In 1991, 35.4 million Americans were uninsured—more than at any time since the passage of Medicaid and Medicare in 1965. An even larger number have seen their insurance coverage deteriorate to the point that they are underinsured.[38] Not surprisingly, low-income families are more likely to be uninsured than middle- or high-income households. However, **84 percent of the uninsured are employed or lived in families where the head of the household is employed**.[39] Only 51 percent of those in households without a working adult had medical insurance.[40]

Although the proportion of Americans in the labor force has been growing recently, the percentage receiving health benefits has been dropping. Many of the new jobs created in the last several years have been in the retail and service industries where the greatest increases in the uninsured occurred.

[35] It is possible that, when billing was always a retrospective accounting based upon fee for service, physicians and hospitals worked on a Marxist principle of payment based upon the maxim "From each according to their ability and to each according to their needs." Charges were shifted to insurers to pay higher amounts for services to subsidize care given to the poor and uninsured.

[36] Beth C. Fuchs, "Mandated Employer-Provided Health Insurance," (Washington, DC: Congressional Research Service, October 13, 1992), p. 2.

In 1987, the Department of Health and Human Services found that 11.4 percent of the population under 65 was uninsured **for the entire year**. And almost the same proportion (11 percent) gained or lost coverage for some period during the year. So more than one out of five Americans had no insurance coverage for at least part of the year. See P. Short, *Estimates of the Uninsured Population, Calendar Year 1987: National Medical Expenditure Survey Data Summary 2* [U.S. Dept of Health and Human Services Pub. No. (PHS) 90-3469] (Rockville, MD: Agency for Health Care Policy and Research, 1990), pp. 4–5.

[37] David U. Himmelstein et al., *The Growing Epidemic of Uninsurance: New Data on the Health Insurance Coverage of Americans* (Cambridge, MA: Harvard Medical School, The Center for National Health Program Studies, December 1992).

[38] Emily Friedman, "The Uninsured: From Dilemma to Crisis," vol. 265, no. 19 (May 15, 1991), p. 2492. The underinsured are more difficult to define, because the diagnosis of an illness may determine whether or not a patient has sufficient coverage while a survey of whether patients have insurance is not likely to reveal certain gaps in protection. Questions regarding where and how long a patient can be treated, the types of treatment allowed, and whether there is a dollar cap or time limit for insurance coverage determine the sufficiency of insurance.

[39] Friedman, "The Uninsured," p. 2492.

[40] P. Short, A. Monheit, and K. Beauregard, *A Profile of Uninsured Americans* [DHHS Publication No. (PHS) 89-3443] (Rockville, MD: Public Health Service, September 1989), p. 7.

The proportion of the Americans receiving coverage through another family member's employment has been declining. An increasing percentage of employers are dropping health care as a fringe benefit. Other employers are providing coverage for the worker only and dropping any contribution for the cost of dependent insurance. In 1980, 72 percent of medium and large firms paid the entire cost of coverage for their workers and 51 percent paid the full cost of dependent coverage. By 1989 only 48 percent of such firms paid full coverage for their workers and only 31 percent included full coverage for dependents.[41]

Young adults between the ages of 19 and 24 are the most likely to be uninsured. One study found that 20 percent of this group was uninsured for all of 1987, and an additional 18 percent of this age group was uninsured for part of the year.[42] Children under 18 are the next most likely to be uninsured. According to the National Health Interview Survey, 10.7 million children under 18 (about 1 in 6) were uninsured for all of 1987. Most were children of working parents who did not have employer-sponsored health insurance. They made up two-thirds of uninsured children, while another 18 percent were children of working parents who were enrolled in a group plan but chose not to enroll their children; 16 percent of the uninsured children did not have access to employer-sponsored insurance because their parents did not have access to insurance at work or were unemployed. Statistics also indicated that only about 20 percent of black children and 3 out of 10 Latino children had insurance for the entire year. Current Medicaid coverage leaves millions of children and hundreds of thousands of pregnant women without insurance because the women's

---

[41] Beth Fuchs, "Mandated Employer-Provided Health Insurance," p. 3. Workers who had coverage through employment did not cover their spouses in about 3 percent of the cases, while about 8 percent of the children of insured workers were uninsured. There were also an increasing number of households with older children who did not meet the eligibility definitions in insurance coverage rules.

[42] See P. Short, *Estimates of the Uninsured Population*, p. 7. Also cited in Friedman, "The Uninsured," p. 2491.

CHILD HEALTH AND POVERTY

There is a clear correlation between childhood poverty and health problems. The National Health Interview Survey of 1988 found the following:

1 Children under age 5 living in families with annual incomes under $10,000 were one-third less likely than children in families with an annual income of more than $35,000 to be in excellent health.

2 Children aged 5 to 17 in families with annual incomes under $10,000 were only half as likely to be in excellent health as their cohorts in families with incomes in excess of $35,000 (36 percent versus 63 percent).

3 Children in these low-income families were twice as likely to have chronic health problems, or mental or physical disabilities.

incomes are above the Medicaid eligibility level, yet too low for their families to be able to afford private health insurance.

The issue of health care for children is of special concern to public policy makers since children cannot make the choices that affect their access to medical coverage. By the same token, there is more societal support for government programs that benefit children than for those that benefit adults.

Insurance coverage climbed dramatically for individuals aged 25 to 54. Yet 19.8 percent of this group was also uninsured for all or part of 1987. And 13.6 percent of those aged 55 to 64 were uninsured all or part of the year. Thus, approximately 50 million Americans were uninsured for part of 1987.

Rates of coverage are also correlated with income, gender, race, and ethnic characteristics. Men are somewhat more likely to be uninsured than women. Those with family incomes below $25,000 now account for 62 percent of the uninsured population. Those earning between $25,000 and $50,000 show a significant loss of insurance coverage.

In 1987 23.8 percent of men were uninsured for at least part of the year compared to just 21 percent of women.[43] This was due to the fact that women are disproportionately represented among the population living in poverty (see Chap. 6). Since Medicaid covers most of that population, more women are likely to have coverage. Medicaid now provides coverage for pregnant women with incomes up to 185 percent of the poverty level.

Data from the Census Bureau's Current Population Survey taken in 1991 found that a disproportionate percentage of black and Hispanic Americans tend to be uninsured. While about 12.9 percent of non-Hispanic whites were uninsured for all or part of 1991, nearly 21 percent of black Americans and nearly 32 percent of Hispanic Americans lacked coverage. Table 11-5 shows data on those uninsured for the years 1989 and 1991.

The number of middle-income Americans without health insurance is also growing at an alarming rate. In 1991, according to the Census Bureau, the number of Americans with family incomes between $25,000 and $50,000 who lost their insurance rose by 1.07 million, over twice the rate of the preceding year. About 8.3 million people in that income group were without health insurance some time in 1991. About 452,000 employed workers lost their insurance in 1991, while 448,000 unemployed and laid-off workers lost their coverage. There were 2.6 million Americans who gained insurance in 1991 because their incomes dropped so drastically they qualified for Medicaid. The increase in the Medicaid case load has caused total Medicaid expenditures to increase from $58 billion in fiscal 1989 to $117 billion in 1992.

The situation has been made worse by the lingering recession in which many employers have replaced full-time positions with part-time or temporary employees without the fringe benefit of health insurance. Approximately 75 percent of full-time employees have access to some minimal level of employer-sponsored health

---

[43] The Census Bureau's March 1992 Current Population Survey found that in 1991 the proportion of males uninsured at any one time rose to 15.8 percent, while the figure for women was 12.5 percent.

TABLE 11-5
PERCENTAGES OF AMERICANS WITHOUT
HEALTH INSURANCE IN 1989 AND 1991, BY
SEX, RACE, INCOME, AND AGE

	1989	1991
Male	14.8	15.8
Female	12.4	12.5
Whites	12.5	12.9
Blacks	19.2	20.7
Hispanics	33.5	31.9
Income		
<$25,000	21.6	22.6
$25,000–50,000	8.3	10.2
>$50,000	7.5	6.9
Age		
<18	13.3	12.7
18–39	19.0	20.9
40–64	12.1	12.6
>64	1.0	0.9

Source: Himmelstein et al., *The Growing Epidemic of Uninsurance.*

insurance, while only about 25 percent of part-time workers have health insurance coverage.

There are some middle-income Americans for whom insurance premiums are not unaffordable, but who nevertheless choose to remain uninsured. Thirty-two percent of the uninsured in 1991 had incomes at least twice that of the poverty level.[44] Presumably a choice by a head of household not to buy insurance is because its opportunity cost is too high compared to other goods needed by the household. Such a decision may have consequences for society. The uninsured may rely on the safety net of emergency rooms, along with the poor, in the event of medical need. In those cases, taxpayer dollars may subsidize the decision. Unfortunately, the decision by the worker also has consequences for spouses and children, who may not have participated in making it.

The Consequences of Being Uninsured

Critics of the American health care system point out that medical services are currently rationed in a manner that is both inhumane and needlessly expensive in the long run. The reality is that the uninsured are usually not able to pay for most of their health care needs. They must find someone else to pay or forgo health care

[44] M. Susan Marquis and Stephen H. Long, "Uninsured Children and National Health Reform," *JAMA*, vol. 268 (December 23/30, 1992), p. 3475.

services. The uninsured are more likely to be in poorer health than those with health insurance. In many cases they are uninsured precisely because their high health costs resulted in their exclusion from medical coverage or in their premiums becoming too costly.

One study found that the uninsured use 37 percent fewer physician services and 69 percent fewer hospital services when compared with the insured population.[45] Some of the difference in physician and hospital service utilization may reflect those services of low marginal value frequently utilized by those with comprehensive coverage. But many of the uninsured cannot avail themselves of important preventive health care such as prenatal care in pregnancy.

Another recent study found that the uninsured are at higher risk to receive poor-quality care when they attempt to get medical help from hospitals or physicians. The study also found differences associated with payer status, indicating that those with less generous reimbursement plans, and especially those without insurance, suffer substandard care.[46] Uninsured patients in New York are more likely than insured patients to receive negligent care and suffer adverse effects. Uninsured patients experience a different process of care and have worse hospital outcomes, including higher death rates, than privately insured individuals.[47]

The poor find their health care is rationed because they are unable to buy access to it and public programs are insufficient for them to obtain mainstream medical care. Physician visits for low-income Americans decreased 8 percent during the mid-1980s, while visits for others, even controlling for the lower use expected with better health status of the more affluent, increased by 42 percent. Visits by the elderly poor decreased even more than that for other low-income Americans (by 20 percent).[48] Those who cannot afford to pay for routine care usually wait longer before seeking care, frequently in a hospital emergency room. By waiting, they are more likely to develop a more serious illness—for example, a viral infection can

---

[45] Stephen H. Long and Jack Rodgers, *The Effects of Being Uninsured on Health Care Service Use: Estimates from the Survey of Income and Program Participation* [Survey of Income and Program Participation (SIPP) Working Paper No. 9012] (Washington, DC: Bureau of the Census, October 1990).
   A 1986 National Access Survey conducted for the Robert Wood Johnson Foundation reported that the uninsured had approximately 40 percent fewer physician visits and 19 percent fewer hospitalizations than the insured. The uninsured were also found to be more likely to delay seeking medical care, and when they did seek it their illnesses were generally more serious and costly to treat.

[46] Helen R. Burstin, Stuart R. Lipsitz, and Troyen A. Brennan, "Socioeconomic Status and Risk for Substandard Medical Care," *JAMA*, vol. 268, no. 17 (November 4, 1992), p. 2383. See also M. Wenneker, J. S. Weissman, and A. M. Epstein, "The Association of Payer with Utilization of Cardiac Procedures in Massachusetts," *JAMA*, vol. 261 (1990), pp. 3572–3576.

[47] See J. Hadley, E. P. Steinberg, and J. Feder, "Comparison of Uninsured and Privately Insured Hospital Patients: Condition on Admission, Resource Use, and Outcome," *JAMA*, vol. 265 (1991), pp. 374–379. They found that patients without insurance are less likely to be given routine diagnostic tests, less likely to have key surgical procedures performed, and are more likely to die while in a hospital. The uninsured were, for example, 29 percent less likely to get coronary bypass surgery compared with insured patients. Uninsured patients in a hospital were 1.2 to 3.2 times more likely to die than were insured patients.

[48] Reported in John M. Eisenberg, "Economics," *JAMA*, vol. 268 (July 1992), p. 344.

lead to a variety of complications such as pneumonia. The poorer health status of the less affluent can also lead to other economic dependencies whose tab must ultimately be paid by taxpayer money. For the poor, health care is usually too little, too late, and too expensive.

PUBLIC DISSATISFACTION: THE GROWING CONSENSUS FOR REFORM

The problems of American health care are clear. Medical costs are soaring. It is not a matter of too little spending. The United States spends more on health care than any other industrialized nation, and costs are still rising faster than the general rate of inflation. Approximately 38 million Americans have no health care coverage and as many more are inadequately covered and live in fear of financial ruin if a medical catastrophe were to occur. Frequently, employees in small businesses have no coverage at work and find private coverage too expensive. An August 1991 *New York Times*/CBS poll revealed that 3 in 10 American workers say they or someone in their household have at some time stayed in a job they wanted to leave mainly to keep the health benefits.[49] This phenomenon of "job lock" was found to most be prevalent in middle-income households, suggesting the increased importance of health care as a political issue. Eighteen percent reported a decline in the last 2 years in the insurance benefits provided by their employer.

Many families face financial indigence if a family member requires intense or long-term medical care. One in six (18 percent) reported that a member of their family has postponed needed health care because of the cost. While two-thirds of those polled were confident that they could meet their current medical expenses, over 60 percent expressed concern they might not have the resources to do so in the future.[50]

CHOICES IN POLICY ALTERNATIVES

All of these factors have led to a consensus that the U.S. health care system needs reform. There is a growing understanding among policy makers that meaningful health care reform must have certain characteristics. It must meet the following goals: **providing access to basic medical care for all Americans, producing real cost containment, and preserving high quality in American health care**. These goals may be accomplished in part by encouraging other secondary goals such as providing greater incentives for physicians to go into areas of primary care, reducing administrative inefficiencies, and encouraging preventive medicine.

What is sometimes puzzling about public attitudes toward health care is that the intense level of support for change on the one hand is not accompanied by great

---

[49] Erik Eckholm, "Health Benefits Found to Deter Job Switching," *The New York Times*, September 24, 1991. A December 1990 Associated Press poll found that 1 in 7 Americans say they have personally changed or remained in a job because of health insurance benefits. See *Concurrent Resolution on the Budget for Fiscal Year 1992*, "Health Care Dimensions of the 1992 Budget," Hearings before the Committee on the Budget, U.S. Senate, 102nd Cong., S. HRG. 102-68, pt. 4, p. 150.

[50] *Concurrent Resolution on the Budget for Fiscal Year 1992*, S. HRG. 102-68, pt. 4, p. 150.

dissatisfaction with personal health care services on the other. In fact, about 80 percent of Americans are very happy with the care they receive personally, while about the same percentage thinks the health care system is in need of major reform. The insecurity of the public on this issue has become identified with economic security, and health care reform has become an essential aspect of guaranteeing economic security to the voting middle class. This seeming paradox means that the public wants to maintain those aspects of health care that it now likes such as the quality of care available, but it wants the system to cost less and to assure coverage in the event of a major medical need.

American support for funding a national health plan decreases rapidly with the increase in taxes necessary to support it. A *Los Angeles Times* poll reported in January 1990 that 72 percent would support a national plan even if it entailed a tax increase. However, only 22 percent would be willing to pay more than $200 per year.[51]

There are a number of proposals on reforming health care that range from minor and very incremental tinkering with the current system to a fundamental restructuring of health care that would involve a universal single-payer system like Canada's. These proposals must be judged by their likelihood of providing health care coverage for everyone while containing prices and maintaining quality.

Option 1: Shoring Up the Current System

The proposals that represent the smallest departure from the current system are those that suggest that the status quo has much to commend it. They point out that most Americans do have health coverage, and most are satisfied with the health care they receive. The free market system has provided patients with access to some of the best trained physicians in the world, and made available the most advanced medical technologies. That such medical care is expensive is not surprising.

But with the building momentum for national medical care reform, some former opponents have endorsed some changes. Major elements of the health insurance industry and the American Medical Association have expressed guarded support for managed competition and for health maintenance organizations.[52] Those who sup-

---

[51] Reported in "Health Care Dimensions of the 1992 Budget," Hearings before the Committee on the Budget, S. HRG. 102-68, pt. 4, pp. 154–155. Other surveys found that the most popular sources of revenues to fund a universal health care system are, in descending order, increases in taxes on cigarettes and liquor, in Social Security taxes paid by employers for each employee, in insurance premiums paid by the individuals, and in income taxes. Surveys have also shown support for an earmarked health-related tax. (See p. 155 of the above source.)

[52] The Health Insurance Association of America proposed standardizing fees that insurance companies pay to doctors and hospitals. This is touted as a way to control costs. Actually it is a way for small insurers to overcome the advantages of large insurers. For that reason several large insurers criticized the proposal and withdrew from the association, which is dominated by small insurers.

The American Medical Association has given its tentative support to managed competition and to health maintenance organizations—ideas it once denounced. But it also supports the right of physicians to join several health care plans. However, if physicians belong to several plans, those plans would have little incentive to compete. This would undermine the whole concept of managed competition.

port this position claim that the current system's shortcomings can be resolved by extending coverage to the uninsured primarily through tax credits for those making up to 150 percent of the federal poverty level or simply through Medicaid. They claim their proposals would promote managed care and greater efficiency in administration through standardized insurance procedures. They maintain that a few reforms such as new regulations to prohibit the exclusion of persons with high-cost illnesses from insurance after initial coverage, and the right to renew policies, are all that is necessary to improve the system. Workers employed at a firm that provides health care as a benefit would be protected against exclusion from coverage for any medical condition if they moved to other companies that also offered employer-sponsored insurance. Supporters of these changes also propose limits on the differences in premiums and the levels of coverage between different policies. Yet another proposed change pushed by small insurers would permit the losses on high-risk patients to be distributed among all insurance premiums.

Supporters of this position also call for major reforms in medical malpractice law. Specifically, they call for revisions in state laws to limit the size of malpractice awards made to patients and lawyers. Lawyers typically earn a percentage of any malpractice award, so they benefit directly from large settlements. Malpractice insurance varies by speciality but averages over $18,000 a year, which is passed on to patients through higher fees. Physicians frequently argue that they are forced to order unnecessary diagnostic tests and practice high-tech defensive medicine to protect themselves from possible legal action, and both of these drive up medical costs.

Supporters of minimal changes in the current system see an advantage to minimal federal government involvement in health care issues. However, most public policy analysts conclude that these changes would do little to resolve the fundamental problems of controlling costs or providing coverage for everyone.

Option 2: Clinton's Managed Competition

Proponents of a second option believe that all Americans have a right to health care coverage, that the extent of basic health care coverage must be clearly defined, and that any proposal to extend coverage to those currently without it should build on the successes and legitimacy of the current system.

Known as "**managed competition**," this option actually consists of several proposals that would achieve universal coverage at some defined minimal level through employer-subsidized and public insurance. Its key elements include guaranteed employment-based coverage for all workers (and their nonworking dependents), replacement of Medicaid with a plan similar to Medicare to cover all those not insured through their jobs and to cover workers whose employers find public coverage more affordable, guaranteed affordable coverage for employers through private insurance reform and through tax credits for small employers with an option to purchase public insurance, and the establishment of a national budget for health expenditures and public- and private-sector initiatives to contain costs.

Proponents of these changes point out that the current system successfully provides coverage for about three-quarters of all workers. Its weakness is that about 75 percent of the remaining 25 percent who have no coverage are full- or part-time workers employed by small firms at low-wage jobs where coverage is not offered. These workers are not poor enough to qualify for Medicaid, so they and their families fall through the cracks of the health care system. Supporters of this second option want to retain the advantages of existing structures that successfully provide coverage for so many, and extend them to everyone.

The Clinton plan would encourage competition among health care providers and insurers, and make health care available to everyone. It is sometimes referred to as a "**play or pay**" system. It would group those currently uninsured into regional alliances, affording small businesses and individuals a better opportunity to bargain for lower medical and insurance prices. It proposes limits on how much premiums can increase annually. But it would also allow employers to "pay" a tax to fund an alternative publicly administered program if they did not wish to provide health care coverage themselves. The plan would provide for a minimum standard of coverage that would constitute acceptable "playing" for employers. It would also make available preventive services that everyone should have on a regular basis.

Politically, this proposal has several advantages. First, it builds on a system that is already operating. Employers already providing insurance benefits for employees could support it because, from their perspective, it would eliminate free-rider employers that have an advantage over competitors already shouldering the financial burden of subsidized health care for their employees. Small firms might prefer to pay a stable and predictable tax and avoid the hazard of annually escalating insurance premiums. It would also make coverage affordable for small firms who maintain that insurers charge them higher premiums for a standard coverage than larger firms because the medical costs of smaller communities are less predictable. The implementation of such a "play or pay" plan would result in an expansion of business purchases of health insurance, which could temper the insurance industry's objections to other features of the plan. Employees and their dependents would be the greatest beneficiaries of the plan. New programs would be created to cover those who are unemployed.

The Clinton administration's form of managed competition owes a great deal to the analysis of the current health care system carried out by Alain Enthoven and Richard Kronick.[53] Central to their analysis is the conclusion that the current system is out of control because it contains more incentives to spend than not to spend. For example, the open-ended fee-for-service system pays physicians for doing more even if more is not appropriate. Allowing the insured the "free choice of provider" blocks the insurance companies' ability to exercise bargaining power when dealing with physicians or other health care providers. Preferred provider insurance rules help to regulate prices but are not effective in controlling the volume of services provided. Other aspects of the current system such as Medicare, Medicaid, and tax subsidies for employer-provided health care coverage are all open-ended and encourage providing excessive services. The tendency to provide ever more care is reinforced by a medical culture that highly regards the most

[53] See Alain C. Enthoven and Richard Kronick, "Universal Health Insurance through Incentives Reform," *JAMA*, vol. 265, no. 19 (May 15, 1991), pp. 2532–2536.

advanced technology and that fosters high patient expectations of successful treat-ment and the threat of a lawsuit if those expectations are not met.[54] So contrary to a widely held view, Enthoven and Kronick maintain that America has not yet tried competition in health care delivery in the normal economic sense, i.e., in terms of **price competition** to serve a cost-conscious demand for health care. Nor, accord-ing to these authors, does the current market for health insurance produce fair or efficient results. It is troubled by problems of biased risk selection, market seg-mentation, and inadequate information. To overcome these problems, Enthoven and Kronick propose that large employers and public sponsors (state and local govern-ments) manage the demand side of the health care market by acting as active, col-lective purchasing agents, that is, manage a process of informed cost-conscious consumer choice of "managed care" to reward those who provide high-quality eco-nomical medical care.[55]

The Clinton administration's plan proposes three methods of paying for the sys-tem. All employers would be required to contribute to the health care of their employees. This would cover not only those already insured but those working Americans who currently account for 85 percent of the uninsured. It would guar-antee insurance to all dependents as well. This would reduce the cost shifting that occurs when uninsured people go to emergency rooms and utilize high-cost med-ical care.

A second method of payment would be through new taxes: a cigarette tax of $0.75 a pack (a sin tax), and a 1 percent tax on the payrolls of large corporations to underwrite medical research.

The third method would be expected savings from higher efficiency in health care delivery, preventive care, and means testing of Medicaid and Medicare recipi-ents.

These policies, according to the Clinton plan, would result in a transformation of the American health care system in which everyone would be covered either pub-licly or privately. And the problems inherent in the fee-for-service system would be overcome by encouraging price competition among HMOs competing for contracts from the sponsors. Each insurance plan would be forced to compete to attract both subscribers and health care providers.

Since HMOs offer coverage through prepaid premiums, they create a strong incentive to keep patients healthy while avoiding wasteful treatments. Advocates of the Clinton plan also argue that HMOs have built-in incentives to systematically study and improve treatment practices and outcomes. Fee-for-service insurers, who have no relationship with health care providers other than a contractual obligation to pay bills, have neither incentives nor the ability to do this.

---

[54] Enthoven and Kronick, "Universal Health Insurance through Incentives Reform," p. 2532.

[55] Sponsors would manage competition through such techniques as an annual open-enrollment process, providing information to ensure full employee consciousness of premium differences, seeing that a standardized benefit package was offered by each insurer, establishing risk-adjusted sponsor contributions so that plans attracting higher-cost subscribers were compensated, monitoring quality on an ongoing basis, and providing consumer information. See Enthoven and Kronick, "Universal Health Insurance through Incentives Reform," pp. 2534–2535.

For the Clinton plan to work, competition must be structured by defining basic benefits, and by federal legislation requiring states to assure that a basic benefits package is available to every resident for an affordable premium. The federal government would subsidize premiums for the poor.

Supporters of the plan point out that it retains and extends job-related coverage for most workers, and provides public programs for those not covered by their employers to achieve universal coverage. The government's primary role would be to provide rules that would actually improve the freedom and fairness of the current system: It would be fairer to workers who would feel free to seek jobs based on their personal preferences and abilities, since a standard health care package would be available regardless of where they worked. And it would be fairer to employers because no firm would be at a competitive disadvantage as a result of providing health care coverage for its employees.

However, critics of the Clinton plan note that rising health care costs have been a major factor in rising labor costs in recent years. Government-mandated employer coverage, whether in the form of insurance premiums or an additional payroll tax, would hit smaller firms the hardest and would do nothing to stop driving up the costs of labor. Moreover, payroll tax payments would have to be steadily increased to prevent employers from dropping their own insurance plans in favor of paying into the cheaper public program. The cost of new employees would begin to exceed their marginal benefit to employers, leading to job losses and a higher unemployment rate. And increasing the costs of coverage for those already employed would come at the expense of wage increases.

Some critics of the plan also object to the further intrusion of government into the health care sector that would be necessitated by the increased regulation. They argue that the tradeoffs involved have not been adequately considered. They point out that managed competition will result in reduced choices for some patients, who will not have as wide a range of doctors to choose from within the HMO structure. They also point out that while some will gain more access to health care, it must come at the expense of others who will lose some of their current access. For example, HMOs to be successful must keep patient costs below the level of prepaid fees. That means some tests and treatments may be "underutilized" to keep costs down.

Still others argue that the idea of managed competition is an oxymoron. On a macro level a managed economy is very different from a competitive economy. Managed competition is based upon the notion that the health care industry in America is a model of imperfect competition. But its introduction into health care will merely prolong the current system by preserving some of its inefficiencies (over 1500 health insurance firms) while doing away with its high quality of care.

Critics also argue that employers have no inherent obligation to provide health insurance for their workers. Rather it is the responsibility of individuals or of the government to do so. If we conclude that health care is a public good to which everyone should have an equal right, then health insurance should not be provided through employers, but through a tax-financed system that provides the same level of care to all.

Option 3: National Health Insurance

The third choice for the nation is to replace the current system based on private insurance with government-sponsored national health insurance (NHI) program. The Canadian model is of special interest to the United States because of the similarities between the two nations. Two aspects of the Canadian system are especially of interest: First, it makes health care a right, and removes the insecurity regarding its availability and cost. Second, Canada has been much more successful in containing the proportion of its GDP devoted to health care than the United States.

Americans tend to have mistaken notions about several aspects of the Canadian health care system. First, contrary to popular opinion in the United States, **Canada does not have a socialized system of health care**. Most of the Canadian health care resources are in the private sector. As in the United States, a third party pays private health care providers. A second misconception concerns the freedom of choice. George Bush asserted in the 1992 Presidential debates that since Americans like freedom of choice, they would find the single system of health insurance in Canada unacceptable. In fact there is more freedom in the doctor-patient relationship in Canada than in the United States. **Canadians choose their own private physicians who receive their incomes based on fees for service**. Physicians are also free to accept or reject patients. Ninety percent of the hospitals in Canada are private, nonprofit corporations. The other 10 percent are almost entirely federal veterans' hospitals and provincial psychiatric hospitals. The Canadian system has preserved the right to choose one's physician, which public opinion polls reveal is very important to Americans.

A third misperception concerns the view that shortages of health care personnel and equipment in the Canadian system result in excessive waiting periods for care, and significant usage of U.S. health care facilities. It is true that Canadians must wait for some elective services longer than Americans. But provincial governments have been successful in shortening the waiting periods significantly in the last several years. Their method of controlling hospital costs has resulted in limiting the use of esoteric and expensive diagnostic and treatment procedures. So although emergency cases are treated immediately, there are queues for some nonemergency and elective services. Waiting lists are necessary because some forms of medical technology are less available in Canada (especially magnetic resonance imaging and lithtripters). Some American observers suggest that such waiting would not be acceptable in the United States. But many Canadians defend this egalitarian aspect by pointing out that you have to wait your turn for nonemergency procedures even if there are two poor people ahead of you. In the United States, they point out, if you are affluent or have comprehensive insurance you can get immediate treatment, but if you are poor or uninsured you may not get any treatment. Americans dependent on Medicaid must wait for many types of health care if they receive it at all. In the vast majority of cases, Canadians argue, the delays do no harm. The major portion of Canadian expenditures on health in the United States are incurred by Canadians on extended stays there—such as those spending the winter in Florida—and not those who cross the border to avoid delays in Canada.

Canada has publicly funded its universal health insurance since 1972 through shared financing by the federal government and the 10 provincial and two territorial governments. Each province and territorial authority administers its own program through a public agency according to federal standards. It covers all legal residents in all provinces for necessary physician and hospital care.

The provincial governments are the single payers of doctors and hospitals in Canada, in contrast to the American system in which reimbursement may be from the national or state governments, insurance companies, self-insured companies, or private payers. Since there is universal coverage, doctors are confident of reimbursement without wrestling with eligibility criteria, a bewildering variety of forms, and different rules for different situations or locations. In this single-payer system there are no deductibles or copayments for covered services.[56] Nor is coverage in Canada linked to employment. It is portable, and this enhances job mobility.[57] The single-payer system eliminates the costs of marketing competitive health insurance policies, evaluating and pricing insurance risks, and billing and collecting premiums. This has kept its administrative costs very low, which account for just under 2 percent of Canadian health expenditures compared to about 7 percent of U.S. health expenditures. According to a study by the American federal government's General Accounting Office (GAO) of Canadian health insurance:

> If the universal coverage and single-payer features of the Canadian system were applied in the United States, the savings in administrative costs alone would be more than enough to finance insurance coverage for the millions of Americans who are currently uninsured. There would be enough left over to permit a reduction, or possibly even the elimination, of copayments and deductibles, if that were deemed appropriate.[58]

Since everyone is guaranteed access to medical care on the same terms and conditions, they are treated much more equitably than in America where ability to pay is a major factor in determining treatment. There is no means testing for eligibility as there is for Medicaid in the United States. Private health care insurance in Canada is often a corporate benefit for those levels of benefits not covered under the NHI program such as dental services or semiprivate rooms in hospitals.

---

[56] User charges and extra-billing are forbidden by law to make certain that patients will not be forced to forgo care because of out-of-pocket expenses.

All residents are entitled to insured health care services. A province may not require a residency period of more than 3 months for entitled coverage. And Canadians moving from one province to another must continue to be insured by their home province during any waiting period imposed by the new province. Canadians with health problems requiring care while traveling in other provinces are covered by the insurance plan of their home provinces during that period.

[57] It also benefits employers who can hire employees who best fit their needs without regard to whether someone is a high-health-risk hire or has a preexisting medical condition that might affect the company's insurance costs.

[58] General Accounting Office, *Canadian Health Insurance: Lessons for the United States* (Report to the Chairman, Committee on Government Operations, House of Representatives) (Washington, DC: U.S. Government Printing Office, June 1991), p. 3.

Canada has achieved universal health care coverage while spending about 31 percent less per capita than in the United States.

Interestingly, physicians in Canada make individual medical decisions for their patients with fewer constraints than physicians in America, who often need second opinions, utilization reviews, and managed care determinations. The supply of physicians in Canada is approximately the same as in the United States.[59]

Rapid increases in health care costs and rapid growth in managed care plans' costs have accompanied efforts to strengthen competition in health care delivery along with an upward spiral in the number of uninsured. This has led many to conclude with The Center for National Health Program Studies at Harvard Medical School that

> Bill Clinton should abandon the failed pro-competition policy of the past decade, and its reincarnation, managed competition. He should instead embrace a single payer national health program similar to Canada's. Without further bankrupting the states or the federal government, this could eliminate the shameful spectacle of tens of millions of uninsured Americans despite annual health expenditures of $817 billion.[60]

Critics of the Canadian system generally acknowledge its impressive accomplishments, but argue that some of its claimed successes are somewhat exaggerated. In particular, they suggest that part of the success in holding down medical costs in Canada is due to demographic characteristics such as a lower poverty rate and a younger average age for the population. Critics also point out that per capita spending on health care is rising about as fast in Canada as in the United States.[61]

---

[59] There are actually slightly more physicians per capita in Canada than in the United States. The medical education and training in Canada is so similar to that in America that U.S. graduates of Canadian medical schools are not considered "foreign medical graduates" on their return to the United States. Canadians make more physician visits per year (5.5 versus 4.6) and have longer hospital stays (14.4 days versus 7.2 days in 1987) than in the United States. Physicians in Canada receive high incomes. In 1984 their income was roughly five times that of the average industrial worker (U.S. physicians' incomes were about five and a half times the average industrial wage). However, between 1971 and 1985 Canadian physician fees decreased 18 percent while U.S. physician fees rose 22 percent. As GAO has pointed out, lower physician fees do not necessarily mean lower net incomes under the single-payer system. Canadian physicians do not maintain office staffs for insurance record keeping, patient billing, or collecting bad debts, so that in 1987 Canadian physicians on average spent 36 percent of their gross income on professional expenses, compared to 48 percent for their American counterparts. Also, malpractice insurance premiums for U.S. physicians average 10 times those for Canadian physicians. See GAO, *Canadian Health Insurance: Lessons for the United States*, pp. 5, 37.

[60] Himmelstein et al., *The Growing Epidemic of Uninsurance*, p. 5.

[61] In comparing international health care expenditures, analysts often use real per capital health care costs and the percentage of GDP going to health care. If growth in real health care expenditures per capita is used, then Canada and the United States have had similar degrees of success in controlling costs. If we use the percentage of GDP going to health care as the measure, Canada has been much more successful than the United States.

Which measure is more meaningful for public policy analysts? Analysts generally measure success in containing health care costs as a percent of GDP. Since health care spending will generally increase at the same rate as GDP, the higher rate of growth in Canadian GDP should have resulted in higher rates of growth in real health care spending than in the United States. Since this has not occurred, it suggests that Canada has successfully controlled its costs. But in the United States, health care has been absorbing an increasing share of a more slowly growing GDP. See The Urban Institute, "Measuring Health Care Costs in Canada and the United States," *Policy and Research Report*, vol. 22, no. 1 (Winter/Spring 1992), pp. 23–24.

The United States could adopt the Canadian model essentially by extending Medicare to all Americans (although even Medicare has deductibles and copayments), but it would not be an easy task because of the low level of trust in public programs in America. Government control in America is perceived generally as undesirable and an unnecessary shift from private to a public responsibility. Canadian culture stresses the common welfare in contrast to the American emphasis on individualism. President Clinton acknowledged the dilemma when he said,

> If you want universal coverage, you could go to the Canadian system. The problem is that no one I know thinks you could pass that in Congress, which means you basically replace all the health insurance sector of the country with a tax.[62]

Adoption of an NHI plan would result in income redistribution in favor of those who are mostly poor and have no health coverage. Instituting NHI would relieve employers of the health insurance premiums they now pay. While employers would be the initial beneficiaries, economic theory suggests that those gains would eventually shift to workers in the form of higher wages and fringe benefits. In turn, those gains would be offset by higher taxes on businesses and individuals to pay for NHI. Many people would feel that they were being taxed for what they had previously considered a fringe benefit. The shift from employer to tax-financed health insurance is a major stumbling block to adopting national health insurance in the United States.

CONCLUSION

1 The current debate over health care is about values and priorities in America. A primary question is whether we as a nation should recognize health care as a **right** and not a **privilege** for those who can afford it. As noted, almost all industrialized nations recognize health care as a right. If there is a consensus that health care should be a **right**, then society has a collective **obligation** to provide some agreed-upon standard level of care. The market forces in health care are unable to provide the access that a **right** demands. Nor do market forces provide the cost control that the economic well-being of society requires.

2 There are many who are apprehensive about whether government can run a more efficient system and maintain control over costs. Others point out the success of the public sector in running programs ranging from defense to police protection. Seeking government action to implement the collective will in health care is no different, they claim—in fact, government inaction, as in the savings-and-loan scandal, is the problem. They think the remedy is for government to shoulder its responsibility, not shirk it.

3 Most Americans have health insurance that relieves them of significant out-of-pocket expenses when they are sick. They are inclined, therefore, to overutilize health services. Health care providers also have an incentive to provide every service available. The use of low-benefit high-cost services encourages the develop-

---

[62] Remarks by the President to the Annual Conference for Business and Social Responsibility, Washington, DC, October 21, 1993.

ment of increasingly costly high-tech medicine that drives up health care costs. The result is that growing numbers of Americans are uninsured or underinsured and worry about their economic security being threatened by an unpredictable need for expensive health care. Many others with adequate insurance are fearful that it could be lost.

4 Americans are clearly concerned about rising health care costs, especially in light of recent declines in private coverage and levels of medical insurance benefits. Any change will require compromise on the part of the interests of the health care providers, insurers, and health care consumers. Changes in health care delivery, which currently constitutes over 13 percent of GNP in the United States, will create winners and losers. The major players involved vigorously defend their interests so they will not be any worse off after changes are adopted. While most Americans support the ideal of health care as a right, they are distrustful of government's ability to manage such a system, nor do they want taxes raised significantly to pay for it.

5 The logic of incrementalism means that comprehensive reform along the lines of the Canadian model has little likelihood of passage, despite its promise of overall savings while providing universal coverage. Reform proposals that build on the current system of private insurance have the greatest chance of success. But any meaningful extension of coverage will require more government involvement in the regulatory process.

6 An initiative to expand health care coverage to the unemployed and the poor must be paid for by new financing mechanisms such as a value-added tax. This must of necessity be accompanied by effective cost-containment measures. Ultimately, payments for the services of physicians and other health care providers will have to be restrained. Hard decisions will eventually have to be made concerning which health care procedures produce benefits too negligible for the costs involved.

7 Managed competition, if fully implemented, provides hope for realistic cost controls through negotiations by insurers with providers on behalf of large groups. Any program that covers those who are currently uninsured will initially require additional government spending. The greatest danger is that mild tinkering with the present system will retain its inefficient aspects while abandoning some of its strengths.

QUESTIONS FOR DISCUSSION

1 Should health care be a right or a privilege? Why?
2 Why are health care costs rising faster than the rate of growth in the GNP?
3 Why have market forces reduced health care access for the poor and driven health care costs up?
4 Why have insurance companies shifted from risk sharing to risk avoidance?
5 How would you define the goals of national health care policy? If you were a benevolent dictator, how would you try to achieve your goals?

KEY CONCEPTS

Adverse selection

Community rating

Cost shifting

Diagnostic-related groups (DRGs)

ERISA

Experience rating

Fee for service

Health maintenance organizations
  (HMOs)

Independent practice associations
  (IPAs)

Managed care

Managed competition

Medicaid

Medicare

Medigap

Moral hazard

Play or pay

Preferred provider organizations
  (PPOs)

Resource-based relative value scale

Self-insured

Third-party payer

SUGGESTED READINGS

Henry J. Aaron, *Serious and Unstable Condition: Financing America's Health Care* (Washington, DC: The Brookings Institution, 1991).

Congressional Budget Office, *Selected Options for Expanding Health Insurance Coverage* (Washington, DC: Government Printing Office, 1991).

David U. Himmelstein et al., *The Growing Epidemic of Uninsurance: New Data on the Health Insurance Coverage of Americans* (Cambridge, MA: The Center for National Health Program Studies, Harvard Medical School, December 1992).

M. Susan Marquis and Stephen H. Long, "Uninsured Children and National Health Reform," *Journal of the American Medical Association*, vol. 268, no. 24 (December 23/30, 1992), pp. 3473–3477.

Mark Merlis, *Controlling Health Care Costs* (Washington, DC: Congressional Research Service, January 26, 1990).

Mark Merlis, *Health Insurance: Summaries of Legislation in the 102d Congress* (Washington, DC: Congressional Research Service, 1992).

Wendy E. Parmet, "The Impact of Health Insurance Reform on the Law Governing the Physician-Patient Relationship," *Journal of the American Medical Association*, vol. 268, no. 24 (December 23/30, 1992), pp. 3468–3472.

Report of the Harvard Medical Practice Study to the State of New York, *Patients, Doctors, and Lawyers: Medical Injury, Malpractice Litigation, and Patient Compensation in New York* (Cambridge, MA: President and Fellows of Harvard College, 1990).

Frank A. Sloan, Randall Bovbjerg, and Penny Githens, *Insuring Medical Malpractice* (New York: Oxford University Press, 1991).

12

ENVIRONMENTAL POLICY: DOMESTIC AND INTERNATIONAL ISSUES

Until recently, many environmentalists have directed their efforts to persuading the public that there is in fact an environmental crisis. The increase in public concern about environmental issues is nothing less than a major change in attitudes. Measurable degradation of air and water quality, oil and sewage spills, and contaminated beaches and drinking water have served to dramatically focus our attention on growing stresses on the environment. Public opinion polls now regularly reveal that overwhelming majorities of Americans think more should be done to protect the environment.

Environmental policy is distinctive because of the scientific nature of the fundamental questions raised. Environmental issues are complicated and multifaceted. Environmental choices are often intertwined with consequences for energy policy. The technical nature of scientific debates may discourage some from trying to inform themselves on the issues. Nevertheless, energy and environmental issues have a very real impact on the average person's daily life. Those who support major initiatives typically want assured energy resources at reasonable prices with acceptable environmental consequences. This is very difficult to accomplish in fact.

INTRODUCTION

During the last two decades, the deterioration of the environment has moved from an issue of personal inconvenience to a major issue on the public policy agenda. People have become aware that population growth and the accompanying growth of industry and traffic congestion contribute to environmental damage. Air quality has deteriorated because of auto and industrial emissions. Smog has become a major problem not only for Los Angeles, but for most major cities of the nation.

Despite increased awareness and scattered efforts since the 1960s to pass legislation to protect the environment, environmental disruptions have surfaced with increasing frequency and urgency. Environmental issues have emerged in different forms, including projected scarcities of energy resources, damage from acid rain, deforestation and soil erosion, water shortages, depletion of the ozone layer which protects life from harmful ultraviolet radiation, and concerns about whether a "greenhouse effect" has started a long-term global warming trend.

EMERGING ENVIRONMENTALISM

The present-day concern with environmental issues has its roots in the conservation movement that began in the 1880s. The conservation movement was led by President Theodore Roosevelt and a few scientists and politicians who were largely motivated by a concern for resource conservation and management. It was driven by a fear of resource exhaustion and a need to manage natural resources before they were destroyed. This approach tried to make rational choices based upon utilitarian principles of "the greatest good for the greatest number," from an economic perspective. This movement did not have significant public support, and was largely viewed as elitist and antipopulist.

The Sierra Club and the Audubon Society were organized at that time to call attention to the environmental destruction caused by the unrestricted and destructive exploitation of the nation's resources. The preservationist movement had an interest in preserving the natural state of wilderness and scenic areas by creating national and state parks, and these groups began waging battles to create and maintain parks in resource-rich areas. Few political elites got involved, but neither did most Americans seem to take seriously the damage that unregulated growth and development was inflicting on the environment.

The publication of Rachel Carson's *Silent Spring* in 1962, warned of the effects of the concentration of toxins as they move up the food chain, and argued that a fragile balance in nature was being upset by the excessive use of pesticides like DDT—for example, on bird reproduction. She articulated the concerns for many who were troubled by environmental degradation and were struggling to comprehend its implications for our future.

Then in 1962 President Kennedy convened a White House Conference on Conservation. Kennedy and a Democratic Congress passed the Clean Air Act of 1963 despite fierce opposition led by the business community. The act had a complicated enforcement procedure that relied upon state action to initiate lawsuits against polluters. The Johnson Administration passed The Water Quality Act of 1965, which established national standards for water quality. Federal grants were made available to states for sewage treatment plants to improve water quality. But again conservatives wrote provisions into the law allowing states to formulate plans to meet the federal standards. Prior to 1970 the federal government provided technical advice and assistance and funding for specific environmental projects, while deferring to state governments as possessing the primary enforcement responsibility.

The increased public concern about the environment resulted in the passage of several pieces of legislation in the early 1970s. Both Republicans and Democrats vied with each other to prove themselves as the real champions of the environment.

Congress passed the National Environmental Policy Act of 1969 (signed by President Nixon on January 1, 1970), which required an Environmental Impact Statement (EIS) for any major federal construction. The EIS must show that government projects either will not significantly impact the environment or that satisfactory steps can be taken to mitigate damage. The Environmental Protection Agency (EPA), was created in 1970; prior to that, many different agencies in several federal departments, such as Interior and Agriculture, had responsibility for monitoring and regulating air and water pollution. The EPA was given the responsibility to enforce environmental laws ranging from toxic waste and air and water pollution to regulation of solid waste and pesticide use.

In 1970 Congress renewed the Clean Air Act and set national standards for ambient air quality. Congress also set a timetable for the reduction of auto hydrocarbon, carbon monoxide, and nitrogen oxide emissions. The 1970 act was intended "to protect and enhance the quality of the Nation's air resources so as to promote the public health and welfare."[1] The EPA was directed to promulgate National Ambient Air Quality Standards (NAAQS), in an effort to limit the amount of certain pollutants in the atmosphere that adversely affect public health. The pollutants cited were sulfur oxides, particulates, carbon monoxide, hydrocarbons, nitrogen oxides, and photochemical oxidants. The act required states to adopt plans to meet NAAQS requirements. After approval by the EPA, each state was required to enforce its plan. The EPA was given the authority to prepare and enforce a state plan if it did not meet federal requirements. The EPA was also to set exhaust emission standards for the auto industry and require the use of catalytic converters and the use of fuels with reduced lead.

The Water Pollution Control Act Amendments of 1972, passed over President Nixon's veto, attempted to limit the discharge of pollutants into navigable waters by 1985. It provided $25 billion in grants for local governments to build waste treatment plants and to install the best available technologies by 1983. The Clean Water Act of 1977 allowed for more flexibility in meeting compliance deadlines and effluent limitation requirements.

Industrial expansion after World War II resulted in the disposal of enormous amounts of solid and hazardous wastes into the atmosphere and water and on land. The potentially dangerous impact on the atmosphere and groundwater of hazardous waste dumping was apparent. Since the states controlled waste disposal, some industries were encouraged to shop for states with the weakest regulatory controls. Congress finally responded with the Resource Conservation and Recovery Act of 1976, which required that hazardous waste storage and disposal be regulated so as

---

[1] Pub. L. 91-604, 84 Stat. 1713 (1970).

to minimize the threat to public health and the environment. The EPA was authorized to establish standards for the disposal of hazardous waste.

The spate of environmental legislation in the 1970s was impressive in its magnitude and scope. One serious drawback in several pieces of legislation was that the EPA had to negotiate with states and local governments to obtain compliance. The agency did not have the personnel or the budget to force compliance in an efficient manner.

Nonetheless, many states began to complain that they were overburdened by these environmental laws. By the late 1970s, critics began complaining that environmental legislation was causing inflation and slowing down economic growth. Business and conservative groups began mounting a counterattack against environmentalists. They ultimately argued that, while the excesses of the past could not continue, "reasonable" future controls would allow the environment to purify itself. They pointed out how a certain amount of pollution is inevitable in a growing economy. Therefore, they claimed, the benefits of any environmental regulation must be balanced against the economic costs to business. There was general acceptance of the view that little additional legislation to protect the environment was necessary. Ronald Reagan wove these views into his campaign for President in 1980; he was not opposed to "reasonable" environmentalism, he said, but the government had gone too far. Government bureaucrats, especially at EPA and the Department of the Interior, were out of control on environmental issues, he claimed.

Ronald Reagan's campaign theme to get government regulators off the backs of business was a significant factor in his victory in 1980. He interpreted his victory as clear support for a reversal of the federal government's role in environmental protection. His administration moved immediately to repeal several regulations approved by the Carter administration. He appointed individuals, such as Ann Gorsuch Burford to EPA and James Watt as Secretary of the Interior, who were openly hostile the federal government's role in environmental policy.[2] Several thousand employees of the EPA were fired, including many attorneys experienced in environmental law. The entire staff of the President's Council on Environmental Quality, whose views were unapologetically proenvironment, was fired.

---

[2] Ann Burford had been a vocal critic of all environmental regulation from Colorado before going to EPA. Under her leadership, the EPA routinely approved states' requests for more autonomy from federal regulation in managing environmental programs. She was forced to resign in 1983 after evidence was made public that strongly suggested clandestine collusion between EPA and the industry it was to regulate. For example, the amendments to the Clean Air Act of 1977 regulating lead content in gasoline was based on public health concerns. Agency records showed that there had been 30 meetings between officials at the highest levels of EPA and the petroleum industry before setting leaded gasoline standards required by the 1977 amendments. However, EPA officials did not meet with public health officials or even request data on the effect of lead levels on health.

James Watt was a leader of the "Sagebrush Rebellion," which was an effort by businessmen, lobbyists, and state officials to pressure the federal government to ease federal regulation, and thereby the costs, of public land used by cattle, mining, and real estate interests. As Secretary of the Interior, he antagonized environmentalists by selling and leasing federal lands at a fraction of the commercial market value to mining and timber interests.

The reluctance of the Reagan administration to fulfill its obligations to enforce environmental law, and the uproar leading to and accompanying the eventual coerced resignations of Ann Burford and her assistant Rita Lavelle, forced Reagan to become more conciliatory toward environmentalists. Although his administration took a less hostile stance toward the environment, it did not propose any new initiatives.[3] It was less interested in protecting the environment than in encouraging industrial growth through reduced regulation.

In 1988 George Bush campaigned for vigorous action to improve the environment. He indicated that he wanted to be known as "the environmental President." Indeed, one of his more famous charges against his opponent, Michael Dukakis, was that he had not done enough to clean up the pollution of Boston Harbor. During the first two years of his term, President Bush supported amendments to the Clean Air Act, put areas of the U.S. coastline off limits for oil exploration, approved an increase in the EPA budget, and was generally supportive of other environmental issues.

Bush introduced a clean air proposal in 1989 which helped members of Congress whose clean air proposals had been beaten back by the previous administration. Ultimately Congress approved the Clean Air Act Amendments of 1990, which provided far stricter and more costly regulations for industry than those proposed by Bush. The legislation was signed into law by Bush and was designed to ensure that air quality throughout the United States would meet certain standards by reducing emissions from industry and motor vehicles, including pollutants that cause acid rain. It also set standards for phasing out chemicals that reduce ozone in the stratosphere.

Environmentalists became disenchanted during the last two years of George Bush's term, however. They charged that his administration undermined the most dynamic provisions of the Clean Air Act. A coalition of cities and business interests claimed that the costs of compliance with environmental regulations were too high. Vice President Quayle's Council on Competitiveness allowed businesses to appeal for a relaxation of environmental regulations if they were shown to raise costs. Based upon the council's recommendations, the government waived rules that would have restricted pollutants from the automobile, chemical, and pharmaceutical industries.

In addition, Bush refused to support an environmental treaty at the "Earth Summit" held in Rio de Janeiro in June 1992 until its provisions designed to slow global warming were watered down. He also refused to sign a second treaty at the same meeting designed to protect endangered species.

In the 1992 Presidential campaign, Bush dismissed his Democratic opponents, Bill Clinton and Al Gore, as dangerous "environmental crazies." Then candidate Clinton campaigned on a pledge to be an activist on the environment. Gore had

---

[3] Congress passed the Water Quality Act of 1987 over Reagan's veto. It required states to identify waters that are not expected to meet water quality standards and approve tactics for reducing pollution in such waters. The Hazardous and Solid Waste Amendments of 1984 called for banning all land disposals of untreated hazardous waste.

already written a book, *Earth in the Balance*, in which his basic premise was that the choice presented between jobs and the environment is false. Gore argued that American industry's failure to invest was the primary cause of job loss, and that environmental problems demand serious attention. This reversed Reagan-Bush administration arguments that most government environmental regulations are excessive and unwarranted impediments to economic growth.

MARKET FAILURE AND THE ENVIRONMENT

Government has a function of providing the legal framework within which economic activity takes place. **Governments also have a role to play when markets fail to produce efficient outcomes**. Here we focus primarily on negative externalities and their relation to energy resource consumption and the closely related concern of environmental protection. One of government's primary policy roles is to provide remedies for the inefficiencies resulting from externalities. In an earlier chapter we noted that **externalities exist when a producer or a consumer does not bear the full cost (negative externality) or receive the full benefit (positive externality) of economic activity**. Externalities result in costs or benefits for third parties.

Keep in mind that externalities do not pass through the market system. Thus the market cannot allocate them. The fact that externalities, whether positive or negative, do not pass through the market system, results in some of our most intractable problems.

This point is worth emphasizing since the American preference for markets is based upon the principle of consumer sovereignty. But the production of certain goods and services has significant effects on people other than those directly involved in buying or selling the goods, since certain of their costs are being transferred to unwilling consumers.

Pollution is the obvious example of an externality problem. Pollution is the production of wastes that we do not want, such as industrial wastes, smoke, congestion, or noise. These externalities exist for two reasons. The first is technical: We do not know how to produce some goods without waste products. Second, even if we do know how to produce goods without waste, their production or consumption may be very expensive without those externalities. For example, an automobile manufacturer may find it cheaper to drain industrial waste into a nearby river than to ship it to a waste dump or detoxify it. Neither the factory owners nor their customers pay for this use of the river. The river is a scarce resource, however, and degrading it does not take into account the rights of those downstream to use it to fish, swim, or enjoy it for other forms of recreation or aesthetic beauty. Consequently, the cost of the pollution is borne by the public at large.

This is an **external cost**—a cost not reflected in market prices. **That cost, moreover, is imposed on the public without its consent**. In the example given above, since the cost of such pollution is not reflected in the price of the automobile, the factory will tend to produce more cars (and pollution) than is socially desirable.

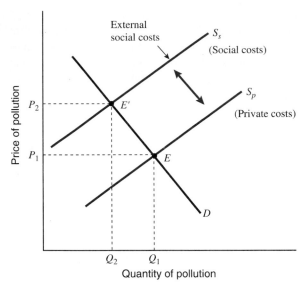

FIGURE 12-1
Equilibrium of a market with negative externalities (pollution).

The inefficient allocation of resources caused in this way is shown in Fig. 12-1. A market with external costs (negative externalities) allocates resources inefficiently. P_1, the **private marginal cost** of producing cars, the cost borne only by the producer, does not include all opportunity costs of production. The **social marginal costs**—the marginal costs of pollution—exceed the **private marginal cost**. Although the market price is at E, the efficient allocation of resources is found at Q_2 and the price at E'.

Thus there arise demands for the government to intervene and change the market outcome through laws and regulations. Those who argue against government intervention to control externalities emphasize that business is, or can be, socialized to be responsible through voluntarism. But there are many instances where feelings of social responsibility and voluntarism are not sufficient. In the early 1960s despite mounting public pressure to reduce auto pollution, car manufacturers lobbied against legislation to mandate pollution control devices. The auto makers in a public relations campaign gave assurances that they were conducting research, but solving the problem was extremely difficult. In 1963, California passed a law requiring pollution control devices on all new cars sold in California 1 year after a state board certified that at least two systems were available at reasonable cost. California certified four devices, made by independent parts manufacturers, and mandated their requirement on 1966 model cars. Although automobile manufacturers had insisted that they would not be able produce such devices before 1967 at the earliest, they announced that they would be able to install emission control devices on their 1966 model cars.[4]

[4] Lawrence White, *The Regulation of Air Pollutant Emissions from Motor Vehicles* (Washington, DC: American Enterprise Institute, 1982), p. 14.

We have already seen how positive externalities, such as those resulting from education, will tend to be undersupplied in the market. In such cases government may respond to raise output to a socially optimal level by subsidizing their cost through student loans or research programs. Likewise, government must oversee solutions to negative externalities. As Fig. 12-2 suggests, economic efficiency requires greater expenditures on environmental protection than would occur in a free market. The equilibrium price (E) does not include the positive benefits received by others. If a firm installs pollution control equipment in its smokestacks, it will have a social marginal benefit higher (E') than its private marginal benefit. A firm that takes only its private interests into account will operate at point E, and not voluntarily install equipment to provide a situation where marginal social benefits equal the marginal costs for society (E').

A major public policy role for the government, then, is to correct for market inefficiencies that result from externalities.

ENVIRONMENTAL PROTECTION AND RATIONAL CHOICE

Policy Debates on Environmental Issues

As with other public policy issues examined in this book, there is spirited debate regarding what role, if any, the government should play in environmental policy. Most people admit to being concerned about environmental degradation at some threat level. But individual views differ markedly about the perceived level of threat to the environment from different sources (such as global warming, ozone depletion, or deforestation). Experts often differ regarding the nature of the threats as

FIGURE 12-2
A market with positive externalities will be undersupplied.

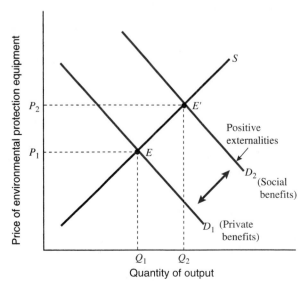

well as the most effective responses to the threats. Frequently, there is sufficient scientific uncertainty to allow people to reach different conclusions based upon the same evidence.

Global Warming: Clear Facts and Hazy Conclusions

For well over a century scientists have speculated about the potential for worldwide climatic changes brought about by the effects of human activity on the composition of the earth's atmosphere. Results from the scientific study of the environmental effects of greenhouse gas (GHG) concentrations have entered the policy debate of the 1990s. **Greenhouse gases refer to atmospheric gases that are almost transparent to incoming solar energy, but trap infrared energy reflected from the earth's surface**. There are about 20 such gases, but scientists primarily focus on carbon dioxide (CO_2), methane, nitrogen oxides, and chlorofluorocarbons (CFCs).[5]

As solar radiation, or heat from the sum, approaches the earth, a fraction is absorbed by the atmosphere and by the earth's surface; the rest is reflected back into space. GHGs permit solar radiation to pass relatively freely to the earth's surface, but then trap significant amounts of solar heat in the atmosphere that would otherwise be reflected back into space. About 30 percent of the solar radiation that reaches the earth is absorbed and the rest is reflected back into space. Without atmospheric gases to prevent some radiation from escaping, the earth would be about 0 degrees Fahrenheit. The GHGs produce the greenhouse effect, which warms the earth's temperature to an average of about 60 degrees Fahrenheit.

Scientific studies confirm that GHG concentrations in the atmosphere are rising due to a variety of human activities. This suggests the **global warming theory**, which holds **that the earth is being warmed because of an increase in carbon dioxide and other trace gases in the atmosphere. This increase is caused by the burning of fossil fuels, deforestation, and other industrial practices**.

Global warming theory is based on undisputed scientific information, and the world's climate scientists share a consensus that the greenhouse effect, magnified by human activity, will lead to global warming. The Intergovernmental Panel on Climate Change (IPCC) issued an "early warning" of this view in May 1990. The IPCC met again in early 1992 to consider whether its "early warning" could be verified. Although the scientists concluded that "global warming" was substantiated, negotiations on a Global Climate Convention ended in stalemate. This occurred largely because the United States and several oil-producing countries insisted that sufficient doubt about global warming had been raised making the effort to set limits on carbon dioxide emissions too drastic. Some scientists, although a minority, criticized the IPCC for putting forth a global warming **worst-case scenario**. In

---

[5] The scientific evidence is clear that the concentration of these gases in the atmosphere is rising due to a variety of human activities. GHCs absorb and radiate heat back to earth at different rates. Carbon dioxide is the major GHC, entering the atmosphere through the burning of fossil fuels in automobiles, aircraft, home heating fuel, and factories. Chlorofluorocarbons make up a much smaller portion of GHGs, but have radiative properties giving them a warming potential several thousand times greater than CO_2.

ACID RAIN

Acid rain refers to the process by which sulfur dioxide and nitrogen oxides are pumped into the atmosphere by coal-fired electric utilities, industrial furnaces, and motor vehicles, where they combine with water vapor and return to earth either as acidic rain or in a dry form. While electric utilities are responsible for over two-thirds of all sulfur oxides, motor vehicles are responsible for over 40 percent of all nitrogen oxide emissions in the United States. Sulfur dioxide is about twice as acidic as nitrogen oxides. Predictably, NO_x emissions are more evenly dispersed around the nation than sulfur oxides, which are concentrated in the Ohio Valley. However, by building high smokestacks, electric utilities and industries in the Ohio Valley have reduced local sulfur oxide concentrations. These oxides are then usually carried by the prevailing winds for hundreds of miles in a northeasterly direction before returning to earth in precipitation.

Acid rain contributes to the deterioration of metal and stone in buildings and statues. It has also been linked to health problems like asthma, emphysema, and chronic bronchitis. The New England states and Canada have linked the acidity of rivers and lakes with the destruction of aquatic life and the killing of many forest trees to emissions originating in the Ohio Valley. Canada has expressed its exasperation with what it considers to be American insensitivity over the need to reduce sulfur oxide emissions.

The amendments to the Clean Air Act of 1990 did establish goals and deadlines for a two-phase reduction in sulfur dioxide emissions, reduced NO_x emissions, and "caps" on future sulfur dioxide emissions; they also created a system of marketable "allowances" for allocating reductions from different emissions sources.

Source: This account relies heavily on Thomas H. Moore, "Acid Rain: New Approach to Old Problem," *Editorial Research Reports*, no. 9 (March 9, 1991). *Note:* Acidity is measured by a pH scale which ranges from 0 to 14. A reading of 0 is most acidic, while 7 is neutral. A pH reading above 7 indicates alkalinity. Unpolluted rainfall is slightly acidic and has a pH level of about 5.6. "Acid rain" is considered to be precipitation with a pH reading below 5.6. Some acid rain falling in the eastern United States has a pH in the range of 3.5.

response, scientists arguing the case for global warming insisted that the minority advancing the **best-case scenario** was getting ample media coverage simply by advocating the minority view.[6]

What are the scientific arguments associated with global warming? To effectively assess the risks involved, we need to examine several questions. How accurate are the climate models? For those scientists concerned about the potentially dangerous aspects of global warming, what is their worst-case scenario? If global warming is occurring, is it primarily the result of human activity? What is the best-case scenario? In the range between the two extremes, what is a best-estimate scenario?

There is no dispute about the upward trend in the concentration of GHGs in the atmosphere over the last century. It is also accepted that, all other things being

[6] Jeremy Leggett, *The Bulletin of the Atomic Scientists* (June 1992), pp. 28–33.

equal, an increase in the amount of GHGs in the atmosphere would be expected to raise the average temperature of the earth. But the amount of increase is not certain. Some models suggest that increasing concentrations of GHGs over the next century will raise the earth's average temperature between 2.5 and 5.5 degrees Celsius.

Scientific efforts to verify the theory face difficulties. For example, the average temperature appears to have risen in the United States over the last century by less than 1 degree Celsius. Yet even this is not certain.[7] Scientists question the accuracy of thermometers in the past. Temperature readings around cities are suspect as cities retain more heat. Consequently, over time official temperature readings have been moved from urban areas to weather stations located in airports outside of cities.

Other data provide strong evidence of long-run climatic fluctuations. Yet skeptics suggest that the trends are **inconclusive**.[8] Other critics point out that some of the computer-based climatic models are still too primitive to provide accurate extrapolations into the future. Ice core samplings taken from Greenland and Antarctica reveal that the earth's climate has fluctuated much more rapidly in the past although what caused the fluctuations is not clearly understood.

Global warming may represent an environmental threat of catastrophic proportions. If alpine and polar glaciers melted from higher temperatures, sea levels would rise. Higher temperatures would also expand the world's surface waters, increasing the volume of seawater. Estimates indicate that by the year 2100 a global-warming-induced rise in the sea level of 1 meter is likely.[9] Bangladesh, Egypt, Indonesia, Thailand, and India have already suffered significant land erosion of low-lying regions from rising sea levels. Even higher sea levels would result in more destructive hurricanes, storm surges, and greater land erosion.

The International Geophysical Union commissioned a survey which revealed that erosion is particularly widespread along the world's sandy coastlines. Over 70 percent of them have receded in the last 25 years. Greater erosion in coastal areas will weaken natural storm barriers while simultaneously decreasing the effectiveness of natural and artificial drainage. Much larger portions of coastal cities in the United States like Miami, New Orleans, and Charleston, South Carolina, will lie within the 10-year floodplain.

Rising sea levels present grim choices for policy makers. They are very stark and clear: Retreat from the sea's encroachment, or try to fend it off. Over the years homes and businesses have been built closer to the ocean. Estimates of the cost to

---

[7] An effort to calculate the uncertainties is found in William D. Nordhaus, *Uncertainty about Future Climate Change: Estimates of Probable Likely Paths* (New Haven: Yale University, Department of Economics, January 1990).

[8] Others suggest the burden of proof should be reversed. They cite, for example, the fact that six of the seven warmest years on record have occurred since 1980. James Hansen of NASA's Goddard Institute for Space Studies states that the relationship between the greenhouse effect and global warming is becoming harder to deny.

[9] Predictions are wide-ranging because so much remains unknown. For example, other studies suggest that the increase might be less, because a warmer Antarctica would actually result in more snowfall there. That would actually enlarge the Antarctic ice sheets and offset melting glaciers in other areas and result in a sea level rise of about 2 feet. See Richard Monastersky, "Predictions Drop for Future Sea-Level Rise," *Science News* (December 16, 1989).

POLLUTION AND PUBLIC HEALTH

Many pollutants are a serious threat to health. Over 2000 deaths per year from cancer are attributed to air pollution. The Harvard School of Public Health calculates that over 50,000 deaths a year are caused by particle pollution (particles of soot 10 microns or less in diameter that are inhaled). These particles are so small that they fall within legal limits of particulate pollution. The deaths occur mostly among asthmatics, children with respiratory problems, and the elderly with bronchitis, emphysema, and pneumonia.

Ozone pollution has reached levels dangerous to health in many cities in the last several summers. Ozone is produced at ground level when volatile organic compounds (VOCs), primarily from auto emissions, solvents, and industrial facilities, react with NO_x and sunlight. Since ground-level ozone is created by a chemical reaction in the atmosphere, the amount of it created is closely related to the weather. Ideal weather conditions for the formation of ozone include dry stagnant and hot conditions with intense solar radiation.[10] Ground-level ozone is acrid-smelling and toxic when it is a part of the smog around us.

Love Canal has come to symbolize the dangers associated with toxic waste, when chemicals including benzene, dioxin, and trichlorethylene contaminated the soil of school and housing areas along the canal in Niagara Falls.

Despite the dangers of pesticides highlighted by Rachel Carson and others, their use continues to grow. About 1 pound of pesticide for every person on the earth (5.6 billion people) is applied on farm crops every year. According to the UN World Health Organization (WHO), over 1 million people per year suffer health problems such as dermatitis, nervous disorders, and cancers. The U.S. National Cancer Institute has established a link between farmers who use a herbicide, 2,4-D and lymphatic cancer. The use of insecticides is often lethal to various animal species as well. For example, carbofuran, a toxic granular insecticide used on crops in the United States, kills well over a million birds that ingest the granules. Pesticide runoff kills well over 2 million fish in waterways.

The greatest health danger may come from nuclear waste. The civilian nuclear power industry has been unable to find a safe way to dispose of such waste. The problem is that it remains dangerous for hundreds of thousands of years. No permanent storage system has yet been devised that can isolate radioactive waste from the rest of the environment and that is satisfactory to those who support or oppose nuclear power.

[10] Susan L. Mayer, *Air Quality Trends: Effects of New Data on Compliance with Standards* (CRS Report for Congress, 92-783 ENR) (Washington, DC: Congressional Research Service, October 30, 1992), p. 8.

Sources: Shirley A. Briggs, "Silent Spring: The View from 1990," *The Ecologist*, vol. 20, no 2 (March/April 1990); Jack Lewis, "Superfund, RCRA, and UST: The Clean-up Threesome," *EPA Journal* (July/August 1991).

protect the current U.S. coastline against a 1-meter rise in the sea level are about $300 billion. Even then there are no guarantees the protective measures would work. Measures designed to be permanent frequently turn out to be only temporary. Efforts to protect one beach often displace the ocean's energies to a different coastal area. The alternative is to limit coastal development, and require property owners to bear the costs for property damage due to storms and flooding.

In regard to assessments of global warming overall, those supporting the best-case scenario argue that the earth has certain automatic stabilizers built in to counter the effects of rising levels of GHGs. They suggest that warmer temperatures will result in a greater cloud cover which will reflect more solar radiation back into space before it reaches the earth's surface. An analysis of ice extracted from deep in the Greenland ice sheet suggests that global warming could even unexpectedly trigger the rapid onset of cold spells. Scientists have generally assumed that there have been patterns in the earth's climate that changed only over long periods of time. They thought that ice ages were characterized by long periods of increased glaciation that gradually evolved into long periods of warmer weather. However, studies of ice core samples taken from Greenland and Antarctica now suggest that weather cycles were much less stable than previously thought. The samples show that there were wide temperature swings at surprising speeds for periods lasting from 70 to 5000 years. Perhaps as glaciers advanced, they reflected more solar radiation back into space and chilled the planet even more.[11]

Finally, those supporting the best-case scenario argue that global warming, if it does occur, may have several benefits. The evidence collected thus far indicates that global warming is causing warmer winters, while summers are practically unchanged. Also, the warming is greater the farther one moves from the equator. It is greater over land than over oceans and appears greater in the northern hemisphere. Demand for air conditioning would rise and demand for heating fuel would fall. The net effect of such warming would be to extend the growing season in some areas. Scientists also suggest that plants may respond to higher levels of carbon dioxide in the atmosphere by increasing their rate of photosynthesis and absorbing more CO_2 in the process. In effect, increasing CO_2 concentrations would have a fertilization effect on some crops and actually raise crop yields.[12] Consequently, while most analysts think that global warming is taking place, many do not think its effect will be entirely negative.

Policy Choices

If we wait until the global warming evidence is incontrovertible, **it may be too late** to prevent highly negative consequences.

On the other hand, some analysts conclude that the best available **data is too inconclusive** to justify drastic and expensive measures to stop global warming at

[11] David Dickson, "British Voters Force Rethink of Global Warming Strategy," *Nature*, vol. 364, no. 6437 (August 5, 1993), p. 472.

[12] See Clark S. Binkley, "A Cast Study of the Effects of CO_2-Induced Climatic Warming on Forest Growth and the Forest Sector: B. Economic Effects on the World's Forest Sector," in M. L. Parry, T. R. Carter, and N. T. Konijn (eds.), *The Impact of Climatic Variations on Agriculture* (Dordrecht, Netherlands: Kluwer Academic Publishers, 1988), Vol. 1, pp. 197–218.

A worst-case scenario counterargument is that the CO_2-induced fertilization may suffer because of lower levels of moisture in the soil, a larger number of forest fires, and higher levels of ultraviolet-B radiation due to ozone depletion.

the present time. It is nonetheless prudent to adopt policies that reduce global warming if these policies also provide economic benefits. The most obvious policy action would be to better monitor the environment and increase scientific research.

Raising public awareness of the potential environmental changes global warming may cause, their effects in human terms, and the costs to ameliorate them is also needed. Encouraging public debate on the implications of global warming builds support for moderate measures that would tend to reduce global warming at a relatively low cost. For example, policy makers might build a consensus for higher fuel taxes to check the wasteful use of fossil fuels.

Many scientists believe that the stakes are so high that a worst-case scenario is the only prudent policy perspective. They argue that policy makers typically design programs based upon a worst-case analysis when evaluating military threats, because if they do not and the worst case happens the results could be disastrous. They feel the same perspective should be adopted to reduce global warming so that situations do not arise which are irreversible. However, best-case scenario advocates point out that since scientific efforts to measure global warming have yielded ambiguous results, demand for government to "do something" are largely based on emotional arguments.

Ozone Depletion

The debate about ozone depletion is much more certain than global warming. Ozone is not discharged into the air by any source. **It is produced when ultraviolet (UV) sunlight splits an oxygen molecule and the resulting single oxygen atom combines with two-atom oxygen molecules forming a molecule with three-oxygen atoms (O_3).** Ozone is primarily **produced** over the tropics, where solar radiation is strongest, and then **diffused** through air circulation toward the polar regions. Therefore, ozone tends to be spread thinner at the poles. Ozone is an unstable atom. The only reason it exists in the upper stratosphere (12 to 25 miles above the earth's surface) is because, until the last several decades, generally it did not come into contact with other highly reactive elements. Although we often refer to an "ozone layer," what actually exists is a diffusion of O_3 throughout the upper reaches of the stratosphere, not a "layer" of pure ozone. If the ozone in the stratosphere were compressed to surface pressures, the ozone layer would be less than $\frac{1}{2}$-inch thick.

The ozone in the upper stratosphere, however, is vital to life on earth. It filters ultraviolet-B (UVB) rays. While ultraviolet radiation is necessary to synthesize vitamin D, it also damages DNA, which is the protein code necessary for cell reproduction. Animal and plant life on earth has adapted to "natural" levels of UVB. Without the ozone layer, much higher levels of UVB would reach the earth's surface, wiping out most life on the planet.

In 1985, a team of British and American scientists confirmed the existence of a hole in the ozone layer over the Antarctic which lasted for several weeks of the Antarctic spring. The following year Canadian scientists discovered a dangerous thinning of the ozone layer over the Arctic. Studies by the National Aeronautics and Space Administration (NASA) found by 1988 that the ozone layer around the entire globe was decreasing by 8 percent, a rate much faster than had been previously suspected.

The cause of ozone depletion has been known for several years.[13] **Chlorofluorocarbons (CFCs) are the great offenders**. CFCs enter the atmosphere from human-made products like refrigerants in refrigerators, aerosol sprays, solvents like carbon tetrachloride and methyl chloroform used primarily as cleaning agents in the electronics industry, and the materials used to make insulating plastic foam expand in products like styrofoam, food packaging, and foam cushions. Chemicals like Halon, used primarily in fire extinguishers, have a much greater ozone depleting potential than other CFCs.

CFCs, unlike ozone, are very stable and have expected lifetimes of 25 to 30 years per molecule before they disintegrate. They are insoluble and therefore unaffected by rainfall. Scientists estimate that it takes between 6 to 10 years for the average CFC molecule to reach the stratosphere by convection and diffusion. Once there, **UV radiation decomposes the CFCs, producing chlorine which acts as a catalyst in breaking down ozone**. The resulting chlorine atom is not used up in the process. Regenerated it can break down well over 100,000 molecules of ozone before it is destroyed.

Because of the long life cycle of CFCs and the time lag before they get to the stratosphere, the full effects of ozone depletion will not be felt for decades. Even if the production of CFCs were to end by the year 2000, the level of chlorofluorocarbons in the stratosphere would continue to increase until about the year 2015 when peak levels of UVB radiation would strike the earth. The persistence of CFCs in the atmosphere will prevent the "hole" in the ozone layer from filling in for at least 45 years. Ozone levels will not be restored before about 2075.

The discovery of ozone depletion led to predictions of sharply increased incidents of skin cancer and resulting deaths worldwide.[14] Data indicate that an increase in UVB will reduce plant yields especially of soybeans, the world's leading protein crop. Other studies have concluded that phytoplankton at the bottom of the food chain is susceptible to destruction by increased UVB exposure. Reduction of phytoplankton will reduce the food available to other fish and sea mammals.

In 1991, satellite data indicated that ozone was being depleted from the stratosphere at twice the rate reported only 3 years earlier. And in 1992, NASA released a study indicating that a "hole" in the ozone, comparable to that which has already appeared over the Antarctic, could appear over the northern hemisphere.

---

[13] Actually, as early as 1974 Sherwood Rowland and Mario Molina predicted that compounds called chlorofluorocarbons emitted into the atmosphere at ground level could drift up to the stratosphere where solar radiation would release chlorine which then would destroy ozone. Each chlorine molecule can destroy over 100,000 ozone molecules.
[14] Skin cancer is manifested in basal and squamous cell carcinomas. These nonmelanoma skin cancers are linked to the ultraviolet rays absorbed throughout a lifetime. They are usually disfiguring rather than fatal. Melanoma is less common, but is often fatal. The skin, the largest human organ, defends itself by producing melanin when exposed to the sun's rays, which acts to filter out UV.

Policy Choices

Ozone depletion, like global warming, is a problem of global proportions. As such it requires a response that includes not only a national commitment, but international efforts. CFCs come primarily from the wealthier nations of the northern hemisphere. Poorer nations produce only a small portion of the CFCs but they share the social costs. Thus the wealthy nations are imposing a negative externality on the rest of the world.

In 1978, CFCs in aerosol spray cans were banned by the Environmental Protection Agency. Intense lobbying by industry and a reluctant Reagan administration precluded any further regulatory activity. The 1985 discovery of the ozone "hole" over Antarctic alarmed scientists and aroused environmentalists around the world. Overwhelming pressure to take action resulted. The Montreal Protocol of 1987 represented an agreement by 34 countries to reduce the production of CFCs by 50 percent by the year 2000. In 1988, NASA announced that research indicated the ozone layer was being depleted at a faster rate than previously thought. The Montreal Protocol was amended to **completely phase out the production of most CFCs by the year 2000**. The protocol provided funding of $250 million, provided by the developed countries to assist the developing nations in their switch to non-CFC-producing products. This protocol has now been signed by over 100 countries.

The Clean Air Act Amendments passed by Congress in 1990 represented a major break with the "benign neglect" attitude that previously characterized the policy toward ozone depletion. The bill required the EPA administrator to identify and, within 2 years of enactment, bar the sale of distribution through interstate commerce of nonessential products that release Class I substances into the environment.[15] It also barred any person (effective January 1, 1994) from distributing or selling any aerosol product that contains any Class II substance or plastic foam product. It established a national policy of ending the production and use of CFCs and carbon tetrachloride by the year 2000. Methyl chloroform must be phased out by 2002. The EPA also issued a rule requiring car repair shops to use equipment that captures and recycles CFCs. Technicians servicing auto air conditioners must use EPA-certified equipment and be trained in the proper procedures for its use.

The commotion caused by the scientific findings of ozone depletion provided a momentum that overwhelmed the lobbyists working for the industries producing CFCs. Events conspired to keep them on the defensive, despite expressed concerns that environmentalists were magnifying the potential harmful effects of ozone depletion. All the evidence was not in, they argued, and the net result of these scare tactics would be to cause harm to American business.

However, supporters of the legislation argued that there was enough convincing evidence to take action. In this case, they pointed out, absolute proof was not necessary when the worst-case consequences could be catastrophic.

---

[15] Class I substances were defined in the Clean Air Act Amendments as all fully halogenated chlorofluorocarbons (CFCs), halons, carbon tetrachloride, and methyl chloroform.

Class II substances include those having a reduced ozone depletion potential, which means they can be used during a transitional phaseout period of all CFCs.

POPULATION

The sheer numbers of the world's population growth raises the specter of a collision between the expanding needs of human beings and the limits on the human ability to increase production. Understanding the relationship between population, pollution, and poverty is necessary before one can consider policies to deal with these issues.

Throughout most of human history, the population has grown very slowly with the net death rate nearly equal to the birth rate, both of which were high. *The crude birth rate minus the crude death rate equals the increase in population for that year.* Mortality has declined just as life expectancy has increased beginning in the late seventeenth century in Europe. Improving infant survival rates lead to potentially much larger populations to produce the next generation of children.

The world's population reached 1 billion around 1830. It took an entire century for it to reach 2 billion. Forty-five years later, in 1975, it doubled again to 4 billion. It now stands at 5.6 billion, and is growing by about three people every second, or more than **a quarter of a million people every day**. As an illustration, the world is adding a city the size of New York every month. Between 90 and 100 million people—roughly equivalent to the population of Mexico—will be added each year of this decade. A billion people, almost the population of China, will be added over the decade. Population growth tends to be much greater in the poorer countries. In some countries, the rate of increase is over 3 percent per year, which means the population will double within 20 years. The result is that social dislocations caused by population growth are more severe in the poorer countries, which also tend to have the fewest natural resources.

Poor countries have traditionally sustained high levels of population growth to support agricultural production. But the modernization of agricultural production in those countries has displaced labor-intensive sharecropping systems in favor of mechanized farms using seasonal wage labor. As a result, urban areas have grown rapidly as unemployed farm workers search for jobs in cities. Continued population growth in many poorer countries has led to overcultivation and the destruction of rain forests in a search for new arable land. Desperately poor people are often driven to further ravage the environment in their struggle to survive. In many cases, the consequence is an actual decline in per capita agricultural production and a further increase in poverty. The gap between rich and poor widens. Hence, all to often, agricultural development has not only failed to eliminate poverty but has increased it, with unfortunate consequences for population growth and the environment.

Almost one-third of the world's 5.8 billion people are age 14 or less. These potential parents are already alive and reaching their reproductive years. An international environmental disaster characterized by starvation, unemployment, poverty, and civil unrest is not idle speculation. The basic concern regarding population growth has been put forward by the U.S. Academy of Sciences and the U.K. Royal Society as follows:

> If current predictions of population growth prove accurate and patterns of human activity on the planet remain unchanged, science and technology may not be able to prevent

either irreversible degradation of the environment or continued poverty for much of the world.[16]

Because population growth rates are not evenly distributed around the world, there will be significantly altered population densities. For example, Europe and North America made up about 22 percent of the world population in 1950, but by 2025 they will make up less than 9 percent. By contrast, Africa, which made up 9 percent of the world's population in 1950, will make up approximately 20 percent in 2025. Over 90 percent of the global population growth over the next 35 years will occur in the developing countries of Africa, Asia, and Latin America.[17] The sheer numbers indicate that there will be an increasing impact on the environment.

There are two views of the ability of developing countries to adjust to changes in the environment and population growth to avoid economic decline. One is the **"Cornucopian"** position of Julian Simon, who opposes all attempts to restrain population growth. He believes that **people are the highest resource**, so it is unbelievable that a society can have too many people. According to Simon, people will use their creativity to develop technologies to provide for ever growing population. Cornucopians historically have been right in that technological progress has allowed most Western economies to avoid the dire warnings of Malthus because output grew faster than population.[18] Unfortunately many less-developed agrarian countries have not been able to avoid Malthusian predictions because of diminishing marginal productivity. As more people live on a fixed amount of land, the output per worker declines. Even though the economies are growing, per capita growth is negligible or even declining.

The other view is known as **"neo-Malthusian,"** and as its name implies, its proponents believe that in the long run population will exceed the means of subsistence. Populations will increase to the limit that natural resources can support.

Paul Ehrlich is a leading exponent of the neo-Malthusian view. He developed an "Impact Equation" to explain the relationship between human beings and their environment: $I = P \times F(P)$, *in which I is the total impact, P is the population, and F is a function which measures the per capita impact*.[19] The larger the population,

---

[16] U.S. National Academy of Sciences and the Royal Society of London, "Population Growth, Resource Consumption, and a Sustainable World" (Joint statement, February 27, 1992).

[17] Nafis Sadik, "World Population Continues to Rise," *The Futurist* (March/April 1991).

[18] In developed societies, food production has increased faster than expected because of technological improvements, and populations have grown more slowly than anticipated. Higher standards of living and improved health care have increased life expectancy and reduced infant mortality. These factors have contributed to population growth. They have been offset, however, by the fact that children become an economic liability in developed societies. This has encouraged family planning and has contributed to the stabilization of populations in developed countries.

Developing countries have also benefited from improved health care. There are fewer incentives for family planning in developing agrarian societies. In agrarian societies children are an economic asset as a source of labor. In countries without pension programs or social security, children may also be a source of support for parents in old age. As a result, family planning is not as popular in developing countries, and their populations are growing much faster than those in developed countries.

[19] Paul R. Ehrlich and John P. Holdren, "Impact of Population Growth," *Science*, vol. 171 (March 26, 1971), pp. 1212–1217.

the greater the impact on the environment. A world population of less than 1 billion people in the 1600s had less of an environmental impact than a population of 6 billion people at the end of this century. A larger population puts more stress on clean water and air than a smaller population.

In addition to the size of the population, lifestyles have an impact on the environment. The lifestyle of an individual in an affluent country like the United States creates more of an environmental burden than the lifestyle of the typical Ethiopian. Americans make up about 5 percent of the world's population but are responsible for producing over two-thirds of the world's atmospheric carbon monoxide and almost one-half of its nitrogen oxide emissions.

Many charge that there are ethical implications for such affluence. They argue that if Americans ate less meat, more land could be used to raise grain to feed hungry people abroad.

During the 1970s, the United States encouraged developing countries to voluntarily limit population growth before it began to seriously erode living standards. However, in the 1980s, Reagan-style conservatism opposed national family-planning programs.[20] The United States had been the major donor to the United Nations Population Fund (UNFPA) and the International Planned Parenthood Federation (IPPF) until the Reagan and Bush administrations withheld financial support from both. By withholding funds from the UN organizations, the United States refused to cooperate with multilateral efforts to reduce population growth. Some nations that are usually closely allied with the United States, such as Canada, the United Kingdom, Japan, and Germany, actually increased their donations to UNFPA to try to fill the void.

There are several reasons why the threat of population growth fails to attract our attention as a critical problem. The world's population grows by over *250,000 people a day, every day*. What networks report as **news** usually involves climactic occurrence rather than daily happenings. Nevertheless many of the consequences of overpopulation such as deforestation, malnutrition and starvation, and toxic waste do make the news on a daily basis.

Another reason overpopulation does not seem a serious threat is that Thomas Malthus' dire warnings of economic collapse resulting from growing populations have so far failed to materialize. While many aspects of the Malthusian analysis have proven wrong, Malthus did focus on at least two important points: that growing populations could be a problem, and that there is a relationship between the numbers of people and poverty. A growing population within a nation means that the national economy must grow by at least the same rate just to maintain the same standard of living. A country with a population growth rate of 2.7 percent a year must maintain economic growth of 2.7 percent just to maintain the status quo. Continual economic growth rates above that level are very difficult to maintain. It is rather like running up a down escalator. Since much of the population growth rate is occurring in underdeveloped countries, it means that their industrial revolutions

---

[20] See Garrett Hardin, "Sheer Numbers: Can Environmentalists Grasp the Nettle of Population?" in *E, The Environment Magazine*, vol. 1, no. 6 (November/December 1990), pp. 40–47.

can be undone by a Malthusian revolution. Another factor that militates against the perception that population growth is a problem is that many individuals and businesses benefit from population increases. Landlords, banks, manufacturers, and merchants all stand to benefit by providing a growing population with goods and services.[21]

Policy Choices

Population, poverty, and pollution are related in complicated ways. World population has grown beyond an optimal level of "carrying capacity" at the present stage of technological development. At least 1.5 billion people today, over 1 in 5, live in absolute poverty. Population growth rates tend to be much greater in poorer countries than in the developed countries.

People do create wealth and earn incomes. Without people there would be no wealth or income. But the more people there are, the greater the impact on the environment. And larger populations often reduce the income per person and the output of economic goods produced per worker. A country can reduce poverty (increase per capita income) by increasing income while holding its population constant, or by holding income steady while decreasing its population.

The commitment to work to reduce poverty is seen by many policy makers as a moral obligation. It is also necessary for the preservation of the environment and the health of the world economy. A healthy environment can more easily support the present or growing population than a devastated one. Policies to protect the environment are necessary to reduce poverty. Pollution and poverty are twin problems. **Economic development programs to reduce poverty must take into account the necessity of environmental protection. But it is not easy to work toward the seeming antithetical goals of reducing pollution while promoting economic development**. Poorer countries have few incentives to limit greenhouse gases. They do have an incentive to transfer the added costs of pollution to the global environment as an externality, giving themselves a cost advantage in the process.

Threats to the environment are global and thus require international cooperation. However, political power often lies with the wealthier members of society who have much at stake in accommodating the current economic interests of business leaders. Political leaders in most countries tend to remain fixated with narrow aspects of sovereignty and feel they are accountable solely to their domestic constituents. Moreover, nations differ in their contributions to environmental degrada-

---

[21] Hardin, "Sheer Numbers," p. 43. Lester Milbrath took a survey in which respondents were asked if they would prefer a society that emphasized environmental protection **over** economic growth or a society that emphasized economic **growth** over environmental protection. Business leaders were more likely to choose economic growth over environmental protection. In contrast the U.S. public chose environmental protection over economic growth by a ratio of 3 to 1 in 1982. When people were asked if they would prefer to live in a society that emphasized economic growth versus one that **limited** economic growth, they overwhelmingly chose economic growth. See Lester Milbrath "The World Learns about the Environment," *International Studies Notes*, vol. 16, no. 1 (Winter 1991), p. 15.

tion. The wealthier nations of the north make a greater per capita contribution to environmental degradation by emissions of GHGs through the burning of fossil fuels. In poorer countries overpopulation contributes to environmentally unsound deforestation. The destruction of watersheds by bringing less arable land under cultivation threatens many ecologically fragile areas, along with the economic viability of the countries in question.

The Clinton administration holds that population stabilization policies must have a high priority to stop environmental degradation. Improving the status of women is a part of this strategy. Women who are given a choice will have fewer children. The recent tribal violence in Rwanda occurred in a country with one of the highest fertility rates in the world. Its population grew at the rate of 3.6 percent per year between 1980 and 1990. There are more than 8 children for every adult female in Rwanda. The arable land has been so depleted that between 1980 and 1990 food production fell by 20 percent. Tribal and religious conflict is aggravated by a rapidly growing population in poverty. The poor have little to lose by violence.

To reduce world poverty, per capita income in poor countries must be raised. However, there is no realistic way poor countries can achieve the economic development needed for them to significantly raise their standards of living unless their population growth rates are decreased. During the Reagan-Bush years, the United States rejected the policy solution of encouraging birth control efforts in poor nations through the UN. The Clinton administration has since reversed that position and encouraged UN efforts to reduce high population growth rates.

Population control is an important first step in reducing poverty levels, but others are needed also. One possibility would be to encourage technology transfers of low-population, energy-efficient production procedures to poorer countries. In addition, subsidizing the investment costs of installing the equipment needed to implement those procedures would be beneficial.

POLICY RESPONSES

Politics is said to be the art of the possible. The task of the political scientist engaged in policy analysis, then, is to devise solutions derived from principles that different interests share. Policy responses that result in non-zero-sum solutions are generally to be preferred. For example, many businesses view environmentalists' concerns with alarm, fearing that any regulatory measures will drive costs up to intolerable levels. Business leaders tend to dismiss negative externalities as inevitable byproducts of market forces. Environmentalists, for their part, tend to view businesses as callous for pursuing profits without sufficiently considering the needs of the environment. The ideal solution would accommodate the needs of both sides, not sacrifice one set of needs to the other.

Command and Control

Diametrically opposed views such as those just described lead to bitter struggles and political polarization. Simply put, government finds itself pressured to outlaw a negative externality, even though many oppose any regulation. Thus the government may adopt **direct regulation in which it determines permissible levels of pollution, and may fine or shut down firms that exceed them** while allowing pollution by other firms that remains within the defined limit.

This regulatory technique is usually referred to as the **command and control** approach because it requires such heavy government involvement. It requires the government to determine the maximum safe level of emissions and then set uniform standards for every smokestack or waste pipe. Policy analysts are uncomfortable with it because the standards promulgated are usually "all or nothing" in nature and do not necessarily reach their stated goals as efficiently or as fairly as possible. The standards require every company to meet the same target regardless of differing costs. This is inefficient because some businesses may have to use more expensive technologies to control pollution than others. Perhaps more importantly, businesses have no incentives to reduce pollution below the standards set by the government. They have no incentives to develop or utilize technologies to exceed the regulated targets. Money that might be used to develop technologies to further reduce pollution is often diverted to fighting the standards or getting an exemption based on the threat of eliminating jobs if the standard is imposed.

Market Incentive Programs

Years of huge budget deficits, anemic economic growth, and sharp foreign competition have inspired searches for policies that reduce bureaucratic intrusion into business decisions. At the same time, policy makers wish to be sensitive to the need for cost-effective solutions to get a high rate of return for the regulatory effort.

Political scientists recognize that pollution externalities represent a failure of the market in which the production of a good exceeds the optimal level. Business and consumers tacitly agree to pass some costs on to the public. Since firms can pass the costs of pollution on to society, they have little incentive to consider them in business decisions. To the contrary, any firm that unilaterally tried to reduce external costs would be less competitive in the market. However, rather than rejecting market mechanisms as a source of help in favor of direct regulation, or forsaking pollution control by returning to laissez-faire economic policies, policy analysts recognize that market incentives might suggest creative solutions. **Market incentive programs try to make the market price of a good include the cost of any negative externality**.

There are several ways to ensure that environmental costs are included in *choices* made by firms and individuals.

Tax Incentives   **A tax incentive program uses taxes to provide incentives for individuals to pattern their behavior in a way that achieves the desired goals**. This tactic charges a fee (tax) on the amount of a good consumed that generates pollution, or imposes effluent charges. The threat of taxes are a stick to encourage the desired behavior to protect the environment.

For example, suppose that 100 gallons of gasoline are consumed each month in a society consisting of just three people. And suppose they mutually agree that total gas consumption should be reduced by 15 percent. Let us assume Mrs. A uses 50 gallons per month, Mr. B uses 35 gallons, and Ms. C uses 15. **Direct regulation** would require that each decrease their consumption by an equal amount (5 gallons each) or by an equal percentage (15 percent each) to achieve the reduction. The difficulty with this approach is that it does not reward anyone for saving more than he or she is required to save. It may be that Mrs. A could easily reduce her consumption by 10 gallons with little inconvenience, and Mr. B can easily reduce his by 15 gallons, while Ms. C has always been frugal and would find it difficult to reduce her consumption by more than $1\frac{1}{2}$ gallons (10 percent) per month.

On the other hand, if they agree to levy a tax of 25 cents per gallon on the gasoline they consume, each will have an incentive to reduce consumption. Mrs. A will likely reduce her consumption by 10 gallons (20 percent) and pay $10 in taxes, Mr. B will reduce his by 15 gallons (42 percent) and pay $5 in taxes, while Ms. C will reduce her consumption by $1\frac{1}{2}$ gallons and pay $3.38 in gas taxes each month.

In this illustration, the tax achieves the goal more efficiently than direct regulation. Since the incentive to conserve is included in the price, each person has to choose how much to reduce their consumption. Each is influenced by the marginal utility of consuming an additional gallon. Those who consume less pay less in taxes. The tax gives individuals an incentive to reduce their consumption as much as possible, and to find new ways of reducing consumption. For example, they may buy more fuel-efficient cars, use carpools, consider public transportation alternatives, or consider walking short distances instead of driving.

A variation on this market-based incentive is to provide a subsidy (a carrot rather than the stick). For example, a business could receive a tax credit for installing pollution abatement equipment, such as a scrubber, in a smokestack. Society is still better off, with less pollution, since the gap between the market price and the social costs is reduced. Businesses almost invariably will prefer subsidies to taxes. Policy analysts typically prefer tax incentives because they encourage companies to seek greater efficiency in reducing consumption or reducing pollution rather than just achieving a defined standard.

Marketable Permits   In the marketable permit approach, the government establishes an upper limit of allowable pollution and gives permits to businesses to emit some fraction of that total. If companies reduce their pollution (or consumption) below the level allocated to them, they receive a permit they can then sell to another firm that has chosen not to reduce its emissions to less than its allowable amount. For example, a utilities firm may want to expand production but under an emissions cap may be unable to do so unless it can purchase permits to increase its emission of pollutants.

This method is aimed at encouraging firms to significantly reduce their pollution in order to generate marketable permits for other firms that for one reason or another do not find such a reduction worthwhile. The 1990 Clean Air Act explicitly uses this market incentive to deal with pollution. The act provides for a 10-million-ton reduction in sulfur dioxide emissions from the 1980 level by the year 2000. Nitrogen oxide emissions must be reduced by 2 million tons under the 1980 level by the year 2000. The law also provides a cap limiting emissions to about 50 percent of 1990 levels by 2000. To meet these goals by the year 2000, the permits issued by the EPA are designed to reduce the amount of pollution allowed each year. Utilities will be forced to take a number of actions to reduce the levels of emissions: install scrubbers, switch to low-sulfur coal, implement conservation measures, close down obsolete plants, use renewable energy sources such as hydroelectric power where feasible, build new more efficient utilities and transfer the emission allowances to the new plant. The act also contains a system of pollution "allowances" that encourages utilities to exceed their required reduction of pollutants and recover their costs by selling their marketable certificates to other companies.

Assessing Policy Approaches

Market incentive policies like taxes, subsidies, and marketable permits are attractive to policy analysts for many reasons. They reduce the market inefficiency of pollution by discouraging undesirable activities that produce externalities. Pollution charges require businesses to share the burden of the costs of externalities, and therefore to include them in their daily business decisions. Firms for which pollution reduction is cheapest will reduce pollution more, while those for whom reduction is expensive will have to reduce it less. Such policies also make the price consumers pay for an externality more closely reflect its cost.

Since pollution cannot be reduced to zero, many see market-based incentives as a pragmatic approach to achieve the **optimal level of pollution. The optimal level of anything produced from a purely economic perspective is the point at which its price reflects the marginal costs of its production**. The difficulty is in accurately determining the marginal social cost of pollution and setting the incentives appropriately. If properly set, firms will pursue pollution abatement to the point that the marginal cost of pollution abatement equals the marginal social benefit control. If the tax is too low, firms will commit to insufficient environmental protection, while if it is too high, production of the good will be cut back too much.

Market approaches to controlling pollution are rapidly gaining acceptance among many involved in policy making. For example, many states have instituted market-based incentives known as "bottle-bills": A deposit must be made on the purchase of beverages in aluminum or plastic bottles, which is refunded when the empty containers are returned. The effect has been to reduce litter and promote recycling.

The Clinton administration has announced new land management policies requiring miners to begin paying royalties for mining gold and other metals on U.S. government-owned land. Timber companies will have to pay close to market prices to cut timber on federal land. Monthly grazing fees for farmers who wish to graze their cattle on federal land will be increased over a 3-year period from $1.86 per grazing unit (which is defined as a cow and a calf or five sheep) to $4.28. This is still a significant subsidy since the rate for grazing on private land ranged from $5 to $15 in 1993, depending on the quality of the land. The use of pesticides by farmers on U.S. land will be curtailed, and grazing leases can be terminated if ranchers violate the terms of the agreements.

Nevertheless, there is still significant skepticism regarding market-based incentives, for several reasons. Many environmentalists oppose them because it seems that selling permits to pollute legitimizes pollution. Many business firms oppose market approaches because they involve taxes which are associated negatively with government interference. Also businesses and their lobbyists often prefer direct-market regulation because they have become very effective at countering this approach. For example, they can appeal for a delay in the implementation of regulatory rules citing economic hardship and the possibility of layoffs due to increased costs, and often get what they want.

ETHICS AND ENVIRONMENTALISM

The appeal of market approaches to encourage environmentally sound policies is their efficiency. The market provides a framework in which trade takes place based upon the choices of individuals between a given supply and demand for goods. Through cost-benefit analysis the government can try to set policy while relying upon the *efficiency* of the market to be reproduced even as centralized government decisions aimed at protecting the environment are incorporated into the market process. This is built on the assumption that the policy goals embody an ethical *consensus* that can be promoted better by market mechanisms than by any other means.

There are problems with this utilitarian approach. Cost-benefit analyses are carried out by individuals, and individual preferences may provide a weak foundation for policy making. Individual preferences are the result of personal experiences, which are necessarily limited and based on incomplete information. Even if we were willing to accept individual preferences, we may have a problem in translating the aggregate conflicting preferences into a single policy decision. Another major objection to this form of utilitarianism is that it may result in decisions that are an affront to our sense of justice. Cost-benefit analysis would permit the loss of income of 30 families at $30,000 per year each rather than the loss of one person's income at $1 million. That is, cost-benefit analysis does not require (or preclude) us from taxing distribution. Cost-benefit analysis then cannot be the sole guide to decision making on environmental matters.

There are several ethical principles that should be included in any evaluation of costs versus benefits in policy making.

There should be a preference for policies that are not irreversible. Many policy choices will make it very difficult to go back and choose an alternative that was rejected. But policy choices should not be of the sort that irrevocably close out other options. For example, many conservationists feel that policies aimed at preserving endangered species from extinction should rank above those aimed at maintaining jobs since new jobs can be created but once a species is extinct its loss is irreversible.

Policies should give special consideration to those most vulnerable to the consequences of policy choices. For example, the poor may find themselves at the mercy of decisions made by the more economically powerful members of society. Dolphins, whales, or spotted owls are affected by human choices. And later generations will have to live with the results of decisions made today regarding the use of fossil fuels versus nuclear energy.

Policies should give a preference to strategies that provide the maximum sustainable yield of benefits. The most obvious application of this principle is setting maximum levels of fish catches. When no one owns the ocean, the fish, or the mammals such as whales that live within it, everyone has an incentive to exploit those resources but no incentive to manage or conserve them. The problem of the commons may be dealt with by setting up regulations and incentives to encourage the management of the common stock in question to its maximum sustainable yield. This principle is consistent with the goal of protecting those most vulnerable to the spillover effects of policy choices as well. Since later generations are vulnerable to present-day choices, setting maximum sustainable yields would guarantee that succeeding generations would be provided with benefits roughly equal to those enjoyed by those making the decisions today.

This principle would also encourage renewable energy sources such as solar, wind, and wave energy over the use of scarce nonrenewable forms of energy.

CONCLUSION

1 Environmental issues are often quite complex, involving substantial disagreement among scientists about the nature of the problems related to them. Political scientists have to be cautious when recommending specific solutions to such problems in part because of technical controversies.

2 Markets do not provide an efficient outcome when negative externalities exist because business firms have a market incentive to not take the marginal social costs into account in their business decisions. To do so would put them at a competitive disadvantage.

3 Political scientists involved in analyzing public policy typically prefer market-based incentives that encourage the desired behaviors over direct regulation by the government. Market incentive policies are more efficient than direct regulation in achieving policy goals.

4 The crucial problem in devising market-based programs is to determine the level of incentives needed to achieve the optimal policy outcome, which is where the marginal cost of the program equals its marginal benefit.

QUESTIONS FOR DISCUSSION

1 Why do the negative externalities of pollution occur?
2 What are the possible solutions for the market failure represented by pollution?
3 How can a business enterprise achieve both its own goals of greater productivity and

resulting higher profits and society's goal of protecting the earth against the negative consequences of individual and business activity?

4 How would a political scientist respond to the following suggestion: "Pollution is unacceptable and must be eliminated?"

5 Should governments try to reduce their nations' population growth rates? If so, what policies would you recommend?

KEY CONCEPTS

Acid rain
Chlorofluorocarbons
Clean Air Act
Cornucopian
Direct regulation
Environmentalism
Externalities
Global warming

Greenhouse effect
Marketable permits
Market failure
Market incentive programs
Merit goods
Neo-Malthusian
Population

SUGGESTED READINGS

Wilfred Beckerman and Jesse Malkin, "How Much Does Global Warming Matter?" *Public Interest*, (Winter 1994).

R. J. Berry (ed.), *Environmental Dilemmas: Ethics and Decisions* (New York: Chapman & Hall, Inc. 1993).

E. Bromley and M. Cernea, "The Management of Common Property Natural Resources: Some Conceptual and Operational Fallacies" (World Bank Discussion Paper No. 57) (Washington, DC: World Bank, 1989).

Lester Brown, *The Twenty-Ninth Day* (New York: W. W. Norton, 1978).

John Byrne and Daniel Rich, *Energy and Environment: The Policy Challenge* (Energy Policy Studies, Vol. 6). (New Brunswick, NJ: Transaction Publishers, 1992).

Paul R. Ehrlich, *The Population Bomb* (New York: Ballantine Books, 1968).

Paul R. Ehrlich and Anne E. Ehrlich, *Healing the Planet: Strategies for Resolving the Environmental Crisis* (Redding, MA: Addison-Wesley, 1991).

Albert Gore, *Earth in the Balance: Healing the Global Environment.* (Boston: Houghton Mifflin, 1992).

Garrett Hardin, *New Ethics for Survival* (New York: Viking Press, 1972).

Michael W. Hoffman, Robert Frederick, and Edward S. Petry, *Business, Ethics, and the Environment: The Public Policy Debate* (New York: Quorum Books, 1990).

Michael J. Lacey, *Government and Environmental Politics* (Baltimore: The Johns Hopkins University Press, 1991).

Francesca Lyman, "As the Ozone Thins, the Plot Thickens," *The Amicus Journal*, no. 13 (Summer 1991).

Patrick Michaels, *Global Warming: Failed Forecasts and Politicized Science* (St. Louis, MO: Center for the Study of American Business, July 1993).

Linda Starke (ed.), *State of the World, 1994: A Worldwatch Institute Report on Progress Toward a Sustainable Society* (New York: W. W. Norton, 1994).

13

AMERICAN FOREIGN POLICY

Foreign policy making has usually been studied in the United States as a field of specialization separate from the making of domestic public policy. The distinction builds on the idea that foreign policy concerns higher "national" rather than lower "special" interests. It further rests upon the notion that foreign policy questions frequently involve governmental organizations that focus primarily on foreign issues which elicit different political reactions. Indeed a "primacy" for foreign policy as the most important area of public policy has been claimed.

Economic issues today are increasingly replacing international political and military strategies as dominant issues on the foreign policy agenda. With the collapse of the Soviet Union, economic development and international trade questions have replaced the concern with possible nuclear military conflict. The clear distinction between foreign and domestic policy is less apparent. This shift has been accompanied by an increased participation by Congress in the debate and more involvement by the general public.

INTRODUCTION

This chapter examines the characteristic traditions of American foreign policy. Why did the United States pursue a policy of containment from 1947 through the early 1990s? How will the end of the Cold War impact the future of U.S. foreign policy? What is the effect on foreign policy of the increasing interdependence in the world community? The chapter also takes a look at the tools of foreign policy, a short history of foreign policy since World War II, and some major challenges to American foreign policy in the future.

THE SETTING OF AMERICAN FOREIGN POLICY

As the last years of the twentieth century approach, the United States now must reexamine its foreign policy. To confront the challenge of communist expansion, Harry Truman reorganized the national security structure in 1947 and developed the "containment policy" which endured for over 40 years. Now that the communist threat has been removed, many of the basic premises that guided foreign policy since World War II must be reexamined.

At the conclusion of World War II, the U.S. economy was largely immune to the effects of economic conditions around the world. This is no longer the case in the mid-1990s. At the end of World War II, the United States was committed to the reconstruction of the economies of war-ravaged Europe and Japan. But today Americans feel the stress of the economic challenge from the European Community and Japan. The United States is thrust into a dominating role by virtue of its being the sole remaining superpower, while its military and economic ability to influence world politics has declined.

Continued leadership by the United States will depend on its ability to deal with issues concerning free trade, protection of the global environment, support for democracies, promotion of worldwide economic development, and prevention of weapons proliferation.

Foreign policy may be defined as actions the government takes or attempts to achieve its goals, in its relationships with other nations. Foreign policy, then, is the product of how government officials, who represent the state, act. The **foreign policy process** refers to how the decision makers identify, choose, and implement external policy.

Most Americans pay attention to foreign policy only when it fails, although expectations about what foreign policy can achieve are often unrealistically high. Many specific issues of foreign policy are less predictable than domestic policy problems. Much of foreign policy is made in **reaction** to what happens in other parts of the world. Over 180 nations are simultaneously pursuing their own foreign policies, which impacts U.S. decisions. As a result, policy issues may suddenly make a public appearance without long gestation periods, appearing like thunderclaps as lead stories on the evening news.

Considerable attention is focused on high policy issues like **crisis management**, or dealing with surprise situations that appear to threaten **the national security**. Economic policy and foreign policy are increasingly intertwined, as are the links between domestic and international economic issues. Such policy issues are often called **"intermestic" policies because they involve a mixture of *inter*national and do*mestic* policies**.

CHARACTERISTICS OF AMERICAN FOREIGN POLICY

The American approach to foreign policy reflects the nation's unique historical experience as a country geographically isolated from Europe, its views of foreign affairs formed primarily by its domestic experiences.

AN AMERICAN SENSE OF DESTINY AND MORAL SUPERIORITY

The United States has traditionally perceived itself as the world's first modern democracy espousing the principles of egalitarianism. European concepts of nobility and hereditary titles had no place in this new nation. Americans believed that individual freedom and social justice would lead immigrants to improve their stations in life. The lack of hereditary status or rank placed responsibility for one's station in life squarely upon the individual. Status and prestige would be measured by one's financial success. Power, in this new society, was the natural consequence of the possession of money. In the old world status, money, and prestige were the consequence of one's inherited position, not of intelligence or merit. Thomas Paine pointed out in *Common Sense* that the natural result of such a system was that ignorance and stupidity prevailed in affairs of state in Europe.

The United States was the first "new" nation born in a revolution championing democracy. Americans, from the earliest days of the Republic, have believed that they have a special destiny to be a beacon of hope to the rest of the world. A system based upon freedom, opportunity, social justice, and faith in the goodness and rationality of all human beings was thought to be obviously morally superior to European concepts based upon hierarchy, exploitation, and war. John Quincy Adams depicted it most vividly:

> Wherever the standard of freedom and independence has been or shall be unfurled, there will be America's heart, her benedictions, and her prayers. But she goes not abroad in search of monsters to destroy. She is the well-wisher to the freedom and independence of all. She is the champion and vindicator only of her own.[1]

Americans have believed it their obligation to encourage the spread of freedom and social justice throughout the world. **The challenge for the United States has been to find a way to serve as an example of freedom and justice in an environment in which problems are resolved through power.**

PRAGMATISM

An additional consequence of being a "new nation" with an emphasis on "**individualism**" was that there was no set pattern or traditional way of doing things. Americans quickly established a penchant for inventiveness and creativeness in solving problems. This utilitarian approach led to the conclusion that whatever works is good. Americans were admired for their "Yankee ingenuity" and their ability to get things done.

Historically, foreign policy has been seen as distinct from domestic policy and generally secondary to individual concerns regarding domestic policy such as jobs, inflation, or taxes. Foreign policy did not seem very important to most Americans

---

[1] Quote from George Kennan, Testimony before the Senate Foreign Relations Committee, February 10, 1966, in *Supplemental Foreign Assistance Fiscal Year 1966—Vietnam: Hearings before the Senate Foreign Relations Committee, 89th Cong., 2nd Session* (Washington, DC: Government Printing Office, 1966), p. 336.

until after World War II. Presidents have therefore had considerable discretion in formulating their foreign policies.

What has resulted is a foreign policy that is reactive to external pressures and characterized by discontinuity. These ad hoc policies emphasize short-term rather than long-term goals. This approach was reinforced by the fact that U.S. foreign policy had never suffered a serious reversal until the late 1960s.

Isolationism and Moral Interventions

During most of the nineteenth and early twentieth centuries, the United States was protected from external threats by two oceans and weaker neighbors to the north and south. This long isolation allowed the nation to concentrate on the domestic aspects of nation building: exploring and settling its expansive territory, developing its national identity, strengthening its governmental institutions, and encouraging participation by its population in the industrial revolution.

During this period America felt secure in the Western Hemisphere and largely maintained its isolation from involvement in the intrigues of European politics. Forays into the international arena were typically justified as being necessary deviations from isolationism to defend the national security.

The United States was decidedly more involved in the politics of the Western Hemisphere however. President James Monroe warned European nations, in the Monroe Doctrine enunciated in 1823, that further colonization of the hemisphere would not be tolerated, and declared a special right of the United States to exercise hegemony in North and South America.

Geographic isolation allowed American democracy to develop without the threat of invasions. By contrast, nations like Germany, France, and Russia were repeatedly both aggressors and victims of aggression. Highly centralized governments, in contrast to the decentralization of American politics, became the norm in Europe. European governments were also often authoritarian. Not surprisingly, Europeans frequently emphasized the subordination of the rights of the individual, such as free speech and other individual liberties, to those of the state in the interests of national security. Rather than the American notion of the state being the servant of the people, European thinking often stressed individual responsibility to the state.

One result of the American experience has been to define foreign policy and security goals in broader terms than just physical security. They include a preference for democratic over nondemocratic states and a belief that freedom should follow the American flag. The Mexican-American War of 1848 was justified as necessary to fulfill America's "Manifest Destiny" of building a democratic state from the Atlantic to the Pacific and therefore seen as part of America's domestic policy. American involvement in international politics was typically seen as a response to an outside provocation against the American will. When the German government decided to wage unrestricted submarine warfare in 1917, the United States was forced to enter World War I. That involvement then became a **crusade** "to make the world safe for democracy." But after the war, the United States rejected membership in the League of Nations and pursued a self-conscious "return to normalcy" in the form of a renewed isolationism.

Franklin Roosevelt justified his foreign policy in the late 1930s as a need to "quarantine" the disease of totalitarian Nazism. Aid to England was justified as necessary after the defeat of France in 1940 because the United States could not survive alone in a totalitarian sea. However, it was the catastrophic blunder of the Japanese attack on Pearl Harbor followed within hours by Hitler's declaration of war against the United States that **forced** a declaration of war by the U.S. Congress. American involvement in both world wars occurred as a result of decisions made abroad.

AMERICAN FOREIGN POLICY MAKING

Who has responsibility for the conduct of foreign policy? And how is foreign policy made in America? This chapter can only briefly consider the primary policy makers and some of the more important instruments they have to implement their policies.

The President and Congress

The Founding Fathers were fearful of the accumulation of too much power in any branch of government. They were especially careful to circumscribe the powers given to the President to ensure against the acquisition of dictatorial powers. Article II of the Constitution gives the President the right, with the advice and consent of the Senate, to make treaties and to appoint ambassadors. The Founding Fathers also designated the President as the Commander in Chief of the military and indicated that the executive could receive foreign ambassadors. These powers do not justify the conclusion that those at the Constitutional Convention thought the President should dominate in making foreign policy. In fact, foreign policy was viewed as a minor matter to the framers. The new nation was thousands of miles from the European cauldron. And George Washington's well-known warning in his farewell address to **avoid entangling alliances** is indicative of the framers' attitudes.

The President was designated the Commander in Chief of America's armed forces, but only Congress was allowed to declare war. And the drafters of the Constitution specifically gave Congress the responsibility to "provide for the common defence." They further gave Congress a role to play in the confirmation of all high-level diplomatic and military officials. Finally, they gave Congress the authority "To make all Laws which shall be necessary and proper for carrying into Execution the foregoing Powers, and all other Powers vested by this Constitution in the Government of the United States. . . ."

The Constitution's grant of authority to the President had the potential for an expansive interpretation by Chief Executives as opportunities presented themselves. The Constitution is silent on many aspects of foreign policy. For example, if Congress has the authority to declare war, should it also be responsible for negotiating peace? Various Presidents have taken the position that the specific Constitutional grants of authority to the office, although meager, include "implied powers" to take whatever actions holders of the office think necessary in new circumstances; this has established precedents for future Chief Executives. The result has been the accumulation of far more power in the hands of the President in the area of foreign affairs than the Founding Fathers contemplated. Yet a President's authority is very sensitive to the individual's ability to persuade the public and Congress to support Presidential positions.

There is a distinctly different perception regarding how **domestic and foreign policy should be made**. The Founding Fathers carefully separated governmental authority among the three branches and placed checks on the exercise of power, and particularly on the President's power, on the theory that too much power is likely to be abused. However, some critics argue that in foreign policy **executive power should be concentrated**. A weak Chief Executive is unable to act with dispatch to protect the nation's vital interests. These critics believe that foreign policy should be made differently than domestic policy, especially in crisis situations like war. During World War II, Congress ceded to the President emergency powers for the duration of the war. Almost immediately after the war ended, the United States found itself involved in the Cold War. Some believed that this situation required the President to continue to exercise emergency powers as long as required by these new circumstances.

However, if a President acquires sufficient power to act almost unilaterally in foreign affairs, there is the danger that restraints on domestic Presidential authority will wear away. Congress, particularly through various of its committees, has exercised considerable influence on foreign policy. Unfortunately, when Congress asserted a greater role in foreign policy making because of the collapse of a consensus on foreign policy goals during the Vietnam War, many complained of "Congressional interference."

What is the proper Congressional role in foreign policy making? Should public opinion play a significant role, or is the public too uninformed?

In the past, the foreign policy process involved only a small elite group that provided input based upon its members' supposed expertise. This is in contrast to the formulation of most domestic policy issues, where the emphasis is on a broad democratic participation in the process. Most problems involving "crisis management" issues require the formation of quick responses and are dealt with by experts at the top of the executive branch's foreign policy bureaucracy. Presumably they formulate the "best" strategy to deal with each such problem.

Longer-term security strategies frequently involve the need for Congressional approval and funding. They require an expanded number of players in the planning and negotiation stages of their adoption.

When a policy question involves **intermestic issues**, it is more likely to resemble domestic policy formulation. That is, it involves a wide spectrum of interest groups claiming a right to be heard. The recent Congressional debate involving NAFTA and the involvement of interest groups with the issue greatly expanded the scope of the conflict and encouraged negotiations and compromises.

The President has foreign policy institutions to advise him on foreign and military issues. The Department of State is the oldest of all the cabinet departments, which makes the Secretary of State (Thomas Jefferson being the first) the ranking cabinet member. Its primary objective is to carry out foreign policy to promote the long-range security goals of the country. American ambassadors, along with over 8000 foreign service officers who work for the State Department, represent the United States at American embassies and international organizations around the world.

The Secretary of State is the President's primary foreign policy adviser. Secretaries of State have only as much policy-making authority as the President chooses to delegate. Presidents like Eisenhower and Reagan gave their Secretaries of State broad discretion to make foreign policy decisions. Others, like Kennedy, Carter, and Bush, took a more active part in foreign policy decision making. Some contend that this has resulted in reducing the State Department to managing routine affairs, with important foreign policy matters being run out of the White House.

Some recent administrations have appointed National Security Advisers with offices in the White House to provide advice on foreign policy matters. Such an arrangement bypasses the more formal institutional provisions of government. National Security Advisers have access to military, intelligence, and diplomatic sources of information and have become very influential in establishing foreign policy. For instance, Richard Nixon and Jimmy Carter relied primarily on Henry Kissinger and Zbigniew Brzezinski rather than their Secretaries of State for advice. Communication technology now permits Presidents to have direct access with foreign heads of state or to speak directly to their own military commanders in the policy-making process.

The National Security Organizations

National Security Council (NSC)   This was created in 1947 to help Presidents integrate the "domestic, foreign, and military policies" that affect national security. The NSC's statutory membership includes the President, Vice President, Secretary of State, and Secretary of Defense. The director of the Central Intelligence Agency (CIA) and the chairman of the Joint Chiefs of Staff (JCS) serve as advisory members. The President's assistant for national security affairs serves as the day-to-day director of the NSC. Technically the agency does not make decisions since that is the responsibility of the President, but it does offer policy guidance and advice. Its statutory authority indicates that it has **advisory** authority only. It does not have any **operational authority**.

Department of Defense (DOD)   The **Secretary of Defense** officially presides over the Department of Defense and is the President's main military adviser. The Defense Department comprises all the military services and is responsible for about 70 percent of the government's equipment purchases. The commanding officers of each of the services and a chairman comprise the **Joint Chiefs of Staff (JCS)**, who advise the Secretary of Defense as well as the President. Friction fre-

IRAN-CONTRA: A FAILED ATTEMPT AT FOREIGN POLICY MAKING

In an effort to obtain the release of American hostages held in Lebanon and to provide aid to the Contras in Nicaragua, the Reagan administration decided upon a plan that used the NSC. Despite being limited legally to an advisory role, the NSC staff became involved in covert operations. The plan was to secretly sell arms to the Iranians in exchange for their assistance in gaining the release of six American hostages being held by terrorists in Lebanon. There were three different shipments of arms to Iran, and one American hostage was released after each delivery. The terrorists maintained their supply of hostages to trade for arms by capturing three more Americans.

Lt. Col. Oliver North diverted the funds from the sale of U.S. government property, which should have gone to the U.S. treasury, to Swiss bank accounts where some of the money was used to support the Contras in Nicaragua. This was done without the knowledge of Congress. Congress had passed the Boland Amendment to prevent the sale of weapons to terrorist organizations and to prohibit any U.S. government aid from going to the Contras. The administration solicited confidential donations from wealthy American citizens and from foreign governments so that the President could continue to aid the Contras despite the Congressional ban. These funds were to be under the control of "The Enterprise" to avoid the Constitutional check of Congressional control of funding. The Constitution provides that foreign policy is to be made by the president and Congress working together. But the Reagan administration was attempting to privatize foreign policy since Congress was not acceding to the President's will.

In November 1986 the Lebanese newspaper *Al-Shiraa* reported that the U.S. government had been selling HAWK missiles to Iran. An executive order by Reagan had officially listed Iran as a government which sponsored terrorism, and the Arms Export Control Act prohibited arms shipments to states so identified. President Reagan had publicly stated his opposition to negotiating with terrorists and discouraged other nations from selling arms to Iran. Reagan claimed that he had not been informed of the diversion of funds. The action was also alleged to be in violation of the requirement of the President to provide notification to the appropriate intelligence oversight committee in Congress before implementing covert operations.

quently develops between the members of the JCS as they try to strengthen the roles of their respective services in military planning.

The Intelligence Community   **Intelligence refers to the process of collecting, analyzing, protecting, and using information to further the national interests**. Prior to the surprise attack on Pearl Harbor, the United States had no centralized agency for intelligence gathering. Then during World War II President Roosevelt created the Office of Strategic Services (OSS) to gather and analyze intelligence to aid in military planning. The OSS also conducted covert operations against enemy forces and their war-making capabilities.

Lt. Col. North readily admitted his involvement in the affair, and that he had lied to Congress concerning these activities. National Security Adviser Robert McFarlane and Oliver North accompanied the first shipment of arms to Iran, bringing additional gifts of a cake baked in the shape of a key (to symbolize the key to friendship between the two nations) and a Bible signed by President Reagan. North also admitted to efforts to deceive Congress and to destroy incriminating evidence. He defended his actions by saying that he was given to understand his superiors were aware of the full range of his activities and approved of them. He contended that he believed President Reagan was also aware of what he was doing. He indicated that he would do whatever asked by the President.

Admiral John Poindexter claimed full responsibility for the decision to siphon the money to the Contras. He said that he thought the President would have approved, but that he had not informed him, so Reagan had no knowledge of the operation. Poindexter claimed that the "buck stops here with me."

The experts on Iran and foreign policy planners from the Departments of State and Defense and the CIA were never included in the policy process. Their involvement in such activities was very explicitly prohibited by the Boland Amendment. The Secretary of State, George Shultz, implied that the State Department would not involve itself in such amateurish schemes. Then Vice President George Bush also explained that he "was out of the loop" despite his position on the NSC.

The policy was a failure on every score. Constitutional procedures and laws were violated. There were as many hostages at the end of the debacle as at its beginning. Those involved showed contempt for democratic principles and procedures. The result was bad policy administered incompetently. Publicly proclaiming an uncompromising policy of not giving in to terrorist blackmail exposed some hypocrisy in the administration and yet secretly doing so damaged the credibility and authority of the President.

Source: Report of the Congressional Committees Investigating the Iran-Contra Affair, with Supplemental Minority and Additional Views, S. Report No. 100-216 (Washington, DC: U.S. Government Printing Office, November 1987).

After World War II, the OSS was disbanded and a small Central Intelligence Group provided information to the government. Soviet control of Eastern Europe and concern over communist expansion suggested a need for accurate up-to-date information about the capabilities and the intentions of other national leaders. The CIA was created by the National Security Act of 1947 to advise and make recommendations to the departments of the government about issues and situations related to national security.

The new CIA was to collect and analyze intelligence about foreign countries and disseminate the resulting intelligence reports to those in the American government who needed the information in their decision making. The intelligence community makes use of classified sources of information, but most information is collected from open sources such as news stories, public documents, and diplomatic reporting. Intelligence is distinguished, however, by its sources and methods, which are not available to everyone.

The most controversial aspect of intelligence has to do with **covert action, which involves the secret operations designed to influence events in other countries while attempting to conceal the sponsoring government's involvement**. Covert actions may include propaganda, political, economic, or paramilitary operations.

Many scholars argue that covert action is not intelligence per se. However, it is a function that most governments assign to their intelligence branches because their organizations for clandestine information collection makes them well suited to many forms of covert action. CIA covert action has ranged from funneling money to finance anticommunist political parties in Italy's national elections in 1948, to helping overthrow foreign governments, such as the one in Iran in 1953 or the government in Guatemala in 1954. CIA covert action launched U-2 flights over the Soviet Union in the 1950s, and the invasion of Cuba at the Bay of Pigs in 1961. The CIA was involved in the destabilization of governments in Indonesia, Chile, and Vietnam. It was also involved, in violation of its charter, in efforts to infiltrate and disrupt the student protest movement against the U.S. involvement in Vietnam.

Congress was concerned about problems created by intelligence organizations within the U.S. democratic structure. Democracies are based upon openness and a free flow of information, while intelligence organizations are relatively closed and place restrictions on access to information. Therefore, Congress provided that the agency would have no police, law enforcement powers, or internal security functions. The CIA was prohibited by law from collecting information about U.S. citizens.[2] The statute creating the CIA provided that nothing in the law was to be construed as authority to withhold information from the intelligence committees on the grounds that providing the information would constitute unauthorized disclosure.[3]

During the early years of the Cold War, Congress did not appear to want to be fully informed about what the intelligence community was doing. But when the national and government consensus on foreign policy began to erode during the Vietnam conflict and rumors began to surface about CIA violations of its charter, Congress began to assert its authority over intelligence operations. Since the 1970s, the role of Congress in intelligence matters has increased dramatically. The intelligence community has become like the rest of government. And the House and Senate permanent Select Committees on Intelligence have become, like other committees, the patrons as well as the overseer of "their" government agencies.[4] The

---

[2] Counterintelligence activity within the United States is carried out by the Federal Bureau of Investigation.

[3] National Security Act of 1947, Title V—Accountability for Intelligence Activities.

[4] Thomas E. Mann (ed.), *A Question of Balance: The President, the Congress, and Foreign Policy* (Washington, DC: The Brookings Institution, 1990), p. 70.

CIA AT THE CROSSROADS

Intelligence is basically a dedicated support service for government policy makers. In theory, intelligence should gather and process information from a variety of sources and present it in an objective fashion. However, intelligence is irrelevant without policy. Its purpose is to provide foreign policy makers with accurate information upon which to base their decisions. A major difficulty is that policy makers prefer that intelligence findings support their goals. Conversely policy makers are unhappy with intelligence that undermines a preconceived policy. In such cases the information is often discounted or ignored by policy makers. But if the intelligence community shades its analysis to please a policy maker, it risks policy and intelligence failures.

Unfortunately the CIA has been drawn into partisan politics more frequently in recent years, which undermines its credibility. The agency rebuffed Richard Nixon when he tried to use it in his efforts to cover up the Watergate scandal. A few years later, Gerald Ford appointed George Bush as Director of Central Intelligence (DCI); Bush was a former Chair of the Republican National Committee—an inherently partisan position—and had no experience in intelligence. When Ronald Reagan appointed William Casey, who had managed his campaign, as the new Director of Central Intelligence, any semblance of nonpartisanship was removed. Casey cooperated with the turning over of covert operations to "The Enterprise" to avoid Congressional control. In 1991, President George Bush nominated Robert Gates, who had worked closely with William Casey during Iran-Contra, to the post. His nomination was also controversial because analysts in the CIA charged that he presented the White House only with intelligence supportive of administration policy. President Clinton appointed Admiral James Woolsey as DCI.

Much of the criticism of the intelligence community centers around covert action. Is covert action an appropriate policy tool to be used by democratic governments? How can its drawbacks be minimized so that it is worth continuing? What controls should be placed on covert action? Should the CIA's covert action be limited to political, propaganda, and economic operations? Should paramilitary covert operations be separated from the CIA and placed with some other group like the military?

Economic intelligence is an increasingly important aspect of information collection. In addition to studying economic trends or trade policies, some governments see nothing amiss in using intelligence organizations to steal U.S. corporations' proprietary secrets. A serious debate is taking place whether the CIA should provide proprietary help to American corporations since many foreign companies receive assistance from their governments. There are great risks involved. Business relationships with companies in other countries might be soured by suspicions that American firms have an unfair advantage. There is also the increasing problem of defining an American company, as many companies have overseas subsidiaries, or are international holding companies.

Reagan and Bush administrations and conservatives, not used to Congress vigorously exercising its prerogative in this area, claimed that intelligence gathering is an executive function and that Congressional meddling in the area weakened national security. It was this misguided sense of executive prerogatives that led ultimately to Iran-Contra.

Although the precise figure is classified, the intelligence community's budget for fiscal 1994 is about $27.7 billion.[5]

With the end of the Cold War, the CIA is having to shift its focus to global problems of nations trying to buy or build nuclear weapons, international terrorism, and international economic trends. The products of American intelligence gathering have been increasingly made available upon request to the United Nations to support peacekeeping operations in areas like Somalia, Croatia, and Rwanda.

THE GLOBAL ACTORS

Nation-States

A nation consists of individuals usually bound together by shared history, culture, and language, and who live in a geographic area that provides them with a uniqueness that distinguishes them from others. When people organize themselves into a political group as a means of defense of their identity or other interests, they may claim to be a nation-state. Not surprisingly, nation-states, like individuals, see the world from their own perspectives.

The number of nation-states has expanded more in the last half of the twentieth century than in any comparable time in world history. In 1945 there were 67 nations. The end of colonialism saw the emergence of new nation-states. And more recently the disintegration of the Soviet Union saw the reemergence of the Baltic states as well as other former Soviet republics which proclaimed their independence. By the mid-1990s there were 187 sovereign states.[6] The number has increased recently as the result of the recent phenomenon of failed states like the Soviet Union or Yugoslavia. Other states like Somalia are collapsing and Canada is threatened with disintegration.

The nation-state, or simply state, exists in a world populated by other states each pursuing its own "national interests." The sovereign state is the main political actor in the international system. Each state lays claim to **sovereignty**. **Sovereignty means that a state's government has supreme control over the body politic and that it is free from any external control**. The highest purpose of the state is to defend itself against external challenges to its sovereignty. Every state claims the right to pursue its own interests at the expense of others, limited only by the constraints of international law.

---

[5] Tim Weiner, "C.I.A. Is Rebuffed on Spying Budget," *The New York Times*, July 17, 1993, p. 7. The CIA receives about $3 billion. About $23 billion goes to various military intelligence agencies, including the National Reconnaissance Office, which is responsible for the design and procurement of all reconnaissance satellites and for their management once in orbit; the National Security Agency, which conducts electronic eavesdropping, decryption, and encryption of U.S. codes; the Defense Intelligence Agency, which analyzes military intelligence; and the intelligence branches of the military services. The remainder goes to the intelligence bureaus of the Departments of State, Justice, Energy, and the Treasury.

[6] *Statistical Abstract, 1992*, pp. 820–822. In addition, there are 37 "Areas of Special Sovereignty and Dependencies."

Sovereignty means that the government has the legal right, and presumably the power, to require citizens to comply with its policies. From an international perspective, sovereign equality means that states are equal in their legal status despite differences in size or economic power. Therefore, no government can require other states to agree to a policy. As in other areas of foreign policy, the ideal is for international problems—say of an economic nature—to be resolved through negotiation.

In practice, governments may find themselves challenged for control of the state by internal as well as by external forces. No state's sovereignty has ever been absolute. Today, states cannot control information or capital flows across their borders, and international economic integration nibbles away at what once were their sovereign prerogatives. Even advanced powerful nations like the United States find aspects of their sovereignty evaporating. Meanwhile, new nations insistent on sovereignty discover that it does not give them the independence for which they struggled.

The environment of the state system in which nations still must coexist as the primary political actors constrains states to be vigilant to any threat to their political, military, and economic security. Survival in a world where states still claim the right of independence and self-defense among other attributes of sovereignty means that states must still ultimately rely upon "self-help." Many policies stem from the nature of the current international system in which there is, as yet, no international organization that can protect states from the hostile acts of other nations. States must ultimately try to advance their interests as a way to increase their security against the possibility of attack. Thus many claim that foreign policy is a product of the state system and not of the existence of states themselves.

Nonstate Actors

States were perceived to be the sole actors in the international system until well after World War II. Although other organizations and groups, such the International Telegraphic Union [now the International Telecommunications Union (ITU)], had been around for well over a century, they were not thought of as having any independent power. Such organizations, known as **intergovernmental organizations (IGOs)**, are voluntary associations of states in which there is a perceived mutual advantage to be gained by cooperation. IGOs may be regional, such as the Organization of American States (OAS) or the European Economic Community (EEC), or global, such as the United Nations (UN). They can in turn be classified according to their goals, which may be very narrow, such as the North American Free Trade Agreement (NAFTA), or all-encompassing, such as the United Nations.

These organizations, of which the best known is the United Nations, may have political, military, economic, or humanitarian purposes. The United Nations was founded in 1945 as the successor to the League of Nations, which was the first attempt at a permanent international organization designed to maintain the peace,

THE EUROPEAN ECONOMIC COMMUNITY

Some parts of the world are experiencing the reemergence of nationalism. This is especially true where nationalism had been suppressed by the division of the world into bipolar camps during the Cold War. While ethnic and minority groups demand the right to self-determination in many of these cases, there are other examples of states moving in the direction of giving up their independence to form larger economic and political unions.

This can be seen most clearly in Europe with the establishment of the European Economic Community (EEC; usually referred to as the Common Market). The EEC is a customs union, with free trade between the members. This stimulus provides a larger marketplace and greater competition for companies within the bloc. Originally consisting of six member states, it has since grown to 12 members—in 1993 members included Ireland, the United Kingdom, Belgium, Netherlands, Luxembourg, Denmark, Germany, France, Spain, Portugal, Italy, and Greece. In 1967 the European Atomic Energy Community (EURATOM), the ECSC, and the EEC joined together to form the European Community (EC).

In 1985, the member states committed themselves to work toward a more integrated Europe by 1992, at which time they would undertake to eliminate all barriers to internal European trade. In December 1991 at the EC meeting in Maastricht, Netherlands, the members agreed among other things to a goal of monetary union by the end of the 1990s. The treaty proposed a common foreign and defense policy as well. A common currency (the European Currency Unit, ECU) was to be in place by 1997 if political problems could be overcome.

Economic integration induces pressure for political integration. The Maastricht Treaty proposed significant political and economic integration. The treaty included a "European citizenship," which would guarantee rights to Europeans in any other European country including voting rights and the right to seek office. But financial strains caused by German deficits incurred to reunify the country give evidence that the nations still have political obstacles to overcome to bring the final monetary union about.

A continuing sense of national and cultural identity and language differences retard the movement toward larger political union. Another major obstacle to the appeal of union

created after World War I. Founders of the UN hoped to provide for world order based upon the rule of law and cooperation rather than conflict and the law of the jungle. It embodies the determination "to save succeeding generations from the scourge of war which . . . has brought untold sorrow to mankind." These words in the preamble to the Charter are based on the conclusion that warfare has long since outlived its usefulness as a tool of diplomacy. The UN Charter is a treaty to which the U.S. Senate has given its advice and consent, and as such its provisions are presumably binding on the United States, as well as on all its members. All members of the UN agree under Article 2 "to fulfill in good faith the obligations assumed by them in accordance with the present Charter." In particular, Article 2, paragraph 4, provides the following:

with a larger community is the reality that the individual nation-state is still responsible for education, housing, health care, and maintaining employment in its labor force through economic policies. These policies differ between nations and in their comprehensiveness, level of funding, and tax rates. Without greater parity between these national policies, a common currency will be extremely difficult to achieve. The movement toward a larger association is clear, but overcoming these last impediments will not happen quickly.

As it is, the European Community poses an impressive economic challenge to the United States. The nations of the EC have a combined total production slightly larger than U.S. GDP and a larger population. There is concern that the effort to develop European economic unity will lead to additional growth of about 5 percent in the next 10 years. Policy makers in the United States are concerned that a single market within the EC could become a tool to increase trade within Europe while reducing trade with the world beyond the EC's boundaries. The United States has argued against high EC protective tariffs. This is an important concern for trade policy since approximately 25 percent of all U.S. exports and imports go to or arrive from EC countries.

The move toward market economies in Eastern Europe and the former Soviet Union have also opened up potential markets for which the United States and the EC will compete. The European Community has not only the obvious geographic advantage over the United States in this competition, but its members also have cultural ties as well.

Because of the economic challenge of the EC, the United States negotiated the North American Free Trade Agreement with Canada and Mexico. President Clinton won Congressional approval for the treaty only after making several trade concessions. The goals of NAFTA are to (1) increase the efficiency of the economies of Canada, Mexico, and the United States; (2) remove barriers to trade between the three; and (3) promote competitiveness with outside countries.

Sources: Walter Goldstein, "Europe After Maastricht," *Foreign Affairs,* vol. 71, no. 5 (Winter 1992); Peter Ludlow, "The Maastricht Treaty and the Future of Europe," *The Washington Quarterly*, vol. 15, no. 4 (Fall 1992); Jorge G. Castaneda, "Can NAFTA Change Mexico?" *Foreign Affairs*, vol. 72, no. 4 (September/October 1993).

All Members shall refrain in their international relations from the threat or use of force against the territorial integrity or political independence of any state, or in any other manner inconsistent with the Purposes of the United Nations.[7]

[7] The purpose of the Article is to outlaw the aggressive use of force by states, which was acceptable in the classical period of international law that did not recognize any authority above the individual nation-state. The Charter does allow the use of force by states in their self-defense, as Article 51 provides: "Nothing in the present Charter shall impair the **inherent** right of individual or collective **self defense** if an armed attack occurs. . . ." (emphasis added)

Article 2 obviously has not prevented the threat or use of force by states against other states. The major difference since the startup of the UN has been that countries try to defend their use of force either as self-defense or as being otherwise consistent with the purposes and principles of the UN.

The Charter gives the Security Council the primary responsibility for the maintenance of international peace and security.[8] Article 42 provides that the Security Council may take "such action by air, sea, or land forces as may be necessary to maintain or restore international peace and security" by using the military forces of UN members.

Nongovernmental Actors

While nongovernmental actors are not new in the international system, the surge in their numbers and their development as major players in the international community since World War II is remarkable. Unlike IGOs, which are creatures of the states they represent, nongovernmental or **transnational organizations (NGOs)** are private groups that have programs in more than one country. Such organizations usually downplay nationality. NGOs have their own interests that they pursue in different states' territories.

The International Committee of the Red Cross (ICRC) is an example of an NGO that supports humanitarian projects in many countries. Its success has been based on its strict impartiality in pursuing its goals of humanitarian relief, which allowed it to operate in all the belligerent nations during World War II. The ICRC has been a major player in drafting treaties on the laws of war.

A nongovernmental organization that predates the modern nation-state and wields global influence is the Catholic Church. It is involved in social issues around the world. In developed Western countries, the Church hierarchy has taken positions on the need for governmental action to reduce social and economic inequalities through programs to help those in poverty. In the United States, the National Conference of Catholic Bishops (NCCB) opposed the 1991 Gulf War, and opposed aid to the Contras in Nicaragua in the 1980s. The NCCB has supported an increase in foreign aid to less developed countries, while at the same time it has opposed the sale of military weapons abroad. The Bishops have also expressed their opposition to the view that the use of nuclear weapons could be an ethical defense strategy. Domestically, they have supported a redistribution of wealth toward the poor, support for gun control, and opposition to abortion. Catholic Relief Services, an overseas aid program sponsored by American Catholic Bishops, is one of the largest NGOs that distributes food provided by U.S.A.I.D. (U.S. Agency for International Development). In the developing world, many of the Catholic clergy have been actively involved in social justice issues. Governments must use a great deal of circumspection in dealing with such a large organization having worldwide membership.

Multinational corporations (MNCs) are the most noteworthy flood of new NGOs in the post World War II period. Increasingly, corporations transcend national boundaries. Many of them have branches involved in production and sales located throughout the world. Such corporations develop a multinational rather than a national orientation.

---

[8] Article 24.

MNCs offer tremendous benefits by creating jobs, helping to train labor forces, bringing new technologies to countries, and providing competition. MNCs also work to reduce international tension. A company with operations in different countries wants friendly relations between them. However, multinational corporations cause problems for national governments. Unlike a domestic corporation that can be dealt with through domestic policies, if an MNC does not like the policies of a particular government, such as taxes or environmental regulations, it can move its operations to a country it finds more hospitable. Nations often compete with each other to influence multinationals to locate within their countries by offering very attractive economic conditions. For example, American investors might form a holding company with a subsidiary for cargo ships incorporated in Honduras to avoid U.S. maritime laws and high wages. Their financial transactions and profits might be handled by Bahamian banks to circumvent American financial disclosure laws.

Many MNCs have greater sales and profits than the gross domestic products of many states. Large corporations have a profound impact on politics in America. It is not surprising, then, that MNCs can threaten the stability of governments in some countries where they operate. In many instances the multinationals can use their leverage to control governments rather than the governments controlling the multinationals. American multinational corporations are spread out across the world, so that, when an American buys a Pontiac from General Motors, over half the money paid goes to Germany, South Korea, Japan, Taiwan, the United Kingdom, and Singapore. In the process, the world is becoming more cosmopolitan, and somewhat Americanized.

In a defensive reaction against MNC penetration, many nations have created their own "corporate champions." Some countries proceeded to develop an industrial policy in which they consolidated whole industries. For example, Britain consolidated its automobile manufacturers into British Leyland and its steelmakers into British Steel. France supported Renault as its automobile manufacturer and Unisor and Sacilor as its steel manufacturers.[9] In some cases these corporations were owned outright by their governments.

Foreign corporations, usually aided by their home government's policies toward business, began to challenge the United States in high-quality, high-volume production of standard goods. As patents expired, less developed countries insisted on coproduction agreements, and as foreign nations improved their educational systems, U.S. technological advantages began to shrink. By the beginning of the 1990s, the United States, which has about 22 percent of the world's GDP, imported over 45 percent of the manufactured exports from all of the developing countries.

Many foreign MNCs, to reduce transportation costs and to avoid any effort to keep cheaper foreign products out of the American market, began buying and building plants in America. Not surprisingly, Honda, Toyota, and Mercedes were aggressively courted by U.S. state governors who hoped new plants would be located

---

[9] Robert Reich, *The Work of Nations* (New York: Vintage Books, 1992), pp. 66–67.

within their borders. MNCs also contribute heavily to political candidates through political action committees (PACs).

Increasingly MNCs operate in disregard of international boundaries. Consequently, business decisions made in one nation will affect employment in other countries.

The Global Village

The rapid pace of political and economic change taking place throughout the world is rearranging the international landscape. American foreign and military policy is being deeply affected by the shift from the old divisions between developed industrialized societies and developing, primarily agrarian, Third-World states to the new situation of industrialization cropping up all over the world. During the last quarter of the twentieth century, some advanced nations have been driven toward high-skill, information-intensive jobs, with lower-skill agrarian and manufacturing jobs being exported to Third-World nations. But the shift taking place is uneven and has many observable overlaps. Even the most technically advanced nations, like the United States, have manufacturing sectors where low-skill labor predominates. Opposition to the North American Free Trade Agreement was a futile effort to prevent more of these jobs from slipping away to Mexico. And there are countries like China and Brazil that are primarily agrarian with some smokestack manufacturing centers that have enclaves of high technology.

Technical societies need many dependable connections with other nations. The change from agrarian to industrialized and high tech economies around the world has been accompanied by a rapid growth of IGOs from about 200 on the eve of World War I to over 4000 by the early 1990s. Over 30,000 treaties have been registered with the United Nations since 1945. In 1991 the United States was party to over 1000 treaties and over 12,000 international agreements.[10] The irony is that the most powerful and advanced state in the world is the most constrained by treaties and other agreements, and the least able to act recklessly. By contrast, the least developed are the least connected. Weak economies, often with only natural products or resources to sell, do not need many external links.

COMING IN OUT OF THE COLD WAR

The Cold War has ended, but a brief summary of the major events of that period is in order to clarify the new challenges the new era presents.

---

[10] According to the *Yearbook of International Organizations* (Munich: K. G. Sauer Verlag, 1993), Vol. 1, p. 1667, the total number of international organizations grew from 10,437 to 14,147 between 1981 and 1992.

T.I.A.S. (*Treaties and International Agreements Series*) published by the State Department, which contains all treaties and agreements in force to which the United States is a party, contained over 283 pages listing bilateral treaties and over 138 pages listing multinational treaties in its 1993 edition.

American-Soviet Competition

The wartime alliance between the United States and the Soviet Union began to show severe strains by the end of the war in 1945. From 1945 until the collapse of the Soviet Union in 1991, American foreign policy was dominated by two fundamental principles: **The first was the primacy of national security**. The threat of an expansionist Soviet communism forced all other issues into a subordinate position relative to national security. Thus U.S. initiatives such as the Marshall Plan, which had humanitarian and economic stabilization aspects, were mainly driven by enlightened self-interest to increase Western security. The roughly equal bipolar distribution of military power between the United States and the Soviet Union became the single most defining aspect of international politics after World War II.

The clear division between East and West led each superpower to construct alliances to better defend itself against threats from the other bloc. The United States ringed Russia with the North Atlantic Treaty Organization (NATO), the Australia, New Zealand, and the United States Treaty (ANZUS), and the U.S.-Japan Security Treaty. The Soviet Union created the Warsaw Pact to counter NATO. Each side tried to convince other states to join their bloc. The bloc antagonisms convulsed universal international organizations to which both belonged such as the United Nations, as each superpower tried to get those organizations to support its own goals.

The second major American foreign policy principle, supportive of the first, consisted of the development of an ideological commitment to market capitalism and opposition to any deviation as socialistic and evil. Repressive dictatorships fending off democratic demands to hold elections quickly learned to denounce their domestic opponents as communist-inspired. They were oftentimes hailed as courageous leaders who had to take repressive measures against ruthless communist opponents. They might receive aid and support from the United States to train their police against opposition forces, as the Shah of Iran did for many years.

As World War II ground to an end, the United States anticipated a new era of cooperation with the Soviet Union that would provide for a stable peace in Europe. Territory of the Soviet Union had suffered catastrophic invasions over the last couple of centuries by Napoleon, by Germany in World War I, by Western powers during Russia's civil war after World War I, and again by Germany in World War II. Although the Soviet Union narrowly escaped defeat at the hands of Germany in the war, it emerged as the major European power by the end of the war. But Western hope that the several years of wartime cooperation would convince Stalin of the peaceful intentions of Britain and the United States was short-lived. To increase Soviet security, the Soviet army imposed control over the nations of Eastern Europe. After World War II elections were never held in those countries or their democratically elected leaders were overthrown; Eastern European nations were reduced to satellites of the Soviet Union.

The United States and the Soviet Union emerged from World War II as the two dominant powers in the world. This bipolar division in which the two superpowers confronted each other extended the competition even to Third-World countries. Each side perceived themselves to be in a zero-sum game in which the slightest gain in power for one was seen as a loss of power and reduced security for the other.

The Soviet army's seizure of authority over Eastern Europe led President Truman to initiate a policy of **containment** in 1947.[11] Under this policy, which was followed on a bipartisan basis until the disintegration of the Soviet Union in 1991, the U.S. goal was to block and contain any expansionist effort of the Soviet Union. In its application, it assumed that communism was a unified subversive force directed and controlled from the Kremlin. Truman felt that the realities of the distribution of international power left the United States no choice but to act to counter communist initiatives anywhere in the world.

Peaceful Coexistence

After the death of Josef Stalin in 1953, Nikita Khrushchev eventually succeeded to the Soviet leadership. Khrushchev said nuclear war would leave no winners and that the Soviet-American military rivalry was too dangerous. He proposed that both sides agree to **peaceful coexistence in which both major powers would compete by economic rather than military means**. Nevertheless, Khrushchev viewed assistance to struggles against colonialism as a central element of Marxist principles which he could not renounce.

President John F. Kennedy accepted the concept of peaceful coexistence, and offered as a peaceful challenge to the Soviet Union a race to put a man on the moon within the decade of the 1960s. But this did not mean that Kennedy intended to compromise the policy of containment. In his 1961 inaugural address, he promised that America would "pay any price, bear any burden, meet any hardship, support any friend, oppose any foe to assure the survival and success of liberty."

All too frequently during the Cold War, the United States came to the aid of authoritarian regimes claiming that their democratic opponents were communist sympathizers. In other instances, the United States helped overthrow democratically elected governments such as Guatemala in 1954, if it was thought that they were less anticommunist or pro-American than their opponents.

The Cold War modified the traditional mistrust of foreign intervention. Victory in World War II led to an overconfidence in the ability of the United States to intervene in any foreign dispute and achieve whatever goal it desired. Many Americans abandoned their preference for isolationism in favor of the "higher goal" of containing communism. Even so, significant interventions against communism—such as Korea and Vietnam—produced widespread domestic opposition. This also resulted in the United States deviating from its historic principle of siding with

---

[11] Actually George Kennan is given credit as the architect of the containment policy. The proposed policy appeared in an article entitled "The Sources of Soviet Conduct," in the journal *Foreign Affairs*. Writing under the pseudonym "Mr. X," Kennan stated that the Soviet strategy was based upon convenient ideology and the conditions inside Russia. Its goal was not world domination, but rather that all governments bordering Russia should be favorably disposed to itself. Kennan proposed a long-term policy of containment of Russian expansionism to buy time for internal changes to occur within that country. He favored a political strategy of containment. He was opposed to the militarization of the concept and therefore opposed our involvement in Vietnam.

democratic regimes against undemocratic regimes. The imperative of containing communism was the justification for aiding unsavory governments while failing to aid democratic forces.

Cuba

Fidel Castro came to power in Cuba in January 1959 when he overthrew the dictator Fulgencio Batista. Castro immediately began to consolidate close relations with the Soviet bloc. In 1961 the new Kennedy administration was presented with a plan put together under the Eisenhower administration by the Central Intelligence Agency to overthrow Castro. The CIA plan assumed that a small group of Cuban exiles would be able to establish a beachhead in Cuba, which would lead to large defections from Castro's army and a popular uprising. It was implemented, and the exiles landed at Cuba's Bay of Pigs. But the invasion was an unmitigated disaster.

The failure of the United States to overtly intervene with its own forces when the covert intervention failed led Khrushchev to miscalculate Kennedy's determination to fight communism. Khrushchev began building launching sites in Cuba for medium- and intermediate-range Soviet ballistic missiles. If Kennedy failed to respond, it would indicate to our NATO allies what some were beginning to fear, that once the United States was vulnerable to attack, it would not risk nuclear war to protect Europe from the Soviets. Failure to respond once the missiles were in place would reinforce Khrushchev's boast that world power was shifting toward the Soviet Union.

The Soviet move in Cuba was predicated on the belief that the United States did not possess the will to use force in the defense of its interests. Kennedy knew that allowing such a misperception to stand was dangerous because it would lead the Soviets to carry out additional challenges to Western security such as Khrushchev threatened over Berlin. So Kennedy stood firm during the Cuban missile crisis: He placed a "quarantine" around Cuba against the shipment of additional missiles there, and demanded the removal of all missiles already in Cuba before they became operational. The overwhelming conventional military superiority of the United States in the Caribbean and its nuclear superiority, along with Kennedy's determined stance, left Moscow little choice but to back down.

Shortly after the Cuban missile crisis, both the Soviet Union and the United States were distracted from their aggressive direct rivalry with each other. The embarrassing blunder in Cuba was a major factor in Khrushchev's ouster by Leonid Brezhnev in 1964, and Brezhnev himself felt forced to concentrate on a massive buildup of conventional and nuclear forces. At the same time, the United States became preoccupied with domestic issues and the war in Vietnam.

Vietnam

After the Cuban missile crisis, the United States two years later faced the shock of Kennedy's assassination in November 1963. Kennedy's successor, Lyndon Johnson, whose main interest was domestic policy, wanted to undertake progressive social reforms, many of which had been proposed by Kennedy, that he termed the

Great Society. But even as he worked toward that end, and started pushing civil rights bills through Congress, he became increasingly involved in the unraveling of the situation in Vietnam.

The logic that ensnared the United States in Vietnam was the dubious **domino theory**: If South Vietnam fell to communist forces, it would be like a falling domino that would cause other dominoes in Southeast Asia, such as Laos and Cambodia, to fall in succession. During World War II, Franklin Roosevelt adamantly opposed any suggestion that France should be allowed to reclaim its colony in Indochina after Japan was defeated. But when communists after the war seized power in the northern part of Vietnam, every President from Truman to Nixon felt compelled to incrementally increase American aid first to the French and then to successive noncommunist regimes in the south of the country in an effort to prevent a communist victory there also. The strategy never worked, however. The autocratic rule of several leaders in South Vietnam provided fertile ground for the recruitment of South Vietnamese into guerrilla activity against the American effort—guerilla activity directed by Ho Chih Minh's communist forces from the north.

The Vietnam War resulted in the deaths of over 55,000 American troops and about 600,000 North Vietnamese. As the conflict dragged on, many Americans began to question the morality of their country's use of force in Vietnam. The traditional American view that democratic principles were incompatible with power politics began to reassert itself. **Vietnam challenged the notion that the policy of containment could be used to justify military intervention regardless of cost in lives and material**. The consensus in support of containment policy remained, but for the first time serious questions were raised concerning how to most effectively pursue the policy.

The intervention in Vietnam subordinated domestic politics to foreign policy issues. The decision to invest resources in fighting the war diverted their being used to deal with the nation's domestic problems in the areas of health, education, pollution, and crime in the streets.

Supporters of the war argued that those who complained that military expenditures shifted resources away from more pressing social issues were prolonging the war by encouraging the enemy while discouraging the American soldier in the field. In fact, as H. R. Haldeman's diaries make clear, President Nixon concluded by late 1970 that the war was unwinnable. He was concerned that a pullout in 1971 would result in an adverse reaction in the 1972 elections. Haldeman noted in his diary that he planned "a continued winding down and then a pullout right at the fall of '72 so that if any bad results follow they will be too late to affect the election."[12] The United States withdrew the last of its ground troops in 1973. The end of the South Vietnamese government was by that time inevitable, although its final collapse occurred in 1975.

---

[12] H. R. Haldeman, *The Haldeman Diaries: Inside the Nixon White House* (New York: G. P. Putnam's Sons, 1994), p. 221.

Detente

By the end of the Vietnam War, the illusion of omnipotence possessed by the United States in 1962 was gone. The optimism of the early 1960s that U.S. power and moral righteousness could encourage democracies and justice throughout the world collapsed with the fall of South Vietnam to the communists in 1975. It was replaced by a new awareness of the difficulties involved in democratic nation-building abroad and a fear that the wielding of international power could corrupt the nation using it. Americans became disillusioned and weary with their nation's Cold War role and the rationale that justified intervention based merely on anticommunism. The strains resulting from the war showed that the nation was not invincible militarily nor invulnerable economically.

By the early 1970s, the failure of U.S. policy in Vietnam led the United States to pursue a policy of **detente**. **Detente** refers to a relaxation of tension between the United States and the Soviet Union during the Nixon, Ford, and Carter administrations. Detente was begun during the Nixon administration with an attempt to use trade to encourage friendlier relations with the Soviet Union. It was not a rejection of the Cold War or the policy of containment so much as a tactical shift in the pursuit of American interests when the strategic superiority of the United States was gone and many Americans were demanding that more attention be paid to domestic issues.

Detente was also useful to the Soviet Union. During the first 20 years of the Cold War, the United States embargoed the shipment of products that might have any military application or promote the economic strength of the Soviet Union. The effect was to encourage the Soviet economy to remain self-sufficient and independent. The Soviet economy was stagnating by the early 1970s due to the diversion of so many resources to its military needs. The communist government was unable to deliver on its promise of more consumer goods, including food. Since Brezhnev considered the structural reforms later undertaken by Gorbachev as too radical, he needed detente to import Western consumer goods, technology, and food. Henry Kissinger and subsequently President Jimmy Carter used trade to reward or punish Soviet foreign policy. The hope was that Soviet need for American wheat and computers would result in the Soviets exercising self-restraint in foreign policy to avoid a cutoff in American trade. Events revealed the limitations of using trade as a foreign policy tool. But the use of economic carrots and sticks under detente did encourage the Soviet economy to become more dependent upon the American economy.[13]

During the 1970s several agreements between the United States and the Soviet Union on arms control, trade, and technology transfer issues were concluded. Detente continued despite strains created over issues like Angola and Ethiopia until late in 1979. In November of that year, militant elements in Iran seized 52

---

[13] John Spanier, *Games Nations Play*, 7th ed. (Washington, DC: The Congressional Quarterly Press, 1990), p. 392.

Americans at the U.S. embassy in Teheran, and a month later the Soviet Union invaded Afghanistan. President Carter began taking a tougher stand toward the Soviets. He embargoed shipments of grain to the Soviet Union, and began giving military aid to forces in Afghanistan fighting the Soviet occupation.

All this caused difficulties for detente and shifts in American attitudes. The situation of the hostages in Iran prevented a retaliatory strike against the Iranian militants and seemed to symbolize the impotence of a policy that emphasized accommodation when dealing with revolutionary fundamentalists. Nor was the wheat embargo popular. Sanctions against the Soviets hit American business with the prospect of lost sales, and workers with lost jobs. Also trade embargoes can be effective only if an adversary cannot obtain the commodities elsewhere. The Soviet Union learned very quickly how to encourage competition between nations seeking markets for their products. Upset over the hostages and over lost trade because of Carter's embargo encouraged a major shift in public attitudes away from detente and toward a more assertive international role for the United States.

Ronald Reagan, who had long espoused a firm stance on foreign policy issues, benefited from the mood swing. Many believed that detente enabled the Russians to advance their interests at the expense of the United States. In the 1980 Presidential campaign, Reagan supported significantly increased defense spending and indicated a greater willingness to use military force in pursuit of containment. He also promised American farmers that if elected he would end President Carter's embargo on wheat to the Soviet Union.

Gorbachev and the Disintegration of Soviet Communism

Leonid Brezhnev's foreign policy, which sought nuclear parity with the United States, had been achieved at the cost of a stagnant Soviet economy. When Mikhail S. Gorbachev came to power in the mid-1980s, he was unlike any other Soviet leader since the communists came to power in Russia in 1917. He was far more sophisticated and less ideological than his predecessors. He, like Reagan, benefited from a changing mood among the Russian people, who were beginning to press for improved living standards. Several years of bad harvests had resulted in the rationing of some basic foods like meat and sugar. Food had been imported from the United States since the 1970s. By the end of that decade, the Soviet economy had literally come to a standstill.

When Gorbachev became General Secretary of the Soviet Communist Party in 1985, he quickly learned the severity of the economic crisis that the Soviet Union faced. He immediately began a series of economic reforms known as *perestroika* or a "restructuring" toward a market system. His reforms included the introduction of civil liberties known as *glasnost* ("openness") within Soviet society. He encouraged the removal of the privileged position of the communist party and allowed competition in elections. He even permitted the Supreme Soviet to initiate actions rather than merely act as a rubber stamp to the communist party leadership's decisions.

To accomplish his political and economic reforms, Gorbachev needed to shift spending from the military to the civilian sector of the Soviet economy. His actions unleashed a pent-up demand for more political and economic freedom, while hard-line communists tried desperately to maintain control. His emphasis on the priority of domestic affairs required pursuit of a conciliatory foreign policy, especially in reducing strategic military forces. The burden of Cold War spending had caused the Soviet Union to divert so many resources to military spending that its economy was falling further and further behind the West.

Gorbachev changed several long-held doctrinaire foreign policy positions of the Soviet Union. For example, he indicated that the value of peace would take prece-dence over the class struggle, and repudiated the Brezhnev Doctrine by stating that socialist countries had no right to intervene in one another's affairs. "Sufficiency" would be the basis for determining the level of Soviet military preparedness. Soviet forces in Eastern Europe would be reorganized into a defense posture that would preclude the possibility of offensive military moves against the West to reassure NATO. To this end, he promised to withdraw six tank divisions and bridging units and their equipment from Warsaw Pact countries.

Gorbachev wanted to slow down the arms race in order to divert more resources to domestic Soviet economic policy. He proposed a strategic arms treaty to slow Reagan's Strategic Defense Initiative (SDI) and limit intermediate nuclear forces (INF) to include nuclear missiles based in the United States and Europe and strate-gic bombers. Gorbachev believed that if Reagan signed such a treaty, his strongly anticommunist record would make it very difficult for conservative senators in the President's own Republican Party to continue their opposition, as would be likely if the President was a Democrat. The Senate ultimately gave its consent to the treaty negotiated under Reagan and Gorbachev by a vote of 93-4 as conservative opposi-tion to it crumbled. In 1988 Gorbachev committed the Soviet Union to a unilateral 10 percent reduction in its military budget.

The Reagan administration, which began by characterizing the conflict between the United States and the Soviet Union as one between good and evil, by 1988 espoused detente and warmly supported Gorbachev's attempts at domestic reform. By the end of the Reagan administration, American-Soviet relations were closer than under any other President since World War II. The Cold War effectively ended the year after Reagan left office.

Gorbachev's reforms gave a great deal of freedom to the peoples of Russia and the Eastern Bloc countries. His limited democratization and the restraints he placed on the communist party led to shifts in power both in Russia and elsewhere in the Soviet sphere of control. Communist governments in Eastern Europe, which had been maintained only by the threat of bayonets, were quickly swept away. The Baltic states, which had been incorporated into the Soviet Union during World War II, regained their independence in 1990. Mikhail Gorbachev refused to use force to suppress the fragmentation of the Soviet empire as his predecessor Leonid Brezhnev surely would have. Gorbachev was himself a victim of the revolution he started. Overtaken by the tide of change, he was forced to resign in December 1991 and with that the Soviet Union essentially collapsed.

The Cold War thus came to an end with the Soviet empire collapsing in upon itself. Rather than a violent battle between communists and counterrevolutionaries in which the losing forces vowed to continue the struggle, the change was surprisingly swift and peaceful. Most of the inhabitants of the communist countries celebrated the victory of the values of the West over communism.

In place of the Soviet Union there is now the Commonwealth of Independent States (CIS), which facilitates cooperation among the independent republics that formerly made up the Soviet Union. Russia, led by President Boris Yeltsin, is merely the largest of the former Soviet Republics.

Although George Bush was in the White House at the time, he was unable to effectively claim credit for the unraveling of the Soviet Union. **The containment policy initiated by President Truman in 1948 and pursued on a bipartisan basis by the United States was an important ingredient in the West's victory over communism. But the failure of Soviet domestic policy and the corruption of the Soviet system was a greater ingredient.**

FOREIGN POLICY AFTER THE COLD WAR

The policy of containment that became an integral part of the Cold War began as a pragmatic reaction to a very real threat. Over time, this anticommunist sentiment defined a major value in the outlook of Americans. The Cold War provided a reaffirmation of the values of freedom and democracy over the antithetical system represented by communism, as well as the need to guarantee the peace through military power. This East-West struggle led most Americans to identify themselves as strongly anticommunist. Winning the Cold War suddenly deprived American foreign policy of the galvanizing sense of purpose that had been its fixed star since the Truman administration. In the middle 1990s Americans no longer share a need to unite to oppose a common enemy. There is little likelihood that another common enemy will emerge to equal the potential threat of international communism and to concentrate our will and spirit in defense of "the American way."

The lack of a unifying foreign threat means that **American foreign policy will become more partisan.** Presidents will no longer be conceded the right to take almost whatever action they deem necessary on behalf of the nation's interests as they were during the extraordinary circumstances of the Cold War. **American foreign policy issues will be more controversial than in the past. This will reduce support for defense programs, economic or military aid, or any other proposal that may be perceived as excessive concern for foreign affairs at the expense of American taxpayers.** The end of the Cold War means that there will be greater attention paid to domestic policies at the expense of foreign and military policies.

The collapse of the Soviet Union left the United States as the only legitimate superpower. **This does not mean the end of international conflict.** On the contrary, the decline of Soviet power breathed new life into nationalistic rivalries in Eastern Europe.

The end of the Cold War will result in greater Congressional challenges to Presidential leadership in foreign policy. For decades the preeminence of the role of the President in conducting foreign policy was aided by the tensions of the Cold War. It allowed Presidents to exercise leadership in foreign affairs with far less interference than could usually be done in domestic policy. This was especially true when Republican Presidents occupied the White House, and Democrats controlled Congress.

It should be noted that President Eisenhower had warned of the growing alliance between military and industrial interests, a military-industrial complex, influencing Congress to fund the military and defense industries quite apart from national security needs. Cold War logic justified and even required huge expenditures for exotic and expensive military weapons systems. These expenditures overwhelmingly reward affluent business interests engaged in military production. Many conservatives found this "higher" policy of national defense also proved to be an effective justification to keep social welfare spending low. Liberals wanted to show that they were patriotic pragmatic realists and also supported the diversion of funds for national security.

Traditionally Democrats have had a more activist foreign policy than Republicans. In fact, Republicans have frequently accused the Democrats of recklessness in foreign policy, noting that Democrats were in the White House when the nation became involved in both world wars, Korea, and Vietnam. However, the Democrats' convention in Chicago in 1968 revealed serious divisions between the party's anticommunist hawks and its doves. For the next 25 years Democrats have, to their disadvantage with voting Americans, generally been perceived as being weaker on foreign and defense issues.

Prior to World War II, Republicans and conservatives tended to be the most isolationist in opposition to Roosevelt's activist foreign policy. But after the war, the menacing specter of communism united the Republican party in a demand to counter communism wherever it appeared. The most damning charge against a political opponent during the postwar period was that he or she was "soft on communism."

Postwar Republican Presidents, while inclined to deemphasize the role of government in domestic policy in favor of market solutions, emphasized the need for a "strong" leadership role by the U.S. government in foreign policy. Richard Nixon, who was forced to resign the Presidency in disgrace after Watergate, salvaged his reputation to some extent later on and made a modest comeback in some circles based on his reputation as a foreign policy expert. Reagan's willingness to switch from an oppositional stance to accepting arms control agreements resulted in solid advances in the conditions for world peace. George Bush, who wanted to be known as the "foreign policy President," gained high marks for his foreign policy efforts. His interest in foreign policy was so great that after the collapse of the Soviet Union and the conclusion of the Gulf War in early 1991, he was perceived to have no domestic policy, and this went a long way toward costing him the 1992 election.

However, the unexpectedly swift end to communism in the early 1990s shattered Republican unity concerning an interventionist foreign policy. Opposition to communism had been perceived to be in our vital national interests, but current problems in Somalia, Bosnia, or Haiti are not. Many Republicans had long been uncomfortable with the contradiction of supporting "big government" intervention abroad in the form of major international political and military actions while arguing that "big government" at home is incapable of solving domestic problems and solutions should be left to the marketplace. A new consensus has yet to be reached.

FUTURE CHALLENGES AND FOREIGN POLICY

The end of the Cold War has reduced the threat of a global nuclear catastrophe. However, without the international bipolar competition, and the discipline it imposed, the world is reverting to greater anarchy that characterized the pre World War II period. The Cold War provided a simple test to distinguish allies from adversaries, or good guys from bad guys. It was based upon which camp a nation or its leaders leaned toward, capitalism or communism. But such simplistic distinctions, which aroused strong support for decades, are now obsolete.

In the post Cold War world, it is far more difficult to determine exactly what an American national policy interest is, as well as to distinguish allies from adversaries. For this reason alone, it is much more difficult to obtain steadfast support for foreign policy. This is especially true since so few trouble spots are or will be perceived as a threat to America's vital interests.

Starting with the Clinton administration, America must begin the complicated task of redefining its role in the international community. The basic foreign policy questions are: **What are the new goals of U.S. foreign policy? What are the obstacles to realizing these goals? How can the United States best achieve its interests?**

With the collapse of communism, Americans clearly want more attention paid to long-neglected domestic problems. Foreign policy challenges must be perceived in the national interest in order to receive broad public support. But the American public also believes that the United States has great responsibilities and cannot withdraw from world affairs. And while it is important to maintain military strength in an unstable world, the country cannot go it alone without friends and allies.[14] There is clear support for an active involvement in nonproliferation and arms transfers. Support also exists for U.S. involvement with the UN to expand peacekeeping efforts, to eliminate chemical and nuclear weapons around the world, to clean up the environment, and to suppress illegal international drug trafficking.[15] Emphasizing domestic priorities and supporting a major proactive foreign policy are not mutually exclusive positions. Nor is an activist international role inherently liberal or conservative.

ETHICAL CONCERNS AND FOREIGN POLICY

The U.S. emphasis on supporting democratic governments is related to the goal of encouraging human rights and social justice. The United States prefers to support constructive change through the ballot box rather than change brought by bullets.

---

[14] Daniel Yankelovich, "Foreign Policy after the Election," *Foreign Affairs*, vol. 71, no. 4. (1992), pp. 6–7.

[15] Norman J. Ornstein, "Foreign Policy and the Election," *Foreign Affairs*, vol. 71, no. 3 (1992), p. 14.

During the Cold War, when policy makers perceived our national security or economic needs diverging from the goals of encouraging democracy and justice, they swallowed their scruples. This was unfortunate because support for human rights can be an effective tool of foreign policy that strengthens democratic principles and American leadership.

Promoting democratic principles is both morally right and in accordance with our national heritage. Oftentimes the national interest and morality support the same policy decision, such as the goal of defeating Nazi Germany. The choice is more difficult when moral principles appear to diverge from political reality. For example, in Operation Desert Storm, the United States used force to dislodge Iraqi forces from Kuwait. We restored a nondemocratic government to power without pressing for democratic reforms. And in Saudi Arabia, we have supported the monarchy of King Fahd against the threat of an Iraqi invasion. The Islamic world denies the basic principle of gender equality. To pressure countries in that region of the world to change, however, would undoubtedly result in greater instability and political turmoil than supporting the status quo.

Many are disappointed that the moral principles enunciated by the Founding Fathers in the Declaration of Independence have not been taken as a firmer guiding principle in America's foreign ventures. It is clear, however, that democracy requires favorable conditions to take root. It is easy to forget that the evolution of self-government has a longer pre- than postrevolutionary history even in the United States.

A current major policy problem for the United States is how to ensure that democratic principles and free market reforms are cultivated in Russia and Eastern Europe. Democratic nation building in the former Soviet republics and in Eastern Europe would permit even lower levels of U.S. defense expenditures. It would also provide a major investment opportunity for business firms if those countries developed stable democratic processes. But the success of democratic governments is far from certain in the 15 independent states that formerly made up the Soviet Union.

It has proven far easier to pressure friendly states to undertake democratic reforms and secure human rights than states with whom relations are strained. It is easier to foster democratic reforms in states that are dependent on the United States like the Philippines than in more hostile states like the People's Republic of China.

The tools available range from quiet diplomacy to the withholding of military and economic aid. Many critics believe that now that Third-World leaders are unable to seek communist support, the United States should encourage democracy and human rights more forcefully than in the past. The difficulty is that supporting democracy and human rights in ambiguous circumstances is not in itself a guide to effective policy. If not done carefully, pressuring nondemocratic states too hard may inadvertently result in a more repressive regime gaining power.

President Clinton stated in a speech in Milwaukee in October 1992 that the United States should pursue a "prodemocracy foreign policy." However, he did not advocate a foreign policy focusing narrowly on that principle. He said, "We know there may be times when other security needs or economic interests will diverge from our commitment to democracy and human rights." Idealistic goals must be tempered with the pragmatism of the realist. However, a foreign policy that tries to nurture democratic development should place a priority on economic and political methods rather than military means.

NATIONALISM AND ETHNIC CONFLICT

Unfortunately, the disintegration of the Soviet Union did not result in an international surge in favor of peaceful democratic forms of government. Instead, the breakdown of the East-West conflict has facilitated a resurgence of older conflicts reined in for decades by Cold War rivalries. In some former communist countries where the authority of the nation-state itself is weak, many people have reverted to precommunist national, racial, ethnic, and religious identifications. The oppressive communist regimes in the former Soviet Union and Yugoslavia, whatever else their failures, did repress the fratricidal ethnic and religious rivalries now raging in Georgia and Bosnia.

During the Cold War the superpowers could also control client states on the periphery of their blocs. While Moscow's leverage to coerce client states has vanished, the ability of Washington to force compliance has also tapered off. In the Middle East and sub-Saharan Africa, in particular, imperialistic European nations earlier in this century created colonies by drawing lines on maps in disregard for ethnic, linguistic, or economic factors. The peace in these areas was often maintained only out of necessities imposed by the Cold War. Without the discipline of superpower rivalry to suppress regional and border conflicts, such problems are becoming much more numerous. The result is frequently the creation of millions of refugees and mass migrations on a scale previously unknown, as in Rwanda.

Many of the problems appear all but insoluble even with superpower intervention. For example, Iraq has made territorial claims on Kuwait since London created the Kuwaiti protectorate in the 1920s. Most Iraqis do not regard the border with Kuwait as either just or permanent. The inability of Saddam Hussein to enforce Iraq's claim over the area in the Gulf War does not lessen the righteousness of the cause in the eyes of Iraq's citizens. The United States has merely replaced British imperialism as the enemy. This impression is reinforced by America returning a nondemocratic government to power in Kuwait, which has led to cynicism regarding how important democracies are to the United States even in a post Cold War world.

Territorial disputes, civil wars, ethnic conflicts (several of which have spilled across international borders) as well as the collapse of governmental authority in some states threaten world peace. While such conflicts may not threaten American national security, their effect cannot be ignored. The United Nations has tried to play a constructive role by mediating disputes and the use of neutral peacekeeping troops interposed between warring factions. The Clinton administration has tried to prod the UN to take action to prevent governments from destroying its own citizens. Sovereignty does not include the right to commit genocide against one's own nationals. The Nuremberg Tribunals settled that issue. As this book goes to press, the UN is cooperating in the gathering of evidence to be used to prosecute individuals who have committed atrocities in Bosnia and Serbia. It is the obligation of the international community, not of the United States or any other state, to prevent genocidal policies.

The U.S. policy may be most effective when prodding the UN to take action. The United States can provide logistical and material support for such operations. The use of U.S. troops for peacekeeping operations present a unique set of problems. Canada, Sweden, and Ireland among others have long experience in peacekeeping operations and are not as likely to be targeted by a faction seeking notoriety as American troops.

The Clinton administration announced a policy of considering U.S. personnel participation in a given peace operation if it advances American interests and if the unique risks to American personnel have been weighed and are considered acceptable. American participation must be considered essential for the operation's success, and there must be clear objectives and an identifiable endpoint for U.S. participation.

ECONOMIC THEMES

Military Spending and Economic Power

There is an unusual relationship between military power and economic power. A nation that would be a military superpower must make significant investments in military production and spending. This must ordinarily be done at the expense of investment in consumer goods. The United States can have the status of a military and an economic superpower only if its citizenry exercises a greater propensity to save and invest in civilian research and development (R&D). Historically there is a tendency for economic powers to invest heavily in military spending. Exorbitant military spending undermines economic power. But in the long run, as Gorbachev found out, military power requires a sound economic structure.

During the Cold War the United States diverted about 6 percent of GDP from consumer production to military spending. This is one reason the American economy has lagged behind those of Japan and Germany for the last couple of decades. About 70 percent of R&D money in the United States was spent on the military. Most of the best engineers and scientists in America during that time worked in military rather than consumer goods research. In Japan the emphasis was the reverse.

International Trade

International trade has become a significant part of the U.S. economy only in the last half of the century. Sales of goods and services abroad, or **exports**, now amount to 10 percent of what the American economy produces. **Exports are goods produced domestically but sold in foreign markets**. The goods and services purchased in the United States but produced abroad, or **imports**, have increased dra-

COMPARATIVE ADVANTAGE

Why do people engage in international trade, which has so many potential difficulties? Would it not be easier if each country relied on the productive capacity of its own economy? The answer is that Adam Smith's reasoning that applied to a domestic economy was shown by David Ricardo to also apply to international trade. National economies differ because they have different comparative advantages. **A comparative advantage exists when a country can produce a good at a lower opportunity cost (give up less production of other goods) than another country**. For example, suppose that in the United States it costs $150 to produce a leather jacket or a portable disc player. Suppose in Japan it costs $150 to produce a leather jacket but only $100 to produce a portable disc player. In the United States, the opportunity cost of producing a leather jacket is equal to that of producing one disc player. Since the cost is the same, the United States must reduce its production of leather coats by one to get one more disc player. Japan has a comparative advantage in producing disc players because its opportunity cost is only two-thirds of a leather jacket. This gives the United States a comparative advantage in the production of leather jackets. Notice that if one country has a comparative advantage in one good, the other nation must have a comparative advantage in the production of another good. Comparative advantage is based on the opportunity cost, not total costs.

Free trade between nations results in situations where a nation as a whole is better off, but some workers are worse off. Industries with a comparative advantage will expand and new workers will be hired as products are produced for the export market. Consumers will also be better off, as they can buy imported products at lower prices. Workers in industries without a comparative advantage will face a downward pressure on wages, and may face layoffs.

The areas of comparative advantage for the American economy have been shifting for a number of years, and there have been job losses as some kinds of industry have moved abroad. The Clinton administration has pledged to provide retraining programs for Americans who lose jobs to help them find employment in the job areas where the United States still enjoys a comparative advantage over foreign competitors. It also supported NAFTA on the basis that free trade should result in a net benefit to the American economy since the overall gains it produces exceed any losses.

matically in the last 20 years. **Imports are goods produced in foreign countries but purchased in the United States**. Imports have exceeded exports consistently since 1975.

Whenever nations engage in international trade, there are potential problems. International trade differs from domestic trade in that a foreign entrepreneur's right to sell in another country's domestic market can be limited by **tariffs**, or taxes on imports. Other regulatory restrictions on imports, such as requirements that a percentage of the products must be assembled within the host state, called **nontariff barriers**, may also limit trade. Foreign producers may also find countries impose **quotas**, or absolute limits on the amounts of goods that can be imported. International trade usually requires the business entities involved to find a way to exchange currencies. **Foreign exchange markets**, where traders exchange currencies, provide this service.

Since nations are not self-sufficient they must obtain through trade the goods they are unable to produce or find too expensive to produce themselves, or they must accept a lower standard of living.

One reason policy makers today must be concerned with international trade issues is America's current **balance of trade** situation, or the gap between the value of goods it exports and imports. When the value of exports exceeds the value of imports, a country runs a **trade surplus**. When the value of imports exceeds that of exports, a country runs a **trade deficit**. From the end of World War II until the early 1980s, the United States consistently exported more than it imported. Then in the early 1980s persistent and massive trade deficits emerged. The United States has been running a trade deficit which increased to $170 billion in 1987. Since then the level has declined, but still runs at about $100 billion annually.

Why Worry about Trade Deficits?

Running a trade deficit has similarities to running a budget deficit. It allows a nation to consume (import) more than it produces (exports) by spending past savings, or by borrowing. When the United States runs a trade deficit, the country must make up the difference by selling assets like real estate, stocks, bonds, and even whole corporations. In the more than half a century from World War I until the 1980s, the United States was the major creditor nation of the world. It ran large trade surpluses with other countries, lending large sums abroad and acquiring large amounts of foreign assets in the process. Net American foreign investment reached a peak of $141 billion at the end of 1981. Then, in just 4 years, the total accumulated investments of over 60 years were undone. By the end of 1985, foreign assets in the United States exceeded American-held assets abroad by $112 billion.[16] Since then, the United States has become the world's biggest debtor nation and instead of receiving interest income, we must pay out interest every year while getting nothing in return.

An important factor in determining whether a country runs a trade deficit or surplus is its ability to produce goods more cheaply than other countries. Through the 1950s and 1960s, American workers were highly competitive even though their wages were higher than most foreign workers. American productivity was so great that American goods were of higher quality and lower price, and therefore more desirable than foreign goods. That began to change by the late 1970s as Japan and Third-World countries invested heavily in developing their industrial bases. Foreign governments were not about to allow natural market forces to determine outcomes with so much at stake. Governments intervened to subsidize much of the research and development necessary for business development and manufacturing. In the process, they proved that governmental intervention can strengthen national markets. Foreign manufacturers with new and modern industrial facilities and lower

[16] Paul Krugman, *The Age of Diminished Expectations* (Cambridge, MA: MIT Press, 1992), p. 40.

wages began with increasing frequency to compete effectively with American manufacturers.

Another major cause of America's current trade deficit is the large federal budget deficit, which requires the government to borrow money to pay the interest on the debt. The resulting upward pressure on interest rates makes the cost of investing in U.S. capital plants and equipment high. This makes it relatively less expensive for foreign manufacturers to produce competing goods.

Other trade pressures magnify a trade deficit. When a trade deficit occurs, imports rise and exports fall. A fall in exports means that domestic production falls, which means that domestic workers have less income and consequently demand for goods falls and unemployment rises. Higher unemployment means that workers spend less and incomes fall more. Conversely, in a nation like Japan that exports more than it imports, as production rises, Japanese citizens have more income to spend on consumer goods or investments, resulting in increased demand and high employment levels that ultimately Japanese incomes rise ever further. The effect of Japan's exports on income creates export-led economic growth. That is, Japan's trade surplus stimulates higher incomes.

Pleas for Protectionism

Free trade has its critics who argue that trade restrictions would directly reduce the deficit. It is often claimed that trade is unfair because of low foreign wages, or government subsidies. However, if U.S. producers would benefit from tariffs, consumers would lose. Consumer prices would rise with tariffs while quality of domestic products would fall, lowering the standard of living. Trade restrictions also invite retaliation. If one country erects trade barriers, other countries respond with restrictions of their own.

The economic arguments in favor of free trade are so compelling it is surprising that sentiments for trade restrictions are so strong. The arguments raised in favor of protecting the economy from the effects of free trade include the following: (a) Foreign governments unfairly subsidize their producers; (b) therefore, trade leads to a loss of jobs; (c) trade increases a nation's vulnerability to other countries' agendas, especially in times of war.

The major political risk of massive deficits is that they compromise U.S. sovereignty. We did not worry about this argument when we were the largest creditor nation. Now that we are the major debtor nation, we more clearly understand the position of other net debtor states.

The decade of the 1980s saw a surge in protectionism in the United States. Some blamed the weak American economy on unfair foreign trade barriers that prevented the sale of American goods in international markets, thereby costing American jobs. Protectionism, it was argued, would save American jobs from such unfair practices and strengthen the economy. While President Reagan talked about the virtues of unfettered market forces, protectionism spiraled. In 1980 about one-eighth of all imports into the United States were affected by protectionism; by 1990 that figure was 25 percent. By the end of the 1980s, about 40 percent of Japan's exports to the United States were limited by some form of protectionism. Japan was persuaded to "voluntarily" limit its exports of cars to the United States or face the possibility of quotas.

President Clinton has committed himself to the reduction of all trade barriers. His commitment to win Congressional approval of NAFTA over sharp opposition by labor is significant in this regard. He has also indicated his commitment to support a reduction in trade barriers at the Uruguay round of the General Agreement on Tariffs and Trade (GATT) negotiations. In addition, he has announced as a goal reforming domestic institutions to improve the competitive performance of the U.S. economy, including its international trade and financial position. Reducing the federal budget deficit, he has indicated, is one component in reducing the trade deficit.

The issue is no longer a zero-sum attempt to combat communist enemies, but a non-zero-sum economic competition among international partners to achieve domestic and international economic growth. There is an important link between domestic economic policy and foreign policy. A robust American economy based upon principles of justice provides a better opportunity for the United States to encourage human rights and democratic approaches along with open market systems. Any effective foreign policy must be based on an improvement in the international competitiveness of the American economy.

CONCLUSION

1 Foreign policy making by the American government is characterized by a unique set of political actors and processes. The Constitution ultimately provides that the President and Congress share responsibility in foreign policy. Actors involved in crisis situations in foreign policy tend to be limited to the President, leading members of Congress, and heads of executive agencies such as the Departments of State and Defense and the Central Intelligence Agency. Long-term national security issues, while generally formulated by the President, traditionally involve Congressional involvement and bipartisan support through the need for funding. Such issues have not typically required major involvement by the American public. A decline in the consensus that the policy in Vietnam was either wise or necessary in opposing communism resulted in a more independent minded Congress in regard to foreign policy.

2 From 1945 until the collapse of the Soviet Union in 1990, American foreign policy was based on the policy of containing communist expansionism. This bipolar rivalry with the Soviet Union provided discipline and restricted foreign policy options for over 40 years. It also reduced funding available for domestic needs such as housing, education, and poverty programs.

3 With the end of the Cold War many nations, particularly in Europe, have been freed from the constraints of superpower rivalry and have more freedom to pursue their national interests. The drive for further European integration has been slowed by the end of the Cold War.

4 The international system is in a state of transition. While international integration is occurring in some areas, nationalism, political turmoil, and even civil war have reemerged in others. Workable foreign policy tools for handling these situations have yet to be developed.

5 Economic and technical changes in international economic systems are eroding some of the sovereign political authority traditionally enjoyed by nation-states. Ideological confrontations between capitalism and communism are being replaced by competition between different models of market economies. Nations are competing to create favorable conditions for economic prosperity. Some governments play a far more active role as coordinators of their domestic economies than others.

QUESTIONS FOR DISCUSSION

1 Is the United States in decline as a superpower despite the collapse of the Soviet Union? Why?
2 Is there evidence that declining hegemonic powers like the Soviet Union create political instability and economic disarray?
3 Is the U.S. economy in disarray because the United States is the largest debtor nation in the world? Why or why not?
4 Why do most political scientists oppose trade restrictions?
5 Why is all voluntary international trade mutually beneficial?

KEY CONCEPTS

Comparative advantage
Containment policy
Covert action
European Community (EC)
Exports
Global village
Imports

Intergovernmental organizations (IGOs)
National Security Council (NSC)
Nongovernmental organizations (NGOs)
Sovereignty
Trade deficit
Trade surplus

SUGGESTED READINGS

C. Fred Bergsten, "The Primacy of Economics," *Foreign Policy* (Summer 1992), pp. 3–25.
Peter Drucker, *Post-Capitalist Society* (New York: Harper Collins, 1993).
Paul Krugman, *The Age of Diminished Expectations: U.S. Economic Policy in the 1990s* (Cambridge, MA: MIT Press, 1992).
Edward J. Lincoln, *Japan's Unequal Trade* (Washington, DC: The Brookings Institution, 1990).
Thomas E. Mann (ed.), *A Question of Balance: The President, the Congress, and Foreign Policy* (Washington, DC: The Brookings Institution, 1990).
Jerel A. Rosati, *The Politics of United States Foreign Policy* (New York: Harcourt, Brace, Jovanovich, 1993).
Theodore Rueter (ed.), *The United States in the World Political Economy* (New York: McGraw-Hill, 1994).

John W. Spanier and Eric M. Uslaner, *American Foreign Policy Making and the Democratic Dilemmas*, 6th ed. (New York: Macmillan, 1994).

John D. Steinbruner (ed.), *Restructuring American Foreign Policy* (Washington, DC: The Brookings Institution, 1989).

Lester Thurow, *Head to Head* (New York: William Morrow, 1992).

Alvin Toffler and Heidi Toffler, *War and Anti-War: Survival at the Dawn of the 21st Century* (Boston: Little, Brown, 1993).

Martin Tolchin and Susan Tolchin, *Buying into America* (New York: Times Books, 1988).

Martin Tolchin and Susan Tolchin, *Selling Our Security* (New York: Alfred A. Knopf, 1992).

INDEX

Acid rain, 383, 391
ACLU (*see* American Civil Liberties Union)
Adams, John, 101, 117
Adams, John Quincy, 411
Adjusted gross income (AGI), 344
Adverse selection, 361
AFT (*see* Bureau of Alcohol, Tobacco and Firearms)
Agenda setting, 39–43
    (*See also* Policy-making process)
Aid to Families with Dependent Children (AFDC), 145, 173, 213, 215–222, 271, 347
    AFDC-UP, 216–217
AIDS, 360, 362
Alzheimer's Association, 52
Alzheimer's disease, 52, 332
American Academy of Family Physicians, 332
American Civil Liberties Union (ACLU), 244
American College of Physicians, 332
American Medical Association (AMA), 332, 337
Americans with Disabilities Act, 89
Aristotle, 95*n.*
Arnold, Roger A., 11
Arrow, Kenneth, 72*n.*
Articles of Confederation, 96–100
Assumptions and theory, 32–34
Audubon Society, 383

Balance of trade, 441
Balanced Budget Amendment, 166–167

Batista, Fulgencio, 429
Bennett, W. Lance, 48
Bennett, William, 221
Bentham, Jeremy, 207
Bernard, Thomas B., 233
Berry, Jeffrey M., 43
Best-case scenario, 391, 395
Black box, 5
Blecker, Robert, 242
Blinder, Alan, 138, 212
Blockbusting, 277
Blumstein, Alfred, 242
Boland Amendment, 91, 417
Bork, Robert, 92
Bourdieu, Pierre, 297
Brady bill, 249
Brezhnev, Leonid, 429, 432
Brzezinski, Zbigniew, 415
Budget deficit, 136, 139
    and uncontrollable elements, 164
Budget Enforcement Act (BEA), 168
Bureau of Alcohol, Tobacco and Firearms (AFT), 248
Bureaucracy, 83–85
Burford, Ann Gorsuch, 385
Burns, James MacGregor, 113*n.*
Burt, Martha, 273
Bush, George:
    appeal to Democrats, 91
    criminal justice, 238
    domestic program, 89
    education as symbolic politics, 119
    education goals, 51, 291–292
    environmental policy, 386, 419, 435
    federal deficits, 157
    health care, 332, 376
    housing policy, 283

Bush, George (*Cont.*):
  no new tax pledge, 50, 161, 170, 185
  pardon of administration officials, 92
  percentage of vote, 122
  reduced role of government, 110,
    141
  and term limits, 114
  and unemployment, 137
  victory margin, 67
  voodoo economics, 94*n.*, 153

Canadian health care system, 376–379
Capital gains:
  defined, 14*n.*, 182–183
  (*See also* Taxes)
Capital investment, 135, 305
Capital punishment, 244–245
Capitation fee, 364
Capture theory of government, 63
Carlyle, Thomas, 132, 206
Carson, Rachel, 383, 393
Carter, Jimmy:
  environmental policy, 385, 415, 431
  housing policy, 282, 283
  negative income tax, 222
  policy shifts, 66
  unified government, 113
Castro, Fidel, 429
Catholic Church and transnational
  organizations, 424
CBS, 358, 370
Census Bureau, 277, 367
Central Business Districts (CBDs), 259
Central Intelligence Agency (CIA),
  417–420
Charlesworth, James, 25*n.*
Checks and Balances, 96–98
Chlorofluorocarbons (CFCs), 390,
  396–397
Choice, 2
  social, 4
Chrysler Corporation, 66, 119, 145
Chubb, John, 314, 317

Civil Rights Act of 1968, 277
Civil rights struggle, 108
Civil War, U.S., 105, 106
Class conflict model, 298
Clean Air Act, 89, 384
  and amendments of 1990, 386, 404
Clearance rates, 228
Clinton, William:
  attempts to embarrass, 92
  crime policy, 253
  deficit reduction, 93
  environmental policy, 386–387, 402,
    405
  foreign policy, 436–440, 443
  health care, 332–333, 336–337,
    372–375
  industrial policy, 40
  intelligence policy, 419
  and NAIRU, 137
  party divisions, 114
  as perceived by left and right, 77
  political center, 76
  Republican opposition to, 153
  tax increase, 155
  trade policy, 423
  victory margin, 122
  welfare reform, 220–221
Cobb, Roger, 41*n.*, 47*n.*, 49*n.*
Coehlo, Tony, 92
Coinsurance, 348
  (*See also* Insurance)
Cold War, 409
Coleman, James, and school-centered
  focus, 308–313, 316
Comparative advantage, 440
Comprehensive Employment and
  Training Act, 113
Conflict:
  scope of, 42–43
  socialization of, 42
Congress:
  and committees, 54
  and foreign policy, 413–415
  Social Security Disability Insurance,
    56

Congressional Budget Office (CBO), 274

Congressional oversight of intelligence, 419–421

Constitution (U.S.):
budgetary process, 152
design, 95
as policy statement, 55

Constitutional Convention, 96–100, 102, 118

Consumer Price Index (CPI), 211*n*., 212

Consumer Product Safety Act, 113

Containment policy, 428, 430

Convenient logic, 146–147

Cost-benefit analysis, 64–66, 406

Cost containment, 358

Cost shifting, 358

Council on Competitiveness, 386

Courts, 236–238

Crime:
causes, 232–234
criminogenic factors, 234
defined, 232
deterrence, 238–241
incapacitation, 238–239
nonviolent, 228–231
rehabilitation, 238, 239
retribution, 238–239
violent, 228–231
white collar, 251–252

Crime index, 226–229

Cultural deficit, 307

Cultural deprivation, 308

Cultural differences, 308

Cuomo, Mario, 245

D'Amato, Alphonse, 92

Davis, Kingsley, 194*n*.

Debt, national, 156–168

Declaration of Independence, 190

Defensive medicine, 344

Deficits, 155–167
defined, 156

Deficits (*Cont.*):
politics of, 165–168
structural, 159

Deforestation, 389, 390

Demand, aggregate, 154

Democratization, 145

Department of Defense (DOD), 415–416

Department of Interior, 385

Department of Labor, 299

Derrick, Martha, 56*n*.

Detente, 431–433

Diagnosis-related groups (DRGs), 349

Discrimination in housing, 276

Distributive justice, 206

Divided government, 112–122

Dolbeare, Cushing, 271, 272

Domino theory, 430

Dowd, Maureen, 89*n*.

Downs, Anthony, 46–47

Dropout, school, 321
defined, 322–325
policies towards 325–326

Dukakis, Michael, 386

Durkheim, Emile, 233–234

Dye, Thomas, 11, 44*n*.–47*n*.

Earth Summit, 386

Easton, David, 38

Economic growth, 151–152

Education Summit, 291

Egalitarianism, 190, 411

Ehrlich, Paul, 399–400

Eisenhower, Dwight, 112, 415, 435

Elazar, Daniel, 94*n*.–95*n*.

Elder, Charles, 41*n*., 47*n*., 49*n*.

Electronic benefits transfer (EBT), 219

Elite theory, 44–47

Employee Retirement Income Security Act (ERISA), 361, 362

Employment Act of 1946, 151

Engels, Friedrich, 132

Enthoven, Alain, 373–374

Entitlements, 153, 171–173

Environmental Impact Statement (EIS), 384

Environmental Protection Agency (EPA), 384

Equal Employment Opportunity Act, 113

Equality and inequalities, 191–210

Equity, 20–21
distinguished from equality, 191

Escobedo v. Illinois, 237

European Economic Community (EEC), 421

Exclusionary rule, 236
good faith exception, 236

External social costs, 388–389

Externalities, 19, 402
negative, 387
positive, 386

Family Support, Act, 216–217
(*See also* Aid to Families with Dependent Children)

Fannie Mae, 257

Federal Bureau of Investigation (FBI), 226, 236, 248

Federal Gun Control Act, 247–248
(*See also* Gun control)

Federal Housing Association (FHA), 281

Federal Kidnapping Act, 244

Federal Reserve System, 14, 140
Board of Governors, 153

Federalism, 102–111
new, 110

Federalist #78, 101

Federalist party, 111

Fee-for-service, 339, 364

Fenno, Richard, 67*n*.

Filtering-down theory, 260

Fiorina, Morris P., 116*n*.

Fiscal policy, 14, 135, 140, 154

Food and Drug Administration, 62

Food and Nutrition Service (*see* United States Department of Agriculture)

Ford, Gerald, 113, 238

Frank, Barney, 92

Free riders, 18, 80, 125, 148

Friedman, Benjamin, 165

Friedman, Milton, 140, 195, 319

Full employment, goal of, 151–152

Functionalism, 295–296

Functionalist theory of inequality, 194–198
and qualifications 196–198

Furman v. Georgia, 244

Galbraith, John K., 147*n*.

Gallup poll, 326

Gates, Robert, 419

General Accounting Office (GAO), 57, 377

General Agreement on Trade and Tariffs (GATT), 443

Genocide, 438–439

Gerston, Larry, 11

Gideon v. Wainwright, 237

Global actors, 420–426
and intergovernmental organizations (IGOs), 421–422
and multinational corporations (MNCs), 424–426
and nation-states, 420–421
and nonstate actors, 421–424

Global Climate Convention, 390

Global warming, 383, 389–395
and best-case scenario, 391, 395
and worst-case scenario, 390–391, 395, 397

Goldstein, P. J., 246

Goldwater, Barry, 116

Gorbachev, Mikhail, 16, 431–434
and Glasnost, 432
and Perestroika, 432

Gore, Al, 386–387

Government:
capture theory of, 63–64
cynicism regarding, 90–91
declining faith in, 89–92

Government (*Cont.*):
  defined, 62
  failures, 56
  fiscal, 14
  monetary, 14
  promotional policies, 12–13
  public interest theory of, 62–63
  redistributive, 14
  regulatory policies, 13–14
Gramm-Rudman-Hollings Act, 50, 93,
    167–168
Great Depression, 40, 41, 88, 114, 126,
    133–135, 139, 141, 144, 145, 151,
    172, 255, 278
Greenhouse effect, 383
Greenhouse gases (GHG), 390, 394,
    402
Gregg v. Georgia, 245
Gridlock, 121
Gross domestic product (GDP):
  defined, 154
  and efficiency, 195
Group theory (*see* Pluralism)
Gun control, 247–249

Haldeman, H. R., 68–69, 430
Halloran, Richard, 74*n.*
Hamilton, Alexander, 12, 45, 101, 104,
    111
Hampden-Turner, Charles, 26
Hardin, Garrett, 7, 400*n.*, 401*n.*
Head Start, 309
Headen, Alvin E., Jr., 37*n.*
Health and Human Services,
    Department of, 354
Health Care Financing Administration
    (HCFA), 349
Health Maintenance Organizations
    (HMOs), 364, 371
Heilbroner, Robert, 127*n.*, 163–164
Heinz, John, 332
Herrnstein, Richard J., 232, 234
Hobbes, Thomas, 206
Hofferbert, Richard, 45*n.*

Homelessness, 266–273
  causes of, 270–273
  defined, 267–268
Housing Act of 1949, 282
Housing and Urban Development, 262,
    268
Housing policy, 255, 278–287
  and affordability, 274–275
  and segregation in, 276–277
Human capital theory, 290, 300–302
  (*See also* Capital investment)
Hussein, Saddam, 438
Hypothesis, 31–34

Iacocca, Lee, 66
Imperfect information, 19, 148
Imperfect markets in health care,
    337–340
Inciardi, James, 245
Income, real, 140
Income distribution, 129
  and inequality, 195–196
  parade, 198
  trends in, 199–206
Incrementalism, 52–53
  and budgetary changes, 155–156
Independent Practice Association
    (IPA), 364
Individualism, 411
Industrial policy, 40
Inflation, 136–138
Insurance, 338
  Blue Cross and Blue Shield, 360
  copayments, 340
  deductibles, 340
  employer subsidized, 345, 355–366
  experience rating, 360
  loss of coverage, 342
  self-insured, 360–361
  (*See also* Medicaid; Medicare)
Intelligence:
  and Central Intelligence Agency
    (CIA), 417–420
  and covert action, 418–419

Intelligence (*Cont.*):
  and Office of Strategic Services
    (OSS), 416–417
Interest groups, 63, 80, 83, 85, 86, 122
Intergovernmental organizations
    (IGOs), 421–422
Intergovernmental Panel on Climate
    Change (IPCC), 390
Internal Revenue Service (IRS), 356
International Committee of the Red
    Cross (ICRC), 424
International Geophysical Union, 392
International Planned Parenthood
    Federation, 400
International Telecommunications
    Union (ITU), 421
International trade, 439–443
Invisible hand, 127
Iran-Contra, 91, 416–417, 419
  (*See also* Intelligence)
Iron Law of Wages, 131
  (*See also* Malthus, Thomas R.)
Iron triangles, 43–44
Isolationism, 412–413
Issue-attention cycle, 46–47

Jackson, Andrew, 112
Jacobson, Gary C., 115
Jefferson, Thomas, 95, 101, 109–112,
    117, 190, 258–259, 296, 415
Jencks, Christopher, 309–311
Job lock, 370
Johnson, Lyndon, 116, 213, 429–430
  housing, 256
  war on crime, 237–238
  Water Quality Act, 383
Joint Chiefs of Staff (JCS), 415

Kemp, Jack, 221
Kennedy, John F.:
  Conference on Conservation, 383
  economic inequality, 206

  foreign policy decisions, 415,
    428–429
Kennedy, Robert, 247
Keynes, John Maynard, and mixed cap-
    italism, 16, 59, 61, 109, 133–136,
    139, 142–145, 151, 184
Keynesian economics, 160
Khrushchev, Nikita, 428–429
King, Martin Luther, 247
Kingdon, John, 40
Kirk, Russell, 28
Kiser, Larry, 36*n.*
Kissinger, Henry, 68–69, 415, 431
Know-Nothing party, 294
Kotz, Nick, 44
Kronick, Richard, 373–374

Laffer curve, 160
Laissez faire, 16, 41, 132, 138, 142,
    403
Lasswell, Harold, 12
Latham, Earl, 48
Lavelle, Rita, 386
Law Enforcement Assistance
    Administration, 238
League of Nations, 412–413, 421
Liberalism, 95
Lichter, S. Robert, 11
Lincoln, Abraham, 69*n.*, 100, 105
Lindblom, Charles E., 52*n.*
Line-item veto, 52
Lineberry, Robert, 54
Lobbyists, 63
Locke, John, 95, 209
Lorenz curve, 202–203
Los Angeles Times, 371
Lotteries, 181
Love Canal, 393
Lowi, Theodore, 12, 107*n.*

Macintyre, Alasdair, 10*n.*
Macroeconomic goals, 151

MADD, 109
Madison, James, 48, 82, 89, 96–98,
    104*n.*, 108, 111, 195
Magnet schools, 318
Malpractice (medical), 344
Malthus, Thomas R., 130–132, 221,
    399
    and neo-Malthusian, 399–401
Managed competition, 371–374
Manifest Destiny, 412
Mapp v. Ohio, 236
Marbury v. Madison, 101
Marginal cost, 407
Marginal productivity theory, 194*n.*,
    207
Marginal revenue product (MRP),
    301
Marginal utility, 208, 404
Market economy, 15, 129, 131
    system, 134
Market failure, 60, 126, 152, 295,
    387–389
Market incentive programs, 403–405
Market instability, 134, 135
Market signaling, 300–301
Marketable permits, 404–405
Marshall, Alfred, 142
Marshall, John, 101
Marx, Karl, 130, 132–133, 142
    and Marxism-Leninism, 428
McKinney Homeless Assistance Act,
    273
Medicaid, 172–173, 341, 343,
    347–349, 355, 362, 367, 376
Medicare, 172–173, 340–343,
    347–350, 355
    Hospital Insurance (HI), 345–346
    Supplemental Insurance, 345–346
Medicare Catastrophic Coverage Act,
    51, 346
Medigap, 346
    (*See also* Insurance)
Mercantilists, 126
    views of, 130
Merit good, 255

Methods:
    abstraction, 31
    assumptions, 34
    hypothesis, 31–34
    theory, 30–37
    values, 34
    variables, 34
Mexican-American War, 412
Mills, C. Wright, 44*n.*
Minh, Ho Chih, 430
Ministry of Trade and Industry (MITI)
    (Japan), 118
Miranda v. Arizona, 237
Mixed capitalism, 15–16, 59, 61, 109,
    133–136, 139, 142–145, 151, 184
    defined, 15
Moe, Terry, 314, 317
Monetarism, 140–141
    defined, 140
Monetary policy, 14, 135, 140
Monroe, James, and Monroe Doctrine,
    412
Montaigne, Michel de, 33
Moore, Wilbert, 194*n.*
Moral hazards, 340
Morgenthau, Hans J., 25–27
Morin, Richard, 14
Mortgage assistance, 278, 281
Motor-voter registration, 186
Moynihan, Daniel Patrick, 50*n.*
Mueller v. Allen, 319

National Aeronautics and Space
    Administration (NASA), 395–397
National Ambient Air Quality
    Standards (NAAQS), 384
National Cancer Institute, 393
National Conference of Catholic
    Bishops (NCCB), 424
National Environmental Policy Act
    (NEPA), 113, 384
National Health Insurance (NHI),
    376–378
National Health Interview Survey, 366

National Housing Act of 1934, 255
National Industrial Recovery Act
    (NIRA), 282
National Institute of Health, 342
National Research Council, 241
National Rifle Association (NRA), 249
National Security Council (NSC), 415
Nationalism, 438–439
Natural law, 206–207
    and just wage, 206–207
Natural philosophy, 24–25
Natural rate of unemployment (*see*
    Unemployment, natural rate of)
Negative campaigning, 90–92
Negative externalities, 387
Negative income tax (NIT), 221
Nelson, Barbara, 40
New Deal, 40, 88, 205
    (*See also* Roosevelt, Franklin)
New Jersey Plan, 99
New York Times, 358, 370
NIMBY, 282
Nixon, Richard:
    cooperation with Congress, 113,
        222, 238, 415, 430, 435
    new federalism, 110
    policy making, 68–69, 100*n*.
Nongovernmental actors (NGOs), 424
    multinational corporations (MNCs),
        424–426
Non-zero-sum solutions, 402
Normal curve of error, 29
North American Free Trade Agreement
    (NAFTA), 421, 423, 440, 443
North Atlantic Treaty Organization
    (NATO), 427
North, Oliver, 416–417
Nozick, Robert, 10–11, 310–311
Nursing home care, 346

Occupational Safety and Health Act
    (OSHA), 113
Ockham's razor, 35

Office of Management and Budget
    (OMB), 152
Office of Strategic Services (OSS),
    416–417
Okun, Arthur, 207
Olson, Mancur, 82–83
Omnibus Budget Reconciliation Act
    (OBRA), 352
Omnibus Crime Control and Safe
    Streets Act, 238
Opportunity costs:
    defined, 2–3
    and increasing costs, 4
Organization of American States
    (OAS), 421
Organization for Economic
    Cooperation and Development
    (OECD), 205, 242
Ostrom, Elinor, 36*n*.
O'Toole, Laurence, 55
Out of pocket expenses, 346
Ozone layer, 383
    and depletion, 389, 395–397
Ozone pollution, 393

Paine, Thomas, 411
Parenti, Michael, 44*n*.
Pareto improvement, 69–70
Parochial schools, 294, 312–313, 320
Patronage policies, 12
Perot, H. Ross, 76, 122
Pesticides, 383–384, 405
Peterson, Paul, 139
Phillips, A. W., 137
Phillips curve, 137
Philosophy:
    moral, 24–25
    natural, 24–25
Pierce, Samuel, 268
Planned economy, 15–16, 143
Plato, 95*n*.
Play or pay, 373
    (*See also* Managed competition)

Plea bargain, 235
Pluralism, 47–48
Poindexter, John, 417
Police, 236
Policy and theory, 30–37
Policy analysis, 24
    normative, 29
    positive, 27
Policy instruments, 151–152
Policy-making process:
    adoption, 39, 54
    agenda, 39–43
        institutional, 41
        symbols and, 49
    evaluation, 39, 56–57
    implementation, 39, 54–56
    policy proposal, 39
    problem identification, 39
Policy typology, 12
Political culture, 94
Political entrepreneurs, 66
Pollution, 387
    and public health, 393
Poor laws, 132
Population, 398–402
Positive externalities, 386
Poverty, 2
    and crime, 250–251
    defined, 210–213
    feminization of, 214–215
    and food stamps, 218–219
    rate, 212
    workfare, 217
    (See also War on Poverty)
Pragmatism, 411–412
President's Council on
    Environmental Quality,
    385
Prexisting condition, 363
Price:
    market, 127
    natural, 127
    stability, 151–152
Price competition, 374

Private good, 17
    defined, 17
Private marginal cost, 388–389
Private schools, 312–313
Production and resource allocation,
    128
Production possibilities frontier, 3, 64
    and choices, 4
Profit under perfect competition, 128
Prospective payment system, 349
Protectionism, 442–443
Public choice theory, 59–61, 64
Public goods, 17, 65, 125
    defined, 17
Public health, 393
Public interest theory of government,
    62–63

Quasi-public good, 295, 318
Quayle, Dan, 386–387

Rachels, James, 6, 7
Randolph, Governor Edmund, 98
Rational public choice theory (see
    Public choice theory)
Rational self-interest, 5–7, 126
    and altruism, 6, 8
    distinguished from selfishness, 6
    mutual, 142
Rawls, John, 9–11, 184
    and theory of justice, 209–210,
    310–311
Reagan, Ronald:
    administration, 55
    antigovernment views of, 110–111
    appeal to Democrats, 91
    campaign, 66
    deficits, 156
    environmental regulation, 385–386
    foreign policy, 435, 442
    futility of antipoverty programs, 213
    health care, 337

Reagan, Ronald (*Cont.*):
  on homeownership, 256
  ideological banner, 115
  inconsistent initiatives, 113
  laissez faire, 139–141
  law enforcement, 238
  low income housing, 282, 283
  policy agenda, 40
  Social Security Disability Insurance, 55–56
  supply-side economics, 94*n.*, 153, 190
  tax cuts, 159, 185
Real investment, defined, 14*n.*
Redistributive policies, 14
Redlining, 277
Regulatory policies, 12–14, 154
Rent control, 284–287
Resource Conservation and Recovery Act, 384–385
Retrospective reimbursement, 349
Return to normalcy, 413
Ricardo, David, 440
Roe v. Wade, 41
Roosevelt, Franklin, 114, 136
  and foreign policy, 416, 430
  and health care, 342, 413
  and New Deal, 40, 88, 134, 144, 190, 205, 255, 274
Roosevelt, Theodore, 383
Rossi, Peter, 268
  (*See also* Homelessness)
Rousseau, Jean Jacques, 209

Sabatier, Paul A., 39, 55
Satisficing, 53
Scarcity, 2
Schattschneider, E. E., 107*n.*
Schneider, William, 263–264
Scholastic Assessment Test (SAT), 291
School choice plans, 318
Schultz, George, 417
Secretary of Defense, 415

Self-correcting mechanism, 128, 129, 135
Self-interest (*see* Rational self-interest)
Separation of powers, 96–98, 105
Shapiro v. Thompson, 217*n.*
Sierra Club, 383
Simon, Julian, 399
Single payer, 2, 371, 377
Sizer, Theodore, 323
Smith, Adam, 8, 125–130, 142, 300–301
Social contract, 142
Social justice, 8, 9, 145
Social marginal costs, 388–389
Social Security, 173, 212, 342, 345
  (*See also* Medicare)
Social Security Disability Insurance (SSDI), 55–56
Social stratification, 297
Sovereignty, 420–421
Soviet Union, former, 146
Special interest groups (*see* Interest groups)
Squires, Gregory, 298
Stagflation, 136–137
  defined, 137
Stalin, Josef, 428
Starling, Grover, 39
Stockman, David, 153
Suburbs, 258–264
  (*See also* Housing policy)
Sundquist, James L., 111*n.*
Sununu, John, 89
Supplemental Security Income (SSI), 347
Supply-side economics, 160, 190, 206
Supremacy clause, 104
Supreme Court, 55
Surplus value, 132
Symbols, 49

Tariffs, 440
  and nontariff barriers, 440

Tax expenditure, 280, 356
Taxes, 148
  and deductions, 278
  effective tax rate, 184
  function of, 64
  incentives, 358, 403–404
  and income distribution, 175–176
  policy, 173–185
  principles of, 177–178
  revenues, 62
Term limits, 120–121
Third-party payer, 339
Thomas, Clarence, 92
Thornburgh, Richard, 332
Thurow, Lester, 327
Ticket-splitting, 115, 122
Tiebout model, 111, 265
Time horizon, 117–118
Tobin, James, 160–161
Tocqueville, Alexis de, 306
Tollison, Robert, 69*n.*
Trade deficit, 441–443
Trade surplus, 441
Tradeoff model, 263
Tragedy of the commons, 7–8
Truman, Harry, 100*n.*, 114, 430
  and health care, 342
Tuition tax credits, 319

UCR (see *Uniform Crime Report*)
Unanimity, 69–70
Underemployment, 298
Unemployment:
  cyclical, 136
  frictional, 136
  and inflation, 135–138
  natural rate of, 137–138
  structural, 136
Uniform Crime Report (UCR),
  226
United Kingdom Royal Society,
  398–399
United Nations (UN), 421–424

United Nations Population Fund
  (UNFPA), 400
United States Academy of Sciences,
  398–399
United States Agency for International
  Development (U.S.A.I.D.), 424
United States Department of
  Agriculture (USDA), 212
  Food and Nutrition Service,
  218–219
United States v. Leon, 236
Universal coverage, 342
Unorganized voters, 81
Urban Institute, 271
Urbanization, 145
Utilitarianism, 207–209, 406

Values, 34
Van Buren, Martin, 112
Variable, 34–36
Veterans Administration (VA), 281
Vidal, Gore, 69*n.*
Vietnam, 69, 428
Virginia Plan, 98, 99
Vold, George B., 233
Volker, Paul, 141
Voting:
  logrolling, 72–74
  majority, 70–71
  median voter, 74–76
  unanimity, 69–70
Voting paradox, 71–72
Voucher plans, 319

Wages, 139
War on drugs and crime, 243–247
War on Poverty, 213–214, 219–220
Warren, Earl, 101, 236
Warsaw Pact, 427
Washington, George, 12, 117
  and Congress, 413
Water Quality Act of 1965, 383

Watergate, 91
Watt, James, 385
Wealth:
   and concentration, 200
   and trends in, 199–206
   and unequal distribution, 195–196
Weber, Max, 83–84
Whig party, 112
White collar crime, 251–252
White House Conference on
   Conservation, 383
Wildavsky, Aaron, 53
Wilson, James Q., 232–234
Wilson, William Julius, 251
Wofford, Harris, 332
Woodson v. North Carolina, 245

Woolsey, James (DCI), 419
Workfare, 217
World Health Organization (WHO),
   393
Worst-case scenario, 390–391, 395,
   397
Wright, Jim, 92

Yeltsin, Boris, 80

Zeigler, Harmon, 11, 44*n*.–47*n*.
Zero-sum solutions, 22, 126, 443
   and non-zero-sum solutions, 402